COST EFFECTIVE QUALITY FOOD SERVICE

An Institutional Guide

Second Edition

Judy Ford Stokes, F.C.S.I., R.D.

AN ASPEN PUBLICATION®
Aspen Systems Corporation

1985

Rockville, Maryland
Royal Tunbridge Wells

Library of Congress Cataloging in Publication Data

Stokes, Judy Ford.
Cost effective quality food service.

"An Aspen publication."
Includes bibliographies and index.
1. Food service—Cost control. I. Title.
TX911.3.C65S74   1985   647'.95'.0681   85-11124
ISBN: 0-87189-118-2

Editorial Services: Martha Sasser

Library of Congress Catalog Card Number: 85-11124
ISBN: 0-87189-118-2

Printed in the United States of America

1 2 3 4 5

This book is dedicated to Lynn R. Hall and the staff of Judy Ford Stokes & Associates, Inc., whose support and loyalty are unsurpassed, who enabled this book to become a reality.

Table of Contents

Acknowledgments

I would like to acknowledge the invaluable contributions of many individuals, clients, and organizations who have helped me increase insight into the specialized field of food service management. A special appreciation also is given to Bruce A. Barker, senior consultant at Peat, Marwick, Mitchell and Co., for developing Chapter 10, Computers: The Inevitable Food Service Opportunity. The input of John Norback, Ph.D., associate professor of food science at the University of Wisconsin, in developing Chapter 11, Computer Food Service Applications, is especially appreciated. I also would like to thank McNeill Stokes, J.D., senior partner of Stokes, Shapiro, Fussell, and Genberg for drafting Chapter 6, Cost-Effective Labor Relations, and Arch Stokes, J.D., of Stokes, Lazarus, and Watson. I would like to express further appreciation for the assistance of Lynn Reeves Hall, R.D., vice president of Judy Ford Stokes & Associates, Inc., for drafting a substantial portion of Chapters 12 (Energy Cost Management: Dollars and Sense), 13 (Selecting Energy-Efficient Equipment), and 14 (Energy Management Systems: Pros and Cons). Further appreciation is also to be given to Darlene Richard, president, Direct Marketing R. & D.; Judy Rohrbaugh, R.D.; Susan Summe, R.D.; and Linda Mack, R.D., of Judy Ford Stokes and Associates, Inc.

In particular I wish to thank Harvey Ogletree of Laventhol and Horwath for reviewing and providing input into Chapter 7, Labor Costs, and the introduction. I also am grateful to Antoinette Colucci, M.S., R.D., assistant professor of the School of Hotel Administration of Cornell University, for her input into Chapter 8, Improving Productivity: A Results-Oriented Approach.

Appreciation is expressed to John Genova and Emmett Barlow of SunLow, Inc., Atlanta, Georgia, for their assistance with the preparation of Appendix D, Pureed Diet Production Guides.

The continued moral support of Jim McCall and the information provided by Ross Laboratories regarding a fee-for-nutrition services program made an invaluable contribution.

Special appreciation also is given to the Consultant Dietitians in Health Care Facilities, a practice group of The American Dietetic Association, for support and continued confidence.

The love, support, and encouragement of my family—my husband, McNeill Stokes, and my children, Ford and Ashley—made the writing of this book

COST EFFECTIVE QUALITY
FOOD SERVICE

possible. I shall always be grateful to them. A special note of appreciation also is given to my parents, Mr. and Mrs. Charles C. Ford, for their love, loyalty, and continued confidence. Thank you, also, to Mr. and Mrs. Jordan Stokes, III, for their love, support, and guidance.

Preface

Control costs. Deliver service. Maintain quality. Each heralds an ever-demanding challenge for today's food services. *Cost Effective Quality Food Service* provides practical specifics and innovative solutions for food service operators in health care, educational, and correctional facilities to control costs, continue service, and maintain quality.

With food service costs representing one of the highest expenses in most facilities, that field must be recognized as a business. Based on dollar volume alone, commercial food service is a major business. No longer can it be considered only a service entity.

COST CONSTRAINTS

Cost constraints have always challenged the correctional and educational food service industries. With the advent of DRGs (diagnosis related groups) promulgated by the government under the prospective payment system October 1, 1983, the hospital industry has met new economic challenges. Chapter 9, DRGs: Biggest Problem or Greatest Opportunity, provides a detailed discussion of DRGs and their impact on food service. Hospitals must control costs or go out of business. The government has estimated that more than 1,000 hospitals will close their doors by the end of 1987. DRGs can be a hospital's biggest problem or its greatest opportunity. There are two ways to control costs: (1) reduce expenditures, (2) generate revenue.

This book outlines specific methods to reduce costs, maintain quality and generate revenue.

Since change is the only constant, food service operations in all types of settings are besieged with challenge and opportunity. Effectively gathering and interpreting cost data as detailed here, with or without a computer, will guarantee a successfully managed operation. Emphasizing proved methods, practical solutions to improving productivity, reducing costs, computerizing service, conserving energy, maintaining quality, and generating additional sources of revenue are identified specifically.

This book has been written in plain language for both veteran and beginning food service operators to help them solve daily operational challenges.

STRATEGIC PLANNING

Developing solutions to daily challenges while taking advantage of opportunities that result from effective strategic planning as discussed in Chapter 1, Strategic Planning: A Bold Concept in Food Service, identifies the threats and opportunities of the future and makes it possible to minimize the former and maximize the latter. That chapter details the five steps of the strategic planning process: (1) mission statement, (2) situation audit, (3) action plan, (4) implementation, and (5) evaluation.

Sample short-term and long-term goals for administrative and nutrition services also are provided to serve as an initial guideline for developing a facility's own action plan. The primary challenge: "To reduce food service costs by 6 percent within the next fiscal year."

That is not difficult. If the principles and specifics of *Cost-Effective Quality Food Service* are applied in the food service operation, this challenge will be met. In fact, it is amazing how easy it is to meet that minimal goal of a 6 percent reduction. It can be and has been done in many facilities, including hospitals, nursing homes, schools, and correctional institutions.

Achieving this goal begins with analyzing the operation and determining a budget that identifies anticipated revenue and expenditures as outlined in Chapter 2, Budget vs. Cost Comparisons. The various types of budgets are reviewed, with special emphasis on the zero-based model to reflect an educated estimate of anticipated revenue and expenses for the next fiscal year as dictated by the facility's strategic plan.

The trend in hospitals is toward restaurant-style menus, particularly with the advent of DRGs. Production costs can be monitored and controlled; needs can be standardized, and public relations can be improved. The restaurant-style menu is an innovative approach to a combination of the best attributes of the selective and nonselective menu systems. Careful planning of menu items and menu format, as detailed in Chapter 3, Cost Realities: Menus and Nutrition-Related Medical Requirements, will result in an appetizing, cost-effective patient relations tool.

Specific guidelines in Chapter 4 cover Cost Efficiencies in Purchasing, Receiving, Storing, and Inventory Systems to facilitate achieving that goal of 6 percent lower food service costs. Cost effectiveness is a science; it is not luck. The pros and cons of purchasing systems are presented, along with recommendations on how to maximize a facility's purchasing dollar while improving vendor relations.

Evaluating the receiving area and increasing storage at a minimal cost are reviewed in preparation for discussing effective storing and inventory systems. Inventories are more than the money represented by shelved cans in the storeroom; inventories can serve as economic and management indicators, as identified in Chapter 4.

Literally thousands of dollars are saved and generated each year by food service through implementing the specific cost-management techniques outlined in Chapter 5. That chapter emphasizes cost savings to be realized in food-related functions while other chapters discuss specific means to reduce costs in labor, energy, and administrative systems such as purchasing, inventory, etc. Chapter 5 describes how to convert food service from a cost center into a revenue center, a feat most need to accomplish. Food utilization studies, purchasing ceilings, portion control, and monitoring systems of use are invaluable tools to control and expose hidden costs.

LABOR

One of the greatest costs in food service is labor. Cost-Effective Labor Relations (Chapter 6) describes how to establish an effective labor relations program to minimize the threat of unionization. Unions sell management mistakes and this chapter spells out in plain language how to minimize such errors. Chapter 7 discusses labor costs, their ramifications, and how to control them. Chapter 8 reviews an unusual approach to improving productivity and how to make it an integral part of the work culture.

To control costs, food service managers must improve productivity, which means: (1) getting more work from the same number of employees or (2) getting the same amount of work from fewer employees. The purpose of Chapter 8 is to identify specific means to: (1) evaluate current staffing patterns in view of present and projected department productivity and (2) improve personnel productivity.

Chapter 9 on DRGs has been developed especially for the hospital industry. DRGs represent the most widesweeping change in health care since the advent of Medicare. With health care costs representing 10.2 percent of the gross national product, of over $300 billion in the early 1980s, the federal government mandated reimbursement ceilings for hospitals effective October 1983. Chapter 9 provides insight into coping with DRGs, identifying how hospitals can convert this potential liability into an innovative asset.

COMPUTERS AND FOOD SERVICE

Computers are an inevitable and exciting, if not essential, opportunity for all areas of the food service industry, including educational, health care, and correctional facilities in addition to hotels, restaurants, and clubs. Chapter 10 provides specifics on how to select a computer while Chapter 11 reviews how food service could and should benefit from its use.

ENERGY

Chapter 12 provides practical applications of energy conservation principles that produce a saving of more than $40,000 a year. Chapter 13 reviews energy specifics of almost every item of equipment as a guide in making investments of the facility's equipment dollar.

Key components of conserving energy include preventive maintenance programs, active employee participation, and energy management systems. Chapter 14 discusses each of these areas, outlining how a facility can evaluate and apply the benefits of each to meet specific needs.

IN THE APPENDIXES

So many persons expressed an interest in having menus in the book that a set of nonselective nursing home menus (Western United States) and a set of selective hospital menus (Southeastern United States) were developed (Appendix A). A sample restaurant-style menu also is included in response to a major current trend (Appendix E). A sample Purchasing/Production Guide—coordinated with the selective hospital menus—has been developed for a variety of quantities ranging from 20 to 300 meals per item (Appendix B). The Pureed Diet Production Guide for fruits, vegetables, and meats appears in Appendix D. Appendix C deals with practicalities in food preparation.

For the first time, a detailing of hospital diet equivalents is presented (Appendix F) to share more specific means of determining them accurately.

Sample energy audits for a 150-bed nursing home and a 35-bed hospital are included (Appendix G) to help in applying the book's energy information to food service operations. Completing the energy section is Appendix H, detailing how some services have saved and can save more than $40,000 a year on energy alone.

Cost-Effective Quality Food Service has been written for those involved in food service operations to help:

- develop a strategic plan to control costs and improve the quality of food services even further
- expose hidden costs
- improve productivity
- convert food service from a cost center into a revenue-producing center
- evaluate the feasibility and apply the potential of computers
- conserve energy to produce significant operational savings.

Judy Ford Stokes
Atlanta, Georgia

Chapter 1

Strategic Planning: A Bold Concept in Food Service

Strategic planning is a bold concept in food service that enables the manager to affect rather than to accept the future. Food service professionals and administration must be able to see into the future and try to determine what could affect the operation so they can take steps to minimize uncertainty and maximize opportunity. Strategic planning identifies the threats and opportunities of the future and seeks to minimize them.

Strategic planning can be divided into five key areas:

1. mission statement
2. situation audit
3. action plan
4. implementation
5. evaluation.

Typical planning involves development and manipulation of budget, production, and staff within existing systems. However, strategic planning involves detailed evaluation of current and anticipated circumstances, potentially to change segments or an entire system. The strategic planning process is far broader and enables the manager to avoid the "firefighting" behavior so often seen. Without a longer range format plan, daily problems take precedence. Strategic planning is applying a definitive structure to setting goals. Strategic planning provides the insurance to achieve those goals.

FOOD SERVICE AS A BUSINESS

Major businesses—such as the Fortune 500—have used strategic planning for years to reach unlimited heights of success. Food service also is a major business. Those in the field today must reorient their thinking. Food service is a department specializing in service and typically is a cost center. Professionals need to realize the department represents a major business; even a small one manages several hundred thousand dollars a year.

With the advent of diagnosis related groups (DRGs), more stringent regulations, and the uncertainty of the economy, cost control is of paramount importance. An effective means of minimizing costs is maximizing revenue. Food service departments have a golden opportunity to use strategic planning to convert their operation from a cost center into a revenue generator, and strategic planning is the brainstorming mechanism to reach this goal.

Some food service departments are similar to small companies and have a tendency to concentrate only on day-to-day activities and operational problems. The result: individuals tend to wait for opportunities to develop and handle crises as they emerge rather than planning in advance for the future. This is in contrast to large corporations or other industries in which strategic planning is a vital part of management and becomes a key reason for their success. Operating without strategic planning is analogous to steering a ship without a rudder: the helmsman has no control over the vessel's direction.

An effective food service manager needs two primary skills:

1. foresight, or the ability to bind the future to the present
2. lateral sight, or the ability to see current options and how they may be applied rather than relying on how it has been done for the last 20 years. (How many have heard, "This won't work because we have always done it another way," or "We don't want to change anything.")

There is no guaranteed pattern for success but there is one for failure: refusal to change with the changing world. Success is not luck, it is a science. Luck is merely preparation meeting opportunity. Strategic planning provides the opportunity of preparation. The common thread among failing situations is reflected in the rueful comment, "I didn't see it coming." What was right yesterday may be questionable today and even wrong tomorrow. Change is the only constant and it is best to be prepared for it.

The complaint may be raised that there is little time for planning. The answer is that managers cannot afford the luxury of not planning. Inflation, Reaganomics, increased minimum wage, new food products, new food systems . . . all have impacts on the future of the food service department. It is mandatory to plan today to assure tomorrow.

Strategic planning answers three questions:

1. Where are we?
2. Where are we going?
3. How are we going to get there?

Strategic planning identifies the threats and opportunities of the future and seeks to minimize the former and maximize the latter.

MISSION STATEMENT

To begin the strategic planning process, administrators and managers should analyze the purpose of the food service department and identify a mission statement. If it be thought that this is not necessary, consider the mission statement of the railroad industry, that indicated it was in the railroad business, rather than the transportation business. Had its mission statement been identified differently, the railroad industry would not be in the difficulty in which it finds itself today.

The mission statement of a food service department should encompass the following factors:

1. the business the unit is in
2. scope, involving annual dollar volume, general services, and those to whom services are provided
3. general profile of department's services
4. geographical location of services
5. future changes anticipated (services, customers, etc.).

For example, the mission of XYZ Memorial Hospital's food service department is to provide nutritious, appetizing meals within budgetary limitations for the patients, staff, and community of Metropolis. The $2 millon-a-year department is to provide the following to the hospital's patients and staff:

- patient meals, including all types of special diets
- between-meal nourishments
- cafeteria meal (one per day per shift)
- staff coffee
- special meals for emergency medical technicians (EMTs).

The department is to seek menus to maximize the use of equipment and personnel by providing additional sources to increase its revenues. Some of these services are to include:

- special gourmet patient meals
- special between-meal nourishments
- cafeteria service to the community
- special theme meals for the cafeteria
- special periodic cafeteria offerings (customers make their own sundaes, pizzas, etc.)
- luncheons/dinners prepared for the business community
- catering
- retail baked goods for patients (depending on diet), staff, and community
- clinical diet instructions for patients, staff, and community
- Fee-for-nutrition services program
- health-oriented seminars/workshops for the community
- food services to local community facilities as needed, such as Meals on Wheels program, small acute care, long-term care, and day care facilities, etc.

Administrators and managers should ask themselves what the mission statement of their food service is. After it has been identified, the strategic planning process can proceed in the following areas:

1. Situation Audit: all factors internal and external that affect the department
2. Action Plan: goals identified and methods by which they are to be accomplished
3. Plan of Implementation: methods to motivate employees to reach the goals that have been set
4. Plan of Evaluation: feedback mechanism to monitor strategic planning results.

3

SITUATION AUDIT

Before any food service department can develop an effective action plan, it needs to understand its current situation and ask the question, "Where are we?" Abraham Lincoln once said, "If we could first know where we are going . . . we could then better judge what to do and how to do it." It is from this understanding that realistic objectives, service and management programs as well as action plans are developed. The review process entails an examination of the food service operation, the external factors that influence it, and the internal resources available to it. These elements need to be summarized into the entity's strengths, weaknesses, threats, and opportunities. Because of the vast amount of information to be considered and the amount of time it takes to collect, some form of structure is helpful.

A situation audit refers to an analysis of types of patrons (patients/residents, students, staff, inmates, community, etc.), services, financial and professional data, past, present, and future that provide a base for pursuing the strategic planning process. There is no one way to conduct a situation audit. In some food service operations, the process is structured and comprehensive but in many it is loose and unstructured. The more detailed an evaluation, the more insight will be gained into the direction of the services, patrons, and resources. Each food service must analyze its present and project its potential sphere of service. Is it to service only patrons within the confines of its own institution or could it expand its base of revenue by servicing the community surrounding the institution?

A major objective of the situation audit is to identify and analyze the key trends, forces, and phenomena having a potential impact on the operation and its patrons. It should be a systematic assessment because experience teaches that the more systematically managers attempt to perceive changing forces in environments, the more likely they are to avoid being surprised.

The audit should determine the location of present patron and service opportunities as well as future opportunities. The situation audit should spot where and how potential threats might develop. In a service economy such as food, the potential for eliminating some elements exists. The department should then be able to shift into different services (see mission statement) rather than be at the mercy and whims of changing circumstances.

The situation audit should include services that generate the department's primary income. Food departments are well advised to stick with their strengths in patrons and services as a basis for future growth plans. The present service mix might be built upon to exploit underutilized services and clients. Services that may be underutilized and unprofitable may be nurtured or upgraded in quality, volume, and profitability. Unprofitable ones may be important to the service mix as loss leaders to shift patrons to more profitable ones. For example, small services such as initial diet instruction can lead to satisfied patrons who, in turn, can lead to a larger, more profitable business such as catering a large function.

In essence, the situation audit summarizes the department's strengths, weaknesses, threats, and opportunities.

External Forces

Having developed a basic understanding of the nature of the department's current activities, the next step is to review the external environment in which it operates. The major objective of the situation audit is to analyze key trends or driving forces that would have potential impact on the operation.

Administrators and managers should identify external factors that have a material effect but are beyond anyone's control. The processes must analyze current events or driving forces that could have an impact on clients' future services or needs. Driving forces may be demographic, economic, resource-related, competitive, technological, social, political, governmental, or legal. By asking the right questions, the answers will become obvious. (See Exhibit 1–1 for a detailed questionnaire.)

External Factors

External factors—including the economy, governmental intervention, the resources of labor, money, and suppliers in addition to technology and industry trends—all have an impact on the future operation of a food service department. The continuing success of an operation depends on the managers' ability to forecast and plan for the inevitable: change. Change is the only constant.

A number of the basic external factors should be considered, with some of the questions that must be answered including:

- What economic factors affect the food service operation and what changes in strategy do they suggest?
- Who are the major competitors and what changes are taking place in them?
- What alternatives exist for patrons (patients, staff, community) to satisfy the same need this department satisfies?
- What are the trends with respect to the availability and productivity of professional, paraprofessional, and other personnel?
- What governmental and political factors have a bearing on the food service?
- What changes are occurring in the market that the department serves, and how will they have an impact on the operation?
- What changes are occurring within our service markets, and how do they have an impact on our food service operation?
- What technological changes are occurring that impact on food service and how vulnerable is the department to technological change?

Economic

What external or internal factors could affect the food service negatively or positively and what management strategies should be used to meet the department goals? For example, how do economic factors affect the service? If inflation increased or recession set in, what difference would that make to the operation? Such external conditions could provide an opportunity for analyzing the department to establish more effective systems in cost comparison, purchasing/receiving, and food delivery.

One 160-bed health care institution performed such an analysis and identified a savings of more than $24,000 a year on only four food items—$10,000 a year on milk alone.

Other external factors could have an impact as well. On the other hand, what if inflation stabilized or deflation occurred? Additional funds then would be available for investing in energy-conserving equipment to program even greater sav-

Exhibit 1–1 Situation audit questionnaire

External Factors

Economic:

- How do economic factors affect food service?
  A. If inflation increased, how would this affect the department?
  B. If inflation stabilized or deflation occurred, how would the service be affected?

Government:

- What governmental factors affect food service?
  A. Federal and state health care regulations, OSHA, EEO?

Resources:

- What is the availability of labor and management in and outside the department? What is its personnel productivity?
- Who are the major suppliers and is the department limited in alternative food/supply sources?
- How could external factors affect major suppliers and their service to the department?

Technology:

- What technological changes are occurring that could have an impact on food service (computers, electronically operated food delivery carts, etc.)?
- What efforts are being taken to keep up with these changes?
- How vulnerable are the services to technological changes?

Internal Factors

Markets:

- Should new services be developed by the department? What new services should be considered (school breakfast program, fee-for-nutrition services program)?
- What new community segments should the department service (Meals on Wheels)?
- What community segments or services should be eliminated? Has each been evaluated as to its own profitability and importance to the operation of food service?

Customers:

- Who are the department's customers (patients, staff, guests, students, inmates, community)?
- What do these customers buy from the department and why?
- What do the customers think about the food services?
- Who could be customers in the future?

Management Information:

- How effective is the organizational structure of the food service and will it meet the department's future needs?
- What do employees think about food service and its management?

Equipment and Facilities:

- Does the department have the proper equipment to handle the type of services it provides?

ings in the future. (See Chapters 12, 13, and 14 on energy for such potential savings, i.e., warewashing machines now are available that save $3,000 to $10,000 a year.)

Funds also might become available to implement new services. For example, could a community nutrition education program be sponsored by a school or the health care facility? Could a gourmet food selection be offered for patients for an additional charge? Could "theme" meals be provided periodically for cafeteria and patients? Could catering be provided for community functions?

Government

Regulations have had and will continue to have an effect on food service operation, whether it is an educational, health care, or correctional facility. Are administrators and managers involved in shaping future regulations or do they wait to see them published in the *Federal Register*? Everyone must become involved because they can make a difference; their input is needed and is to be encouraged. They should develop a rapport with members of Congress and, if possible, with representatives of the Health Care Financing Administration (HCFA) to become informed on governmental developments. They should let their voices be heard. Congress and HCFA need input from knowledgeable people in the field.

Resources

Labor is a big resource. Increased employee satisfaction could be instituted through wage incentive programs and an effective performance evaluation system. With labor's being 55 to 60 percent of the direct expense of most health care facilities, it obviously is a major cost factor. Food service personnel represents 5 to 7.5 percent of the direct expense of such institutions. The availability of labor and management both in and outside the department are significant factors of concern. Who are the competitors for labor for the department (factories, other health care institutions, hotels, other departments within the institution, etc.)?

Productivity is another important factor in determining the bottom line. Have the labor-minutes per meal or meals per labor-hour been determined for the operation? If additional funds become available, investing in a productivity survey could result in significant savings. One food warehousing company invested $500,000 in a productivity survey and saved $3 million to $4 million in one year.

Economic resources also must be managed. In examining other external resources, is the department limited in the suppliers from which it may purchase? If so, why?

Even though the hospital, nursing home, school, or correctional facility may be relatively small and have minimal storage capacity, quantity buying is effective when integrated or coordinated with other facilities in the same general locale. Volume purchasing talks. If the storage capacity does not permit volume purchasing, cooperative purchasing with weekly drop shipments could save any facility literally thousands of dollars a year.

When there is no cooperative purchasing system, consideration should be given to a comparative pricing system that involves obtaining prices weekly or monthly from several vendors on numerous items. Cost comparisons then are made in analyzing expenses in relation to quality before ordering. It must be emphasized again that there is little incentive for vendors to charge minimal prices when no comparisons are made.

Suppliers are yet another valuable resource. Are there external factors that could affect the service of suppliers to the institution? Could gasoline or diesel prices affect the number of deliveries and, therefore, have an impact on storage capacities?

Suppliers should be provided with a current set of menus and food specifications to be certain they maintain the appropriate food items for the facility's use. Projecting annual usage of various food items is an effective tool in achieving price reductions as well as increasing cooperation from suppliers. If storage capacity is at a premium, there are alternatives to building additional bulk storage. Several manufacturers sell a continuous storage or track shelving system that rolls on wheels in channels embedded in the floor. Aisle space is minimized and the existing capacity storage space can be doubled or tripled at minimum cost.

Technology

External forces affecting the food service industry include regulations, new technology, and many other factors. Helpful guides can be found in the field's historical growth and the expected trend for the future. The changes occurring in the field will change the operation of the department, the facility, and potentially the careers of those involved.

Trends in Commercial Food Service

Current trends in commercial food service are wide and varied and are affecting the equipment industry and food operations. Cost control, virtually mandated by the economy and government intervention, pervades every facet from menus and purchasing the food, preparation and productivity, to merchandising the service of food.

A major trend in the commercial field—because of those cost and quality constraints—is directed toward system concepts as compared with individual equipment items. Cooking to inventory as opposed to cooking to menus represents a major trend. Cooking to inventory (the use of food on hand) can significantly reduce labor, ensure quality, and control costs by eliminating food waste. Fluctuations in numbers served have little impact on such a system since food remains in inventory if it is not needed. Waste obviously is minimized, and food is served at the peak of its palatability. Production in these cook/chill, cook/freeze, and freeze/cook systems is coordinated with the menus. Food is prepared several days, possibly even weeks, in advance, then is pulled from inventory and rethermatized to satisfy menu needs.

The interest in increased productivity, controlled costs, and quality service are thrusting computers into the forefront of commercial food operations. Cost analyses of menu items, food components of cafeteria, patient/student/inmate/patron services, and purchasing options, in addition to staffing analysis and correlation of production with purchasing, represent some of the important computer data managers no longer can operate effectively without. Computers are having a major impact on the industry and are becoming as commonplace as the telephone.

With food service labor costs continually increasing, efficient use of personnel is essential. Therefore, equipment that can assist in redistributing workloads and maximizing current levels of personnel is of significant interest. Articles that actually reduce labor include transporting equipment, cook tanks, and slow-cook ovens that enable meat to be cooked overnight, and those that require no pots and pans (tilting braising pans), etc.

Commercial food service operators appreciate the trend toward flexibility/versatility in equipment such as those just identified. Conveyorized equipment such as conveyor steamers, broilers, and fryers, and dual function items such as combination convection and microwave ovens, assist in maximizing labor while improving the quality of food delivered through the batch cooking process. Controlling costs is of even greater concern with the new reimbursement for hospital regulations that became effective October 1, 1983, and base reimbursement strictly on the 470 diagnosis related groups (DRGs) as compared with actual costs. Therefore, costs must be reduced while maintaining quality. Batch cooking achieves both goals.

Although energy management is not seen of immediate urgency now by the public, it eventually will become a major concern again. Food service designers and equipment manufacturers continue to show their prowess by developing and programming energy management and reutilization systems into their planning. Commercial end users are becoming keenly interested in payback periods or return on investment (ROI) as well as specific energy utilization of equipment. Energy management and utilization systems and some specific equipment items provide such an opportunity.

A minimum of $10,000 to $20,000 a year can be saved in any food service department in energy alone through implementing simple, yet effective, operation procedures.

Each of the areas of cost control, productivity, system concepts, flexibility and versatility in equipment use, energy management, and computerization represents a major trend in strategic planning for commercial food service. Strategic planning can be used no longer only for the Fortune 500 businesses. Strategic planning is a bold concept in food service, yet cost control and quality service mandate this market-based approach to minimize the threats and maximize the opportunities of all types of operations.

Internal Factors

Internal factors also can affect any food service operation. Internal factors include quantity, skill and interpersonal relationships among employees, and how they may affect the services the department may provide. Other internal factors include the markets the department serves—its customers, management data, equipment, and facilities.

Employee Benefits

Determining the economic impact of existing employee benefits can lead to improved personnel morale. Do employees know what their fringe benefits mean to them in terms of actual dollars? In one private psychiatric hospital, the food service director expressed the need for an increase in salary. When the fringe benefits were determined and a dollar figure was placed on them, the executive was amazed to learn that the salary actually amounted to $3,000 to $4,000 more per year and no longer felt a raise was necessary.

In assessing employees of the food service labor force, an effective performance evaluation system is vital. Conclusions from such an evaluation can reflect the training required, new skills that may be needed, factors to reduce turnover rate, steps to improve safety, and sources of personnel replacement, and almost literally can be the salvation for a department.

A dramatic example of the effectiveness of a well-planned performance evaluation system occurred in one health care institution where food service employees were ready to "walk." The new supervisor had been promoted from a cook's position since the head cook had refused the supervisor post. However, the head cook's attitude was seriously affecting the morale of the entire department as she refused to work with the new supervisor, thereby generating a negative influence on the department. When the performance evaluations were reviewed by an outside consultant firm that had been retained, the head cook received all "As"—a model employee. The head cook had so intimidated the food service supervisor that the supervisor had not evaluated her performance objectively.

In coordination with the administrator and food service director, an entirely new performance evaluation system was developed, including the following procedures:

- reviewing job descriptions of each position in the department
- redistributing the workload throughout the day
- developing worksheets for each employee
- developing performance evaluation forms
- establishing a six-week trial period for the initial evaluation process
- apprising the employees of the evaluation process.

The system consisted of two components for each position in the department: (1) general performance standards, including attitude, tardiness, etc., and (2) specific performance standards for each position. A total of 30 points for each component was possible (Exhibit 1–2). The evaluations were to be conducted weekly for the initial six-week trial period. Employees who received a score of 19 or less on either the general or specific evaluation twice within the six weeks were subject to termination. The administrator assured the consultant firm that this policy would be followed, and the evaluation process began. After the first three-week trial period, the entire department was a different operation due to the system that had been initiated by the consultant firm. Employees' attitudes had improved greatly as had the quality and productivity of their work. Evaluations by the administrator and supervisor then were conducted every two weeks for a month, then once a month for two months, and now are quarterly. Annual evaluations are less than effective.

Effective performance evaluations can assure a strong, participative work force to achieve departmental goals.

Markets

Professional food service operators must determine who are the customers and what are the department's services. The financial aspects must be reviewed to determine the historical, profitable sources of revenue and services. Those that do not generate much income now may become the dominant growth services in the future while the traditional "cash cow" services may become static or decline in growth. The situation audit will help identify future cash cows and potential "dogs." Services that are not economically feasible still may be vital to the overall professional work of the department or facility and may lead to more lucrative ones. Before any service is added or eliminated, its economic realities should be compared against its public relations concerns and benefits. An objective evaluation will determine the future viability of continuing the service. (Chapter 5 reviews specific means to convert the food service department from a cost center into a revenue center.)

Name: _____ Position: _____

1. Punctuality:
   1. Frequently late for work.
   2. Usually on time for work.
   3. Always reports for work on time.
Comments: _____

2. Appearance:
   1. Does not wear appropriate uniform, is untidy or messy.
   2. Sometimes needs to be reminded to wear uniform, is usually neat and clean.
   3. Wears appropriate uniform, is clean and neat.
Comments: _____

3. Attendance:
   1. Is frequently absent and/or not in, no call.
   2. Is absent periodically, usually calls in if will be absent.
   3. Rarely absent, always gives appropriate notice.
Comments: _____

4. Attitude with Staff:
   1. Frequently rude, uncooperative, unfriendly.
   2. Periodically rude, uncooperative, unfriendly.
   3. Is courteous, friendly, and cooperative.
Comments: _____

5. Attitude toward patients:
   1. Frequently rude, inattentive, discourteous. Does not adhere to patient food preferences.
   2. Periodically rude, discourteous, inattentive to patient food preferences.
   3. Courteous, pleasant, attentive to patient needs and food preferences.
Comments: _____

6. Ingenuity:
   1. Waits to be told what to do.
   2. Needs frequent instruction.
   3. Is a self-starter.
Comments: _____

7. Willingness to improve.
   1. Refuses training, constructive criticism.
   2. Generally accepts training, constructive criticism.
   3. Accepts training, constructive criticism.
Comments: _____

8. Loyalty:
   1. Is not loyal and supportive, speaks and acts in negative manner.
   2. Generally is loyal and supportive.
   3. Is loyal and supportive of supervisor and nursing home.
Comments: _____

9. Works without supervision:
   1. Unable to work without supervision.
   2. Usually can work without supervision, at times must be reminded.
   3. Knows what must be done and does it whether supervised or not.
Comments: _____

10. Honesty: Trustworthiness
    1. Unable to accept responsibility, must be monitored.
    2. Usually able to accept responsibility, must be monitored at all times.
    3. Able to accept responsibility and also monitor others.
Comments: _____

Total _____

Comments: _____

Evaluated By: _____ Date: _____

Signed: _____

A minimum score of 20 must be attained.

Exhibit 1–2 continued

Cook

Name: _____ Date: _____

1. Food Preparation:
    1. Food rarely meets quality standards of taste and temperature.
    2. Food inconsistently meets quality standards of taste and temperature.
    3. Food meets quality standards of taste and temperature.
Comments: _____

2. Appearance of patient trays:
    1. Food is not garnished and is not presented attractively.
    2. Garnishes are used only intermittently.
    3. Appropriate garnishing is used consistently to enhance appetite appeal.
Comments: _____

3. Portion Control:
    1. Portion control is rarely used.
    2. Portion control is inconsistently used.
    3. Portion control is consistent (i.e., scoops, pre-portioned meats, etc.)
Comments: _____

4. Serving of Special diets:
    1. Special diets are rarely followed.
    2. Special diets are inconsistently followed.
    3. Special diets are served according to approved menu. (Scoops and scale are used.)
Comments: _____

5. Following the approved menus:
    1. Menus are rarely followed.
    2. The approved menus are followed inconsistently.
    3. The approved menus are always followed.
Comments: _____

6. Coordination with Food Service Director:
    1. Coordination with the FSD is rare.
    2. Coordination with the FSD is inconsistent.
    3. Daily coordination of menus, food preparation and operation of the kitchen is maintained with the FSD.
Comments: _____

7. Sanitation:
    1. Sanitation responsibilities are rarely fulfilled.
    2. Sanitation responsibilities are periodically fulfilled.
    3. Sanitation responsibilities are fulfilled as designated.
Comments: _____

8. Supervising Dietary Aides:
    1. Does not assist in guiding work of Dietary aides.
    2. Periodically assists in guiding work of Dietary aides.
    3. Assists with the FSD in guiding of work of Dietary aides.
Comments: _____

9. Food Handling Techniques:
    1. Proper food handling techniques are rarely practiced.
    2. Proper food handling techniques are inconsistently practiced.
    3. Proper food handling techniques are practiced consistently.
Comments: _____

10. Cooperation:
    1. Occasionally demonstrates willingness to work as a team for the good of the whole.
    2. Inconsistently demonstrates willingness to work as a team for the whole.
    3. Consistently demonstrates willingness to work as a team for the good of the whole.
Comments: _____

Total: _____
Comments: _____
Evaluated By: _____ Date: _____
Signed: _____
A minimum score of 20 must be attained.

Dietary Aide

Name: _____Date: _____

1. Appearance of patient trays:
   1. Rarely tries to make trays attractive and uniform. Rarely uses garnishes.
   2. Inconsistent attention is paid to attractiveness and uniformity of trays; garnishes are used inconsistently.
   3. Trays are assembled attractively and uniformly; garnishes are used when appropriate.
   Comments: _____

2. Accuracy of tray assembly:
   1. Often puts inappropriate beverages and dessert on tray; rarely follows diets and food preferences.
   2. Appropriate beverage and dessert are placed on tray inconsistently. Diets and food preferences are observed at times.
   3. Appropriate beverages and desserts are placed on tray; all diets and food preferences are observed.
   Comments: _____

3. Dining Room meal service:
   1. Does not make effort to see that each resident gets appropriate tray; is not courteous or attentive to patient needs.
   2. Inconsistently distributes trays accurately; is not always courteous and attentive to needs.
   3. Ensures that each resident gets the proper tray and is courteous and attentive to needs.
   Comments: _____

4. Clean-up
   1. Rarely uses appropriate dishwashing method or inspects dishes for cleanliness.
   2. Inconsistently uses appropriate dishwashing method and inspects dishes for cleanliness.
   3. Uses appropriate dishwashing method, inspects dishes to ensure cleanliness.
   Comments: _____

5. Cooperation:
   1. Occasionally demonstrates willingness to work as a team for the good of the whole.
   2. Inconsistently demonstrates willingness to work as a team for the good of the whole.
   3. Consistently demonstrates willingness to work as a team for the good of the whole.
   Comments: _____

6. Sanitation:
   1. Sanitation responsibilities are rarely fulfilled.
   2. Sanitation responsibilities are periodically fulfilled.
   3. Sanitation responsibilities are fulfilled as designated.
   Comments: _____

7. Serving of special diets:
   1. Special diets are rarely followed.
   2. Special diets are inconsistently followed.
   3. Special diets are served according to approved menus.
   Comments: _____

8. Food Handling Techniques:
   1. Proper food handling techniques are rarely practiced.
   2. Proper food handling techniques are inconsistently practiced.
   3. Proper food handling techniques are practiced consistently.
   Comments: _____

9. Cleaning of dining areas:
   1. Uses appropriate cleaning techniques rarely.
   2. Uses appropriate cleaning techniques inconsistently.
   3. Uses appropriate cleaning techniques consistently.
   Comments: _____

10. Communication and cooperation with the cooks:
    1. Communicates and cooperates with cook rarely.
    2. Communicates and cooperates with cooks inconsistently.
    3. Communicates and cooperates with cooks consistently.
    Comments: _____

Exhibit 1–2 continued

Total: _____

Comments: _____

Evaluated By: _____Date: _____

Signed: _____

Date: _____

A minimum score of 20 must be attained.

Customers: Past, Present, and Future

Other internal factors include identifying customers and services. Who are the customers and how can they have a positive or negative impact on the department? Does the department receive 80 percent of its complaints from 20 percent of its customers? Should its services then be directed to the 20 percent vocal minority or to the 80 percent silent majority?

A management brainstorming session (including key line personnel) can be of significant benefit in determining what new services and/or new customers could be developed. Some examples: community nutrition programs, breakfast programs for school lunch children, Meals on Wheels, special function catering, vending and/or midnight suppers for the evening shift, etc.

What customers really think of the department can determine its future. A meaningful questionnaire regularly distributed and reviewed can give food service direct input into serving the needs of its clientele. Planning also should consider the potential for future customers, i.e., local business persons or industries such as factories. Special boardroom luncheons for business leaders or volunteer groups or providing factor workers with another luncheon alternative could further improve the bottom line.

Management Data

Administrators and managers must make internal factors work for them. The right management information analyzed and applied properly can make the difference between success and failure for any food service department. (See Chapter 2 for a detailed cost control checklist to assist in analyzing the operation.) Does the department have a:

- budget
- cost-comparison system
- system for costing nutrition-related medical requirements
- system for determining productivity
- wage scale of competitive employers in the area
- performance evaluation system that works
- meaningful inventory cost-control system
- system to cost each food item per portion, cost per patient day of nourishments, raw food, labor supplies, nutritional supplements
- record of the number of meals actually served (including blended diet meal equivalents, double meal portions, etc.).

Is the administration aware of the vast resources that can be provided by the food service manager as head of a significant business, the second greatest cost center of the institution? The administrator needs to be aware of managers' potential and responsibility. The opportunities for their contributions to management and delivery of quality service are unlimited. If this information is available, is it properly applied and is it communicated to the appropriate persons?

Another essential management function is contingency planning. What steps have been taken to ensure continuity in services, management, and support personnel in the event of an emergency? A contingency plan must be devised to continue operations during a strike, a natural disaster, or a large number of unexpected absences. The importance of contingency planning cannot be emphasized enough. It must assume a high priority in any strategic plan.

Equipment and Facilities

Another important internal resource that can have a major impact on costs, labor, and daily operations involves the department's equipment and facilities.

Imagine a food service that could serve 4,000 meals a day with one eight-hour shift of personnel Monday through Friday and with only one four-hour shift Saturday and Sunday. This has become reality through a modified cook chill system in a 1,500 bed correctional facility. The system has saved more than $750,000 in capital expenditure and $125,540 a year in continuing labor expenditure. And what is more important, it works.

Careful analysis of the type, quantity, and location of equipment in the department by a trained professional could increase its productivity and that of personnel while reducing the cost of operation.

External and internal factors influence the future direction and success or failure of the food service department. Strategic planning is the tool to affect rather than accept the future. Managers must become leaders with foresight for their facility by taking active, if not initiating, roles in strategic planning.

The situation audit, if done carefully, should produce an accurate list of weaknesses, opportunities, threats, and strengths. This information is useful, if not essential, in revising mission statements, setting tentative long-range objectives, and devising program strategies.

The identification of major strategies must entail identification and later evaluation of the substrategies into which all strategies must be divided. In all important strategic decisions the ability to ask the right questions, the application of judgment, and the intuition of the professionals are the determinants of the decision. A number of approaches can be used in identifying program strategies. In developing a strategic profile, management should ask, "What are our customer and service strategies? Which ones must be changed? Where do we need new strategies?"

As a key component of the market-based strategic planning process, the situation audit should identify the department's potential strengths and weaknesses. With this information, the situation audit can identify potential threats, opportunities, services, and customers.

ACTION PLAN

Food service departments should develop an action plan to reflect results and projections of the situation audit. Coordinating the two will result in an organized approach to directing the department and establishing a firm foundation for growth. An effective action plan has three goals:

1. identify realistic goals that can be reached
2. involve all apppropriate levels of personnel in implementing the plan
3. provide a feedback or reporting system to evaluate the results of the action plan (budget-cost comparisons, monthly reporting meetings, patient/food service questionnaire, etc.).

Objectives need to be developed that are appropriate, measurable over time, feasible, and understandable. Broad, abstract, and often vague statements need to be redefined in more concrete terms. Only when generalities are made concrete can people in organizations understand exactly what they are trying to achieve. Reducing food service costs by 6 percent within six months is not the impossible goal that it may seem. The only danger in not reaching a goal is in not setting it. If managers do not know where they are going, they are there already. The action plan is the fun part of the strategic planning process.

The action plan outlines the direction of the department, its personnel, equipment, and facilities to achieve its projected results.

As a beginning, *each manager is challenged to reduce food service costs by 6 percent within the next fiscal year*. This is not difficult. If the principles and specifics of *Cost-Effective Quality Food Service* are applied in the department, this challenge will produce results. In fact, managers will be amazed how minimal that 6 percent goal is. It can be achieved, and has been, in many facilities, including hospitals, nursing homes, schools, and correctional facilities.

Administrators and/or managers have an outstanding opportunity to serve as leaders and pioneers by forming the facility's first cost-control team. The establishment of an organizational structure to include a management team, a health care team (potentially nutrition support team), a cost-control team, and an energy conservation team for the food service operation can propel the department to a successful future. This participative form of management will elicit the help of many others in reaching mutually beneficial departmental goals.

The action plan (Exhibits 1–3 and 1–4) forms identify only a few objectives or goals. (Exhibit 1–3 is a blank form for beginning an action plan.) The goals should be divided into two groups, administrative and nutrition services, each of which should be segmented into short-term (six months to a year) goals and long-term (two- to five-year) goals. Exhibits 1–4, 1–5, 1–6 and 1–7 list general approaches to achieve one goal, each of which is broken into numerous approaches and methods. Goals or objectives need to be broadly based, approaches and methods should be more detailed. Approaches outline steps by which to accomplish goals and methods delineate specifics of achieving the approaches.

In developing objectives, it is important that the food department recognize limitations on the scope of its service and/or customers. It cannot be all things to all people. For example, it might establish primary specialization or geographical areas of services. Customers and services outside these areas may not be appropriate.

Identifying a responsible party to accomplish each method and approach is as important a component of the action plan as is the "date to be accomplished." An action plan becomes a viable management tool only when specifics are identified to accomplish the goals.

IMPLEMENTATION

No food service department ever earned a dollar or provided a service by making plans. Only when those plans are set into motion will any services be provided or revenue realized. The goal of strategic planning is to develop superior strategies that realize results. Managers must be more than good paper strategists—they must be able to implement as well.

In transforming the action plan from paper to practice, administrators and managers must determine whether the right organizational structure is adequate and in place. If not, the necessary changes must be made.

One of the biggest problems is the tremendous resistance to change. This may result from the lack of an organizational structure for making decisions. For example, several administrative levels may have to reach a consensus before any change can occur. Although this may be the system, this takes time and patience. It is essential to be well prepared before presenting any proposal for change so administrative levels will be able to make their decisions appropriately and more quickly.

In determining the efficiency of an organizational structure, these points should be considered:

- Do decisions often have to go ''looking for a home?''
- Does the structure put the attention of key people on the right priorities—major decisions, coordination of essential activities, performance, and results?
- Are conflicts within the organization all resolved in a timely and effective manner?

The successful implementation of strategy requires certain procedures. Administrators and managers must shape the formal structure of their organization, its informal relationships, and the process of motivation and control that provides incentives and measures results to meet specific needs of their strategy.

The implementation of strategy consists first of acquiring resources (personnel, economic, physical, and organization). These then must be organized and directed within and outside the food service department. Obtaining resources includes staffing and providing development through educational opportunities and personnel policies. It also includes the functions necessary to provide the essential financial and physical elements in a timely fashion and at an appropriate cost.

A planning system should be established that (1) communicates a well-defined plan of reasonably attainable goals, (2) engages the participation and support of all levels of management and supervisory personnel, and (3) provides feedback through a reporting system for evaluation of results as a basis for appropriate subsequent action.

The most effective action plans are developed and implemented through participative management, utilizing professionals, paraprofessionals, and workers. Their input is invaluable. Plans thus developed are better because there is more diverse input and implementation becomes more effective because of this broadscale involvement. All action plans must be communicated and monitored to be effective.

Once realistic goals are set, they normally are reached. Managers' minds are just like computers: solutions evolve after diligent work on problems. It is particularly important the entire department understands the mission of where its services are designed to go. Without a strategic, formalized marketing approach, as in an organized marketing action, plans should be integrated with the general department action plans, so elements of the department will not be pulling in

Exhibit 1–3 Action plan administrative services (short term)

Facility: _____

Objectives	Approach	Methods	Responsible Party	Date to be Accomplished	Status Evaluation
1. Reduce raw food service costs by six percent by the end of the fiscal year.	1. Evaluate expenditures.	Form food service cost control team. Form purchasing coalition. Institute purchase order system. Obtain price quotations.			
	2. Identify weekly/monthly purchasing ceiling for major food items based on anticipated census.	Coordinate and monitor purchasing ceilings with amount of food pulled for preparation.			
	3. Obtain food market forecasts for menu/cost planning purposes.	Order *Food Marketing Alert.* Confer with vendors.			
	4. Evaluate receiving/storing system.	Identify employees to be trained in receiving. Initiate receiving standards. Institute receiving stamp.			
	5. Evaluate level of inventory.	Establish and monitor monthly cost ceiling of inventory.			
	6. Evaluate production system.	Establish production meetings with production personnel.			
	7. Establish quantity prepared/quantity served comparison.	Monitor use of standardized recipes. Coordinate quantity prepared with quantity served and to be purchased in future with anticipated census.			

8. Evaluate methods of portion control.	Institute and monitor use of portion control scoops, etc.
9. Evaluate use of leftovers.	Establish minimum level of leftovers anticipated per menu item and future use of item. Freeze, date and label selected leftovers for future use.
10. Evaluate energy use in food service.	Conduct energy audit. Form food sevice energy conservation team.
11. Evaluate productivity.	Analyze staffing. Establish productivity standards for each major area of food service. Determine productivity rate for the food service department.
12. Evaluate use of computers for food service department.	Evaluate performance evaluation system, job descriptions, etc. Determine need and research available software versus compatibility with appropriate hardware.

Exhibit 1–4 Action plan nutrition services goals (short term)

Facility: _____

Objectives	Approach	Methods	Responsible Party*	Date to be Accomplished	Status Evaluation
1. Improve delivery of nutrition services to patients/residents.	1. Institute specific procedure to improve quality of charting and patient visitation.	Food Service director is to visit all patients after admission. Progress notes are entered _____ or more often as needed.			
	2. Establish system to ensure dietary assessments are completed for all patients.	Develop written dietary assessments for all patients to be reviewed and evaluated by Dietary Consultant.			
	3. Establish drug/food interaction communication system among food service, pharmacy and nursing service.	Establish conferences with pharmacist. Establish monthly conferences with Director of Nursing. Draft list of potential drug/food interactions to maintain in Dietary Department and at each nursing station. Develop communication form to indicate potential drug/food interactions.			
	4. Establish system to monitor patient food intake.	Evaluate plate waste and develop form to document patient acceptance. Confer with Nursing Service to develop and initiate appetite chart.			
	5. Establish system to be certain all diets are served as prescribed.	Confer with Nursing Service to be certain all diets correspond with coordinated menus.			

Identify *ALL* patient trays with diet card indicating patient name, room number, diet and beverage preference for each meal.

Verify menus are followed and posted for reference on serving line.

Menu substitutions are properly recorded.

Portion control scoops are used.

Entrees for calorie calibrated diets are properly weighed per portion.

6. Develop system to evaluate patients receiving mechanically altered diets.

Confer with Director of Nursing and Food Service Director to evaluate need for mechanically altered diet when patient care plan is reviewed.

7. Evaluate need for patient self-help feeding program and/or devices.

Confer with Director of Nursing as to individual patient evaluation for need for self-help feeding program and/or device.

8. Determine system to evaluate resident's meal environment.

Dietary Consultant to evaluate feeder patient program to determine number of patients fed and ratio of patients to nurses.

Evaluate dispensing medications during meals.

Confer with Activity Director to provide music to be played during meals.

Evaluate use of dining room decorations.

Maximize socialization of patients.

Exhibit 1-4 continued

Objectives	Approach	Methods	Responsible Party*	Date to be Accomplished	Status Evaluation
	9. Monitor system by which bedtime feedings are dispensed and documented.	Confer with Nursing Service.			
	10. Develop list of nutritious, economical snacks to maintain at each nursing station.	Dietary Consultant to draft list for review by Nursing Service.			
2. Improve education to patients/residents and staff.	1. Initiate patient nutrition education programs.	Dietary Consultant to confer with Activities Director to conduct patient nutrition education programs on regular basis.			
	2. Initiate nutrition-related in-service education programs for Nursing Service.	Confer with Director of In-service Education to correlate programs.			
	3. Conduct food service related course for Dietary employees.	Quarterly in-service education programs will be provided to Dietary Department employees on infection control, kitchen safety and accident prevention, fire safety and disaster preparedness, and patients' rights and confidentiality. In addition, a 10 to 12 month course will be provided with monthly lessons presented to the Dietary Department employees by the _____. Courses available include the Food Service Worker, Diet Therapy, Food Preparation, Sanitation, and Energy Conservation. Certificates will be presented to each Dietary Department			

employee successfully completing each course.

4. Establish diet instruction files for the most commonly ordered clinical diets.

Food Service Director to compile files to be maintained in Dietary Department in coordination with Dietary Consultant.

Maintain accurate records of all patients receiving diet instructions.

*Determined per facility need.

Exhibit 1-5 Action plan nutrition services goals (long term)

Facility: _____

Objectives	Approach	Methods	Responsible Party*	Date to be Accomplished	Status Evaluation
1. Improve nutrition education services to the community.	1. Conduct patient/family nutrition education meetings.	Provide buffet for patients and families with program on nutrition concerns for the elderly. Publicize programs through media. Involve local professional associations to participate in program.			
	2. Develop and distribute nutrition education materials for and about nutrition for the elderly.				

*Determined per facility need.

Exhibit 1–6 Action plan administrative services (short term)

Facility: ABC Memorial Hospital

Objectives	Approach	Methods	Responsible Party	Date to be Accomplished	Status Evaluation
1. Reduce raw food service costs by six percent by the end of the fiscal year.	1. Evaluate expenditures.	Form food service cost control team.	FSD		
		Form purchasing coalition.	FSD		
		Institute purchase order system.	FSD		
		Obtain price quotations.	FSD		
	2. Identify weekly/monthly purchasing ceiling for major food items based on anticipated census.	Coordinate and monitor purchasing ceilings with amount of food pulled for preparation.	FSD		
	3. Obtain food market forecasts for menu/cost planning purposes.	Order *Food Marketing Alert.*	FSD or P.A.		
		Confer with vendors.	FSD		
	4. Evaluate receiving/storing system.	Identify employees to be trained in receiving.	FSD		
		Initiate receiving standards.	FSD		
		Institute receiving stamp.	FSD		
	5. Evaluate level of inventory.	Establish and monitor monthly cost ceiling of inventory.	FSD		
	6. Evaluate production system.	Establish production meetings with production personnel.	Head Cook & FSD		

7. Establish quantity prepared/quantity served comparison.	Monitor use of standardized recipes.	Cook
	Coordinate quantity prepared with quantity served and to be purchased in future with anticipated census.	Cook & FSD
8. Evaluate methods of portion control.	Institute and monitor use of portion control scoops, etc.	FSD & Cook
9. Evaluate use of leftovers.	Establish minimum level of leftovers anticipated per menu item and future use of item. Freeze, date and label selected leftovers for future use.	FSD & Cook
10. Evaluate energy use in food service.	Conduct energy audit.	
	Form food service energy conservation team.	
11. Evaluate productivity.	Analyze staffing.	
	Establish productivity standards for each major area of food service.	
	Determine productivity rate for the food service department.	
	Evaluate performance evaluation system, job descriptions, etc.	
12. Evaluate use of computers for food service department.	Determine need and research available software versus compatibility with appropriate hardware.	

Exhibit 1–7 Action plan administrative services goals (long term)

Facility: ABC Memorial Hospital

Objectives	Approach	Methods	Responsible Party	Date to be Accomplished	Status Evaluation
1. Evaluate preparation commissary concept for installation in the next five years.	1. Evaluate cook/chill and cook/freeze systems for applicability.	Contact representatives and conduct on-site surveys of installations.	FSD		
		Consult food service design consultant for feasibility.	FSD		
		Prepare cost/benefit proforma of preparation commissary concept.	FSD		
		Confer with administrator regarding cost/benefit proforma of preparation commissary concept to market/sell facility's food service to other entities.	FSD		

different directions. With an organized action plan and implementation program, all personnel are hitched to pull in the same direction to provide the maximum horsepower

EVALUATION

The most important part of the strategic planning process is evaluation and feedback, which is possible only after:

1. a mission statement is identified
2. the situation audit is conducted
3. the action plan is developed and implemented.

How is the effectiveness of the strategic plan determined? It is tested in actual day-to-day operations. A strategic plan is good only if it accomplishes what it set out to do. Its execution is monitored through evaluation and subsequent feedback.

At times, a review can indicate planning assumptions were wrong; an evaluation may show unexpected events interfered with accomplishing the goals. Management can use such information to take corrective action. A viable strategic plan should be flexible enough to accommodate change.

Feedback can provide answers to such questions as:

- Do changes need to be made?
- If changes are necessary, what are the priorities?
- How should such changes be made?
- What results can be expected with such changes?

Feedback and evaluation lie at the heart of control, supplying data to reflect present status and providing advanced signals of strategic planning results.

This planning should be developed on a regular, yearly basis and as formally as possible so the department will reap the results of the complete process.

During that time, past and present strategies should be analyzed to identify their limitations. The premises upon which they are based then can be reestablished so their effectiveness can be measured.

Strategic planning merely involves applying an effective structure to the process of identifying goals. The only danger in not reaching a goal is in not setting one; strategic planning provides a framework to ensure its achievement. This planning will enable food service professionals to affect rather than simply accept the department's future. Strategic planning is a bold concept that will enable food service professionals to lead their departments into a successful future.

Chapter 2

Budgets vs. Cost Comparisons

Management is defined as the process of planning, organizing, motivating, and controlling in order to formulate and achieve organizational objectives.[1] To accomplish any of these management functions, the food service director must have a scientific approach to determining departmental objectives and a method to evaluate the effectiveness of the approach. Budgets provide the basis for making plans: they organize decision making to make it more systematic, they provide standards for employees to aid in motivation, and they are an essential component of control.

To be effective and efficient managers, food service directors should learn to utilize the same management techniques as used by other industries. The introduction of the diagnosis related groups (DRGs) is stimulating the health care industry to become more efficient. These same principles apply to all areas of food service, since controlling costs is important in all types.

The 470 DRGs mandated by the federal government in October 1983 to serve as a basis of reimbursement for health care facilities have made cost control a high priority. These cost controls were certainly needed. Health care costs in 1960 were only $26.9 billion but rose to $355.5 billion by 1983. Although final figures are not yet compiled at the time of this writing, the Health Care Financing Administration projects health care costs in 1984 at $392.7 billion.[2]

Food service costs generally represent the second highest expenditure of health care facilities, topped only by nursing service. Proper management in the food area requires serious consideration and planning. However, even with inflation, experienced and knowledgeable managers can minimize any cash drain. There is yet to be a food service department that cannot reduce its costs and/or further streamline its operation. Analyzing the department and its operations is the first step toward increased productivity, reduced costs, and improved quality of service. Objectively answering the questionnaire, "Analyzing the Food Service Department" (Appendix 2–A) will provide specific insights into its operations.

Controlling food service costs has always been a challenge but never has it been more vital to the economic viability of health care institutions, so proper management requires serious consideration.

COST CONTROL CHECKLIST

The checklist in Appendix 2–A is a guide to assist in maximizing cost savings and reimbursement of food services so that constraining expenditures can become one of the facility's greatest opportunities, not its biggest problem.

After this analysis and the situation audit have been completed (as detailed in Chapter 1), it is important to set goals and develop an action plan. For virtually any facility, as noted, reducing food service costs by 6 percent in the next fiscal year can become a reality. This chapter identifies specific ways to achieve this goal.

MANAGING THE FOOD SERVICE BUDGET

The budget establishes a definite plan of action and provides specific statements on objectives, business volume, and the necessary resources, program priorities, productivity levels and costs, and accountability for performance. Budgets also can convey financial information to outside agencies such as health planning agencies, the hospital rate review entity, and third party insurance carriers.

Establishing an effective budget that becomes a viable measurement tool is the first step toward reaching the stated goal. It is amazing how few institutions actually have budgets or have communicated such important management information to their food service directors. Food professionals can be a valuable resource for administration and need to increase management's awareness of their capabilities.

As noted, many departments have functioned with an incomplete budget or with none at all. An occasional administrative review may have been conducted to determine whether food service expenditures approximated past costs or deviated too much from those norms. To complicate the situation, many directors procrastinate when it comes to creating a carefully thought out budget. The reasons for such reluctance include:

- the difficulty of predicting future prices
- the difficulty of forecasting labor cost increases
- the difficulty of estimating business volume.

THE OPERATING BUDGET

Establishing a food service operating budget is the foundation for the economic viability of any department. Consistent monitoring and analysis of the budget can save up to 6 percent in operating costs.

Budgets take numerical data from past experience to forecast future expectations. By knowing what has happened, it is easier to predict the success of plans by providing a basis of comparison. If the plans' goals have not been achieved, the budget information can be used to determine whether the problem is in the original plan or in its implementation. With these data, problems can be identified early, before they become unmanageable, thus facilitating planning future budgets.

Budgets enable managers to coordinate operations and plan for the future by providing the means to control expenditures, which can reach hundreds of thousands, if not millions, of dollars a year. The food service budget:

1. serves as the hub of the management wheel
2. reviews the total needs of the department as it relates to the whole
3. exposes hidden costs
4. reveals the financial impact of administrative policies and goals
5. provides a systematic review of the operation.

A budget traditionally is prepared several months in advance for the next fiscal year. It can be helpful to divide the year into smaller time segments, representing weeks, months, or quarters of income and expenditures. All time segments can then be compiled to yield the total budget on an annual basis. Exhibit 2–1 is a suggested work sheet format.

When figuring each monthly cost, managers should look at the variables likely to change, what the operation spent and received each month for each category last year, and what it expects to generate in revenue and to spend this year. For example, in figuring the salary expenses per month, managers should look at when each employee is due a raise and how much it is anticipated that will be. Salary expense for December should be higher than January to reflect the raises, bonuses,

---

Exhibit 2–1 Food service operating budget work sheet

| | Budget | | Actual | | Previous |
	Month	YTD	Month	YTD	YTD
No. of patient meals	———	———	———	———	———
No. of cafeteria meals	———	———	———	———	———
No. of special function meals	———	———	———	———	———
No. of ——— meals	———	———	———	———	———
Revenue	———	———	———	———	———
Raw food costs	———	———	———	———	———
——— % Eggs	———	———	———	———	———
——— % Meats	———	———	———	———	———
——— % Dairy	———	———	———	———	———
——— % Bread	———	———	———	———	———
——— % Staple	———	———	———	———	———
——— % Produce	———	———	———	———	———
——— % Supplies	———	———	———	———	———
——— % Fats & oils	———	———	———	———	———
Labor costs	———	———	———	———	———
Employer costs	———	———	———	———	———
FICA	———	———	———	———	———
Benefits	———	———	———	———	———
Contracted services	———	———	———	———	———
Supply costs	———	———	———	———	———
Equipment Replacement:	———	———	———	———	———
Major equipment	———	———	———	———	———
Minor equipment	———	———	———	———	———
Equipment depreciation:	———	———	———	———	———
Major equipment	———	———	———	———	———
Minor equipment	———	———	———	———	———
Maintenance costs	———	———	———	———	———
Utilities	———	———	———	———	———
Facility depreciation	———	———	———	———	———
Total	———	———	———	———	———

added personnel, or other changes expected for the year. If the facility uses a fiscal year different from the calendar year, the revenue and expenditures are simply allocated accordingly.

An added advantage to developing an annual budget is that it provides more control over how the service is run. An accurate budget is one of the most effective management tools at managers' disposal.

TYPES OF BUDGETS

There are many types of budgets.[3] It does not matter which is used as long as one is used. Here, briefly, are some examples of health care budgets:

- *Fixed Budget* is based on a fixed annual level of volume activity, such as the number of patient days, number of meals served, and number of visits (to nutrition clinics) to arrive at annual budget totals. Usually, these totals then are divided into 12 parts for months of the year.
- *Flexible Budget* is centered on ranges of volume activity, representing the range of business volume of service units (number of meals served) from a low point to a higher point.
- *Variable Expense Budget* is used to adjust the budget plan to the actual performance volume. It establishes a formula to generate a "controlled" budget related directly to volume of activity. It is computed by using predetermined standards or budget rates (labor and cost benefit per meal, food cost per meal, etc.), then multiplying these rates by the actual volume. This type of budget is used when certain factors are subject to change and which are beyond the control of the department. An example is the labor cost of part-time workers used strictly for catering functions. The number of workers varies with the number of catered functions, which depends on a number of factors. In this instance, multiply the labor cost by the number of workers to yield the total labor cost. Naturally, each facility must use its own data.

Part-Time Workers for Catered Functions

	No. Served	No. of Workers	No. of Hours	Cost per Hour/each	Total Cost
Continental Breakfast	100	2	2	$5	$20
Coffee	50	2	3	5	30
Cold Buffet	50	2	4	5	40
Cold Buffet	51–125	2	4	5	
		1*	4	8.50	74
Hot Buffet	50	2	4	5	
		1*	5	8.50	82.50
Hot Buffet	51–125	4	4	5	
		2*	5	8.50	165
Seated Function	50	4	4	5	
		1*	6	8.50	131
Seated Function	51–125	5	5	5	
		2*	5	8.50	
		1**	8	12.50	310

*Skilled worker for Ass't Supervisory level personnel.
**Supervisory level personnel.

- *Appropriations Budget* is used most commonly by government facilities, with the amount fixed by some external body through appropriation of funds after review of an expense estimate on an almost line-by-line basis.
- *Rolling or Moving Budget* is derived from expanding any of the preceding approaches. The most recent month or quarter is deleted and a new projection is added for a corresponding month or quarter, so that the budget continually projects a fixed period of time, usually a minimum of a year.
- *Program Budget* is used to determine the cost per benefit of a specific project or program. This concept should never be considered a replacement for the overall budget system. It restructures the budget elements by accumulating costs by categories.
- *Zero-Based Budget* is based on a decision-making process that requires the manager to justify the entire budget request in detail and reevaluate all programs and expenditures every year, as though starting from scratch—from zero.

A PRACTICAL FOOD SERVICE BUDGET

In establishing an effective budget, it is important to institute a budget in which everything can be cost/benefit justified. The projection should be based on the situation audit already conducted. The situation audit can provide significant insight into projections and increases the opportunity for accuracy. From this point, select the type of budget that best suits the facility's, department's, or program's needs. Do not just take last year's budget and add a factor for inflation to determine next year's fiscal needs.

After an annual budget has been set, it is subdivided into quarters, months, weeks, and potentially even days, depending upon the item involved (i.e., raw food, labor, etc.). The form in Exhibit 2–1 reflects an overview of the food service department, including not only revenue but also raw food, labor, and supply costs as well as equipment replacement and depreciation, maintenance, utilities, and depreciation of the facility. It also indicates the projected percentage of food costs by category.

Exhibit 2–2 itemizes anticipated monthly revenue. Exhibit 2–3 reflects the approximate percentage of food categories, based on a national average. These percentages may vary, as dictated by the menus, but they can be a good beginning point. The percentages serve only as an indication of the cost distribution of food-stuffs as dictated by menu and purchasing and generally are most useful in pinpointing areas out of control.

The best indicator is an effective inventory cost control system (see Chapter 4 for detailed discussion). If monthly inventories are not taken, the year-to-date financial data will be helpful in evaluating performance, although it often is too late at that point. Information needs to be available on a timely basis to serve as an effective management tool.

For years, raw food was the highest single factor in food service costs, but with the ever-escalating minimum wage, labor costs have moved into undisputed first place, with raw food and supplies second and third, respectively.

Employee Input and the Team Approach

In developing a budget, a coordinated team approach is important in encouraging effective, economic management. After an initial budget has been developed, all workers should be included in reviewing it and its potential ramifications. The

Exhibit 2–2 Budget work sheet: anticipated budget by month

	Jan.	Feb.	Mar.	Apr.	May	June	July	Aug.	Sept.	Oct.	Nov.	Dec.	Year Total
Revenue													
Raw food costs													
Eggs													
Dairy													
Meat/poultry													
Produce													
Bakery													
Staples													
Fats/oils													
Dessert													
Nourishments													
Other													
Labor costs													
Payroll													
FICA													
Benefits													
Equipment replacement													
Major equipment													
Minor equipment													
Equipment maintenance													
Contracted services													
Supply costs													
Chemicals													
Other													
Utensil replacement costs													
Utilities													
Other (specify)													

Exhibit 2–3 Raw food cost by category
(Actual cost and percent of total)

	Actual		Budget		Year-to-date	
Month of _____	*Cost ($)*	*% of total*	*Cost ($)*	*% of total*	*Cost ($)*	*% of total*
Eggs	_____	_____	_____	_____	_____	_____
Dairy	_____	_____	_____	_____	_____	_____
Meat/poultry	_____	_____	_____	_____	_____	_____
Produce	_____	_____	_____	_____	_____	_____
Bakery	_____	_____	_____	_____	_____	_____
Staples	_____	_____	_____	_____	_____	_____
Fats/oils	_____	_____	_____	_____	_____	_____
Dessert	_____	_____	_____	_____	_____	_____
Nourishments	_____	_____	_____	_____	_____	_____
Other (supply)	_____	_____	_____	_____	_____	_____
_____	_____	_____	_____	_____	_____	_____
_____	_____	_____	_____	_____	_____	_____
_____	_____	_____	_____	_____	_____	_____
Total cost	$_____		$_____		$_____	
Total budget	$_____ (mo)				$_____ (year)	
Difference						
(+ or −)	$_____				$_____	
% difference						
(+ or −)	_____%				_____%	

importance each individual plays in achieving budgetary goals should be emphasized. Communication is vital. This is an additional opportunity for management to solicit employees as allies, reinforcing a good labor relations program. When employees see how their job performance directly affects the overall cost of operation, they make a greater effort to be efficient. Even dishwashers can have an impact on the amount of hot water, detergent, labor cost, chemical sanitizers, etc. used. If the salad chef is made aware of the amount of money used to purchase fresh ingredients, he or she would probably take greater care not to waste supplies.

Employees who offer good ideas should be rewarded. There are a variety of incentive opportunities: additional time off, free meals, name in the local paper or the facility's paper, gift of a plant or other similar items. The budget should become a management tool, not a paper albatross.

The budget also can serve as a stimulus for increased communication among the departments. For health care facilities, discussing the economic impact of between-meal nourishments in relation to quality patient care can help eliminate unnecessary waste of food and, therefore, money. (The cost of nutrition-related medical requirements is discussed later in this section.)

For all types of institutions providing food service, communication among support departments—maintenance, administration, and accounting—must be initiated before drafting an effective food service operating budget. The increased communication provided by the team approach can result in the ultimate goal of cost effective, yet concerned, quality food service. Without proper communication and support from interrelated departments, the budget can become a meaningless burden.

Budget Results

Establishing a carefully considered food service budget can net many positive results. Since the budget automatically sets goals, it offers incentive and challenge to co-workers, encouraging them to join in the team effort. By communicating employees' role in management goals through a detailed review of the budget, they realize their work is important in achieving these objectives. By minimizing waste—including portion control and leftover use—by reducing breakage, and by cleaning equipment properly, considerable savings can be realized.

Employees should understand that as they share the department's responsibilities, they also will share in the benefits. Managers should confer with administration to assure that at least some of the projected savings realized by a departmentwide teamwork effort will be returned to food service. These funds could be used for additional labor-saving equipment, an employee party, and/or wage incentives. The budget is not meant to strangle spending but should be viewed as a flexible management tool, a control device.

Budget-Cost Comparison

Initiating an operating budget is an excellent move but it is far more effective when coupled with a budget-cost comparison. The budget-cost comparison should be reviewed monthly and at the end of each fiscal year. Differences between the budget and actual spending should be discussed with personnel. Budgets enable the actual operation to be compared with the projected or desired results. Budget-cost comparisons provide the means for control and analysis of current performance. Previous reports must be analyzed in preparing future budgets, to correct any problematic situations that may have arisen and to assure they are not perpetuated. (See Budget-Cost Comparison in Exhibit 2–4).

Exhibit 2–4 Food service budget-cost comparison

Item	Budget	Actual	Differential
Revenue	_____	_____	_____
Raw food cost	_____/Month		
____ % Eggs	_____	____%	
____ % Meats	_____	____%	
____ % Staples	_____	____%	
____ % Dairy	_____	____%	
____ % Produce	_____	____%	
____ % Bread	_____	____%	
____ % Nonfood	_____	____%	
Labor costs	_____/Month	_____	_____
Labor hrs/Wk 1	_____	_____	_____
Labor hrs/Wk 2	_____	_____	_____
Labor hrs/Wk 3	_____	_____	_____
Labor hrs/Wk 4	_____	_____	_____
Labor hrs/Wk 5	_____	_____	_____
Supply costs	_____	_____	_____

Exhibit 2-5 Invoice summary (blanks)

Monthly Budget Estimate:	Meats	Staples	Dairy	Produce	Bread	Supplies	Eggs		
Date	Inv. Total	Inv. Total	Inv. Total	Inv. Total	Inv. Total	Inv. Total	Inv. Total	Inv. Total	Inv. Total

Exhibit 2–6 Invoice summary (partially filled in)

Monthly Budget Estimate:	Meats	Staples	Dairy	Produce	Bread	Supplies	Eggs				
Date	Inv. Total	Inv. Total	Inv. Total	Inv. Total	Inv. Total	Inv. Total	Inv. Total	Inv. Total	Inv. Total	Inv. Total	Inv. Total
Week 1—Total spent											
Difference											
Week 2—Total spent											
Difference											
Week 3—Total spent											
Difference											
Week 4—Total spent											
Difference											

It is important to maintain budget-cost comparison data but it is the interpretation of these data that is most significant. An analysis gives employees a direct way to measure their contribution toward the goals, providing an additional incentive by emphasizing the importance of their role in the management and economic well being of their department.

Budgets are indicators of overall projected departmental operation but can be invaluable when applied to specific areas as well. Examples include controlling labor costs by setting a maximum number of labor-hours per day and/or evaluating expenditures in terms of labor-minutes per meal. Establishing a budget for nonproductive labor costs (i.e., holidays, sick leave, vacations, etc.) is equally important. Nonproductive labor costs also represent a very real expense. (Productive and nonproductive labor costs are explained in detail in Chapter 8.) Generally full-time positions must be multiplied by .55 to determine the number of relief personnel needed because of holidays, sick leave, vacation, etc.

Using the budget-cost comparison form (Exhibits 2–1 and 2–3, earlier) can save thousands of dollars a year and even a month. A private psychiatric facility saved more than $4,000 a month by instituting a cost-comparison system that included such a form (Exhibit 2–4) and an invoice summary form (Exhibit 2–5 has blanks, Exhibit 2–6 is partially filled in).

In using the invoice summary, the projected daily or weekly budget for each of the food categories is placed on the line of each respective column, and the daily invoices are recorded as issued or received. The food service manager then can determine through a continuing tallying procedure how the actual expenditures compare with the projected budget.

For example, if the budget for meats is $500 and the expenditures are $700 the first week, then only $300 will be available for the following week. By the same token, if only $400 is spent on meats with that same $500 budget, $600 will be available for the next week, if required. Breaking down food invoices into specific areas enables the manager to determine almost instantly where costs could increase. Vendors that sell a variety of food categories should be requested to group the items on their invoices to facilitate this process.

Regular cost comparisons of the budget are valuable tools in controlling the bottom line of the food service operation.

NOTES

1. Michael H. Mescon, Michael Albert, and Franklin Khedouri, *Management, Individual and Organizational Effectiveness* (New York: Harper & Row, Publishers, 1981), 21.

2. Health Care Financing Administration. *Health, United States, 1983* (Washington, D.C.: U.S. Government Printing Office, 1983).

3. Faisal Kaud, "Budgets That Work," *Food Management* (February 1980):30–39.

REFERENCES

Hitchcock, Mary J. *Foodservice Systems Administration*. New York: Macmillan Publishing Co., Inc., 1980.

Kaud, Faisal. "Budgets that Work." *Food Management* (February 1980):39ff.

Osgood, William R. *Basics of Successful Business Planning*. New York: Amacom, 1980, 111–170.

Phyrr, P.A. *Zero-Based Budgeting*. New York: John Wiley & Sons, Inc., 1973.

Steiner, George A. *Strategic Planning*. New York: The Free Press, 1979.

Weiss, Steven M. "Food Buying Trends." *Institutions* (September 15, 1980):131.

Appendix 2-A

Analyzing the Food Service Department

Controlling Food Service Costs

	Yes/No	Comments
1. Are food service cost components, including raw food, labor, and supplies, budgeted and compared with actual costs on a monthly basis?	_____	_____
2. Are these costs examined in terms of cost per meal and/or cost per patient day?	_____	_____
3. Has an inventory cost control system been initiated, monitored, and maintained?	_____	_____
4. Is a computer utilized to identify and monitor cost management data in the food service operation?	_____	_____
5. Are revenues generated by the food service reflected in the cost per patient meal or per patient day?	_____	_____
6. Are periodic conferences held with administration and other pertinent departments to compare the actual food service expenditures with its budget?	_____	_____
7. Has a cost control team for the department been formed?	_____	_____

Menu Planning

	Yes/No	Comments
1. Is there a seasonal menu cycle?	_____	_____
2. Is a selective menu essential to maintaining or improving current patient census?	_____	_____
3. Is a selective menu cycle economically feasible?	_____	_____
4. Are therapeutic diets coordinated specifically with the general diet menu to minimize additional preparation?	_____	_____
5. Are menus planned to maximize labor and time efficiency?	_____	_____

Purchasing and Receiving

Yes/No   *Comments*

1. Are firm price quotes obtained on all food purchases? _____ _____
2. Are these prices obtained through a competitive mechanism such as a cooperative buying service? _____ _____
3. Have monthly purchasing ceilings been established for specific food items such as milk, eggs, and bread? _____ _____
4. Are meat and produce weighed to compare the invoiced quantity with the ordered quantity? _____ _____
5. Are invoiced prices checked for agreement with quoted prices? _____ _____

Food Preparation and Service

Yes/No   *Comments*

1. Is portion control consistent and effective? _____ _____
2. Are specific systems monitoring the quantity of food prepared established? (For example, how many cans of vegetables are used for how many meals served?) _____ _____
3. Are leftovers utilized effectively? _____ _____
4. Has the actual cost of nutrition-related medical requirements (including therapeutic diets, mechanically altered diets, evening nourishments, and nutritional supplementation) been determined? _____ _____
5. Are records of the cost of nutrition-related medical requirements kept, monitored, and/or analyzed? _____ _____
6. Is the necessity for all therapeutic and mechanically altered diets evaluated periodically? _____ _____
7. Are ancillary food services (such as supplementary nourishments, special catering functions, and activities) specifically cost detailed? _____ _____
8. Has policy been set for gross cafeteria receipts to reflect accurately the number of meals served? _____ _____
9. Do records reflect the actual cost of meals served in patient food service (hospital and/or hospital-based skilled nursing facility) compared with the cafeteria? _____ _____

Labor Efficiency

Yes/No   *Comments*

1. Have the number of labor-minutes per meal or meals per labor-hour been determined? _____ _____
2. Has the rate of employee turnover been determined? _____ _____

41

	Yes/No	*Comments*
3. Is the employee turnover rate periodically determined and evaluated?	_____	_____
4. Are job descriptions developed and reviewed at least annually with the persons involved?	_____	_____
5. Are detailed duty schedules drafted and reviewed at least quarterly with employees?	_____	_____
6. Are records kept of duties performed for at least two weeks each quarter?	_____	_____
7. Has a rate of productivity been determined for the food service?	_____	_____
8. Is the daily work distribution reviewed periodically to maximize labor efficiency?	_____	_____
9. Are employee and guest meals evaluated periodically for cost effectiveness?	_____	_____

Energy Efficiency

	Yes/No	*Comments*
1. Has an energy management team been formed in the facility?	_____	_____
2. Has an energy audit been conducted of the facility or of the food service?	_____	_____
3. Is energy-efficient equipment planned into future equipment replacement budgets?	_____	_____
4. Has each department been trained in methods of energy conservation?	_____	_____
5. Has an effective preventive maintenance program been established?	_____	_____

Administrative Factors

	Yes/No	*Comments*
1. Are periodic conferences held with administration to review service and cost factors of the department?	_____	_____
2. Are periodic staff meetings conducted with food service personnel to receive their input and communicate progress of the department?	_____	_____
3. Are interdepartmental conferences held to review service and areas of cost control?	_____	_____

42

Chapter 3

Cost Realities: Menus and Nutrition-Related Medical Requirements

The development of appetizing, nutritious, economically feasible menus must be coordinated with the establishment of the financial structure of the food service department.

"The menu is the key to using all resources in a food service as it affects the amount and type of space and equipment needed, the number and type of personnel, food and other materials, and ultimately sales and costs of production and service."[1] The menu determines all aspects of operation and affects the success or failure of the department.

MENU STRATEGY

Menu needs differ with the type of institution served. Health care facilities have very specific diet requirements, while prisons and schools must place more emphasis on food preferences of the specific population and use of government surplus items. The menu planning needs of hospitals, nursing homes, prisons, and schools, colleges, and universities are discussed individually.

Hospitals

In planning hospital menus, consideration must be given to the clinical diets, other hospitals in the area and what they offer, the type of patient served, the budget, equipment available, and skill of the staff. Hospital food costs vary greatly depending on whether the facility uses the food service department as a drawing card to attract patients (as opposed to alternative hospitals available) or provides the basic nutritional requirements without frills. Major metropolitan area hospitals may find it necessary to compete with others for the patient population. On the other hand, regional or inner-city hospitals may put less emphasis on the food served, encouraging the food service director to be creative within extreme budget limitations.

Other planning considerations include selective vs. nonselective menus, coordination of diets, and the cost of nutrition-related medical requirements.

Menu Trends in Hospitals

Current cost effective menu trends in hospitals include:

- reducing the number of selective printed diets to only three or four, with less common ones being available on a nonselective basis
- writing menus that meet clinical diet parameters so that items need be prepared in no more than two ways
- offering a low-calorie option on the regular diet menu
- using a cycle menu at lunch and dinner with a noncyclical breakfast
- placing more expensive items on weekends when census is lower
- placing popular, low-cost items next to higher cost items
- using of restaurant-style menus (one-day cycle), offering "distinctive dining," and charging a premium price for items selected from this special menu.

Nursing Home and Extended-Care Facilities

Nursing homes and extended-care facilities encounter many of the same challenges found in hospital menu planning. In addition to the medical requirements and need for specialized diets, nursing homes also must consider the generally reduced appetite and chewing ability of their residents. Many extended care facilities must work closely with persons who have eating handicaps. Consequently, attention must be given to the types and consistency of foods served.

All of the considerations in hospital menu planning should be reviewed when planning for either of these types of facilities. The same problems often occur—both external and medical factors. In areas where nursing homes are plentiful and a private pay population is served, more sophisticated menus can and must be developed.

Many nursing homes are moving toward a larger noon meal, with soup and sandwiches in the evening as many residents prefer this pattern since they do not want to eat heavily before going to bed. In a 1985 symposium sponsored by the National Citizens' Coalition for Nursing Home Reform, residents stated that they wanted well-prepared, tasty foods made from high quality ingredients. Resident menu planning committees can aid greatly in providing meals well accepted by the whole facility, thereby decreasing waste and increasing menu acceptance.

Another variable in planning nursing home menus is the ability of the elderly population to chew and swallow. Although soft foods are not necessary for every resident, certain foods should be avoided unless special arrangements are made to assist patients in consuming them. For example, a whole apple may be difficult for some residents to bite into, although apple slices generally are well accepted.

Similarly, in the extended-care facility, the residents' eating ability must be considered carefully. If they are relearning to feed themselves (for example, after a stroke), then puddings, toast rather than bread, and foods that already are cut into small bites may be more acceptable.

Managers must ascertain the needs of the population, and consult with a dietitian, in order to ensure the residents' needs are being met well.

High-fiber diets are recommended for many elderly patients who have problems with elimination. Including fresh fruits and vegetables and whole-grain items will help alleviate this concern. Many nursing homes now include bran in at least one menu item per day. Medication costs are reduced and the residents enjoy their meals more because they feel better.

Menu Trends in Nursing Homes

Current cost effective trends in nursing homes and extended-care facilities include:

- providing selective menus for private pay facilities
- including resident input into menus to increase acceptance and reduce waste
- centering activities on food, such as homemade ice cream socials, barbecues, menu contests, and preparing menus of monthly winners for all residents and announcing "Tonight is Ms. Someone's winning menu"
- liberalizing clinical diets
- serving wine with meals (if sanctioned by the physician)
- providing chopped or ground foods in lieu of purees for residents who are able to accept consistency (this reduces costs and increases palatability as well as residents' acceptance of the food)
- garnishing to enhance residents' enjoyment of the food and to minimize waste.

Residents' needs in nursing homes and extended-care facilities are very specific. Menu planning must be responsive to their nutritional, social, physical, and cost requirements.

Correctional Institutions

Correctional food service faces unique challenges such as security, sabotage, special religious group demands, and food used as barter.

Limiting factors affecting menus in correctional institutions are the budget, the cooks' ability, the shortage of civilian supervisors, and the lack of operating equipment, just to mention a few. Food in a prison population should be healthy—and inmates have equally healthy appetites. Food is the highlight of the day. It must be abundant, with variety and as well prepared as circumstances permit. Some institutions also must provide clinical diets—diabetic, low sodium, and bland.

Although selective menus usually are not provided in prisons, the menu cycles must be creative in order not to provide the same foods week in and week out, which can lead to disgruntled inmates. Since the prison population is exposed to the results of the kitchen on a relatively long-term basis, the menu cycle should be longer than that required for hospitals, where most patients have short stays. Taste fatigue can result in loss of appetite and dissatisfaction with the food, which can have disastrous results in a prison setting.

Menu Trends in Corrections

Current cost effective trends in correctional institutions include:

- providing more nutritious menus and greater variety of food (milk is now offered twice a day in many institutions and fresh or canned fruit daily)

- identifying items prepared with pork products on the menu as well as on the serving line to accommodate specific religious groups
- developing systems providing for equity in portioning so food is used less as a punishment or a reward as between inmates serving on the line and those receiving trays
- providing the same food to all types of inmates, including those in administrative segregation or solitary confinement
- using salad bars as a reward for good behavior
- using the preparation commissary concept in food production in which pre-prepared food is either purchased from a civilian commissary or a correctional facility and served to satellite correctional units.

Schools

The types of menu cycle required in a school depends on the budget, the age of the students, the type of school (public, private, parochial), type(s) of meal(s) provided (lunch and/or breakfast), and equipment available.

Utilizing large quantities of government surplus food items necessitates creativity in menu planning. Serving acceptable foods that provide adequate nutrition can be challenging. Although students may accept hamburgers, French fries, and pizza every day, the school food service department must be clever if it is to provide foods that meet minimum nutritional standards. Some schools are using a selective system whereby students may choose between a hot meal or a cold (nutritionally equal) meal. For example, some offer salad carts and sandwich lines. When students are allowed to select their own meals, plate waste is reduced dramatically.

The age of the students served also must be considered in menu planning. Younger children (6–12) prefer familiar foods, and creativity can be confusing to them. Older students (high school or college) may respond to innovation, although the old standbys still win good acceptance. Even with the use of the same foods on a continuing basis, menus should be on a varied cycle so meals will not become classified with days (i.e., every Tuesday, hot dogs).

Whether the menus are planned on a systemwide basis, or within the individual school, the students' needs and tastes must be a primary consideration. Student committees that work closely with the food service director in planning meals are being used in many schools to provide user input. Allowing students to request foods improves acceptance of the meals and also teaches them about nutrition and budgets.

Menu Trends in Schools

Current cost-effective trends in schools include:

- offering-vs.-serving system to minimize plate waste and improve nutrition
- involving student committees in working with the food service manager to include student food preferences
- increasing variety through greater selection of menu items (hot or cold, including soup and sandwich, salad bar)
- providing ethnic meals such as Tex-Mex, pizza, oriental, soul foods, etc.
- offering vegetarian meals.

46

Josephine Martin, past president of the American School Food Service Association, in a phone interview, says that school food service tends to lag about ten years behind current population trends of more nutritious foods. She believes adult restaurant customers are demanding more nutritious menus because of what they learned from school food service as children. Today's children, however, as adults, will reflect the opposite trend since schools are now leaning more toward fast foods.

Colleges and Universities

When the college or university provides on-campus food service three meals a day, seven days a week, taste fatigue can become a main concern so change must become the constant. In order to entice students into the school's eating facilities, colleges and universities are providing settings which rival the upbeat, trendy restaurants so popular with this age group. Along with the change in decor, food quality is also being upgraded to meet local restaurant standards. Marketing and nutrition education is provided through calorie counts on menus, lunch and learn seminars, basket lunches to take to the park, etc., to make eating in the school setting more enjoyable for the student while contributing to his or her overall well-being.

Menu Trends in Colleges/Universities

Current cost effective trends in colleges and universities include:

- offering greater variety in food settings and types of items (including fast food, snack shops, delis, restaurants, and cafeterias)
- using theme meals to add variety
- increasing student participation in menu development
- providing low-calorie items and health foods
- offering cereal bars three times a day—these are low cost, nutritious, and popular with students
- presenting fresh fruit at each meal
- establishing an ice cream bar
- creating a small, tablecloth restaurant for dinner meals.

CYCLE MENUS

Menu planning is always a challenge—at home and in restaurants as well as in hospitals, nursing homes, prisons, schools, colleges, and universities. The use of a cycle menu is the easiest method of providing interesting, well-accepted meals at minimum cost. Cycle menus are defined as carefully planned menus that are rotated according to a definite pattern. Cyclical menus offer numerous advantages, such as:

- minimizing menu planning time
- coordinating preparation
- reducing repetition of menu items
- promoting standardization of preparation procedures
- increasing labor efficiency through improved coordination and organization planned into the menus

- simplifying purchasing
- taking advantage of purchasing seasonal variation of foods
- improving inventory control and cost control
- maximizing utilization of equipment, potentially resulting in reduction of energy expenditures.

Disadvantages arise if the menu cycle is too short and seasonal variation in food availability is not considered. Drafting a good seasonal menu cycle initially can be time consuming yet it will save substantial time since it eliminates the need for planning menus weekly.

Seasonal menu cycles can vary from two to half a dozen or more weeks. However, experience indicates the maximum amount of variety with the minimum amount of repetition occurs in a three-week seasonal cycle. Some institutions prefer four three-week cycles a year while others opt for two three-week cycles (fall/winter, spring/summer). Each menu cycle is repeated (or re-cycled) a sufficient number of times to accommodate the designated "season" for the respective menu cycle.

Another variation involves a specified number of days—18 or 16 in a cycle—any number that is not an increment of seven. This system provides an ingenious way to rotate continuous menu items so they rarely appear on the same day of the week.

The primary difficulty with this system involves Sunday menus. Most institutions prefer to serve "special" food items such as roast beef, ham, or chicken in lieu of meatloaf, chicken casseroles, hot dogs, or other items considered less special. If meatloaf appears on the numbered day cycle for Sunday, supervisors and cooks wishing to please their patients usually will serve a more "Sunday" type of meal instead. Therefore, after they change the Sunday meatloaf to fried chicken, the Monday shift may meet a new challenge if chicken appears on that day's menu as well. Once the game of menu checkers begins, it becomes increasingly complicated, with the patron the ultimate loser. Obviously, such challenges are even more complicated with a selected menu, providing an even greater variety of opportunity for repetition.

SELECTIVE VS. NONSELECTIVE MENUS

One type of menu that continues to be popular is providing patients with a choice of foods. While this may be admirable, it also becomes a challenge to management and to the budget. Whenever a "choice must be made between selective and nonselective menus, carefully appraise the benefits to be gained and compare them with the potential costs to be incurred. This evaluation will vary for each hospital. In some cases it may prove to be wise to retain nonselective menus."[2] The advantages of selective and nonselective menus are reviewed next.

Selective

- Patient satisfaction can be improved since there is a positive psychological impact when the individual has an active role in choosing meals.
- Menu variety can be increased, which can minimize special food orders.
- Special diet orders by physicians can be limited because they can be provided only as a therapeutic measure rather than to cater to a specific patient.

- Knowledge of users' favorite menu items can be improved and used in menu planning. Patient relations can be fostered if the dietitian or food service director offers written guidance in marking the daily menu selection, minimizing confusion and assuring the patient receives exactly what has been selected for each respective meal.
- Food waste can be reduced if menus are tallied carefully and if leftovers can be used on the cafeteria line.
- Patients will show a tendency to eat more of the foods they choose.
- Patient complaints can be reduced.
- Employees can benefit from the greater variety of food available, which can help the facility by promoting better attitudes about their work environment.

Nonselective

- Food and labor costs can be reduced at least 15 percent.
- The demand for skill and quantity of labor can be decreased because of the reduction in number and types of foods to be prepared.
- Time required for meal preparation and service can be reduced, which generally gets the food to the patient at a more optimum temperature.
- Storage and preparation areas required can be reduced.
- Quantity and types of equipment required can be minimized.
- Quantity of supervision required can be decreased.
- Food waste can be minimized since this type of menu makes possible closer control on all aspects of food service.
- Additional costs of menus (paper, typing, printing, staff to distribute and tally) are avoided.
- Meal serving takes less time and perhaps fewer persons.
- Less room is needed for equipment, food inventory, and preparation.
- Fewer labor-hours are required to prepare, fill, and deliver the meals.
- Control over the nutritional needs of patients is improved.
- Menus are less complicated to plan, write, and/or change.

Many of the advantages inherent in the selective menu are labor-intensive and increase food service costs. However, special facility circumstances may dictate and justify the need for such an increased expenditure.

A new approach to health care food service now has been proposed: "kind of a 'medical hotel'." As health costs escalate, patients feel they deserve better care, and not necessarily medically. Santos and Cutlar sum up the concept this way: "Meals must be ordered from a limited menu, 24 hours in advance—something even a healthy person might be reluctant to do. There is no food service on demand: everybody must eat at the same time."[3] They explain that patients not in intensive care or under restrictive diets might appreciate the option to pay for better meals if only they were available. This could thus create a new revenue-generating possibility. (Chapter 5, on cost management, reviews specific ideas on converting food service from a cost center into a revenue center.)

On the other hand, some facilities have been very successful with nonselective menus. Crawford Long Hospital, a major teaching hospital in the Southeast went from selective to nonselective menus to improve public relations. The chief dietitian said patients either changed their minds or did not remember selecting menu items they received. Since the hospital switched to nonselective menus (substitutions are provided on specific request), there have been few patient complaints. The nonselective menu has been a positive public relations tool for this facility.

The facility changed from a selective to a nonselective menu while redesigning its food service. When reviewing the results, the 520-bed hospital found a saving of $100,000 to $150,000, divided evenly between food costs and labor. There were few, if any, complaints from patients about their lack of choice, even though today most expect a selective menu. These patients rated the dietary department at 85 percent to 90 percent: "good to excellent."

A hospital and hospital-based skilled nursing facility might be interested in using menus to widen the cost differential between the two to maximize reimbursement. The institution could provide a selective menu (possibly even restaurant style, with or without gourmet items) for the hospital patients and a nonselective menu for patients in the skilled nursing facility. However, careful documentation of all cost components would need to be maintained. The cost allocations could be subject to negotiation and additional ones still could be incurred because of the selective menu. Selective menus generally cost 15 percent more to provide than do nonselective ones.

Restaurant-Style Menu

A current trend in hospitals is the use of restaurant-style menus in lieu of selective or nonselective ones. Production costs can be monitored and controlled, needs can be standardized, and public relations are improved. The restaurant-style menu is a combination of the best attributes of the selective and nonselective systems. Careful planning of menu items and format will result in an appetizing, cost effective patient relations tool.

Twelve hospitals throughout the country were surveyed in 1984 by the author on menus, cost effectiveness, special food requests, gourmet meal programs, and computerization of their food services. Results of facilities surveyed that use a restaurant-style menu are presented in Table 3–1.

Restaurant-style menus, like selective menus, can be cost effective or ineffective depending on management and on production systems established (see Appendix E). Facilities such as Cedar-Sinai in Los Angeles, which uses a freeze/cook production system, emphasize the cost effectiveness of their method. Items are prepared and frozen, then cooked on request. A short-order approach to production has been effective in controlling costs. Any unused portions are served in the cafeteria or in the vending program the same day, so food waste is virtually eliminated.

Vanderbilt University Hospital in Nashville praises its restaurant-style menus for assuring quality and minimizing waste. Vanderbilt uses primarily convenience foods to simplify production, maintain quality, and minimize labor and energy.

Massachusetts Eye and Ear Hospital in Boston, St. Elizabeth Community Hospital in Lincoln, Neb., and Women's and Infants' Hospital in Providence prepare their restaurant-style menus from scratch. They control costs by carefully planning production, including a variety of items to minimize special requests, and by utilizing unused portions so potential waste is reduced.

Alliance City Hospital in Ohio used a restaurant-style menu for only eight months, then returned to a two-week selective menu. It felt the restaurant-style

Table 3-1 Survey of hospitals using restaurant-style menus

	Massachusetts Eye & Ear Hospital Boston	Cedar-Sinai Hospital Los Angeles	St. Elizabeth Community Hospital Lincoln, Neb.	Vanderbilt Hospital Nashville	Women's & Infants' Hospital Providence	Alliance City Hospital Ohio
Size of facility	180 beds; 95% occup.; 25% modified diets	1,100 beds; 80% occup.; 50% modified diets	208 beds; 75% occup.; 40% modified diets	600 beds; 85% occup.; 80% modified diets	163 beds; 72% occup.; 5% modified diets, 15% liquid	160 beds; 55% occup.; 33% modified diets
Type of menu & information	Restaurant-style menu for regular and therapeutic diets used since 1966.	Restaurant-style menu for regular and therapeutic diets used since 1969.	Restaurant-style menu for regular diet used since 1972.	Restaurant-style menu for regular therapeutic diets used since 1973.	Restaurant-style menu for regular and therapeutic diets used since 1980.	Restaurant-style menus for regular and therapeutic diets used for 8 months.
	Regular menus used for therapeutic diet menus.	Therapeutic diet menus maintained for 14 different diets. Breakfast rotated on seven-day cycle. Lunch & dinner alternate every three days.	Initiated for therap. diet patients for four diets.	Restaurant-style menus developed for nine therapeutic diets.	Restaurant-style menus developed for five therapeutic diets.	Restaurant-style menus developed for six therapeutic diets.
	Lunch & dinner items separated on menu. Six standard items and one "special" for each meal. No numbers are used. Items are circled by patients to minimize confusion.	Lunch & dinner menus combined with approx. 18 entrees offered plus daily special. Menu order form is circled. Only items requested are pulled; unused portions are offered on cafeteria line and in vending.	Lunch & dinner menus combined. Patients indicate numbers of items on menu order form.	Lunch & dinner menus separated. Eight entrees are offered per meal. Menu order form is circled.	Lunch & dinner menus combined, with 26 entrees plus one chef's choice item that is on seven-day cycle.	Lunch & dinner menus combined with 36 entrees. Breakfast selection also offered in same menu. No longer used—2 week cycle menu in effect.
Production system	Conventional, from scratch	Freeze/cook	Conventional, from scratch	Convenience foods	Conventional, from scratch	Cook/freeze

Table 3–1 continued

	Massachusetts Eyes & Ear Hospital Boston	Cedar-Sinai Hospital Los Angeles	St. Elizabeth Community Hospital Lincoln, Neb.	Vanderbilt Hospital Nashville	Women's & Infants' Hospital Providence	Alliance City Hospital Ohio
Special Food Requests	Cafeteria menu different from patient menu.	Cafeteria menu different from patient menu.	Cafeteria menu different from patient menu.	Cafeteria menu different from patient menu.	Cafeteria menu different from patient menu.	Few requests due to large selection available.
Gourmet meal program	No gourmet meal program.	Gourmet meal program "Distinctive Dining" offered at $12 extra per day for three meals.	No gourmet meal program now, but wine is offered as a regular part of meal.	Gourmet meal program "Distinctive Dining" for $10 per meal. Three gourmet entrees (beef, chicken, fish) offered.	Gourmet meal program offered. Four choices at $8 per meal sold in gift shop.	No gourmet meal program.
The stork club	Meals for parents of newborns not offered as there is no obstetrics department.	Meals for parents of newborns not offered.	Stork Club meal of prime rib is provided to parents of newborns at no additional charge.	"Distinctive Dining" menu is available for new parents.	Stork Club is offered on same basis as gourmet meals for $8 per meal. Waitress service is provided at no additional charge. Meals may be purchased in gift shop.	Candlelight meal with selection of T-bone steak, lobster, or chicken cordon bleu, with champagne.
Patient feedback surveys	Food service director conducts patient feedback surveys on semiannual basis. Patient response has been excellent.	Patient feedback surveys taken once-twice/week with quantitative analysis of quality measurements. Patient response has been excellent.	Patient feedback survey taken by food service. Hospital also gives questionnaire on patient dismissal. Patient response has been excellent.	Food service supervisors complete daily patient surveys. Patient Affairs Dept. also conducts survey upon dismissal. Patient response has been excellent.	Patient questionnaires are received through hospital administration. Patient response has been excellent.	Quality Assurance twice weekly; patient survey every two months; daily personal contact.
Computerization of food service	No computer involvement to date.	No computer involvement to date.	No computer involvement to date.	No computer involvement to date.	No computer involvement yet except budget monitoring of food service.	No computer involvement to date.

52

menu was not conducive to controlling costs. However, it had offered 36 entrees and had discarded unused portions.

Based on the survey results, the cost effectiveness of restaurant-style menus depends primarily on management systems established to control them. If production is carefully correlated with patient census and unused portions are used properly, the restaurant-style menu can be cost effective whether a convenience food production system (onsite or commercial), a conventional food production system, or a combination of the two is used.

Hospitals need ways to increase their occupancy rate, and food service—through a well-developed restaurant-style menu—can be helpful.

To enhance patient satisfaction even further, some facilities have developed alternative listings of menu items for frequent and long-term admissions. Still others offer patients a "distinctive dining" experience featuring gourmet items. Meals range from $8 each to $12 extra a day—service and public relations for a price.

In planning a well-accepted, economically feasible seasonal set of cycle menus, several considerations are involved. Exhibit 3–1, the Menu Checklist, provides a listing of these considerations to produce an excellent set of menus. If menu substitutions do become necessary because of delivery failures, etc., it is important that the substitutions be nutritionally equivalent to the original item. Exhibit 3–2 offers guidance in making nutritionally equivalent menu substitutions. Exhibit 3–3 is an example of a form to document menu substitutions.

COORDINATION OF DIETS

As soon as the general diet seasonal menu cycle has been drafted (on a selective or nonselective basis) and approved for nutritional adequacy, patient acceptability, and economic feasibility, it must be coordinated with all therapeutic diets. It is essential to coordinate the therapeutic diet as closely to the general diet menu items as possible for economy in labor and food.

If many different foods are served to comply with therapeutic dietary prescriptions, ignoring menu items included in the general diets, substantial increases in raw food and labor costs can be expected. A set of economically feasible cycle menus with therapeutic diet coordinations is reproduced in Appendix A.

Achieving an Accurate Cost per Meal

As soon as the general diet menus have been developed and the therapeutic diet menus have been coordinated, it is suggested a Purchasing/Production Guide be drafted. (A Purchasing/Production Guide for two sets of menus is presented in Appendix B.) Utilizing such a guide can result in significant savings through correlating purchasing and food production directly with the census.

For example, if eight cans of green beans traditionally have been pulled to serve four-ounce portions to 150 people, instead of the six cans that should have been pulled, an additional two cans of green beans have been purchased, prepared, and served that were totally unnecessary. Only one extra ounce of one vegetable for 800 meals a day results in an overexpenditure of $5,840 a year. Carefully planned menus, developing and maintaining a Purchasing/Production Guide, as well as monitoring portion control are essential steps to assuring cost-effective quality food service.

Exhibit 3–1 Menu checklist

Nutritional Factors

Include the following in menu planning to meet adequate nutritional needs:

1. One serving of a good source of Vitamin C (citrus fruits, cantaloupe, broccoli) or two servings of a fair source of Vitamin C (tangerines, raw cabbage, tomatoes, and turnip greens, collard greens, baked potato in the skin, rutabagas, spinach, sweet potato) daily.
2. One serving of a dark green or deep yellow vegetable or fruit every other day to supply a sufficient amount of Vitamin A.
3. Four or more servings of fruits and vegetables daily.
4. Two cups of milk (as a beverage, on cereal, and/or in cooking).
5. Four to six ounces cooked weight of meat, fish, poultry, and/or substitute daily. (One ounce of meat substitute may be served as one egg, ¼ cup cottage cheese, etc., as an equivalent to one ounce of meat.)
6. Four eggs a week. At least one ounce of high-quality protein (one egg, cheese toast, peanut butter, sausage, etc.) should be served at breakfast and a minimum of two ounces of high-quality protein at the noon and evening meals.
7. Four or more servings of whole-grain, enriched, or restored bread, or cereal daily. Bran should be incorporated into at least one menu item per day—for example, in meatloaf, biscuits, cornbread, cereals, or desserts such as cobblers, cakes, and the icing on cakes.

Factors for Greater Menu Acceptability

1. Try a new menu item at least three times so it will become familiar to the residents and not be regarded as foreign.
2. Maintain variety in foods served during the week and throughout the menu cycle.
3. Vary menu combinations of food according to color, shape, taste, texture, and temperature.
4. Avoid serving more than two starches in one meal. Noodles and potatoes should not be served at the same meal.
5. Use spices creatively to enhance flavor and to reduce the need for salt and sugar.
6. Investigate new tray accessories and patient menus.
7. Be sure food is well prepared and offered at the proper temperature.
8. Take time to interview the patients personally to understand and note their individual food likes and dislikes.
9. Take into consideration the patients' regional, ethnic, and economic backgrounds.

Factors to Increase Labor Efficiency

1. Incorporate at least one menu item that can be prepared the day before.
2. Plan and distribute menu items according to the skill of employees scheduled.
3. Plan menu items to utilize equipment efficiently (that is, surface-prepared, oven-prepared, and refrigerated-stored menu items).

Factors to Maintain Cost Control

1. Use an extended meat, such as chicken with noodles, as the entree for the evening meal if the noon meal provides a solid meat, such as roast beef.
2. Minimize the use of expensive vegetables, including broccoli, asparagus, and brussels sprouts. Depending on the budget, these items could be included a maximum of once a week.
3. Check menus in advance to take advantage of specials—for example, buying in ten-case lots as storage permits. If there is a sufficient savings (more than 10 percent), storage space should be found in some area.
4. Specify portion sizes directly on the menu, including the number scoop, etc., to be utilized (for example, 4 ounce portion, No. 8 scoop). This makes it much more convenient for actual servers.
5. Monitor returned trays periodically to determine how patients are receiving the meal. Does food waste occur in a pattern?
6. Cost convenience food against time, personnel, and actual expense.

Exhibit 3–2 Equivalent menu substitutions

Cost Realities

Following is a list of suggested substitutions for certified menu items, should the need arise. The items within each category contain a general approximation of the equivalent food value of the category. This list has been provided for the convenience of the food service director and is to be utilized only when absolutely necessary. Menus have been carefully developed and approved according to nutrition values and in coordination with color, taste, and texture combinations.

Protein Entrees

The average protein serving generally is 3 ounces, which is about the size of a dollar bill and a quarter of an inch thick. Therefore, a combination of any three items or a triple amount of the quantity listed should be substituted to equal the amount of food value in three ounces of protein entree.

Beef	1 ounce	Frankfurter	1 each
Poultry	1 ounce	Egg	1 each
Lamb	1 ounce	Salmon, tuna	¼ cup
Pork	1 ounce	Cheese, cheddar	
Liver	1 ounce	& American	1 ounce
Fish	1 ounce	Cottage cheese	¼ cup
Cold cuts	1 thin slice	Peanut butter	2 tbs.

Vegetables

All calculations are based on the standard half-cup serving.

1. collard greens, mustard greens, spinach, turnip greens
2. broccoli, tomatoes
3. asparagus, green beans, okra
4. Brussels sprouts, lettuce
5. cabbage, cauliflower, sauerkraut

Fruits

1. watermelon, cantaloupe, apricots
2. peaches, prunes, blueberries, strawberries, raspberries, blackberries
3. bananas, plums, pears, figs, raisins
4. tangerines, oranges, grapefruit
5. applesauce, honeydew melon
6. pineapple, cherries

Starches

1. cereal (cooked), cereal (dry-flaked and puffed)
2. bread, biscuit, muffin, cornbread, graham crackers, saltines, soda crackers, round thin crackers
3. rice, corn, spaghetti (noodles, etc.) cooked, baked beans (no pork), potatoes (Irish, baked, mashed, sweet, or yams)

Is the cost per meal figure accurate? If the total food service budget includes nourishments, nutritional supplementation, cafeteria, special functions, and other similar areas, without separating out each of these cost centers, it may be advisable to assign a specific budget for each to identify an accurate cost per meal. It is only when the whole can be dissected into parts that management can take an effective look at the interrelationships. It often is difficult to determine where a potential excess in cost is hidden unless the expense of each component part is identified.

Exhibit 3–3 XYZ health care facility: Menu substitution form

If menu is served exactly according to the master menu, check "SAME." However, if any menu substitutions are made, they are to be nutritionally equivalent to the original menu item. The reason for the substitution should be noted and initialed by the authorizing party.

DATE	MEAL	SAME	SUBSTITUTIONS	REASON	AUTHORIZED
	Breakfast				
	Lunch				
	Dinner				
	Breakfast				
	Lunch				
	Dinner				
	Breakfast				
	Lunch				
	Dinner				
	Breakfast				
	Lunch				
	Dinner				
	Breakfast				
	Lunch				
	Dinner				
	Breakfast				
	Lunch				
	Dinner				
	Breakfast				
	Lunch				
	Dinner				

Meal Census

A meal census form, which seemingly is innocuous, can become a vital factor in analyzing and obtaining an accurate per meal cost. For example: Are double portions counted as two meals or only one meal? Are pureed diet meals counted as only one meal or is there a pureed diet meal equivalent? This, in itself, can make a significant impact on cost per meal as well as on total food expenditures. (These factors also are discussed later in this chapter in relation to the cost of nutrition-related medical requirements.)

Once economic parameters have been established through a food service operating budget, it is important for reimbursement purposes—as well as for creating an index by which to evaluate costs—to maintain a meal census. A strict head count divided only among patients, employees, and guests could be maintained, but in the interest of maximizing reimbursement a more detailed census form (Exhibit 3–4) is recommended. The cost per meal and/or per patient day can be determined easily once the total food cost and number of meals served have been substantiated.

Exhibit 3–4 Monthly meal census

Month: _____

	Regular	Therapeutic	Mechanically Altered	Tube Feedings	Employee	Guest	Total To Date
1							
2							
3							
4							
5							
6							
7							
8							
9							
10							
1							
2							
3							
4							
5							
6							
7							
8							
9							
10							
1							
2							
3							
4							
5							
6							
7							
8							
9							
10							
11							
TOTAL							

Nutrition-Related Medical Requirements

Even when careful consideration is given to aligning therapeutic diets closely with the general diet, the cost of nutrition-related medical requirements can be staggering. Table 3–2 presents an analysis of the cost of nutrition-related medical requirements incurred by one 168-bed nursing facility. Because of the type of patients admitted, this institution spent more than $25,000 a year above what it would have for those who required fewer nutrition-related medical services. The facility received no additional reimbursement for these expenses.

Indiscriminate use of nutrition-related medical requirements such as pureed diets, evening nourishments, and nutritional supplementation actually can reduce quality patient care while escalating costs. For example, food palatability is enhanced for patients by providing chopped or ground food as compared with the more costly pureed items. Excessive and unnecessary nutritional supplementation can inhibit patients' appetites for meals.

Integrating the clinical and management aspects of dietetics by increasing awareness of costs in delivering quality patient care is the ultimate service provided by any food professional in the health care industry.

Pureed Diets

Details of the additional raw food costs incurred due to pureed diets are presented in Exhibit 3–5. Additional raw food costs alone amounted to $10,515.65. Additional labor costs required by pureed diets in this same facility are shown in Table 3–3. The pureed diets added annual labor costs in this facility of $9,552.74 (based on $3.35 per hour average wage).

Table 3–4 summarizes the costs resulting from pureed diets alone to be $20,068.39, for which the facility receives no additional remuneration.

The size of pureed diet portions must be evaluated. This may vary to some extent with individual patients; however, a standard must be set for the majority. Two-ounce portions of vegetables are standard for most regular diet patients in many geriatric institutions throughout the country. However, a two-ounce portion (#16 scoop) is visually unacceptable for a pureed diet.

Many nursing homes have decided to use a #12 scoop (2.67 ounces) as a standard for pureed diet portions, which means that the patient actually is receiving 3.34 ounces of solid food that has been pureed to produce 2.67 ounces. The nutritional adequacy for the basic four food groups is met through providing half a cup of citrus juice for breakfast, two vegetables at noon and evening, and a minimum of one additional blended fruit at either noon or evening. Typically, blended fruit is offered at the noon and evening meals in addition to the citrus juice in the morning.

Other institutions, such as hospitals, that normally provide four-ounce portions of vegetables as a standard for regular diets, use a #10 scoop (3.2 ounces) for pureed portions. Each institution must evaluate the physical condition and appetite level of each of its patients, regardless of the portions provided for those on the regular diet, to determine the size portion to be provided to pureed diet patients.

Proper planning can assure a nutritionally adequate diet is provided for the pureed diet patient, with, as noted, a #12 scoop. However, if patients are relatively active and have a good appetite, the larger #10 scoop may be necessary. *The Stokes Report* has developed an extensive *Pureed Diet Production Guide*

Table 3–2 Cost of nutrition-related medical requirements

(Average census: 168 nursing home residents)

Item	Additional Raw food Cost/Day	Labor-Hours/Day	Additional Labor Cost/Day +25%*			Total Cost/Day	Total Cost/Month	Total Cost/Year
Therapeutic diets	—	2.5	$3.35 4.50	$8.38 + $2.09 11.25 + 2.81	= $10.47 = 13.43	$10.47 13.43	$318.46 408.50	$3,821.55 4,901.95
Pureed diets	$28.21	3.25	3.35 4.50	10.89 + 2.72 14.63 + 3.66	= 13.61 = 18.29	41.82 46.50	1,272.03 1,414.38	15,264.30 16,972.50
Milkshakes	9.15	1.0	3.35 4.50	3.35 + .84 4.50 + 1.13	= 4.19 = 5.63	13.34 14.78	405.76 449.56	4,869.10 5,394.70
Diabetic snack	2.80	.5	3.35 4.50	1.68 + .42 2.25 + .56	= 2.10 = 2.81	4.90 5.61	149.04 170.64	1,788.50 2,047.65
Total cost per year			$3.35 $4.50	$30.37 $40.16		70.53 80.32	2,145.29 2,443.08	25,743.45 29,316.80

*$3.35/hour = minimum wage plus estimated 25 percent employer costs.
$4.50/hour = average wage plus estimated 25 percent employer costs.

Exhibit 3–5 Additional raw food costs with pureed diets

Meals

Diet meals	62	Single portions/meal
Portions of pureed food (twice daily)	24	Double portions/meal (12 additional single portions × 2)
	86	Total portions/meals

(25 percent more solid food required to yield the same portion per volume of pureed diets, based on mean decrease in volume)

$86 \times .25 = 21.5$ extra portions of solid food required to produce pureed diets

$86.0 + 21.5 = 107.5$ (total portions/noon and evening meal)
   × 2 (noon and evening meal) = 215.0 total portions/noon and evening meals

Raw Food Costs

Raw food costs/meal	$.67
Additional raw food cost/day with pureed diets	21.50×2 (meals/day) $\times \$.67 = \$28.81$
Additional raw food cost/month with pureed diets	$\$28.81 \times 30$ (days/month) $= \$864.30$
Additional raw food cost/year	$\$28.81 \times 365$ (days/year) $= \$10,515.65$

(Breakfast items not pureed)

Table 3–3 Additional labor costs of pureed diets*

	Wages	
Item	$3.35/hr	$4.50/hr
Preparation		
1.0 hour/day	$3.35	$4.50
3.0 hours per day (1.5 hours twice daily)	10.05	13.50
Serving		
2.25 hours per day	7.54	10.13
Total additional labor required 1 day		
6.25 hours per day	20.94	28.13
Total additional labor required 1 year		
2,281.25 hours	7,642.19	10,265.63
25% Employer costs	1,910.55	2,566.41
Total additional labor costs per year	9,552.74	12,832.04

*Breakfast items not pureed, thereby requiring no additional labor for pureed diets for this meal.

Table 3–4 Summary of costs

Additional raw food cost per year (See Exhibit 3–5)	$10,515.65
Additional labor costs per year (See Table 3–3)	9,552.74
Total additional costs per year required by pureed diets	$20,068.39

(Exhibit 3–6) that identifies the quantity of solid food that must be pureed and the quantity of liquid to add to yield the desired number of portions of each food item based on the percent of volume decrease of each.

To reflect an accurate per-patient meal cost, the total number of pureed diets (usually for noon and evening meals only, since breakfast rarely is pureed) should be multiplied by a 1.67 meal equivalent to determine the actual number of meals served to produce the pureed diets:

Std. portion for diets solid food	*Pureed diet portion*	*Meal equivalent*
2 oz. (#16 scoop)	2.67 oz. (#12 scoop) (equivalent to 3.34 oz. of solid food because of 25 percent additional food required)	1.67

(Appendix D presents detailed information and chart.)

MANAGEMENT ANALYSIS CASE STUDY

A 168-bed intermingled (skilled and intermediate care residents) nursing home was serving 62 single-pureed diet portions and 24 double-pureed diet portions for the noon and evening meals (Table 3–5). An evaluation of pureed diets from both clinical and management viewpoints was undertaken in an attempt to reduce food costs while maintaining quality care.

Solution

Costs of pureed diets were reviewed with administration and nursing service and a team approach to solving the problem was used. The food service director and director of nursing evaluated the residents for whom pureed diets had been prescribed:

1. A nutrition assessment was completed for each patient, with nutrition status, height, weight, etc., being discussed by the entire health care team. Team members defined the purpose of the diet and identified the pureed diet prescription as a ''problem'' on the resident care plan. This assured that the problem would be reviewed automatically every three months.
2. All pureed diet residents were observed at mealtime by all health care disciplines. Some residents were unable to feed themselves solid food. Self-help feeding devices were ordered through consultation with the physical therapist. Several of the pureed diet residents ate solid food at times other than mealtimes, e.g., during activities or when families brought food to them.
3. Residents who were admitted with a stroke, had difficulty in swallowing, and were undergoing rehabilitation were prescribed a ''mechanical soft'' diet in lieu of a pureed diet. Meat was ground and served au jus or with gravy.

Exhibit 3–6 Pureed diet production guide

Meats

| Item | 5 Servings | | | | | |
| | #12 Scoop (2.67 ounces) | | | #10 Scoop (3.2 ounces) | | |
	Amt. Solid Food	Amt. Liquid	Amt. Yield	Amt. Solid Food	Amt. Liquid	Amt. Yield
Beef Liver	23.6 oz	2 oz	13+ oz	25 oz	2 oz	16 oz
	3c	2 oz	1c 5 oz	3c 1 oz	2 oz	2c
Breaded Pork Pattie	20.2 oz	3+ oz	13+ oz	24 oz	4+ oz	16 oz
	2c 4 oz	3+ oz	1c 5 oz	3c	4+ oz	2c
Breaded Veal/Beef Pattie	20 oz	5 oz	13+ oz	24 oz	6 oz	16 oz
	2c 4 oz	5 oz	1c 5 oz	3c	6 oz	2c
Chicken	15 oz	7.5 oz	13+ oz	18 oz	9 oz	16 oz
	1c 7 oz	7.5 oz	1c 5 oz	2c 2 oz	9 oz	2c
Cubed Beef/Veal Pattie	20 oz	3+ oz	13+ oz	24 oz	4 oz	16 oz
	2c 4 oz	3+ oz	1c 5 oz	3c	4 oz	2c
Cubed Pork Pattie	20 oz	5 oz	13+ oz	24 oz	6 oz	16 oz
	2c 4 oz	5 oz	1c 5 oz	3c	6 oz	2c
Fish Fillet	20 oz	4 oz	13+ oz	24 oz	5 oz	16 oz
	2c 4 oz	4 oz	1c 5 oz	3c	5 oz	2c
Pepper Pattie	20 oz	5 oz	13+ oz	24 oz	6 oz	16 oz
	2c 4 oz	5 oz	1c 5 oz	3c	6 oz	2c
Salisbury Steak Pattie	18 oz	2+ oz	13+ oz	21 oz	3 oz	16 oz
	2c 2 oz	2+ oz	1c 5 oz	2c 5 oz	3 oz	2c
Stuffed Lamb Breast* *Stuffed w/chopped lamb	25 oz	4+ oz	13+ oz	30 oz	5 oz	16 oz
	3c 1 oz	4+ oz	1c 5 oz	3c 6 oz	5 oz	2c
Veal/Beef Pattie	18 oz	4 oz	13+ oz	21 oz	5 oz	16 oz
	2c 2 oz	4 oz	1c 5 oz	2c 5 oz	5 oz	2c

| Item | 10 Servings | | | | | |
| | #12 Scoop (2.67 ounces) | | | #10 Scoop (3.2 ounces) | | |
	Amt. Solid Food	Amt. Liquid	Amt. Yield	Amt. Solid Food	Amt. Liquid	Amt. Yield
Beef Liver	47.2 oz	4+ oz	27 oz	49 oz	4 oz	32 oz
	6c	4+ oz	3c 3 oz	6c 1 oz	4 oz	4c
Breaded Pork Pattie	40.3 oz	7 oz	27 oz	48.3 oz	9 oz	32 oz
	5c	7 oz	3c 3 oz	6c	9 oz	4c
Breaded Veal/Beef Pattie	40 oz	10 oz	27 oz	48 oz	12 oz	32 oz
	5c	10 oz	3c 3 oz	6c	12 oz	4c
Chicken	30 oz	15 oz	27 oz	36 oz	18 oz	32 oz
	3c 6 oz	15 oz	3c 3 oz	4c 4 oz	18 oz	4c
Cubed Beef/Veal Pattie	40 oz	7 oz	27 oz	48 oz	9 oz	32 oz
	5c	7 oz	3c 3 oz	6c	9 oz	4c
Cubed Pork Pattie	40 oz	10 oz	27 oz	48 oz	12 oz	32 oz
	5c	10 oz	3c 3 oz	6c	12 oz	4c
Fish Fillet	40 oz	8+ oz	27 oz	48 oz	10 oz	32 oz
	5c	8+ oz	3c 3 oz	6c	10 oz	4c
Pepper Pattie	40 oz	10 oz	27 oz	48 oz	12 oz	32 oz
	5c	10 oz	3c 3 oz	6c	12 oz	4c

Exhibit 3–6 Meats, continued

Item	10 Servings					
	#12 Scoop (2.67 ounces)			#10 Scoop (3.2 ounces)		
	Amt. Solid Food	Amt. Liquid	Amt. Yield	Amt. Solid Food	Amt. Liquid	Amt. Yield
Salisbury Steak Pattie	36 oz	5 oz	27 oz	43 oz	5+ oz	32 oz
	4c 4 oz	5 oz	3c 3 oz	5c 3 oz	5+ oz	4c
Stuffed Lamb Breast* *Stuffed w/chopped lamb	50 oz	8+ oz	27 oz	60 oz	10 oz	32 oz
	6c 2 oz	8+ oz	3c 3 oz	7c 4 oz	10 oz	4c
Veal/Beef Pattie	35 oz	8 oz	27 oz	42 oz	9+ oz	32 oz
	4c 3 oz	8 oz	3c 3 oz	5c 2 oz	9+ oz	4c

Item	15 Servings					
	#12 Scoop (2.67 ounces)			#10 Scoop (3.2 ounces)		
	Amt. Solid Food	Amt. Liquid	Amt. Yield	Amt. Solid Food	Amt. Liquid	Amt. Yield
Beef Liver	70.8 oz	6 oz	40 oz	74 oz	7 oz	48 oz
	8c 7 oz	6 oz	5c	9c 2 oz	7 oz	6c
Breaded Pork Pattie	60.4 oz	11 oz	40 oz	72.4 oz	13 oz	48 oz
	7c 4 oz	11 oz	5c	9c	13 oz	6c
Breaded Veal/Beef Pattie	60 oz	15 oz	40 oz	72 oz	18 oz	48 oz
	7c 3 oz	15 oz	5c	9c	18 oz	6c
Chicken	45 oz	23 oz	40 oz	54 oz	28 oz	48 oz
	5c 5 oz	23 oz	5c	6c 6 oz	28 oz	6c
Cubed Beef/Veal Pattie	60 oz	11 oz	40 oz	72 oz	13 oz	48 oz
	7c 3 oz	11 oz	5c	9c	13 oz	6c
Cubed Pork Pattie	60 oz	15 oz	40 oz	72 oz	17+ oz	48 oz
	7c 3 oz	15 oz	5c	9c	17+ oz	6c
Fish Fillet	60 oz	12+ oz	40 oz	72 oz	15 oz	48 oz
	7c 3 oz	12+ oz	5c	9c	15 oz	6c
Pepper Pattie	60 oz	15 oz	40 oz	72 oz	17+ oz	48 oz
	7c 3 oz	15 oz	5c	9c	17+ oz	6c
Salisbury Steak Pattie	53 oz	7 oz	40 oz	64 oz	8 oz	48 oz
	6c 5 oz	7 oz	5c	8c	8 oz	6c
Stuffed Lamb Breast* *Stuffed w/chopped lamb	75 oz	12+ oz	40 oz	90 oz	15 oz	48 oz
	9c 3 oz	12+ oz	5c	11c 2 oz	15 oz	6c
Veal/Beef Pattie	52.5 oz	12 oz	40 oz	63 oz	14 oz	48 oz
	6c 4 oz	12 oz	5c	7c 7 oz	14 oz	6c

Item	20 Servings					
	#12 Scoop (2.67 ounces)			#10 Scoop (3.2 ounces)		
	Amt. Solid Food	Amt. Liquid	Amt. Yield	Amt. Solid Food	Amt. Liquid	Amt. Yield
Beef Liver	94.4 oz	8 oz	53+ oz	99 oz	9+ oz	64 oz
	11c 6 oz	8 oz	6c 5 oz	12c	9+ oz	8c
Breaded Pork Pattie	80.6 oz	14+ oz	53 oz	97 oz	17+ oz	64 oz
	10c	14+ oz	6c 5 oz	12c 1 oz	17+ oz	8c
Breaded Veal/Beef Pattie	80 oz	20 oz	53 oz	96 oz	24 oz	64 oz
	10c	20 oz	6c 5 oz	12c	24 oz	8c

63

Exhibit 3–6 Meats, continued

| Item | 20 Servings | | | | | |
| | #12 Scoop (2.67 ounces) | | | #10 Scoop (3.2 ounces) | | |
	Amt. Solid Food	Amt. Liquid	Amt. Yield	Amt. Solid Food	Amt. Liquid	Amt. Yield
Chicken	73 oz	30+ oz	53 oz	72 oz	37 oz	64 oz
	9c 1 oz	30+ oz	6c 5 oz	9c	37 oz	8c
Cubed Beef/Veal Pattie	80 oz	14+ oz	53 oz	96 oz	17+ oz	64 oz
	10c	14+ oz	6c 5 oz	12c	17+ oz	8c
Cubed Pork Pattie	80 oz	19 oz	53 oz	96 oz	23 oz	64 oz
	10c	19 oz	6c 5 oz	12c	23 oz	8c
Fish Fillet	80 oz	16+ oz	53 oz	96 oz	20 oz	64 oz
	10c	16+ oz	6c 5 oz	12c	20 oz	8c
Pepper Pattie	80 oz	19 oz	53 oz	96 oz	23 oz	64 oz
	10c	19 oz	6c 5 oz	12c	23 oz	8c
Salisbury Steak Pattie	71 oz	9 oz	53 oz	85 oz	11 oz	64 oz
	8c 7 oz	9 oz	6c 5 oz	10c 5 oz	11 oz	8c
Stuffed Lamb Breast*	100 oz	17 oz	53 oz	120 oz	20 oz	64 oz
*Stuffed w/chopped lamb	12c 4 oz	17 oz	6c 5 oz	15c	20 oz	8c
Veal/Beef Pattie	70 oz	16 oz	53 oz	84 oz	19 oz	64 oz
	8c 6 oz	16 oz	6c 5 oz	10c 4 oz	19 oz	8c

| Item | 25 Servings | | | | | |
| | #12 Scoop (2.67 ounces) | | | #10 Scoop (3.2 ounces) | | |
	Amt. Solid Food	Amt. Liquid	Amt. Yield	Amt. Solid Food	Amt. Liquid	Amt. Yield
Beef Liver	118 oz	10 oz	67 oz	123 oz	12 oz	80 oz
	14 c 6 oz	10 oz	8c 3 oz	15c 3 oz	12 oz	10c
Breaded Pork Pattie	100.75 oz	18 oz	67 oz	121 oz	22 oz	80 oz
	12c 5 oz	18 oz	8c 3 oz	15c 1 oz	22 oz	10c
Breaded Veal/Beef Pattie	100 oz	25 oz	67 oz	120 oz	30 oz	80 oz
	12c 4 oz	25 oz	8c 3 oz	15c	30 oz	10c
Chicken	75 oz	38 oz	67 oz	90 oz	46 oz	80 oz
	9c 3 oz	38 oz	8c 3 oz	11c 2 oz	46 oz	10c
Cubed Beef/Veal Pattie	100 oz	18 oz	67 oz	120 oz	22 oz	80 oz
	12c 4 oz	18 oz	8c 3 oz	15c	22 oz	10c
Cubed Pork Pattie	100 oz	24 oz	67 oz	120 oz	29 oz	80 oz
	12c 4 oz	24 oz	8c 3 oz	15c	29 oz	10c
Fish Fillet	100 oz	20+ oz	67 oz	120 oz	25 oz	80 oz
	12c 4 oz	20+ oz	8c 3 oz	15c	25 oz	10c
Pepper Pattie	100 oz	24 oz	67 oz	120 oz	29 oz	80 oz
	12c 4 oz	24 oz	8c 3 oz	15c	29 oz	10c
Salisbury Steak Pattie	89 oz	11+ oz	67 oz	106 oz	13+ oz	80 oz
	11c 1 oz	11+ oz	8c 3 oz	13c 2 oz	13+ oz	10c
Stuffed Lamb Breast*	125 oz	21 oz	67 oz	150 oz	25 oz	80 oz
*Stuffed w/chopped lamb	15c 5 oz	21 oz	8c 3 oz	18c 6 oz	25 oz	10c
Veal/Beef Pattie	87.5 oz	20 oz	67 oz	105 oz	24 oz	80 oz
	10c 7 oz	20 oz	8c 3 oz	13c 1 oz	24 oz	10c

Exhibit 3–6 Meats, continued

| Item | 30 Servings | | | | | |
| | #12 Scoop (2.67 ounces) | | | #10 Scoop (3.2 ounces) | | |
	Amt. Solid Food	Amt. Liquid	Amt. Yield	Amt. Solid Food	Amt. Liquid	Amt. Yield
Beef Liver	141.6 oz	10 oz	80+ oz	148 oz	14 oz	96 oz
	17c 6 oz	10 oz	10+c	18c 4 oz	14 oz	12c
Breaded Pork Pattie	121 oz	18 oz	80+ oz	145 oz	26 oz	96 oz
	15c 1 oz	18 oz	10+c	18c 1 oz	26 oz	12c
Breaded Veal/Beef Pattie	120 oz	25 oz	80+ oz	144 oz	43 oz	96 oz
	15c	25 oz	10+c	18c	43 oz	12c
Chicken	90 oz	38+ oz	80+ oz	108 oz	55 oz	96 oz
	11c 2 oz	38+ oz	10+c	13c 4 oz	55 oz	12c
Cubed Beef/Veal Pattie	120 oz	18 oz	80+ oz	144 oz	26 oz	96 oz
	15c	18 oz	10+c	18c	26 oz	12c
Cubed Pork Pattie	120 oz	24 oz	80+ oz	144 oz	35 oz	96 oz
	15c	24 oz	10+c	18c	35 oz	12c
Fish Fillet	120 oz	20+ oz	80+ oz	144 oz	29+ oz	96 oz
	15c	20+ oz	10+c	18c	29+ oz	12c
Pepper Pattie	120 oz	24 oz	80+ oz	144 oz	35 oz	96 oz
	15c	24 oz	10+c	18c	35 oz	12c
Salisbury Steak Pattie	106 oz	11 oz	80+ oz	128 oz	16 oz	96 oz
	13c 2 oz	11 oz	10+c	16c	16 oz	12c
Stuffed Lamb Breast*	150 oz	21 oz	80+ oz	180 oz	30 oz	96 oz
*Stuffed w/chopped lamb	18c 6 oz	21 oz	10+c	22c 4 oz	30 oz	12c
Veal/Beef Pattie	105 oz	20 oz	80+ oz	126 oz	28+ oz	96 oz
	13c 1 oz	20 oz	10+c	15c 6 oz	28+ oz	12c

Vegetables

| Item | 5 Servings | | | | | |
| | #12 Scoop (2.67 ounces) | | | #10 Scoop (3.2 ounces) | | |
	Amt. Solid Food	Amt. Liquid	Amt. Yield	Amt. Solid Food	Amt. Liquid	Amt. Yield
Beets, Sliced	19 oz	3+ oz	13+ oz	23 oz	4 oz	16 oz
	2c 3 oz	3+ oz	1c 5+ oz	2c 7 oz	4 oz	2c
Carrots, Sliced	19 oz	3+ oz	13+ oz	23 oz	4 oz	16 oz
	2c 3 oz	3+ oz	1c 5+ oz	2c 7 oz	4 oz	2c
Green Beans	19 oz	3+ oz	13+ oz	23 oz	4 oz	16 oz
	2c 3 oz	3+ oz	1c 5+ oz	2c 7 oz	4 oz	2c
Green Peas (3 Sieve)	17 oz	3 oz	13+ oz	21 oz	3+ oz	16 oz
	2c 1 oz	3 oz	1c 5+ oz	2c 5 oz	3+ oz	2c
Mixed Vegetables	12 oz	3 oz	13+ oz	22 oz	4 oz	16 oz
	2c 5 oz	3 oz	1c 5+ oz	2c 6 oz	4 oz	2c
Peas, Blackeyed	15 oz	2+ oz	13+ oz	18+ oz	3 oz	16 oz
	1c 7 oz	2+ oz	1c 5+ oz	2c 2+ oz	3 oz	2c
Potatoes, Whole New	18 oz	6 oz	13+ oz	22+ oz	7+ oz	16 oz
	2c 2 oz	6 oz	1c 5+ oz	2c 6+ oz	7+ oz	2c
Spinach	15 oz	2+ oz	13+ oz	18+ oz	3 oz	16 oz
	1c 7 oz	2+ oz	1c 5+ oz	2c 2+ oz	3 oz	2c

Exhibit 3–6 Vegetables, continued

Item	5 Servings					
	#12 Scoop (2.67 ounces)			#10 Scoop (3.2 ounces)		
	Amt. Solid Food	Amt. Liquid	Amt. Yield	Amt. Solid Food	Amt. Liquid	Amt. Yield
Squash	16 oz	3 oz	13 oz	19 oz	3+ oz	16 oz
	2c	3 oz	1c 5+ oz	2c 3 oz	3+ oz	2c
Tomatoes, (Diced, Crushed or Whole)	13+ oz	—	13+ oz	16 oz	—	16 oz
	1c 5+ oz	—	1c 5+ oz	2c	—	2c
Turnip Greens	16 oz	5+ oz	13+ oz	22 oz	7+ oz	16 oz
	2c	5+ oz	1c 5+ oz	2c 6 oz	7+ oz	2c

Item	10 Servings					
	#12 Scoop (2.67 ounces)			#10 Scoop (3.2 ounces)		
	Amt. Solid Food	Amt. Liquid	Amt. Yield	Amt. Solid Food	Amt. Liquid	Amt. Yield
Beets, Sliced	39 oz	6+ oz	27 oz	46 oz	8 oz	32 oz
	4c 7 oz	6+ oz	3c 3 oz	5c 6 oz	1c	4c
Carrots, Sliced	39 oz	6+ oz	27 oz	46 oz	8 oz	32 oz
	4c 7 oz	6+ oz	3 c 3 oz	5c 6 oz	1c	4c
Green Beans	39 oz	6+ oz	27 oz	46 oz	8 oz	32 oz
	4c 7 oz	6+ oz	3c 3 oz	5c 6 oz	1c	4c
Green Peas (3 Sieve)	35 oz	6 oz	27 oz	41+ oz	7 oz	32 oz
	4c 3 oz	6 oz	3c 3 oz	5c 1+ oz	7 oz	4c
Mixed Vegetables	37 oz	6+ oz	27 oz	44 oz	7+ oz	32 oz
	4c 5 oz	6+ oz	3c 3 oz	5c 4 oz	7+ oz	4c
Peas, Blackeyed	31 oz	5+ oz	27 oz	36+ oz	6 oz	32 oz
	3c 7 oz	5+ oz	3c 3 oz	4c 4+ oz	6 oz	4c
Potatoes, Whole New	37+ oz	12+ oz	27 oz	44 oz	15 oz	32 oz
	4c 5+ oz	1c 4+ oz	3c 3 oz	5c 4 oz	1c 7 oz	4c
Spinach	31 oz	5+ oz	27 oz	36+ oz	6 oz	32 oz
	3c 7 oz	5+ oz	3c 3 oz	4c 4+ oz	6 oz	4c
Squash	33 oz	5+ oz	27 oz	40 oz	7 oz	32 oz
	4c 1 oz	5+ oz	3c 3 oz	5c	7 oz	4c
Tomatoes, (Diced, Crushed or Whole)	27 oz	—	27 oz	32 oz	—	32 oz
	3c 3 oz	—	3c 3oz	4c	—	4c
Turnip Greens	37 oz	12 oz	27 oz	40 oz	13+ oz	32 oz
	4c 5 oz	1c 4 oz	3c 3 oz	4 oz	13+ oz	4c

Item	15 Servings					
	#12 Scoop (2.67 ounces)			#10 Scoop (3.2 ounces)		
	Amt. Solid Food	Amt. Liquid	Amt. Yield	Amt. Solid Food	Amt. Liquid	Amt. Yield
Beets, Sliced	57 oz	9+ oz	40 oz	69 oz	11+ oz	48 oz
	7c 1 oz	1c 1+ oz	5c	8c 5 oz	1c 3 oz	6c
Carrots, Sliced	57 oz	9+ oz	40 oz	69 oz	11+ oz	48 oz
	7c 1oz	1c 1+ oz	5c	8c 5 oz	1c 3 oz	6c
Green Beans	57 oz	9+ oz	40+ oz	69 oz	11+ oz	48 oz
	7c 1 oz	1c 1+ oz	5+c	8c 5 oz	1c 3 oz	6c

Exhibit 3–6 Vegetables, continued

Item	15 Servings					
	#12 Scoop (2.67 ounces)			#10 Scoop (3.2 ounces)		
	Amt. Solid Food	Amt. Liquid	Amt. Yield	Amt. Solid Food	Amt. Liquid	Amt. Yield
Green Peas (3 Sieve)	52 oz	9 oz	40 oz	62 oz	10+ oz	48 oz
	6c 4 oz	1c 1 oz	5c	7c 6 oz	1c 2 oz	6c
Mixed Vegetables	54 oz	9 oz	40 oz	65 oz	11 oz	48 oz
	6c 6 oz	1c 1 oz	5c	8c 1 oz	1c 3 oz	6c
Peas, Blackeyed	46 oz	8 oz	40 oz	55 oz	9+ oz	48 oz
	5c 6 oz	1c	5c	6c 7 oz	1c 1+ oz	6c
Potatoes, Whole New	65 oz	22 oz	40 oz	66 oz	22 oz	48 oz
	8c 1 oz	2c 6 oz	5c	8c 2 oz	2c 6 oz	6c
Spinach	46 oz	8 oz	40 oz	55 oz	9+ oz	48 oz
	5c 6 oz	1c	5c	6c 7 oz	1c 1+ oz	6c
Squash	48+ oz	8 oz	40 oz	58 oz	10 oz	48 oz
	6c	1c	5c	7c 2 oz	1c 2 oz	6c
Tomatoes, (Diced, Crushed or Whole)	40 oz	—	40 oz	48 oz	—	48 oz
	5c	—	5c	6c	—	6c
Turnip Greens	50 oz	17 oz	40 oz	60 oz	20 oz	48 oz
	6c 2 oz	2c 1 oz	5c	7c 4 oz	2c 4 oz	6c

Item	20 Servings					
	#12 Scoop (2.67 ounces)			#10 Scoop (3.2 ounces)		
	Amt. Solid Food	Amt. Liquid	Amt. Yield	Amt. Solid Food	Amt. Liquid	Amt. Yield
Beets, Sliced	76 oz	13 oz	53+ oz	92 oz	15 oz	64 oz
	9c 4 oz	1c 5 oz	6c 5+ oz	11c 4 oz	1c 7 oz	8c
Carrots, Sliced	76 oz	13 oz	53+ oz	92 oz	15+ oz	64 oz
	9c 4 oz	1c 5 oz	6c 5+ oz	11c 4 oz	1c 7+ oz	8c
Green Beans	76 oz	13 oz	53+ oz	92 oz	15+ oz	64 oz
	9c 4+ oz	1c 5 oz	6c 5+ oz	11c 4 oz	1c 7 oz	8c
Green Peas (3 Sieve)	74+ oz	12+ oz	53+ oz	87 oz	14 oz	64 oz
	9c 2 oz	1c 4 oz	6c 5+ oz	10c 7 oz	1c 6 oz	8c
Mixed Vegetables	72 oz	12 oz	53+ oz	87 oz	14+ oz	64 oz
	9c	1c 4 oz	6c 5+ oz	10c 7 oz	1c 6+ oz	8c
Peas, Blackeyed	60+ oz	10 oz	53+ oz	73 oz	12+ oz	64 oz
	7c 4+ oz	1c 2 oz	6c 5+ oz	9c 1 oz	1c 4 oz	8c
Potatoes, Whole New	73 oz	24+ oz	53+ oz	88 oz	29 oz	64 oz
	9c 1 oz	3c+	6c 5+ oz	10c 8 oz	3c 5 oz	8c
Spinach	60+ oz	10 oz	53+ oz	88 oz	29 oz	64 oz
	7c 4 oz	1c 2 oz	6c 5+ oz	11c 1 oz	3c 5 oz	8c
Squash	64 oz	11 oz	53+ oz	77+ oz	13 oz	64 oz
	8c	1c 3 oz	6c 5+ oz	9c 5 oz	1c 5 oz	8c
Tomatoes, (Diced, Crushed or Whole)	53+ oz	—	53+ oz	64 oz	—	64 oz
	6c 5+ oz	—	6c 5+ oz	8c	—	8c
Turnip Greens	66 oz	22 oz	53+ oz	80 oz	27 oz	64 oz
	8c 2 oz	2c 6 oz	6c 5+ oz	10c	3c 3 oz	8c

Exhibit 3–6 Vegetables, continued

Item	25 Servings					
	#12 Scoop (2.67 ounces)			#10 Scoop (3.2 ounces)		
	Amt. Solid Food	Amt. Liquid	Amt. Yield	Amt. Solid Food	Amt. Liquid	Amt. Yield
Beets, Sliced	96 oz	16 oz	67 oz	114 oz	19 oz	80 oz
	12c	2c	8c 3 oz	14c 2 oz	2c 3 oz	10c
Carrots, Sliced	96 oz	16 oz	67 oz	114 oz	19 oz	80 oz
	12c	2c	8c 3 oz	14c 2 oz	2c 3 oz	10c
Green Beans	96 oz	16 oz	67 oz	114 oz	19 oz	80 oz
	12c	2c	8c 3 oz	14c 2 oz	2c 3 oz	10c
Green Peas (3 Sieve)	86 oz	14+ oz	67 oz	103+ oz	17+ oz	80 oz
	10c 6 oz	1c 6+ oz	8c 3 oz	12c 7+ oz	2c 1+ oz	10c
Mixed Vegetables	91 oz	15 oz	67 oz	109 oz	18+ oz	80 oz
	11c 3 oz	1c 7 oz	8c 3 oz	13c 5 oz	2c 2+ oz	10c
Peas, Blackeyed	76 oz	13 oz	67 oz	91 oz	15+ oz	80 oz
	9c 4 oz	1c 5 oz	8c 3 oz	11c 3 oz	1c 7+ oz	10c
Potatoes, Whole New	92 oz	31 oz	67 oz	30 oz	10 oz	80 oz
	11c 4 oz	3c 7 oz	8c 3 oz	3c 6 oz	1c 2 oz	10c
Spinach	76 oz	13 oz	67 oz	91 oz	15+ oz	80 oz
	9c 4 oz	1c 5 oz	8c 3 oz	11c 3 oz	1c 7+ oz	10c
Squash	81 oz	13+ oz	67 oz	97 oz	16+ oz	80 oz
	10c 1 oz	1c 5+ oz	8c 3 oz	12c 1 oz	2+c	10c
Tomatoes, (Diced, Crushed or Whole)	67 oz	—	67 oz	80 oz	—	80 oz
	8c 3 oz	—	8c 3 oz	10c	—	10c
Turnip Greens	84 oz	28 oz	67 oz	100 oz	33+ oz	80 oz
	10c 4 oz	3c 4 oz	8c 3 oz	12c 4 oz	4c 1 oz	10c

Item	30 Servings					
	#12 Scoop (2.67 ounces)			#10 Scoop (3.2 ounces)		
	Amt. Solid Food	Amt. Liquid	Amt. Yield	Amt. Solid Food	Amt. Liquid	Amt. Yield
Beets, Sliced	114+ oz	19+ oz	80+ oz	137 oz	23 oz	96 oz
	14c 2+ oz	2c 3+ oz	10+c	17c 1 oz	2c 7 oz	12c
Carrots, Sliced	114+ oz	19+ oz	80+ oz	137 oz	23 oz	96 oz
	14c 2+ oz	2c 3+ oz	10+c	17c 1 oz	2c 7 oz	12c
Green Beans	114+ oz	19+ oz	80+ oz	137 oz	23 oz	96 oz
	14c 2+ oz	2c 3+ oz	10+c	17c 1 oz	2c 7 oz	12c
Green Peas (3 Sieve)	103+ oz	17+ oz	80+ oz	124 oz	21 oz	96 oz
	12c 7+ oz	2c 1+ oz	10c	15c 4 oz	2c 5 oz	12c
Mixed Vegetables	109 oz	18+ oz	80+ oz	131 oz	6 oz	96 oz
	13c 5 oz	2c 2+ oz	10+c	16c 3 oz	6 oz	12c
Peas, Blackeyed	91 oz	15+ oz	80+ oz	109 oz	18 oz	96 oz
	11c 3 oz	1c 7+ oz	10+c	13c 5 oz	2c 2 oz	12c
Potatoes, Whole New	30 oz	10 oz	80+ oz	132 oz	12 oz	96 oz
	3c 6 oz	1c 2 oz	10+c	16c 4 oz	1c 4 oz	12c
Spinach	91 oz	15+ oz	80+ oz	109 oz	18 oz	96 oz
	11c 3 oz	1c 7+ oz	10+c	13c 5 oz	2c 2 oz	12c
Squash	97 oz	16+ oz	80+ oz	116 oz	19+ oz	96 oz
	12c 1 oz	2+c	10+c	14c 4 oz	2c 3 oz	12c

Exhibit 3–6 Vegetables, continued

| Item | 30 Servings | | | | | |
| | #12 Scoop (2.67 ounces) | | | #10 Scoop (3.2 ounces) | | |
	Amt. Solid Food	Amt. Liquid	Amt. Yield	Amt. Solid Food	Amt. Liquid	Amt. Yield
Tomatoes, (Diced, Crushed	80+ oz	—	80+ oz	96 oz	—	96 oz
or Whole)	10+c	—	10+c	12c	—	12c
Turnip Greens	100 oz	33+ oz	80+ oz	120 oz	40 oz	96 oz
	12c 4 oz	4c 1+ oz	10+c	15c	5c	12c

Fruits

| Item | 5 Servings | | | | | |
| | #12 Scoop (2.67 ounces) | | | #10 Scoop (3.2 ounces) | | |
	Amt. Solid Food	Amt. Liquid	Amt. Yield	Amt. Solid Food	Amt. Liquid	Amt. Yield
Apricots (H.S.)	17 oz	3+ oz	13+ oz	21 oz	3+ oz	16 oz
	2c 1 oz	3+ oz	1c 5+ oz	2c 5 oz	3+ oz	2c
Fruit Cocktail (H.S.)	16 oz	1+ oz	13+ oz	20 oz	2 oz	16 oz
	2c	1+ oz	1c 5+ oz	2c 4 oz	2 oz	2c
Peaches, Halves or Sliced	15 oz	2+ oz	13+ oz	18+ oz	3 oz	16 oz
(H.S.) (L.S.)	1c 7 oz	2+ oz	1c 5+ oz	2c 2+ oz	3 oz	2c
Peaches, Pie Pack	13+ oz	—	13+ oz	16 oz	—	16 oz
	1c 5+ oz	—	1c 5+ oz	2c	—	2c
Pears, Halves (H.S.), (35/40)	16 oz	2 oz	13+ oz	19 oz	3+ oz	16 oz
	2c	2 oz	1c 5+ oz	2c 3 oz	3+ oz	2c
Fruit Mix (L.S.)	13+ oz	—	13+ oz	16 oz	—	16 oz
	1c 5+ oz	—	1c 5+ oz	2c	—	2c
Pear Halves (40/50)(L.S.)	17 oz	3+ oz	13+ oz	21 oz	3+ oz	16 oz
	2c 1 oz	3+ oz	1c 5+ oz	2c 5 oz	3+ oz	2c
Apricots (W.P.)	15 oz	2+ oz	13+ oz	18 oz	3 oz	16 oz
	1c 7 oz	2+ oz	1c 5+ oz	2c 2 oz	3 oz	2c
Fruit Cocktail (W.P.)	13+ oz	—	13+ oz	16 oz	—	16 oz
	1c 5+ oz	—	1c 5+ oz	2c	—	2c
Peach Halves (W.P.)	15 oz	2+ oz	13+ oz	18 oz	3 oz	16 oz
	1c 7 oz	2+ oz	1c 5+ oz	2c 2 oz	3 oz	2c
Pear Halves (W.P.)	19 oz	3+ oz	13+ oz	23 oz	4 oz	16 oz
	2c 3 oz	3+ oz	1c 5+ oz	2c 7 oz	4 oz	2c

| Item | 10 Servings | | | | | |
| | #12 Scoop (2.67 ounces) | | | #10 Scoop (3.2 ounces) | | |
	Amt. Solid Food	Amt. Liquid	Amt. Yield	Amt. Solid Food	Amt. Liquid	Amt. Yield
Apricots (H.S.)	35 oz	6 oz	27 oz	41 oz	7 oz	32 oz
	4c 3 oz	6 oz	3c 3 oz	5c 1 oz	7 oz	4c
Fruit Cocktail (H.S.)	33 oz	3 oz	27 oz	39 oz	3+ oz	32 oz
	4c 1 oz	3 oz	3c 3 oz	4c 7 oz	3+ oz	4c
Peaches, Halves or Sliced	31 oz	5+ oz	27 oz	36+ oz	6 oz	32 oz
(H.S.) (L.S.)	3c 7 oz	5+ oz	3c 3 oz	4c 4+ oz	6 oz	4c

Exhibit 3–6 Fruits, continued

Item	10 Servings					
	#12 Scoop (2.67 ounces)			#10 Scoop (3.2 ounces)		
	Amt. Solid Food	Amt. Liquid	Amt. Yield	Amt. Solid Food	Amt. Liquid	Amt. Yield
Peaches, Pie Pack	27 oz	—	27 oz	32 oz	—	32 oz
	3c 3 oz	—	3c 3 oz	4c	—	4c
Pears, Halves (H.S.), (35/40)	33 oz	5+ oz	27 oz	39 oz	7 oz	32 oz
	4c 1 oz	5+ oz	3c 3 oz	4c 7 oz	7 oz	4c
Fruit Mix (L.S.)	27 oz	—	27 oz	32 oz	—	32 oz
	3c 3 oz	—	3c 3 oz	4c	—	4c
Pear Halves (40/50)(L.S.)	35 oz	6 oz	27 oz	41 oz	7 oz	32 oz
	4c 3 oz	6 oz	3c 3 oz	5c 1 oz	7 oz	4c
Apricots (W.P.)	31 oz	5 oz	27 oz	36 oz	6 oz	32 oz
	3c 7 oz	5 oz	3c 3 oz	4c 4 oz	6 oz	4c
Fruit Cocktail (W.P.)	27 oz	—	27 oz	32 oz	—	32 oz
	3c 3 oz	—	3c 3 oz	4c	—	4c
Peach Halves (W.P.)	31 oz	5 oz	27 oz	36 oz	6 oz	32 oz
	3c 7 oz	5 oz	3c 3 oz	4c 4 oz	6 oz	4c
Pear Halves (W.P.)	39 oz	7 oz	27 oz	46 oz	8 oz	32 oz
	4c 7 oz	7 oz	3c 3 oz	5c 6 oz	1c	4c

Item	15 Servings					
	#12 Scoop (2.67 ounces)			#10 Scoop (3.2 ounces)		
	Amt. Solid Food	Amt. Liquid	Amt. Yield	Amt. Solid Food	Amt. Liquid	Amt. Yield
Apricots (H.S.)	52 oz	9 oz	40 oz	62 oz	10+ oz	48 oz
	6c 4 oz	1c 1 oz	5c	7c 6 oz	1c 2+ oz	6c
Fruit Cocktail (H.S.)	49 oz	4 oz	40 oz	59 oz	5 oz	48 oz
	6c 1 oz	4 oz	5c	7c 3 oz	5 oz	6c
Peaches, Halves or Sliced (H.S.) (L.S.)	46 oz	8 oz	40 oz	55 oz	9+ oz	48 oz
	5c 6 oz	1c	5c	6c 7 oz	1c 1+ oz	6c
Peaches, Pie Pack	40 oz	—	40 oz	48 oz	—	48 oz
	5c	—	5c	6c	—	6c
Pears, Halves (H.S.), (35/40)	48 oz	8 oz	40 oz	58 oz	10 oz	48 oz
	6c	1c	5c	7c 2 oz	1c 2 oz	6c
Fruit Mix (L.S.)	40 oz	—	40 oz	48 oz	—	48 oz
	5c	—	5c	6c	—	6c
Pear Halves (40/50)(L.S.)	52 oz	9 oz	40 oz	62 oz	12+ oz	48 oz
	6c 4 oz	9 oz	5c	7c 6 oz	1c 4+ oz	6c
Apricots (W.P.)	46 oz	8 oz	40 oz	55 oz	9+ oz	48 oz
	5c 6 oz	8 oz	5c	6c 7 oz	1c 1+ oz	6c
Fruit Cocktail (W.P.)	40 oz	—	40 oz	48 oz	—	48 oz
	5c	—	5c	6c	—	6c
Peach Halves (W.P.)	46 oz	8 oz	40 oz	55 oz	9+ oz	48 oz
	5c 6 oz	8 oz	5c	6c 7 oz	1c 1+ oz	6c
Pear Halves (W.P.)	57 oz	10 oz	40 oz	69 oz	12 oz	48 oz
	7c 1 oz	1c 2 oz	5c	8c 5 oz	1c 4 oz	6c

Exhibit 3–6 Fruits, continued

Item	20 Servings					
	#12 Scoop (2.67 ounces)			#10 Scoop (3.2 ounces)		
	Amt. Solid Food	Amt. Liquid	Amt. Yield	Amt. Solid Food	Amt. Liquid	Amt. Yield
Apricots (H.S.)	68 oz	11+ oz	53+ oz	83 oz	14 oz	64 oz
	8c 4 oz	1c 3+ oz	6c 5+ oz	10c 3 oz	1c 6 oz	8c
Fruit Cocktail (H.S.)	65 oz	5+ oz	53+ oz	78 oz	6+ oz	64 oz
	8c 1 oz	5+ oz	6c 5+ oz	9c 6 oz	6+ oz	8c
Peaches, Halves or Sliced (H.S.) (L.S.)	60+ oz	10 oz	53+ oz	73 oz	12+ oz	64 oz
	7c 4 oz	1c 2 oz	6c 5+ oz	9c 1 oz	1c 4+ oz	8c
Peaches, Pie Pack	53+ oz	—	53+ oz	64 oz	—	64 oz
	6c 5 oz	—	6c 5+ oz	8c	—	8c
Pears, Halves (H.S.), (35/40)	64 oz	11 oz	53+ oz	77 oz	13 oz	64 oz
	8c	1c 3 oz	6c 5+ oz	9c 5 oz	1c 5 oz	8c
Fruit Mix (L.S.)	53+ oz	—	53+ oz	64 oz	—	64 oz
	6c 5+ oz	—	6c 5+ oz	8c	—	8c
Pear Halves (40/50)(L.S.)	68 oz	11+ oz	53+ oz	83 oz	14 oz	64 oz
	8c 4 oz	1c 3+ oz	6c 5+ oz	10c 3 oz	1c 6 oz	8c
Apricots (W.P.)	60 oz	10 oz	53+ oz	73 oz	12 oz	64 oz
	7c 4 oz	1c 2 oz	6c 5+ oz	9c 1 oz	1c 4 oz	8c
Fruit Cocktail (W.P.)	53+ oz	—	53+ oz	64 oz	—	64 oz
	6c 5+ oz	—	6c 5+ oz	8c	—	8c
Peach Halves (W.P.)	60 oz	10 oz	53+ oz	73 oz	12 oz	64 oz
	7c 4 oz	1c 2 oz	6c 5+ oz	9c 1 oz	1c 4 oz	8c
Pear Halves (W.P.)	76 oz	13 oz	53+ oz	92 oz	15+ oz	64 oz
	9c 4 oz	1c 5 oz	6c 5+ oz	11c 4 oz	1c 7+ oz	8c

Item	25 Servings					
	#12 Scoop (2.67 ounces)			#10 Scoop (3.2 ounces)		
	Amt. Solid Food	Amt. Liquid	Amt. Yield	Amt. Solid Food	Amt. Liquid	Amt. Yield
Apricots (H.S.)	86 oz	14+ oz	67 oz	103 oz	17 oz	80 oz
	10c 6 oz	1c 6 oz	8c 3 oz	12c 7 oz	2c 1 oz	10c
Fruit Cocktail (H.S.)	82 oz	7 oz	67 oz	98 oz	8 oz	80 oz
	10c 2 oz	7 oz	8c 3 oz	12c 2 oz	1c	10c
Peaches, Halves or Sliced (H.S.) (L.S.)	76 oz	13 oz	67 oz	91 oz	15+ oz	80 oz
	9c 4 oz	1c 5 oz	8c 3 oz	11c 3 oz	1c 7+ oz	10c
Peaches, Pie Pack	67 oz	—	67 oz	80 oz	—	80 oz
	8c 3 oz	—	8c 3 oz	10c	—	10c
Pears, Halves (H.S.), (35/40)	81 oz	13+ oz	67 oz	97 oz	16+ oz	80 oz
	10c 1 oz	1c 5+ oz	8c 3 oz	12c 1 oz	2c+	10c
Fruit Mix (L.S.)	67 oz	—	67 oz	80 oz	—	80 oz
	8c 3 oz	—	8c 3 oz	10c	—	10c
Pear Halves (40/50)(L.S.)	86 oz	14+ oz	67 oz	103 oz	17 oz	80 oz
	10c 6 oz	1c 6+ oz	8c 3 oz	12c 7 oz	2c 1 oz	10c
Apricots (W.P.)	73 oz	12 oz	67 oz	91 oz	15+ oz	80 oz
	9c 1 oz	1c 4 oz	8c 3 oz	11c 3 oz	1c 7+ oz	10c
Fruit Cocktail (W.P.)	67 oz	—	67 oz	80 oz	—	80 oz
	8c 3 oz	—	8c 3 oz	10c	—	10c

Exhibit 3–6 Fruits, continued

Item	25 Servings					
	#12 Scoop (2.67 ounces)			#10 Scoop (3.2 ounces)		
	Amt. Solid Food	Amt. Liquid	Amt. Yield	Amt. Solid Food	Amt. Liquid	Amt. Yield
Peach Halves (W.P.)	73 oz	12 oz	67 oz	91 oz	15+ oz	80 oz
	9c 1 oz	1c 4 oz	8c 3 oz	11c 3 oz	1c 7+ oz	10c
Pear Halves (W.P.)	96 oz	16 oz	67 oz	114 oz	19 oz	80 oz
	12c	2c	8c 3 oz	14c 2 oz	2c 3 oz	10c

Item	30 Servings					
	#12 Scoop (2.67 ounces)			#10 Scoop (3.2 ounces)		
	Amt. Solid Food	Amt. Liquid	Amt. Yield	Amt. Solid Food	Amt. Liquid	Amt. Yield
Apricots (H.S.)	103 oz	17 oz	80+ oz	124 oz	21 oz	96 oz
	12c 7 oz	2c 1 oz	10+c	15c 4 oz	2c 5 oz	12c
Fruit Cocktail (H.S.)	98 oz	8 oz	80+ oz	118 oz	20 oz	96 oz
	12c 2 oz	1c	10+c	14c 6 oz	2c 4 oz	12c
Peaches, Halves or Sliced (H.S.) (L.S.)	91 oz	15+ oz	80+ oz	109 oz	18 oz	96 oz
	11c 3 oz	1c 7+ oz	10+c	13c 5 oz	2c 2 oz	12c
Peaches, Pie Pack	80+ oz	—	80+ oz	96 oz	—	96 oz
	10+c	—	10+c	12c	—	12c
Pears, Halves (H.S.), (35/40)	97 oz	16+ oz	80+ oz	116 oz	19 oz	96 oz
	12c 1 oz	2+c	10+c	14c 4 oz	2c 3 oz	12c
Fruit Mix (L.S.)	80+ oz	—	80+ oz	96 oz	—	96 oz
	10+c	—	10+c	12c	—	12c
Pear Halves (40/50)(L.S.)	103 oz	17 oz	80+ oz	124 oz	21 oz	96 oz
	12c 7 oz	2c 1 oz	10+c	15c 4 oz	2c 5 oz	12c
Apricots (W.P.)	91 oz	15+ oz	80+ oz	109 oz	18+ oz	96 oz
	11c 3 oz	1c 7+ oz	10+c	13c 5 oz	2c 2+ oz	12c
Fruit Cocktail (W.P.)	80+ oz	—	80+ oz	96 oz	—	96 oz
	10+c	—	10+c	12c	—	12c
Peach Halves (W.P.)	91 oz	15+ oz	80+ oz	109 oz	18+ oz	96 oz
	11c 3 oz	1c 7+ oz	10+c	13c 5 oz	2c 2+ oz	12c
Pear Halves (W.P.)	114 oz	19 oz	80+ oz	137 oz	23 oz	96 oz
	14c 2 oz	2c 3 oz	10+c	17c 1 oz	2c 7 oz	12c

Table 3–5 Summary of savings

Comparison item	Present	Proposed	Differential
Number of pureed diets (single portions)	62 noon 62 evening	10 noon 10 evening	52 noon 52 evening
Number of pureed diets (double portions)	24 noon 24 evening	— —	24 noon 24 evening
Total/noon & evening meals	172	20	152
Additional meals required due to solid food factor (25%)	43	5	38
Total meals	215	25	190
Raw food cost/meal ($.67)*	$144.05/ patient for noon and evening meals/day	$16.75/ patient for noon and evening meals/day	$127.30/ patient for noon and evening meals/day

Savings:

$127.30 × 30 = $3,819.00/savings month

$127.30 × 365 = $46,464.50/savings year

*$.67 per meal is used as the documented cost per meal for the facility. With implementation of recommendations, actual costs of pureed diet meal would be $.55.

Result

Residents for whom pureed diets were prescribed were reduced to ten, and no double portions were required after a reevaluation. The facility established a policy requiring that when residents request or need additional food, a notation should be made on the diet card. A periodic evaluation system of large portions was instituted and waste was significantly reduced. Table 3–5 identifies the resultant savings.

In this facility, 168 residents × 3 meals a day × 30 days/month = 15,120 resident meals served/month. Therefore, the facility actually would have served an additional 3,457 meals per month, for a total of 18,577. This difference in number of meals significantly influences the per meal cost. Such management information is essential to a cost-efficient, quality food service operation. The raw food cost per meal, including the pureed diet meal equivalents, would be 55 cents instead of 67 cents. Although this facility had an unusually large number of pureed diets, the same principles will apply to any institution and have an impact on per meal cost.

Given this information, it may be desirable to evaluate the number of skilled care residents the budget can afford to maintain. An important first step is an accurate assessment of pureed diet prescriptions. An extensive evaluation of residents and their diets made it possible to reduce the number of pureed diets to ten, resulting in an actual savings of:

$127.30 × 30 = $3,819.00/month

$127.30 × 365 = $46,464.50/year

73

Pureed diets thus can make a substantial difference in food costs.

Although pureed diets are expensive, they sometimes are necessary. Establishing the cost of such a requirement should encourage reevaluating its use. Some residents who receive pureed diets conceivably could manage foods that are either ground, chopped, or soft. The change would increase the diet's acceptability as well as reduce costs. The maxim to follow is:

> Don't puree the food if ground will do;
> Don't grind the food if chopped will do;
> Don't chop the food when whole will do;
> Do all you can to make them chew.

Pureed foods often are prescribed because of patients' inability to chew, a choking experience, or a stroke. As the resident gets better, ground or chopped foods may be indicated. This is relatively easy to eat and provides the resident with far greater enjoyment. With the exception of tube feedings, food should be liquefied only as a last resort. All other means of improving the resident's nutritional status and enjoyment of meals should be exhausted first.

DIABETIC AND DIETETIC FOODS

By comparison, other therapeutic diets are not as costly as those that are pureed. However, some additional labor is required in the preparation and serving of therapeutic diets as indicated earlier in Table 3–2. With the exception of fresh or water-packed fruits, no special dietary foods should be required for regular patients.

Most foods can be served to diabetic patients, as well, as long as the food has been prepared free of fat and properly measured according to the food exchanges. The appropriate number of "fat exchanges" can be added to the diabetic patient's tray as indicated per caloric calibration. Specially prepared "dietetic" foods may not be appropriate for the diabetic since many dietetic foods contain sorbitol or mannitol that produce metabolic results similar to sugar and, therefore, should not be used by the diabetic. These dietetic foods have been processed primarily for persons trying to lose weight rather than for diabetic patients.

Diabetic snacks, necessary for some patients, can be costly. Although such snacks must be provided, costs should be identified for this nutrition-related medical requirement to maximize third party reimbursement.

NUTRITIONAL SUPPLEMENTS

The cost of milkshakes and nutritional supplements should be documented:

1. to assess the actual need for milkshakes and/or nutritional supplements
2. to maximize third party reimbursement.

Such supplements are excellent for improving the nutritional status of some patients. However, they also can deter appetites at meal time. The health care team should evaluate each patient's needs and review them periodically before any nutritional supplement is prescribed and maintained.

In one facility, it was determined that between-meal milkshakes cost more than $8,000 a year, for which it received no additional remuneration. Nursing service noted that many of the patients were not eating their meals. Although some definitely needed the milkshakes, a majority would have been equally pleased with a less expensive, less filling nourishment between meals. Therefore, nursing service and the entire health care team reevaluated the necessity of such supplements. A program was instituted to monitor and control between-meal nourishments that reduced costs to $3,000 a year—almost a 60 percent saving.

Similar cost-containment measures can make a definite difference in the balance sheet of any health care institution. It is vital to identify and document them. The monthly meal census form is an effective tool for initiating the documentation of nutrition-related medical requirements. Exhibit 3–7 provides yet another way to maintain a more accurate daily diet census record. Institutions and fiscal intermediaries only recently have become aware of the substantial influence nutrition-related medical requirements can have on food service costs. However, to obtain reimbursement, careful records must be kept.

Evaluating Nourishments

The cost of evening nourishments, another requirement, can represent a major, hidden portion of the food service budget. Before reducing these costs, the present system must be evaluated. The following questions should be asked in analyzing the department's nourishment system:

- Do the nourishments provided reflect the health care needs of the patients or the hunger of the staff?
- How much are nourishments costing the facility?
- Are nourishment requisitions used? Are costs of nourishments recorded?
- Has a system of monitoring nourishment utilization been established?
- Does the quantity of nourishments vary with patient census?
- Is the nourishment order built up to a standard quantity per item as coordinated with census?
- Does the nourishment order vary on weekends and holidays?
- Do types of nourishments ordered ever vary?
- Does the nourishment requisition change according to the staff on duty?
- Do the quantities of nourishments ordered consider inventories of the nourishment refrigerator?

Establishing effective nourishment monitoring systems can benefit patients nutritionally as well as add to the facility's economic well-being. In considering maintaining control of nourishment costs, administrators and managers should:

- Improve interdepartmental relationships between nursing and food services; emphasize that the patient is the ultimate beneficiary; stress the importance of the economic viability of each department.
- Initiate a nourishment requisition system with coordination between nursing and food service (Exhibit 3–8). The requisition should be submitted by nursing service once daily at a specific time. Each item sent to the respective

75

Exhibit 3–7 Daily diet census record

Daily Diet Census Record

DATE JANUARY	1	2	3	4	5	6	7	8	9	10	11	12	13	14	15	16	17	18	19	20	21	22	23	24	25	26	27	28	29	30	31
REGULAR	34	34	33	34	34	31	34	34	34	34	34	32	33	31	34	34	34	30	32	32	33	34	33	33	33	33	33	32	33	33	33
SOFT	8	7	8	8	8	7	8	8	8	8	8	8	8	8	8	7	8	8	8	8	8	8	8	8	8	8	8	8	8	8	8
BLAND	1	1	1	1	1	1	1	1	1	0	1	1	1	1	1	1	0	1	0	0	0	1	1	1	1	0	0	0	0	1	0
LOW SODIUM 1000mg	1	1	1	0	1	1	1	1	1	1	1	1	1	1	1	1	1	1	0	0	0	0	0	0	0	0	0	0	0	0	0
LOW SODIUM 2500mg	18	18	18	18	18	18	17	18	18	18	18	17	17	18	18	18	18	18	19	19	19	19	19	19	19	19	18	19	19	19	19
DIABETIC 1000 Cal.	10	10	10	10	10	10	10	10	10	10	10	10	10	9	10	10	10	10	10	10	10	10	10	10	10	10	10	10	10	10	10
DIABETIC 1500 Cal.	5	5	5	5	5	5	5	5	5	5	4	5	5	5	5	5	5	5	5	5	5	5	5	5	5	5	5	5	5	5	5
DIABETIC 2000 Cal.	1	1	1	1	1	1	1	1	1	1	1	1	1	1	1	1	1	1	1	1	1	1	1	1	1	1	1	1	1	1	1
DIABETIC other	2	2	2	2	2	2	2	2	2	2	2	2	2	2	2	2	2	2	2	2	2	2	2	2	2	2	2	2	2	2	2
LOW FAT	0	0	0	0	0	0	0	0	0	0	0	0	0	0	0	0	0	0	0	0	0	0	0	0	0	0	0	0	0	0	0
MECHANICAL SOFT	7	7	7	7	7	7	7	7	7	7	7	7	7	7	7	7	7	7	7	7	7	7	8	8	8	7	8	8	8	8	8
PUREED	10	10	10	10	10	10	10	10	10	10	10	10	10	10	10	10	10	10	10	10	10	10	10	10	10	10	10	10	10	10	10
OTHER (specify)																															
AIDES & WORKERS	8	6	9	5	10	6	8	9	7	9	9	10	10	9	9	8	6	6	5	10	10	9	9	9	8	9	9	9	9	9	9
TOTAL DAILY	105	102	105	102	107	99	104	106	102	105	105	104	105	102	106	104	103	98	99	104	105	107	106	106	105	105	105	105	106	106	106

Courtesy of Progressive Medical Group

Exhibit 3–8 Nourishment requisition form

Date: _____

Item	Unit	Quantity on hand	Quantity ordered	Amount sent	Cost
Apple juice	qt.				
Cranberry juice	qt.				
Grape juice	qt.				
Grapefruit juice	qt.				
Mixed citrus juice	qt.				
Orange juice	qt.				
Pineapple juice	qt.				
Tomato juice	qt.				
Whole milk	½ gal.				
Skim milk	½ gal.				
Buttermilk	½ gal.				
Tube feeding					
Cookies	doz.				
Graham crackers	pkg.				
Bread	loaf				
Prune juice					
Kool-Aid					

Ordered:
Nursing Staff _____

Filled:
Dietary Staff: _____

patient area should appear on the form, then be filled and fully costed by food service.

• Institute a system of monitoring nourishments that each wing uses (Exhibit 3–7).

• Evaluate the type and quantity of nourishments ordered in relation to patients' needs and requests.

Cooperation among departments is essential to achieving economically efficient, yet quality, health care. The process of ordering and monitoring the use of
nourishments is no exception. A budgetary goal on a daily, monthly, or per-
patient-day basis should be established and evaluated periodically. The goal
should reflect projected therapeutic needs based on past and anticipated mix of
future patient census.

Nourishment Costing Forms

When properly used, a Nourishment Requisition Form, coupled with a Summarization of Nourishment Costs Form, can assist in directing policy on nourishment costs and benefits.

Forms are good as long as they are used properly. In analyzing the nourishment
costs of one hospital, it was found that a nourishment requisition was being
completed but not costed. After final tabulation, the 75-bed facility determined
that $14,000 a year was being spent for evening nourishments. Based on 60 per-
cent occupancy, evening nourishments were costing $.85 per patient day. This
was inordinate for a general care institution, and once the exceptional costs were
exposed, appropriate steps for reducing the waste were initiated.

Completing the Summarization of Nourishment Costs Form (Exhibit 3–9) can
prove enlightening. Why does one patient area require $11.39 of nourishments per
day while another needs only $4.24? Therapeutics, patient requests, or an emer-
gency could have demanded such a discrepancy. The significant factor is that the
form identifies the costs so they can be evaluated.

In some instances the evening shift of nursing personnel places a nourishment
order already submitted by the day shift to be certain a sufficient supply is
available. Staff pilferage also can become an identifiable factor. The summarization form (Exhibit 3–9) further reflects the fact that costs can vary, depending on
the staff on duty. Some nursing personnel order more expensive nourishments,
such as cranberry and prune juice, as well as milkshakes. Many reasons can
account for increased costs. The primary point to emphasize is these costs must be
monitored in order to control them. Coordination among administration, nursing,
and food service can produce an effective nourishment costing system.

In anticipating future reimbursement considerations, it is recommended that
nourishments, special catering, and any food-related functions other than three
meals a day be costed separately and documented carefully. More effective
management of thousands of dollars a year and potential increased reimbursement
will result.

For example, a 200-bed nursing home reduced its monthly nourishment expenditure from $800 to $200 by evaluating and monitoring the type and quantity of
items provided.

A private psychiatric institution saved more than $10,000 a year by instituting a
daily nourishment cost ceiling for each cottage. Each was responsible for maintaining nourishments within the established cost parameters; if costs exceeded the
ceiling one day, nursing service reduced ordering below that level the following
day.

The national averages of the evening nourishment cost index from institutions
include:

Nursing homes: 18¢ to 24¢ per patient day
Hospitals: 30¢ to 99¢ per patient day
Private psychiatric hospitals: 75¢ to 95¢ per patient day

Exhibit 3–9 Summarization of nourishment costs form   *Cost Realities*

Facility: _____   Month: _____

Day	Total
1	
2	
3	
4	
5	
6	
7	
8	
9	
10	
11	
12	
13	
14	
15	
16	
17	
18	
19	
20	
21	
22	
23	
24	
25	
26	
27	
28	
29	
30	
31	
Total	

These primarily reflect items ordered for distribution after the evening meal, including juices, milk, crackers, or cookies, etc.

The cost of nutrition-related medical requirements, including pureed diets, therapeutic diets, unnecessary nutritional supplements, between-meal nourishments, and evening nourishments, can significantly affect food service budgets. Administration and managers must monitor and control them to minimize costs while maximizing patient care.

NOTES

1. Mary J. Hitchcock, *Food Service Systems Administration* (New York: Macmillan Publishing Co., Inc., 1980), 37.

2. Elaine E. Cabot, "Selective Menu Raises Satisfaction and Costs," *Modern Hospital* (February 1971):139–140.

3. Lourdes Santos and Kathleen Cutlar, "How Hospitals Implement Selective Menu Systems," *Hospitals, JAHA,* 38:93–96.

REFERENCES

Livingston, G.E., and Chang, Charlotte M. *Food Service Systems: Analyses, Design and Implementation.* New York: Academic Press, 1979, 155.

Packer, Linda. "Nutrition—What Do You Really Need to Know?" *Food Service Marketing* (November 1980), 37–41.

Van Den Haag, Ernest. "How to Make Hospitals Hospitable." *Fortune* (May 17, 1982), 123–129.

Chapter 4

Cost Efficiencies in Purchasing, Receiving, Storing, and Inventory Systems

In his 1979 testimony before the Senate Subcommittee on Health, Joseph A. Califano Jr., then Secretary of Health, Welfare, and Education, estimated that $1.3 billion was wasted in FY 1977 through inefficient buying practices.

Effective purchasing is one, but not the only, cornerstone in providing cost effective quality food service.

> Purchasing and procurement, once considered ho-hum activities, are rapidly becoming the current food service buzzwords. With many facilities spending 35 to 45 percent of their total direct expenses on food alone, it has quickly become apparent that the efficiency with which an organization procures its products has an astounding impact on the bottom line.[1]

Once the essential, preliminary food service goals have been identified—through budget and menu planning—proper purchasing, receiving, and storage of food will enable professional managers to reach those objectives.

Efficient, cost effective purchasing is a science, not guess work. It begins with a realistic budget and economically feasible menus, including proper food specifications and quantities needed to implement the menu cycle. (Appendix B is an example of a Purchasing Production Guide for two three-week menu cycles.) After the approximate quantities per cycle have been determined, they can be further detailed in accordance with delivery schedules and storeroom capacities.

The purchasing department handles a variety of duties besides simply dealing with vendors, including:

- preparing information for vendor negotiations
- supplying current marketing information
- maintaining a price index of products and supplies
- preparing the purchasing department budget
- preparing and/or maintaining the purchasing manual
- administrating or conducting purchasing training programs
- maintaining the purchasing library

- informing other departments of current cost trends
- preparing forecasts of food service trends
- preparing purchasing requirement forecasts
- conducting management audits of purchasing operations
- assembling intelligence information on competitors.

PURCHASING SYSTEMS

The type of food purchasing system selected can mean the difference between profit and loss. The three primary types of purchasing systems discussed in this chapter are: (1) purchasing by item, (2) one-stop shopping, (3) the primary vendor concept, and (4) group purchasing. The advantages and disadvantages of each are analyzed next.

Purchasing by Item

Produce is purchased from a produce company, meat from a meat company, eggs and chickens from a poultry supplier, groceries from one or more grocery suppliers, bread from a bakery, milk and ice cream from a dairy, etc.

Advantages

- Managers can deal with a representative well versed in the particular product being purchased—a specialist in the specific field.
- Managers can take advantage of emergency deliveries and donations for special functions if the vendor is local (but must beware the hidden cost for these services).
- Overhead costs are lower because of the vendor's small size (no computer, fewer trucks on the road).
- It usually is possible to get fresh meat (not frozen) if requested from a meat supplier.

Disadvantages

- Managers can spend too much time placing orders—calling the company, being put on hold, being asked to call back, etc. This costs the facility money.
- Managers spend too much time processing the numerous invoices for payment.
- Smaller companies (produce, meat, poultry, etc.) usually are not on a computer so their invoices often are hard to read. They may have more mistakes, and they cannot offer many services that are available only by computer as provided by large companies (such as a printout of items purchased monthly, nutrient analysis, suggested usage figures based on menu and size of facility).
- Prices usually are higher since no single company receives a significant dollar volume of business.

One-Stop Shopping

In this system, the institution buys every food item needed from one full-line supplier, generally excluding bread and dairy.

Advantages

- Better dollar volume with one company gives purchasers a more advantageous pricing structure.
- Less time is spent ordering, processing invoices, etc.

Disadvantages

- Menu adjustments must be made if the facility is shorted on an item.
- Meats, both frozen and fresh, may not be available. (If food service plans to store its meat frozen, this can be an advantage because quality will be higher if quick frozen by a commercial plant rather than frozen more slowly in the facility's freezer.)
- The supply responsibility is on the shoulders of the vendor; however, the seller also benefits and should not take this responsibility lightly.

Primary Vendor Concept

The facility buys from two companies—a ''primary'' vendor for 75 percent to 90 percent of dollar volume purchased monthly (excluding bread and dairy) and a second company for backup or for shorted items, specialty items, etc. Both vendors should be full-time suppliers.

Advantages

- Enough volume goes to the primary supplier so that the facility gets good pricing flexibility.
- The institution is not limited to the inventory of one company in writing menus or selecting products.

Disadvantages

- Prices usually are higher with the secondary vendor, and the facility may get locked into purchasing from such a company because of menu needs, particular products, etc.
- The secondary vendor must understand the type of system being used so that the institution will not be constantly pressured to purchase more. If purchases from the secondary vendor increase, the drop in sales with the primary vendor may cause the latter's prices to go up.

Group Purchasing

Group purchasing allows smaller facilities to take advantage of lower prices associated with volume discounts. Prices are contained because the supplier is ensured of a large order but is free to quote prices as they fluctuate within the market.

Advantages

- Results in a significant price break
- Streamlines administrative functions
- Improves quality and delivery of products

Disadvantages

- Individual preferences are not considered
- Large facilities often already have a large volume discount
- Good communication among cooperative members is required

A new twist to the group purchasing concept is the addition of computers to improve communication among members and to identify quickly the lowest price. Vendors provide prices on a monthly basis, which are added to the lists stored in the computer. As the prices are updated, the computer identifies the two lowest prices for each item, along with the current price for all vendors. The members of the group purchasing system may then select the prime vendor or cherry-picking method of purchasing.

In theory, most of these systems can apply to any size or type of operation but certain facilities are more likely to go with the one system that works best for them. Three major factors must be considered in making a choice:

1. the operation's purchasing arrangement—whether it is a separate unit or part of a group by ownership, lease, or purchasing agreement
2. the size of the facility
3. the location of the facility

Each of these contributes uniquely to a purchasing system. An independent 50-bed facility in an isolated rural area probably would get better quality and service at a more reasonable price by going with no more than two vendors. If that facility is part of a large chain or a purchasing cooperative agreement, it would benefit from such an association and probably get better pricing than an independent facility in the same area. The independent institution should not expect the same pricing structure as one that is part of a large group.

Conversely, a large metropolitan facility can be served easily and more economically by many vendors and it might choose any system in terms of service, quality, and costs. The major considerations would include the time involved for the purchaser and the accounting costs for maintaining a vendor.[2]

In recent years, many food service operators have consolidated their purchasing. The tendency now is to use considerably fewer supplies than was thought necessary in the mid-1970s.

Regardless of how many suppliers it elects to have, the institution should maintain a file of vendors, both actual and potential. Each supplier card should record name, address, telephone number, categories of food purveyed, terms, sales representatives' names, and information on deliveries, reliability, and special characteristics.[3]

As budgets tighten, even more skill must be used in food purchasing. Comparison shopping may work for the homemaker but an institution is faced with ordering from up to a hundred vendors that can supply some 1,200 line items of inventory. Managers need shortcut methods and practical tips to help. Purchasing need not be complicated, yet specific systems need to be instituted to obtain the lowest possible price.

PURCHASE ORDERS

The purchase order should be the core of any purchasing system. Whether it is a classic order with the identifying number given before the order is placed, or a strictly in-house form, is irrelevant. It is vital to use some type of purchase order form and to obtain quoted prices. Some vendors charge 20 percent to 30 percent more to facilities that do not take the time to get price quotations or comparisons, only 10 percent to 13 percent for those that do have specific purchasing procedures and obtain quoted bids.

Purchase order forms permit verification of the invoiced quantity, quality, and cost against what was ordered. Attaching the invoice to the order form facilitates this procedure. Before any invoice is paid, it should have a signature authorizing the purchase and be verified against the order. Since discrepancies occur, vendors gain respect for institutions that follow these businesslike policies and procedures.

Purchase order forms should contain:

- name and address of purchasing organization
- purchase order number for identification purposes
- date of issue
- name and address of supplier
- delivery date and time
- item description
- brand
- order unit (number per unit)
- price and discount (terms and conditions)
- general instructions
- signature of person(s) authorized to purchase.

Taking price quotations on every order every week can be time consuming. It also may mean putting the cart before the horse in menu planning. Menu writing is a time-consuming but necessary challenge for food service managers. When they try to work in the vendors' weekly specials to take advantage of temporary lower costs, managers may have to sacrifice their well-planned menus. Specials should be incorporated into the food service operation whenever feasible, although they should not dictate production.

Monthly Price Quotes

Monthly quotes can be taken, with the vendors agreeing on fixed prices for a set period of time. Budgeting certainly gets easier with this method because items' cost will be known. However, planners should be sure to keep a close eye on the invoices and check them carefully against the prices agreed upon. This will help in remaining within budget and prevent billing slip-ups.

Unfortunately, in this type of arrangement, pricing generally will not be as competitive. Vendors who agree to a month-by-month system must build in a 1 percent to 2 percent markup to protect themselves from the ever-fluctuating market.

The benefits of market swings when prices drop on an item within the month will not be available in the fixed monthly price quote. In fact, most companies do not hold prices for produce, meat, eggs or poultry longer than one week. However, purchasing staple items and frozen products this way will guarantee price stability for at least a month and possibly more.

Cost and Percentage (Cost-Plus)

This system is simply a contract for purchasing items at cost plus a percentage jointly agreed upon with the vendor to cover overhead. When negotiating this type of contract, it is imperative that both parties agree on the definition of "cost." Does "cost" mean landed or dock cost, the cost of getting the food to the warehouse or dock, or does it include storage, transportation, and inventory costs? Although cost-plus may be an appealing approach to food purchasing and budgeting, the details of what the vendor includes in "cost" could cause trouble if not defined carefully beforehand.

Vendors that agree to "cost and percentage" generally will not hold prices firm longer than seven days. This is especially true if the contract is large and profit is based on volume rather than a high percentage markup. Having the best price on an item that is not delivered on time fails to be a bargain.

Vendor Item Comparison

Vendor item comparisons can save time and assure consistent quality in food produced in the kitchen. As the cooks become accustomed to dealing with specific brands of products, they can anticipate how best to work them into meals.

Some purchasers feel much time is wasted with weekly or even monthly price comparisons on an item-by-item basis. Vendors can be compared every six months to a year by checking individual products.

Once the decision is made on which vendor(s) to buy specific products from, managers will have a reasonable idea of their projected costs for a longer period. They also may try to initiate a ceiling price agreement with vendors under these circumstances. Past quality or recommendations from other users, and reliable service, are factors to consider before selecting any vendors.

With time and experience, vendors become attuned to the institution's specific buying habits and will make sure its desired products are on hand. Some food service managers have been particularly astute in providing their vendors with copies of their facility's menus, along with projected use of each item over a specified length of time. This information helps vendors program their purchasing and warehouse storage to meet these specific needs.

Purchasing Services

There are benefits and some notes of caution in all these approaches to bulk comparison shopping. Managers may find individual or monthly price quotes, cost and percentage, vendor item comparison, or a combination of all these methods works best as they try to stretch their food-purchasing dollar.

In balancing needs, the size of the facility, budget, and staff with managers' time, many of these tips can be useful guidelines to benefit the overall success of the food service department.[4]

A key to quality purchasing is to develop a good relationship with distributors or vendors. Although there are different purchasing systems and many ways to get pricing and bids on items, the key to economical food purchasing lies in communication with and control of the vendors or their sales representatives.

A food wholesale company is a profit-oriented business and it must guard that status carefully if it intends to prosper or even survive. Institutions, as buyers, have the right to expect good quality and service but there are some limitations.

Many buyers have made demands that have jeopardized their relationship with vendors that otherwise would ensure they receive first-class service. Here are some steps for managers in developing cooperative lines of communication or to reestablish those that may be broken or frayed:

1. Do not ask vendors to donate goods to a profit-oriented institution.
2. Do not ask vendor representatives to make special deliveries of items the facility forgot to order. For the most part, vendors do not mind a rare request. On the other hand, they should correct their own errors promptly. A typical food salesperson has 60 to 100 customers. If the vendor made time for on-call deliveries to everyone, there would be little time for anything else.
3. Do not expect weekly visits for orders or personal introduction of new items because the sales rep never could service enough customers. The personal attention may seem beneficial but the facility's budget will suffer. The more customers the vendor serves, the more competitive prices can be.

Some other vital steps are involved to complete ordering. Managers should:

1. Check with staff members or have them, on a consistent basis, submit notes of items needed or that they observe are running low. (Designate a specific place for these to be held.)
2. Evaluate inventory records. Check whether there has been an unnecessary amount of spoilage or waste of an item (be sure to investigate why, later).
3. Project the expected lead times for delivery of items needed. Base the choice of deadlines on the normal, expected delivery time. Be sure to factor in the weeks of inventory being planned.
4. Consider each item. How much is used on a regular basis? Evaluate projected need for the next planned time period, taking into account how much inventory is on hand and how long it should last.

Efficient, cost effective purchasing of food items is a science, not luck. It begins with a realistic budget and carefully planned menus that include proper food specifications and quantities as managers and menu makers have been trained to plan.[5]

Reducing Food Costs

Some common examples of activities to reduce food costs include:

- increased utilization of casseroles
- increased use of vegetables

87

- reduced portion sizes
- increased use of protein extenders
- service of menu items, such as breakfast items, at all meals
- making the facility's own "convenience foods"
- addition of an in-house prefreeze system.

As costs are of such primary concern, management must use every possible way to reduce them. As an example, one hospital and hospital-based skilled nursing facility used a unique means to reduce expenditures. It exercised its right as a county-owned institution to obtain state contract prices normally representing at least a 12 percent reduction in cost. (Any hospital that is owned by a county and/or city may request these prices. The contract prices are in effect for a year, and the state will furnish renewal prices on request.) This institution also conducted a study of actual annual usage of items ranging from medical supplies to paper goods to food items. It then formed a loose purchasing cooperative with other area facilities to order larger quantities and reduce prices further.

The vendor selected could supply quality equal to or better than the state requirements at prices that equalled or bettered the state figure. The facility projected its annual volume of specific items for the vendor while retaining the right to order only the quantity needed per delivery. Each facility agreed to take delivery on a weekly basis and to order only the amount needed or to replace the quantity used during the prior week. This was done by maintaining a reserve stock over and above the amount that actually would be used in any week. By using the state contract prices as leverage and as a guideline, by being able to forecast annual consumption, and by eliciting the participation of other facilities in the area, this institution saved more than $70,000 a year on only 70 items.

Even though a facility may be relatively small (fewer than 100 beds or 200 students or inmates) and have minimal storage capacity, quantity buying is effective when coordinated with other institutions in the same area. Volume purchasing talks. If storage capacity does not permit volume purchasing, cooperative purchasing with weekly drop shipments could save a facility thousands of dollars a year.

An alternative to cooperative purchasing involves obtaining weekly or monthly price bids from several vendors on numerous items. This is known as comparative pricing.

Receiving

An effective receiving system can have a significant impact on profit and loss. The receiving function is one of the most important in any food service establishment and, unfortunately, most often is pitifully neglected. Management spends hours on menus, recipes, purchase specifications, and competitive bids, then fails to check the quantity and quality of delivered goods.

An effective receiving system is another key building block in the pyramid of cost effective quality food service. Improper receiving of goods may actually double purchasing costs. Managers must have an effective way to monitor the orders delivered to protect the facility.

For example, a 200-bed institution received an invoice for 40 pounds of chicken yet only 20 pounds were delivered. This loss was identified through an effective receiving system and by using scales. If the food delivered cost $1.33 a pound, the initial loss of 20 pounds translated into \$26.60; however, the actual loss was \$53.20: the initial \$26.60 in chicken not delivered and an additional \$26.60 for 20 pounds of chicken to replace the missing amount. Therefore, if this occurred only once a week, the result would be an unbudgeted loss of \$2,766.40 in a year.

The importance of instituting a simple yet effective receiving system cannot be overemphasized. To provide such a receiving system, managers should:

- Designate and train one employee to be responsible for receiving food service supplies. (For security, periodically use management and/or a substitute as the "receiving" employee.)
- Establish specific receiving hours (for example, Monday through Friday, 7 a.m. to 4 p.m.). Some institutions have received deliveries as late as 11 p.m. Don't let this happen.
- Maintain purchase orders, food specifications, inventory forms, and other pertinent items near the receiving area.
- Set up a receiving scale and other measuring devices to verify deliveries. Several food service equipment suppliers sell an inexpensive (about \$75) receiving scale that could pay for itself in a short time.
- Provide the receiving area with a written explanation of all procedures. This manual should cover weighing, counting, measuring, physical handling of goods, and routines for receiving tickets. Inspection for quality also must follow established routines.[6]
- Use a receiving stamp. An office supply or rubber stamp company can put the facility's receiving data on an easy-to-use (inexpensive) rubber stamp (Exhibit 4–1). It should be used when an order is checked in and should include the date received, who accepted it, quantity and quality, prices, and who approved the purchase for payment.

Safeguards Against Delivery Discrepancies

Economic loss can occur in ways other than discrepancies in quantities delivered; it can result from discrepancies in quality, as well. Produce and all perishable goods should be checked carefully on delivery. Cases of canned items should be opened to return unusable cans for credit. Expiration dates, particularly on milk, should be verified before accepting delivery.

Indiscriminately signing invoices for the sake of expediency can lead to increased food cost if unusable goods are accepted or undelivered goods are acknowledged as received. Signed invoices represent accepted inventory and money owed. The employee who signs for deliveries should be held accountable,

Exhibit 4–1 Example of a receiving stamp

Date received	Received by ....
	Checked by ....
Quantity	....
Quality	....
Prices	....
Extension	....
Approved for payment by	....

to the extent possible, for the quality and quantity of received goods. The receiving stamp system can facilitate this process.

Receiving forms should be printed and prenumbered in triplicate: one copy goes to the accounts payable bookkeeper, the second to the purchasing department, and the third remains in the receiving area, where it should be filed for reference as necessary.

All food service supplies should be dated and unit cost indicated on the package before storage. This facilitates inventory accounting, regardless of the inventory system used. It also reduces potential theft by demonstrating to employees that management is aware of the receipt and cost of each item. If administration wants further documentation of receiving procedures, a daily report may be appropriate.

Establishing a receiving system is vital to controlling costs. An efficient receiving area facilitates the process. The receiving area can be evaluated by completing the questionnaire in Exhibit 4–2.

Storage Systems

Before actual preparation, proper storage is the final step to ensure quality food service. Bulk purchasing may not be a bargain unless at least 10 percent can be saved on delivered costs of items. Storage space, like food, represents money. It must be used wisely. Appendix 4–A lists specific ways to assure efficient, cost-effective storage.

After the storeroom has been made as efficient as feasible, managers should consider establishing this simple but fool-proof storage system.

Exhibit 4–2 Evaluation of receiving area

	Yes	No
1. Can the facility's dock accommodate two delivery trucks at one time?	—	—
2. Is there a dock extending at least eight feet from the building and 40 inches off the ground?	—	—
3. Is there a load leveler incorporated into the dock?	—	—
4. Is there a roof overhanging the dock to facilitate deliveries during inclement weather?	—	—
5. Is there adequate and appropriate lighting on the back dock?	—	—
6. Are there security lights in the parking areas near the back dock?	—	—
7. Is the Receiving Office near the delivery/receiving area?	—	—
8. Does the receiving area have and use the following receiving equipment?		
Receiving table (at least one)	—	—
Receiving scale	—	—
Area to store:		
Purchase order forms	—	—
Receiving stamp	—	—
Inventory records	—	—
9. Does the facility have an insect control system (fly fan, electronic insect lights, etc.) near the door to the receiving dock?	—	—
10. Is there sufficient storage area for delivery racks (bread racks, milk crates, carbonated beverage tanks, etc.)?	—	—
11. Is there a flushing mechanism (i.e., hose reel) to wash the back dock?	—	—
12. Is there an area adjacent to the back door to store garbage cans or cardboard boxes before pickup?	—	—

All packaged items should be color-coded with a particular color for each quarter of the year. For example, January, February, and March could be color-coded blue; April, May, and June, yellow; July, August, and September, green; and October, November, and December, red. This can be accomplished—with stick-on or colored tabs, magic markers, etc. As time passes, items remaining from previous quarters should be tallied and incorporated into the menu so that most remain in the storeroom no more than two consecutive quarters.

School food service has used a similar storage system for years. It becomes a matter of pride for managers to maintain only current stock in the storeroom. Therefore, they have little, if any, excess ordering. Previously stocked items are not overlooked because of the monthly monitoring process. This system minimizes waste and saves money by mandating a continual monitoring of the FIFO (first in, first out) method of storing. The FIFO system of storage is important in maintaining and protecting the financial and nutrition investment in goods received.

Increasing Storage Capacities

Increasing present storage capabilities can translate into greater purchasing power to minimize cost per item. Emphasis has been placed on the benefits of volume purchasing, but a major additional problem is that storage space is at a premium at most health care facilities. Exhibit 4–3 lists steps to maximize storage at minimum cost.

Proper storage is a key ingredient in producing cost-effective, quality food service.

> Purchasing of food, equipment, and supplies represents about 4 percent to 5 percent of most hospitals' total budgets. It is usually the biggest expenditure by any department other than payroll. The average 300-bed hospital will spend nearly $1 million dollars in the next year for food, equipment, and supplies. For the most part the food service department will be responsible for the buying, receiving and storage of most of that material.[7]

Exhibit 4–3 Ways to maximize storage at minimum cost

- Place extra shelves in reach-in refrigerator and freezer to recapture "lost space" between items stored and the next shelf.
- Use pallets on casters in middle of floor of walk-in refrigerators and the storeroom. (Sanitation codes are met as pallets are easily moved for cleaning.)
- Hang all utensils possible to free drawers.
- Use dividers in drawers to organize space better.
- Hang spice racks on back of storeroom door.
- Utilize space between top of equipment to within 18 inches of ceiling for storage of less-used items.
- Increase depth of shelving from 12 inches to 24 inches, minimizing wide, unnecessary aisles.
- Add shelving between tubular legs of work tables; this provides additional rack storage in dishroom.
- Leave no blank wall space; hang shelves on them or use empty racks for storage.

INVENTORY SYSTEMS

For the food service director, a simple, yet effective inventory cost control system can be the next most important tool for monitoring the operating budget. Monitoring stored items is enhanced through an appropriate inventory system. Some facilities operate strictly on a cash accounting basis, with no "credit" being given to the food service department for the thousands of dollars of stored items. Shelves filled with such supplies actually represent packaged, processed dollars, not supplies. Although the cash method can be effective for fiscal purposes, the accrual basis of accounting (including inventory of items on hand) provides a more accurate reflection of actual departmental operating costs.

Inventory cost control systems serve as an effective monitoring tool. The system selected to meet a particular facility's needs should provide:

- a mechanism to determine the amount and kind of food service supplies maintained and the economic value of each
- a means to identify how much and how often each item per product category is used
- a format to determine progression and/or regression of prices and use of each item.

There are several types of systems to be considered.

Perpetual Inventory Systems

Perpetual inventory systems are the most informative but also are the most costly to maintain in terms of time and labor. Exhibit 4–4 is a perpetual inventory card that can be coupled with Exhibit 4–5, the storeroom checkout sheet. However, there is a simplified version of the perpetual inventory system that also should be considered. The results are similar in that the quantity purchased can be compared with the quantities prepared, yielding the value on hand. The modified version requires less time and labor yet it provides numerous services. It:

Exhibit 4–4 Perpetual inventory card

Item:

Date	On hand	Received	Unit cost	Total cost	Amount used	Cost	Value on hand
6/10	2 cans		$1.90	$3.80			$3.80
6/12		2 cases (12 #10 cans)	$2.00	$24.00			$27.80
6/13					2 cans	$3.80	$24.00

Exhibit 4–5 Storeroom checkout sheet

Cost Efficiencies

Facility _____   Date_____

Quantity	Food Item	Cost/Unit	Total

1. reflects quantity on hand
2. reflects quantity used
3. indicates progression or regression of prices
4. guides purchasing
5. provides a current value of items on hand.

Computerization of inventories can further enhance this process. (See Chapter 11 on computers.) Computers are becoming a standard tool in the management of food service operations.

Modified Perpetual Inventory System

If a computerized perpetual inventory system is not an immediate option, administration and managers should consider initiating a modified perpetual inventory system (Exhibit 4–6). This reflects the beginning inventory as well as the progression and/or regression of prices and enables the food service director to maintain a current account of stock with the storeroom checkout sheet. Information on the quantity as well as the cost of the items remaining on hand can be maintained.

Beg. Inv.	Item	Unit	Receiving Weekly Prices																End Inv.	Total Cost
			1st				2nd				3rd				4th					
			Qty.	Cost	Unit Cost	On Hand	Qty.	Cost	Unit Cost	On Hand	Qty.	Cost	Unit Cost	On Hand	Qty.	Cost	Unit Cost	On Hand		
1 cs	Apple Rings	6/10	1 cs	15.88		1 cs													1 cs	15.88
1 cs	Applesauce	6/10	1 cs	11.00	11.00	1 cs					2 cs	22.00	11.00	2 cs					1 cs	11.00
2 cs	Fruit Coctail	6/10					1 cs	13.60	13.60	1 cs					1 cs	13.60	13.60	1 cs	1 cs	13.60
1 cs	Peach Halves	6/10	1 cs	11.77	11.77	1 cs	2 cs	24.00	12.00	3 cs									1 cs	12.00
1 cs	Peach Slices	6/10	1 cs	11.77	11.77	1 cs					1 cs	12.00	12.00	1 cs	1 cs	12.00	12.00	2 cs	1 cs	12.00
1 cs	Pineapple Sl	6/10									1 cs	15.50	15.50	1 cs					—	

Exhibit 4-6 Modified perpetual inventory system

The modified perpetual inventory system provides the same basic five information elements as the standard system. It is relatively simple to initiate. Administration and managers should:

- Arrange the storeroom items as much as possible in accordance with various categories in the order shown on the inventory form.
- Take an inventory at the end of one month that subsequently becomes the beginning inventory of the next month.
- Record food service supplies as they are received, indicating quantity as well as cost. These entries are made in the respective weekly columns.
- Note the cost per unit directly on the item when shelving, which facilitates taking inventory and tallying the monetary value.
- Initiate the storeroom checkout sheet (Exhibit 4–5).

For inventory as well as security purposes, food items should be pulled only twice a day. Foods needed to be prepared for the noon meal could be pulled immediately after breakfast and those for the evening meal and breakfast the following day could be retrieved after the noon meal. Perishable items naturally would be stored in one section of the refrigerator designated for subsequent meal preparation. Periodic supervision by the food service director and a direct comparison of the items pulled against the storeroom checkout sheet should be made for verification purposes. The storeroom should remain locked between official pulling times unless specifically authorized by the director or other recognized authority. Since the items have been recorded on the storeroom checkout sheet, the inventory form (Exhibit 4–6) can then be updated in the column indicating food on hand. Naturally, food is subtracted from the on-hand column when pulled and is added as newly delivered goods are received.

These forms are maintained throughout the month. To complete the system for maximum effectiveness, an ending inventory at the close of the month is taken as final verification of balance-on-hand. The subsequent figures are entered on the inventory cost control report (Exhibit 4–7). Total purchases are added to the beginning inventory of the month as the closing inventory is subtracted from that total, leaving the total cost of raw food and supplies consumed. This form further identifies specific segments of cost that can facilitate exposing hidden, excess expenditures.

Inventory Levels

Setting goals to maintain appropriate inventory levels cannot be overemphasized. The determination of requirements should be based on the following:

1. Customer Participation Forecast: Prior experience will indicate what effect weather conditions, special function preregistration, seasonal or holiday trends, or other changeable factors will have on the number anticipated at each meal during the week.
2. Menu Plan: Customer preferences should be considered in choosing items. In estimating quantities of raw materials needed, the recipe file should be consulted for a listing of ingredients for each item.
3. Previous Food Production Records: Past records can guide forecasting customer participation and required product quantities.[8]

Exhibit 4–7 Monthly cost control report

Month of _____ :

Raw food cost
    Beginning inventory ....$_____
    Plus total purchases ....$_____ $_____
    Less closing inventory ....$_____
    Total cost of raw food consumed ....$_____

Supplies
    Beginning inventory ....$_____
    Plus total purchases ....$_____ $_____
    Less closing inventory ....$_____
    Total cost of supplies consumed ....$_____

Summarization of expenses
    Nourishments ....$_____   _____ Per pt. day
    Nutritional supplements ....$_____   _____ Per pt. day
    Supplies ....$_____
    Special functions:
        Patient services ...._____
        Staff services ...._____
    Labor: Labor hrs./mo._____ $ _____
    Other operating expenses........$_____
    Total ....$_____
    Less revenue ....$_____
    Net cost ....$_____

Number of meals served
    Patient days/month ...._____No. of pt. meals/mo. _____
    Staff ...._____Meals/mo.
    Guests ...._____Meals/mo.
    Total number of meals served ...._____

Total food cost
    Raw food _____ + Supplies _____ + Net cost _____ = Total food cost $_____
    Total food cost _____ ÷ No. of meals/month $_____
        = $_____ Total food cost per meal
    Total food cost $_____ ÷ No. of patient days/month _____
        = $_____ Total food cost per patient day

Each facility should adopt a maximum monthly inventory ceiling, with specific accountability to administration if the level exceeds the ceiling. Inventory ceilings generally reflect the minimum that should be maintained on hand at any one time to assure compliance with regulations and efficiency. Thus, the necessary minimum should be considered as the maximum ceiling since there usually is no need to overstock the storeroom. Occasionally, there may be specific reasons for exceeding the maximum, including special purchasing opportunities or unexpected increases in patient census. However, justification and documentation of deviations should be made.

Maximum inventory ceilings should be established by each institution according to its patient and staff needs. Coordinating purchasing capabilities and storage capacities with regulations requiring a minimum three-day supply of food and ancillary items also can facilitate cost control. In states requiring a full week's supply of food, the maximum ceiling levels would increase accordingly. "It is necessary to measure costs versus savings on large nonperishable quantity purchases. This is especially true when such purchases are in excess of the normal

Exhibit 4–8 Evaluating inventory *Cost Efficiencies*

1. Has the inventory been studied to optimize quantity on-hand and the size of orders?
2. If the formulas for inventory optimization are not used, have minimum and maximum levels been established? (Minimum level is the reorder point.)
3. Are purchases made at optimum quantity levels to take advantage of quantity discounts? (Many vendors do not advertise quantity discounts when available; the purchaser must ask. Arrangements often can be made for warehousing on the supplier's premises. The "carrying cost" of inventory should be evaluated against the quantity discount benefits.)
4. Is there any excess inventory on hand that can be returned to vendors for credit? (Purchasing policies should be reviewed to verify (a) existing return arrangements and (b) return conditions in the current purchase contracts.)
5. Has the inventory been evaluated to determine what slow-moving items might be dropped from regular purchase?
6. Has consideration been given to selling slow-moving items at reduced prices to purge inventory and allow for inventory write offs?
7. Are staff discussions held to determine ways to help move slow-moving or obsolete items?

Source: Adapted from "Keep Inventory in Check by Following This Plan—Part 1" by Harvey Ogletree, *The Stokes Report*, October 1981, pp. 7–8.

usage requirements. The cost to carry inventory from one year will vary from 25 percent to 30 percent of total cost of the inventory."[9]

Inventory requires a large cash investment. Therefore, it is necessary to keep to the minimum levels needed to meet the facility's needs. To reduce inventory levels, careful analysis and planning must be done.

To determine whether the facility's inventory is at optimum level or whether potential savings may be available, the questions in Exhibit 4–8 must be answered positively.

Economic Indicators

Inventories are more than money represented by shelved cans in the storeroom; they also can be economic and management indicators. Although it is important to determine the value of items in the storeroom, it is even more significant to evaluate the data in terms of food inventory turnover. Turnover is derived by dividing the value of food on hand into the cost of the food used per month.

$$\frac{\text{Cost of food used per month}}{\text{Approximate value of food inventory}} \quad \frac{\$5,000}{\$1,200} \quad = \quad 4.17$$

Optimally, food inventory turnover of three to five times a month by needs is indicative of efficient storeroom management. The number of times a particular inventory turns over in a year can point up overstocking and speculation in inventories when prices look "right" at the moment—two practices that should be avoided.[10] A high turnover rate can imply minimal quantity buying and the inability of the facility to afford volume purchasing. Although the turnover rate may go undetected by administration as pertinent to the economic well-being of the department, maintaining a policy of purchasing small quantities can be self-defeating and can significantly escalate expenditures and cost per patient day.

The opposite side of the coin—too low a food inventory turnover—can be equally dangerous economically because the assets shelved in the storeroom are essentially being ignored. This requires additional goods to be purchased and increases the storage cost. Thus, both administration and managers should evaluate food inventory turnover, particularly in terms of how it reflects the purchasing/ storing policies of the food service operation.

Cost efficiencies can be achieved by establishing effective purchasing, receiving, storing, and inventory systems for the food service department.

NOTES

1. "Purchasing," *Restaurants and Institutions* (February 1, 1981):21.

2. Sharon Davidson, "Stretch Your Food Dollar Further By Focusing on Purchasing System," *The Stokes Report* (July 1982):1–2.

3. Kenneth I. Solomon and Norman Katz, *Profitable Restaurant Management*, 2nd. ed. (Englewood Cliffs, N.J.: Prentice-Hall, Inc., 1981), 37.

4. Sharon Davidson, "How to Get The Most From Your Food Dollar," *The Stokes Report* (August 1983):1–2.

5. _____, "Increase Your Food Service Purchasing Power," *The Stokes Report* (September 1983):7.

6. Solomon and Katz, *Profitable Restaurant Management*, 43.

7. McLaren, "The Art of Prudent Buying," 61–122.

8. Ray Pedderson, "Purchasing Pointers from a Pro," *Restaurants and Institutions* (February 1981): 154–155.

9. Harvey Ogletree, "Keep Inventory in Check By Following This Plan—Part 2," *The Stokes Report* (November 1981):8.

10. Solomon and Norman Katz, *Profitable Restaurant Management*, 218.

REFERENCES

Buchanan, Robert D. "Purchasing Research Projects Focus on Vendors Supply Sources." *Food Service Marketing* (October 1980).

_____. "Purchasing Research is Focused on Various Subjects." *Food Service Marketing* (November 1980).

Driscoll, Robert. "The Unethical Bidder." *Hospital Purchasing News* (January 1982).

Keiser, James K., and Kallio, Elmer. *Controlling and Analyzing Costs in Food Service Operations*. New York: John Wiley & Sons, Inc., 1974.

Livingston, G.E., and Chang, Charlotte M. *Food Service Systems: Analysis, Design and Implementation*. New York: Academic Press, 1979, 155.

Weiss, Steven. "Food-Buying Trends." *Institutions* (September 1980).

Appendix 4–A

Cost Effective Storage

1. Evaluate the use of storage space carefully. Does the facility use more canned and dried food items, or more convenience, preprepared foods? Obviously, canned goods will require more dry storage and convenience foods will need more cold storage area.
2. How often are deliveries scheduled? This will help determine the maximum space required.
3. Analyze the volume of business in the facility. Is it stable? Storage needs should be planned accordingly, taking into consideration peak delivery periods.
4. Establish a "par" inventory for most food items. Simply set a maximum level of items to be stored and the minimum needed to be maintained. (For example: Worcestershire sauce: 12 bottles minimum, 45 maximum.)
5. Maintain about 25 percent of the raw food cost expenditures in inventory. Minimum space requirement can be estimated by determining one-half square foot per meal served daily.
6. Consider good lighting, proper temperature, and effective air circulation when designing an efficient storeroom.
7. Take appropriate measures to prevent freezing of stored food items if the facility is located in the northern part of the United States. If it is in the southern area, maintain safe storage temperatures (no higher than 85 degrees), with perishable food products kept in refrigerated storage.
8. Use fluorescent lighting in storage areas where lights are to be left on for extended periods since it is 90 percent more efficient in lumens (brightness) per watt than incandescent lighting. Two to three watts per square foot of floor space are needed for dry storage areas. Fluorescent lighting is recommended for walk-in coolers but freezers must have incandescent lighting because of extreme temperatures.
9. Make sure every storeroom has an exhaust fan; proper air circulation also can be helped by using the right type and size of shelving.
10. Consider, in determining the type and size of shelves to be used, the variety of operations in food service. Efficiency can be increased by estimating storage needs on the percentage of #10 cans, gallon jugs, #2 cans, boxed food products, etc., to be stored. For example, #10 cans and gallon jugs

will store 4 deep per 24-inch-wide shelf and 2 deep per 14-inch-wide shelf; #2 cans will store 6 deep per 21-inch-wide shelf.

11. Use shelving made from steel, wire, or wood. Metal shelving is preferred since it is durable and easy to clean. Price quotations should be compared on all types of shelving before a final decision is made. Wooden shelving constructed on site may be even more expensive than wire shelving. If wooden shelving is installed, it should not be painted; instead it should be sealed with clear varnish. Painted shelves require continuous and expensive upkeep. Wire shelves can be very efficient in a dry storeroom but are not recommended for refrigerated storage as they are difficult to keep clean.

12. Design shelving so as to permit proper air circulation through louvers or other ventilation slits to allow air beneath and around food products.

13. Plan aisles in the storeroom just as carefully as the shelving. A minimum of 30 inches between rows of shelves is enough unless a hand truck or dolly is to be used; then, at least 42 inches of aisle space is required.

14. Look for innovations in storage. Two commercial systems currently available will increase the efficiency of storage areas. These systems provide track shelving that rolls on wheels in tracks installed in the floor. The system will increase storage space by at least one-third. (Essential side and end shelf guards must be ordered.) Also, a cost feasibility study should be conducted to determine whether the costs of this type of system will save enough to make it profitable.

Chapter 5

Food Service Cost Management

Every food service can save at least 6 percent of food costs within the next fiscal year. Chapter 1, on strategic planning, identified this as a primary goal. This goal can become reality. As noted, the only danger in not reaching a goal is in not setting it.

Literally thousands of dollars are saved and generated each year by food services through implementing the specific cost management techniques detailed in this chapter. The emphasis here is on savings in food-related functions; other chapters detail means to reduce costs in labor, energy, and administrative systems such as purchasing, inventory, etc. This chapter also discusses how to convert a food service operation from a cost center into a revenue center.

PREPARATION, SERVING, PURCHASING

The preparation and serving of food offers a golden opportunity to satisfy all factions of the food service operation, from cost management to patron service. Properly executed, it can provide patrons (patients, residents, students, inmates, community) with appetizing, highly nutritious food that offers three stimulating interludes eagerly awaited each day. Effectively planned food preparation and serving represents the culmination of all administrative efforts—an ultimate tribute to the food service manager—and virtually assures the goals of patron satisfaction and economic reality.

Purchasing guidelines, production sheets, and standardized recipes are three tools basic to economically efficient quality food service.

Exhibit 5–1 and Tables 5–1 and 5–2 indicate approximate quantities of food to be ordered for the number of meals served. As a guideline, they provide parameters for purchasing and/or for establishing a monitoring system of food utilization. (Appendix B provides specific Purchasing/Production Guidelines for each set of seasonal cycle menus in this book.)

FOOD UTILIZATION STUDIES

Food utilization studies have proved one of the most effective ways to save money. For example, food utilization studies enabled a Florida-based, 168-bed health care facility to identify more than $24,000 a year in savings on four food items alone. To conduct food utilization studies, the institution need only establish monthly purchasing ceilings for key items and correlate them with the number of meals expected to be served. This quantity can be based on the average historical census for the time of year for which the ceiling is being established. This may not be necessary in all facilities because the census of such places as nursing homes, correctional facilities, and potentially schools may not fluctuate. (Appendix C provides tips on preparation practicalities.)

Eggs

As an example, a purchasing ceiling is established for eggs (based on average census) and compared with the number of eggs currently purchased.

Eggs can break an institution. If eggs are served every morning to 100 patients, 120 eggs (including double portions), or four flats (30 eggs in a flat), will be needed just for breakfast. With 12 flats per case, one case, or 30 dozen, should last three days. Thus, the monthly order will be easy to calculate (Exhibit 5–1). In the example cited there, the institution saved $1,512 a year on eggs alone by establishing a purchasing ceiling and monitoring the quantity bought each month.

Exhibit 5–1 Egg purchases

	(per 100 people)
Breakfast use only	10 cases/month
Cooking and other uses	2 cases/month
	12 cases/month

or,

Estimated cases/month

Beds:	100	300	500	700	900	1,500	2,000
Cases	12	36	60	84	108	180	240

Example:

(120 eggs/a.m. per 100 meals served)
4 flats × 30 days/month—120 flats*

Breakfast	10 Cases/month
Cooking purposes	2 Cases/month (per 100 beds)
Total =	12 Cases/month

19 Cases/month
− 12 Cases/month
7 Cases/month

Present	*Proposed*	*Differential*	*Savings/Year*
19 Cases	12 Cases	7 Cases (210 dozen @ 60¢/dozen)	$1,512

*30 eggs/flat, 12 flats/Cases

In controlling costs on eggs, managers should:

- Establish monthly purchasing ceiling and follow closely.
- Use medium eggs only (in lieu of large). Medium eggs are almost always cheaper. There is only a ¼-ounce weight difference between medium and large yet the average cost differential is 7 to 11 cents per dozen. (Table 5–1 shows the differences.) Do the cooks use eggs by the ounce or individually? One medium egg scrambled will yield one standard 2-ounce (#16 scoop) portion. It is not necessary to use more medium eggs to provide the volume of portions required. To achieve the number of servings projected, be sure to use one #16 scoop per serving of one egg.
- Allocate the distribution of eggs rather than leaving this to the discretion of a cook.
- Portion scrambled eggs with a #16 scoop. (One #16 scoop will yield one medium egg scrambled. If the patron requests two eggs, then two #16 scoops should be provided.)
- Evaluate the number of eggs used in cooking. Excessive numbers can be used and go almost unnoticed (until the invoices are paid). A vital question: how many eggs are used in cooking in the facility? Standardized recipes can save money as well as yield a standard product. If the cooks are not using standardized recipes, dozens of extra eggs could be added unnecessarily. It is essential to evaluate the standardized recipes as well as the actual preparation of casserole items, meats, vegetables, salads, etc., to determine the proper quantity of eggs that should be included. The cooks should be asked how many eggs they use per product—they should be members of the cost control team, too.
- Lock the kitchen after it is closed in the evening and keep the refrigerators locked throughout the day with the exception of twice a day when food supplies are pulled for actual preparation. This procedure is not as difficult as it sounds when coordinated with a Purchasing/Production Guide (Appendix B).

Oleo

Evaluating the quantity and type of oleo purchased can result in cost savings. It is worthwhile considering whipping oleo solids, as many restaurants do; whipping increases oleo's volume by 33 percent and is excellent for spreading. If whipped oleo is to be used for cooking, one and one-half cups should be used to one cup of

---

Table 5–1 Savings using medium instead of large eggs*

Beds	100	300	500	700	900	1,500	2,000
	$388.80 (144 cs/yr)	$1,166.40 (432 cs/yr)	$1,944 (720 cs/yr)	$2,721.60 (1,008 cs/yr)	$3,499.20 (1,296 cs/yr)	$5,832 (2,160 cs/yr)	$7,776 (2,880 cs/yr)

*Based on average cost difference of 9 cents a dozen between medium and large.

Table 5–2 Savings realized by whipping oleo solids

Beds	100	300	500	700	900	1,500	2,000
	$129.60	$388.80	$648.00	$907.20	$1,166.40	$1,944	$2,592

unwhipped oleo. A 30-pound case of oleo can be increased by 15 cups in volume through whipping:

unwhipped $10.90/60 cups = 36 cents/lb. (2 cups)
whipped: $10.90/75 cups = 29 cents/lb. (2 cups)

The whipped oleo solids should be used primarily for general cooking purposes, as in glazing rolls, adding to hot cereals, and buttering toast.

With an estimated five pounds of oleo used per day per 100 meals (for cooking), a maximum of 150 pounds of oleo a month should be ordered. That represents 2.5 teaspoons per individual per day. Only four cases of oleo solids a month would be needed for a 100-bed facility if oleo solids are whipped. At 36 cents per pound and a minimum saving of 30 pounds a month, $129.60 a year per 100 beds could be saved. Although this is a small amount at this level, Table 5–2 shows how the savings increase in value in larger facilities from merely whipping oleo solids.

Milk

Establishing a monthly purchasing ceiling for milk has represented a significant cost saving for many institutions. In doing so, managers should be sure to monitor the quantity used to assure that a sufficient supply is ordered. With milk, for example, the Recommended Daily Dietary Allowance for adults, as established by the National Research Council, is a minimum of 16 ounces of milk per patient per day. That equals 12.5 gallons per day per 100 people, or 375 gallons per month.

At one 100-bed institution, the administrator and food service director were shocked when a milk utilization study showed that an average of 600 gallons a month had been ordered—225 gallons more per month than the recommended level. Careful analysis determined that patients were not receiving the extra milk, so the quantity purchased could be reduced significantly. The extra milk may have been used excessively in cooking or could have been ''removed'' from the premises. Table 5–3 lists recommended usages.

In determining purchasing ceilings, managers should base their figures on the average (not peak or low) percent of occupancy.

The following procedures are recommended to assure a cost saving in milk. Managers should:

- Establish a specific monthly purchasing ceiling for milk (based on average census).
- Submit a specific order to the milk delivery person in lieu of permitting a build-up to a ''standard.''
- Monitor the quantity and charges per gallon of milk delivered. Discrepancies can and have occurred.
- Consider utilizing 2 percent rather than whole milk. There is little difference in taste, it is comparable nutritionally to whole milk, and the savings can be

Table 5–3 Milk order ceilings

Estimated Gallons/Month (Adult Facilities)*

Beds	100	300	500	700	900	1,500	2,000
Gal.	375	1,125	1,875	2,625	3,375	5,625	7,500

Example: Food utilization study, 700-bed unit
Purchasing ceiling to meet RDDA: 2,625 gallons/month

Present	Proposed	Differential	Savings/Yr.
3,238	2,625	613	$14,712/yr.
gal./mo.	gal./mo.	gal./mo.	
		(7,356 gal./year @$2/ gal.)	

*Based on two eight-ounce servings of milk per person per day for 700 individuals based on 100 percent occupancy.

---

substantial. Another benefit of 2 percent milk is the lower cholesterol level. For example:

Whole milk (3.5% fat)	$1.92/gallon
2% milk	1.82/gallon
Saving	$ .10/gallon

The savings-per-year advantage of using 2 percent milk (and assuming each person receives the minimum of 3.75 gallons a month) are shown in Table 5–4.

Milk packaging also can affect expenditures. The cost/gallon equivalent should be determined. Half-pint cartons could be cheaper in the long run because they provide increased portion control. Comparing prices and establishing an annual milk contract can be of real assistance in achieving cost savings.

The type and quantity of milk used in cooking should be evaluated. Nonfat dry milk powder should be used. It generally is a fraction of the cost of whole milk. For example:

Present	Proposed	Cost Difference
$1.92/gal.	$.35/gal	$1.57/gal.
homogenized	nonfat dry	

If an average of three gallons of milk/day/100 beds were used, the saving per year from using nonfat dry milk in cooking instead of homogenized, liquid milk would be $1,719 (Table 5–5).

The institution should prepare its own buttermilk for cooking purposes. When a recipe calls for its addition, it can make its own: Add one-half cup of commercial buttermilk to one quart of reconstituted nonfat dry milk. This can cut costs in half

---

Table 5–4 Savings per year using 2% milk

Beds	100	300	500	700	900	1,500	2,000
Saving	$450	$1,350	$2,250	$3,150	$4,050	$6,750	$9,000

Table 5–5 Savings using nonfat dry milk in cooking

Beds	100	300	500	700	900	1,500	2,000
Saving	$1,719.15	$5,157.45	$8,595.75	$12,034.05	$15,472.35	$25,787.25	$34,383

for this product without sacrificing quality. (This can only be used for cooking, not beverage, purposes).

Employees can be charged for milk (2.5 times the actual cost). If half-pint milk cartons cost the facility 20¢ each, employees should pay 50¢ apiece in order to approximate the overhead, labor, and energy costs of receiving, storing, and serving. However, cafeterias in most health care and educational institutions are considered subsidized and typically take less than the 2.5 times markup.

Coffee

Coffee is this nation's national drink, and a significant amount is spent every year on it. However, institutions can save 40 percent by evaluating and utilizing a coffee enhancer—which also reduces caffeine 50 percent. The Georgia Department of Offender Rehabilitation saved thousands of dollars a year. Some estimates for GDOR run as high as $33,000 a year. There are several coffee enhancers on the market, but a taste test and cost comparison should be conducted before one is selected.

To stretch the coffee dollar, it is advisable to evaluate the type being used:

- Compare the cost per pound of coffee as sold in two-ounce, one-pound, and three-pound packages: 2 oz.,$3.13/lb.; 1 lb., $2.86/lb.; 3 lb., $3.05/lb. (Prices provided by National Institutional Food Distribution Association (NIFDA) headquarters, Marietta, Ga. for NIFDA coffee)
- Halt losses of small (two- to three-ounce) packages used for drip-type brewers, which are convenient to drop into purses and pockets. Instead, buy coffee in bulk (one- to five-pound packages) and use a dispenser (usually provided free by the coffee purveyor) to measure coffee into filters.
- Do not forget the cost of filters. Store them with other paper supplies under lock and key, issuing them only as needed.

Managers should take advantage of new products, such as coffee flavor enhancers. These are calcium-based formulas that strengthen coffee flavor without adding caffeine. The amount of coffee used can be reduced by half, cutting costs 40 percent. This could mean thousands of dollars in savings. At least four coffee enhancer products are currently available. Samples should be obtained and "double-blind" studies conducted with the institution's clientele. (Coffee is served both with and without enhancer.)

Managers can conduct their own taste tests and weigh the public relations and economic benefits of using enhancers when making the final decision.

A Management Case Study

When budget cuts forced the administrator of a 300-bed hospital to examine costs, he was shocked to discover he had been providing his staff with coffee to the tune of $32,302.50 a year. Good coffee is a cornerstone to any food service but uncontrolled coffee costs can mount to surprising levels.

This hospital calculated coffee use at 100 2½-ounce packages (at $3.05/lb.) for patient use and 30 one-pound packages (at $2.95/lb.) for staff. Exhibit 5–2 details the cost per year of each and the resultant savings.

Coffee use can be reduced in any facility. These questions should be asked to analyze the operation, first in tracking coffee usage to staff and visitors:

- Is coffee provided in an unlimited supply? Keep a close count of "free" coffee in visitor lounges, lobbies, administrative offices, doctor and staff lounges, dining areas, and meetings.

Exhibit 5–2 Cost analysis of coffee use

Current use
Patients:
$$\frac{100 \times 2\frac{1}{2} \text{ oz.} \times \$3.05/\text{lb.}}{16 \text{ oz.}/1 \text{ lb.}} = \$47.66/\text{day} = \$17,395.90/\text{yr.}$$
Staff:
30×1 lb. $\times$ $2.95/lb. = $88.50/day = $32,302.50/yr.
Total coffee costs = $136.16/day = $49,698.40/yr.

Recommended solutions:

1. Use one-pound packages for patients as well as staff to save at least $.10/lb.:
   Current Use: $47.66/day
   Proposed:
   $$\frac{100 \times 2\frac{1}{2} \text{ oz.} \times \$2.95/\text{lb.}}{16 \text{ oz.}/1 \text{ lb.}} = \$46.09/\text{day}$$
   Saving: $1.57/day = $573.05/yr.
2. Use a dispenser (usually free from the vendor) to measure 2-ounce rather than 2½-ounce portions:
   Current Use: $47.66/day
   Proposed:
   $$\frac{(100 \times 2 \times \$3.05)}{16 \text{ oz.}/1 \text{ lb.}} = \$38.13/\text{day}$$
   Saving: $9.53/day = $3,478.45/yr.
3. Use coffee enhancer to cut costs 40 percent:
   Current Use: $136.16/day
   Proposed:
   $136.16 (60% of current use) = $81.70/day; $54.46/day (40% savings)
   Saving: $19,877.90/yr.
4. Reduce total use:
   Current Use/Day:
   $$\frac{(100 \times 2\frac{1}{2}\text{-oz. pkgs.})}{16 \text{ oz.}/1 \text{ lb.}} + 30 \text{ lbs.} = 46 \text{ lbs./day}$$
   46 lbs. $\times$ 80 cups coffee/lb. = 3,680 cups/day
   Proposed:
   (300 patients $\times$ 2 cups/day) plus
   500 cups/day for staff = 1,100 cups/day
   Saving:
   $$\frac{2,580 \text{ cups/day} \times \$2.95/\text{lb.}}{80 \text{ cups/lb.}} = \$95.14/\text{day} = \$34,726.10/\text{yr.}$$

- When is coffee being used? Compare amount of coffee used for day and night shifts. The facility may be providing more coffee than it knows for sleepy evening-shift personnel.
- Who delivers the staff coffee supply? Is it a food service employee or does the staff have ready access to the food service department?
- Is coffee provided at nursing stations intended for patient use? Monitor closely to be certain that "patient" coffee is not consumed by the staff.

Then, take action:

- Set a per-day ceiling on coffee usage. Calculate the total number of pounds to be used per day and distribute coffee for this amount throughout the day.
- Let employees know how much the facility spends for coffee each day, month, and year. Colorful graphs and posters can illustrate and emphasize the importance of controlling coffee waste.
- Prepare a predetermined quantity per day for staff. When it runs out, no more is prepared.
- Have staff establish a "coffee kitty" with funds donated monthly, or designate a Coffee Committee to collect money and furnish coffee.

Tea

The use of one-ounce tea bags should be evaluated. One food service director was impressed with employees' taking used, one-ounce tea bags home with them, reportedly for use as mulch for their garden. Actually, they were brewing tea: One-ounce bags can—and should—be used twice. By doing so, tea expenditure can be reduced 50 percent. The tea bags should be wrapped in dampened paper towels for use at the next meal. This doubles their use and should reduce ordering of large tea bags by 50 percent.

ECONOMIC IMPACT OF DECISIONS

Calculating the cost of administrative decisions means evaluating the cost/benefit ratio of potential results before taking action. The economic impact of a simple administrative decision such as the number of times to serve bacon or sausage per week can make a significant difference.

Before bacon is bought, it should be determined how often it will be served and how many strips should constitute one portion. The economic result and the public

Table 5–6 Quantity vs. cost: Bacon servings

Quantity/month	Cost/lb.	Cost/month	Cost/year
1. 300 lbs.	$1.50	$450.00	$5,400
2. 150 lbs.	1.50	225.00	2,700
3. 75 lbs.	1.50	112.50	1,350
4. 43 lbs.	1.50	64.50	774

1. 2 strips bacon/100 patients/each morning
2. 1 strip bacon/100 patients/each morning
3. 1 strip bacon/100 patients/every other day
4. 1 strip bacon/100 patients/twice weekly.

Exhibit 5–3 Cost comparison of serving frequency of sausage

	Present			Proposed			
	1-1½-oz. sausage patty served twice a week for breakfast			1-1½-oz. sausage patty served once a week for breakfast			
			Savings/Year				
Meals	100	300	500	700	900	1,500	2,000
	$338	$1,014	$1,690	$2,366	$3,042	$5,070	$6,760
	Present			Proposed			
	2 1-oz. sausage links served twice a week for breakfast			2 1-oz. sausage links served once a week for breakfast			
			Savings/Year				
Meals	100	300	500	700	900	1,500	2,000
	$494	$1,482	$2,470	$3,458	$4,446	$7,410	$9,880

relations value of each potential decision should be known or estimated before the final determination is made. Table 5–6 and Exhibit 5–3 illustrate the potential economic impact of an administrative decision.

This information is not provided to recommend the number of times a facility should be providing bacon or sausage to its patients, nor the portion size. It does reflect the economic ramifications of such decisions.

The following recommendations are offered in making the administrative decision on the quantity and size serving of bacon and/or sausage:

- Evaluate the cost of bacon and/or sausage, comparing it against the intangible but real benefit of public relations.
- Verify the number of servings actually received per pound in either bacon or sausage.
- Consider using sausage links instead of sausage patties, yet realize usually two links are needed to equal the portion of one 1½-ounce sausage pattie (Exhibit 5–3).
- Consider obtaining meat from a local slaughtering house rather than a meat purveyor.

After all these areas have been evaluated, then—and only then—can the appropriate administrative decision be made.

ECONOMIC IMPACT OF RECEIVING

Purchasing and bottom line costs also are affected by receiving.

One facility discovered that for six months it had been receiving 12 slices of bacon a pound instead of the 18 to 22 ordered. That meant 3.34 more pounds of bacon were needed to feed 100 patients. The additional cost (@ $1.50 per pound) per year for 3.34 additional pounds of bacon each day of such an undetected error is shown in Exhibit 5–4.

It is essential to weigh and count all deliveries to verify that the facility is receiving exactly what was ordered. An exciting afternoon really can be spent

Exhibit 5–4 Additional costs per year for bacon

(12 slices per 1 pound instead of 18 to 22 slices per pound)

Beds	100	300	500	700	900	1,500	2,000
Meals	$1,828.65	$5,485.95	$9,143.25	$12,800.55	$16,457.85	$27,429.75	$36,573.00

weighing and counting bacon. Other items to consider include comparing the cost per serving of different food products. With bacon and sausage, for example, the less expensive of the two should be served more often. Proof of the value of this can be obtained by working up a comparison, as in Exhibit 5–5.

Identifying appropriate purchasing ceilings, portion sizes, systems, etc. is important. Yet all efforts are moot unless coordinated with both production and portion control.

PORTION AND PRODUCTION CONTROL

How many cans of green beans do the cooks really prepare per meal? The production sheet (Table 5–7) used with the Purchasing/Production Guidelines (Appendix B) offers simple yet effective tools for the food service director to prepare and for the cooks to use.

The portion size of all foods to be served should be determined before preparation so that an accurate number of portions can be prepared to minimize waste. Simple as this may seem, few facilities make a conscious effort to forecast the actual number of servings to be prepared.

Coordinating proper portion control with careful food preparation translates into major savings. Portion control scoops are paramount because serving spoons provide inaccurate portions at best. Portion control scoops (#16 = 2 oz.; #8 = 4 oz.; #10 = 3.2 oz.) with holes to drain liquids, provide accurate control for most items. Exhibit 5–6 illustrates the economic impact of how much only one extra ounce of one vegetable twice a day can cost an operation.

Portion control scoops also are one of the most effective ways to maintain equity in portioning. To determine the size portion per the scoop number used, divide 32 ounces by the serving size. For example, to determine the scoop number of a two-ounce portion:

$$\frac{32 \text{ ounces}}{2 \text{ ounces}} = \#16 \text{ scoop}$$

Exhibit 5–5 Cost comparison per portion

Bacon	Sausage Patties	Sausage Links
Avg. 20 slices/lb.	10 ⅔ servings/lb.	2 1-oz. unit
$1.50/lb.	(at 1½ oz./serving)	$8.34/box of 96
7.5¢/slice	$1.50/lb.	17¢/serving
	14¢/serving	

Bacon vs. patties cost difference = 6.5¢/each
Bacon vs. links cost difference = 9.5¢/each

Table 5–7 Purchasing/production guide form

Item	Size of purchase unit	Portion control size	Service utensil used*	#Serv./ purchase unit	# Times offered on: Cycle week 1	Cycle week 2	Cycle week 3	Serving extensions 50	150	300
Meat/entree*										
Beef										
Chicken										
Fish										
Pork										
Other										
Vegetables										
Canned (gr. beans)	6 #10	4 oz.	#8 scoop*	25	3	2	3	2 cs. + 4 cans (16)	8 cs. (48)	16 cs. (96)
Frozen										
Fresh										
Dry										
Breads/Starches										
Bread										
Cereal										
Fruits										
Canned										
Water packed										
Frozen										
Fresh										

*Evaluate the portion size appropriate. A #16 scoop is generally recommended in nursing homes.

Exhibit 5–6 Extra cost of vegetables

Meals	120	200	400	600	800	1,000	1,500	2,000
	$1,941.80	$3,236.33	$6,472.66	$9,709.00	$12,945.33	$16,181.66	$24,272.50	$32,363.33

Example: If one case of a vegetable costs an average of $8 ($1.33/can), and the following number of portions yielded:

20 three-ounce portions/can = 6 cans or $7.98
(120 3-ounce portions)
30 two-ounce portions/can = 4 cans or $5.32
(120 2-ounce portions)
Total additional cost/meal 2 cans or $2.66
(resulting from at least one extra ounce per serving because of lack of portion control)
$2.66 × twice/day = $5.32 × 365 = $1,941.80 additional cost per year because portion control is lacking.

To determine the size portion a specific scoop yields, divide the number of the scoop into 32:

$$\frac{32 \text{ ounces}}{\#8 \text{ scoop}} = 4\text{-ounce portion}$$

Portion control scoops can even by used for serving liquid-retaining vegetables such as spinach or peas by drilling holes in the bottom of the scoops to permit the drainage of liquid. With these scoops, the server is always aware of how much constitutes one serving. If a patient requests double or triple servings, these can be provided accurately and included in the number of servings to be prepared.

When there are discrepancies between what should have been prepared (i.e., vegetables) with what actually was prepared, food service professionals have the cooks check samples of portions of the product with them, using a portion control scoop. With this method the cooks convince themselves there really are "x" number of "y" ounce portions per can; therefore, there is no need to pull the extra cans of product, as they always had done.

Standardized Recipes

Standardized recipes, those that continually produce good products, are as important to controlling costs and assuring patron satisfaction as is portion control (Table 5–8). Although some cooks may pride themselves on not needing recipes, standardized ones offer the following undisputed benefits to all. They

- eliminate guess work
- guarantee repeated quantity and quality of product
- require less skill from employees
- reduce the amount of supervision required
- serve as a continuing cost-control procedure.

Standardized recipes and experienced cooks are an incomparable combination but both require time to develop. Some computerized systems provide a cost and

Table 5–8 Example of a standardized recipe

DISH: Au gratin potatoes with paprika   DAY: Friday

Pan Size: 12 × 20 × 4"   Temperature: 350

Portion Size: ½ Cup (#8 scoop)   Time: 45 minutes

Ingredients	50 Portions	60 Portions	70 Portions	80 Portions	90 Portions	Method
Potatoes, sl. dehyd.	2 lb	2⅓ lb	2⅔ lb	3 lb	3½ lb	1. Reconstitute potatoes in boiling salted water in cooking pans.
Water, boiling	2 gal	2⅓ gal	2⅔ gal	3 gal	3½ gal	
Salt	½ T	½ T	2 tea	2 tea	1 T	2. Sprinke parsley over potatoes; stir carefully.
Parsley flakes	2 T	2 T	7 tea	8 tea	3 T	
Margarine	1 C	1¼ C	1⅓ C	1½ C	1¾ C	3. Melt margarine, add flour, stir until smooth. Add salt, then hot milk gradually. Stir until smooth and thick (15–20 minutes).
Flour	1 C	1¼ C	1⅓ C	1½ C	1¾ C	
Milk	1 gal	4¾ qt	5½ qt	6½ qt	7 qt	
Salt	½ T	½ T	2 tea	2 tea	1 T	
Cheese, grated	2 lb	2½ lb	3 lb	3½ lb	4 lb	4. Pour sauce and cheese over potatoes.
Dry bread crumbs or cornflakes	1½ C	1¾ C	2 C	2¼ C	2½ C	5. Mix margarine and crumbs.
Margarine	¼ C	⅓ C	⅓ C	½ C	½ C	6. Sprinkle over potatoes.
						7. Sprinkle paprika on top.
						8. Bake until lightly browned, about 45 minutes.

113

nutrient analysis that facilitates, as well as emphasizes, the importance of standardized recipes correlated with cycle menus.

Stealing

Food service cost management would not be complete without a discussion of stealing. ''Forty-seven percent of all people will steal.'' That's an amazing—and alarming—statement. It was made in a telephone interview by Carl Klump, criminologist at The Stanton Institute.

In the food service industry, unfortunately, that 47 percent figure may be low. Years of experience have taught those in the field that food service operations seem to stimulate employee ingenuity with regard to theft.

For example, how often have one or more of the following been discovered?

- the carefully wrapped roast, ham, or turkey at the bottom of the garbage can being taken to the dumpster
- a continuing increase in leftovers that employees then are permitted to take home
- one-ounce tea bags that have only been used once being taken home. (As noted earlier, one supervisor had thought they were being used as mulch for employees' gardens.)
- a continuing loss of flatware that necessitates hundreds, if not thousands, of dollars a year for replacement
- cash register receipts that never seem to equal anticipated revenue.

Occasionally, food service designs encourage theft. For example, when plans for the kitchen at one 300-bed institution were presented for review, amazingly the main kitchen area opened directly into the employees' locker area, which in turn opened directly into the storeroom, which then opened directly onto the back dock. The first comment to the president of this corporation was, ''For a potential thief, this is one of the most considerate kitchen plans ever.'' The kitchen subsequently was redesigned.

Three factors lead to stealing:

1. when management sets the stage for pilferage by failing to provide security systems
2. when employees see how easy it is to steal
3. when greed sets in.

What can be done to deter theft?

First, the magnitude of the problem must be assessed. Exhibit 5–7 illustrates the potential economic impact.

There are two kinds of food service operations: Those that have been hit by theft and those that are going to be hit by theft. There are several reasons for that unfortunate fact, among them high turnover of low-skill workers, low wages, low supervisor-to-employee ratios, and lack of adequate internal control systems.

An effective security system begins with good hiring practices. Those who do the hiring must not depend solely on hunches; they must check thoroughly with all former employers and personal references. Employees handling cash should be bonded—the small cost may be money well spent.

47 percent of all employees steal. Of 100 employees:

27% are borderline—steal $45/year	$1,215
20% are significantly dishonest—steal $175/year	3,500
53% are basically honest—steal $5.50/year	291.50
Loss from theft per year	$5,006.50

If a ratio of four employees per patient were used, even a 100-patient facility could lose $1,252 in one year alone.

Evaluation of Current Procedures

A detailed evaluation should be made of current procedures in receiving, storage, preparation, serving, storing/utilizing leftovers, and cash register check-and-balance systems. Precautions that can significantly reduce employee theft include the following:

- Establish a receiving system that includes one or two employees who are trained in proper receiving; however, without notice, the food service manager should periodically assume receiving and storing responsibilities.
- Institute a receiving stamp system that maintains accountability by the individual who accepts the quantity and quality of incoming goods. Never allow the same employee who received food items to store them as well.
- Date all supplies with a unit cost directly on the package before storage. This facilitates inventory accounting, regardless of the system used, and will reduce potential theft by demonstrating to employees that management is aware of the receipt and cost of each item.
- Maintain a procedure of keeping the storeroom and bulk chilled storage locked except for pull times for items required for preparation.
- Maintain a tight control of access to keys. Have locksmith stamp on keys "Do Not Duplicate."
- Do not allow the manager's work schedule to become an accepted routine with employees. The manager should appear at unannounced times on the morning, evening, and weekend shifts. Employees should always expect the manager to appear, even though the schedule does not so indicate.
- Locate employee parking away from the back door.
- Provide small lockers for the storage of purses, and permit only small purses.
- Do not permit packages to leave the institution without specific authorization from an individual in authority or a code that is specifically identified and changed frequently.
- Designate one exit only for employees on a per-shift basis and station a responsible management-oriented employee at the exit. Rotate the person in this position periodically.
- Prevent traffic through the food service department by nonauthorized individuals from within the facility or from outside sources.
- Lock the food service department after the evening meal.

- Maintain specific records on cash register tapes that must balance with the number of meals served. Any shortages should be reported to the department head. The cashier must be held accountable.

Testing

The Stanton Corporation of Chicago has developed a three-step method of tightening security against employee pilferage.[1] Stanton produces three booklets:

1. The Stanton Survey, for screening job candidates
2. The Stanton Inventory, for pinpointing security violations and identifying the culprit(s)
3. The Stanton Case Review, for determining guilt after an incident has occurred.

The Stanton Survey

The Stanton Survey is a test designed to determine whether a prospective employee is basically honest or dishonest. It costs $8 to $12 a copy, depending on the quantity ordered. The cost includes a telephone report obtained from a toll-free number and a written summary.

The survey was developed to supplement the application form and to be administered in the "second interview" situation. Although a prospective employer may have a "gut feeling" about a person's honesty, a routine application or interview will not indicate whether a person is in fact honest.

In an effort to reduce discrimination, it now is illegal to ask whether a person has ever been arrested, because many members of minority groups are arrested on inadequate grounds and never charged or convicted. It is legal to ask if a person has ever been convicted of a crime, but this is of little use, as innocent people sometimes are convicted and many guilty ones are never caught.

Inventory and Case Review

The two other booklets, The Stanton Inventory and The Stanton Case Review, are designed to be administered to employees rather than applicants.

The Stanton Inventory is distributed when management suspects something is going on (i.e., cash flow is suddenly down or inventory is missing) but is not sure of the incident or the culprit(s). All employees involved are given the test, which they return in a sealed envelope. The results usually will pinpoint the security violation and the guilty party(ies).

The Stanton Review is given to any group of employees who are suspects in a known incident. These test results almost always provide management with the guilty person(s).

Through intensive research and years of experience, Stanton criminologists have found distinct patterns in the responses of basically honest or dishonest people. According to Carl Klump, criminologist at the Stanton Corporation, "It's as if all the dishonest people read the same book on how to take these sorts of tests." Guilty people usually try to make themselves appear innocent.

For example: the Survey asks if the person has ever thought about taking anything from the place of work; 80 percent of honest people say no, 66 percent of dishonest people say yes. (Apparently dishonest people think this is a trick question. They believe their behavior is normal so they try to "fake the graders out" by answering yes.) Of course, one question alone can't determine basic honesty or dishonesty but a combination of questions can. Another example: basically honest people tend to answer the essay question asking why they are honest, dishonest, or a bit of both with the statement that they take pride in their integrity. Dishonest people say "they are what they are."

These tests cost $25 per booklet (including the final reports), much less expensive than a polygraph, which costs as much as $500 per test. The Stanton booklets are intended to be used instead of a polygraph, although many who try them disbelieve the results and use a polygraph as well. In most cases, employers drop the polygraph after a short time.

Use of a polygraph is restricted in many states; in fact, in some states, an employer is guilty of a misdemeanor for even asking an employee or applicant to take a polygraph. In other states, the employer can ask but, if the person refuses, cannot fire the person on that basis. Therefore, it is imperative to check state laws.

The three Stanton tests are only guidelines. An employee cannot be dismissed solely on the basis of the tests, either. However, the booklets have passed tests designed to eliminate discriminatory language bias so, if a rejected applicant charges discrimination, employers can fall back on the Stanton test as at least partial proof they were not discriminating.

In the case of a suspected guilty employee, an employer should try to get a confession: "The results of this booklet indicate you've been doing XYZ. How many times have you done this?" If employees confess, they can be dismissed if their offense violates company policy.

Steeling themselves against theft not only is a challenge to managers but also can provide a significant opportunity in cost control. One institution that initiated a receiving system that followed the recommendations of the first edition of this book in inventory and the locking of storerooms and coolers saved more than $20,000 in one year. Other institutions can save significant amounts in the same way.

When management provides an opportunity for employees to steal and they see how easy stealing can become, greed sets in. Managers must be security smart.

INNOVATIONS

Effective cost management demands innovation. Food service must be looked at as a business, not only a service. This motivation facilitates innovation. The health care industry is particularly challenged to innovate with the changing federal intervention.

Innovations such as shared services and converting the food service department from a cost center to a revenue center are becoming a necessity. Sharing services enables facilities to maximize labor resources, reduce costs, and improve patient care.

Increased revenue sources can be created by providing additional services to immediate and surrounding communities. Another source is the purchasing and selling of services from and to other facilities. Such activities reduce, if not eliminate, the escalating cost of in-house personnel, equipment, and support services.

Through dispersing services to, and sharing their strengths with, a broader spectrum, public relations are enhanced for each participating facility. That could

117

translate into (1) an increased patient count, (2) a reinstatement of services cancelled because of current onsite production costs, and (3) a reduction of interdepartmental friction caused by an overload and fragmentation of duties.

The specific programs fall into five primary areas. Facilities could share:

1. Purchasing

   - food purchasing, which could conservatively reduce cost at least 10 percent (Chapter 4), with additional savings through coupons and the discount-payment system

2. Education

   - educational materials for patients and staff, to minimize printing and development costs
   - training sessions for all levels of personnel, to reduce instructional time and effort
   - ideas and solutions to operational problems, to lower cost as well as improve patient services, merchandising techniques, and methods of motivating personnel

3. Personnel/Services/Equipment

   - savings of at least 30 percent in labor costs alone, plus other services with facilities in the same locale
   - registered dietitians, among facilities that are unable to justify such a full-time equivalent (FTE) position
   - professional maintenance engineers, to develop a preventive maintenance program and to instruct personnel in the care, cleaning, and operation of equipment
   - nursing personnel, when full-time equivalent positions are not indicated
   - consultation services for all areas of the facilities, to improve the skills of in-house personnel and to offer an objective approach to operational problems
   - existing catering equipment, to avoid purchasing expensive units

4. Data

   - computer information, on purchasing, cost comparisons, economics, and specifications, etc.
   - administrative information, energy-management results, and methods to improve purchasing/production guidelines
   - cost/benefit data, for each type of service provided by the food service department

5. Product

   - Food products, themselves, i.e., baked goods, dietetic baked goods, formulae, salads, and potentially full meals produced and distributed to participating hospitals in bulk to dispense by existing food delivery systems.[2]

The following example dramatizes the importance of shared-services food production facilities.

The Dayton, Ohio, Mental Health Center saved $253,000 a year in a program involving six mental-health and/or mental retardation facilities. These represent 1,700 meals, with projections in the near future to 5,000 meals.

The shared-services program of the six institutions began operating December 1, 1981, after it was conceived in 1975. The production facility is operating on a three-week menu cycle with a Cryovac packaging system that enables food to be held at 28° to 32° for four to six weeks. Food is sent in bulk to the facilities daily.

Advantages

- greater ability to adhere to menus that are carefully planned for patient acceptance, nutrition adequacy, and economic feasibility
- consistency in food product
- elimination of the need for skilled food service workers
- reduction in the number of FTEs for all facilities

In just the initial stages, 13 FTEs were eliminated. As production increases, with additional facilities participating in the shared facility, the savings in FTEs also should grow.

Disadvantage

- The central production facility reports no serious disadvantages yet the institutions have experienced some disappointment in the loss of control at their own levels. Consistency in the quality of food and the reduced need for menu substitutions are positive trade-offs for such loss of control.

Savings

- Approximately $253,000 a year is being saved with only six institutions participating.

Marion Motter, director of food services, and Bill Amirante, assistant food service director of the Mental Health Center in Dayton, Ohio, conceived and implemented this system.

CONVERTING FOOD SERVICE TO REVENUE CENTER

Today's food service department is under pressure to save money while maintaining quality. It has always been considered as a cost center. Any administration would be delighted if its food department began to bring in revenue. That income could provide a fund for renovating, adding or repairing equipment, or the opportunity to take advantage of an exceptional employee training program. These are only a few of the benefits the department can enjoy when it generates revenue.

The key to reaching any goal is attitude. The food department should be considered a business, not a service that is expected to lose money. This is especially important at budget time. Only if administration and managers know exactly how much they spend, and on what, can they be prepared and plan future budgets well. Following are three guidelines. Administration and managers (directors) should:

1. Develop a service standard for patients, residents, and customers and charge for everything above and beyond that standard. Just as all patients must pay for medications and laboratory services, so also should services such as nutrition assessments and diet instructions be remunerated. These are services all patients do not require. When facility policy is consistent, the department's additional services will be paid for fairly and the patients/customers will not be paying for services they do not need in the general bill for meals.

2. Charge everything that is used to someone, even if it is only on paper. This will help develop a realistic idea of where the department's money goes. Charge meals and services to the patients, nourishments to the nursing floors, and staff meals to the cafeteria account. Be able to present this information to the administrator. This should lead to an even fairer budget next year.

3. Make sure to know what part of labor, food, utilities, dishwasher time, etc., are going toward the cafeteria. This will make it possible to charge food items more appropriately. Beware of undercharging visitors and employees. If an employee discount is given, be sure to include its cost in the employee fringe benefits allowance.

In the following seven specific ways to assure their food service departments bring in revenue, directors should:

1. Offer gourmet meals in the gift shop for patients and/or their guests. Give visitors the opportunity to select this as a gift as an alternative to flowers or candy. A menu can be provided for visitors to choose from; it can even offer such delicacies as steak and lobster, depending on the patient's diet restrictions.

2. Expand the service. Cater functions inside the facility—auxiliary group teas and luncheons, staff dinners, board meetings, etc. School food service can serve kindergarten children, offer school breakfasts, participate in Meals on Wheels, contract with day-care centers to provide meals or snacks, or provide meals for the elderly at the school. (In addition to a nutritious lunch, both children and adults who do not have extended families nearby benefit from the social contact.)

3. Hold seminars at the facility for surrounding area workers. Use the fees to help the food service department by purchasing needed labor-saving equipment, etc.

4. Invite government agencies to expand their services and bring in revenue. State departments can offer nutrition counselling to community nutrition groups, food co-ops, and other nonprofit groups. If the facility meets the criteria to receive government food allotments, use ingenuity to negotiate processing agreements with the state department of agriculture to make sure the food is in the form that can be used best. It is less expensive to buy the food processed than to process it in-house and incur high labor costs. For example, if the facility receives flour allotments, negotiate to buy processed products from approved providers instead of taking the commodity flour in bulk. Make agreements with bread and pizza companies to take the com-

modity allotment in their products. In one case such an agreement resulted in saving nearly $1 a pound when the commodity meat was centrally processed instead of using facility labor. North Carolina's Department of Mental Health, Mental Retardation, and Substance Abuse Services received a commodity turkey allotment from the government of 30 pounds per person of the population eligible to receive commodities. A facility that processed its own turkey had high labor costs and received only 40 percent of its commodity allotment in edible meat. Its cost per pound of edible meat was $1.91. A facility that had its meat centrally processed received 70 percent of its allotment in edible meat, had no labor costs, and spent only 96¢ per pound of edible meat. By using this creative method, the facility that used central processing saved 95¢ a pound, or $28.50 per eligible population for this program.

5. Operate a bakery. Bake extra breads and pastries and market them to the community. This works especially well for metropolitan facilities. (At one Florida hospital, people line up every day to buy its baked goods.)
6. Market the department's services (if that is within the facility's policies and procedures). Let the downtown business lunch group know about the coffee shop, cafeteria, or private dining facilities. Put flyers out that list the baked goods.
7. Consider establishing a fee-for-nutrition services program if the facility is a health care institution. (See Chapter 9 on DRGs.)

A food service department's main objective is to provide cost effective, quality food service to its patients/clients. These suggestions for producing revenue are not intended to detract from that goal; rather they are designed to provide additional ways to achieve it.

NOTES

1. The Stanton Corporation, 5701 Executive Center Drive, Suite 302, Charlotte, NC 28229.
2. American Hospital Association, *Shared Food Services in Health Care Institutions* (Chicago: American Hospital Association, 1976).

Chapter 6

Cost Effective Labor Relations

Labor is typically the greatest concern of food service directors. There are three major components of labor: (1) managing the work force, (2) labor costs, and (3) personnel productivity. Of these, labor relations or managing the work force often demands the most of the food service director's time.

Food service employers are in the people business, and successful ones must learn and practice human engineering. To maintain good labor relations, it is important that management establish a reputation for truthfulness, predictability, and fairness with employees. Respected employers resist expedient solutions and operate on a fixed policy. Thus, recurring problems will be handled consistently. Good employee relations start with basic courtesy and good human relations.

NLRB AND PREVENTIVE LABOR RELATIONS

With labor problems in health care facilities escalating, Congress expanded the power of the National Labor Relations Board to provide for boards of inquiry and collective bargaining in that field. All private health care institutions were included in the jurisdiction of the NLRB (U.S.C.A. §151 et seq. and the Health Care Amendment of 1974, P.L. 93-360). The intent of the legislation reflected two primary Congressional goals:

1. extending NLRA benefits to employees
2. giving appropriate notice of strikes or picketing to provide for patient care in the event of work stoppage.

This chapter is not intended as a legal treatise on labor; rather, it is designed to emphasize the importance of developing a good labor relations program that will minimize the threat of unionization. It also discusses the detailed specifics of how to establish a good labor relations program in the food service operation.

Unions sell management mistakes. Unions do not organize employees; employees organize employees. A union cannot sell its service and organize a happy ship. Once the seeds of discontent in food service are sown, it is easy for a union to harvest the fruit.

123

Food service employees have a choice under the law to join or not to join a union. Employers have broad rights of free speech, including expressing opinions in meetings, letters, posters, etc., so employees have the facts about the terms and conditions of their employment. A food service employer that is nonunion should answer these questions:

- Does the facility have a rational wage policy that pays jobs at adequate competitive levels?
- Are employees' wages and fringe benefits keeping pace with inflation and the competition?
- Are supervisors trained and performing well?
- Do employees have a feeling of job security and a sense of affiliation?
- Is management processing and settling all legitimate grievances fairly?
- Is management dealing impartially, candidly and unemotionally with employees?

If these can be answered with an objective "yes," the facility is a long way down the road in preventing employees from selecting a union to represent their interests. Organizing campaigns often are symptoms of undiagnosed or untreated employee problems.

Most employers probably choose to keep an operation nonunion because they feel they can run their food service without the union's interfering as a business partner. The employer can hire people as wanted and needed and there are no unnecessary restrictions on work assignments, pace of production, and other vital matters. Nonunion food service employees work as a team and take satisfaction in their jobs and their work. They feel closer to the facility and their employer than to their union.

GRIEVANCES AND AUDITS

There is little more important than to discuss grievances employees want to talk about. No matter how small this may seem to management, employees' grievances are very important to them. Food service supervisors must be trained to discuss gripes and grievances in a fair and even-handed manner. Providing an outlet for grievances can be critical in remedying employee relations hot spots. Procedures should be developed to ensure that grievances are dealt with fairly. Job conditions must be safe and in compliance with the law and normal employee conveniences must be satisfactory.

Some means should be established for monitoring employee relations periodically. Labor-wise attorneys suggest semiannual audits covering wages, fringe benefits, job conditions, supervisors, and, generally, privileges for employees as keys to morale. A definite plan should be designed to correct deficiencies and steps should be implemented to make certain the plan works.

A good labor relations program is founded on the solid philosophy of the Golden Rule: "Do unto your employees as you would have them do unto you." Each facet of the program builds productivity and helps avoid the management mistakes that can "earn" the facility a union. Exhibit 6–1 presents a dialogue of preventive labor relations principles.

Exhibit 6–1 10 Principles of preventive labor relations

First Principle: Put policies in employee handbook.

Second Principle: Determine the status of the personnel department or function.

Third Principle: Document all employment decisions, favorable or unfavorable to the employees.

Fourth Principle: Coordinate the implementation of employment decisions with and through the personnel department or the executive responsible for the personnel function.

Fifth Principle: Always suspend pending investigation—never precipitously or summarily discharge or fire employees.

Sixth Principle: Fight when right—do not capitulate unless there are legitimate reasons to do so.

Seventh Principle: Train employees and promote from within whenever practical to do so.

Eighth Principle: Quantify labor costs—personnel executives should know what labor costs, including all wages and benefits, and their trends.

Ninth Principle: Know the employees—personnel should ensure that management knows all employees as individuals.

Tenth Principle: Maintain a union-free environment.

Source: Reprinted from *The Wage and Hour Handbook for Hotels, Restaurants and Institutions* by Arch Stokes, published by CBI Publishing Co., Inc., 1979.

KEY EMPLOYEE NEEDS

Food service employers must establish their labor relations program and improve productivity through effective employee management. There are several key employee needs basic to maintaining satisfied employees.

Security

Managers are in the day-to-day business of human engineering that can develop into an effective labor relations program. Employees need a feeling of security. Therefore, managers must communicate that employees' jobs are secure and that steady work is available at the facility, barring unforeseen circumstances. Unless such a point is stressed, a union could organize employees by promising to provide such job security. In reality, unions sell only job insecurity, since they introduce the elements of strikes, union policies, etc.

Affiliation

Another important human need is a sense of affiliation, to feel like a part of the team. When employees lack a sense of loyalty and close identity with the facility (hospital, nursing home, university or correctional institution), unions seek to provide the affiliation within their "brotherhood."

Self-Esteem

Employees need to have their self-esteem built up. This is an incentive element that can increase productivity, enabling workers to carry tasks through from beginning to end, thus enlarging their sense of recognized accomplishment. Of course, food service employers must be careful not to give employees more responsibility than they can handle comfortably or conveniently.

Self-esteem also can be increased by involving food service employees in the decision-making process. How can workers relate to overall departmental goals?

125

Periodic brain-storming sessions could be held with them to obtain their input. Increased self-esteem and improved productivity are natural byproducts. One large teaching hospital in the Northeast saved more than $80,000 after requesting employees' input and after implementing their recommendations.

Employee Sensitivity

Employers who are sensitive to the needs of employees and their complaints are generally the ones who have more contented employees. Without such sensitivity, unions certainly can make employers listen to grievances. More fundamentally, food service employers should listen to grievances in the first place to build up employee morale, improve productivity, and, incidentally, avoid unionization.

Encouraging employees to talk constructively with management about their problems further reinforces their self-esteem and sense of affiliation.

Hiring

Next to discharges, the most frequent employment decision that has the potential for generating labor cases is the hiring of workers. Accordingly, following these simple rules in the recruitment and selection of personnel is fundamental to prevention of labor cases.

Hiring should be nothing more than a common-sense decision that a certain person fits a certain job. The hiring process should get top priority. After all, hiring is the first step toward good personnel management—including productivity, employment stability, and employee morale. Good productivity begins with the hiring of a labor force that is skillful and responsive. The bottom line is improved productivity. Putting a maximum effort into the hiring procedure, therefore, is cost effective.

Employers first must understand the position to be filled as a basis for better evaluating candidates and selecting those best qualified.

Step 1

With complex jobs, an employer may need the periodic input of existing employees, asking them to list the tasks they perform and how important the work is to the position. By involving co-workers, supervisors, and other knowledgeable persons in the evaluation process, a workable position description can be developed. This then defines exactly what kind of employee is needed and the candidates will know just what they are being asked to do.

Step 2

Next is assessing candidates' potential for the job. A job evaluation list (Exhibit 6–2) can be used as a checklist for qualifications. This evaluation may be matched with such conventional sources of information as references, resumes, and military or past employment records to develop a detailed picture of candidates.

A great deal of time should be spent getting information on applicants. Each should be screened through an appropriate form to learn about skills, experiences, and employment history. Each should be interviewed by persons familiar with the skills required of the candidates. They should name their immediate past employer and several previous ones so references can be checked to determine the individuals' work habits before hiring.

Exhibit 6–2 Job evaluation list

*Cost Effective
Labor Relations*

Cook: A.M. Shift

Rate tasks on a scale of 1–3 in order of importance to the position (with 1 being the most important).

Preparing breakfast items	_____
Coordinating with food service manager	_____
Estimating production requirements	_____
Utilizing and storing leftovers	_____
Preparing lunch entree items	_____
Supervising assistant cooks and other pertinent personnel	_____
Cleaning work area, equipment, and utensils	_____
Providing the line with adequate supplies of food	_____
Preparing clinical diet food items	_____

Only by knowing the details of the position can an effective evaluation be made of candidates through a written questionnaire and/or an oral interview. The important thing is the information received about the person's qualifications for the job. The employer thus should know the candidates in detail before hiring them. A job to which they are not suited will not be satisfying to them or the employer and productivity will suffer.

Careful hiring practices have the side effects of reducing absenteeism, minimizing employee wrong-doing, and avoiding other potential labor troubles. Certainly, in this day, prevention of such troubles is well worth consideration.

Step 3

Next, fitting the employee to the job is largely completed if the first two steps are followed carefully. If the right questions are asked, the best candidate usually will be found.

Step 4

One additional factor can improve hiring: Check the procedure to make certain it is efficient. For this purpose, written general criteria will improve hiring results. The employer may be wasting time if more than five candidates are interviewed for each position filled below the supervisory level; not enough candidates may be seen if there are fewer than three for each position.

Orientation

Food service employers should have an orientation program to bring employees into the work force and explain clearly what is expected of them. The orientation program also informs new employees what to expect from the employer. A comprehensive orientation policy can be an extremely important investment in time and money toward upgrading and maintaining a proficient work force. Much of the orientation is done on the job by supervisors who understand the necessity for setting an atmosphere to make employees thoroughly familiar with their jobs, explaining and demonstrating each step. The employees then are permitted to perform the job and the supervisors follow up to determine whether the new workers actually are oriented and performing their jobs efficiently.

The importance of proper orientation cannot be overemphasized. New employees must be given orientation covering personnel policies, especially labor relations. They must be introduced to the job and the supervisor (and higher levels as appropriate) must be introduced to them. Without such a formal program, new employees will learn about company policies via the rumor mill, which can be extremely damaging to everyone.

Employees should not be allowed to learn the facility's policies and be oriented by osmosis. This could lead them to adopt poor work habits. The institution's policies should be reviewed with all personnel at the outset and periodically thereafter. A confused mind leads to unhappy employee morale, which can lead to unsound labor relations programs and, potentially, even to a union organizational drive.

JOB INTRODUCTION

Employers must introduce the new workers to the job, particularly emphasizing how it integrates with the overall picture. This formal introduction must include the information employees need to know immediately, for example:

- when to report to work
- how to keep track of hours worked
- provisions for lunch
- uniform requirements
- employee benefit programs
- payroll procedures
- employee entrances
- employee disciplinary procedures.

Fellow workers need to be introduced so new employees feel comfortable as quickly as possible in their new surroundings. The fundamental benefits to employers of a good orientation are high employee morale, productivity, and a good start in cost effective labor relations.

Training

Employee training normally is task oriented. Task training has become an extremely important exercise for most employers. Some of the most successful in food service have extensive training programs in the special aspects of the job and have enhanced their employees' ability in several areas. Not only does the possibility of growth offer the potential to increase earnings but learning additional skills increases job opportunities. Task training also can bring into the work force disadvantaged youths who have difficulty finding jobs.

For example, simple orientation and training slide shows are helpful in ensuring uniformity and proper orientation of all employees. It also is important to reorient older employees since policies may change and the new ones need to be explained and reaffirmed.

A cornerstone in building an effective labor relations program is the development of a positive, complete, specific employee handbook. A handbook is essential to employee communications, particularly on basic personnel policy.

Personnel policies are practiced at all management levels in food service. They are not confined to the personnel department but should be practiced daily. These policies must consider creative self-expression and the building up of human assets. They should be couched in positive terms.

For example, if there is a food service policy against smoking, it should not state: "Employees are prohibited from smoking except in designated areas." Instead, it should say, "You may smoke but please do so only in areas so designated."

Similarly, the facility should develop personnel policies with information on:

- wage and salary compensation programs and policies
- promotion and transfers
- sick leave
- all forms of leaves of absence
- holiday policies
- shift scheduling
- vacations and vacation scheduling
- complaint procedures.

On the other hand, handbooks and the policy manuals are no substitute for supervisors' day-to-day communication with employees. Thus, it is essential that supervisors know all personnel policies and procedures and can explain them extemporaneously to employees. This is vital to good labor relations.

SETTING WAGE POLICIES

Many employers do not set a wage policy; instead, they fall into the trap of paying individuals what they think they are worth. Wage practices based on ad hoc decisions on raises almost certainly will lead to employee dissatisfaction and ultimately to the formation of a union. The lack of a wage policy can only promote employee dissatisfaction. How the employer pays is more important than how much is paid.

A pay policy consists of establishing logical wage classifications, paying employees in each classification the same rate, and letting them know they will get annual increases. However, if someone in management plays "God," dealing out wages on a catch-as-catch-can basis and paying varying rates to employees in the same category, there is no wage policy. Such an institution would be ripe for union organization.

An employer may be smart enough to explain the difference in the worth of employees in the same job classification but will not be able to convince those making less in the same type of job that the higher paid individuals are better employees.

Unions learned long ago that the only way to keep workers happy is to establish job classifications in their collective bargaining agreements and pay employees in the same classification the same wage rate. However, some employers never have learned this lesson. They insist on paying individuals instead of classifications—and that policy usually earns them a union.

A consistent wage policy saves management time. With a system of ad hoc raises, the employer constantly has to fend off employees who want increases. Little time is left for management.

As noted, employers pay the job classification, not the individual. The cornerstone of an appropriate wage compensation plan is developing the proper job descriptions (Exhibit 6–3) and job specifications (Exhibit 6–4). Once the job descriptions are written, the job classifications can be constructed by comparing certain jobs with others—for example, comparing cooks with dietary aides. Rates of pay can then be assigned to each job classification based on its relative worth.

Of course, entrance level workers may be kept as probationary employees below the job classification rate until they have learned their duties. Probation should not be longer than it takes to master the job.

Food service employers must pay the competitive wage rate for employee skills in their geographic area; otherwise, they will become merely a training ground for other employers. It is good business to pay the competitive wage rate or above to maintain employee continuity. It also is good business to pay wages that enable them to live comfortably within their economic stratum.

Before an annual wage raise, an employer should survey other employers in the area who compete for the same work force to determine what they are paying. An annual raise should be determined with an eye on yearly cost-of-living increases. Employees who are given a specific date on which to expect an annual raise thus have assurances they have a future with the organization and that they will be rewarded regularly.

Employers should not yield to the temptation to chisel on wages. A few cents an hour more can provide a stable work force and reduce turnover, which is much cheaper than paying a few cents less and continually investing in training and always having inexperienced employees. Employers should conduct annual wage and benefit surveys and communicate the results to the employees if favorable and competitive in the marketplace. (If they are unfavorable, the institution should act promptly to eliminate variances.)

JOB PERFORMANCE STANDARDS

Job performance standards should be measurable and objective. Utilization of evaluation standards such as those presented earlier in Exhibit 6–2 provide the basis for an objective assessment of employees and prevent arbitrary ratings.

For example, the food service employees of a 300-bed hospital were ready to walk off the job because of arbitrary performance evaluations. When an objective, measurable system was established (see Chapter 8), productivity and job satisfaction improved. There is no room for arbitrary wage rates or performance evaluations in a food service operation.

Effective Supervision

An incompetent food service supervisor can virtually destroy productivity and may leave the employer a sitting duck for a union. The effectiveness of any effort

Exhibit 6–3 Job description

*Cost Effective
Labor Relations*

COOK: A.M. Shift

Job Description

Requirements, Qualifications and Promotional Opportunities

Educational Requirements: Sufficient education and knowledge to meet the performance requirements outlined. Specialized training in the preparation of food for therapeutic diets would be desirable.

Training and Experience: Experience as a cook in an institution is preferred.

Physical Demands: Stands and walks short distances most of the working day. Stoops and reaches for, lifts, and carries food and kitchen equipment. Tastes and smells food to determine quality and palatability. Needs hand dexterity to prepare food. Must have an annual physical examination accompanied by a health card as designated by the facility.

Special Demands: Willingness to work for best interest of institution. Ability to supervise and work cooperatively with others. Considerable initiative and judgment involved in setting up meals, seasoning food, estimating food requirements, utilizing leftovers, and presenting food in an attractive and palatable manner. Works under general supervision. Follows standardized recipes and menus. (If appropriate: must have a genuine interest in geriatric work.)

Job Knowledge: Must be able to cook a variety of foods in large quantities and be familiar with seasoning required and cooking time involved. Must have first-hand knowledge of cooking characteristics of various cuts of meat and know names and contents of various types of dishes. Must be able to make simple estimates of quantities of food required.

Working Environment: Works in clean, well-lighted, ventilated kitchen. Atmosphere is warm and humid from hot food preparation. Cook is exposed to sudden temperature changes when entering refrigeration equipment and subject to burns from hot foods and utensils and cuts from knives. Possibility of injury from falls on slippery floors.

Knowledge of Equipment and Machines: Must know how to operate and clean all equipment properly in the kitchen.

Promotional Opportunities: Possible promotion to Food Service Director if education and abilities warrant.

Job Summary

1. Checks certified menu for the day and confers with Food Service Director as necessary.
2. Supervises and proceeds in the preparation of all menu items for the breakfast and noon meals with the aid of the A.M. Dietary Aide.
3. Responsible for seeing that all food is prepared and ready for serving for breakfast and lunch.
4. Responsible for seeing that the cleaning schedule is followed on the A.M. shift.
5. Makes certain that all menu items are well supplied on the steam table throughout the serving time.
6. Checks certified menu with the Food Service Director for the following day.
7. Supervises Dietary Aides as necessary in the preparation and serving of food under the general supervision of the Food Service Director.
8. Relation to other jobs: Directly responsible to the Food Service Director.
9. Is in charge of the Dietary Department in the absence of Food Service Director as designated.
10. Although specific duties have been outlined above, each employee is to complete any additional responsibilities assigned by the supervisor.

I, _____, have read the above job description and fully understand the conditions set forth therein, and if employed as COOK, I will perform these duties to the best of my knowledge and ability.

Date: _____   _____

Signature

Exhibit 6–4 Standard job specification

Job Title:	A.M. Dietary Aides
Hours:	7:30 A.M.–2:30 P.M., 5 days per week
Total Hours Per Week:	40 Days off: 2 per week
Vacations:	2 weeks after one year's service
Educational Background Needed:	None _____ Read and write X
	High School _____ College _____
Personality:	must meet public well
Supervisor:	head cook
Age Range:	18–65
Experience required:	desirable
Physical qualifications:	good health
Special skills required:	interpersonal skills

Special responsibilities of the job (description): The job requires that the dietary aide be efficient in gathering, organizing, and delivering supplies; work well with other employees; work required on Sunday two times per month.

to improve job productivity or control costs ultimately depends on the effectiveness of the supervisors. It is through them that management instructions are transmitted and work rules are enforced.

Employers should look for leadership traits when they select supervisors. These individuals must develop a thorough knowledge and mastery of the job skills and equipment used by their employees. A good record by a supervisor in handling a job gives the employees confidence the person knows the job and can supervise or direct them.

Supervisors must have the respect of their co-workers. They enthusiastically lead by example, practicing good work habits, and such admirable qualities then are adopted by other employees. Subordinates are as good as the standards set and maintained by their supervisors.

A supervisor also must be able to organize, anticipate problems, adjust to change, and give comprehensible instructions to employees before job tasks begin. Supervisors must concentrate, thinking as an assistant in a teamwork effort to help food service workers get the job done, smooth the way, see they have what they need, make suggestions, and give support.

The supervisor also is in the people business and must understand and practice "human engineering," which is nothing more than good personnel relations. The individual must be sensitive to identifying signs of employee discontent and must take appropriate action to deal with grievances.

A supervisor needs to consult with employees when problems arise. Sometimes there is a good reason for poor job performance, so compassion and assistance in rectifying any problems can result in the best solution.

Harsh and inflexible enforcement of work rules can lead to diminished employee morale and lower productivity. On the other hand, inexcusable absences from work, late starts and early quits, insubordination, and shoddy workmanship should never be tolerated. Failure to enforce these rules in a strict and evenhanded manner, when appropriate, will erode employee effectiveness and, consequently, lessen productivity.

Food service supervisors must be able to motivate employees to work more efficiently. In part, motivation to perform well is built by giving them a feeling of involvement, responsibilities they can handle, results they can show, and recognition for what they accomplish.

It is important that the supervisor state the reasons for plans set forth and seek suggestions concerning possible alternatives. One food service supervisor explains success: "I try to put everybody in business for himself. Each one of my people is in charge of some part of the job. I just hang around to keep them out of trouble. When the work gets done, they get the credit. When it does not, they get the blame, and they know it. Mostly, they blame themselves."

Employers must instruct and control supervisors as to responsibilities. The supervisors should arrive in advance of the employees to coordinate the work for the day, anticipate potential problems, and schedule work assignments. They also must make certain all food, supplies, and equipment are readily available. It is essential that supervisors know the employees so they can allocate jobs to the individuals best able to perform them. Supervisors also must train new employees, ascertaining their special qualifications, making sure they know all aspects of the new jobs. It is essential that supervisors be on hand so that unforeseen problems that arise may be resolved expeditiously.

A weak food service supervisor, or one who is playing favorites with employees, not only produces poor productivity but also invites a union to organize the facility. Employers cannot afford to keep supervisors who are incompetent or who abuse authority. Remember, unions sell management mistakes.

Employee Grievances

Administrators, managers, and supervisors must become good listeners. It will pay off in harmonious employee relations. To an employee, a grievance can be all-important. And no matter how insignificant the grievance may seem to employers, they must hear the employee out. Allowing employees an outlet for their problems can be helpful in cooling employment relations hot spots.

Essentially, paying attention to grievances is nothing more than practicing good employee communications, helping workers realize they can talk to management. Some employers have even retained ombudsmen to act as mediators.

In listening to problems, managers must get the facts and make the decision so the employees get the feeling of having had a fair hearing. They must come away with the knowledge that management understood and weighed the decision carefully.

The grievance procedure must be fair and must be conducted and communicated to employees with the appearance of fairness. Managers should be empathetic and tactful, must listen well, acquire the facts and make a well-considered decision.

Unions sell and can deliver an organized grievance procedure. Employers must meet this challenge. If the facility has a grievance procedure that employees perceive as fair, they will not seek a union for redress. Only food service supervisors or other top managers should handle grievances, not an employee committee. An employee grievance committee could easily become the organizing committee for the union.

Managers and supervisors must maintain an open-door policy. They must go to the employees to let them know such a policy is in active operation. Employees may not have the courage to come forward with their problems until the issues have festered to the breaking point.

There must be mechanisms for bringing grievances to a satisfactory conclusion and there must not be a lack of communication between employees and employer. Being genuinely interested in employees' problems affords an excellent opportunity to gain their respect and confidence. Grievances may be minimized by being alert to potential causes. In other words, the best procedure in handling grievances is a preventive labor relations program. (Exhibit 6–5 is a chronology of grievance procedure for a nonunion facility.)

Discharge of Unproductive Employees

One of the most difficult things for food service supervisors and managers to do is fire employees who are not measuring up to a realistic, minimum standard. Those who are falling behind usually are those who seek a union to shore up their own insecurity. No one likes to fire employees, for two reasons: (1) it is distasteful and, (2) it may not be possible to hire anybody better.

Therefore, there are three elements to providing a good disciplinary procedure. Managers should:

1. make sure all employees understand the standards of job performance necessary to remain employed
2. give the employees notice of any failing on their part

Exhibit 6–5 Sample chronology of a grievance procedure

	Days lapsed between events	Total days elapsed
Incident giving rise to grievance takes place	0	0
Step 1: Informal discussion between supervisor and grievant	1	1
Step 2: Written grievance filed	1	2
Step 3: Conference between grievant and company management (no more than 3 working days)	3	5
Step 4: Written decision on grievance, appeal filed (no more than 5 working days)	5	10
Step 5: Vice president of personnel for the company issues written decision on appeal (no more than 3 working days)	3	13
Step 6: Executive vice president of the company issues written decision on appeal (no more than 3 working days)	3	16

3. give the employees an opportunity to explain their side of the story fully before final discharge; in short, suspension pending investigation prevents major lawsuits.

Documentation Can Mean Economic Salvation

When an employee has consistently disregarded facility policies or work rules or commits a serious breach of conduct that cannot be tolerated, such as gambling, drinking, or fighting on the job, the employer should be quick to terminate the person. It is essential to get witnesses and statements from those who have knowledge that an employee has violated a facility rule.

Work rules must be written in facility policies (Employee Handbook) and should be enforced fairly and consistently. To keep an employee who regularly does not measure up or to enforce rules sporadically will have a devastating effect on the morale of other workers. Except in the case of a flagrant violation of company rules, no one should be discharged until a supervisor has counseled the employee in an effort to correct a work habit or an attitude. The result of such a discussion should be noted in the employee's records or personnel file or folder for future reference. Obviously, the supervisor should interview the individual during a pretermination investigation. The supervisor should be patient, fair, and honest in dealing with the employee.

Should discharge become necessary, the termination notice should show the specific reason the action has been taken: nonproduction, tardiness, irregular attendance, drinking, use of drugs, gambling, disregard of safety and/or health rules, abuse of food service equipment, theft, horseplay, physical incapacity to perform the job, leaving the worksite without permission, violation of coffee or lunch break rules, fighting, etc.

If the employee had been warned previously, the date of the warning should be shown on the notice. The specific cause should be stated. Listing a general reason for termination, such as "personal" factors, could damage the employer in subsequent unemployment pay claims.

Cut Unemployment Pay Claims by Keeping Good Records

Supervisors must "put it in writing." That bit of advice could save the facility a lot of money if it later wants to oppose an unemployment compensation claim. Management should oppose all claims it feels are unjustified. Unemployment compensation is financed through taxes contributed by the employer in every state except Alabama, Alaska, and New Jersey. Obtaining a reduction in paying unemployment tax by winning a compensation case is an opportunity the institution cannot afford to miss. However, it requires proper documentation of all facts relating to an employee's termination. Here are some steps to take. Management (including supervisors) should:

- Begin documentation at the time of hiring. Advise all management personnel of the importance of keeping careful records on each employee's conduct and job performance. In particular, note any incidents in which it was necessary to correct an employee.
- Fill in all forms, particularly separation forms. State laws require employers to complete a separation notice form for each terminated employee, regardless of the reasons for departure. Failure to do so may jeopardize chances of showing an employee was either terminated for cause or quit voluntarily. It is imperative to detail every incident leading to the separation.
- Determine whether an employee could be placed in another job if termination is caused by lack of work. If the person chose a layoff when work was available in another department or position at a similar rate of pay, that fact must be documented on the separation form to preserve the institution's right to protest the payment of benefits. Employers are not responsible for unemployment compensation benefits if an employee quits voluntarily.
- State the exact reason the employee gave for leaving and the amount of notice of that decision in all cases of voluntary separation. If an employee reported the reason for leaving was "to accept another job," carefully record that fact. Obtain a written resignation and place it in the employee's personnel file. Employees often quit for personal reasons. However, the purpose of unemployment compensation is to provide financial assistance to individuals who lose their jobs through no fault of their own and are unable to find other employment. The facility should protest the payment of benefits as a result of separation due to voluntary retirement, family or personal illness, job dissatisfaction (including unhappiness with the job, supervisor, or other employees, and/or earnings, hours, working conditions, or commuting time), marriage, pregnancy, child care, education, moving, or various other personal reasons. Employers are not responsible for unemployment compensation if an employee quits for any of these reasons so it is imperative to make sure the specific cause for the separation is documented and submitted to the employee on the respective state department of labor form. Contact your local state department of labor office for the specific procedure and time frame. Management should protest the payment of benefits that are charged to the facility's reserve account if an employee leaves for personal reasons and then receives benefits.
- List all facts and details of an employee's dismissal for misconduct in the remarks section of the separation form. Explain exactly how the person was neglectful or behaved improperly in the performance of work. Detail the policy the employee violated. It is extremely important to include details of

prior warnings, disciplinary measure(s), or suspension(s) that relate to the separation. Indicate all dates of absences and tardiness. Document poor attendance, violation of company rules, unauthorized absences, failure to report for work, excessive tardiness, refusal to follow instructions, or any other examples of gross misconduct. Do not give conclusions but do report facts. Do not say an employee was "unsatisfactory," rather, tell exactly how the person was unsatisfactory. If an employee was insubordinate, detail exact conversations that reflect that conduct. Careful documentation of all facts leading to a dismissal will enable the institution to avoid having a claim for benefits charged to its account, thereby decreasing its unemployment compensation taxes.

- Note the exact date and time of receiving a hearing notice and be sure to be present at the session. Take all documentation necessary to show that an employee either quit voluntarily or was terminated for cause. Bring witnesses who can support management's position and can testify concerning the employee's separation. Only first-hand testimony will be acceptable, and it is the manager's responsibility to make sure it is provided.

Prevent Union Organizing

Employees who are not measuring up are always a possible source of union organization. The first thing managers should do to avoid organization is to fire the person they have been meaning to dismiss for months. Who is this employee? This is the one who never quite measures up to expected productivity and who never complies with the institution's rules. This employee typically is late, often absent, and cannot admit to any fault.

Therefore, poorly performing employees seek out a union to aid in their personal cause. All a union organizer has to do to organize a poorly run food service operation is to wait for a telephone call from a disgruntled employee. The organizer then makes that individual the head of the organizing committee to expand the sphere of union influence, planting seeds of discontent by focusing on management's mistakes. Retaining poor employees merely lowers the common denominator of other workers' performance.

The bottom line is that food service employers cannot afford to keep poor employees, from the standpoint of productivity or possible union organizational potential.

What Constitutes a Poor Employee

Documentation of any of the characteristics listed next provides legitimate grounds for termination:

- drinking or being under the influence of alcoholic beverages, drugs, and/or narcotics—or possessing any of these—during working hours
- insubordination (including failing to follow supervisors' instructions as defined in *Webster's Dictionary*)
- stealing (includes adding tips)
- fighting on the premises
- violation of any house rules or regulations of which the employee has been notified

- insolence or lack of courtesy to supervisors, department heads, managers, fellow employees, or patients
- failure to perform the service required by the employee's position
- lack of proper personal appearance, sanitation, and cleanliness—especially critical in food service
- inefficiency
- physicial condition that endangers the health of fellow workers or of the employee
- failure to report for work, except in the case of established illness, which must be attested by a medical certificate or other verified emergency, when requested by the employer, except that a medical certificate will not be requested when not practical
- improper cash, money, or credit card handling procedures, including failure to follow established procedures.

As noted earlier, unions are opportunists. If a supervisor is playing favorites, if someone is playing ''God'' with wages, or if the food service manager does not listen to legitimate grievances and does not give employees the feeling of fair dealing, then the facility can become an easy mark for union organization.

DEALING WITH EXISTING UNIONS

Food service employers who already are organized by a union must maintain the right to run their business. Management should proceed to act and assume its rightful leadership role unless in managing its business or in dealing with a specific situation the union contract expressly prohibits the action. In other words, management should act and let the union react to greivances or complaints. Management should not seek advance permission from the union to do something not covered by the contract. Unions do not give advance permission for something that is not, or they believe is not, in their interest.

Management can be a leader and at the same time consult with the union. Disputes often arise as to whether a certain work practice is permitted or required under the contract, and meetings between a supervisor and a business agent can produce a quick resolution that is satisfactory to both sides. However, the job must be run as the supervisor sees fit, letting the union bring a grievance if a dispute cannot be settled in management's favor. It should be kept in mind that if the labor agreement has a no-strike provision and mandatory arbitration of disputes, the employer may get an injunction against a union work stoppage and have the dispute settled by an arbitrator. Employers stand a better chance of victory at arbitration when business economy and efficiency are on their side.

A union operates as a political organization. Union officials must be reelected periodically, and the employee members of the union are their political constituents. This may explain why some meritless complaints and grievances are presented to management by a business agent, who may be responding to union members' wishes rather than exercising independent judgment. Even though the union may not win the grievance, the business agent fulfills a role by discussing it with management. If the business agent does not win, the employees can blame management, not the agent.

The job steward or business agent cannot serve as a second boss. The employer and the employer's supervisors alone must run the job. The union's function is to protect employees and not to join with management in managing them. Employers should not abdicate authority to union stewards or agents by allowing them to dictate how a job should be done. Management also should encourage long-term employees to attend union meetings. In this way, union meetings will have meaningful input from loyal company employees as opposed to being run by hotheads who float from employer to employer.

It is essential that the employer and supervisors read and become familiar with the labor agreement in order to administer it properly. Many employer committees have won a point at the bargaining table and then lost it because other food service facilities in the area have allowed a practice to develop that was not clearly set forth in the labor agreement. Employers should be alert to dangers inherent in establishing past practices that add to or subtract from the contract and should not allow compromise.

Management must not fall into the trap of permitting a union to demand organized coffee breaks when they are not provided in the agreement. It should insist upon eight hours' work for eight hours' pay. Late arrivals, tardiness, or extended lunch hours should not be tolerated. Management negotiators may have fought hard for an issue the union may try to avoid by various excuses. The collective bargaining agreement, itself, already is a package of compromises for which the management committee may have paid dearly in the course of negotiations.

In summary, unions sell management mistakes. A good labor relations program, based on the Golden Rule, will improve productivity and will help the institution avoid the management mistakes that can "earn" it a union.

Chapter 7

Labor Costs

The cost of labor is a major consideration in planning and controlling food service expenses—50 to 60 percent of the total. The upward pressure on wage increases indicates labor will continue to be the major cost component.

LABOR COST FACTORS

Although two major factors constitute the bulk of labor costs, numerous other hidden elements contribute either directly or indirectly. The time required to perform a job and the rate of pay designated for the task represent only the tip of the labor cost iceberg. Other factors include type of service, productivity, benefits, turnover, overtime, and absenteeism.

When evaluating a food service to determine any of the labor costs, the following types of information must be obtained:

1. Menu Information

   - type of menu offered
   - menu pattern to be followed
   - form in which food for the menu is purchased
   - number and type of diet modifications
   - number and type of nourishments
   - type of service (self-service, centralized bulk service, ambulatory patient service, any other special menu services), and length of daily operations' service times

2. Physical Plant Information

   - amount of labor-saving equipment available
   - layout of the food service facility
   - working conditions of the facility

141

3. Service Information

- type of service ware (permanent or single service)
- maintenance of service performance standards and food quality standards
- service distribution logistics (specifically, who will be responsible for service of food and what method or system of delivery is to be used)

4. Statistical Data

- number of meals served per day
- seating capacity
- maximum patient/customer capacity
- percentage of therapeutic diets
- quantity of intermittent meals or nourishments
- current wage rate
- rate of employee turnover
- personnel productivity
- employee benefits

5. Human Resources Information

- training programs
- amount and adequacy of supervision
- employee morale
- skill of employees.

A clear picture of the department's labor costs will emerge in determining this information. This chapter identifies potential hidden labor costs and specific, practical means of controlling them.

DETERMINING ACTUAL LABOR COSTS

It is important to remember the hourly employee wage rate is only the beginning of actual labor costs. Although this expense may be considerable, it can become the least costly component when hidden costs are considered.

The payroll wage cost is determined by two factors: (1) the compensable employee working time and (2) the employee's rate of pay. It states the amount of the employee's gross wages, but that is not the real cost. The real cost of the work performed must be considered with two additional factors: (1) employer costs, and, (2) employee productivity, which is determined by dividing total wages and employee costs by the actual number of meals produced (see Chapter 8 on productivity).

The list in Exhibit 7–1 identifies many of the hidden expenses on an hourly basis per employee. As the exhibit indicates, the minimum wage employee is an expensive commodity to the employer. The basic state and federal taxes and compensation requirements in addition to a variety of benefits can almost double the "actual" hourly labor cost.

These figures do not indicate additional employer costs for supervision, pilferage, payroll preparation, bookkeeping, overtime, institutional maintenance for employees, life insurance, or other employee benefits. A total of $2.12 must be added to the hourly base rate to present an accurate picture of employer costs per minimum wage employee per hour. This is 63 percent of the base labor hourly

Exhibit 7–1 Actual hourly employer costs to employee   *Labor Costs*

Benefit	$3.35/hr (minimum wage-base rate)	
FICA	$.20	
Worker's compensation	.07	
Employment compensation	.11	
Medical and hospital insurance	.13	
Uniform allowance	.65	
Meals (two, costing employer $1 each)	.27	
Meal break time	.24	
Coffee breaks (two of 15 minutes each)	.24	
Vacation (one week)	.07	
Time off for sickness—7 days	.07	
Holiday pay—7 days	.07	$2.12
Total cost per hour		$5.47
		+ 5.47
Total production cost per hour (50% productivity):		$10.94

rate. Exhibit 7–1 does not include a variety of individual employer expenses that must be considered when calculating an institution's actual labor costs. It is important to include data specific to a facility when evaluating labor costs for its food service department.

With a revised actual hourly employer cost per employee (the base rate of $3.35 plus the extras and benefits of $2.12), the actual total cost per hour of $5.47 is determined. Factoring in the 50 percent productivity results in a total cost of ($5.47 × 2) $10.94 per employee.

These calculations represent only minimum wage workers. Skilled employees at higher rates could become expensive labor liability costs if that 50 percent productivity rate were allowed to continue.

LABOR TURNOVER

Employer costs escalate with labor turnover. The cost of replacing employees is one of the greatest expenses the employer incurs. Evaluating the turnover rate and taking action to reduce it will lead to greater cost efficiency.

Labor turnover is a ratio of "leavers" to "stayers." The relative frequency rate is the number of employees who have left divided by the total number employed during the year (Exhibit 7–2).

These are approximate rates, obscuring differences in length of service and dissimilarities in characteristics of personnel. Therefore, food service employers should calculate the instability rate as well. The instability rate (Exhibit 7–3) is the number of employees who leave divided by the number who stay, plus the total number employed during the specified time.

The institution in Exhibit 7–3 has a slightly better rate of stability than of turnover. However, figures above 10 percent in either employee turnover or rate of stability bear further analysis of the operation and policies.

The greatest employee turnover occurs between 14 days and 90 days of employment. Some leave of their own accord while in other cases, where a union exists, the employer may release a worker within a 90-day probationary period after hiring.

Exhibit 7–2 Labor turnover

$$\text{Turnover rate*} = \frac{\text{Total terminations}}{\text{Average number of persons employed in specified time}} \times 100 = \underline{\hspace{1cm}}\%$$

For example:

$$\frac{6 \text{ terminations}}{30 \text{ food service employees in one year}} \times 100 = 20\%$$

*The optimum turnover rate is 10 percent or less a year.

COST OF EMPLOYEE TURNOVER

The following costs are associated with turnover of employees:

- Break-in cost: the cost incurred because of new employees' substandard performance as they are learning
- Breaking-in cost: the cost of time lost by supervisors as they train new workers
- Lost production and extra burden cost: the cost of running a food service operation on low or below-normal staffing as well as overtime costs
- Extra Social Security tax cost: the employer's cost when tax payments are resumed with each new employee
- Extra unemployment tax cost: the cost when a former employee collects unemployment insurance and the increased burden of insurance for each new employee
- Bookkeeping cost: the cost to complete necessary paperwork when an employee is terminated or hired.

Formalized training programs will help offset the break-in and breaking-in cost by allocating training expenses to a specific budget line that may or may not be considered when assessing total labor expense attributed to employee turnover. Since this may be charged to the personnel department, these two aspects could be

Exhibit 7–3 Stability rate

Rates of stability:

$$\frac{\text{Total terminations}}{\text{Number who stay} + \text{Total number employed during specified time}} \times 100 = \underline{\hspace{1cm}}\%$$

For example:

$$\frac{6 \text{ terminations}}{26 \text{ (who stay)} + 6 \text{ (new hires in 1 year)}} \times 100 = 18.75\%$$

deleted from consideration in the food service turnover rate. Estimates of the cost of hiring, employing, and training even one minimum wage employee range from $1,200 to $3,000. Better hiring means less firing and reduced costs.

Reduced Turnover by Improved Employee Satisfaction

It is evident that turnover is a major cost, so food service employers must look at what causes employees to leave. Sometimes the fault lies with the person responsible for hiring: an applicant's work record, qualifications, and recommendations may not have been examined well. Extensive examination of work records and discussions with former employers can prove invaluable in this time-consuming yet critical stage.

A qualified employee well matched to the position is the beginning of a healthy work experience. On the other hand, a mismatch causes high frustration levels for both worker and employer. The orientation program may not have explained the job and its requirements adequately, leading new employees to misunderstand what was expected of them. A well-organized, well-defined, structured orientation of the worker to the institution is imperative in developing a valuable long-term employee, which in turn increases the return on the facility's investment (ROI).

Well-written, easily understood position descriptions are invaluable in the orientation process as well as throughout the term of employment. The orientation leader or immediate supervisor should ensure the chain of command (outlined in an organization chart) is presented in such a way as to facilitate understanding. If the employee does not know or comprehend the position and company expectations, misunderstandings, poor performance, and eventually turnover may result.

Supervision

Poor or inadequate supervision also is a cause of employee failure. If turnover and/or rate of instability have been high, management should evaluate the current orientation and training process to determine its potential weaknesses, consulting with both supervisors and workers. How could the orientation and training programs be improved?

Wage Policies

Wage structures must be reviewed. If new employees are hired at higher wages than current workers are paid for doing the same job, morale of the latter will fall. If a grievance outlet is not available, employees may become discontented. Frustration also may occur because of an apparent lack of supervisory interest. As noted in Chapter 6, this can be prevented by providing a way employees can communicate with supervisors or their representatives.

Lack of motivation may result if a definite means of advancement or financial incentive is not apparent. For many employees, periodic wage increases are not enough to satisfy their potential as productive leaders of the organization, and a definite path toward more responsibility is necessary.

Creature Comforts

The working environment, although optimal in many food service facilities, may cause considerable employee dissatisfaction. Many times, the facility is designed by individuals who will not work (and in some instances never have worked) in a kitchen. Certain equipment design features can serve as daily irritants. The variety of human factors of engineering that must be considered in commercial food service departments often exceeds those for other production industries.

Temperature, humidity, and ventilation all play critical parts in employees' ability to perform their tasks efficiently. A relative humidity of 25 to 50 percent with ambient room temperatures of 65°–70° F (winter) and 70°–75° F (summer) have proved the most acceptable.

Many persons think a food service kitchen is supposed to be noisy because of the equipment. This is a fallacy since too high a noise level (80 to 90 decibels) causes fatigue, decreased productivity, and has deteriorative effects on the hearing if continued over a long period. Teaching employees to place rather than drop heavy pots and pans, insulating or remotely locating noisy equipment, and scheduling motorized equipment usage to minimize worker exposure are ways to reduce noise, fatigue, and dissatisfaction.

In a commercial kitchen, glare caused by direct lighting on shiny stainless steel surfaces may cause a variety of eye irritations, consequent fatigue, and ultimate decrease in productivity. Where economically feasible, a finish of brushed stainless steel, color coded, or wood-grain type is recommended. Since lighting is inescapably related to color, it is important to realize that a highly reflective background (e.g., white) in a room requires less light from the fixture to provide an adequate and comfortable level of lighting to the work surface. It has been recommended that 30 to 50 FC (foot-candles) are acceptable for the types of tasks in food production areas. On the other hand, 70 FC are recommended at the clean end of the dishmachine to permit proper inspection of colorless residues that may be on the articles.

The nature of the work in the department lends itself to excessive standing or walking. Although many managers have felt an employee is not productive while sitting, studies have proved that muscle fatigue is reduced significantly when the back and leg muscles are supported properly. The use of resilient flooring, antifatigue mats, stools with footrests, and footstools on wheels are highly recommended for repetitive tasks done in one location over a long period. The use of one or more of these items tends to relieve fatigue and maintain productivity levels.

Since 70 percent of all the work in kitchens is done on tables, it is necessary to ensure they be at a proper height for the majority of the employees. Anthropomorphic considerations recommend comfortable working heights for women at 38 to 39 inches from the floor and for men 39 to 41 inches. Table feet that adjust the height between 37 and 42 inches will best meet the needs of both men and women. Heavy work (breaking down meat carcasses or kneading bread) requires a height of 34 to 36 inches for both men and women. Employees who are physically exhausted at the end of the day will be in no hurry to return to work the following day.

The old axiom, "If you can't stand the heat, get out of the kitchen," should not apply when addressing turnover and employee satisfaction. The state of the food service equipment industry has progressed to such a level of complexity and sophistication that heat production can be regulated. More and more heat-producing pieces of equipment are better insulated and capable of short heat-up periods with quick cool-down times. There also now are systems to recover equipment heat for alternate uses. These features, coupled with air conditioning and/or ventilation systems, all contribute to employee comfort, reduced turnover, and increased productivity.

An area overlooked by management and frequently of major concern to employees is the specific equipment in the kitchen. The placement of gauges and dials so they can be read and/or set easily and accurately, the type of handle on a broiler or oven, and the location of the locking device on a chopper are but a few of the areas that cause employee irritation. Malfunctioning equipment aggravates employees, causes frustration, and leads to poor work habits and bad attitudes about management and the organization.

Advancement

Finally, a clear career progression for advancement in the position or within the organization must be identified. By citing examples of those who have been promoted to more responsible positions, the supervisor helps to encourage employee self-development. This final recommendation should be a major consideration since it has been the crux of the low morale problem in the entire food service industry. All too many employees eagerly enter a new job, only to discover quickly that it is a dead end, with little or no opportunities for advancement. Employees reach a level of diminishing return of job satisfaction, resulting in decreased productivity and ultimately turnover.

Employee Attitude Survey

Employee dissatisfaction and turnover are caused by a variety of factors. Determining these factors while the worker is on the job is accomplished best through the use of an anonymous employee attitude survey (Exhibit 7–4). The survey is designed to maintain anonymity because the response need only be checked; no written comment is necessary. Exhibit 7–5 on administering the survey, highlights the do's, don'ts, and methods of converting the results for comparison purposes.

Periodic use of this survey (once every six to 12 months) will provide management with insight into the dimensions of the work force, the work life, and the workplace. Management's adjustment of those factors will help reduce turnover, thereby cutting labor cost and increasing productivity.

Exit Interview

Since turnover is such an important expense to control, its causes must be discovered to reduce this unnecessary outlay of funds. However, there are instances in which turnover is inevitable. In such cases the use of an exit or termination interview will: (1) determine reasons why the employee is leaving and (2) generate data that can be used to improve the work life and workplace to prevent additional turnover. In some instances, a termination may be prevented because the employer may be able to correct employee dissatisfaction at that time.

For example, an employee ready to resign revealed at a termination interview he was leaving because the organization did not provide a clean uniform daily. Management was able to correct this for the individual and for the other food service employees, preventing the termination and improving employee satisfaction. A termination interview or evaluation, besides serving as a means of gaining information about employee satisfaction, is also a good management tool. Exhibit 7–6 is provided for both purposes.

Exhibit 7–4 Employee attitude survey

Please complete the following questions by marking the answer that most closely represents how you feel about your job. This information will be used to improve working conditions for you and to increase your job satisfaction. Since we want honest answers, PLEASE DO NOT PUT YOUR NAME ON THIS SURVEY.

1. Do you feel you are treated fairly by your supervisor?
   _____ Always _____ Usually _____ Seldom _____ Never

2. Does your supervisor criticize you in front of other people?
   _____ Always _____ Usually _____ Seldom _____ Never

3. Does your supervisor know and understand your job?
   _____ Always _____ Usually _____ Seldom _____ Never

4. Do you have any conflicts because of too many supervisors?
   _____ Always _____ Usually _____ Seldom _____ Never

5. Does your supervisor express a sincere interest in your problems?
   _____ Always _____ Usually _____ Seldom _____ Never

6. Do you feel free to go to your supervisor with a complaint?
   _____ Always _____ Usually _____ Seldom _____ Never

7. Do you have enough time to do a good job?
   _____ Always _____ Usually _____ Seldom _____ Never

8. Do you thoroughly understand how your job should be performed?
   _____ Always _____ Usually _____ Seldom _____ Never

9. Did you receive adequate training in your job?
   _____ Always _____ Usually _____ Seldom _____ Never

10. Do you like doing your job?
    _____ Always _____ Usually _____ Seldom _____ Never

11. Do you feel your work is appreciated?
    _____ Always _____ Usually _____ Seldom _____ Never

12. Do you have the equipment, supplies and tools needed to do your job?
    _____ Always _____ Usually _____ Seldom _____ Never

13. Are assignments handed out fairly by your supervisor?
    _____ Always _____ Usually _____ Seldom _____ Never

14. Do you like your co-workers?
    _____ Always _____ Usually _____ Seldom _____ Never

15. Do your co-workers pull their share of the load?
    _____ Always _____ Usually _____ Seldom _____ Never

16. Are you assigned the type of work you do best?
    _____ Always _____ Usually _____ Seldom _____ Never

17. Do you feel your talents are wasted?
    _____ Always _____ Usually _____ Seldom _____ Never

18. Do you have an opportunity to make suggestions to improve your job?
    _____ Always _____ Usually _____ Seldom _____ Never

19. When you make suggestions, are they appreciated?
    _____ Always _____ Usually _____ Seldom _____ Never

20. Do you believe your pay is in line with your co-workers?
    _____ Always _____ Usually _____ Seldom _____ Never

21. Do you believe your pay is in line with similar jobs in this area?
    _____ Always _____ Usually _____ Seldom _____ Never

Exhibit 7–4 continued *Labor Costs*

22. Are your raises in line with what you expect?
_____ Always _____ Usually _____ Seldom _____ Never

23. Do you understand facility and department policies and procedures?
_____ Always _____ Usually _____ Seldom _____ Never

24. Are you proud of the place you work?
_____ Always _____ Usually _____ Seldom _____ Never

25. Is your workplace safe and comfortable?
_____ Always _____ Usually _____ Seldom _____ Never

Turnover and its costs can be controlled. Managers should brainstorm with their supervisors and turn this problem into a project. The results may prove astounding:

- increased morale of workers and supervisors
- increased productivity

Exhibit 7–5 How to administer the employee attitude survey

1. Have a competent person outside of the department (outside of the facility, if possible) administer and interpret the results of the survey.
2. Be sure there are no managers or supervisors anywhere in the vicinity of the survey site. If it is necessary to have a management person explain the reason and basis of the survey, that person should leave before administration of the survey begins. In order to receive honest answers, the employees must be certain they will receive no reprisal for their answers. Strict anonymity is essential.
3. Explain fully the purpose of the survey. Stress that names or handwritten answers are not allowed. Provide the pens or pencils with which to answer the survey.
4. Do not allow talking or discussion during the survey. Move the employees as far apart as possible during the survey to assure privacy of answers. Do not encourage employees to discuss the survey after it has been administered.
5. The person administering the survey should not watch the employees while they are answering the questions. This person may want to sit in the front of the room and read a paper or otherwise busy himself or herself so as to allow the employees a complete feeling of privacy.
6. The survey sheet should be folded and dropped in an enclosed box upon completion (similar to an election box).
7. An objective person should tally the results and carefully study the responses to determine where improvements are needed. Percentile ratings of the responses facilitate review of the information. Areas of general employee satisfaction should also be carefully noted.
8. Analysis of the responses should reveal areas that need improvement, as well as areas in which employees are generally satisfied. Some employees will give the best answer in all instances; some will give the worst. Disregard these responses, but take a hard look at the answers which have a 75% to 80% response rate.
9. Have the person who administers the survey prepare a report to be presented to both the management and the employees. Recommendations should be included in the report.
10. Use the survey to formulate policies to improve employee job satisfaction. Be sure the employees *see* the results of their input and that action is being taken because of their answers to the survey.
11. Once a program to improve employee satisfaction has been implemented, another survey should be administered in three to six months to evaluate the program's effectiveness.

Exhibit 7–6 Termination interview

Name: _____   Termination Date: _____

Position: _____   Department: _____

Rating at termination

	Superior	Above Average	Average	Below Average
Ability				
Quality of Work				
Attendance				
Physical Health				
Emotional Disposition				
Appearance				
Attitude				

Comments: _____

_____

Reason for leaving: _____

_____

_____

Recommended for reemployment: Yes_____   No_____
Comments: _____

_____

Forwarding address: _____
Forwarding telephone: _____

Date: _____   Signed: _____
                                                                    Supervisor

- improved quality of performance
- reduced turnover
- reduced costs.

Communication

Other factors that affect employee satisfaction, and therefore quality of performance, productivity, and costs, include channels of communication as noted earlier. A channel of communication both up and down the organization chart must exist and be accessible to all pertinent parties. Employees are concerned with knowing what is going on in the department as well as within the facility.

Management has an obligation to provide information about major departmental or facility changes.

On the reverse side, management should maintain and encourage channels of open communication from employees. This may be an outlet for grievances or a simple open door. When employees feel they have no recourse to a problem or receive no encouragement to speak about their position, unrest frequently results. Another more open method of encouraging this type of participation is the use of employee staff meetings.

Quality Circles

Quality circles relate directly to channels of communication and are used primarily to improve the quality of the product. An employee who has repeatedly done the same or a similar job for an extended time knows more about the quality of the product and the steps necessary for its completion than does the manager. By questioning the employee about how to improve the product or the process, a twofold function (communication and improved quality assurance) is being accomplished.[1]

Today's employees are more aware of the quality of work life and the workplace. Reinforcing the positive factors that contribute to the improvement of their quality will enable management to realize two results: (1) open channels of communication and (2) employees' participation in the organization. As management identifies problems, challenges, and opportunities to the employees, it encourages continued, if not improved, involvement in the organization.[2] Of course, it is mandatory to the success of such programs that management make a conscientious effort to implement all practical solutions and improvements recommended by the employees as well as give appropriate credit for such suggestions.

Specific and successful techniques that improve the quality of work life and mandate involvement include the following: flextime (flexible hours), flexible time off (instead of regularly scheduled vacations and sick leave), job sharing, input on job design, personally designed development programs, use of permanent part-time employees and leaves of absence for educational or other job-related purposes.[3]

It is important to note that any of these techniques must be tailored to the individual organization. The very nature of food service organizations, with specific demands for product and service at regulated times during the day, further complicates the possibility of readily adapting some of these techniques.

However, some solutions do exist. Creativity, flexibility, and sensitivity to cost have proved successful for some food service organizations. These factors coupled with some redesign of the menu and delivery systems have contributed to improved efficiency, productivity, and quality of work life in several institutions.[4]

Absenteeism

Absenteeism is another labor cost factor that must be considered. Absenteeism has reached chronic, nationwide proportions in the public and private sectors of both the production and service industries. It seems to flourish precisely where it is ignored. Too many employers consider sick days that employees take off as part of the cost of doing business. Whether or not absent employees receive compensation, their work must be allocated to others, who may do it begrudgingly. Low morale develops quickly when this type of behavior persists.

An absentee rate should not be allowed to exceed 2 percent. The following calculation can be used to calculate the absentee rate for the food service department:

$$\frac{\text{Number of daily absentees during pay period}}{\text{Average number of employees} \times \text{number of working days in pay period}} \times 100 = \underline{\hspace{1cm}}\%$$

For example:

$$\frac{4}{30 \times 14} \times 100 = 1\%$$

Since employees will come to work regularly only if it is to their advantage, management should not tolerate nor condone frequent absences; instead, it should monitor them closely. The most common causes of absenteeism are:

- job-related problems (poor morale, supervision, working conditions)
- community-related problems (poor transportation, inadequate police protection, lack of child care facilities)
- personality-related problems (illness, alcoholism, family responsibilities, psychological problems).

The decision to stay away from work is a symptom something is wrong. The most effective way managers can combat absenteeism is to show concern and to be committed to attendance. The management staff should be attendance oriented and, when setting an example using the following guidelines, should:

1. explain to the employees that attendance rates are considered seriously in raises and performance review
2. check on the absentee and communicate that the absence affects co-workers
3. give recognition to those who report to work every day
4. utilize preventive medicine approaches by requiring annual physical check-ups
5. demonstrate flexibility with on-time rules; a five-minute lateness should not be a bigger offense than a sick day—that merely promotes employees' use of sick days
6. show people the importance of their work; employees must be made to feel that their job is significant and critical to the working of the whole
7. interact with community agencies relating to needs of child day care, the handicapped, parolee, etc., to check on chronic absenteeism or to facilitate the coordination of community support services.[5]

A program maximizing the use of these seven key points should be made public to the employees and any existing union in order to eliminate misinterpretation of actions taken by management.

Overtime

Unauthorized and uncontrolled overtime will quickly pyramid already high labor costs. The keys to controlling overtime are knowledge of the tasks, estimated time of completion, and constant awareness of the cost. Normally, overtime is the hourly rate plus half again the wage rate. An accurate comparison of the cost of allowing one employee to work four hours of overtime at the minimum wage of $3.35 (overtime wage rate of $5.03) receiving $20.10, with the part-time employee working the same four hours at the minimum wage rate ($3.35), receiving $13.40, quickly reveals the substantial cost differential. Finally, the additional 30 percent to 40 percent employer cost (employee benefits) need not be paid for the part-time employee.

All overtime should be authorized properly by some responsible level of management. To allow an employee to decide overtime is needed to complete a task is a poor practice. Two methods have been developed for use in controlling overtime: (1) requisitioning overtime in advance when absence because of illness or vacation is anticipated (Exhibit 7–7) and (2) requiring an authorizing signature and explanation within 24 hours after it has been incurred. With the use of either method, responsibility for authorization and, consequently, control of overtime labor costs still rests on the shoulders of management.

Labor costs are significant in any food service operation. They must be controlled. Administration and managers must evaluate their labor costs and expose potential problem areas. They should:

- set goals (for example, reduce turnover rate to 10 percent within six months)
- develop a plan of action
- consult department employees for their input
- implement the action plan
- evaluate the action plan periodically for any needed modifications
- reap the results
- reward employees when goal(s) are achieved.

Exhibit 7–7 Report of overtime or extra wages

Facility _____

Department: _____
Date overtime occurred: _____
Number of persons required for overtime: _____
Total number of hours overtime: _____

Employee	Hours overtime incurred	Rate

Reason for overtime: _____

Signature, Department head

NOTES

1. Kathleen Marshall, "Quality Circles: Are They For You?" *Restaurants and Institutions* (June 1, 1982):133.

2. Edward Glaser, *Productivity Gains Through Worklife Improvement* (New York: Amacom, 1980).

3. Hermine Lagat Levine, "Consensus—Efforts to Improve Productivity," *Personnel* (January-February 1983):4–11.

4. Ronald C. Wacker, "Value Driven Management," *Hospitals* 57 (April 1, 1983):81–84.

5. James Hayes, "The Death of Productivity," *Restaurant Business* (June 1, 1980):74.

Chapter 8

Improving Productivity: A Results-Oriented Approach

As noted earlier, labor represents 50 percent to 60 percent of total food service costs. Controlling and improving productivity are keys to managing labor costs. Employees are not responsible for improving productivity—employers are. Improving productivity cannot be a one-time effort. Systems must be set in place to encourage productivity on a daily basis. This chapter reviews how to help make productivity an integral part of the work culture in the food service operation.

To control costs, managers today must improve productivity, which means:

- getting more work from the same number of employees, or
- getting the same amount of work from fewer employees.

This chapter identifies specific means by which managers can:

- evaluate current staffing patterns in view of present and projected departmental productivity
- improve productivity of food service personnel.

A food service department is productive if it achieves its goals at the lowest possible cost. Consequently, productivity is concerned with both efficiency and effectiveness. A good general definition of productivity is input divided by output—for example, the amount of labor (input) necessary divided by the number of meals (output) served, yielding the number of labor-hours required to serve one meal.

If 1,200 meals per day are served with 80 hours of labor, .06 labor-hours per meal are required and represent one initial index of productivity. Conversely, another measure of productivity is meals per labor-hour, which results from output (meals) being divided by input (labor). In this example of 80 hours of labor required to serve 1,200 meals, the initial productivity index is 15 meals per labor-hour. Other important factors that affect indexes of productivity are discussed in detail later in this chapter.

155

FACTORS AFFECTING PRODUCTIVITY

Three primary areas affect productivity and, therefore, labor costs:

1. Behavior: motivating employees in their work and encouraging them to increase their efficiency
2. Technical: type of equipment, its usage, layout, and measurement systems
3. Marketing: influences the number of people the department services.

Productivity of 100 percent is also defined as employees' working 100 percent of the working time at 100 percent capacity. General industry averages 80 percent productivity, food services generally at 50 percent, so there is plenty of opportunity for improvement. For example, if the employees are performing productive work only 70 percent of the time, and while they are working they are at 70 percent capacity, their rate of productivity would be 49 percent (70% × 70% = 49%). However, determining the exact rate of productivity can be subjective and exceedingly complicated, utilizing industrial engineering methods. This chapter sets forth a practical, unique approach to improving food service productivity that managers can implement immediately.

Thoughts about productivity rarely begin with the aim of improving it. The issue normally arises as the result of a review of a profit-and-loss statement, balance sheet, or departmental budget. More often than not, some sort of crisis (usually financial) precipitates the questions. Administration may view increased productivity as a goal for the entire facility. An alert food service director or manager may want to improve productivity in that entire department. Overall evaluation for accreditation, complaints about service, and a financial crisis all may inspire developing a productivity program.

Improved productivity can be accomplished in varying degrees as illustrated in Exhibit 8–1 by the productivity pyramid.

INPUT/OUTPUT INDEX

The input/output calculation (labor-hours/meal or meals/labor-hour) is a good beginning index of productivity, yet it is far from definitive of the operation. This productivity index, when compared with similar data of other facilities, can serve to measure efficiency of the food service. However, such comparisons are far from meaningful because of the variables of type, size, age, and location of facility; services offered; type of equipment; skill and number of personnel, etc.

Exhibit 8–1 Steps to improve productivity

Input/Output Index
Management Commitment
Productivity Study Committee
Productivity Index
Priorities in Productivity
Productivity Audit

The input/output index certainly can serve to stimulate further interest in proceeding with more defined information to result in meaningful productivity improvement. The specific means to determine an accurate productivity index is demonstrated later in this chapter. The index can be compared with any other facility as long as the same calculation procedure is followed.

Before jumping blindly into a project designed to increase efficiency, it is necessary first to review the existing operation to determine its strengths and weaknesses. In making this assessment, it is mandatory to be objective. Including the employees as part of the assessment team is invaluable. The assessment may lead to the formation of quality circles.

Quality circles are a Japanese management tool in which the employees form small groups of five to ten persons to identify problems and recommend solutions. Generally, 30 minutes to an hour per week are allocated to quality circles. Although they offer a good way to involve employees in improving productivity, it is important to be familiar with the circles' procedures, advantages, and disadvantages before hastily implementing them as a solution to any and all food service problems. Common signs that a quality circle plan (or other quality of work life program) may be needed include:

- higher than average absenteeism, turnover, or tardiness
- a sharp upswing in grievance rate
- sabotage
- inattention to maintenance
- increased accident rate
- drop in employee suggestions
- poor schedule compliance
- disputes over time standards needed to do a job
- poor communication between or within departments[1]

Methodology aside, the stronger the thrust of commitments by management and employees to work improvement, the easier the involvement of other key personnel and, ultimately, the greater opportunity for overall success of the productivity improvement program.

MANAGEMENT COMMITMENT

The single most important factor in improving productivity is management commitment. If management is convinced productivity increases can be achieved, they generally will be; if management is not convinced, then they probably will not be. As someone once commented, "When food service work is slow, you can't afford to make changes; and when it is really busy, you don't have time to." Inaction is easy, but the plain fact is no change will occur unless management believes in and is committed to change.

Commitment to improving productivity results from the food service director's understanding of two factors: (1) the point that benefits outweigh the costs, and (2) the specifics of how to improve productivity. Since both the goals and the means to achieve greater productivity are unclear, improved productivity remains a laudable and often unattainable goal. Commitment to change requires planning and staff participation.

157

Myths of Productivity

Before discussing productivity, it is worthwhile dispelling some of the myths about the subject.

A happy employee is a productive employee. Do managers believe this? Although employee satisfaction was once considered important in improving workers' effort, numerous studies have not provided conclusive support for this belief. Even in instances where studies support this theory, the correlation is low. No general statement can be made relating job satisfaction and productivity.[2,3]

Another myth concerning job satisfaction is that unhappy employees are more likely to be frequent absentees. Recent studies assert that organizational (managerial) commitment is a more important factor in absenteeism than is employees' job satisfaction.[4]

Perhaps the greatest myth is that financial rewards increase productivity. A raise in pay or bonus may produce a short-term increase in productivity, but studies have shown that performance is improved by payment only when the two are directly linked (as in piecework, where payment depends on number of items produced).[5] For the hourly or salaried employee this link is difficult to achieve. Therefore, an employee of this type who receives a pay raise often perceives it as well deserved for past performance rather than as an incentive for future efforts.[6]

Quality of Work Life

For most individuals, employment provides more than just a job. It offers important socialization opportunities, the chance to achieve satisfaction through achievement, and/or the respect of other people. Management expert J. Lloyd Suttle defines the quality of work life as "the degree to which members of a work organization are able to satisfy important personal needs through their experiences in the organization."[7]

Important methods for improving employees' quality of work life involve reassessing reward systems (pay raises, bonuses, fringe benefits, incentives such as employee of the month, etc.), and assessing job design. In some cases, the job's design may need to be changed to increase either its scope (number of different operations performed) or its depth (the relative influence the employee has over the work itself). Both of these motivational factors allow employees to feel they are important members of the food service department and that administration recognizes this fact. If employees believe managers and the institution are loyal to them, administration can be assured of the workers' loyalty in return.

Specific methods for increasing employees' quality of work life include establishing a productivity study committee, providing a job support analysis, reviewing the productivity factors, and analyzing motivation, work methods, and the work environment. Each of these methods is discussed in depth to help managers implement a program that will improve the productivity of their department.

It must always be remembered, however, that productivity is not just a "program" but is a continuing process. The ideas suggested here should become an integral part of the department's work culture to ensure continuing productivity.

PRODUCTIVITY STUDY COMMITTEE

Outside consulting services can provide expert control and management of a work improvement program, and the return on investment may result in significant savings. For example, a large grocery wholesaler spent $500,000 on a productivity survey that saved more than $3 million a year. However, an effective productivity survey need not be in the five-figure or six-figure category. An in-house team, such as a quality circle, can be quite successful in accomplishing the aims of the department while maintaining high sensitivity to the goals of the organization as a whole. This group becomes the ''action committee'' to oversee the implementation of productivity goals that evolve.

Key food service staff persons including supervisors and potential employee leaders, should be made members of the productivity committee. Once the committee is in place, it should be charged to:

- appoint a chairperson
- delineate responsibility
- maintain a timetable for achieving the project
- identify the method of reporting the results.

A key part of this charge is the timetable for achievement. It is not advisable to allow work improvement studies to continue ad infinitum. The committee could quickly tire of repetitive information and lose interest. Achievement of small but meaningful goals will serve as an impetus to accomplish larger and even more productive ones. The committee should begin its evaluation and assessment by conducting a productivity audit.

CONDUCTING A PRODUCTIVITY AUDIT

Six specific steps can be used to conduct an effective productivity audit of the food service department:

1. Divide the operation into major areas of responsibility (see Exhibit 8–2, Productivity Priorities Questionnaire).

   - Conduct both a general and a focused review of the operation.
   - Audit first the three areas of highest priority.

2. Interview and observe employees on a one-on-one basis in each of the three areas of highest priority.
3. Continue the productivity audit by completing the analysis forms for Job Support, Productivity Factors, Motivation and Work Methods, and Work Environment (Exhibits 8–3, 8–4, 8–5, 8–6, and 8–7 later in this chapter). Divide each of the three areas of operation into specific jobs. For example, if dishwashing were one of the areas, some of the jobs this could be divided into include

   - scraping dirty dishes
   - racking dirty dishes
   - pulling clean dishes
   - storing clean dishes.

4. Determine the actual number of meals served (use forms in Exhibits 8–8, 8–9, and 8–10, also later in this chapter).

5. Determine the actual labor-hours worked, the actual labor worked, and the actual labor-hours paid, including vacations, sick leave, holidays, etc.
6. Develop productivity indexes (Exhibits 8–11 through 8–18).

After all the data have been gathered and the productivity indexes have been developed, managers should identify and prioritize the specifics to improve productivity in the department. By asking the questions raised by the productivity audit, the answers will become obvious.

General Review

Conducting a food service productivity audit results in information collected from all areas, including managers' own knowledge of their department and interviews with food service, nursing, and other pertinent personnel. Managers should note the areas that seem to need the greatest productivity improvement and compare them with the results of the focused review (discussed next). How did they compare?

The general review should include the following information, as well as other statistical data about the department:

- normal patient census
- average patient stay
- number of modified diets ordered
- trays assembled per minute (including error ratios)
- number of late or unserved meals
- quantity of intermittent meals or nourishments
- cost per meal
- labor-hours per patient meal
- meals per labor-hour
- overtime hours by employee skill types
- number of full-time equivalents (FTEs) in the department.

Focused Review

Once all the general data have been reviewed, a focused review evaluates the intricacies of each area of the operation by completing the questionnaire on productivity priorities (Exhibit 8–2).

The focused review should highlight the potential problem areas that affect productivity adversely. In evaluating the operation, managers should review these initial areas and rank these and others, as they apply, in order of those in greatest need of improved productivity (number 1 should indicate the area of highest priority).

As is the case with many problem areas, all productivity problems may not be attributed directly to the food service department alone. Some may be symptoms of systematic problems in other departments. Delayed or inaccurate census systems, late admissions, and test scheduling are but a few examples of the types of factors with which food service must interact, yet over which the manager can

Exhibit 8–2 Productivity priority questionnaire

Facility ————————————————————
Department ————————————————————

| Priority | Yes | No | Area |

Receiving
Are food service suppliers properly received with verification of quantity, quality, and price?
Is the right type of receiving equipment consistently available and maintained?

Storing
Are food service supplies stored promptly and correctly, using the FI-FO system of storage?
Is the inventory system properly maintained in a timely manner?

Production
Are production sheets maintained and correlated with purchasing and the census?

Preparation
Are sufficient foods prepared in a timely manner to correlate with meal serving times to maximize nutrient retention and minimize leftovers?
Is there sufficient, trained staff to prepare all menu items, including special diets if indicated?
Is the right type and quantity of equipment available and maintained in operating order to prepare all menu items (including therapeutic diets if indicated)?

Serving
Are foods portion controlled to provide equity in portioning?
Are sufficient portion control utensils available?
Is hot food served hot and cold food served cold?
Are meals served in a timely and efficient manner?
Is there the proper quantity and type of serving and delivery equipment available and maintained to facilitate the serving process?

Sanitation
Is the sanitizing process of pots, pans, and dishware accomplished promptly and effectively?
Is sufficient staff available for sanitizing pots, pans, dishware, and all work areas of the food service department?
Are sufficient supplies available to accomplish the sanitizing process properly?
Is the equipment available for sanitizing appropriate in size, quantity, and kind to facilitate the sanitizing process?
Other areas

List, in order of priority, the three areas to conduct a productivity audit:

1. ————————————————————

2. ————————————————————

3. ————————————————————

exert little authority. A large number of therapeutic diet orders may be the result of insufficient education of the medical staff about clinical indications for and implications of such diets. When and where possible, it is recommended that the total number of diets be kept to a minimum so the benefits of mass production can be realized to increase the speed of plating patient meals.

EMPLOYEE INTERVIEWS

Members of the productivity committee should interview employees of each of the three key food service areas identified in the questionnaire on a one-on-one basis. Interviewers must remember to put employees at ease and interview them on neutral territory, i.e., the dining room, as opposed to the food service director's office or the kitchen. The productivity audit analysis forms can be used as a basis of discussion to encourage the employee to share with the committee member areas that could have a positive impact on productivity. The employees are the experts in the job and hence are valuable resources for the productivity team.

Interviewers should emphasize this is a teamwork effort and each employee will benefit directly from the results of the improved productivity. In order to make improved productivity effective, managers should have a firm understanding with administration that at least some of the funds resulting from improvements will be channeled back into benefiting the employees of the food service department.

How will the employees benefit? Improved productivity can make additional funds available for labor-saving equipment such as slicers, food choppers, commercial blenders, perhaps even to air-condition the kitchen if it is not already. Interviewers should ask employees what benefits they would like to see (initially, exclusive of wage increases) from improved productivity.

The interview process is divided into two components: (1) interviewing supervisors and (2) interviewing employees.

Each group will provide different perspectives and insight. Supervisors responsible for the areas of operation being evaluated should be interviewed first using Exhibits 8–3, 8–4, and 8–5. Exhibit 8–6 is used by employees and Exhibit 8–7 by supervisors to estimate time lost per job evaluated.

JOB PLANNING: THE MANAGERS' ROLE

Managers should ask themselves whether they are satisfied with the present level of job planning or whether they see ways to improve it. And what about the supervisors? Could they benefit from some additional training in the art of job planning? Here are important things managers/supervisors should be doing.

If people in the department do not know what is expected of them when it comes to planning a job, then plans will be inconsistent and incomplete. If there is no standard checklist for job planning, one should be created. Then everyone should be told specifically how to use it and what a good plan looks like when it is done.

The first step is to start with the institution's general job plan, adding notes on how its specific items apply to food service positions in as much detail as possible. It then is retyped and others read and comment on it, adding what they think are important items.

When managers are satisfied the plan is something everyone can use, they should distribute it but, even more important, gather employees together to explain what it is and how to use it. An hour or so of training will go a long way toward improving productivity. Also, the time spent with employees lets them know managers care about and are accessible to them.

Once the job so designed is instituted, managers should use a job plan checklist to note problems (Exhibit 8–8). Why did they come up? Was something omitted from the checklist? Was it something that should have been foreseen? Activities that did go smoothly should be noted. Was it because of the plan? These notes

Exhibit 8–3 Planning and job support analysis

Facility _____
Department _____
(For supervisors to use in interviewing employees)

Instructions: The 12 statements below apply to any food service job. The statements assume answers, given by someone in charge of the job (i.e., Food Service Supervisor). The statements apply to only ONE job (i.e., washing dishes, preparing salads, etc.). So pick a specific job now in progress and write it in here:

(To assure effectiveness, use the statements more than once, selecting a different job each time you go through the statement.) For each statement, mark the ONE answer that BEST fits the job being evaluated.

Job: _____   Date: _____

	Always	Usually	Often	Sometimes	Seldom	Not sure	N/A
1. Work proceeds in the best sequence, with few delays caused by interferences among workers and tasks.							
2. Each work task has the right amount of labor, with neither too many nor too few workers on the job.							
3. Work tasks are clearly defined so that both supervisor and workers know exactly what the job is and what is takes to complete it.							

163

Exhibit 8–3 continued

	Always	Usually	Often	Sometimes	Seldom	Not sure	N/A
4. Instructions (and/or production sheets) are clear and complete and supervisors have no trouble interpreting them for their workers.							
5. When unexpected delays arise and workers cannot do the work planned for them, alternative work is available, and little time is lost.							
6. Regular communication between the Food Service Manager and supervisors ensures that decisions requiring higher authority are made on time.							
7. Good communication and cooperation between supervisors and among workers avoids many potential problems.							
8. Workers have the right equipment when they need them.							
9. Repetitive tasks are assigned to specially trained workers.							
10. Supplies needed for the job are available on time.							
11. Supplies are stored onsite close to the work place yet are secure from theft and/or vandalism.							
12. Attention to working conditions protects workers from unnecessarily harsh or uncomfortable conditions.							

Job support analysis

Each of the following 12 statements describes an important factor that affects onsite productivity of the food service operation. Each statement refers to one important aspect of job planning. Failure to plan ahead for these items creates unnecessary problems for those who do the work. Does the score show planning support for the jobs evaluated?

1. Work Sequence. On most jobs, there seems to be a logical order to the sequence of tasks. Clearly, dirty dishes must be washed before they can be stored. However, do dishes need to be rinsed before they are racked prior to washing? Supervisors know too well the horror stories that come from work being out of sequence. Do the work plans follow the best sequence? Do they account for possible interferences to allow supervisors to "work around" the obstacles to job accomplishment?

2. Task Manning. Labor requirements are not always planned by management. Increase or decrease in labor requirements can also be mandated by unanticipated increase or decrease in patrons. Overall scheduling and work assignments are part of management's planning concern, however. Supervisors should seek to fit workers to the tasks at hand or fit tasks to the workers at hand. Extra labor reduces productivity. Too often food service jobs can be overstaffed to be sure they stay on schedule. Such practices show poor management skills. Not only does the job waste labor-hours, it also fosters an attitude among the work force to accept wasted time as okay.

3. Task Definition. When making plans, how clearly does the supervisor define the tasks to be done? Each job should be divided into small pieces that can be fitted to individual workers. How small each task is will depend on the operation. Defining tasks in such small pieces lets supervisors think through the work and find the potential problems that need to be avoided, resulting in a realistic staffing plan and schedule.

4. Instructions. It is important to take the time to explain a job fully, providing productivity schedules, training, and coordination with coworkers and/or supervisors to save lost time in the future. This one simple step will go a long way to assuring the productivity level required.

5. Contingency Plans. No job proceeds exactly as planned. Something usually develops to disrupt and delay it. How carefully do supervisors look ahead to find the most likely problems? Do they include contingency plans on what to do if and when problems evolve? It is necessary to pay close attention to the most critical points in the operation because if something can go wrong, it probably will happen there.

6. Decision Making. As much as managers rely on the ability of their supervisors, questions are bound to arise that demand decisions by higher-ups. How quickly do those decisions get made? Do supervisors know what information to collect and pass along so the decisions can be made

165

Exhibit 8–3 continued

intelligently? Since many of the decisions requiring top administration involve crisis management, how could better communication and planning have avoided the situation in the first place?

7. Onsite Coordination. Infighting among supervisors and between food service workers can destroy productivity quickly. Productivity depends on good cooperation.

8. Tools and Equipment. Everybody talks about the importance of having the right equipment for the job when it is needed. Yet somehow something's always missing or broken or in the shop just when it is needed most. Equipment shortages not only reduce productivity, they also undermine the workers' attitude toward the job—if management does not care enough to supply the equipment, why should they care either? This includes such overlooked items as being sure the knives are sharp enough for the job to be performed.

9. Repetitive Tasks. Task definition in No. 3 above will reveal jobs that are repetitious. Fitting special workers (or special equipment) to such tasks can save time and money. Does the job planning include attention to such items or do managers hope their supervisors will find and organize the repetitive tasks? Planning for repetitive tasks must not be left to chance.

10. Delivery. Like tools and equipment in No. 8 above, workers deserve the proper materials when they need them. Suppliers do not always deliver when expected. Do operational plans lay out a delivery schedule, note alternative suppliers, and mark critical checkpoints along the way for following up on the status of orders for supplies?

11. Storage of Supplies. Once supplies arrive, where are they stored? Has the most efficient location been designated to store each type of food service supply or are cleaning supplies always stored near the back dock? Storing materials close to specific work locations minimizes movement. Yet it also is imperative to pay attention to security needs. Damaged or stolen materials may be worse than no materials at all. Storage locations must be evaluated.

12. Working Conditions. What are the working conditions in the food service location? Is it hot and humid or cool and dry? Obviously, some thought in your planning is given as to how kitchen conditions will affect equipment but is consideration also given as to how the same conditions will affect workers' productivity? How can these plans protect workers from unnecessarily harsh or uncomfortable conditions?

How many of the 12 statements were marked "not sure" or "not applicable?" Those who work at the supervisory level should have first-hand knowledge of most of these areas. Any "not sure" checks may indicate that plans are incomplete or that they are not being carried out. Any "not applicable" checks should be reviewed to be sure they do not apply to this job. Under what circumstances would they apply?

Exhibit 8–4 Productivity factor analysis

Facility _____

Department _____

(For supervisors to use in interviewing employees)

The 10 statements below apply to any food service operation. Check the one answer that best describes the impact of each of the factors on a specific job (with lost time excluded). Keep in mind one job and one set of work methods in making judgments.

Job: _____

Date: _____

	Yes	No	N/A	Comments
1. Employees have the right equipment in good working condition available to them at all times.				
2. Work performance depends upon the skills and experience of individual employees.				
3. Sequence of work is carefully planned and laid out so employees can move from one task to another without problems or delay.				
4. Work is assigned to specific individuals with special skills or experience for particular tasks.				
5. The right equipment operated by skilled employees is readily available when needed.				
6. Supplies are near at hand when employees are ready to use the materials.				

Exhibit 8-4 continued

	Yes	No	N/A	Comments
7. Supervisors provide regular feedback concerning employee performance at specific tasks.				
8. Employees receive complete instructions and information.				
9. Additional training is needed to contribute to higher productivity rates for individual employees.				
10. Top management is always available for timely decision-making when problems arise.				

Productivity factor analysis

Each of the ten factors is important to the food service operation. For any given task, however, one or two will stand out as being more important than the others. Factors that have the most impact need special attention, perhaps being reviewed several times a week to make sure they are not interfering with work accomplishment.

1. Tools. Everyone needs equipment on the job. But how important is equipment to the job the work force does? Do sharp blades and full brushes count or can the workers get by with worn tools/equipment? How often do their tools/equipment need repair and replacement? Who sees that it is done? Who tries new electric tools/equipment to measure their effectiveness?

2. Skills and Experience. People acquire skills through experience. How can managers and supervisors make sure their workers have the skills they need to do the job? It must not be assumed that everyone knows the best way to do a job. Supervisors must make a point of checking everyone out. The importance of training cannot be overemphasized.

3. Work Sequence. Whenever a job requires the sequence and coordination of many subtasks, supervisors must make sure they do their planning homework. When a worker can move smoothly from one task to another, the rhythm of the job builds a productive pace.

4. Work Assignment. Because everyone has different strengths and weaknesses, no two workers have the same ability. Do worker assignments try to take these differences into account? Do managers/supervisors look for the key tasks and critical points to assign to the best workers?

5. Equipment. When workers must wait for equipment, they experience lost time. When they have the equipment, but it is poorly operated or inadequate for the task at hand, their productivity drops. How critical is equipment to productivity in food service? Do workers have the equipment they want when they need it?

6. Supplies. Transporting supplies from one end of the operation to the other causes lost time. Excessive handling, searching for the right supplies, and onsite fabrication all may be adding unnecessary labor-hours. How can materials handling and placement be streamlined?

7. Feedback. Much has been said about the importance of feedback. How much feedback do the workers get? Is it enough? What do they do with it when they get it?

8. Work Methods. Since supervisors usually know of several ways to do a job, how do they go about selecting the best one for a particular job? Even when they are sure they are using the best work methods, they should experiment some more—they may surprise everyone.

9. Training. Both supervisors and workers can benefit from additional training. Do managers/supervisors take time to train workers in the most productive work method when a new or unusual job comes up? It is tempting to overlook training, thinking that it does not pay because the employee who is trained will only end up working for someone else. Training can pay off when managers start to add up the extra hours they would have to pay for to do the job with an untrained worker or supervisor.

10. Management. One of the biggest factors affecting productivity is management input. When everyone knows exactly what to do, the job moves smoothly. When problems arise and decisions are not made, work slows and people wonder what to do next. They lose confidence in what they are doing. Is a strong management presence maintained in food service?

169

Exhibit 8–5 Motivation and work methods analysis

Facility _____
Department _____
(For supervisors to use in interviewing employees)

The food service management team takes prime responsibility for motivating personnel and using the best work methods. If good performance here means keeping unit labor costs down, do onsite managers perform well? Do they know what standards are expected of them? For the job being evaluated, check the ONE box that best applies to each statement below.

	Always	Usually	Often	Sometimes	Seldom	Not sure	N/A
1. Does management set clear standards as to the quality and quantity of work expected of all food service workers?							
2. Does management evaluate finished work and make a point to spot employees who have performed well at specific tasks on a weekly or bi-weekly basis?							
3. Do you, as an employee, receive regular information on their performance?							
4. When supervisors identify poor work performance, do they quickly inform you, as an employee, (provide feedback) of what must be done to improve?							
5. Does top management reward employees for performance above expected standards and "come down hard" on employees who fail to meet standards?							

6. Does management include representatives from the work force in meetings to plan and analyze work methods and procedures?

7. Does management use the work force effectively so that you feel your time as an employee is valuable to the job?

8. Are food service employees encouraged to suggest ways to improve methods they use to work?

9. Do you feel your work as an employee is organized so as to make the best use of equipment and labor?

10. Do management and the work force run experiments to find the best method to complete the job the most effectively?

11. Does management closely follow equipment needs to provide the best support possible for employees?

12. What changes would you, as an employee, make to make your work more productive?

Exhibit 8–5 continued

Motivation and work methods analysis

1. Performance Standards. To achieve the desired employee performance, managers/supervisors first must set the standards they expect everyone to meet. No one can perform well consistently if they do not know what good performance is. The first five questions above score the standards. Marks that fall in the fourth and fifth columns ("Sometimes" and "Seldom") indicate standards are not clear; marks in the first and second columns ("Always" and "Usually") should indicate standards indeed are set. The most important standards for managing productivity concern communicating information about what needs to be done and what has been done.

2. Feedback. Having standards will not help people know how well they are doing. Feedback means telling people how well (or poorly) they do. The responses to these questions indicate how much feedback employees get. If there is more than one mark in the fourth and fifth columns, the workers probably lack the information they need to rate their own performance. How was Question 4 answered? Although any feedback is better than none, giving feedback about poor work rather than good work can undermine motivation. Praise, not criticism, is the stronger management tool. How much feedback information does management give supervisors? (And how much do they give back?)

3. Reinforcement. Besides knowing how well they do, employees need reinforcement to continue to do well. Sure, they are paid—what else motivates people to perform well? In Question 5, was the first or second column marked, meaning you, as management, "come down hard" on employees who fail to meet the standards? Constant use of such "negative reinforcement" can produce only mediocre performance. The other questions in this set identify positive reinforcers—things that make an individual feel good about participating on the job. However, positive reinforcement does not mean lack of accountability. All members of the work force should take responsibility for doing their job.

4. Task Interference. The last six questions score the support provided to people on the front line, actually in the kitchen performance specific task responsibilities. Management must take responsibility for removing the things that interfere with getting the job done. What about all of the other interferences that slow the job? Weekly meetings are helpful in identifying interferences and in developing plans to avoid them in the future. Supervisors should watch supplies and equipment needs to make sure employees have what they need for the job. Managers/supervisors must plan work sequences and can involve the work force in finding better ways to do various jobs. How does the pattern of marks compare to what they should be? How many marks in the fourth and fifth columns indicate that supervisors could do better?

Exhibit 8–6 Work environment analysis

Facility _____

Department _____

(For employees to provide information to supervisor and/or employee interviewers. If interviewed by supervisor and employee, as recommended, compare results.)

The 12 statements below apply to any food service operation. Check the one box that best describes your situation. Keep in mind a single job when making judgments; review the list again for a different job to build a broader profile or to make comparisons.

Job: _____   Date: _____

	Always	Usually	Sometimes	Seldom	Never
1. Work rules on the job are clear and are understood.					
2. Job plans are complete and a realistic schedule guides work progress.					
3. Standards for work quality are clear and each employee knows the quality expected.					
4. Each individual, including all supervisors, receives some information on the quality of finished work.					
5. Performance of new employees on the first few days is monitored carefully and reviewed with them.					
6. Employees are complimented for cooperating and helping solve problems.					
7. Outstanding performance by an individual is recognized and acknowledged quickly.					

Exhibit 8–6 continued

8. Suggestions are welcomed, and employees receive feedback, whether or not their suggestions are used.

9. Supplies and equipment are available when needed.

10. Changes in plans and schedules are coordinated with pertinent employees and supervisors.

11. Efforts are made to protect employees from uncomfortable working conditions.

12. Parking, dining facilities, and toilets for the work force are above average.

Work environment analysis

1. Teamwork. Each of the items checked has an impact on motivation. When people feel they are part of a team and that their contribution counts, they are motivated to do well. On the other hand, when they feel that no one really cares about them or how they perform, they are not motivated. Often the same factor that serves to motivate people can demotivate them if neglected. How well does the "motivation profile" show employees are doing?

2. Clarifying Standards. The first three statements refer to setting up and clarifying expectations. Standards for work quality and work methods must be high enough to foster pride in the completed job. When work rules, plans, and work quality standards are clear, people know what is expected of them. They can make sure their work meets these standards. When employees are unsure of what is expected of them or believe the standards are too low, their motivation fades. Managers/supervisors should talk over the standards with the workers expected to meet them, making sure they understand what is wanted and agree the standards are reasonable.

3. Feedback. Employees should be given feedback as to their performance. They will feel good about their work and continue to work hard when they can see their progress. Special pains should be taken to make sure new employees know exactly how their performance stacks up against what is expected of them. Good feedback starts workers on the right foot and gives them a positive attitude toward the job. They know their superiors care about the work they do. Continuing communication with employees shows management's belief that they are an important part of the job. Feeling they are a part of a team motivates workers to work well.

4. Reinforcement. Statements 7, 8, and 9 relate to the reinforcement managers/supervisors give to employees. When the "system" fails to recognize individual performance, much of the incentive to continue to perform well disappears. As food service departments grow in size, they tend to lose the personal touch with their employees. They unwittingly create a system that gives supervisors more independence while taking away many of the personal reinforcers from the employees. The belief that the system does care can provide a powerful, positive reinforcement to the work force to perform well.

5. Support. The last four statements probe how well management supports employees. Are they given what they need to do the job expected of them? Managers/supervisors should put themselves in employees' shoes once in a while; if asked to do the job with what they have, would managers be motivated to do well? Workers are paid to perform their job, not to worry about support. The support burden should be put on competent supervisors. When workers know they are being supported fully, they are more likely, in turn, to support management fully by doing the job.

Exhibit 8–7 Lost time questionnaire

Facility _____

Department _____
(For supervisors to use in evaluating job performance)

Job: _____   Date: _____

Employee Interviewed _____   Interviewer _____

Estimated lost time/day

How much lost time per day is generally experienced to wait
for:

1. Instructions on work?   _____

2. Work from other personnel
   a. within the food service department   _____
   b. from other departments (nursing, admissions,
      housekeeping, maintenance, etc.)   _____

3. Equipment
   a. to use   _____
   b. because of malfunctioning   _____

4. Supplies   _____

5. Other reasons
   _____   _____
   _____   _____

6. Redo work
   a. lack of instruction   _____
   b. lack of understanding direction   _____
   c. lack of ingredients/supplies   _____
   d. lack of appropriate work performance (burned
      product, etc.)   _____
   e. lack of properly functioning equipment   _____
   f. lack of other skilled/trained personnel   _____

Total estimated lost time per day   _____

provide feedback to everyone who worked on the plan, trying to find ways to do the job better next time. The marked-up plan and the checklist can be used as an after-action report to compare what was expected with what actually happened.

A job plan checklist should not be used to beat people for not meeting the criteria. Such criticism usually causes everyone to avoid helping design a plan the next time around. No one wants to do something for which they get criticized. Parts of the plan that worked well should be praised; weaknesses should be identified and questions asked as to how it could be done better next time. Good planning should produce good jobs and increased productivity.

Good planning requires time. Too often, jobs start too quickly. Managers should give themselves and others time to prepare the plan right and provide the individuals and information they need to do it right.

If plans are not being made in spite of developing a checklist and setting a standard, it is crucial to find out why. Obstacles must be removed so the plans can be made and can improve productivity.

Those four troubleshooting categories—standards, feedback, reinforcement, and interference—play a central role in productivity management.

Exhibit 8–8 Job plan checklist   *Improving Productivity*

	Yes	No	Comments
1. Did you list each step of the job?	____	____	_____
2. Are the steps in logical order?	____	____	_____
3. Did you list all necessary supplies?	____	____	_____
4. Did you list all necessary equipment?	____	____	_____
5. Did you include the amount of time necessary to complete each task?	____	____	_____
6. If necessary, did you provide a brief description of how to complete the task?	____	____	_____
7. Did you have someone who is unfamiliar with the task read the description to see if they could understand it?	____	____	_____
8. Did you have someone who is unfamiliar with the task perform the task from your written description?	____	____	_____
9. Did you sign your name to the plan?	____	____	_____

NOTES: _____
_____
_____
_____

DEVELOPING A PRODUCTIVITY INDEX

In lieu of conducting an industrial engineering productivity study, which may not be feasible economically nor practical from a time point of view, this chapter offers a new approach to evaluating the productivity level of the food service department that is based on documented figures that are easily attainable. Two primary methods of determining a productivity index are discussed, each of which provides a basis for future comparisons of the department's productivity.

Method I

$$\frac{\text{Input}}{\text{Output}} = \text{Productivity Index}$$

$$\frac{\text{Labor-hours}}{\text{Meals}} = \text{Labor-hours/meal} \times 60 = \text{Labor-minutes per meal}$$

Method II

$$\frac{\text{Output}}{\text{Input}} = \text{Productivity Index}$$

$$\frac{\text{Meals}}{\text{Labor-hours}} = \text{Meals per Labor-Hour}$$

177

Developing a productivity index by either method in the manner discussed here will provide practical, accurate information to evaluate department productivity. These indexes also provide a means to compare the productivity as circumstances change. It should be remembered that the only constant is change. How will the food service department measure up? If the level of labor remains the same and extra meals (through increased census or additional services) are initiated, i.e., Meals on Wheels, cafeteria service to the community, etc., productivity will be increased—more work will be performed by the same number of employees.

Work responsibilities are evaluated, offering an opportunity to combine some positions. When normal attrition occurs, it may not be necessary to refill a position, thus improving productivity: The same amount of work is accomplished with fewer employees.

Determining Actual Meals

Determining the number of actual meals served is important in achieving an accurate cost per meal and is equally important in determining the productivity index. Exhibit 8–9 illustrates the Patient Meal Equivalent Index for accurately calculating the actual number of meals the department has been responsible for preparing and serving.

Exhibit 8–9 Patient meal equivalent index

Based on 2,000 calories for a regular diet meal, equivalents listed below were developed based on the accepted types and number of food items for each clinical diet as coordinated with the regular diet.

	Meal equivalents	
Diet	Hospital	Nursing home
Regular (approximately 2,000 calories)	1.0	1.0
Soft	1.0	1.0
Bland	1.0	1.0
Low residue	.9	1.0
High residue	1.0	1.0
Salt restricted	1.0	1.0
Fat restricted	1.0	1.0
Clear liquid	.4	.4
Full liquid	.5	.6
Diabetic		
800	.4	.6
1,000	.6	.9
1,200	.6	.9
1,500	.9	1.0
1,800	1.0	1.2
2,000	1.0	1.3
Protein restricted	1.0	1.0
Pureed	1.25*	1.25*
Tube feeding	.25	.8

*See Chapter 3 on pureed diet meal equivalents.

Table 8–1 Patient meal equivalent census

Meal Equiv.	Diet	Days:	1	2	3	4	5	6	7	8	9	10	11	12	13	14	15	16	17	18	19	20	21	22	23	24	25	26	27	28	29	30	31	Total
1.0	Reg.																																		
1.0	Soft																																		
1.0	Bland																																		
1.0	Low residue																																		
1.0	High residue																																		
1.0	Salt restricted																																		
1.0	Fat restricted																																		
	Clear liquid																																		
	Full liquid																																		
	Diabetic																																		
.4	800																																		
.5	1,000																																		
.6	1,200																																		
.75	1,500																																		
.9	1,800																																		
1.0	2,000																																		
	Protein restricted																																		
1.25	Pureed																																		
	Tube feeding																																		

Total _____

Table 8–2 Meal equivalent summary

Meal Service Component	Days:	1	2	3	4	5	6	7	8	9	10	11	12	13	14	15	16	17	18	19	20	21	22	23	24	25	26	27	28	29	30	31	Total
Patient meals																																		
Cafeteria																																		
Meals on Wheels																																		
Between-meal feedings																																		
Evening nourishments																																		
Nutritional supplements																																		
Activities																																		
Catering																																		
Other																																		

Total _____

Exhibit 8–10 Factor for nonproductive paid time *Improving Productivity*

Based on 10 production employees

10 vacation days/year/employee × 10 employees	= 100 days/year
8 holidays/year/employee × 10 employees	= 80 days/year
7 sick leave days/year/employee × 10 employees	= 70 days/year
	250 days/year

Monthly basis

$\dfrac{250 \text{ days/year}}{12 \text{ months/year}}$ = 20.83 days/month × hours paid per day to be added to total labor-hours actually worked in month

Example: 20.83 × 8 = 166.64 extra labor-hours paid per month

Two-week-pay-period basis

$\dfrac{250 \text{ days/year}}{26 \text{ pay periods/year}}$ = 9.62 days/two-week pay period × hours paid per day to be added to total labor-hours actually worked in pay period

Example: 9.62 × 8 = 76.96 extra labor-hours paid per pay period

Weekly basis

$\dfrac{250 \text{ days/year}}{52 \text{ weeks/year}}$ = 4.81 days/week × hours paid per day to be added to total labor-hours actually worked in week

Example: 4.81 × 8 = 38.48 extra labor-hours paid per week

Daily basis

$\dfrac{250 \text{ days/year}}{365 \text{ days/year}}$ = .68 extra days/day × hours paid per day to be added to total labor-hours actually worked in day

Example: .68 × 8 = 5.44 extra labor-hours being paid per day

All meals cannot be considered as one; that is, equivalent to the quantity of food or labor required to prepare and serve a regular diet. In a hospital, nursing home, correctional institution, or extended care facility, the meal equivalent of a modified diet must be calculated since the raw food cost varies from the norm. An 800 calorie American Diabetes Association (ADA) diet simply does not require as much food as a regular diet, while a blended diet requires more.

Based on a regular diet of 2,000 calories, the soft, bland, low and high residue, salt restricted and fat restricted diets all require about as much food and labor as the regular diet, so essentially, these all are equal. However, a clear liquid diet requires only about 40 percent of the food and labor costs of the regular diet. A 2,000-calorie diabetic diet calls for 1.3 times as much food and labor cost because of the added expense of carefully preparing, portioning, and using special foods. Hence, modified diets should be recorded carefully so the facility can calculate actual food and labor costs based on meal equivalents.

If the food and labor cost for a regular diet is $3.90, then preparation of the clear liquid diet will cost $1.56 and the 2,000-calorie diabetic diet $5.07. Calculated for a nursing home meal equivalent, these figures are:

$$\$3.90 \times 0.4 = \$1.56$$
$$\$3.90 \times 1.3 = \$5.07$$

Exhibit 8–11 Determining actual input and output

Facility: 300-bed acute care hospital

Personnel: Food service workers – 42 FTEs (full-time equivalents) = 28 positions

   Food service management – 3 FTEs   = 3 positions

Input[a]

A. Determining actual labor-hours (input) of food service workers
  1. 28 employees on duty per day × 8 hours per day × 7 days per week = 1,568 labor-hours per week
  2. 1,568 labor-hours per week × 4.33 weeks per month = 6,789.44 labor-hours per month

B. Determining actual labor-hours (input) of food service management
  1. Food service director (administrative dietitian
    or food service administrator):   8 hours per day × 5 days per week =   40 labor-hours per week
    2 assistant food service directors: 8 hours per day × 5 days per week =   80 labor-hours per week
    Dietitian[b] (clinically oriented)

                                                                             120 labor-hours per week

  2. 120 labor-hours per week × 4.33 weeks per month = 519.6 labor-hours per month
    Total food service labor-hours worked per month   = 6,789.44 workers
                                                         +519.60 management
                                          Total labor hours = 7,309.04

C. Determining nonproductive paid time[c]

10 vacation days/employee/year × 45 employees = 450 × 8 labor-hours paid/day = 3,600 extra labor-hours paid per year divided by 12 months per year = 300 extra labor-hours per month

8 holidays/employee/year × 45 employees = 360 × 8 labor-hours paid per day = 2,880 extra labor-hours paid per year divided by 12 months per year = 240 extra labor-hours per month

7 sick leave days/employee/year × 45 employees = 315 × 8 labor-hours paid per day = 2,520 extra labor-hours paid per year divided by 12 months per year = 210 extra labor-hours per month

25 paid nonproductive days/year × 45 employees = 1,125 × 8 labor-hours paid per day = 9,000 extra labor-hours paid per year divided by 12

D. Input summary

    7,309.04 labor-hours worked in month
  + 750.00 extra labor-hours paid (nonproductive per month)
  ─────────
    8,059.04 actual labor-hours in month

[a]Use hours actually recorded on time cards.
[b]It is not necessary to calculate these hours since this is a clinically oriented position unless management elects to include it in total department labor.
[c]These calculations for nonproductive paid time have been developed for an evaluation based on figures per month. As detailed in Exhibit 8–9, similar calculations can be determined for a two-week pay period, weekly, and daily.

Output

Determining Actual Meals (Output)

Item		Meals per month
Patient meals	300 beds (75% occupancy = 225 patients) × 3 meals per day × 30 days per month including meal equivalents (see Exhibit 8–8 and Appendix F)	20,250.00
Cafeteria meals	Average daily receipts for month being evaluated = $1,000 divided by $3.90 (meal cost equivalent) = 256.4 × 30 days per month	7,692.00
Staff coffee	$800 per month divided by meal cost equivalent of $3.90	205.13
Nutritional supplements	$1,200 per month divided by meal cost equivalent of $3.90	307.69
Between-meal nourishments	$2,500 per month divided by meal cost equivalent of $3.90	641.03
Special functions	$600 per month divided by meal cost equivalent of $3.90	153.85
Total actual meals (output) in month:		29,249.70

Obviously, the clear liquid diet saves money while the 2,000-calorie diabetic diet greatly increases costs.

Appendix F provides the meal equivalents of the average price per serving in hospitals and nursing homes and how to determine them. Based on those examples, food costs per one meal (raw food cost × 2.5) are divided into the economic (including monetary) value of any additional services provided by the food service department.

The Patient Meal Equivalent Census (Table 8–1, page 179) provides a sample form to facilitate tabulating the actual number of meals prepared and served by the department. Although such meals represent part of the result of the department's productivity, the figure does not reflect the many additional services for which food service must employ labor, i.e., evening nourishments, nutritional supplements, activities, food service operations, Meals on Wheels, coffee to nursing service, etc. All of these affect the productivity index.

If the evening nourishments for a 200-bed acute care facility cost $100 a day, and the cost per meal equivalent was determined to be $3.90, the number of meals represented by the $100 would be $25.64 (100 ÷ 3.90 = 25.64). The actual number of meals represented by the economic value of each of the services the department provides should be determined because food service is held responsible for purchasing, preparing, and serving food for each of these services. Ancillary services can have a significant impact on the department's productivity. This information must be included in determining its Productivity Index.

Table 8–2 (page 180) provides a meal equivalent summary form to total all meals actually prepared and served by the department. This information is vital to providing an accurate output figure to produce a true productivity index.

Determining Actual Labor

In determining the actual labor (input) paid by the facility to provide the various food services, two factors must be considered:

1. productive time: labor-hours on the job
2. nonproductive time: labor-hours not worked, including days off, vacation time, holidays, sick leave, emergency leave, etc., for which the facility must pay someone to replace services not provided.

Productive Time

Productive time is easily determined. Time cards for the period being evaluated (one day, one week, two weeks, etc.), are used to add up all time spent by all workers (excluding management personnel). Smaller facilities may use cook-managers. In this instance, the hours allocated for production or nonmanagement purposes would be included. Hours worked in a management capacity are omitted.

Nonproductive Time

The inclusion of only productive time does not provide an accurate picture of the department's labor obligations. Someone must fill in to offer services not provided because of days off, vacations, holidays, sick and/or emergency leave. Although meals must be served 365 days a year, full-time employees are available an

Exhibit 8–12 Productivity index—Method I

Improving Productivity

$$\frac{(Input)}{(Output)}$$

Based on the figures in Exhibit 8–10, the productivity index (using Method I) is calculated for this 300-bed acute care hospital as follows:

$$\frac{8,059.04 \text{ actual labor-hours}}{29,564.46 \text{ actual meals}} = .27 \text{ labor-hours/meals}$$

.27 labor-hours/meal × 60 minutes/hours = 16.2 labor-minutes/meal

average of only 236 days a year, so the number of full-time positions must be multiplied by .55 to determine the number of relief persons necessary:

days per year	365
days off (2 days a week)	104
vacation days a year	10
holidays	8
sick leave days	7
Total number of days actually worked/year	236

For food services responsible for providing continuous service throughout the year, relief personnel must be available. Therefore, this information must be included in determining an accurate productivity index. Days off are included automatically with relief personnel but the time paid but not worked such as vacations, holidays, sick leave, and potential emergency leave must be added to the time actually worked to establish an accurate productivity index. Therefore, a standard factor for nonproductivity, paid time can be developed on a per-month, per-two-week-pay-period, per-week, or per-day basis as needs dictate (Exhibit 8–10, page 181).

Productivity Index Calculation

With all data gathered—actual meals (output) and actual labor (input)—a productivity index now can be determined. The period of time to be evaluated (month, pay period, week, or day) is identified. Exhibits 8–11 (pages 182-183), 8–12, and 8–13 illustrate methods for determining a productivity index (input divided by

Exhibit 8–13 Productivity index—Method II

$$\frac{(Input)}{(Output)}$$

Based on the figures in Table 8–1, the productivity index (using Method II) is calculated for this 300-bed acute care hospital as follows:

$$\frac{29,564.46 \text{ actual meals}}{8,059.04 \text{ actual labor-hours}} = 3.67 \text{ meals/labor-hours}$$

Exhibit 8–14 Determining actual input and output

Example: 120-bed nursing home (100% occupancy), 10 full-time employees including food service director.

Input

A. Determining actual labor-hours (input)

6 employees on duty per day × 8 hours worked per day × 7 days/week + 8 hours per day worked by food service director × 5 days worked per week = 366 total labor-hours per week

366 total labor-hours per week × 4.33 weeks/month = 1,584.78 labor-hours worked per month + 166.64 extra labor-hours (nonproductive) paid per month (Exhibit 8–11) = 1,751.42 total actual labor-hours/month (input)

Output

B. Determining actual meals (output)

Item		Actual[a] meals/month
Patient meals: 120 beds × 3 meals/day × 30 days/month	=	10,800
Staff meals:[b] 30/day × 30 days/month	=	900
Staff coffee: $\dfrac{\$250/month}{\$1.50\ cost/meal\ equivalent^c}$	=	167
Nutritional supplements: $\dfrac{\$300/month}{\$1.50\ cost/meal\ equivalent}$	=	200
Evening nourishments: $\dfrac{\$720/month}{\$1.50\ cost/meal\ equivalent}$	=	480
Meals on Wheels: $\dfrac{\$1,125/month}{\$1.50\ cost/meal\ equivalent}$	=	750
Total actual meals/month (output)		13,297

[a]Figures are rounded off to the nearest digit.
[b]Staff meals are included as either a fringe benefit or a nominal charge; therefore, it is not appropriate to determine a cost-per-meal equivalent for nursing home staff meals.
[c]The average of $1.50 total food cost/meal includes raw food, labor, and supplies.

Exhibit 8–15 Productivity index—Method I

$$\frac{(Input)}{(Output)}$$

Based on the figures in Exhibit 8–13, the Productivity Index (using Method I) is calculated for this 120-bed nursing home as follows:

$$\frac{1,751.42\ \text{actual labor-hours}}{13,297\ \text{actual meals}} = .13\ \text{labor-hours/meal}$$

.13 labor-hours/meal × 60 minutes/hour = 7.8 labor-minutes/meal

Exhibit 8–16 Productivity index—Method II

Improving Productivity

$$\frac{(\text{Output})}{(\text{Input})}$$

Based on the figures in Exhibit 8–13 the Productivity Index (using Method II) is calculated for this 120-bed nursing home as follows:

$$\frac{13{,}297 \text{ actual meals}}{1{,}751.42} = 7.59 \text{ meals/labor-hours}$$

output) for a 300-bed acute care hospital. Exhibits 8–14, 8–15, and 8–16 present methods for determining the productivity index for a 120-bed nursing home.

After the productivity index (meals per labor-hours or labor-minutes per meal) is determined, the data gathered from interviewing employees are evaluated. What specific steps can management take to improve productivity? Can the amount of time lost by employees be reduced? If so, what can be done to minimize lost time and increase efficiency?

The steps to be taken to improve productivity then are categorized into short term and long term (Exhibit 8–17). Each item is prioritized in the two categories, paving the way for improved productivity in the food service department. Labor-saving techniques are listed in Exhibit 8–18.

After sufficient time has elapsed to implement some of the suggestions to improve productivity, a new productivity index should be developed and compared with the earlier one. The results should be shared with the food service workers to keep them updated on progress. If the improved productivity warrants, employees should be rewarded with one of the incentives promised. Seeing a tangible benefit will motivate them to continue participating in the productivity program. Do they have other ideas that would improve productivity even further or make their job easier?

Implementing the productivity program outlined in this chapter will help improve productivity in food service without conducting extensive industrial

---

Exhibit 8–17 Suggestions to improve productivity

Short term

1. Evaluate interrelationships between work areas and implement employee suggestions to streamline workflow.

2. Implement work method improvements recommended by employees and supervisors for work areas evaluated (see Exhibit 8–18 for specific labor-saving techniques).

3. Evaluate location of equipment and relocate as feasible to improve workflow.

Long term

1. Evaluate intradepartmental workflow relationships to streamline process.

2. Evaluate need for additional labor-saving equipment. Schedule purchases.

3. Evaluate current system of food production to determine efficiency in view of newer systems. Determine cost effectiveness of new food production systems.

Exhibit 8–18 Labor-saving techniques

1. Balance out workload in tray makeup so everyone takes the same time to do their part of the operation.
2. Place the materials around the tray lowerator in the same relative position they occupy on the tray in making up the initial layout. Use both hands to place the menu and silver on the rear of the tray and the bread and butter plate and the saucer on the front.
3. Fill time can be reduced and be more accurate if gallonages are marked on sides of steam-jacketed kettles or paddle; a water meter is a wise investment.
4. Use a cart to take all cooked food to serving line at one time.
5. Use portable tables to provide table space beside equipment that is fixed in place but does not have sufficient adjoining table spaces, such as fryers, griddles, and steamjacketed kettles.
6. Place a pot under the front of board when chopping vegetables and meat so that drop delivery can be used without having to lift the product.
7. Use scissors as superior to knives in cutting up dates, marshmallows, sticky foods, and vegetables for salads and bite-size foods.
8. Use egg slicers not only for slicing eggs but also for slicing mushrooms, cooked carrots and potatoes, margarine, bananas, and other soft foods.
9. Use pastry brushes not only for greasing pans but for buttering toast, french toast, pancakes, frying pans, and steam table pans.
10. Dip a knife in hot water to speed the cutting of cakes, salads, and desserts.
11. Roll biscuit dough into rectangular shapes smaller than the sheet pan, then cut out biscuits with a knife on the pan in shapes of squares, triangles, and diamonds and separate them to save biscuit-making labor.
12. Use pie markers for pies and bulk cake slicers to save cutting time and labor.
13. Invert two large steamer pans and wash on top of them in pot sinks that are too low.
14. Shred directly into a plastic carrying bag when using a mechanical shredder.
15. Turn potato with one hand while twisting scraper type peeler the other way when peeling potatoes by hand. Peel will be longer and peeling time shorter. When peeling by hand, it shortens the time to remove eyes and blemishes before peeling.
16. Reduce volume of sauces without stirring by placing pan in the oven at 225°–250° F.
17. Reduce oven cleanup by roasting meat in special bags such as Reynolds ''Brown in Bag,'' Drackett's ''Cooking Magic,'' and ''Reveal.'' A small amount of flour must be placed in bag first to avoid bursting.
18. Make hamburger patties by placing scoops of meat over surface of sheet pan, covering with waxed paper, then pressing another sheet pan down until hamburgers are proper thickness.
19. Cook rice by placing it in proper amount of water, oil, and salt in a deep steam table and roasting in a preheated 350° F oven for 30 minutes. Use four quarts of boiling water to three pounds of rice, one tablespoon salt, and one tablespoon oil. It can be served directly from the pan without draining or transferring.
20. Run a few crusts of bread through meat grinder after grinding to ease job of cleaning.
21. Use pastry bags to help fill souffle cups with tartar sauce, mayonnaise, or applesauce.
22. Separate egg yolks from whites quickly by using a small funnel.
23. Make dried bread crumbs or nut meats easily by placing them in a paper bag and rolling them with a rolling pin.
24. Lift loads with the legs rather than the back to help prevent torn back muscles. Do not carry things that can be slid or rolled.
25. Put vegetables directly into steam table pans and reheat them in the steamer rather than in steamjacketed kettles.
26. Portion muffin mix and meatballs with an ice cream scoop.
27. Bring eggs to room temperature before hard cooking them in hot simmering water. It helps when removing the shells. Separate yolks when eggs are 60° F or warmer.
28. Prepare potatoes for baking by turning on water in peeler, dumping in potatoes, and running for six seconds, then letting potatoes out; they are washed and skins pricked but they should be inspected.
29. Eliminate peeling hard-cooked eggs when chopped eggs are required. Crack eggs into a greased hotel pan and steam until hard. Cool. Remove from pan and chop with knife on board or in food chopper.

engineering productivity studies involving job task analysis and time/motion studies that divide each movement into Therbligs. Such studies are productive but costly and complicated. Implementation of the recommendations in this chapter will enable administrators/managers/supervisors to (1) get more work from the same number of employees, or (2) get the same amount of work from fewer employees.

NOTES

1. Paul Bernstein, "Using the Soft Approach for Hard Results," *Business* (April–June 1983):14.

2. Stephen P. Robbins, *Organizational Behavior, Concepts, Controversies, and Applications* (Englewood Cliffs, N.J.: Prentice-Hall, Inc., 1983).

3. Chapman, J.B. and R. Ottemann, *Employee Preference for Various Compensation and Fringe Benefit Options* (Berea, Ohio: ASAP Foundation, 1979).

4. Michael H. Mescon, Michael Albert, and Franklin Khedouri, *Management, Individual and Organizational Effectiveness* (New York: Harper & Row, Publishers, 1981), 601–602.

5. Glueck, William. *Personnel* (Dallas: Business Publications, 1978).

6. Lawler, Edward E. *Pay and Organizational Effectiveness: A Psychological View* (New York: McGraw-Hill, 1971).

7. Hackman, J.L. and J. Lloyd Suttle. *Improving Life at Work* (Santa Monica, CA: Goodyear, 1977).

Chapter 9

DRGs: Biggest Problem or Greatest Opportunity

The decade of the eighties is seeing major changes in the approach to health care in the United States. In the previous two decades, access to quality health care was extended to a majority of the population through federal legislation. In the 1960s, Congress enacted bills specifically designed to compensate institutions for costs incurred in providing medical services for the indigent through reimbursement from Medicare and Medicaid programs. The health care industry has since been laboring under the consequences of waste, mismanagement, and excesses of otherwise well-intentioned programs.

Consumers, as well as legislators, viewed with alarm a total health care spending bill that reached a staggering $286.6 billion in 1981 (compared with $155 billion in 1977 and $20 billion in 1960). The latest figure represents 10.2 percent of the Gross National Product, or, in more specific terms, $1,400 for each man, woman, and child in the country. These increases in medical expenses are three times greater than costs in general, stirring worries about Medicare solvency.

In his State of the Union Address in 1979, President Carter declared: "We must act now to protect Americans from health care costs that are rising one million dollars an hour—doubling every five years."

A program comparable to the current diagnosis related group system (DRGs) was implemented in New Jersey in 1980. Although its effects still were being evaluated at the end of 1984, it appeared that costs were being contained. According to the New Jersey Department of Health, hospital costs increased 14.6 percent in that state as compared with 17 percent nationally. During the 1980–1981 period, New Jersey's total operating expenses increased 13.8 percent while operating expenses increased 18.7 percent nationally. Average lengths of stay in hospitals also declined in New Jersey 1980–1981. Even though costs still increased in the New Jersey facilities, the rate was less than other institutions without such a program.

Because of spiraling costs, coupled with the view that health care institutions were doing little to control spending, Congress changed the method of Medicare reimbursement to a program called Prospective Payment System (PPS), which is based on DRGs. Beginning in October 1983, instead of receiving the actual cost of services to patients, health care facilities were paid a standard fee based on one of 470 DRGs. Reimbursement applied only to Medicare patients but many industry

191

analysts predicted private insurers would follow suit quickly. With the advent of DRGs, the health care industry today had to control costs.

INCREASES IN HEALTH CARE COSTS

Starting with the liberal social ideals of the 1960s, medical costs skyrocketed—three times greater than costs in general—leading to serious concerns about the potential for bankruptcy of the Medicare Hospital Insurance Trust Fund. The Congressional Budget Office in 1985 projected the fund's outlays for 1985 would exceed its income. However, the fund is to show a net gain in 1986, to be followed by a deficit in 1988.[1]

The Health Care Financing Administration estimated that national health expenditures would reach $456 billion by 1985 and $690.4 billion by 1990. These figures were in line with HHS predictions that total health care costs would exceed $2 trillion by the end of the century. National health expenditures rose 146.2 percent since 1974, the last year price controls for health services were in effect.

Putting this into human terms, the national average for health care was $1,225 per person in 1981. By 1985, this figure was expected to reach $1,881 per person, a 54 percent increase. Nationally, $286.6 billion was spent on health care in 1981.

PPS AND DRGs

To combat this threat, on April 20, 1983, President Reagan signed the law establishing the Prospective Payment System and identifying 467 diagnosis related groups on which reimbursement to hospitals would be based. Three more diagnosis related groups were added. (See Exhibit 9–1 for a complete listing of DRGs.) This was regarded as the most significant alteration in the system since its origin in 1965. Exhibit 9–2 lists the ten most frequently reported DRGs.

The PPS goals are to:

- reduce, if not eliminate, additional billing of beneficiaries by hospitals
- maintain access to quality care
- reduce reporting requirements
- establish efficiency incentives
- contain costs
- predict costs
- expedite implementation
- ease administration.

Reaction to the program in its first 18 months indicated ultimate success for these goals was possible to a large extent. As of September 1984, 81 percent of all hospitals were operating under PPS. The average length of stay has been reduced from 9.4 days (November 1982 to August 1983) to 7.5 days (October 1983 to August 1984) during the period between November 1982 to August 1984.

In the beginning, the PPS affected only inpatient hospital services covered by Medicare. The DRGs classified all acute illness and health care problems into 470 categories based on primary and secondary diagnoses, complicating factors, treatment procedures, and the patient's age. The DRGs then are weighted and calculated based on regional and hospital variances.

Exhibit 9–1 List of diagnosis related groups (DRGs)

DRGs

DRG	MDC		Title
1	1	SURG	Craniotomy Age >17 Except For Trauma
2	1	SURG	Craniotomy For Trauma Age >17
3	1	SURG	Craniotomy Age <18
4	1	SURG	Spinal Procedures
5	1	SURG	Extracranial Vascular Procedures
6	1	SURG	Carpal Tunnel Release
7	1	SURG	Periph + Cranial Nerve + Other Nerve Syst Proc Age >69 +/OR c.c.
8	1	SURG	Periph + Cranial Nerve + Other Nerve Syst Proc Age <70 w/o c.c.
9	1	MED	Spinal Disorders + Injuries
10	1	MED	Nervous System Neoplasms Age >69 and/or c.c.
11	1	MED	Nervous System Neoplasms Age <70 W/O c.c.
12	1	MED	Degenerative Nervous System Disorders
13	1	MED	Multiple Sclerosis + Cerebellar Ataxia
14	1	MED	Specific Cerebrovascular Disorders Except TIA
15	1	MED	Transient Ischemic Attacks
16	1	MED	Nonspecific Cerebrovascular Disorders With c.c.
17	1	MED	Nonspecific Cerebrovascular Disorders w/o c.c.
18	1	MED	Cranial + Peripheral Nerve Disorders Age >69 and/or c.c.
19	1	MED	Cranial + Peripheral Nerve Disorders Age <70 w/o c.c.
20	1	MED	Nervous System Infection Except Viral Meningitis
21	1	MED	Viral Meningitis
22	1	MED	Hypertensive Encephalopathy
23	1	MED	Nontraumatic Stupor + Coma
24	1	MED	Seizure + Headache Age >69 and/or c.c.
25	1	MED	Seizure + Headache Age 18–69 w/o c.c.
26	1	MED	Seizure + Headache Age 0–17
27	1	MED	Traumatic Stupor + Coma, Coma >1 Hr
28	1	MED	Traumatic Stupor + Coma, Coma <1 Hr Age >69 and/or c.c.
29	1	MED	Traumatic Stupor + Coma <1 Hr Age 18–69 w/o c.c.
30	1	MED	Traumatic Stupor + Coma <1 Hr Age 0–17
31	1	MED	Concussion Age >69 and/or c.c.
32	1	MED	Concussion Age 18–69 w/o c.c.
33	1	MED	Concussion Age 0–17
34	1	MED	Other Disorders of Nervous System Age >69 and/or c.c.
35	1	MED	Other Disorders of Nervous System Age <70 w/o c.c.
36	2	SURG	Retinal Procedures
37	2	SURG	Orbital Procedures
38	2	SURG	Primary Iris Procedures
39	2	SURG	Lens Procedures
40	2	SURG	Extraocular Procedures Except Orbit Age >17
41	2	SURG	Extraocular Procedures Except Orbit Age 0–17
42	2	SURG	Intraocular Procedures Except Retina, Iris + Lens
43	2	MED	Hyphema
44	2	MED	Acute Major Eye Infections
45	2	MED	Neurological Eye Disorders
46	2	MED	Other Disorders of the Eye Age >17 With c.c.
47	2	MED	Other Disorders of the Eye Age >17 w/o c.c.
48	2	MED	Other Disorders of the Eye Age 0–17
49	3	SURG	Major Head + Neck Procedures
50	3	SURG	Sialoadenectomy
51	3	SURG	Salivary Gland Procedures Except Sialoadenectomy
52	3	SURG	Cleft Lip + Palate Repair
53	3	SURG	Sinus + Mastoid Procedures Age >17

Exhibit 9–1 continued

DRG	MDC		Title
54	3	SURG	Sinus + Mastoid Procedures Age 0–17
55	3	SURG	Miscellaneous Ear, Nose + Throat Procedures
56	3	SURG	Rhinoplasty
57	3	SURG	T + A Proc Except Tonsillectomy +/or Adenoidectomy Age >17
58	3	SURG	T + A Proc Except Tonsillectomy +/or Adenoidectomy Age 0–17
59	3	SURG	Tonsillectomy and/or Adenoidectomy Only Age >17
60	3	SURG	Tonsillectomy and/or Adenoidectomy Only Age 0–17
61	3	SURG	Myringotomy Age >17
62	3	SURG	Myringotomy Age 0–17
63	3	SURG	Other Ear, Nose + Throat O.R. Procedures
64	3	MED	Ear, Nose + Throat Malignancy
65	3	MED	Disequilibrium
66	3	MED	Epistaxis
67	3	MED	Epiglottitis
68	3	MED	Otitis Media + Uri Age >69 and/or c.c.
69	3	MED	Otitis Media + Uri Age 18–69 w/o c.c.
70	3	MED	Otitis Media + Uri Age 0–17
71	3	MED	Laryngotracheitis
72	3	MED	Nasal Trauma + Deformity
73	3	MED	Other Ear, Nose + Throat Diagnoses Age >17
74	3	MED	Other Ear, Nose + Throat Diagnoses Age 0–17
75	4	SURG	Major Chest Procedures
76	4	SURG	O.R. Proc on the Resp System Except Major Chest with c.c.
77	4	SURG	O.R. Proc on the Resp System Except Major Chest w/o c.c.
78	4	MED	Pulmonary Embolism
79	4	MED	Respiratory Infections + Inflammations Age >69 and/or c.c.
80	4	MED	Respiratory Infections + Inflammations Age 18–69 w/o c.c.
81	4	MED	Respiratory Infections + Inflammations Age 0–17
82	4	MED	Respiratory Neoplasms
83	4	MED	Major Chest Trauma Age >69 and/or c.c.
84	4	MED	Major Chest Trauma Age <70 w/o c.c.
85	4	MED	Pleural Effusion Age >69 and/or c.c.
86	4	MED	Pleural Effusion Age <70 w/o c.c.
87	4	MED	Pulmonary Edema + Respiratory Failure
88	4	MED	Chronic Obstructive Pulmonary Disease
89	4	MED	Simple Pneumonia + Pleurisy Age >69 and/or c.c.
90	4	MED	Simple Pneumonia + Pleurisy Age 18–69 w/o c.c.
91	4	MED	Simple Pneumonia + Pleurisy Age 0–17
92	4	MED	Interstitial Lung Disease Age >69 and/or c.c.
93	4	MED	Interstitial Lung Disease Age <70 w/o c.c.
94	4	MED	Pneumothorax Age >69 and/or c.c.
95	4	MED	Pneumothorax Age <70 w/o c.c.
96	4	MED	Bronchitis + Asthma Age >69 and/or c.c.
97	4	MED	Bronchitis + Asthma Age 18–69 w/o c.c.
98	4	MED	Bronchitis + Asthma Age 0–17
99	4	MED	Respiratory Signs + Symptoms Age >69 and/or c.c.
100	4	MED	Respiratory Signs + Symptoms Age <70 w/o c.c.
101	4	MED	Other Respiratory Diagnoses Age >69 and/or c.c.
102	4	MED	Other Respiratory Diagnoses Age <70
103	5	SURG	Heart Transplant
104	5	SURG	Cardiac Valve Procedure with Pump + With Cardiac Cath
105	5	SURG	Cardiac Valve Procedure With Pump + w/o Cardiac Cath
106	5	SURG	Coronary Bypass with Cardiac Cath
107	5	SURG	Coronary Bypass w/o Cardiac Cath
108	5	SURG	Cardiothor Proc Except Valve + Coronary Bypass With Pump

Exhibit 9–1 continued

DRGs

DRG	MDC		Title
109	5	SURG	Cardiothoracic Procedures w/o Pump
110	5	SURG	Major Reconstructive Vascular Procedures Age >69 and/or c.c.
111	5	SURG	Major Reconstructive Vascular Procedures Age <70 w/o c.c.
112	5	SURG	Vascular Procedures Except Major Reconstruction
113	5	SURG	Amputation For Circ System Disorders Except Upper Limb + Toe
114	5	SURG	Upper Limb + Toe Amputation For Circ System Disorders
115	5	SURG	Permanent Cardiac Pacemaker Implant With AMI or CHF
116	5	SURG	Permanent Cardiac Pacemaker Implant w/o AMI or CHF
117	5	SURG	Cardiac Pacemaker Replace + Revis Exc Pulse Gen Repl Only
118	5	SURG	Cardiac Pacemaker Pulse Generator Replacement Only
119	5	SURG	Vein Ligation + Stripping
120	5	SURG	Other O.R. Procedures on the Circulatory System
121	5	MED	Circulatory Disorders With AMI + C.V. Comp. Disch. Alive
122	5	MED	Circulatory Disorders With AMI w/o C.V. Comp. Disch. Alive
123	5	MED	Circulatory Disorders With AMI, Expired
124	5	MED	Circulatory Disorders Exc AMI, With Card Cath + Complex Diag
125	5	MED	Circulatory Disorders Exc AMI, With Card Cath w/o Complex Diag
126	5	MED	Acute + Subacute Endocarditis
127	5	MED	Heart Failure + Shock
128	5	MED	Deep Vein Thrombophlebitis
129	5	MED	Cardiac Arrest
130	5	MED	Peripheral Vascular Disorders Age >69 and/or c.c.
131	5	MED	Peripheral Vascular Disorders Age <70 w/o c.c.
132	5	MED	Atherosclerosis Age >69 and/or c.c.
133	5	MED	Atherosclerosis Age <70 w/o c.c.
134	5	MED	Hypertension
135	5	MED	Cardiac Congenital + Valvular Disorders Age >69 and/or c.c.
136	5	MED	Cardiac Congenital + Valvular Disorders Age 18–69 w/o c.c.
137	5	MED	Cardiac Congenital + Valvular Disorders Age 0–17
138	5	MED	Cardiac Arrhythmia + Conduction Disorders Age >69 and/or c.c.
139	5	MED	Cardiac Arrhythmia + Conduction Disorders Age <70 w/o c.c.
140	5	MED	Angina Pectoris
141	5	MED	Syncope + Collapse Age >69 and/or c.c.
142	5	MED	Syncope + Collapse Age <70 w/o c.c.
143	5	MED	Chest Pain
144	5	MED	Other Circulatory Diagnoses With c.c.
145	5	MED	Other Circulatory Diagnoses w/o c.c.
146	6	SURG	Rectal Resection Age >69 and/or c.c.
147	6	SURG	Rectal Resection Age <70 w/o c.c.
148	6	SURG	Major Small + Large Bowel Procedures Age >69 and/or c.c.
149	6	SURG	Major Small + Large Bowel Procedures Age <70 w/o c.c.
150	6	SURG	Peritoneal Adhesiolysis Age >69 and/or c.c.
151	6	SURG	Peritoneal Adhesiolysis Age <70 w/o c.c.
152	6	SURG	Minor Small + Large Bowel Procedures Age >69 and/or c.c.
153	6	SURG	Minor Small + Large Bowel Procedures Age <70 w/o c.c.
154	6	SURG	Stomach, Esophageal + Duodenal Procedures Age >69 and/or c.c.
155	6	SURG	Stomach, Esophageal + Duodenal Procedures Age 18–69 w/o c.c.
156	6	SURG	Stomach, Esophageal + Duodenal Procedures Age 0–17

Exhibit 9–1 continued

DRG	MDC		Title
157	6	SURG	Anal Procedures Age >69 and/or c.c.
158	6	SURG	Anal Procedures Age <70 w/o c.c.
159	6	SURG	Hernia Procedures Except Inguinal + Femoral Age >69 and/or c.c.
160	6	SURG	Hernia Procedures Except Inguinal + Femoral Age 18–69 w/o c.c.
161	6	SURG	Inguinal + Femoral Hernia Procedures Age >69 and/or c.c.
162	6	SURG	Inguinal + Femoral Hernia Procedures Age 18–69 w/o c.c.
163	6	SURG	Hernia Procedures Age 0–17
164	6	SURG	Appendectomy With Complicated Princ. Diag Age >69 and/or c.c.
165	6	SURG	Appendectomy With Complicated Princ. Diag Age <70 w/o c.c.
166	6	SURG	Appendectomy w/o Complicated Princ. Diag Age >69 and/or c.c.
167	6	SURG	Appendectomy w/o Complicated Princ. Diag Age <70 w/o c.c.
168	6	SURG	Procedures on the Mouth Age >69 and/or c.c.
169	6	SURG	Procedures on the Mouth Age <70 w/o c.c.
170	6	SURG	Other Digestive System Procedures Age >69 and/or c.c.
171	6	SURG	Other Digestive System Procedures Age <70 w/o c.c.
172	6	MED	Digestive Malignancy Age >69 and/or c.c.
173	6	MED	Digestive Malignancy Age <70 w/o c.c.
174	6	MED	G.I. Hemorrhage Age >69 and/or c.c.
175	6	MED	G.I. Hemorrhage Age <70 w/o c.c.
176	6	MED	Complicated Peptic Ulcer
177	6	MED	Uncomplicated Peptic Ulcer >69 and/or c.c.
178	6	MED	Uncomplicated Peptic Ulcer <70 w/o c.c.
179	6	MED	Inflammatory Bowel Disease
180	6	MED	G.I. Obstruction Age >69 and/or c.c.
181	6	MED	G.I. Obstruction Age <70 w/o c.c.
182	6	MED	Esophagitis, Gastroent, + Misc. Digest. Dis Age >69 +/or c.c.
183	6	MED	Esophagitis, Gastroent, + Misc. Digest. Dis Age 18–69 w/o c.c.
184	6	MED	Esophagitis, Gastroenteritis + Misc. Digest. Disorders Age 0–17
185	6	MED	Dental + Oral Dis. Exc Extractions + Restorations, Age >17
186	6	MED	Dental + Oral Dis. Exc Extractions + Restorations, Age 0–17
187	6	MED	Dental Extractions + Restorations
188	6	MED	Other Digestive System Diagnoses Age >69 and/or c.c.
189	6	MED	Other Digestive System Diagnoses Age 18–69 w/o c.c.
190	6	MED	Other Digestive System Diagnoses Age 0–17
191	7	SURG	Major Pancreas, Liver + Shunt Procedures
192	7	SURG	Minor Pancreas, Liver + Shunt Procedures
193	7	SURG	Biliary Tract Proc Exc Tot Cholecystectomy Age >69 +/or c.c.
194	7	SURG	Biliary Tract Proc Exc Tot Cholecystectomy Age <70 w/o c.c.
195	7	SURG	Total Cholecystectomy With C.D.E. Age >69 and/or c.c.
196	7	SURG	Total Cholecystectomy With C.D.E. Age <70 w/o c.c.
197	7	SURG	Total Cholecystectomy w/o C.D.E. Age >69 and/or c.c.
198	7	SURG	Total Cholecystectomy w/o C.D.E. Age <70 w/o c.c.
199	7	SURG	Hepatobiliary Diagnostic Procedure For Malignancy
200	7	SURG	Hepatobiliary Diagnostic Procedure For Non-Malignancy
201	7	SURG	Other Hepatobiliary Or Pancreas O.R. Procedures
202	7	MED	Cirrhosis + Alcoholic Hepatitis
203	7	MED	Malignancy Of Hepatobiliary System Or Pancreas
204	7	MED	Disorders Of Pancreas Except Malignancy
205	7	MED	Disorders Of Liver Exc Malig. Cirr. Alc Hepa Age >69 and/or c.c.

Exhibit 9–1 continued   *DRGs*

DRG	MDC		Title
206	7	MED	Disorders Of Liver Exc Malig. Cirr. Alc Hepa Age <70 w/o c.c.
207	7	MED	Disorders Of The Biliary Tract Age >69 and/or c.c.
208	7	MED	Disorders Of The Biliary Tract Age <70 w/o c.c.
209	8	SURG	Major Joint Procedures
210	8	SURG	Hip + Femur Procedures Except Major Joint Age >69 and/or c.c.
211	8	SURG	Hip + Femur Procedures Except Major Joint Age 18–69 w/o c.c.
212	8	SURG	Hip + Femur Procedures Except Major Joint Age 0–17
213	8	SURG	Amputations For Musculoskeletal System + Conn. Tissue Disorders
214	8	SURG	Back + Neck Procedures Age >69 and/or c.c.
215	8	SURG	Back + Neck Procedures Age <70 w/o c.c.
216	8	SURG	Biopsies Of Musculoskeletal System + Connective Tissue
217	8	SURG	Wnd Debrid + Skn Grft Exc Hand. For Muscskeletal + Conn. Tiss. Dis
218	8	SURG	Lower Extrem + Humer Proc Exc Hip, Foot, Femur Age >69 +/or c.c.
219	8	SURG	Lower Extrem + Humer Proc Exc Hip, Foot, Femur Age 18–69 w/o c.c.
220	8	SURG	Lower Extrem + Humer Proc Exc Hip, Foot, Femur Age 0–17
221	8	SURG	Knee Procedures Age >69 and/or c.c.
222	8	SURG	Knee Procedures Age <70 w/o c.c.
223	8	SURG	Upper Extremity Proc Exc Humerus + Hand Age >69 and/or c.c.
224	8	SURG	Upper Extremity Proc Exc Humerus + Hand Age <70 w/o c.c.
225	8	SURG	Foot Procedures
226	8	SURG	Soft Tissue Procedures Age >69 and/or c.c.
227	8	SURG	Soft Tissue Procedures Age <70 w/o c.c.
228	8	SURG	Ganglion (Hand) Procedures
229	8	SURG	Hand Procedures Except Ganglion
230	8	SURG	Local Excision + Removal Of Int Fix Devices Of Hip + Femur
231	8	SURG	Local Excision + Removal Of Int Fix Devices Except Hip + Femur
232	8	SURG	Arthroscopy
233	8	SURG	Other Musculoskelet Sys + Conn Tiss O.R. Proc Age >69 +/or c.c.
234	8	SURG	Other Musculoskelet Sys + Conn Tiss O.R. Proc Age <70 w/o c.c.
235	8	MED	Fractures Of Femur
236	8	MED	Fractures Of Hip + Pelvis
237	8	MED	Sprains, Strains, + Dislocations Of Hip, Pelvis + Thigh
238	8	MED	Osteomyelitis
239	8	MED	Pathological Fractures + Musculoskeletal + Conn. Tiss. Malignancy
240	8	MED	Connective Tissue Disorders Age >69 and/or c.c.
241	8	MED	Connective Tissue Disorders Age <70 w/o c.c.
242	8	MED	Septic Arthritis
243	8	MED	Medical Back Problems
244	8	MED	Bone Diseases + Septic Arthropathy Age >69 and/or c.c.
245	8	MED	Bone Diseases + Septic Arthropathy Age <70 w/o c.c.
246	8	MED	Non-Specitic Arthropathies

Exhibit 9–1 continued

DRG	MDC		Title
247	8	MED	Signs + Symptoms Of Musculoskeletal System + Conn Tissue
248	8	MED	Tendonitis, Myositis + Bursitis
249	8	MED	Aftercare, Musculoskeletal System + Connective Tissue
250	8	MED	Fx, Sprns, Strns + Disl Of Forearm, Hand, Foot Age >69 +/or c.c.
251	8	MED	Fx, Sprns, Strns + Disl Of Forearm, Hand, Foot Age 18–69 w/o c.c.
252	8	MED	Fx, Sprns, Strns + Disl Of Forearm, Hand, Foot Age 0–17
253	8	MED	Fx, Sprns, Strns + Disl Of Uparm, Lowleg Ex Foot Age >69 +/or c.c.
254	8	MED	Fx, Sprns, Strns + Disl Of Uparm, Lowleg Ex Foot Age 18–69 w/o c.c.
255	8	MED	Fx, Sprns, Strns + Disl Of Uparm, Lowleg Ex Foot Age 0–17
256	8	MED	Other Diagnoses Of Musculoskeletal System + Connective Tissue
257	9	SURG	Total Mastectomy For Malignancy Age >69 and/or c.c.
258	9	SURG	Total Mastectomy For Malignancy Age <70 w/o c.c.
259	9	SURG	Subtotal Mastectomy For Malignancy Age >69 and/or c.c.
260	9	SURG	Subtotal Mastectomy For Malignancy Age <70
261	9	SURG	Breast Proc For Non-Malig Except Biopsy + Loc Exc
262	9	SURG	Breast Biopsy + Local Excision For Non-Malignancy
263	9	SURG	Skin Grafts For Skin Ulcer Or Cellulitis Age >69 and/or c.c.
264	9	SURG	Skin Grafts For Skin Ulcer Or Cellulitis Age <70 w/o c.c.
265	9	SURG	Skin Grafts Except For Skin Ulcer Or Cellulitis With c.c.
266	9	SURG	Skin Grafts Except For Skin Ulcer Or Cellulitis w/o c.c.
267	9	SURG	Perianal + Pilonidal Procedures
268	9	SURG	Skin, Subcutaneous Tissue + Breast Plastic Procedures
269	9	SURG	Other Skin, Subcut Tiss + Breast O.R. Proc Age >69 +/or c.c.
270	9	SURG	Other Skin, Subcut Tiss + Breast O.R. Proc Age <70 w/o c.c.
271	9	MED	Skin Ulcers
272	9	MED	Major Skin Disorders Age >69 and/or c.c.
273	9	MED	Major Skin Disorders Age <70 w/o c.c.
274	9	MED	Malignant Breast Disorders Age >69 and/or c.c.
275	9	MED	Malignant Breast Disorders Age <70 w/o c.c.
276	9	MED	Non-Malignant Breast Disorders
277	9	MED	Cellulitis Age >69 and/or c.c.
278	9	MED	Cellulitis Age 18–69 w/o c.c.
279	9	MED	Cellulitis Age 0–17
280	9	MED	Trauma to the Skin, Subcut Tiss + Breast Age >69 +/or c.c.
281	9	MED	Trauma to the Skin, Subcut Tiss + Breast Age 18–69 w/o c.c.
282	9	MED	Trauma to the Skin, Subcut Tiss + Breast Age 0–17
283	9	MED	Minor Skin Disorders Age >69 and/or c.c.
284	9	MED	Minor Skin Disorders Age <70 w/o c.c.
285	10	SURG	Amputations For Endocrine, Nutritional + Metabolic Disorders
286	10	SURG	Adrenal + Pituitary Procedures
287	10	SURG	Skin Grafts + Wound Debride For Endoc, Nutrit + Metab Disorders
288	10	SURG	O.R. Procedures For Obesity
289	10	SURG	Parathyroid Procedures
290	10	SURG	Thyroid Procedures
291	10	SURG	Thyroglossal Procedures
292	10	SURG	Other Endocrine, Nutrit + Metab O.R. Proc Age >69 +/or c.c.

Exhibit 9–1 continued

DRGs

DRG	MDC		Title
293	10	SURG	Other Endocrine, Nutrit + Metab O.R. Proc Age <70 w/o c.c.
294	10	MED	Diabetes Age >36
295	10	MED	Diabetes Age 0–35
296	10	MED	Nutritional + Misc. Metabolic Disorders Age >69 and/or c.c.
297	10	MED	Nutritional + Misc. Metabolic Disorders Age 18–69 w/o c.c.
298	10	MED	Nutritional + Misc. Metabolic Disorders Age 0–17
299	10	MED	Inborn Errors of Metabolism
300	10	MED	Endocrine Disorders Age >69 and/or c.c.
301	10	MED	Endocrine Disorders Age <70 w/o c.c.
302	11	SURG	Kidney Transplant
303	11	SURG	Kidney, Ureter + Major Bladder Procedure For Neoplasm
304	11	SURG	Kidney, Ureter + Maj Bldr Proc For Non-Malig Age >69 +/ or c.c.
305	11	SURG	Kidney, Ureter + Maj Bldr Proc For Non-Malig Age <70 w/o c.c.
306	11	SURG	Prostatectomy Age >69 and/or c.c.
307	11	SURG	Prostatectomy Age <70 w/o c.c.
308	11	SURG	Minor Bladder Procedures Age >69 and/or c.c.
309	11	SURG	Minor Bladder Procedures Age <70 w/o c.c.
310	11	SURG	Transurethral Procedures Age >69 and/or c.c.
311	11	SURG	Transurethral Procedures Age <70 w/o c.c.
312	11	SURG	Urethral Procedures, Age >69 and/or c.c.
313	11	SURG	Urethral Procedures, Age 18–69 w/o c.c.
314	11	SURG	Urethral Procedures, Age 0–17
315	11	SURG	Other Kidney + Urinary Tract O.R. Procedures
316	11	MED	Renal Failure w/o Dialysis
317	11	MED	Renal Failure with Dialysis
318	11	MED	Kidney + Urinary Tract Neoplasms Age >69 and/or c.c.
319	11	MED	Kidney + Urinary Tract Neoplasms Age <70 w/o c.c.
320	11	MED	Kidney + Urinary Tract Infections Age >69 and/or c.c.
321	11	MED	Kidney + Urinary Tract Infections Age 18–69 w/o c.c.
322	11	MED	Kidney + Urinary Tract Infections Age 0–17
323	11	MED	Urinary Stones Age >69 and/or c.c.
324	11	MED	Urinary Stones Age <70 w/o c.c.
325	11	MED	Kidney + Urinary Tract Signs + Symptoms Age >69 and/or c.c.
326	11	MED	Kidney + Urinary Tract Signs + Symptoms Age 18–69 w/o c.c.
327	11	MED	Kidney + Urinary Tract Signs + Symptoms Age 0–17
328	11	MED	Urethral Stricture Age >69 and/or c.c.
329	11	MED	Urethral Stricture Age 18–69 w/o c.c.
330	11	MED	Urethral Stricture Age 0–17
331	11	MED	Other Kidney + Urinary Tract Diagnoses Age >69 and/or c.c.
332	11	MED	Other Kidney + Urinary Tract Diagnoses Age 18–69 w/o c.c.
333	11	MED	Other Kidney + Urinary Tract Diagnoses Age 0–17
334	12	SURG	Major Male Pelvic Procedures With c.c.
335	12	SURG	Major Male Pelvic Procedures w/o c.c.
336	12	SURG	Transurethral Prostatectomy Age >69 and/or c.c.
337	12	SURG	Transurethral Prostatectomy Age <70 w/o c.c.
338	12	SURG	Testes Procedures, For Malignancy
339	12	SURG	Testes Procedures, Non-Malignant Age >17
340	12	SURG	Testes Procedures, Non-Malignant Age 0–17
341	12	SURG	Penis Procedures
342	12	SURG	Circumcision Age >17
343	12	SURG	Circumcision Age 0–17

Exhibit 9–1 continued

DRG	MDC		Title
344	12	SURG	Other Male Reproductive System O.R. Procedures For Malignancy
345	12	SURG	Other Male Reproductive System O.R. Proc Except For Malig
346	12	MED	Malignancy, Male Reproductive System, Age >69 and/or c.c.
347	12	MED	Malignancy, Male Reproductive System, Age <70 w/o c.c.
348	12	MED	Benign Prostatic Hypertrophy Age >69 and/or c.c.
349	12	MED	Benign Prostatic Hypertrophy Age <70 w/o c.c.
350	12	MED	Inflammation of the Male Reproductive System
351	12	MED	Sterilization, Male
352	12	MED	Other Male Reproductive System Diagnoses
353	13	SURG	Pelvic Evisceration, Radical Hysterectomy + Vulvectomy
354	13	SURG	Non-Radical Hysterectomy Age >69 and/or c.c.
355	13	SURG	Non-Radical Hysterectomy Age <70 w/o c.c.
356	13	SURG	Female Reproductive System Reconstructive Procedures
357	13	SURG	Uterus + Adenexa Procedures, For Malignancy
358	13	SURG	Uterus + Adenexa Proc For Non-Malignancy Except Tubal Interrupt
359	13	SURG	Tubal Interruption For Non-Malignancy
360	13	SURG	Vagina, Cervix + Vulva Procedures
361	13	SURG	Laparoscopy + Endoscopy (Female) Except Tubal Interruption
362	13	SURG	Laparoscopic Tubal Interruption
363	13	SURG	D+C, Conization + Radio-Implant, For Malignancy
364	13	SURG	D+C, Conization Except For Malignancy
365	13	SURG	Other Female Reproductive System O.R. Procedures
366	13	MED	Malignancy, Female Reproductive System Age >69 and/or c.c.
367	13	MED	Malignancy, Female Reproductive System Age <70 w/o c.c.
368	13	MED	Infections, Female Reproductive System
369	13	MED	Menstrual + Other Female Reproductive System Disorders
370	14	SURG	Cesarean Section With c.c.
371	14	SURG	Cesarean Section w/o c.c.
372	14	MED	Vaginal Delivery With Complicating Diagnoses
373	14	MED	Vaginal Delivery w/o Complicating Diagnoses
374	14	SURG	Vaginal Delivery With Sterilization and/or D+C
375	14	SURG	Vaginal Delivery With O.R. Proc Except Steril and/or D+C
376	14	MED	Postpartum Diagnoses w/o O.R. Procedure
377	14	SURG	Postpartum Diagnoses With O.R. Procedure
378	14	MED	Ectopic Pregnancy
379	14	MED	Threatened Abortion
380	14	MED	Abortion w/o D+C
381	14	MED	Abortion With D+C
382	14	MED	False Labor
383	14	MED	Other Antepartum Diagnoses With Medical Complications
384	14	MED	Other Antepartum Diagnoses w/o Medical Complications
385	15		Neonates, Died Or Transferred
386	15		Extreme Immaturity, Neonate
387	15		Prematurity With Major Problems
388	15		Prematurity w/o Major Problems
389	15		Full Term Neonate With Major Problems
390	15		Neonates With Other Significant Problems
391	15		Normal Newborns
392	16	SURG	Splenectomy Age >17
393	16	SURG	Splenectomy Age 0–17
394	16	SURG	Other O.R. Procedures Of The Blood + Blood Forming Organs
395	16	MED	Red Blood Cell Disorders Age >17

Exhibit 9–1 continued

DRGs

DRG	MDC		Title
396	16	MED	Red Blood Cell Disorders Age 0–17
397	16	MED	Coagulation Disorders
398	16	MED	Reticuloendothelial + Immunity Disorders Age >69 and/or c.c.
399	16	MED	Reticuloendothelial + Immunity Disorders Age <70 w/o c.c.
400	17	SURG	Lymphoma Or Leukemia With Major O.R. Procedure
401	17	SURG	Lymphoma Or Leukemia With Minor O.R. Proc Age >69 and/or c.c.
402	17	SURG	Lymphoma Or Leukemia With Minor O.R. Procedure Age <70 w/o c.c.
403	17	MED	Lymphoma Or Leukemia Age >69 and/or c.c.
404	17	MED	Lymphoma Or Leukemia Age 18–69 w/o c.c.
405	17	MED	Lymphoma Or Leukemia Age 0–17
406	17	SURG	Myeloprolif Disord Or Poorly Diff Neoplasm W Major O.R. Proc + c.c.
407	17	SURG	Myeloprolif Disord Or Poorly Diff Neopl W Major O.R. Proc. w/o c.c.
408	17	SURG	Myeloprolif Disord Or Poorly Diff Neopl With Minor O.R. Proc.
409	17	MED	Radiotherapy
410	17	MED	Chemotherapy
411	17	MED	History of Malignancy w/o Endoscopy
412	17	MED	History of Malignancy With Endoscopy
413	17	MED	Othr Myeloprolif Disord Or Poorly Diff Neopl Dx Age >69 +/or c.c.
414	17	MED	Othr Myeloprolif Disord Or Poorly Diff Neopl Dx Age <70 w/o c.c.
415	18	SURG	O.R. Procedure For Infectious + Parasitic Diseases
416	18	MED	Septicemia Age >17
417	18	MED	Septicemia Age 0–17
418	18	MED	Postoperative + Post-Traumatic Infections
419	18	MED	Fever Of Unknown Origin Age >69 and/or c.c.
420	18	MED	Fever Of Unknown Origin Age 18–69 w/o c.c.
421	18	MED	Viral Illness Age >17
422	18	MED	Viral Illness + Fever Of Unknown Origin Age 0–17
423	18	MED	Other Infectious + Parasitic Diseases Diagnoses
424	19	SURG	O.R. Procedures With Principal Diagnosis Of Mental Illness
425	19	MED	Acute Adjust React + Disturbances Of Psychosocial Dysfunction
426	19	MED	Depressive Neuroses
427	19	MED	Neuroses Except Depressive
428	19	MED	Disorders Of Personality + Impulse Control
429	19	MED	Organic Disturbances + Mental Retardation
430	19	MED	Psychoses
431	19	MED	Childhood Mental Disorders
432	19	MED	Other Diagnoses Of Mental Disorders
433	20		Substance Use + Subst Induced Organic Mental Disorders, Left AMA
434	20		Drug Dependence
435	20		Drug Use Except Dependence
436	20		Alcohol Dependence
437	20		Alcohol Use Except Dependence
438	20		Alcohol + Substance Induced Organic Mental Syndrome
439	21	SURG	Skin Grafts For Injuries
440	21	SURG	Wound Debridements For Injuries
441	21	SURG	Hand Procedures For Injuries
442	21	SURG	Other O.R. Procedures For Injuries Age >69 and/or c.c.

Exhibit 9–1 continued

DRG	MDC		Title
443	21	SURG	Other O.R. Procedures For Injuries Age <70 w/o c.c.
444	21	MED	Multiple Trauma Age >69 and/or c.c.
445	21	MED	Multiple Trauma Age 18–69 w/o c.c.
446	21	MED	Multiple Trauma Age 0–17
447	21	MED	Allergic Reactions Age >17
448	21	MED	Allergic Reactions Age 0–17
449	21	MED	Toxic Effects Of Drugs Age >69 and/or c.c.
450	21	MED	Toxic Effects Of Drugs Age 18–69 w/o c.c.
451	21	MED	Toxic Effects Of Drugs Age 0–17
452	21	MED	Complications Of Treatment Age >69 and/or c.c.
453	21	MED	Complications Of Treatment Age <70 w/o c.c.
454	21	MED	Other Injuries, Poisonings + Toxic Eff Diag Age >69 and/or c.c.
455	21	MED	Other Injuries, Poisonings + Toxic Eff Diag Age <70 w/o c.c.
456	22		Burns, Transferred To Another Acute Care Facility
457	22		Extensive Burns
458	22	SURG	Non-Extensive Burns With Skin Grafts
459	22	SURG	Non-Extensive Burns With Wound Debridement + Other O.R. Proc
460	22	MED	Non-Extensive Burns w/o O.R. Procedure
461	23	SURG	O.R. Proc With Diagnoses Of Other Contact With Health Services
462	23	MED	Rehabilitation
463	23	MED	Signs + Symptoms With c.c.
464	23	MED	Signs + Symptoms w/o c.c.
465	23	MED	Aftercare With History Of Malignancy As Secondary Dx
466	23	MED	Aftercare w/o History Of Malignancy As Secondary Dx
467	23	MED	Other Factors Influencing Health Status
468			Unrelated OR Procedure
469			PDX Invalid As Discharge Diagnosis
470			Ungroupable

Exhibit 9–2 The ten most frequently occurring DRGs reported for PPS discharges

FY 84 Rank	DRG	Discharges	% of PPS
1	127 Heart failure and shock	168,290	4.8
2	039 Lens procedure	130,598	3.7
3	182 Esophagitis, Gastroenteritis miscellaneous digestive disorders	129,880	3.7
4	089 Simple Pneumonia and pleurisy	110,857	3.2
5	014 Specific Cerebrovascular disorders	105,057	3.0
6	140 Angina Pectoris	102,417	2.9
7	088 Chronic Obstructive pulmonary disease	72,185	2.1
8	243 Medical back problems	70,094	2.0
9	138 Cardiac Arrhythmia	69,665	2.0
10	096 Bronchitis and asthma	63,061	1.8

This weighting factor takes into consideration the estimated costs of hospital resources used in comparable groups. Each discharge is assigned only one DRG regardless of the number of conditions treated or services provided. Regional variations are based on nine census divisions established by the Bureau of the Census as well as differences between rural and urban locales.

The PPS was being phased in over a three-year period. During the first year, 75 percent of a facility's Medicare payment was based on the actual cost and 25 percent on DRGs; in the second year, 50 percent on facility cost and 50 percent on DRGs; and by the third year, 75 percent and 25 percent; and in 1987 to 100 percent on DRGs. After four years, DRGs were to be based on a national figure. Based on the amount specified by the DRG, the hospital is reimbursed at a flat rate rather than at actual cost. If the hospital can provide services below the DRG amount, then it can "pocket" the difference; on the other hand, if its cost is above the DRG rate, then it must absorb the difference, providing the potentially biggest problem or greatest opportunity health care institutions have ever encountered. Hence, the incentive to control costs is urgent.

COST CONTROLS

Cost controls at the hospital level include shorter lengths of stay, fewer tests, fewer services, greater specialization, bulk and discount buying, shared services arrangements, and possible reduction in personnel and hospital staff.

The food service department in a hospital or nursing facility is considered a support department and its cost is allocated to revenue-producing departments. A support department is one that services one or more revenue-producing departments. Generally, food service services the routine patient care areas of a facility as food is served to the patients. It also furnishes service to the special units such as intensive care, coronary, or other similar units.

The food department also services ancillary departments such as laboratory, x-ray, and pharmacy through the cafeteria. In most hospitals the employees eat in the cafeteria. The cost of a food service department generally is allocated between strictly patient food and cafeteria, based on the number of meals served. The cost of the cafeteria is then allocated to the ancillary departments, based either on the number of meals served to employees of each or, if almost everyone eats there, on the number of employees in each department.

External Cost Factor

Even though food service departments can cut some costs internally to slow the rate of inflation, many of the external cost variables cannot be controlled. Goods and services must be purchased from suppliers; if their prices are increased, the facility must either increase its charges or absorb the higher cost, which in turn may affect the level of service.

DRGs are designed to increase efficiency, thereby decreasing costs, so institutions must develop a plan of action to cope with both the internal and external factors. The DRG rates are based on reported costs and estimated increases. In 1984 and 1985 the rates were to be calculated to reflect inflation plus 1 percent. After 1985, however, rate increases would be revised upon the recommendations of the Prospective Payment Assessment Commission (ProPAC).

Whether or not external factors would be considered in these future increases was unclear, but provisions had to be made at once to ensure they could implement plans whenever changes occurred. Unfortunately, such external factors usually are difficult to predict. Furthermore, because the health care industry's rate of inflation historically has been greater than for the general economy, aggressive plans of action were needed for food service departments.

Governmental Actions

As mentioned, DRGs are either the biggest problem or the greatest opportunity since the advent of Medicare, depending on how dedicated to efficiency an institution is or will become. It was imperative that controls be increased if the food service department, or even the institution itself, were to survive. However, the Prospective Payment System also could be viewed as an opportunity to improve the quality and efficiency of food services. Funds must be managed, saved, and potentially redistributed in order to deliver patient care under these reimbursement parameters. Quality patient care cannot be separated from economic reality.

According to Richard S. Schweiker, then Secretary of HHS, in his 1982 Report to Congress, "The ultimate objective of the Prospective Payment System (PPS) is to set a reasonable price for a known product." The unknown variables were being factored out of health care and were being replaced with good business practices that have been proved themselves in other industries.

Obviously, the first step in preparing for any changes in the food service department precipitated by DRGs is to define the operation specifically. Helpful guidelines are provided in Chapters 1 and 2. Once needs and services have been determined, efficient methods of providing them must be implemented.

The DRG system is not the only governmental action to consider in health care. Rising minimum wage standards, Social Security (FICA), and state and local taxes all increase the cost of operating a food service department. The federal trend of transferring the costs of many social programs to the states has resulted in imposing greater responsibilities on state and local governments. Many of these found it necessary to increase their tax base to meet the new responsibilities.

FOOD SERVICE ACTION

In light of the fact that food service costs are second only to nursing in any health care facility, the PPS had a strong impact. Failure to adapt could result in layoffs, closure of departments (and contracting of food service with other facilities), elimination of Registered Dietitians (RDs) and even possible hospital closings. The PPS requires new approaches to cost control in both the food service and clinical areas of the dietary department and creates an incentive to generate revenues. This chapter details specific, day-to-day operational steps to reduce costs and increase food service revenues.

Reducing food costs, while maintaining high quality, is the challenge facing all hospital food service operations. Funds must be managed, saved, and redistributed in order to deliver quality patient care under today's reimbursement policies.

Some hospitals instituted cost containment programs early, so DRGs and PPS had little effect. For hospitals that had not already prepared for these stringent controls, the DRGs offered a unique opportunity to begin cost control programs.

There are two ways to control costs: (1) reduce costs, (2) increase revenue. Cost control should be initiated in both the administrative and clinical areas of food service. In analyzing the operation to get the most for the budget dollar, administration and food service directors should:

- establish a results-oriented budget
- evaluate purchasing procedures
- establish an effective receiving system
- expose hidden food service costs
- evaluate the menu for cost, acceptability, and energy requirements
- compare the benefits of selective vs. nonselective menus
- improve productivity and evaluate current staffing to eliminate overtime
- implement energy conservation measures.

These steps have resulted in significant savings for many health care facilities in food service. This chapter identifies practical steps to control costs, converting the prospective payment system (a potential problem) into a golden opportunity.

Budget

Establishing a budget that is a viable measurement tool is the first step toward reaching the goal of reducing costs. Once the game plan or budget has been established, a budget-cost comparison system should be developed and evaluated weekly. This system will reflect budget overages that can be controlled before they become problems. One private hospital saved $4,000 the first month a budget and budget-cost comparison system was initiated for its food service.

The food service budget, which represents hundreds of thousands, if not millions, of dollars, per year:

- serves as the hub of the management wheel
- reviews the total needs of the department as it relates to the whole
- exposes hidden costs
- reveals the financial impact of administrative policies and goals.

Budgeting should identify the costs associated with patient meal preparation as opposed to foods served in the employee cafeteria. Zero-based budgeting is an effective, if not essential, method for setting up a cost benefit analysis. This assumes beginning with no historical data and projecting department revenues and expenses for the next fiscal year. This provides a far more accurate management tool than the traditional method of developing a budget, then adding an inflation factor to last year's expenses and revenues. After an annual budget has been set, it is subdivided into quarters, months, weeks, and potentially even days, depending upon the item involved (i.e., raw food, labor, etc.) so the information can be truly "managed."

Purchasing

Additional savings can be realized by evaluating purchasing procedures (see Chapter 4). Purchasing need not be complicated, yet specific systems must be instituted to obtain the lowest possible prices. By using state contract prices as leverage and as a guideline, by forecasting annual consumption, and by eliciting the support of other facilities in the area, one combination of a 28-bed hospital and a 60-bed nursing home saved more than $70,000 on only 70 items in one year.

Another deterrent to overspending is to develop a purchase order system. This need not be anything fancy—simple in-house purchase orders will do. The purchase order is an invaluable tool in establishing effective buying procedures. With such documentation, quoted prices of goods before they are delivered can be checked against the invoiced prices for discrepancies. Privately, vendors have said they can (and do) charge higher prices to institutions that have not taken the time to get quoted prices.

Cooperatives also are useful in obtaining quantity discounts. They can project the annual volume of specific items for the vendor, retaining the right to order only the quantity needed per delivery. In a purchasing cooperative, each facility agrees to take delivery on a weekly basis and orders only the quantity needed per delivery. This can be done by maintaining reserve stock over and above the amount that actually would be used in any week.

Receiving

An effective receiving system (Chapter 4) can have a significant impact on profit and loss. For example, a 200-bed institution was invoiced for 40 pounds of chicken and received only 20 pounds. This loss was identified through an efficient receiving system and by utilizing receiving scales. If the food delivered cost $1.33 per pound, the initial loss of 20 pounds translated into $26.60; however, the actual loss was $53.20. That resulted from the initial $26.60 loss in nondelivered plus an additional $26.60 in 20 pounds of chicken to replace the amount lost initially. Therefore, if such losses occurred only once a week, they could total $2,766.40 in a year.

An effective receiving system is another key building block in the pyramid to control costs. All supplies should be closely checked against the invoice to ensure that the price, quantity, and quality of items specified are received as ordered. Receiving scales can more than pay for themselves if they are used consistently in weighing in meats and produce upon delivery. Purchases should always be counted and visually inspected before the delivery receipt is signed; items that are less than perfect items should not be accepted.

The importance of instituting a simple, yet effective, receiving system, cannot be overemphasized. Such a system can result if the institution:

- designates and trains one primary employee to receive food and supplies for the food service department

- establishes specific receiving hours to ensure that supplies are not delivered during the busiest part of the day when employee(s) are too tied up to check in the order correctly

- maintain purchase orders, food specifications, inventory forms, and other pertinent items near the receiving area to facilitate the receiving process

- obtain and use a receiving scale (a Pelouze U-250A is an inexpensive, yet effective receiving scale).

If menus have not been evaluated recently, now may be a good time to do so (see Chapter 3). Although it is imperative to serve nutritious and appetizing food in an institution, some items are simply not accepted by patients and/or staff. Plate waste should be monitored not only to ascertain which foods are not being consumed but also to look for trends to identify potential and costly problem areas in tray delivery (such as patients' returning their plates untouched). (Chapter 3 provides an in-depth review of menus.)

Selective vs. nonselective menus vs. restaurant-style menus also should be evaluated objectively. One hospital found the selective menu actually was cheaper in the long run because the patients were able to choose their items, resulting in reduced plate waste. Less expensive sources of protein often were chosen over the more expensive meats.

However, selective menus are labor intensive and energy intensive, generally being 15 percent more expensive than nonselective ones. The present menu system should be evaluated in view of costs, public relations, and wastes. Restaurant-style menus have been found to be as cost effective as any systems.

EXPOSING HIDDEN FOOD SERVICE COSTS

Exposing hidden food service costs can reveal ways to save literally thousands of dollars a year. For example, if only two patient trays are prepared with incorrect diet orders five times per day, and the average hospital meal cost is $2.80, the hospital is losing $5,110 a year ($14 a day) in food and revenue. This is one of many hidden and unnecessary costs in food service.

Today's computerized census offers an up-to-the-minute count of patients and meal needs. If food service is not receiving a patient census before each meal, it should work with the data processing department to set up such a system. It is imperative the diet order for each meal be the most recent, so only one tray per patient is prepared per meal.

Foods not delivered to the patient at the right temperature often are wasted. If trays are delivered by nursing service, it is important to emphasize and verify their speedy delivery. Cold trays result in dissatisfied patients—plus uneaten food and potential lost revenue if the tray must be prepared again or if the patient selects another hospital for future treatment.

With DRGs and PPS, hospital food service is reevaluating staffing needs. Many have turned to flexible staffing with the use of part-time help, consultant dietitians, or rescheduling the permanent staff to avoid hiring new employees or incurring overtime. One facility saved $18,000 a year by conducting a productivity audit that led to redistributing the workload more evenly throughout the day.

The food service operation should be analyzed to determine which activities could be done in advance to redistribute the workload; presetting trays and preparing food during off times of the day are examples. Employee productivity must be improved since this increased labor efficiency can make this factor of cost control become a reality.

CLINICAL

Food service is not the only area in which costs can and must be controlled—clinical areas also should work toward reducing overall costs and generating revenue. Cost containment is appropriate in many areas without compromising the quality of care. This chapter identifies specific means to reduce costs in several nutrition-related medical requirements.

Pureed Diets

Thousands of dollars a year in food costs can be saved or recaptured by evaluating the costs, number, and portion control of pureed diets. One long-term care facility saved more than $26,000 a year by reevaluating its pureed diet policy. Although institutions may not have many such diets, these still can represent excessive hidden costs.

Recognizing the economic impact of such hidden costs, *The Stokes Report* surveyed pureed diets to establish control guidelines and standards for providing consistency and nutrition. When vegetables and fruits were pureed, their mean decrease in volume was 25 percent; in other words, the department had to purchase, prepare, and serve 25 percent more solid food to yield the same portion, per volume, of pureed diet food than for regular diets. This affects overall food costs and per-meal costs.

All pureed orders should be evaluated to determine that such a diet actually is needed; in some instances, a mechanical soft diet would be more appropriate. Pureed diets are generally not as appetizing as diets using solid foods, and the probability is low that a patient will consume all of a serving—especially when a mechanical soft diet would suffice. Any food not consumed is wasted. That increases costs, quality care suffers, and patients do not receive the nutrition necessary.

A 168-bed long term care facility saved $7,238 a year on pureed diets alone by:

- evaluating patients on pureed diets and providing chopped or ground food to those capable of accepting its consistency
- establishing and monitoring the specific portion size (#12 scoop) for single servings of pureed food (two #12 scoops for patients requesting large portions).

This results in:

- improved patient acceptance and enjoyment of the food
- reduced feeding time required by nursing personnel
- reduced food costs.

Nourishments

Uncontrolled nourishments can have significant impact on costs. One private hospital saved more than $10,000 a year by implementing the recommendations set forth here. Do the quantities of nourishments ordered reflect the health care needs of the patients or the hunger of the staff?

Effective systems of monitoring nourishments can benefit patients nutritionally as well as streamline food service. To control nourishment costs, institutions should:

1. Improve interdepartmental relationships between nursing and food service; emphasize that the patients are intended to be the ultimate beneficiaries and that the economic viability of each department is important.
2. Initiate a coordinated nourishment requisition system in which nursing submits its order once a day at a specific time. Each item sent to a patient area must appear on the requisition, then be filled and fully costed by food service.
3. Institute a nourishment monitoring system for each wing.
4. Evaluate the type and quantity of nourishments ordered in relation to patient needs and requests. (One acute care facility with six patients on the surgical wing submitted a requisition calling for $85 in juices and snacks for one day.) Reimbursement under PPS will not accommodate such unchecked costs.

Evaluation of nourishments includes ensuring that supplements provided are actually what are needed. In some instances, commercially prepared supplements are used when a milkshake would be just as effective, and patients almost always prefer milkshakes. The clinical dietitian should personally evaluate all orders for supplements to be sure not only that those ordered are the ones needed but also that the patient's condition will enable the patient to tolerate them.

Nutrition Assessments

Studies have indicated that patients who are nutritionally at risk have a greater incidence of mortality and morbidity. Hospital malnutrition is a concern that has not gone away in spite of the improvements. Consequently, these patients should be identified as soon as possible in order to increase their recovery chances and shorten hospital stays, thereby lowering costs.

The admission procedure could include such questions as height, weight, age, weight changes, home diet, and family history of diabetes, hypertension (or whatever is appropriate for the institution). If the facility uses diet aides or diet technicians, they should visit each patient as soon as possible upon arrival to perform the initial assessment and identify those who are at risk. Once they are identified, the clinical dietitian should conduct a more in-depth assessment and make recommendations as necessary.

Surgery Patients

Patients who are not at optimum nutritional status before surgery are said to have a greater incidence of mortality and complications, so all such individuals should undergo nutrition assessments before surgery.

Upon arrival, patients often are anxious about surgery, do not feel well, and probably have not been eating well before being admitted. If they are admitted a day or two before the operation and given nothing but clear liquids while tests are being performed, their nutrition status is depleted even before the stress associated with surgery comes into play. Low-residue supplements during this day or two can help the nutrition status substantially, resulting in fewer complications and speedier recovery.

Complications translate into longer hospital stays. At the average cost per day of $203 in 1984 for a semiprivate room, it is important to keep stays as short as possible. Since the DRG reimbursement rate is a set amount regardless of the expense incurred, hospitals can survive only by providing the maximum care at minimum cost. Every department in the hospital must work together in delivering this care and in helping hold costs down. The food service department's contribution should include helping patients reach optimum nutritional status before surgery.

GENERATING REVENUE

Food Service Menu

The selective menu can produce added revenues. Some institutions use their menu like a restaurant's, allowing patients to select their foods by preference and cost. Expensive items such as lobster and steak can be added when patients agree in advance, by their menu marking, to pay for them. Hospital gift shops can offer gift certificates that can be purchased as a get-well wish in lieu of flowers or candy. The dietary department must monitor patients' food selections closely so they will receive adequate nutrients.

Cafeteria/Coffee Shop

Some hospitals have found that a restaurant-style coffee shop is a good drawing card to attract physicians and nurses, to provide patients' friends and families with a nice place to wait or visit, and to improve the institutions' public image. Salad bars, potato bars, freshly baked breads, fancy desserts, and coffees served in enhanced surroundings can increase sales while minimizing costs. Lessons learned in restaurants apply to any food service operation, and the ability to provide what the public wants is a key to success. Staff members should be asked what foods they would like served and their comments solicited when experimenting with new foods or menu.

One hospital purchased a pizza oven and prepared take-out pizza that could be bought ready to eat or partially baked. This type of convenience is appreciated by nurses who have spent eight or nine hours on their feet. Other facilities sell leftovers or prepare special orders of baked goods for the staff and/or community.

Catering

Catering also can bring monies into the hospital food service department. Examples include day care centers, senior citizens congregate feeding (presenting this population with an opportunity to socialize as well as to become familiar with the hospital and its food), smaller hospitals, church functions (especially if the facility has a religious affiliation), school functions, Meals on Wheels, etc.

Departments that utilize the quick-chill method of food production can look for an even greater variety of possible clients. One hospital proposes to prepare airline meals. Large offices and industries are potential clients. Sources for generating revenue are limited only by the imagination.

Gift Shop

Fruit baskets, freshly baked breads and pastries, gift certificates for a special meal, birthday cakes, cookies, and even specialty items all are possible sources of revenue that can be distributed through the hospital gift shop. A gift cart that sells throughout the hospital is another good marketing tool for food service products.

CLINICAL

Fee-for-Nutrition Services Program

Clinical dietetics departments need to be progressive in implementing a fee-for-nutrition services program. Generally, these services include inpatient, outpatient, and diabetic diet instructions and classes as well as community education programs. Increased involvement with industry and businesses as well as the surrounding community can provide an additional community service while generating revenue. Wellness and good nutrition, i.e., weight loss clinics, after-school programs for children, nutrition during pregnancy, and sodium control diet ideas are topics of interest to the community and to businesses and industries. Classes on these and other topics could be provided to increase revenue generated by the clinical dietetics department.

Classes

As wellness and preventive nutrition continue to increase in popularity, hospitals find that classes on these topics are well received by the public. Charges depend on the facility, the number of people in the class, materials needed, and the dietitian's teaching fee. A $10 charge, paid by 10 participants, yields $100 for a class that usually only lasts one to two hours. Continuing classes, such as weight reduction, can provide a steady source of income.

Along with the obvious revenues, these classes indirectly provide income by increasing public awareness of the institution, improving its image, and potentially increasing the number of future patient days. If it can be thought of as a place to go when well rather than just when sick, its other services (i.e., the public cafeteria) also can benefit.

Examples of classes that could be taught include:

- the American Hospital Association's Culinary Hearts Cooking Class
- diabetes control
- hypertension control
- weight loss
- maternal and infant nutrition
- how to survive in the kitchen until Mom comes home
- cooking for children and teens.

Diet Instruction

Hospital clinical dietetics departments provide routine nutrition assessments and diet instructions for specified patients. Fees could be charged for dietary consultation and nutrition assessments as ordered by physicians and for patients identified to be at risk nutritionally, including burn, oncology, diabetic, and cardiac patients.

211

The implementation of a fee-for-nutrition services program must include plans for extensive communication with other departments and professionals, including nursing service, medical staff, and bookkeeping. Other hospitals initiating such a system have charged these services as diagnostic nutrition analyses and intake analyses. The clinical dietetics department would need to establish levels of nutrition care, include simple and comprehensive diet instructions, follow-up instructions, and basic and comprehensive nutrition assessments so a fee structure can be identified.

Fee structures for each of these categories should be based on the professional time involved. For example, a basic nutrition assessment may involve a calorie count and brief patient interview, taking 30 minutes, while a comprehensive assessment could involve a thorough evaluation of the patient's history, lab values, diet history, and interview, with frequent follow-up visits. After the establishment of fee structures, coordination with the accounting department to determine billing is necessary. Thereafter, biweekly revenue summaries can indicate numbers and types of services as well as income generation from the clinical dietetics department, and a revenue-to-cost ratio can be developed.

Outpatient or clinic consultation is an excellent source of revenue. For example, if only $20 per session is charged, then five patients per day results in an extra $500 a week or $26,000 a year. Many dietitians (as well as many unqualified "experts") have found that weight loss consultation represents an unlimited economic opportunity. The public should be receiving nutrition information from the qualified resource, the registered dietitian. Other outpatient consultation with a large potential population involves diabetes and hypertension.

Some hospitals are beginning to charge for inpatient consultation or patient education. This provides additional revenue for the dietary department and helps it justify the number of dietitians when administration begins looking at personnel cutbacks.

Proper accountability is based on appropriate documentation such as reliable data collection, recording and analyses of variables as they affect nutritional status, such as changes in treatment (i.e., chemotherapy) or drug/nutrient reactions. Any dietary intervention, including calorie counts, counseling, and diet histories, assessment of clinical data, and recommendations must be documented as proof of professional input.

Beyond providing a source of income and cost justification for the clinical dietetics department, documentation of the time it spends per diagnosis is invaluable in identifying the service cost. Implementation of DRGs may necessitate an administrative review of patient mix as well as identification of the cost of services for specific diagnoses. The clinical dietetics department should provide accurate input as to the cost of nutrition services in this regard.

Enteral Feeding

Consideration should be given to establishing a cost center for enteral feedings. (A new category of medical and nutritional supplies may need to be developed for this purpose.) Enteral products other than standard formulary could be specified by name in the billing process and a unit dose type of charging system with a cost factor added per unit could be devised with three classes of enteral products: (1) that need nothing other than affixing a label, (2) that require some processing, and (3) that require extensive mixing. Patients' accounts would, of course, be credited for the return of unused tube feeding formulas.

A standard house formulary should be determined as part of the hospital's treatment base. This will decrease the currently required large inventory of enteral products and would be a cost effective means of handling these products.

Survey Results

A survey of six hospitals in different parts of the country was made in 1984 by the author to evaluate the components and functions of nutrition support teams (Table 9–1). The services of the nutrition support team varied by facility. For example, at Baptist Medical Center, Little Rock, Ark., it serves as a consultation team with six physicians, a dietitian, nurse, pharmacist, and assistant administrator making rounds under a physician's written order. The team at Children's Memorial Hospital, Chicago, consists of clinical dietitians who make rounds with physicians and residents to offer input as to providing appropriate nutrition. It develops prototypes for nutrition intervention, screening, and assessment to provide standardization of quality care and to limit the number of required consultations. The team at the Ochsner Foundation Hospital in New Orleans provides clinical dietitians who work with physicians when nutrition intervention is requested.

Lack of cooperation among participating departments can destroy this approach. The nutrition support team at New Hanover Memorial Hospital in Wilmington, N.C., was established through the pharmacy department yet was disbanded within two years because physicians did not refer patients to it.

At St. Mary's Hospital, Saginaw, Mich., the nutrition support team serves only as a communication conduit among physicians, dietitians, pharmacists, and nursing as needed and to sponsor education programs.

University Hospital in Boston designates patients seen by the team as part of the clinical nutrition unit and they receive separate billing for these services.

To initiate a nutrition support team and a fee-for-nutrition services program it is recommended that a task force be established to investigate the possibility of initiating the team as a physician-directed nutrition intervention service composed of a physician, dietitian, nurse, and pharmacist. The team would function as a consultation service for nutritionally at-risk patients and direct the hospital's efforts in the area of parenteral and enteral nutrition support. An evaluation of the types of enteral and parenteral nutrition currently utilized as well as an interdisciplinary audit of potential candidates for referral to the team should be identified. Interviews at hospitals listed in Table 9–1 indicated patient groupings typically benefiting from intense nutritional support include low-birthweight infants, those with gastrointestinal disorders, oncology patients, and preoperative and postoperative patients.

The effectiveness of nutrition support has been well documented (see References at the end of this chapter). It can help reduce the incidence and complications of malnutrition, resulting in decreased patient stay and reduced need for readmission. Hospital clinical dietetics departments generally complete basic and comprehensive nutrition assessments, in addition to presurgery evaluations, for many patients that help identify those who are nutritionally at risk. However, without identification of team members for accounting and cost-allocation purposes, all patients must help pay the expense of a service received by only a few.

Developing such a support team and a fee-for-nutrition services program is an effective way of delivering quality patient care, identifying the cost of nutrition services per diagnosis, and generating revenue.

213

Table 9–1 Nutrition Support Teams

Facility	Baptist Medical Center Little Rock, AK	Children's Memorial Hospital Chicago, IL	Ochsner Foundation Hospital New Orleans, LA	New Hanover Memorial Hospital Wilmington, NC	St. Mary's Hospital Saginaw, MI	St. Francis Peoria, IL
Size	700 Beds	265 Beds	600 Beds	400 Beds	240 Beds	800 Beds
Components of Nutrition Support Team	6 Physicians 1 RN 1 RD 1 Pharmacist 1 Asst. Adm.	4 Physicians 1 Pharmacist 2 RNs 2 RDs	2 Physicians 6 RDs	1 Pharmacist 1 RD 1 RN	1 MD 1 Pharmacist 3 RDs 2 RNs 1 Physician	1 MD ½ Pharmacist 1 RN 1½ RD
Services of NST*	Consultation is provided for patients only upon physician's written order. Team tries to make rounds together and confer among each other as to recommendations for nutrition support.	Dietitians make rounds with physicians and residents. All patients are seen. Recommendations for nutrition intervention are made.	Consultation provided for patients upon doctors' written orders. Dietitians visit patients and provide recommendations to the physician.	Team was organized for two yrs. but disbanded due to poor physician support.	Team provides general information on nutrition support and organizes seminars. No rounds are made as a team.	Consultation provided by physician's orders. Perform routine and follow-up on TPN & tube feeding; provide home instruction.
Patients	Average 15 pts./day (2.5%)	All (100%)	6–8 pts./day (1.6%)	NA	5%	30/day
Cost Accountability of NST	Services are not billed. Staff keeps log of patients seen. No documentation of costs or payback.	Two cost centers maintain a nutrition lab. Charge of $35 for nutrition assessment and	Only team charge is physician fee. Clinical Dietetics Dept. charges for instruction (Avg.	No records kept.	No charges assessed.	Billed by service. Initial consult charge depends on degree of service. Plan to go to cost plus basis.

214

(continued)	personnel costs include RDs and diet clerks. Lab pays for less than half the cost of department.	$16.50). No cost as to total revenue information.				
Origin of NST	Physician interest generated the NST in 1982. Committee of six physicians remains actively involved in policy making.	Nutrition committee of hospital approved for formulary and team protocols.	Dietitians requested more involvement. "Team" organized in 1982.	Pharmacist organized without support of MDs or RDs.	Physicians and pharmacist initiated team formation.	Physician interest generated team formation.
Other	Large number of patients are seen due to the size of hospital and acute care setting.	Clinical Dietetics developing protocols for intervention, screening and assessment.	Plan to identify time requirements.	Physicians were reluctant to request patient visits due to fear of losing patients to other physicians.	Communication conduit for pharmacy, dietary and physicians. Team was initiated due to high number of oncology, burn and nutritionally at-risk patients admitted.	Plan to take over nutrition lab production and go computer billing.

*NST—nutrition support team.

215

As for cost accountability by nutrition support teams, this varied considerably in the survey. Most of those surveyed billed patients only for physician's fees as required; however, Children's Memorial Hospital in Chicago identified a nutrition lab cost center for revenues from nutrition assessments. Boston's University Hospital indicates its clinical nutrition unit is revenue producing, although its departmental structure is more extensive than that of a nutrition support team.

DOCUMENTING DIFFERENCES

One of the difficulties that hospitals and skilled nursing facilities encounter is their inability to document the difference, if in fact there is any, in the cost of preparing and delivering meals to patients as compared with those served in the cafeteria. In larger facilities this can be done a little more easily since they have employees who spend 100 percent of their time preparing and serving meals in the cafeteria and others whose time is 100 percent related to patients. However, in smaller facilities, where an employee's time is used in preparing both cafeteria and patient meals, this can prove to be a major costing problem. In many instances the food served in the cafeteria and to patients is the same.

The major cost differential would be delivering meals to the patient rooms and returning plates and utensils to the food service department. A consultant dietitian with experience in many facilities could help to design, conduct, and analyze tests to document the difference between patient and cafeteria costs. It sometimes is difficult to convince hospital personnel that the small amount of time spent performing a small duty is important. As an example (Table 9–2), a chore that takes a food service employee only five minutes a meal to perform for a specific area in the hospital translates into 5,460 minutes (91 hours) or 2¼ weeks' salary and benefit costs that should be allocated to that particular area. Five minutes a meal on a particular duty does represent a substantial cost.

The exhibits in this chapter can be adapted for gathering data to be used in allocating food service costs. Table 9–3 provides the means to cost out servings of raw food. It is simply a list of food served for that meal, indicating whether to hospital patients or in the cafeteria to visitors or employees. The cost per serving of each menu item can be determined by the dietitian and/or the food service director. The latest invoices should be used for costing. These expenditures should be extended and totaled for all meals served during the day at the end of each day rather than permitting them to accumulate. After the cost of each item has been determined, totaling can be accomplished by clerical personnel.

Table 9–4 can be used to develop ratios of how personnel labor cost can be divided between the cafeteria and patient food service. It lists all employees responsible for a specific duty. Each individual routine should be on a separate

Table 9–2 Per annum cost of 5-minute task

Time	Minimum Wage Rates		
Number of minutes per year	$3.35/hr.	$4.50/hr.	$5.50/hr.
5,460 (91 hrs.)	304.85	409.50	500.50
25% benefit cost	76.21	102.33	125.12
Total	381.06	511.83	625.62

Table 9-3 Cost per serving of raw food

FOOD ITEM	CAFETERIA				HOSPITAL				NURSING HOME			
	Size/Serving	No. Serving	Cost/Serving	Total Cost	Size/Serving	No. Serving	Cost/Serving	Total Cost	Size/Serving	No. Serving	Cost/Serving	Total Cost
Orange juice					4 oz.	25	.050	1.25	4.oz.	60	.050	3.00
Egg					1	20	.047	.94	1	65	.047	3.06
Cereal					4 oz.	20	.050	1.00	4 oz.	55	.050	2.75
Toast					1	22	.025	.55	1	70	.025	1.75
Milk					8 oz.	20	.094	1.88	8 oz.	60	.094	5.64
Coffee												
Fried Chicken	4 oz.	35	.31	10.85	4.oz.	15	.31	4.65	2 oz.	46	.155	7.13
Baked Chicken					4 oz.	5	.29	1.45	2 oz.	14	.145	2.03
Rice	4 oz.	25	.03	.75	4 oz.	20	.03	.60	2 oz.	55	.015	.83
Carrots	4 oz.	29	.110	3.19	4 oz.	20	.123	2.46	2 oz.	60	.055	3.30
Roll	1	34	.04	1.36	1	17	.04	.68	1	50	.04	2.00
Banana Pudding	4 oz.	28	.10	2.80	4 oz.	15	.10	1.50	2 oz.	45	.05	2.25
Banana						5	.106	.53		15	.106	1.59
Swiss Steak					4 oz.	15	.51	7.65	2 oz.	46	.255	11.73
Plain Steak					4 oz.	5	.41	2.05	2 oz.	14	.206	2.88
Mashed Potatoes					4 oz.	20	.04	.80	2 oz.	60	.020	1.20
Mixed Vegetables					4 oz.	20	.104	2.08	2 oz.	60	.046	2.76
Roll					1	17	.04	.68	1	46	.04	1.84
Fruit Cup					4 oz.	15	.163	2.44	2 oz.	45	.081	3.65
Diet Fruit Cup					2 oz.	5	.214	1.07	2 oz.	15	.214	3.21
TOTAL				$18.95				$34.26				$62.60

Note: Breakfast and evening meals are not served to cafeteria clients in this institution. Nursing home patients may receive additional servings on request.

Table 9–4 Documentation of labor hours per duty

DATE _____

ROUTINE: Washing Dishes

MEAL: Breakfast

Employee	Hrly Wage	Cafeteria			Hospital			Nursing Home		
		Start	Stop	Total	Start	Stop	Total	Start	Stop	Total
Jane Doe	3.35	9:00	9:10	:10	9:10	9:40	.30	9:45	10:30	:45
John Doe	3.45	9:00	9:35	:35				9:45	10:30	:45
Mary Smith	3.55				9:00	10:20	1:20	10:20	11:00	:40
Sally Jones	3.45	9:30	9:45	:15	9:45	10:10	:25	10:15	11:00	:45

sheet for each meal. Employees should be made aware of the importance of these tests and shown how to complete the form properly. (Exhibit 9–3 can help in developing Table 9–4). Table 9–5 is simply a means to compile and summarize the labor cost.

Hospitals or other facilities that do not have employees who work in and cook solely for the patient or cafeteria food service will find that these will cost meals more accurately between the cafeteria and patients than merely dividing the cost of meals served in the two areas. It is recommended that two-week tests be conducted in each quarter of the year and that they be at different times in each quarter. It should be noted that it is suggested that the total labor cost be allocated, based on the ratios developed during these tests, since they do not account for down time. The fiscal intermediary will insist that down time costs be allocated as well since that is the purpose for documenting time spent in each. It is essential that time spent in each separate area be documented in order to receive appropriate reimbursement.

CAFETERIA COSTS

If the tests prove that cafeteria meals cost less, the hospital will benefit from the higher rate in the patient areas in a cost-reimbursed program. However, the cafeteria poses some special problems.

Employees often pay less for cafeteria meals than do visitors and guests. The discount generally is offered to encourage them to eat their meals in the facility, which encourages shorter lunch breaks. It also is advantageous to the facility because the employee is essentially "on call" should an emergency arise.

The difference between the actual meal cost and the charge to employees can be allocated to their health and welfare. Whether this would be advantageous would not be clear until the cost report is worked out using both methods. It can be beneficial when an institution's payroll cost in departments with a high Medicare involvement is much greater than the ratio of employees who work in other areas. This is because employee health and welfare generally is allocated on gross salaries, and the cafeteria cost is allocated on either the number of employees in its various areas or on the number of meals it serves to employees of the departments. In a free-standing facility there will be less chance for any cost differential. Patients who generally are more mobile are encouraged to go to a common eating area where their meals are served along with any guests, visitors, and/or employees.

Exhibit 9–3 Work schedule form

DRGs

Name:

Position: Food Service Aide I (position #3)

Hours on Duty: 6:00 a.m. - 2:30 p.m.

Days off: Saturday and Sunday

Relieved by: Part-time Food Service Aide
(weekends)

Supervisor: A.M. Cafeteria Superivsor

Time	Duties
5:55	Clock in, in correct uniform
6:00	Assist cooks as necessary in breakfast preparation
6:45	Set breakfast trays
7:00	Help dish up breakfast
7:15	Take breakfast carts to floors
7:30	Break - 15 minutes
7:45	Wash pots and pans
8:15	Set up trays for lunch
8:30	Assist cooks in lunch preparation
9:45	Break - 15 minutes
10:00	Clean: Refer to assigned duties on cleaning schedule
11:30	Assist cooks in setting up steamtable for lunch
12:00	Help dish up for lunch
12:15	Take carts for floor
12:30	Wash pots and pans
1:00	Lunch break - 30 minutes
1:30	Sweep and mop dining room
2:30	Clock out

➤ Any other duties as assigned by supervisor.

REIMBURSEMENT TO NURSING FACILITIES

The hospital and hospital-based skilled nursing facility probably offer the greatest opportunity for reimbursement savings. Normally, Medicare utilization in a skilled nursing facility is far less than in a hospital. This results mainly from

219

Table 9–5 Summary of time spent

DATE _____

Routine	Cafeteria	Hospital	Nursing Home
Washing Dishes*	2:15	2:15	3:00
Preparing & Checking Menus	0:35	1:45	2:00
Cooking Food	1:45	3:45	2:45
Preparing Salad	1:15	2:00	1:30
Baking	1:20	3:05	2:30
Cleaning	2:02	3:35	4:30

*More time is required to wash dishes in a nursing home as there is a larger and more stable census than in a hospital.

tightened regulations on skilled nursing care and the stringent limitations Medicare places on the length of stay in such facilities.

The Medicare program states that a patient is entitled to a maximum of 100 days of skilled nursing care for each spell of illness. Once these days have expired, the patient no longer is a Medicare patient. If, during this time, the patient no longer needs "skilled nursing care," then the individual no longer is covered under Medicare. The program does not pay for any level of care except skilled nursing. It requires that a physician certify the need for skilled care before the patient enters the facility. This certification and treatment plan must be submitted before the end of the second day after admission. The certification must include an estimate of how long the patient will require skilled care. A recertification is required as of the last day of the presumed period of coverage. Subsequent required recertifications are reevaluated periodically by a utilization review committee.

Therefore, the more cost retained in the hospital, the higher reimbursement it generally receives. Since there normally is very high Medicaid utilization in skilled nursing facilities, and since both programs are essentially cost reimbursed, it might be thought that if Medicare did not pick up the hospital cost, it would in the nursing facility.

However, it is not quite that simple. Although Medicaid and payment levels vary radically from state to state and even within rural and urban areas within a state, states have set ceilings on the amount per day that they will pay for skilled nursing care during an interim period. In many instances, there is no retroactive settlement for Medicaid. This is why it is vital to document any differences in cost between meals served in the hospital and those in the skilled nursing facility. Some states set limitations on the routine costs per day that they will pay to nursing facilities regardless of the cost to the institution. If the facility has a high Medicaid utilization, the state is basically setting the price for the institution. For this type of institution, controlling costs is critical. The unreimbursed costs would have to be made up by private-pay patients or the facility eventually would have to close.

DRGs have given everyone in hospital food service a new and exciting challenge, a golden opportunity not to be ignored. Costs can be controlled. Revenues can be increased. Imagination is the only limitation. This is a rare opportunity to demonstrate the food service department's value to the patients, to the health care team, and to the institutions served. It is vital to be equal to the challenge and realize the opportunity.

NOTE

1. HCFA Background Paper, Department of Health & Human Services, November 1984.

REFERENCES

Collins, J.P.C., B. Oxley and G.L. Hill. "Protein Sparing Therapy After Major Surgery—A Controlled Clinical Trial of Intravenous Amino Acids and IV Hyperalimentation." *Lancet* 1 (1978): 788.

"Establishing a Nutrition Support Service." Abbott Laboratories and Ross Laboratories.

Freeland, Mark. "Health Spending in 1980's: Integration of Clinical Practice Patterns with Management." Nation Cost Estimates Group, *Health Care Financing Review,* Spring 1984.

"Nutrition Services Payment System." ADA's Coding and Terminology Task Force.

O'Keefe, S.J.D and D.M. Sender. "Catabolic Loss of Body Nitrogen in Response to Surgery." *Lancet* 2 (1974): 1035.

Powell-Tuck, J. et al. "The Effect of Surgical Trauma and Insulin on Whole Body Protein Turnover in Parenterally-Fed Undernourished Patients." *Human Nutrition: Clinical Nutrition* (January 1984): 11.

"SDR's Information Systems Data Book." Arthur Young and Company, Shared Data Research.

Seltzer, M.H. et al. "Instant Nutritional Assessment: Absolute Weight Loss and Surgical Mortality," *Journal of Parenteral and Enteral Nutrition* (May–June 1982): 218.

"The Source Book of Health Insurance Data." Health Care Insurance Association, 1984 update.

Stokes, Judy Ford. "Blended Diet Survey and Production Guide," *The Stokes Report,* (February 1982).

Stokes, Judy Ford. "Exclusive Study Never Before Published: Convert DRGs into Real Opportunity, Part III," *The Stokes Report* (December 1984): 94.

Young, G.A. and G.L. Hill. "Assessment of Protein Calories Malnutrition and Surgical Patients from Plasma Protein and Anthropometric Measurements," *American Journal of Clinical Nutrition* (1978): 429.

Young, Gerald A., et al. "Plasma Proteins in Patients Fed Intravenously After Major Surgery," *American Journal of Clinical Nutrition* (June 1979): 192–99.

221

Chapter 10

Computers: Opportunity for Food Service

Industry has long recognized the value of computers in increasing productivity, managing inventory, analyzing costs, and countless other functions. Food service is one of the last businesses to embrace computerized data management and its benefits.

Many automation alternatives are available to the food service industry: full-scale (mainframe) computers, minicomputers, microcomputers, and service bureaus. Each performs its functions in different ways, such as batch processing, real-time processing, and distributed processing. This chapter briefly defines these terms, then concentrates on one of the newest and most affordable options—microcomputers.

AUTOMATION ALTERNATIVES

One of the most common questions among those not familiar with computers is: "What is the difference between different sizes of computers?" The best answer is that it does not matter (e.g., whether it is a minicomputer or a microcomputer) as long as it gets the job done. However, this answer often is not satisfactory. More detailed responses are discussed later.

Full-Scale (Mainframe) Computers

These computers are used by large organizations with massive data processing needs. They are very expensive, usually more than $1 million, and require special rooms, special air conditioning, special power connections, and trained personnel to operate them. While they have significant capabilities, they usually have even more important demands placed on them.

This means that normal turnaround time (the time between submitting a processing job and receiving the results) can be several hours or, in unusual circumstances, even days. The time required to have a new function (program) installed on the computer can range from months to years. These delays are a primary reason why smaller computers are rapidly becoming fixtures in many organizations that already have full-scale computers.

223

Minicomputers

Minicomputers are probably the most difficult type to define. The most expensive and complex units look and act very much like full-scale computers. At the other end of the market, some minicomputers are out performed by microcomputers. In general, minicomputer systems begin in the $25,000 range.

Many minicomputers work best under conditions similar to those required by full-scale computers: special air conditioning, power connections, and trained operating personnel. Minicomputers generally are oriented toward real-time processing (defined later) and, in some cases, the operating personnel are more receptive to new functions than their counterparts using full-scale computers. For these and other reasons, it sometimes is possible to make effective use of existing minicomputer facilities.

Microcomputers

Microcomputer systems suitable for commercial use begin in the $3,000 to $4,000 range. Typically, they are single-user, desktop machines meant to process one function (program) at a time. Microcomputers do not need the supporting personnel and facilities required by their larger cousins. This makes them ideal for functions that cannot be run satisfactorily on larger existing computers. As noted, their growth rate in business is accelerating as more people discover the functions they can perform.

Microcomputers have placed the computerization of the largest retail industry—food service—within reach. As the leading retail employer and the fourth largest industry in terms of sales, the need for computerization is essential in order to accommodate food services' tremendous industry growth. It is difficult to get through the day without encountering an advertisement for some kind of microcomputer. From Apple to Xerox, everybody claims to have the ultimate solution to users' commercial computing needs. How does a food service director know which microcomputer is best for a specific operation? Is one even needed? Where should the search for information about microcomputers begin?

This chapter explores these and other questions typically asked by first-time microcomputer buyers. The objective is to develop a structured acquisition approach. This assumes most first-time buyers want and can find existing programs that fit their needs. Modifications to such programs and custom programs require a somewhat different and more complex approach.

Service Bureaus

Service bureaus, also known as timesharing services, are companies that supply computer services on a part-time, as-needed basis to other companies that cannot justify an in-house computer. Service bureaus range from comparatively small local firms to major international organizations. The services they provide vary as much as their size and include:

- Batch Services: In this mode, the customer completes data entry forms that are delivered to the service bureau, which enters them into the computer. The results are printed and delivered back to the customer. Turnaround for this process ranges from overnight to several days, depending on the contract.

- On-Line Services: In this type, the customer has one or more terminals at its location. The customer enters data at the terminal and, depending on the agreement with the service bureau, can receive reports back immediately.
- Custom Programming: Many service bureaus offer services that allow users to customize the bureaus' standard programs to meet their own needs. Service bureaus also will help customers design and write completely new programs.

A service bureau can be a cost effective alternative to an in-house computer. However, institutions should analyze the initial and recurring costs carefully before committing to use a service bureau.

Computer Operating Methods

Each of these alternatives can operate in one of three different ways. In some cases, a particular function will use each of these methods at one time or another. The questions of choosing among these methods is beyond the scope of this chapter; the purpose here is to define these common terms briefly:

- Batch Processing: This involves entering data and holding it until later before updating permanent files. This method can appear to the user as keypunching computer cards or as a terminal entry screen. Its objective is to verify data accuracy before moving into permanent files.
- Real-Time Processing: This involves entering data at a terminal and immediately updating permanent files. The objective is immediate processing of results.
- Distributed Processing: The only way to use a computer until recently was by a device connected directly to some central computer. Many computers now have the capability of processing data at smaller units, located nearer the user, and feeding the information into the large central computer where it can be merged with data from other users and shared by other appropriate remote computers.

BASIC COMPUTER COMPONENTS

Computers have two basic components: hardware and software. Hardware refers to the computer itself, software to the program(s) required to make the computer function. This chapter provides a foundation in both areas to help the food service department reap worthwhile results.

When the technical jargon is stripped away, all microcomputers perform four basic functions:

1. Input: The microcomputer must have some means of knowing what information it should act on. The input mechanism can be as mundane as a keyboard like a typewriter or as exotic as a microphone for talking directly to the microcomputer.
2. Storage: The microcomputer must have some means of remembering what it must do. This involves two types of memory, random access memory (RAM) for remembering tasks it must perform immediately and mass storage for remembering tasks it may perform later.

3. Processing: The microcomputer must have some means of manipulating the information users provide. For this purpose every microcomputer has a central processing unit (CPU). This is the unit's brain and, like a person's brain, it controls the action of the other microcomputer devices.

4. Output: The microcomputer must have some means of reporting the results of its efforts. This can be done on a device similar to a television screen, on a device that prints the results on paper, or on other more exotic machines.

Every computer, from the smallest pocket model to the largest room size system, must have at least one device for performing each of the four functions; some may have multiple devices.

Before beginning a detailed look at microcomputer components, a word of warning is in order. A microcomputer system is a combination of equipment and programs whose sole purpose is to satisfy customer requirements. The evaluations and comments here about specific devices are useful for comparing similar combinations of equipment and programs. However, equipment specifications should not be used as the only criteria when evaluating a microcomputer system.

Central Processing Unit (CPU)

When evaluating a computer's brain, there are five important features that can differentiate one model from another:

1. How Many Brains Does the Computer Have? If two heads are better than one, two or more brains should be better than one. While one brain usually is adequate, a microcomputer with multiple brains (called microprocessors) can assign specific tasks to each brain, thus working more efficiently through specialization. For example, some microcomputers use one brain for performing the basic calculations and other brains for communicating with the input, storage, and output devices. This multiple brain arrangement can improve the speed of entering and receiving information and is particularly useful in applications, such as hospital admissions, where input and output demands are significant.

2. How Large Is the Computer's Brain? Microcomputer brains come in different sizes and, all other factors being equal, the larger the brain the more versatile the microcomputer. The difference involves the amount of information that can be processed at one time. In technical jargon, this capacity is measured in bits (binary digits). It is not important to know what a bit is. The important thing to remember is that, as a general rule, more bits mean more versatility. Microcomputer brains come in three sizes.

   a. 8 Bit: Microcomputers with 8-bit brains are adequate for many applications in which one person performs one task at a time. If a single microcomputer will never be used for more than one task at a time, this smaller brain often is more cost effective than larger brains; is a stable, time-proved device; and has a much wider range of prewritten programs available for use.

   b. 8/16 Bit: Microcomputers from major companies such as IBM and Apple have the capacity to support up to three or four persons simultaneously using one CPU with the use of a hard disc. Each station can share the data stored and input information which can be obtained by each station. They

can access more internal storage and thus process more complex programs at a faster rate than 8-bit microcomputers. A note of caution is
appropriate when comparing microcomputers advertised as ''16-bit.''
While microcomputers using microprocessors such as models 8086 and
8088 are ''16-bit'' in some definitions of the term, they still share some
technical characteristics of their 8-bit ancestors. That is why they are
referred to as 8/16-bit. Microcomputers with the 8086 and 8088 model
microprocessors in 1985 include: the AT&T Personal Computer, Model
6300, Hewlett-Packard HP110, IBM PC, IT&T XTRA Model II, and
IBM PC XT. As a general rule, 8/16-bit microcomputers do not have the
growth capacity of the 16/32-bit models. If requirements do not call for
more than four simultaneous users, the 8/16-bit units can represent a
good value.

c 16/32 Bit: Microcomputers with this brain size represent the top-of-the-
line in terms of processing ability available as of 1985. While there are
microcomputers with larger brains, they typically cost more than the
16/32-bit units. Microcomputers with this brain size have the potential to
handle four to eight users simultaneously, thus allowing more growth
than their smaller cousins. As might be expected, these usually cost more
than their smaller counterparts. Prices vary according to various models
so comparative shopping is essential. Potential growth requirements
should be evaluated before extra money is spent to buy microcomputers
using the 68000 microprocessor and other similar models.

3. How Much Internal Storage Can the Brain Access? More internal memory
permits more complex tasks to be performed at a faster rate. This is because
the microcomputer can find information in its internal memory many times
faster than it can using mass storage. Most 8-bit microcomputers can access
about 64,000 characters of internal memory, although some manufacturers
are using programs that permit accessing up to 128,000 characters. This is
not the same as the larger brain microcomputers that have the ability (not
used by some manufacturers) to access more than 1 million characters of
internal memory directly. If the requirements call for multiple simultaneous
users or processing complex applications such as engineering calculations,
large ''what-if'' financial models, or certain accounting functions, increased
internal memory capacity is more important.

4. How Many Free Expansion Slots Does the CPU Have? Many models permit
the addition of devices by plugging printed circuit boards into the microcomputer. The number of boards that can be plugged in is an important measure
of how much a microcomputer can grow. For example, one popular model
has eight expansion slots; however, once the video display, mass storage
control, and printer boards (all required for most commercial purposes) are
added, only five slots are actually available for future growth. When planning requirements, it is imperative to make sure to understand what additional devices might be needed and how many slots these devices require.
Examples of such devices include: color display capabilities, additional
memory (in excess of 256,000 characters, depending on the microcomputer), additional terminals and printers, and telephone connection devices
(modems).

5. How Fast Is the Computer's Brain? Many microcomputer store salespeople
can be put off balance by asking them how fast the microprocessor operates.
The technical jargon is ''clock speed.'' This is a general measure of how

many program instructions can be processed each second. Like EPA mileage estimates for automobiles, this performance measure is potentially misleading. However, when comparing two microcomputers using the same model microprocessor and the same operating system (defined later), the faster microcomputer brain will be able to process jobs in less time.

Terminals (Video Displays)

Almost all microcomputers have some kind of typewriter-style keyboard for entering information and a device similar to a television screen for displaying the results of its work. Together these are referred to as a terminal. Other common synonyms are CRT (for cathode ray tube, the technical name for the TV type of screen) and VDT (for video display terminal).

For most customers, the terminal is the primary point of contact with the microcomputer. It is important, therefore, that users feel comfortable working with the keyboard and viewing the terminal. A poorly designed terminal can cause eye strain, back problems, fatigue, and generally lower productivity. Following are important features to look for in a terminal:

1. Screen Size: Just as a small television screen is more difficult to see, a small terminal screen is more difficult to work with. While small screens have valid uses in portable microcomputers, units used several hours a day should have a screen size of at least 12 inches, measured diagonally.

2. Display Size: Microcomputers vary widely in the maximum number of characters they can display on the screen at one time. As a general rule, fewer characters means more inconvenience for the user. The industry has been moving toward a standard of 80 horizontal columns by 24 vertical rows. Although screen size varies from 9-14 inches models with a smaller display size may cost less but may cause operating inconveniences in the long run. If the requirements include word processing and electronic spreadsheets, an 80 × 24 display size is the minimum that should be considered.

3. Color Graphics: Studies show that most people can receive more information in a shorter time from graphs than from numbers alone. If the requirements include analysis of statistical or accounting information, color graphics capabilities may prove to be a sound investment. However, color is optional on most microcomputers and can cost more than $1,000 extra. When comparing color graphics capabilities, two features are important:

   a. Density: How many individual points are available on the screen? More points means better looking graphs. Density is measured by the number of pixels (points) on the screen. Like the display size, the measure is expressed in terms of vertical and horizontal points.

   b. Number of Colors: How many different colors are available? More colors means more display flexibility (and higher cost). The number of colors is not as important as density.

4. Fixed or Detachable Keyboard: Several microcomputers have keyboards that can be detached from the CPU. This is a useful feature because it permits users to adjust their seating position from time to time. This helps increase productivity by making users more comfortable.

5. Keyboard "Feel": People who type know they can do so faster on some typewriters than on others. One reason for this is a good keyboard. Primary users of the microcomputer should test the keyboard for overall layout and comfort. While keyboard "feel" to a large extent is based on individual preference, some general beneficial features include the following.

   a. Firmness: The keys should require a light but firm touch. They should not wobble from side to side.
   b. Response: Some acknowledgement that a key has been depressed is useful. This can occur as a soft click sound or as a slight hesitation when a key is depressed.
   c. Key Layout: Some microcomputer programs require special keys, such as "BREAK" or "CONTROL." Are these keys easy to reach? Is the "RETURN" (also marked as "ENTER") key easy to reach?

6. Calculator (10-Key) Pad: If the requirements include entering numeric data, a separate calculator style set of keys is useful. Some manufacturers implement this by having the pad set in the regular alphabetic keys and creating the number function using a shift or control key. This is not normally as useful as a separate 10-key pad, particularly for persons experienced using 10-key calculators.

7. Function (Soft) Keys: Many microcomputer programs, such as word processing programs, have single operations requiring several keystrokes. Function keys allow a programmer to combine several frequently used keystrokes or other operations and execute them automatically when a single function key is pressed. This increases productivity and ease of use. Keyboards with more function keys permit more combining of repetitive tasks.

Mass Storage

As discussed earlier, most microcomputers have two ways of remembering what they must do. When instructions or information are not available in the computer's internal memory, it can go find what it needs in mass storage. As a general rule, the more mass storage available to a microcomputer, the more versatile it is.

Following are the characteristics, advantages, and disadvantages of the two primary mass storage devices used by commercial microcomputers:

Floppy Discs

These in many ways resemble a phonograph record in its cover. They appear as 5¼- or 8-inch squares with a hole in the center and a slot along the bottom. They are the most common form of mass storage for commercial microcomputers. Important characteristics: (a) they are random access devices, permitting the microcomputer to find information quickly at any point on the disc without reading it sequentially; (b) they can store 80,000 to 1.2 million characters on a disc; (c) they can be removed from the disc drive (the device that reads the disc for the microcomputer), permitting storage of more information on additional discs than could be stored on nonremovable discs; and (d) they are easy to copy (back up) and store to protect against equipment failure or other problems.

Floppy disc drives are relatively inexpensive. The discs themselves generally cost $3 to $8 each, depending on size and quantity purchased. If the requirements do not include processing more information at one time than can be stored on a floppy disc, and if the microcomputer is to be used to process one task for one user at a time, floppy discs are an inexpensive and reliable alternative for mass storage.

Winchester Drive

This is a relatively new mass storage device that brings large capacities into the microcomputer buyer's price range. The Winchester drive was introduced to microcomputer buyers as early as 1980 at a very high price. However, in 1983, the IBM PC XT gave microcomputer purchasers an opportunity to obtain hard disk storage at an affordable price. IBM has additional models available also, such as the PC AT, which entered the market in 1985. Unlike the floppy disc, this device is sealed and the disc cannot be removed. The storage capacity of Winchester drives generally begins around 5 million characters and can exceed 70 million per drive. Additional drives provide significant storage capacity.

The initial cost of a Winchester drive is greater than a floppy disc drive; however, on a cost-per-character-stored basis (number of characters divided by purchase price) it often is less expensive. Again, prices vary depending on the model, number of floppy disc drives, and memory capacity. Winchester drives usually can find and transfer information to the CPU faster than a floppy disc and, because they are sealed, generally are more reliable. If the requirements call for large storage application programs or multiple simultaneous users, serious consideration should be given to a Winchester drive.

If the question is asked: "Why doesn't everyone use a Winchester drive?" there is a good reason. Besides the higher initial cost, its backup sometimes is difficult and expensive. Because backup is so important, it should be understood in more detail.

Backup is the process of copying information in mass storage and storing the copy away from the microcomputer. This is necessary because a number of mechanical and human problems can destroy information in mass storage. These problems range from power failures during the time you are writing to the mass storage, to sabotage of the information by an angry employee. Unless you have a copy of the information from which you can recover the lost information, you may suffer significant financial loss by manually recreating the lost information.

If your requirements include processing accounting or other sensitive information, you should seek professional advice on backup and recover strategies before you acquire a microcomputer.

Now that we understand what backup means and why it is important, we can briefly discuss Winchester drive backup problems. Unlike floppy discs, which you can copy and remove from the disc drive, Winchester drives are not removable. It is necessary, therefore, to copy the material from the sealed Winchester drive to some removable medium. Some manufacturers copy the information from the Winchester drive to floppy discs. This may sound good, but consider how many 300,000 character floppy discs would be required to back up a 10,000,000 Winchester drive. Consider that this process could take about one hour or more. Some manufacturers copy the information onto a magnetic tape cartridge similar to an eight-track stereo cartridge. This usually is better than floppy disc backup but adds several hundred dollars to the purchase price.

There are many ways to back up, store, and recover information (copy it from the backup medium) when using Winchester drives. As discussed, it is important to devise a workable method before buying any microcomputer.

Most commercial microcomputer systems require some means of recording information on paper for distribution to other persons. This task is handled by a printer. General printer features and two common types used by commercial microcomputers are discussed next.

Common features of concern to microcomputer users include the following.

- Character Set: This refers to the different symbols a printer will print. Some less expensive printers are limited to uppercase letters, numbers, and some math symbols. Some printers provide a wide range of symbols, type fonts, pitches (spacing between characters), and other capabilities.

- Noise: Printer noise can be very distracting—and some produce more than others. It is essential to listen to the printer in operation and consider where it will be situated before purchasing. Sound reduction options are available for some printers. These are often good investments for the sanity of persons using the machines.

- Bidirectional Printing: This speedup feature permits printing a line from left to right and right to left. It avoids the time required to return the print head to the home position (left) before typing another line. This greatly increases throughput (number of lines printed per minute) and reduces wear on the printer. This is a highly desirable feature.

- Mean Time Between Failure (MTBF): With the possible exception of disc drives, printers are the most likely components in a microcomputer system to fail. MTBF is a measure of the general reliability of a printer (or disc drive). A higher MTBF rating usually indicates a more reliable piece of equipment.

The features we have discussed apply to all types of printers. We will now discuss these features in terms of the two most common types of printers used in commercial microcomputer systems.

1. Dot Matrix Character Printers: These printers derive their name from the way they print characters on a page. Characters are formed one at a time by altering the pattern of dots that are printed. If you look closely at the printing from this kind of printer, you will see a series of tiny dots forming the individual characters. These printers are typically used where typewriter quality printing is not required, such as internally distributed reports. In general these printers offer higher print speeds, larger carriages, larger character sets and less noise, at a lower cost than word quality printers. Most microcomputer systems have at least one dot matrix character printer. If the requirements do not include word processing, this type of printer is the best bet.

2. Letter Quality Printer: These printers derive their name from the typewriter quality of print they produce. Rather than forming characters from patterns of dots, they produce characters more like a typewriter. They are almost a necessity in word processing applications. In general they are much slower (30 to 80 characters per second), have more limited character sets, and are somewhat noisier than a similarly priced dot matrix printer. Letter quality printers are costly. If word processing will not be performed on the microcomputer, there probably is no need to invest in this type of printer.

231

Other Devices

In addition to the basic equipment components in a commercial microcomputer system, a multitude of other devices can be attached to the microcomputer. The laser printer hit the market in early 1985 and represents the top-of-the-line in terms of speed. It produces 325 characters per second with a high resolution and with minimal noise factors. These printers are available for microcomputers; however, the price is high (almost as high as the computer itself).

Modem

This device permits the microcomputer to communicate with others over standard telephone lines. This is useful when there is a need to transfer information between parts of an organization located in different areas of the city, different cities or parts of the world.

Another common use for modems is access to collections of information called databases. These databases allow access to stock quotations, headline news, research information, games, and many other useful services. Modems are useful devices, and many people eventually purchase one.

However, it is important to be aware that communication between microcomputers is a complex subject and more detailed information should be sought before buying a modem, in particular on the following points:

1. A modem may require an expansion slot in the CPU.
2. Communication requires special software (microcomputer programs) to make it work.
3. The other microcomputer must be compatible in terms of the information transmission speed (called baud rate) and method of coding the transmitted data (called protocol).

Joystick (Mouse)

These devices permit moving the cursor (the light on the screen that indicates where the microcomputer is looking for information) to any point on the screen. These are similar to the devices that control home video games. Their original use was in games but some microcomputers now provide these devices as a supplement to keyboards.

Plotter

This device draws on paper the charts and graphs that appear on the screen. It is useful when creating presentations and reports. These originally were extremely expensive but have come down to the price range of many commercial microcomputer buyers. Like most microcomputer devices, plotters require software (microcomputer programs) to make them work. It is essential to make sure the use of the plotter software can be learned before buying the plotter.

SOFTWARE

Software refers to a set of instructions that tells the microcomputer to do something. A microcomputer without software is like a car without fuel. It may have plenty of potential but nothing to make it go. Everything a microcomputer does requires some kind of software. This includes basic tasks, such as adding two numbers or finding information in mass storage, and more advanced tasks such as displaying a pie chart on the screen or printing on paper, using a plotter.

Most microcomputers require three types of software to perform useful tasks. This section is designed to help potential buyers understand what each of these software types does and make them aware of some of the options available. Some specific products are mentioned but only as examples of common items available. This is not necessarily to recommend these products or to express an opinion about their relative merits.

Operating Systems

At any one time, every microcomputer must have one operating system resident in internal memory. The software controls the most basic functions required to make the machine work. The operating system tells the microcomputer where to look for information in internal memory and mass storage, controls the operation of devices such as terminals and printers, and performs many other routine functions too numerous to mention.

In most well-designed microcomputer systems, the operating functions are not seen by the average user. Indeed, most users do not know or care how or why an operating system works. Why, then, is it worth mentioning here? The reason is that different operating systems have different features that a nontechnical user can and should understand. With many manufacturers offering a choice of operating systems, the question of which one to buy becomes increasingly important.

Important general features of operating systems are discussed next.

Available Application Software

This important feature deals with an operating system's acceptance in the marketplace. If the operating system is used by many vendors of application software (defined later) there will be available a wider selection of tasks that can be performed with the microcomputer. In 1985, the operating system called CP/M80 (from Digital Research) was by far the most widely supported operating system for 8-bit microcomputers. No single leader has emerged for the 8/16- and 16/32-bit microcomputers. CP/M-86 (Digital Research) and MS-DOS (Microsoft) are popular in the 8/16-bit market and UNIX-based operating systems (Bell Labs) such as XENIX (Microsoft) seem to be increasingly popular in the 16/32-bit microcomputers.

Single or Multiple User

This feature deals with the ability to accommodate one (single user) or more than one (multiple user) customer simultaneously. If the requirements call for simultaneous use of more than one terminal connected to one CPU, then a multiple-user operating system is necessary; otherwise a smaller, less complex, and less expensive single-user operating system should suffice.

Among single-user operating systems, CP/M, CP/M-86 (Digital Research), and MS-DOS (Microsoft) are popular. Among multiple-user operating systems UNIX (Bell Labs) and MP/M (Digital Research) are popular.

Multiple Tasks

This involves the ability of a user to perform different tasks independently and simultaneously. For example, a multiple task operating system would alphabetize a list of vendor names and addresses while the user is entering invoices at a terminal. The microcomputer can interrupt the user at the terminal when the alphabetizing is complete. Multiple task operating systems are useful when performing functions that are processing oriented—functions requiring no user intervention at the terminal.

Two points about multiple task operating systems sometimes are puzzling. Multiple tasking should not be confused with print spooling. Print spooling is an important and useful feature in which a printing job is sent to a disc drive for later printing. Print spooling looks like multiple tasking but it is not. Multiple-user capability should not be confused with multiple tasking. The two features can occur together in one operating system, but not always. Concurrent CP/M (Microsoft) is an example of a multiple-task, single-user operating system.

Portability

This deals with the ability to transport application programs and information between and among different microcomputers. This is useful when users outgrow a microcomputer. A portable operating system will help ease the conversion of programs and information from the old microcomputer to the new. At best, little or no modification to programs or information will be required.

This is an important point when considering how to deal with the growth in processing demands that normally occurs when people discover how microcomputers help make their jobs easier. The USCD-P operating system is an example of a generally portable operating system.

Programming Languages

Between the operating system and the application program (defined later) is the programming language. This type of software permits a person who writes application programs to do so in a human-oriented rather than machine-oriented form. The programming language takes a statement such as "ADD AMOUNT TO TOTAL" and converts that instruction to a series of codes that the microcomputer can understand.

As with the operating system, the programming language is of little or no concern to the average, nontechnical user. However, like the operating system, there are many choices of programming languages and the quantity and type available directly affect a microcomputer's overall versatility.

Some of the most common microcomputer programming languages are discussed next.

BASIC

This is a generic name for a number of similar programming languages. As a group, BASIC is by far the most popular microcomputer programming language. It is easy to learn, easy to work with, and, depending on the type, can perform many useful programming functions. While all BASIC programming languages are similar, they can and do differ greatly from one another. The ways in which they differ are important for the operating efficiency of the microcomputer; however, the details are best left to the many books on the subject.

The most important question potential buyers can ask is, "How many companies write application programs for this version of BASIC?" Having more companies supporting a version of BASIC means a wider range of application programs will be available. One of the most widely supported versions of BASIC is produced by Microsoft.

FORTRAN

This programming language is more standardized in form and capabilities than is BASIC. FORTRAN is a mathematically oriented language used primarily in scientific applications. It is available on many microcomputers but it is not widely supported with application programs.

COBOL

This is the primary business programming language on large computers. COBOL was written specifically for business use and can perform many of the tasks required in accounting-oriented applications. Like FORTRAN, it is far more standardized in form and capabilities than is BASIC.

COBOL programs tend to use more internal memory than BASIC or FORTRAN. For this reason it is not widely supported on microcomputers, particularly on the 8-bit models. However, some application software vendors are converting COBOL programs, written for large mainframes, to run on larger microcomputers. This could prove a good source of well-tested accounting-oriented application programs.

Other Programming Languages

Many other programming languages are available on microcomputers. A few are mentioned briefly so they will be recognized when they appear in a microcomputer's specification sheet.

PASCAL is a general-purpose language well suited for a wide variety of applications. It is becoming increasingly popular on the 8- and 8/16-bit microcomputers.

"C" and "M" are BASIC-like languages that are gaining popularity with UNIX-based operating systems on the 16/32-bit microcomputers.

FORTH, PILOT, and LOGO all are languages used primarily as tools for teaching microcomputer programming skills and their commercial applications generally are limited.

LISP is a specialized language used primarily by persons interested in a branch of microcomputer science known as artificial intelligence. Its commercial applications are limited. APL is a multipurpose programming language and is especially useful for tables of numbers. The APL language permits the operation to be completed in a whole matrix at one time rather than a row or a column at one time. This is an effective language to use to facilitate programming quickly.

Application Programs

These are the programs that perform a set of tasks directly beneficial to users. Persons operating a microcomputer interact directly with application programs, unless, of course, they know how to program and are actually writing the programs. Application programs for microcomputers are as diverse as the needs of individuals.

Chapter 11 is devoted to application programs oriented specifically toward the commercial food service industry. This section discusses more generic applications.

Electronic Spreadsheets

These application programs, sometimes referred to as "Calc" programs, help users who must manipulate large quantities of numeric information. They permit entering numbers into an electronic version of a multiple column accountant's spreadsheet, define the mathematical relationship between the numbers, and have the microcomputer calculate the totals for each column and row.

These programs also are useful in forming "what-if" analyses. For example, if serving sizes are increased by a certain amount, how much more food will be needed and how much will it cost. By simply changing a few numbers, all totals are recalculated automatically. These "Calc" programs go by many trade names: Lotus 1-2-3, VisiCalc (VisiCorp), Multiplan (Microsoft), WonderCalc (Businessoft International), and SuperCalc (Sorcim).

Word Processing

These programs permit users to enter letters, reports, and the like into the microcomputer, edit the material as many times as required (changing only the edited material), and print out perfect originals every time. Fancy versions of this application have features such as spelling verification, merging mailing lists with letters to create "personalized" form letters, math capabilities (for financial reports), and merging financial information, such as overdue accounts receivable, into letters, thereby creating past-due notices.

Word processing is most useful in situations where: (1) documents go through multiple drafts, (2) documents are used a number of times with minor changes, and (3) lengthy documents are produced. Word processing is least useful when typing consists primarily of short, unique documents. Word processing can use large amounts of disc storage and other microcomputer resources and, as stated earlier, letter quality printers are expensive.

Learning to use all the capabilities of a good word processing package takes a lot of effort. Word processing can be very useful. Many people who try it refuse to return to regular typing. However, it has costs beyond simply buying a word processing application program. Those costs and needs should be evaluated before investing. Examples of word processing programs include Wordstar (Micropro), Easy Writer II (Information Unlimited) and Superwriter (Sorcim).

Accounting Applications

The first and probably the largest commercial application of microcomputers is accounting: general ledger, accounts payable, accounts receivable, payroll, and fixed assets. Of these "Big Five" accounting applications, the first three are the most common for microcomputers.

In general, payroll is best left manual or contracted to a company specializing in computerized payrolls. The costs and risks involved in computerized payroll seldom are exceeded by the benefits derived by small organizations. Most microcomputer users do not have sufficiently numerous or complex fixed asset structures to warrant computerizing fixed asset accounting. It would require an entire book to explain how to select and install general ledger, accounts payable, and accounts receivable accounting applications.

The best advice in selecting applications is to seek professional assistance from an accountant or consultant experienced in computerized applications. If an institution wants to acquire accounting applications by itself (many individuals do it successfully), it should carefully analyze how its accounting information is processed. The normal flow of transactions through the present accounting system should be determined as well as, perhaps more important, abnormal events that occur. As a general rule, 20 percent of the transactions in an accounting system will cause 80 percent of the problems. Requirements analysis is discussed in the next section.

Databases

These programs fall somewhere between application programs and programming languages. Their main purpose is to help establish relationships among various kinds of information and, using other programs, manipulate the information in various ways. Databases might be thought of as electronic filing cabinets. By arranging a system of file drawers, file folders, and paper within folders, information can be arranged in a way that suits user needs. Then, with other application programs, selected drawers and folders can be opened to add, manipulate, change, replace, or delete various pieces of information.

For example: Assume it is necessary to know the dietary needs of a number of people. A database can be used to maintain information about those persons. When important attributes are defined, such as food allergies, and disease conditions such as diabetes, hypoglycemia, and the like, the microcomputer can be asked to print a list of all individuals in the database with an allergy to a certain food. This simple example illustrates their many potential uses.

Several companies market databases for microcomputers. Two of the most popular are dBase II (Ashton-Tate) and 1-2-3 (Lotus). Other companies market helpful application programs, training aids, and other materials.

STRUCTURED ACQUISITION APPROACH

By this point, there should be an understanding of some basic facts about microcomputer equipment, microcomputer software, and basic functions that can be performed. Next is a sequence of steps to follow in acquiring microcomputer equipment and software. This is a time-proved method and, when completed properly, greatly increases the odds in favor of a successful computerization project.

As stated earlier, this method is oriented toward off-the-shelf equipment and software. Custom applications require a somewhat more complex approach so they are not discussed here.

Determining Feasibility

This step answers the question: "Do you need a microcomputer or just want one?" This is an important question because it helps set realistic expectations early in the process. If there are undefined expectations about benefits desired from computerization, the odds of achieving those benefits are small and the odds of disappointment from unfulfilled expectations are high. If expectations are specific, then knowing what they are will help guide purchasing efforts and increase the odds of achieving them.

Completing the following four steps will help determine realistic expectations about microcomputers.

1. Deciding on General Functions for the Computer: With an understanding of some functions a microcomputer can perform in a commercial environment, it is possible to select from them or define some specific others. If possible, these functions should be quantified and rank ordered. For example: On a scale of 1 to 10, it may be decided that database functions are very important and they may be assigned a 10; electronic spreadsheets may get a 7 as somewhat important, and word processing may be assigned a 3 as "nice to have." It is advisable to avoid making "wish lists." These confuse the process. The function list should be restricted to those that have the potential to provide real benefits.

2. Conducting Initial Research: A well-informed buyer usually is a better, more successful buyer. There are many sources of more specific information about microcomputers. General publications such as *Byte Magazine, PC World, Compute,* and the weekly newspaper, *Infoworld,* are good sources of information about new products, product reviews, and microcomputer trends. *Datapro Research* publishes good comparisons of microcomputer equipment and some types of software. Friends who have microcomputers can be good sources of information; however, their opinions sometimes are biased for a number of reasons. Some money should be spent on this task: $50 to $100 invested in good reference material can help prevent a several thousand dollar mistake.

3. Rethinking General Tasks: Original tasks should be added, changed, reordered, or deleted, based on the research.

4. Setting Objectives and Benefits: It is essential to identify specific problems to be solved, situations to be improved, and general benefits the microcomputer should produce. Objectives and benefits should be quantified where possible to provide some means of determining whether or not they have been achieved. A quantified objective might read: "Reduce food waste by 10 percent through more accurate demand forecasting." The food service director may want a microcomputer simply for self-education and to experiment with. If that is the objective, it is certainly valid. The point is, there should be an objective.

Deciding Whether to Proceed

This decision depends on the food service director's own personal situation and the capital asset acquisition criteria of the institution. If the director or facility are financial analysis-oriented, there are many ways to estimate rate of return on the computer investment. The less financially oriented may rely on a gut feeling about the overall feasibility of the project. It probably is advisable to discuss the situation with an accountant or consultant experienced in these matters. Whatever the decision, if it is to move forward at this point, the project can always be aborted later. There still are several steps to complete before buying hardware or software.

This probably is the most important step in the process because unless the director knows exactly what features the microcomputer system should have, it is unlikely they will be included. Requirements definition is a complex topic. The exact method for defining requirements depends on the application program. For example: Requirements definitions for word processing differ from those for accounts payable. The following general tasks illustrate the basic requirements definition process.

Gather Examples of Documents in Present System

This will help determine specific functions the application program must perform, data it must store, and information it must report to management. It is important to be as specific as possible about all required inputs, functions, and outputs. The 80/20 rule discussed earlier applies here: 80 percent of problems are caused by 20 percent of transactions. It is advisable to concentrate on the unusual things that happen.

Estimate Volumes

This task is critical to acquiring a microcomputer large enough to meet the needs. For many microcomputer users, the input, storage, and output volumes are most important.

Input volumes deal with how many terminals will be needed. To calculate this, it is necessary to estimate the quantity of input documents that must be entered each day. The vendor should help calculate the total document entry time required. If the time exceeds about five hours a day, multiple terminals may be required.

Storage volumes deal with the disc storage capacity needed. The information to calculate this depends entirely on the application program, and meaningful general guidelines cannot be provided.

Output volumes deal with the size and speed of the printer(s) needed. Again, the information to calculate this depends heavily on the application program. One general rule to consider is: "Estimate volumes on peak demand, not average demand." Estimating volumes on average demand can cause a crisis during peak operating periods because the microcomputer may not have the capacity to accommodate such volumes. Another general rule is: "Estimate growth in volumes." Equipment purchased should accommodate present volumes and those expected over the next three to five years.

Document Requirements

A detailed list of requirements with examples of present system documents will help buyer and vendors decide whether a particular microcomputer and application program will satisfy the needs.

Finding and Evaluating Vendors

Armed with a clearly defined set of objectives and requirements, the buyer is ready to go forth boldly into the world of microcomputer vendors. The following general guidelines will help locate hardware and software that will satisfy all objectives and requirements.

239

Locate Software First

The finest microcomputer equipment in the world is useless without software that satisfies the requirements. In many cases equipment is bought to accommodate the software.

Buy Locally When Possible

Most first-time microcomputer users need assistance in installing their system. A local store usually is in a better position to offer that support than is a mail-order house.

See Software Running on Desired Hardware

It is essential to determine whether the software meets important requirements. If it does not, the buyer must decide whether to change the requirements or find a way to compensate for a missing element. It is advisable to look for these general characteristics: (a) Does the software reject user errors? (b) Does it use available function keys? (c) Are there "HELP" functions at difficult points in the program?

Review the Operator's Manual

Software is one area where it sometimes is possible to judge a book by its cover. A professional looking instruction manual often accompanies software. Some characteristics of a good manual are: (1) it is well indexed; (2) it contains sample problems; (3) it uses pictures and graphics; (4) it is readable, using little jargon; and (5) it defines jargon when it is used.

Size the Equipment Properly

It is important to consider the effect of growth in present volume and the possibility of adding new application programs. As a general rule, present peak volume estimates should not exceed two-thirds of the capacity being purchased. This means that terminal, internal memory, mass storage, and printing capacities should have the capability of handling about a 50 percent growth in volume without buying more equipment.

There also should be room to add memory, mass storage, terminals, and printers if the need for such growth can reasonably be foreseen. As a general rule, it is unwise to buy a maxed-out configuration. This means that if there is no room to add more devices, particularly mass storage, the director should consider purchasing a low-end model of a larger microcomputer.

Address Special Accounting Software Issues

Accounting application programs have some special issues to be considered:

- Programs should be in compliance with Generally Accepted Accounting Principles (GAAP). A statement of compliance should be obtained from the software vendor, particularly if the organization is subject to independent audits. It may be advisable to have the regular auditors review the programs because they will have to use the information from them during the audit.
- Programs should provide adequate audit trails. An audit trail permits tracing a balance on a financial statement back to the transactions that created it and

tracing a transaction to a balance on a financial statement. This is important even if no audit is conducted.

- The buyer should understand how to restart the microcomputer and recover from malfunctions or mistakes. This is critical when all business information is stored on a disc.
- Programs and equipment should provide adequate security against unauthorized access to sensitive business information. Security might include key locks on power switches, passwords for entry into application programs, and security checks at sensitive points in the program.

Ask for References

The best references are people running the same or similar application programs on the same or similar hardware. These sources should be asked about their good and bad experiences, how well the vendor supports them, whether they know of others who purchased from this vendor. These secondary references should be contacted. They often are more valuable than the vendor-supplied references simply because vendors typically give the names of people they expect will provide a good word.

Ask the Vendor About Support

The availability and cost of postsale support and service is an important factor in the purchase decision. Questions should include:

- What kind of training related to hardware and software is available? How much is free and how much does extra training cost?
- What kinds of service are available if the equipment breaks? Is onsite service available? Does the vendor service onsite or ship to a repair facility? Are loaners available? What is the average length of time a customer is down because of equipment failure? Is the vendor willing to warrant a minimum down time? How much does service cost?
- What are the warranty terms on equipment? What is covered under warranty? Are loaners available for warranty service? Where is warranty service performed? What is the software warranty? Can the software and/or hardware be returned for a full refund if not satisfactory? How can software be modified and upgraded? How much does the upgrade service cost? What help will the vendor provide to install upgrades? How much will the vendor's help cost?
- What kind of assistance does the vendor provide during installation of the equipment and application programs? Does the software vendor provide telephone support for answering questions? Is there a charge for this? Does the software vendor have an "800" number?

Obtain a 'Drive-Away' Price

This is the price including everything needed to get started. It is imperative to make sure the following items are included, as appropriate: cables and connectors, diskettes and tapes, paper, power line filters (if in an area with "dirty power" or electrical power surges that may affect computer function), furniture (if there is no sturdy place to put the microcomputer and printer), and, of course, all equipment

241

Exhibit 10–1 Evaluation matrix for microcomputer acquisition

Feature	Weighting factor	Raw score	Extended score
Software			
Fit with requirements	20	6	120
Optional features	1	3	3
Installed base	3	5	15
Documentation quality	10	7	70
Maintenance support	7	8	56
Hardware			
Fit with requirements	15	7	105
Growth in equipment	2	10	20
Growth in family	2	10	20
Maintenance support	7	7	49
Installed base	3	5	15
Cost			
Initial costs	10	5	50
Recurring costs	10	4	40
Vendor			
Experience in industry	2	0	0
Time in business	1	2	2
Financial stability	3	0	0
Reference reports	1	10	10
Degree of support offered	3	7	21
	100		560

Source: Reprinted with permission of Bruce Barker.

components, application programs, operating system, programming languages, and instruction manuals.

Evaluating vendors can be difficult. There are tangible factors such as cost and degree of fit with requirements. There are intangibles such as trust and vendor experience. One way of quantifying the tangible and intangible factors is a vendor evaluation matrix such as in Exhibit 10-1. To use this matrix, buyers should:

1. Identify Important Features: Decide about what features and attributes are most important to them. Use general categories like those on the sample matrix or identify very specific features from the requirements definition. Make the choice based on needs and penchant for analysis.
2. Determine Weighting Factor: Decide the relative importance of each feature selected, with all weighting factors totaling 100. A weighting factor of 20 means the feature is 20 times more important than one with a factor of 1.
3. Assign a Raw Score: Decide how each vendor compares with the others in terms of the features selected. On a scale of 1 to 10, a 0 indicates no fit with requirements and a 10 a nearly perfect fit. Different vendors can have the same raw score for a feature; this part is very subjective so try to be as objective as possible. Beware of inflating raw scores for vendors liked personally.
4. Calculate an Extended Score: Multiply the weighting factor by the raw score to yield the extended score. Total the extended score column. This is the

vendor's rating. By completing a matrix for each vendor and comparing the scores, it is possible to quantify to some extent the impressions and evaluation of each vendor.

Negotiating with the Selected Vendor

The results obtained from this step will vary greatly. If a relatively small system is being acquired from a large national vendor, negotiating success may be limited to a free box of diskettes; if a relatively large system from a locally owned microcomputer store, negotiating may produce more significant concessions. Some of the items to negotiate include:

- written commitments about the type and extent of training
- written commitments about the type, extent, location, and cost of equipment maintenance
- written commitments to refund some or all of the purchase price if the buyer is not satisfied
- written commitments as to the type, extent, and cost of installation support.

Even if it is not possible to negotiate concessions from the vendor, it is mandatory to reduce all understandings and agreements to writing and get the vendor to sign it. This process produces three benefits:

1. It identifies potential misunderstandings before purchase so the buyer can either resolve them or select another vendor.
2. It places the vendor on notice that the buyer is serious about the issues discussed.
3. It is useful to have something in writing if problems arise.

Planning Conversion to New System

Conversion means taking the information and manual procedures from the old system and adapting them for use with the new microcomputer. In the case of a completely new application program, such as an electronic spreadsheet, conversion may involve no more than establishing the formats. For example, where the new application replaces existing programs and procedures in an accounting situation, conversion is much more complex.

A detailed explanation of conversion planning is beyond the scope of this chapter. The purpose here is to provide an overview of some common steps to be taken in conversion planning.

Plan for Training Personnel

When numerous persons are going to use the new microcomputer, they must be trained. An effective method is to select a lead operator who will receive any vendor training and in turn teach others. A training plan should deal with questions such as:

- Who should be trained?
- How will they be trained (on the job, in the classroom, etc.)?

- When will they be trained?
- What topics should each person learn?

Plan for Converting Old Data

When replacing an existing system (manual or automated), historical data such as opening balances and open transactions must be converted for use by the new system. A data conversion plan should deal with questions such as:

- What data must be converted?
- How will it be converted?
- When will it be converted?
- How will the accuracy of the converted data be ensured?

Plan for Parallel Operation

Parallel operation involves running the new microcomputer system with the same data used by the old manual or automated system. The objective is to ensure the new microcomputer is processing data accurately. If discrepancies between the old and new systems are discovered, they must be reconciled. A parallel operation plan should deal with questions such as:

- When will parallel operation occur?
- How long should it run?
- How will discrepancies between systems be identified and resolved?
- What results are required to decide parallel operation is successful?
- Who is responsible for conducting parallel operation?

Plan for Conversion of Manual Procedures

Microcomputers often require changing the workflow of an office. If this is the case, it is necessary to deal with questions such as:

- Who will perform new tasks?
- How should they perform the tasks?
- Who is responsible for controlling and reviewing information entered into the microcomputer?
- How will old tasks change?
- How will work be allocated?
- How will the new procedures be documented?

In general, conversion plans should be written and agreed to by all persons involved. This will help assure the commitment of those charged with the conversion process. Conversion is not easy under ideal conditions. Unplanned conversions have a high probability of failure or at least a significant increase in difficulty. Anyone converting accounting systems, particularly partially automated accounting systems, might wish to consult with someone experienced in conversions.

The nature and extent of user training depends on the complexity of the application program(s) involved. Some may require only a few hours with the instruction manual and some practice problems for entry into the microcomputer. More complex applications may require formal training sessions complete with overhead slides, procedure manuals, sample forms, and practice exercises. Between these extremes are a wide range of techniques.

The important point to remember is that no users should be turned loose on the microcomputer in a live operating environment without the minimum level of training. The confusion and frustration felt by untrained persons can influence their perception of the microcomputer for many months or perhaps permanently. If most or all users have a negative perception of the microcomputer, a successful conversion is severely jeopardized. Also, untrained users are more likely to make errors and less likely to find them. In summary, untrained users cost money through mistakes, inefficiency, and poor acceptance of change. At a minimum, new users should be provided with:

1. time to read, study, ask questions about, and understand the instruction manual
2. sample problems with sample solutions for them to enter into the microcomputer
3. instructions about who to ask if problems or questions occur
4. an opportunity to feel comfortable with the microcomputer before being introduced to a live operating environment.

These minimum training requirements apply to every user, including the person responsible for installing the microcomputer. In this case, that person should have already arranged with the vendor for some training and support that will allow completion of these minimum requirements.

Converting to the New System

Anyone who has understood and completed the steps outlined in this chapter has accomplished more than most first-time microcomputer users: they have learned the basic facts about microcomputers, set realistic objectives and expectations, defined requirements, selected hardware and software using a logical and thorough approach, planned how to install the microcomputer and trained self and employees. Now it is time to begin using the microcomputer, secure in the knowledge that the odds for success are greater than average.

Most people who fear microcomputers simply do not understand them. As this chapter has shown, there is no real magic behind these machines. By understanding some simple principles and applying common sense, most people can deal with them. By applying a little more effort, most can learn to write their own simple programs, although this is by no means necessary for those who just want to enjoy the practical, time-saving benefits a properly selected microcomputer can provide.

Food service operations represent a fertile field of applications for microcomputers. This topic is explored in Chapter 11.

245

REFERENCES

Blumenthal, Howard J. *Everyone's Guide to Personal Computers*. New York: Ballantine Books, Inc., 1983.

Bradbeer, Robin, et al. *The Beginner's Guide to Computers*. Reading, Mass.: Addison-Wesley Publishing Company, 1982.

Coan, James S. *Basic Basic*. Rochelle Park, NJ: Hayden, 1978.

Datapro Research Corporation. ''The Top Microcomputer Systems at a Glance.'' Datapro Research Corporation, February 1985.

National Restaurant Association. *1984 Food Service Industry Pocket Fact Book*.

Osborne, Adam. *Business Systems Buyer's Guide*. Berkeley, Calif.: Osborne/McGraw-Hill, 1982.

Vles, Joseph M. *Computer Fundamentals for Nonspecialists*. New York: Amacom, 1981.

Zaks, Rodney. *Introduction to PASCAL*. Berkeley, Calif.: Sybex, 1981.

Computer Food Service Applications

Those in the food service industry often can justify a microcomputer simply on the basis of the general application programs discussed in Chapter 10. Add the functions and capabilities of the current food management and nutrition analysis programs and an even better justification is possible. Although computers cannot provide a solution to every management problem, they can be a useful tool to help in solving the problems.

Often, the speed with which computers assist in problem solving allows the food service department to find even more uses for them. The time that is "freed" for the director or manager because the computer is performing the routine calculations, gives more time to manage and more time to invent new uses. The computer can put managers on an upward spiral whereby the more they use the machine to assist in problem solving, the more uses they will find for it.

Food service is the second greatest cost center in any health care institution after nursing. Computers can provide more effective management of the resources of time, money, and labor, thus controlling costs while preserving quality. Gone are the days when costs could take a back seat to quality of service. They are of at least equal importance today.

COMPUTING CATEGORIES

There are five categories of computing (their applicability to food service is discussed next):

1. Data processing, which includes billing, accounts payable, accounts receivable, inventory control, etc., is in wide use.
2. Numerical calculations that result in answers to mathematical problems such as analyses of cost and labor could have infinite uses in food service.
3. Logical processing, which is still being developed, enables computers to appear "smart;" examples include programs that translate languages and play chess.
4. Control processing that determines the next action to be taken from prior information given to the computer has unlimited potential for some indus-

tries. An example of this type of process is the design computers used by architectural and engineering firms.

5. Word/text processing for writing letters, storing information, and editing text provides a valuable service for virtually every type of business.

FOOD SERVICE APPLICATIONS

These five categories provide the basis for numerous specific uses for the computer in food service:

- Ingredient Management: Permits entering and maintaining costs, unit size, and other information about each food item used.
- Recipe Management: Permits building and maintaining different recipes based on the ingredients used.
- Menu Management: Permits building and maintaining menus based on recipes.
- Recipes and Menu Costing: Calculates cost per recipe and menu based on ingredient costs.
- Diet Management: Permits appropriate recipes to be assigned to diets, which helps prevent preparing a particular recipe for the wrong diet.
- Menu Planning: Helps automate this function by extending a menu cycle throughout a selected period.
- Purchasing Assistance: Indicates what ingredients to order based on the menu plan.
- Ingredient Pull List: Calculates and prints, based on the menu plan, a list of ingredients that should be pulled from food storage areas.
- Individual Profiles: Calculates various nutrition and caloric requirements for a person based on the individual's needs. Permits dietary changes to be recommended, if indicated.
- Recipe and Menu Analysis: Analyzes the nutrients available in a serving, recipe, or menu and compares them to the Recommended Daily Dietary Allowances.

MICROCOMPUTER POTENTIAL IN FOOD SERVICE

Perhaps the biggest failing of computers is that they must be programmed. Humans must give them explicit instructions or they will not perform. This is not really a computer failing at all, since the machines are performing as designed.

One advantage of microcomputers is that they are relatively easy to program, compared with bigger machines. Most of the small machines are intended to be used interactively. This mode involves a "conversation" between the machine and the user, as the user digs the information wanted out of the computer's memory. While bigger computers have large memories and are good at producing stacks of printouts, that often is a clumsy way to retrieve information. If the microcomputer is programmed properly, it can be used conversationally to determine the information the manager needs.

In a good food service applications program the machine will "prompt" the user in a way that will guide the search for information. The user responds in such a way as to continue the search until the exact desired information is found, or until the search is abandoned. A typical dialogue might be:

MICRO: What information do you need?
USER: Cost (this is punched in at the keyboard).
MICRO: Cost of what?
USER: Menu item.
MICRO: Enter the code of the menu item.
USER: ABC123
MICRO: There is no menu item with this code. Please enter the code of the menu item.
USER: ABC124
MICRO: Cost information for APPLESTRUDEL, code ABC124 . . .

The program provides a series of prompts or cues, to which the user responds with a limited set of words recognizable to the computer. A good program will not require the user to develop a different way of conducting business. Instead, it will conform to the way a food service operates, using words and ideas familiar to the manager. What the user has to learn is the limited language to which the computer can respond. If this limited language consists of words ordinarily used in food service management, this should not be difficult.

Organizing and Integrating Data

When viewed as a business, food service is one of the most complicated to manage, primarily because it must manufacture and serve a large number of different products, each in very low volume. The food service decision maker is faced with integrating information about hundreds of products, hundreds of ingredients, and many other factors when planning or implementing plans.

To be effective, software applications in food service should integrate menu planning material with information pertinent to the decision at hand so that the ripple effects can be displayed for the manager. For example, substituting one menu item for another happens regularly in many facilities. Some questions that then occur to the manager are:

- How does this change affect the budget?
- How does this change the inventory?
- How does this change procurement?
- Is there holding space for the new item?
- How does this affect labor utilization?
- How does this change affect the nutrient content of the menu?

Good computer software for food service will incorporate the intended changes in such a fashion that these effects can be anticipated.

'What-If' Ability

The ability to simulate the consequences of a decision is termed the "what-if" ability. The computer can answer the question, "What if we make this change?"

The main difficulty with most existing software for food service is that it applies to only one aspect of the operation, such as procurement, when the manager needs information that treats the entire operation as a single system. Some software packages allow the user to pose "what-if" questions, but the scope of the answers generally is limited by the program.

Until the last two years, microcomputers were unable to treat the entire food service as a single system effectively. The main problem was the large data storage requirement. Newer microcomputers, however, offer enhanced on-line storage as well as very large capacity through peripherals such as hard disc drives. A properly configured microcomputer (one with adequate on-line storage) could be used effectively for treating the food service as a system. The many interrelationships among menu planning, budgeting, labor scheduling, nutrition assessment, inventory management, and other important factors can be retrieved and displayed in an integrated fashion for consideration by the manager when programming is in place.

Data Gathering and Structuring

To take advantage of the power of the machine to organize and integrate food service information, the data describing the department's activities must be collected and entered into the machine. Since the chief product is the menu item, that is the focal point of the data-gathering efforts. Ingredients are related to the menu item by recipes, which should be standardized so that the same information is available consistently for every menu item.

The computer is literal minded. It does not differentiate between a recipe involving 12 ingredients and three hours baking from a container of milk. It may not be customary to have a "recipe" for one serving of milk but it is important for the computer to have data about the ingredients and other resources necessary to provide this menu item (one serving of milk) to the customer.

What is easy for the flexible brain of a human to comprehend and adjust is impossible for a literal-minded machine. Even though trivial recipes are not important to humans, they are critical for giving the computer a systematic picture of the food service operation. If the operation does not customarily keep this kind of information standardized and available, the manager should develop it so the software packages can function properly.

Coding Structure

Since there are so many potential menu items, most software uses some kind of coding structure for identifying and distinguishing among them and for ingredients. Although such codes may seem to be unnecessary "computerese," they are necessary for many reasons. Quite often menu items and ingredients have the same name and cannot be distinguished by inflexible machines. Milk, eggs, and rice are examples. In other cases the names of items are very similar, even though the items themselves are different—"milk, chocolate" and "milk chocolate" for example.

To distinguish between these items a code is a more reliable device than names. A code is more convenient to the user as it is easier to punch five or six characters on the keyboard than an entire menu item name. Finally, codes allow the computer to search for information more quickly. Instead of having to compare all the letters in the name of an item, it needs to compare only the characters in the code.

Codes can be structured to help the user identify the menu item sought. If the code is mixed letters and numbers, i.e. ABC123, the letters can represent menu item categories and the numbers can give the final identification. MBC004 might mean Menu item, Beef, Casserole, number 4.

Because of the many similar names, the software must be able to distinguish menu item codes from ingredient codes in some unmistakable way. An example ingredient code might be IVG003 or simply VG003 to distinguish it from menu item codes. Some codes consist entirely of numbers. This has the advantage of allowing entry on a numeric keypad, which an experienced user can do very rapidly. This extra speed is not much advantage unless large amounts of data are entered regularly. In most cases a combination of letters and numbers is remembered and used more easily.

Units and Unit Problems

Other data that may be required include price information about the ingredients and other inputs to menu items. In some cases suppliers may have price data on electronic media that a microcomputer can read directly. It will save time and money if this is possible, but this information may require special augmentation of the computer as well as special programming. Software also must deal with the "units problem." Often the purchase unit for an ingredient (a case of number 10 cans, for example) is not the same as the issue unit (one number 10 can) which is not the same as the recipe unit (one cup). The software should convert recipe units to purchase units in order to cost menu items properly.

Some investigation is warranted to determine whether the software can in fact handle units. The units problem gets more complicated when ingredients (weiners, for example) are purchased and issued by the pound but the recipe calls for "one." An important question about any software is how it computes weight-to-item or weight-to-volume conversions in these situations.

Because of these conversions, it is not realistic to expect that every system will cost every menu item exactly the same. The important thing about any system is that it handles the costing procedure consistently from menu item to menu item. The manager then can compare costs of items and understand what the comparison means. The use of such a system over time will allow valid comparisons to evolve when the numbers displayed by the machine are factored through the judgment of the manager.

Menu Plan

Other information that may be entered is a plan for the entire menu cycle. This usually is a specification, meal by meal or hour by hour, of the expected number of menu items of each type that will be served. Just what planning periods are chosen will depend on the food service. Patient feeding may require planning meal by meal, while a coffee shop may wish to plan day by day or even week by week. Software should allow the choice of different types of planning periods.

Nutrient Data

If a software package promises nutrient information for meals or menu items, it is important to investigate the data entry requirements. If nutrient data must be entered for hundreds of menu items whose ingredient composition may shift from time to time, it may be advisable not to use the software. There are, however, nutrient data bases on electronic media that are readable by microcomputer. Most of these are based on USDA *Handbooks 8* and *456*.[1,2] If the software requires the use of one of these data bases, it is important to make sure the microcomputer chosen can access and use that data base.

Much information about nutrition may come self-contained in a program. Although such programs can provide useful information, it is not integrated with other food service information to help in decision making. Until such integration occurs, nutrient information will not be as important as cost to the manager.

Data Structure

For these data to be used by a microcomputer, it is important they be structured properly. A food service manager may be required to determine the cost of the noon meal in a hospital facility without the aid of a computer. If the data are well organized, they can be retrieved from filing cabinets and reports, and—after tedious calculations—the meal cost can be produced. To accomplish this at all, the information must be organized for easy retrieval.

The same is true for electronic computation. The information describing menu items and ingredients must be organized so it can be retrieved quickly and used easily for computation and display. Inefficient organization can make programs slow and cumbersome to use. Proper organization not only will make the computer response quicker but also can help integrate a systems approach. The organization that works on a large computer may not be efficient or even possible on a microcomputer. If a program has been adapted from a large computer to a micro, it should be tested thoroughly to determine whether it still is convenient to the user.

Much software has been written for food service that deals with some specific concerns of the manager. Even though a package integrating the entire food service and treating it as a single system is not yet available, it is important that the programs employed fit into the service's managerial schemes.

The manager may be able to use bits and pieces of output from existing programs to aid in decision making as long as the entire system is kept in mind. The key to good decision making is having the right information at the right time. Where the amounts of information are large, as in a food service operation, a properly programmed microcomputer can be an invaluable aid to the manager.

According to *The Stokes Report*'s July 1982 survey in which more than 200 responses were received, nearly a quarter of those responding already were using computers, with the largest percentage of these in nonprofit hospitals with more than 200 beds. The facilities are using computers for many things, as detailed in Exhibit 11–1.

MICROCOMPUTER APPLICATION CHALLENGES

As with every microcomputer application, food service offers potential areas of challenge. Here are a few to consider:

- Large Disc Storage Requirements: These programs are based to a large extent on nutrient information from various sources. These databases (not related to database applications discussed earlier) could exceed several million characters. Disc storage sizing is critical in this situation.

Exhibit 11–1 Uses of computers in food service

Use	Percent
The top ten:	
1. Budget updates	57
2. Cost accounting	54
3. Current inventory	40
4. Billing	31
5. Ordering	26
6. Purchasing inventory	20
7. Meal card printing	17
8. Food production plan	14
9. Ingredient issue	14
10. Precosting	3

Other uses mentioned include:

- Diet orders
- Admissions, transfers, and discharges
- Patient information
- Communication from floors
- Documenting resident intake
- Payroll
- Program reporting
- Accounting
- Menu tallies
- Menu price groups
- Nutrient analysis
- Calorie counts
- Meal price groups
- Policies and procedures
- Job descriptions
- Files
- Unit stock orders from nursing units

- Frequent Database Maintenance: Accurate costing reports will require constant updating of price information in the ingredient file. Careful consideration should be given to the clerical effort required.

- Nonintegration with Other Applications: In general, these applications appear to stand alone, with no automatic feedthrough of information to general ledger or accounts payable applications. This lack of integration results in duplicate data entry if stand-alone food service programs are used with accounting applications.

NOTES

1. Watt, B.K. & Merril, A.L. et al. *Composition of Foods*, Agriculture Research Service, USDA, Washington, D.C.: 1975.

2. Adams, Katherine S. *Nutritive Value of American Foods in Common Units*, Agriculture Research Service, USDA, Washington, D.C.: 1975.

Chapter 12

Energy Cost Management: Dollars and Sense

As energy costs continue to climb, the advantages of conservation translate into significant dollars saved. The cost of utilities has become a major portion of any facility's operating budget and, depending on its size, service, and geographical location, the food service operation can demand 20 percent to 50 percent of the total energy bill. According to Secretary of Health, Education, and Welfare Joseph A. Califano, Jr., in FY '79 health care facilities wasted $1.3 billion in energy cost.[1]

Every food service department can save at least $10,000 a year in energy conservation alone. Simple techniques, many of which require little or no investment, provide opportunities for significant cost savings. For example, the Desert Terrace Nursing Center in Phoenix, Ariz., realized a 16 percent reduction in such costs within six months of implementing noninvestment energy-saving techniques in the food service department.

Energy management programs must begin with administrative commitment. The concept of conservation usually is appealing; however, sincere commitment in identifying funds available and support for necessary policy changes are key factors in developing a successful program. An active desire for the organization and follow-through of an energy management program must come from the highest levels of administration.

STRATEGIC PLAN FOR ENERGY SAVINGS

The strategic planning approach (Chapter 1) is an excellent method by which to establish an efficient energy management program. This systematic, step-by-step effort can assure the clear definition of goals as well as provide a workable outline for implementation. The mission statement, or purpose, must be identified first. The purpose of the program must be defined in terms that can be understood easily by successive administrations yet are definitive enough to encompass the facility's overall goals. For example, a clearly identified mission statement for an energy management program might be "to establish and perpetuate energy conservation techniques throughout the facility to result in a savings of 10 percent annually in total energy costs." Definite guidelines for the program enable its success to be measured objectively.

255

Methods of achieving this goal, or mission statement, can then be explored. The scope of the program will depend on many factors:

- The facility size (total conditioned square feet, total operating efficiency in layout and design, and scope of service provided) is of primary importance. Each of these factors could have significant impact on the amount of energy used.
- The older the building, the greater the opportunities to reduce the energy used. Approximately 80 percent of the hospitals in the United States were built before 1973, and therefore were not designed with energy efficiency in mind.
- Additions, expansion, or other structural changes may affect energy efficiency.
- Food services utilize significant amounts of energy, and older equipment may show deterioration, affecting operating efficiency. Nearly all manufacturers emphasize energy efficiency in most of their recent equipment designs.
- A monetary commitment from administration is vital. Many energy conservation opportunities require little, if any, investment; however, equipment replacement or additions can prove cost effective if funds are available.

Energy Management Team

The most efficient means to identify the scope of the program, as well as the needs of the facility, is through the establishment of an energy management team or committee.

Administration and department heads may be hesitant to form another committee, yet the multidisciplinary character of energy management makes interdepartmental communication essential. While it is not essential that department heads be involved directly, committee members must be given the authority to make policy decisions affecting the entire facility. They must be able to act quickly, without the delays caused by the need to seek authority to make decisions.

The size of the committee will depend upon the size of the facility; however, the following types of participants are recommended:

- Administrator or Assistant Administrator: It is important that a representative of administration chair the group to guide the decisions of all departments. Some facilities have designated the director of engineering as chair. It is recommended, however, because of the multidisciplinary authority held by administration, that the administrator or assistant be the leader.
- Finance: In some institutions, the administrator may represent the financial department; however, in large facilities, the controller will be helpful in identifying available funds. Plans for expansion or monetary commitments may influence energy management decisions.
- Director of Engineering: If the facility has a building and grounds committee, a representative may be needed. The director of engineering is an essential team member as this position alone has a working knowledge of heating, air conditioning, ventilation, and water heating equipment throughout the facility.
- Director of Nursing: Nursing service, which usually is the largest department in a health care facility, should be represented by the director or assistant

director of nursing. Daily routines that involve equipment, water, and other utilities can significantly affect energy costs.

- Food Service Director: This individual, or the assistant director, should represent food service, as it is one of the most energy-intensive departments of the health care facility. Preparation, refrigeration, and ventilation require significant amounts of energy, and proper use can result in significant savings.

These participants are essential, although other departments may be included as needed, such as laundry and housekeeping; physician, especially if energy-intensive equipment is used regularly; public relations department; security; an energy consultant; and a board member.

The function and goals of the committee involve a three-step approach: (1) identifying current energy utilization, (2) defining opportunities for energy conservation, and (3) implementing ideas to reduce energy utilization.

IDENTIFYING ENERGY UTILIZATION

The simplest yet most effective means to evaluate energy utilization is through a hands-on review of utility bills. All such bills (and other energy-related costs such as water and sewage fees, etc.) should be assembled for a 12-month period. Actual utilization will be available on utility bills. Monthly records (Exhibit 12–1) should then be charted on a master work sheet so that usage of electricity, gas, and oil can be tracked easily.

A graph illustrating energy utilization over a 12-month period is an excellent means of displaying months of highest usage. Actual percentages and dollar figures can then be assigned as conservation goals.

Exhibit 12–1 Energy use record

BTU utilization	*Electricity*	*Gas*	*Steam*	*Oil*	*Total*
January					
February					
March					
April					
May					
June					
July					
August					
September					
October					
November					
December					

To provide a basis for an equivalent comparison, all energy utilized, whether it be kilowatt hours, cubic feet of natural gas, gallons of oil, or pounds of steam, must be converted to BTUs (British Thermal Units):

Source	Measure	BTUs
Electricity	KWH (kilowatt hour)	3,413
Natural Gas	Cubic foot	1,000
Oil	Gallon	140,000
Steam	Pound	1,000

For example, 120 kilowatt hours converts to (120 KWH $\times$ 3,413) = 409,560 BTUs.

Peak Loading

The concept of peak loading is an important consideration. Many utility companies base a facility's rate on the maximum energy utilized at any given time. If, for example, a hospital simultaneously used major energy-consuming equipment, such as is in the operating rooms, x-ray, and food service, the surge of power required would determine the rate scale for months to come. Load-shedding devices are available to avoid unnecessary peak loads by reducing the energy available to certain pieces of equipment when a predetermined utilization level is approached.

For example, when a large amount of energy is required at one time, the load shedder lowers the total electricity required by arbitrarily turning off designated equipment requiring power. Equipment to be turned off briefly by the load-shedding device is most often "non-critical," such as air-conditioning units. Therefore, the danger of food service equipment being turned off indiscriminately is negated. Other systems provide an alarm when the peak usage limit is approached. Load-shedding devices do, however, indicate accurately the highest demand periods and billing rates by measuring kilowatts used through a power meter. Employee education on this issue is essential. By careful production scheduling and menu planning, food service equipment use can be maximized while eliminating the need for all of it to be used simultaneously. Supervision must be an integral part of an energy management program.

Building Survey

When actual utilization has been identified, the energy management team can conduct an onsite review of consumption throughout the facility. Survey or energy audits can be as complex as to involve computerized monitoring systems, or they can be as basic as a walk-through evaluation of the building. Depending on the funds available, experienced energy consultants may be hired to increase the effectiveness of the building survey and identify changes to improve conservation. Federal and state grants may be available for some energy audits, although strict guidelines may need to be identified to conform to detailed government standards to receive such funding.

The Energy Policy and Conservation Act and the Energy Conservation and Production Act require energy audits to establish criteria for determining whether the installation of a particular modification meets certain requirements for designation as an Energy Conservation Measure. Meeting these criteria can qualify the energy conserving as a tax benefit or make it eligible for federal financial assistance. Energy audits must include:

- a visit to the building by an auditor qualified by the state for a technical, mechanically oriented audit (Class A audit) or completion of a workbook provided by the state (Class C audit). (A Class B audit also exists, but is almost as technical as a Class A; most facilities choose to complete a Class A audit if a technical audit is selected.)
- recommendations and an analysis of energy and cost savings likely to result from energy conservation measures
- a building profile, indicating location; climate; site conditions; configurations, construction; heating, ventilating, air-conditioning, and lighting systems; energy consumption; and cost of energy for the preceding 12 months.

The following items must be evaluated before a walk-through survey:

- Building blueprints and layouts; if blueprints are unavailable, coordinate with the director of engineering in making drawings of the building's layout and the heating and ventilation system.
- Any plans for renovation or other changes that will affect long-range planning and energy management policy.
- Persons who are to conduct the walk-through; these should not include individuals who may be biased, such as the original designer or representatives of engineering firms who may have an interest in future construction. Include only essential team members, as large groups may become less efficient as the survey is conducted.
- Applicable codes, such as (1) state and local fire codes; (2) local electrical, mechanical, and plumbing codes; (3) local elevator codes; and (4) federal pollution control regulations.

Preorganization cannot be overemphasized. The actual onsite observations should be succinct and accurate, with minimal disturbance to daily operation. The following tools are recommended:

- tape recorder, preferably hand-held type
- camera, including flash attachment and extra film
- light meter (available at camera dealers)
- thermometers, including refrigerator thermometers; holding thermometers, which maintain the highest temperature reached to test dishmachine rinse temperatures; food thermometers; and surface thermometers, which indicate the temperature of flat surfaces, such as heated bases.

A checklist is a helpful guideline on the actual onsite survey. Appendix G is a review of food service equipment utilization. All checklists must be modified to reflect the needs and functions of each individual facility and should reflect the types of equipment there. Before the onsite evaluation, all equipment should be identified as to manufacturer/model number, serial number, date purchased, and energy required for operation. Recent repairs or part replacements also should be identified. Some of this information can be found on a metal place affixed to the equipment. Manufacturers can be helpful in clarifying model numbers and energy requirements.

The food service department survey should evaluate equipment for the following:

1. Proper utilization: Is equipment being used for the purpose for which it was designed? For example, one survey revealed that a convection oven was being used solely to heat plates.
2. Proper maintenance: Is all equipment evaluated regularly to make adjustments before major repairs or replacements are required? A preventive maintenance program is essential for health care facilities complying with Joint Commission on Accreditation of Hospitals regulations but also is important in saving time and money in major equipment repairs.
3. Equipment efficiency: Is current equipment working well? Energy efficiency has increased substantially with new designs in equipment. Some replacement equipment may pay for itself in energy savings.

DEFINING CONSERVATION OPPORTUNITIES

The following areas should be observed during the building survey; they can lead to the identification of energy conservation opportunities (ECOs). The survey should look particularly at the operation and utilization of equipment.

Lighting

Lighting in the food service area should be evaluated. A simple pocket light meter, held 30 inches from walls and windows and 30 inches from the floor, is an accurate measurement of illumination as stated in foot-candles. Each area should be measured, including walls, work surfaces, etc., both with lights on and with several or all lights off.

Traditionally, incandescent bulbs are used for most general lighting purposes. These bulbs are rated at an efficiency of 17.5 lumens per watt and produce 90 percent of their energy as heat rather than light. Fluorescent lights are more than four times as efficient, providing 80 lumens per watt, and are ideal for institutional food service settings. Regulations under the Occupational Safety and Health Act require fluorescent light bulbs in food service areas to be covered.

The Illuminating Engineering Society recommends 30 to 70 foot-candles for the overall kitchen area, 15 to 20 foot-candles for informal dining areas and 10 foot-candles for storage areas. The age of the bulbs should be checked as older ones are weaker and less efficient.

The following suggestions can help achieve maximum efficiency in lighting. The department should:

- Replace nondecorative incandescent lights with more energy-efficient fluorescent lights.
- Disconnect nonutilized fluorescent ballasts to save energy and prevent damage.

260

- Paints walls and ceilings in light colors to reflect light. Clean walls regularly to maximize reflection of natural light.
- Clean lamps and fixtures regularly.
- Use timers in areas generally unused to be certain that lights do not remain on after the department is closed.
- Install signs instructing users to turn off lights when finished.
- Reorganize task areas to eliminate unnecessary illumination.
- Install light sensors or dimmers to compensate automatically for varying lighting conditions.
- Consider small area switching where an individual task area may be used only intermittently.

Innovative techniques for controlling the amount of light required for optimum working conditions have been developed. For example, Controlled Environment Systems, Inc. of Rockville, Md., produces a system by which room light level is read by a sensor and the arc current of standard fluorescent lamps and ballasts is adjusted accordingly. Thus, a standard light level is maintained within a given area. The sensor adjusts the lights for daylight as well as the intensity of other lights. It is estimated the system could pay for itself in two to four years from energy savings throughout a building.

Although fluorescent bulbs are indeed much more efficient than incandescents, they become inefficient in light output over time. Dust accumulation, phosphor decay, and erosion of cathode material reduce output. Some areas thus may be subject to overlighting; that is, more than enough lights are provided to allow for system deterioration. Simply removing every other fixture is not an accurate means of determining optimum light requirements since a 50 percent reduction in wattage reduces illumination by only 40 percent. The use of automatic light determining systems can prevent overlighting, reducing the number of fixtures required and lengthening the life of existing fluorescent lamps.

Refrigeration

Refrigeration equipment operates 24 hours daily and is an essential part of any food service operation. Energy consumption should be evaluated in terms of compressor running time—how long the compressor has to run to maintain the proper internal temperature, as compared with compressor off time.

National Sanitation Foundation (NSF) standards are based on 100° ambient temperature, nonload conditions, with no door openings: storage refrigeration, compressor runs 70 percent of the time to maintain proper temperature; short-term and display refrigerator, compressor runs 100 percent of the time to maintain proper temperature; storage freezers, compressor runs 80 percent of the time to maintain proper temperature.

Actual running time will far exceed the standard under normal conditions because of loading, door opening, etc. Refrigeration capacity needed for optimum food service operation should be determined; storage that is too large wastes energy. Inadequate refrigeration results in overcrowding, poor air circulation, and consequently increased compressor running time. Compressors should be sized to have just enough power to handle maximum daily heat loads. The area of the country and the location of the refrigerator and compressor are significant factors when considering size.

261

Insulation

Energy savings are directly attributable to insulation. Thermal conductivity is measured in numerical terms as "K" factor. The lower the number, the better the material resists the flow of heat and acts as a good insulation.

$$H = \frac{K \times A \times T \times 24R}{W}$$

where

H = heat transfer
K = thermal conductivity
A = sq. feet of area
T = temperature differential
R = hours
W = thickness of walls

For example, fiberglass has a K factor of .32, and expanded urethane, R11, has a K factor of .17, making polyurethane the better insulation material.

Walk-in refrigeration insulation traditionally has been three and a half to four inches thick; however, insulation now available is five inches thick, which is recommended for outdoor or high-temperature applications.

Magnetic gaskets should always be used to ensure tight closing. Large doors may require a cam-lock device that closes tightly to prevent loss of cool air. Self-closing hinges provide a positive seal and prevent air leakage. Strip curtains—overlapping strips of thick, translucent plastic—prevent heat from entering the refrigeration unit. Research by the Indianapolis Power & Light Co.[2] has proved that strip curtains reduced cool air loss to less than 3 percent a day and KWH use more than 40 percent, and increased the life of refrigeration equipment more than 150 percent.

Operational Efficiency

The following symptoms indicate potential operating problems:

- A noisy condensing unit may indicate loose parts, bent fan blade, or worn motor bearings.
- Temperatures that are too high may mean a thermostat setting that is too high, or improper air circulation.
- Condensing units that operate for prolonged periods can signal a refrigerant shortage or leak, control contacts that have frozen closed, an excessive heat load in the cabinet, open doors, ice blockage of the evaporator coil, or a dirty condenser or air filter.

The following recommendations can be helpful in improving operational efficiency. Food service (and its employees) should:

- Maximize refrigeration space by filling to capacity. Fully loaded refrigerators use energy more efficiently. Schedule deliveries to avoid overloading or creating underutilization.

- Open doors only when necessary and be certain that self-closing hinges and latches are working. Every time the door is opened, heat enters the cabinet, requiring the compressor to run longer.

- Set thermostats at the highest point possible while maintaining proper food storage temperatures (35 to 40° F. for refrigerators, 0° F. for freezers). Every 1° F. temperature rise reduces energy consumption by 5 percent. Freezers should be maintained at 0° F. to maximize shelf life. However, maintaining the freezer at − 10° F. increases energy consumption and operating costs by nearly 15 percent, at − 20° F. by nearly 25 percent, and at − 30° F. by 33.5 percent. These significant cost increases result in only minimal efficiency improvements. Maintaining the freezer at 0° F. also increases the life of the equipment and reduces maintenance and repair costs.

- Avoid placing items within four feet of the compressor as they may restrict airflow.

- Load food items carefully, allowing for air circulation between products. Remove unnecessary packaging materials, which not only take up space but retard cooling. Avoid jamming items against doors where they may damage gaskets and create air leaks. Cover or wrap all foods in moisture-proof wraps or containers to avoid dehydration of exposed food surfaces.

- Discard leftovers more than 48 hours old.

- Clean refrigerators and freezers at least weekly to maintain sanitation.

- Clean condenser and coils monthly to avoid buildup of dirt and lint.

- Feel the outer walls of refrigerators and/or freezers for cold spots, which may indicate a settling of insulation and subsequent poor temperature retention.

- Schedule times when refrigerator and freezer doors are open. Labeling stored items helps, as does planning times when workers take several items out. This increases security as well.

- Cover all liquids stored in the refrigerator. Moisture is drawn into the air from the uncovered liquid, making the refrigerator work even harder as moisture from the liquid raises the temperature. Storing items improperly in front of coils may restrict airflow; unrestricted airflow to the coils is essential to the cooling process.

- Do not refrigerate foods that do not require it—unopened catsup, mustard, pickles, salad oils, etc.

- Place frequently used items near the front of the refrigeration unit.

- Close doors immediately after items have been removed from the refrigerator. Do not use cooler to store individual portions of products because that requires opening the door every time a portion is needed, e.g., salads, desserts, etc.

- Keep all gaskets and seals in good condition and the blower coil free of ice buildup. Replace worn or damaged compressor belts.

- Plan ahead so that a worker entering the walk-in cooler can fill many needs at one time. Prepare a schedule for use.

- Turn off lights in the walk-in when leaving. Unit should have pilot light or light switches to indicate that lights are on.

- Allow food to cool for a few minutes before placing in the refrigerator. However, do not permit food to remain at room temperature for too long to avoid the temperature danger zone (45° to 140° F.) (8° C. to 60° C.) in which bacteria grow the most readily.

- Check refrigerators for short cycling and loss of temperature control. Maintain a record of refrigeration temperature forms (as indicated in Exhibit 12–2). Check refrigerant level if abnormal operation exists.
- Place compressors in cool areas rather than near heating units.
- Clean freezer fan periodically and check compressor regularly. These procedures should be scheduled as a regular maintenance item.
- Consolidate refrigeration and freezer floor space where possible.
- Schedule food deliveries, whenever possible, to avoid overloading refrigeration facilities or using them below capacity.

Exhibit 12–2 Record of refrigeration temperatures

Record of Refrigeration Temperatures

Equipment: _____

DATE	MONITOR	A. M. TEMPERATURE	MONITOR	P. M. TEMPERATURE

- Expedite receiving and prompt refrigeration of frozen and perishable foods.
- Defrost freezers frequently. Ice should not be allowed to build up more than one-eighth of an inch on the wall and shelves.

Ranges

The range (including the oven) can be one of the most energy-intensive pieces of equipment in the food service department. Operational practices are the key to efficient use, and effective control can result in significant savings. Food service should:

- Heat units to the lowest temperature required. Food service employees sometimes may preheat the ovens to the highest temperature available, thinking that they will heat faster.
- Consider calibrating thermostats to 350°-400° F. to prevent excessive energy use.
- Load ovens to capacity, with a two-inch clearance around pans for proper air circulation.
- Limit preheat times to no more than 15 to 20 minutes. Warm-up times can be used to begin cooking food.
- Open oven doors only when necessary. Use timers to prevent frequent openings, as the internal temperature drops 10° every second the oven door is opened. If it is not done automatically, turn the fan off in a convection oven before opening the door to prevent hot air from being blown out.
- Plan menus to maximize oven efficiency. Cook as many menu items as possible in the oven when it is in use.
- Group pots and pans together on the range top to use as little area as possible. Cover them with lids to reduce heating times.
- Be sure to keep heating elements clean and free from grease buildup. Oven interiors also should be cleaned regularly.
- Make sure doors seal tightly to retain heat.
- Consider turning the oven off before the cooking period is finished to reduce the amount of heat lost when the oven is empty. Most ovens are well insulated and retain heat long after they are turned off.
- Cook meat slowly at low temperatures. Cooking a roast for five hours at 250° F. (122° C.) could save 25 to 50 percent of the energy that would be used in cooking for three hours at 350° F. (176° C.).
- Schedule baking or roasting so that oven capacity can be utilized fully, thereby reducing operating hours.
- Insert metal skewers lengthwise in potatoes to speed cooking. If foil is necessary, wrap the potato after it is baked.
- Place weight on bacon and sausage to quicken their cooking time but be aware this may alter the characteristics of the product.
- Close open dampers on a deck oven to prevent heated air from escaping out the back, resulting in an excessive intake of cold air through the breather space at the front below the door. Open dampers will cause the product to be unfinished at the front of the oven and overdone at the back. Dampers on deck ovens should never be opened except when baking foods that contain an

265

excessive amount of moisture, such as fruit pies and cobblers. Moisture on the glass or at the top of the oven door indicates an excessive level and the damper should be opened enough to eliminate it.

- Do not place pans too close to the sides, back, or front of deck or convection ovens since this results in poor circulation of hot air inside and produces crippled runs.
- Clean fans on convection ovens to provide maximum air delivery, to assure even heating throughout the oven capacity, and to prevent crippled runs. Regular cleaning and maintenance of filters also is necessary.
- Check the fuel-air ratio on all gas burners and adjust to the most efficient mixture.
- Consult the local gas utility about using pilot lights. Adjustments made by persons not thoroughly familiar with the equipment could be dangerous.
- Huddle food on griddle close together whenever possible and heat only the portion of the griddle being used for cooking.
- Clean griddle every shift after use. Remove deposits, being careful to prevent loose deposits from falling on hot area and creating air pollution by formal degradation. Excessive buildup of burned-on food particles in spots on a griddle will cause uneven heat transfer and result in crippled food products. Unnecessary or excessive cleaning by burning off of the heating elements on fryers will waste energy and energy dollars.
- Cover pans with lids; foods cook faster when covered.
- Control flame tips so they are only touching utensil bottom, not engulfing it.
- Place foil under range burners and griddles to improve operating efficiency and make equipment easier to clean. Electric range burners should always be smaller than the kettle or pot placed on them.
- Place kettles and pots close together on range tops to decrease heat loss. With preheat time of 10 to 15 minutes for electric ranges, only the section in use needs to be heated. Place pots in use specifically in this area. Gas open burners need no preheating.
- Turn off electric surface for a short period before the food is done as the cooking will continue from stored energy.
- Choose the pot and pan carefully for the surface unit. To assure efficient heat transfer from hot plates, french plates of ranges, and hearths of deck ovens, use only heavy, flat-bottomed pots and pans. Pans that are bent or warped not only waste energy because of inefficient heat transfer but may also finish products unevenly. The bottom should cover the heating element while not extending more than one inch (2.5 centimeters) over the edge.

Dishwashing

The task of cleaning dishes, flatware, and preparation equipment is often neglected; however, it can be one of the most costly and most technical aspects of food service. Dishwashing systems, in fact, account for 10 to 40 percent of the department's total energy bill. Heating and water costs can mount even higher if efficiency is ignored.

The National Sanitation Foundation has approved chemical sanitization, meaning that dishes are sanitized by means of a chlorine solution rather than heat. Rinse temperatures need not be higher than 120° to 140°F, negating the need for an expensive booster heater. Annual energy saving can be as much as $4,000 a year for a single tank machine and $10,000 for multitank machines. Chlorine, which is easily injected into the rinse water with automatic controls, has been proved to be more sanitation effective than heat in terms of controlling bacteria. (Low-temperature machines are discussed in detail in Chapter 13.)

To assure maximum dishwashing results, equipment must be maintained properly. Regular temperature checks should be made. If the machine is designed for 180° F. rinse, it should not simply be converted to a low-temperature machine by adding chlorine to the final rinse. While the U.S. Food and Drug Administration (FDA) has approved this procedure, the NSF has not. Bacteria culture counts and proper dispensing equipment, among other items, are required to meet sanitation standards set by state and federal agencies. On the other hand, if the final temperature is higher than 180°F, water is being heated unnecessarily.

When evaluating temperatures of low-temperature machines, the manufacturer's suggestions of 140° to 160°F should be followed. Lower temperatures cannot effectively sanitize, and higher temperatures dissipate the chlorine.

Water pressures should be checked often. The recommended level is 15 to 25 PSI. Higher water pressure levels not only use more hot water but cause vaporization of rinse water, reducing its effectiveness. The booster heater should be as close to the dishmachine as possible, as water loses heat the more it has to travel.

Energy Saving Devices

Many cost-saving devices are available to increase dishwasher effectiveness. Conveyor and detergent cutoffs stop the conveyor and washing system when the machine is empty. Such devices can pay for themselves within weeks through energy savings. Many of these systems often are provided free of charge by chemical companies.

Low-water cutoff devices also are important. One food service department spent more than $500 in one year replacing booster heaters that had burned out when operators failed to turn them off. By installing a low-water cutoff device, the payback was realized in less than six months. Energy consumption also can be reduced on flight type and conveyor machines with plastic strip curtains as they prevent heat and steam from escaping through machine entrance and exits.

Chemical Products

Dishmachine efficiency also is affected by lime deposits. Minerals such as calcium and magnesium are released from solution when water is heated, creating a deposit along pipelines and machine surfaces. About 85 percent of the United States and Canada has "hard," mineral-laden water and could benefit from water softening. Many products are available, including ion exchange resins, semipermeable reverse osmosis membranes, detergents formulated for hard water, and deliming agents.

To determine the best product for food service, the grains per gallon (gpg) or parts per million (ppm) of mineral content in the area's water should be checked against the following:

1–3 gpg = slightly hard water
3.5–7 gpg = moderately hard water
7–12 gpg = hard water
12 + gpg = very hard water

267

Softened water not only increases machine efficiency, it also reduces spots and stains on dishes and glasses. A half-inch of scale reduces dishwashing efficiency by 28.5 percent, wasting 480 cubic feet of gas per 1,000 cubic feet, doubling energy expenditures and potentially costing thousands of unnecessary dollars a year.

Employees must be trained to operate dishwashing equipment effectively. Only full racks of dishes should be run and the machine should be drained, cleaned, and turned off between meals. Spray arms and nozzles should be cleaned daily, removing clogs of debris and lime. Gas burner efficiency, heater operation, and possible steam leaks should be evaluated regularly.

The following recommendations can prove cost effective. Food service departments should:

- Use the lowest temperature appropriate to the use intended.
- Keep distribution runs as short as possible. Hot water boosters should be located within 48 inches of dishwasher to avoid heat loss in the run.
- Use spring-operated valves on the hand levers and foot pedals to save water.
- Consider wetting agents versus power drying.
- Operate dishwasher exhaust only when dishwasher is in use.
- Check local sanitary codes to ensure that water is supplied at the lowest possible temperature.
- Install pressure regulators if not already present.
- Replace water jets that allow too much water to flow through the dishwasher.
- Insulate heating pipes and hot water lines.
- Stop leakage, check pipes and faucets.
- Caution personnel to avoid letting faucets run unnecessarily.
- Keep heater coils free from lime accumulation.
- Turn off electric booster heaters on dishwashers when kitchen is closed.
- Turn off equipment heat boosters after most dishwashing is over and accumulate dishes until next rush period.
- Obtain water pressure for the hot water line to dishwasher to reduce wasted hot water. Set regulator to operating pressure required by the machine; make sure power rinse turns off automatically when a tray has gone through the machine.

Vent Hoods

Ventilation is essential to any food service and can be quite expensive. Heated, grease-laden air must be removed from working areas to provide safe, sanitary, and tolerable conditions. The extent to which ventilation must be provided depends upon the type of preparation equipment used. Griddles, broilers, fryers, and range tops require the most efficient ventilation.

Innovations in vent hoods providing significant cost savings are discussed in detail in Chapter 13. However, any vent hood must be kept clean to operate efficiently and safely. It is recommended that airflow and fan efficiency be evaluated regularly by a ventilation engineer to assure proper operational efficiency.

By evaluating how and when food service equipment is used—from lighting to refrigeration and ranges to dishwashers and vent hoods—literally thousands of dollars can be saved each year.

How to Save Over $40,000 in Energy in Your Food Service, the extensive survey of energy conservation opportunities developed by *The Stokes Report*, identified more than $47,000 a year savings that could be realized in some operations. Every food service can save at least $10,000 a year in energy (see Appendix H).

A thorough survey of the food service area can identify energy conservation opportunities that can save any such department literally thousands of dollars annually.

NOTES

1. U.S. Congress, Senate, Committee on Finance, 96th Congress, 13 and 14 March 1979. Califano in hearings before the subcommittee on Health.

2. H.E. Halcolm. "Summary of Test of Effectiveness of Plastic Strip Curtain on Fork Truck Door of Large Freezer in McFarling Brothers' Plant," Indianapolis Power and Light Company, March 25, 1976.

REFERENCES

"Automatic Lighting Output System," *Energy Engineering* 79, No. 1.

Borsenek, Frank. "Refrigeration Equipment Operating and Energy Characteristics." *Turtle Tracks* (May-June 1983): 1.

Federal Energy Administration. *Guide to Conservation in Food Service*. Washington, D.C.: Author, 1975.

Federal Energy Administration. *Energy Management Workshops: Restaurants*. Washington, D.C.: Author.

Hospitals, 54, no. 20 (October 1980).

Janco, John W.; Krouner, Robert D.; and McConnell, Charles R. *The Hospital Energy Management Manual*. Rockville, Md.: Aspen Systems Corporation, 1980.

Chapter 13

Selecting Energy-Efficient Equipment

The purchase of food service equipment is a major economic consideration. Equipment not only is a substantial initial capital investment, it also must function dependably for years. Food service equipment generally is divided into three categories:

Equipment I: Major, permanent equipment (example: walk-in refrigeration)
Equipment II: Major, movable equipment (example: food carts)
Equipment III: Small equipment (example: pots and pans)

The considerations discussed here must be evaluated carefully for every piece of equipment purchased.

UTILITIES AVAILABLE

Most facilities have both gas and electricity available; some large institutions also may have direct steam. Of the utilities available, recent bills should be evaluated to determine which is the most economical in the area. Any indispensable preparation or storage equipment that is electric should be connected to an emergency generator. Gas equipment also requires electric connections for thermostats, spark ignition, or other features. These must be identified and coordinated with the contractor and/or engineer before installation.

Electrical Capability

When evaluating utility needs, the facility's capabilities should be discussed with a knowledgeable engineer. The type of voltage available (for example, 120, 208, 240, 480, etc.) is an essential component of the equipment specification. Some facilities have limited power capacities. It should be determined with the engineer whether the wiring available in the department is sufficient for additional equipment. Circuit breakers should provide overcurrent protection to prevent burnout. Some items require special receptacles because of plug configurations. It is essential to designate the number of plugs needed and where they should be located (36 inches or 48 inches above the finished floor, etc.).

Gas Considerations

If gas has been determined to be the fuel of choice, natural or propane gas must be identified in the equipment specification. All gas equipment should be evaluated upon installation by a professional engineer from the gas company so that accurate fuel-to-air ratios can be determined. Specifics on the total BTU (British Thermal Unit) load are necessary to assure proper installation and size and type of piping.

STANDARDS

Several regulatory agencies regularly inspect and evaluate the manufacture and use of food service equipment. Their respective seals of approval should be designated as part of the equipment specification to ensure quality.

The National Sanitation Foundation (NSF), a voluntary organization, inspects equipment as it is manufactured, giving its seal to items complying with its standards on factors such as:

- ease of cleaning
- types of materials and finishes (nontoxic, food grade)
- manufacturing techniques (coved corners, screws and nuts that are not exposed, etc.)
- performance standards
- thermometers provided.

Underwriters' Laboratories (UL) tests electrical equipment for fire and safety standards and bestows its seal on products meeting its standards. Participation in this product testing program also is voluntary.

The American Gas Association (AGA) evaluates gas equipment for safety and also provides a seal of approval. Its Canadian counterpart, the CGA (Canadian Gas Association) conducts similar product testing services.

Pressure equipment is tested and evaluated by the American Society of Mechanical Engineers, whose ASME seal indicates that safety and quality standards have been met. This program is voluntary and also indicates a manufacturer's willingness to identify quality in a product.

All safety standards for food service employees are under the regulatory jurisdiction of the Occupational Safety and Health Administration (OSHA), which has investigative powers to evaluate operations for safety. Equipment must be in proper working condition, with appropriate warning labels and necessary protective devices to ensure employee safety.

ENERGY

Energy efficiency has been identified as a major consideration when operating equipment. It is equally essential to identify equipment as energy efficient before it is purchased. Evaluation of different manufacturers should include the number of BTUs or KWs their equipment requires. For example:

Gas Convection Ovens

Manufacturer	Blodgett	Garland	Wolf
Model No.	DFG–100	TTG–2	AFS–100
BTUs Req./Hr.	60,000	70,000	81,000

Generally, the most energy-efficient equipment requires the least amount of power for its size. Other factors to consider when evaluating energy include: (1) the amount of water required (if applicable), (2) the insulation in heating and refrigeration equipment, and (3) the purpose of the equipment. Buyers should try to identify equipment that can be used for multiple purposes, i.e., tilting braising pans rather than several types of single-purpose equipment items.

EMPLOYEE CAPABILITIES

Buyers should identify training necessary for employees to utilize the new equipment effectively. Manufacturers' representatives often are available to conduct initial inservice training in cleaning and operation but regular followup and supervision are essential. Employees not only must be aware of proper equipment operation, they also must be trained in proper care and maintenance. Neglect in cleaning can lead to energy inefficiency, decreasing the life span of equipment and increasing repair costs.

WRITING SPECIFICATIONS

Whether specifications are written for an entire kitchen or for a single piece of equipment, the basic fundamentals remain the same. The following are essential components of any specification:

- Name of equipment: Use the conventional, well-understood name of equipment, such as "rotary oven" or "fryer."
- Utilities required: Specify gas, electric, or steam identified in BTUs, KWs, or PSI, respectively.
- Description of materials: Include details on metal thickness and type (for example, 14 gauge, type 18-8 stainless steel), finishes, special instructions regarding welds, soldering, fasteners, etc. (i.e., stud-bolting should be underbraced to table top). Most food service equipment uses welding; any soldering must conform to NSF standards.
- Controls or other displays: Describe exactly what controls are needed, such as "power on" indicators, timers, thermostats, thermometers, pressure gauges, etc. Controls should be located where they can be seen easily, such as at eye level, yet not subject to abuse. Figures should be large, clear enough to be read easily, and not obstructed by indicators or pointers.
- Performance requirements: Emphasize performance in high-volume operations that require rapid product turnover. Keep in mind future expansion and clientele needs when forecasting the uses of planned equipment. Describe in detail the needs of the equipment; for example: "Fryer must be able to fry ten pounds of chicken (eight-piece cut) per hour."
- Certification requirements: Include approvals from such organizations as NSF, UL, AGA, or ASME.
- Dimensions: Include exact dimensions of every piece of equipment, especially when space in existing facilities can be a critical factor. Include height, depth, width, and/or thickness.
- Quality assurance indicators: List any requirements for product presampling and evaluation, such as onsite reviews at the dealer or factory, onsite

273

inspections before or after installation, and minimum standards of acceptance upon delivery. If performance tests are to be run, the types of tests and who is to conduct them should be identified.

- Warranty: Indicate in detail the warranty required. Rather than simply listing "one year parts and labor," include indications as to the parts to be replaced and under what conditions they are to be considered defective. Identify clearly what is to be considered "operator abuse" and what is to be considered defective merchandise. Labor should be defined as to whether it covers onsite repairs as well as travel and travel time.

- Delivery requirements: Write marking, delivery date, and place of delivery clearly. Include a penalty clause so that the buyer is compensated if delivery dates are missed. Be very specific as to place of delivery; simply including the address of the facility may mean that the equipment is unloaded onto a dock rather than delivered to the food service area.

- Installation: Identify the person or persons responsible for installation and give specific details as to when and how the equipment must be listed. Be certain before any equipment purchase that factors such as plugs, wiring, gas lines, drains, etc., are available so that it can be installed upon delivery.

- Options: List carefully all optional or additional features required. Include as an essential part of the specifications an isometric drawing or three-dimensional layout of the equipment as it is intended, if any special manufacturing techniques are required.

- Include any administrative qualifications necessary, including special payment schedules or contract handling details. Be certain that the name and address of the individual preparing the specifications is available should questions arise. To maintain fairness, exceptions should not be granted to one bidder without extending the courtesy to all bidders.

EQUIPMENT SELECTION

This section discusses a number (but not all, for space reasons) of types of equipment found in the food service department.

Ranges

- When considering hot tops vs. open burners, remember that hot tops require more energy because the heating plate must be heated before the pot or pan can be heated. It is estimated that 20 to 30 percent more energy is used for a hot top than an open burner. However, hot tops do offer versatility in providing a large area for several pots and pans, while burners are limited to one pot or pan each. A unit combining a hot top and open burners could give maximum flexibility.

- Grease traps should be easily removable for cleaning and maintenance.

- Oven interiors should be made of material easy to clean, such as porcelain. Removable sides and bottom also facilitate cleaning.

- Continuous-clean ovens must be wiped daily to preserve their effectiveness. When sides become encrusted with deposits, the oven cannot be cleaned properly and the continuous-clean option is negated.

- Floating, or three-piece, handles prevent heat conduction and possible burns.

- The thermostat capillary tube should be in the cool zone, away from heating elements, to measure oven temperature accurately.
- Doors should be heavy duty and counterbalanced to prevent unpredictable slamming or opening.
- Controls should be easy to reach and mounted away from the hottest part of the range, usually the center front.

Convection Ovens

Gas-fired convection ovens have been revolutionized in recent years by the advent of air recirculation devices. These mechanisms have resulted in significantly reduced BTU consumption. Energy savings of 29 to 40 percent have been reported with the use of snorkels or tubes to recirculate hot air. Electric convection ovens also have heat recirculating devices. BTUs and KWs must be carefully compared to determine actual energy consumption. These other points should be considered:

- Motors are available in various sizes, but adding more horsepower increases energy consumption.
- All ovens have a stainless steel front and most offer stainless steel exterior (sides, top, and back) as an option. A complete stainless steel exterior or a louvered rear panel may be necessary when the oven is visible to patrons or vulnerable to abuse.
- Most oven doors have a glass vision panel. When a large amount of roasting is done or cleaning is irregular, solid doors may be best. The appearance of a solid door is preferable to that of a soiled glass panel. Solid doors also conserve energy more effectively.
- Manufacturers generally provide five oven racks; however, for a large amount of baking and more efficient utilization, extra oven racks should be ordered to provide greater flexibility.
- Control panels are located on the right front of ovens; however, if location of the oven prevents this application, the placing of the panel can be specified.
- Automatic control assures that a fan will cease operation when the oven door is opened.
- Two interior lights provide optimum visibility and increase assurance of visibility if one light malfunctions.
- Ovens can be provided on legs, above an open rack with angle guides for extra racks, or above a cabinet base with doors for enclosed storage.
- A two-speed motor offers the flexibility of baking light items, such as meringue, without airflow's disturbing it.

Fryers

Deep fat fryers should be chosen with production needs in mind. Rate of volume and turnover must be evaluated to determine the size and energy usage required:

- Preheat times should not exceed 15 minutes.
- The thermostat should be located to maximize reading of the fat capacity of the frypot.

275

- Signal lights should be specified to indicate readiness for use or overheating.
- Element configuration should maximize energy efficiency. Tubular or stacked elements improve fryer operation.
- Swing-up elements can aid in cleaning but can cause a fire hazard when the elements are burning.
- The "cold zone" is the area in which crumbs and sediment fall. If the cold zone is in the center of the unit, crumbs and sediment will not carbonize, thus increasing energy utilization.
- The automatic fat filtering system is a labor-saving device that increases the life of the shortening by removing carbon and free fatty acids that break down the usable shortening.
- The short melt cycle control is a solid-state fat melter that acts quickly to avoid scorching of heating elements or fat.
- The frying computer is a time/temperature sensing device set to identify proper cooking temperatures in a limited area of the fryer. Solid state sensors can more accurately control oil temperature, thereby reducing energy used. Conventional thermostats may permit wide variances in temperatures above and below the temperature designated on the dial. This requires more energy. Higher temperatures may burn the fat and shorten its life and that of the fryer while the lower temperatures allow more fat to absorb into food, resulting in a greasier product.

Pressure Fryers

Pressure fryers are gaining widespread use as an alternative to traditional methods of deep fat frying. Rather than simple immersion of food in hot fat, pressure fryers have a sealed cover that, when closed, traps vapor created by heated food to produce 10 to 20 pounds of pressure. Atmospheric or open air frying results in foods' rising to the top of the fat when the cooking is completed. Pressure fryers cook the food under timed conditions while it is totally immersed in fat. Following are points to note:

- Cooking time with pressure fryers is generally shortened and always timed. The unit automatically turns off after each cooking cycle, preparing product uniformly and assuring quality control. Losses from overcooking are minimized, and the need for relying upon a cook's judgment as to when the product is fully done is negated. Because products are cooked for a specified time under pressure, the cooking cycle cannot be interrupted to add to the product load. Production planning is essential to forecast needs because the cooking cycle of 10 to 20 minutes plus the pressurization time must be completed before another batch can be prepared.
- Heat output from the pressure fryer usually is less because hot fat is not exposed to air. Ventilation systems and air conditioners may be used less. Generally, pressure fryers use a temperature setting 10 to 15 percent lower than that for atmospheric fryers.
- Pressure frying results in a higher degree of moisture retention in the cooked product, reducing shrinkage. Moisture from the product vaporizes when it is immersed in hot fat, preventing it from absorbing much of the fat. The food is totally submerged in hot fat so all exposed sides of it are cooked at the same

temperature for the same length of time. A controversy continues as to the effect of pressure on the cooking fat. Proponents of pressure frying indicate that because the fat is not exposed to air, oxidation does not occur as quickly, so fat breakdown is slowed. Makers of traditional deep fat fryers contend that pressure causes fat to break down into free fatty acids, reducing the life of the shortening. Users of both methods report no notable difference in fat consumption.

- Pressure fryers require specialized cleaning techniques to assure that breading and other debris do not coat the heating elements. Special brushes, tools, or cleaners may be required. Cleaning techniques and cooking procedures must be demonstrated when evaluating a possible purchase.
- The labor skill of employees, the menu items, and the clientele must be evaluated carefully when considering the purchase of a pressure fryer to assure all production needs will be met.

Tilting Braising Pans

The tilting braising pan originally was designed and used in Europe. This can be the most versatile piece of equipment in the food service operation. It can be used to boil, stew, braise, grill, or even moist-heat roast. Training of employees is the key in maximizing its benefits. Creative uses include grilling hamburgers, roasting turkey, and scrambling or boiling eggs. Other important factors:

- Open-leg models of tilting braising pans generally are easy to clean and provide maximum access to operating parts. Counter and cabinet models also are available.
- Distance between the gas or electric burners and the cooking surface defines the pans' efficiency. Heat content of the cooked product as well as energy expended by the heating elements should be evaluated.
- A condensate vent in the lid allows steam to be released without raising the cover.
- Manual tilt is managed easily for pouring off liquid and/or draining the pan. A power tilt option also is available.

Microwave Ovens

Microwave ovens have been used in commercial food services for 25 years to cook or reheat food products quickly. Microwave ovens offer versatility, flexibility, speed, and economy for rethermalization when thawing or reheating prepared food products.

Basically, the microwave oven operates through an electronic device known as a magnetron inside the oven. The magnetron produces high-frequency energy waves similar to radio or television transmission waves. Microwaves are stirred by a propeller to produce an even pattern of wave energy. This wave energy is absorbed by liquids, and the electrons bounce around creating friction and heat. The longer the food is exposed to microwaves, the hotter it becomes. Microwaves cook through vibration rather than radiant heat so they do not create excess heat. The food itself may become hot; however, the oven and nonmetal serving dishes remain cool.

277

Capacity limitations currently preclude the use of microwave ovens for preparing large quantities of food. Items weighing more than six to eight pounds take about the same amount of time to prepare by microwaves as by radiant heat or conventional methods. New systems offer microwave cooking teamed with precooking and postcooking by convection ovens.

A microwave oven requires minimum floor space, no ventilation, and small energy use. Reheating in a microwave oven rather than a range or oven can result in 40 percent to 50 percent savings in energy cost.

The following factors should be considered when evaluating their use:

- Unevenness in the microwave energy pattern can cause hot and cold spots in the oven but rotating bases can lead to more even distribution. Otherwise, periodic stirring of dishes, especially of layered casseroles, helps heat the entire dish.
- Bulk and thickness of the food affect heating. Microwaves penetrate food approximately one inch, depending on the moisture content and type being cooked or heated. This limits the direct heating effect to a maximum of two inches of total product thickness (assuming the dish being cooked is on a shelf in the oven or in a glass container to allow penetration from all sides). Anything thicker than two inches or in an uneven shape is more difficult to heat. Conversely, very thin items such as thin cuts of meat may become dry very quickly.
- Frozen foods must absorb additional energy to melt the ice first. This tends to cause a breakdown in the food structure, so it is better to use refrigerated, not frozen, items in the microwave. A defrost cycle is preferable when thawing is required. If a defrost cycle is not available, it is preferable to turn the oven on and off several times (on 15 seconds, off 15 seconds) to produce proper thawing. A frozen product will take about twice as long to heat as a refrigerated one.
- The amount of energy is constant. If it takes 15 seconds to heat a particular product from the holding temperature, it will take 30 seconds to heat two similar portions of the same product. Cooking too many portions at once can result in uneven heating as items must be located farther from the center of the oven.
- Different food types absorb and react to microwave energy at different rates. This generally is caused by the molecular structure and moisture content of the food. When heating dissimilar products in the microwave oven (such as a preplated hospital meal), cooking time should be gauged so that all products are cooked correctly. This may mean putting some of the meal in first, adding items that do not require as much cooking time later.
- Microwave energy normally does not brown or caramelize food although many newer ovens contain a heating element that does brown. Browning in an oven without this option can be achieved using commercial glazing preparations.[1]
- Baking items with a high sugar content (i.e., angel food cake, pie, etc.) may crystallize the sugar because of the high microwave energy.
- Meat or packaged items require ventilation so heat does not build up pressure within them. Baking potatoes must be pierced with a fork and plastic bags must have a hole or steam release. For this reason, it is difficult, if not

impossible, to cook eggs in their shells in a microwave oven without their bursting.

- It is important that regular preventive maintenance be maintained for all microwave ovens, including proper cleaning and regularly scheduled service. All such units must meet the safety requirements of the U.S. Department of Health and Human Services.[2]

Soft-Serve Ice Cream Freezers

Soft-serve ice cream has become a popular menu item, not only in restaurant and fast-food establishments but in schools, hospitals, and nursing homes as well. Soft-serve ice cream freezers can be used not only for soft ice cream but for frozen fruit drinks, slushes, and milkshakes. Soft-serve ice cream mix is available in liquid form and as a powder to blend with water before use. The many formulas all basically contain mix, fat, milk solids, sweeteners, stabilizers, and emulsifiers. The quality of mix is important in order to maintain a smooth, textured ice cream that does not melt quickly.

Soft-serve mix is poured into a hopper through which it descends into a freezing cylinder by one of two methods: gravity, where the liquid flows through a tube, and pressure, where an electric beater regulates the flow. There, it is held at temperatures from 17° to 20° F. Most small units are gravity fed. For larger volumes requiring strict quality control, pressure-fed freezers generally provide a more consistent product. Gravity-fed machines do not regulate the rate of flow as effectively because mix viscosity and ambient temperature create longer variables. Pressure-fed units also create a colder freezing temperature.

As the ice cream mix freezes, crystals form, and the mix combines with the air to create product expansion known as overrun. Soft-serve ice cream with too little overrun will be heavy and will melt quickly; however, with too much overrun, the product will be too light and have little flavor. Most food service operations utilize an overrun between 35 percent and 60 percent. Although some freezers regulate the rate of freezing through temperature alone, others measure product viscosity to control the variables more effectively. Other factors to consider:

- Soft-serve machines are available in a large range of sizes, from countertop models that produce four to six gallons an hour to floor models that make up to 30 gallons an hour.
- Options include milkshake spinner attachments, cleaning faucets, and topping trays, although these elements may not be available for small countertop units.

Ice Makers

Ice machines are an essential part of any food service operation. Unwanted breakdowns can create havoc in any facility. Key factors involved include the following:

- Ice machines can draw large amounts of energy unless they are placed properly in the kitchen area. Proximity to point of use should be considered. Since freezing compressors require adequate ventilation, they should be located in a cool, dry area.

- Many types of cubes are available. The cube shape should adequately fill the type of glass used and melt slowly. Flaked or crushed ice melts the fastest. Some manufacturers have designed unusual shaped cubes to melt more slowly. Proper liquid displacement for maximum profitability also is a consideration in determining cube shape.
- Air-cooled condensers are less expensive as an initial expenditure and can be used outdoors or indoors. They are the most effective when used in temperate climates. Although air-cooled condensers require regular maintenance to keep the fans free of dust and debris, they are efficient. Water-cooled condensers generally are more efficient because water temperature can be controlled more effectively in cooling the condenser. These condensers also are more expensive and require a steady flow of water, increasing operational costs. Water-cooled condensers are especially effective in hot climates such as Arizona, Southern California, or Florida.
- Ambient water temperature affects ice production. Most ice machines are based on 70° F. ambient water temperature; higher temperatures will reduce efficiency.
- Proper maintenance, including the use of a water softener, is necessary to prevent mineral buildup. Regular cleaning of the condenser vent to permit proper air circulation is essential.

Steam-Jacketed Kettles

Steam-jacketed kettles have long been a mainstay of conventional food service preparation. An outer hemisphere of stainless steel encloses chemically pure water and rust inhibitors that, when heated either electrically or with direct steam, cook the food in the kettle. The principle is the same as a double boiler. The kettle should be constructed of stainless steel for both ease of maintenance and appearance.

Regular preparation of high-acid items such as tomatoes may pit or otherwise damage the interior stainless liner, requiring a higher gauge steel. Most conventional preparation units will not experience this problem. Maximum working pressure is the top level the self-contained steam source can safely reach. The higher the maximum working pressure, the more efficiently the steam can be produced. Other factors involved:

- Tilting kettles provide a safe and easy way to remove heavy food items from the bowl. Many kettles have the option of tangent drawoff that allows food to be released through a faucet at the bottom into a pot. The method is efficient and safe. However, a drawoff of more than two inches is not recommended as the velocity with which the food emerges may make control of the flow difficult.
- A reliable thermostat and pressure gauge are essential parts of a well-equipped steam kettle. Covers, either lift-off or counter-balanced hinge, are excellent when items such as vegetables are to be steamed. Lift-out basket inserts are available for immediate draining when cooking such items as pasta. For easy filling of the container, a pantry faucet provides direct water access.
- Powered agitation involves an attached mixer unit and is an efficient way of preparing large quantities of soups, stews, and sauces. This feature is expen-

sive, however, and the cost of labor must be evaluated. Units with powered agitation may cost twice as much as a conventional kettle.

- Reinforced rim (a heavy steel bar inserted into the rim of the kettle) is recommended since the outer rim receives wear and tear from contact with pots, pans, and stirrers.
- Closed lids are recommended to reduce energy utilization during cooking.

Griddles

Griddles have become increasingly popular with the rise in the fast-food concept. They may be gas or electric, flat or sloped, grooved or smooth, but all operate on the same principle: Heat is transferred from a burner to the griddle surface to the food. These points should be considered:

- Thickness of the griddle is important when considering menu items. Placing frozen or partially thawed items on the steel surface may eventually cause warping. Frozen items need a steel plate at least one inch thick. Griddles that do not supply such a plate as standard equipment usually have them available as options.
- A splash guard is especially needed if the griddle is next to other equipment such as open-burner ranges or fryers.
- A grease trough that is easily accessible permits more thorough cleaning and draining.
- Grease drawer capacity should reflect menu needs. High-volume cooking or preparation of beef patties and other high-fat foods requires large grease drawers.
- Proper burner configuration (placement beneath the griddle surface) increases efficiency.
- Sloped griddles facilitate grease runoff and may reduce smoke production.
- Multiple thermostats provide greater heat control and promote energy efficiency by allowing the use of several griddle areas.
- Stainless steel sides and back are available but most manufacturers prefer they be enamel coated when they are well protected.
- Legs are recommended as an aid in cleaning.
- Gas and electric connection locations should be well protected yet easy to service and maintain.

Convection Steamers

Convection or ''pressureless'' steamers are a fairly recent innovation in the food service industry. The following factors should be considered:

- Steam is supplied continuously to a closed compartment to create a uniform flow and a consistently cooked product. Since there is no pressure buildup, the door of the convection steamer can be opened at any time during the cooking cycle.
- Convection steamers provide a uniform temperature (212°F. or 100°C.) directed across the food at high velocity. The steam, generated by a boiler,

blows condensation off cooking food instantly, thus transferring far more heat than is possible with a conventional pressure steamer.

- This method of cooking is especially advantageous with frozen food as it results in a consistently cooked product in faster preparation time. Fewer seasonings are necessary, and steamed vegetables retain 10 to 20 percent more solid matter and 10 to 15 percent more protein and minerals. Quick cooking time permits flexibility in production forecasting and food can be cooked to order, minimizing plate waste.

- Convection steamers maintain a constant pressure so energy use is higher than that of pressurized steamers, which automatically turn off when a specified pressure is reached. Cooking time for frozen vegetables is decreased, and the quality of the final product usually is excellent. For fresh, canned, or defrosted products, cooking time and product quality are not measurably different from those of a pressurized steamer. Menu composition, number of meals served, and available labor are major considerations when evaluating the purchase of a convection steamer.

Pressure Steamers

Pressure steamers are available with one, two, or three compartments and usually operate with five to seven pounds of pressure. Safety valves release pressure if it exceeds eight pounds. These are other points:

- Automatic timers are recommended to prevent overcooking of food.
- Boilers must be adequate to heat the size of the unit. Boilers rather than direct steam are recommended to ensure the sanitation of ''clean'' steam.

Disposers

The following must be evaluated for each individual application:

- The first step is to identify the major type of waste to be disposed of, i.e., plate waste, vegetable or salad preparation, meat preparation or butcher shop, or pot sink waste.
- The volume of waste to be disposed is evaluated in terms of peak load, including the maximum amount of waste to be disposed at any given time.
- The frequency of waste disposal—i.e., daily, hourly, continuously—is determined.
- The body construction of the unit, as well as the rotor size, should be adequate to handle peak loads.
- The motor size (horsepower) should be sufficient to handle waste volume. Light, bulky waste such as bakery items requires a small (1 to 1½ horsepower) motor. Standard food service use normally requires at least a 2-horsepower motor, and heavy-duty applications, such as butcher shop, require up to 3. Special applications may warrant even larger motors.
- Each disposer has a different rotor action; cutaway models at the manufacturer's or retailer's make it possible to evaluate them.
- The disposer's jamming prevention properties must be checked. Jams usually occur as the machine is slowing to a stop. A reversible motor permits turning

the rotor disc alternately clockwise or counterclockwise each time the motor is turned on. The double action prevents jamming as well as ensures longer life for the motor and other wear parts.

- The water supply should be adequate. Flow restrictors are available to decrease water consumption; however, care must be taken to avoid clogged water lines.

Coffee Urns

Coffee urns use heated water, which is sprayed over coffee grounds and through a paper, cloth, or fine aluminum screen filter. Water is maintained in two ways:

1. A water pump is used to force hot water kept in a holding area to the spray head.
2. Heat exchangers maintain water in a coil and a flow regulator alters the pressure, forcing hot water to the spray head. Water pressure can be adjusted for accurate flow.

Some other factors to consider include the following:

- Evaluation of capacity should consider that coffee should be brewed to last no more than 30 minutes. Coffee kept warm for longer periods becomes bitter.
- Energy requirements must be evaluated; lower amp and BTU requirements mean less energy usage.
- Liners should be durable and removable to facilitate cleaning.
- Low-water cutoff can prevent heater burnout.
- Insulation can reduce energy requirements.
- Recovery time is instantaneous for urns using the heat-exchange coil.

Toasters

Commercial toasters provide high-quality toast efficiently and with minimal energy usage. Pop-up toasters usually are the least expensive type of institutional toaster; however, conveyor toasters can provide up to twice the capacity. Production needs must be evaluated when deciding on the type to use. Feeding large numbers of persons within a short time calls for a high production conveyor toaster. Other factors to consider:

- Conveyor toasters rotate the bread past a series of elements that heat the entire slice but toast only one side. The degree of doneness is determined by varying the speed of the conveyor. Pop-up toasters have heating elements on both sides of the slot to toast both sides of the bread and a color-selector knob to determine crispness.
- Ovens used for toasting bread draw excessive energy and provide an unreliable product. A standard oven uses approximately 11 KW/hr ($.05/hour), a conveyor toaster 4 KW/hour ($.02/hour), and a pop-up toaster only 2.5 KW/hour ($.01/hour).
- Incoloy—a heat-conducting metal alloy—coats most heating element tubes for efficient heat transfer. Quartz-sheathed tubes produce instantaneous heat but the tubes are breakable and have a shorter life span.

• One conveyor toaster offers the option of rear delivery, enabling the operator to load the toaster on one side of the serving line and have the finished toast dispensed on the customer side.

Slicers

The base of most slicers is of anodized aluminum, which is durable under normal operating conditions. This sometimes is advertised as "stainless" but care should be taken to determine whether it is stainless steel or stainless aluminum. Other important factors:

• Stainless-steel blades or knives must be durable and maintain their sharpness.
• Blade width should be determined by needs. Large blades may be unnecessary in small operations and often require a "fence" guard attachment.
• Most slicers are available with automatic or manual feed.
• Safety factors should be determined by having demonstrations of blade guard removal and cleaning procedure.

Mixers

Mixers provide a versatile preparation tool for facilities of all sizes. A thorough review of menu items is needed to evaluate potential uses. Other elements to consider:

• Motors should have grease-packed ball bearings for low maintenance and should be ventilated for heat release and safety. Horsepower is not always an indication of durability as motors often are made for different purposes. Load capacity charts are available from manufacturers' representatives and should be evaluated for the facility's needs.
• Revolutions per minute (RPMs) should be evaluated to determine the ability of the motor to handle the capacity of food in the mixer. The higher the RPMs, the greater the capacity of the mixer motor.
• A gear-driven transmission is reliable, more efficient, and longer lasting.
• A capacitor start feature is needed for single-phase mixers to provide a surge of electricity to start under a heavy work load.
• A squirrel cage fan housing to which the motor is attached is more efficient than a blade fan.
• Open-rim bowl design facilitates easy handling and cleaning. Tinned bowls are less expensive but less durable.
• Mixer motors offer the variety of attachments for chopping, grinding, and slicing. Large production use would warrant a separate piece of equipment for these functions; however, for small facilities, attachments are a relatively inexpensive way to provide versatility.

Vent Hoods

Traditional vent hoods operate by exhausting 100 percent of the air above cooking equipment. This conditioned heated or cooled air that is pulled to the outside must be replaced by "makeup" air, usually from outside the kitchen area.

Unless the air that is exhausted is replaced, a vacuum will result in the kitchen area. Costs rise when "makeup" air must be conditioned (heated or cooled) at significant expense, only to be reventilated once again to the outside.

Compensation type vent hoods that provide makeup air are economical and efficient. The makeup air from the outside can be circulated just within the vent hood itself or can be released at ceiling level from the front of the hood. During winter months in most areas of the country, this makeup air must be reconditioned.

Heat recovery systems that capture the heat ventilated from the preparation equipment are available from several manufacturers and can significantly reduce the energy requirement of reconditioning the makeup air during colder months. Heater coils can be located in the vent hood to recondition makeup air. (Reconditioning is unnecessary in spring and summer in most areas of the country.) Each of these systems is more efficient than the traditional vent hood design that exhausts and requires reconditioning of 100 percent of the makeup air (see Figure 13–1).

An innovation in vent hood design requires only 20 to 30 percent of the air above the cooking equipment to be exhausted. A fan is located in the hood to force outside air into the hood at high velocity, creating a jet stream. This air attracts the hot, grease-ladened air above the cooking equipment into the hood and forces it to the outside, so only 20 percent of the air in the preparation area is removed. Consequently, only this 20 percent must be air-conditioned again. Since 70 to 80 percent of the makeup air does not have to be conditioned, significant savings in energy, and therefore dollars, result. It is easy to see that most 80/20 vent hoods can pay for themselves within two years.

Ventilation is measured in cubic feet per minute (CFM). Evaluating the number of total CFMs saved is one of the first steps in reducing utility costs by using more efficient systems. For example, a 12-foot-by-4-foot hood requires 4,800 cubic feet of air to be made up each minute of use. With an 80/20 vent hood, 4,200 CFMs are saved. Thus, when heating air in winter, BTUs and dollars are saved.

Conditioning air to accommodate a 30° temperature difference results in the following demand for energy:

$$1.08* \times 4,800 \text{ CFM air replacement} \times 30° \text{ temperature} = $$
$$\text{differential } 155,520 \text{ BTU utilized per hour}$$

An average cost of $.47 per therm (100,000 BTUs) translates into $.73 per hour, or $7.30 for ten hours of use. A four-month winter could cost $876 in vent hood makeup air alone.

Ventilating systems deserve careful consideration before purchase. Types of cooking equipment and hours of operation dictate the type of hood best suited for a facility. Large amounts of frying and broiling require careful calibration of exhaust and supply air to assure efficient and reliable ventilation.

Vent hoods can be made by a metal fabricating company. However, because of continued developments in energy conservation and other innovations in vent hoods, it is recommended that ventilation systems be purchased from manufacturing companies specializing in such equipment. Ventilation designs, such as the 80/20 concept, are essential to efficient operation. Qualified manufacturers can provide a total package system, including vent hood body, collar, calibration of air velocities, controls, and wash-down systems.

---

*Standard ventilation conversion factor

Figure 13–1 Examples of vent hoods

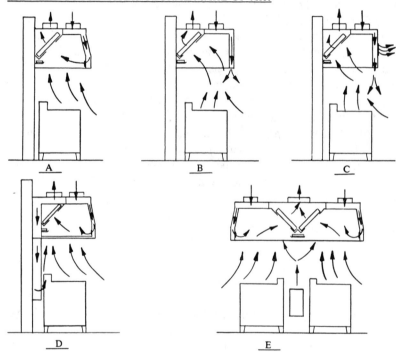

CANOPY WALL HOOD - NO MAKE UP AIR

WALL HOOD | WALL HOOD | ISLAND HOOD

CANOPY HOODS WITH INTEGRAL MAKE UP AIR

A | B | C

D | E

Notes:
A—Makeup air provided internally.
B—Makeup air discharged vertically at vent hood.
C—Makeup air discharged vertically and horizontally.
D—Makeup air provided internally and behind cooking battery.
E—Makeup air provided internally for island-type hood.

Source: Courtesy of LDI Manufacturing Company, Logansport, Ind.

A food service operation need not wait for a kitchen renovation to benefit from the 80/20 vent hoods. Conversion packages are available to convert existing 100 percent exhaust hood to the 80/20 vent hood. The cost is approximately $1 per CFM, which can be recouped in six months to two years.

Other factors to consider:

- Grease extraction methods differ with each manufacturer. Cartridges and filters provide a screen to filter grease, while baffle-type hoods remove grease through centrifugal force, swirling the exhausted air through a series of baffles. Each type is unique and should be observed in action. Filters must be removed and cleaned regularly, and cartridges require replacement periodically. Baffles are nonremovable but also require regular cleaning to ensure effectiveness.

- Each type of hood is available with a water-wash option, which provides automatic cleaning with hot or cold water and detergent. The additional expense of self-cleaning hoods must be weighed against labor costs. Many areas provide reduced fire insurance costs for hoods with automatic cleaning systems. Cleaning systems vary with each manufacturer; however, most systems work on the principle of a limited (three-minute to five-minute) wash, with water and detergent injected throughout the grease-extracting chambers at a preset time. Manual controls also are available. Most systems use hot (140° F.) water; however, some manufacturers have cold water applications available. Hot water is recommended for maximum cleaning ability. Potential buyers should ask to see a working example of ventilators being considered.

- Air extraction, as noted, is measured in cubic feet per minute and the CFM needed depends on heat and grease generation in the preparation area. Equipment such as broilers and fryers, which produce large amounts of heat and grease, require a much higher CFM. The more CFMs required, the larger the fan(s) required, so more energy is needed. Types of equipment and hours of use must be evaluated when purchasing a ventilation system.

- Static pressure is the amount of pressure required at the entrance of the vent hood to exhaust the required number of CFMs. Static pressure varies with the length of the ductwork, the number of turns in the ductwork as it proceeds to the outside, and the number of CFMs required. High static pressures may require modifications in hood design, larger fans, and increased energy costs.

- Damper closing systems should be analyzed closely for safety, as fires can spread throughout the ductwork if dampers do not close adequately. Dampers should close with airflow when fire extinguishing systems are in operation (rather than depending on mechanical or hard-to-reach systems that may expose the ventilator interior to fire).

- All vent hoods used in food service areas must be NSF and UL approved and must meet No. 96 codes of the National Fire Protection Association (NFPA). While all ventilation systems must meet such national codes, state and local standards may supersede other codes. Before investing in any ventilation system, the CFM and fire protection requirements in the area must be checked.

- Fire dampers are standard on some hoods; however, because of code variations, some manufacturers make this item optional. It is imperative that any contract with a ventilation manufacturer includes a provision that all state and local codes will be met.

Exhaust CFM rates, determined by fan size, also are subject to local codes. Factors that determine the CFM rate include the length of hood, type of equipment

287

beneath it, and use of the equipment. For example, CFM exhaust rates for charbroilers and fryers, which are used for many hours, are much higher than those for steam equipment. A qualified mechanical engineer should assist in determining CFM requirements for each application. The direction of makeup air supply also is critical in evaluating hood efficiency.

Supply-to-exhaust ratios are rated by Underwriters' Laboratories and tested under maximum conditions. These ratios vary according to equipment use, and much is dependent on hood sizing, location of other HVAC equipment, and proper maintenance of the hood itself (cleaning, etc.).

Warranties vary with each manufacturer. Many hoods have no moving parts and maintenance is minimal.

Refrigeration

Refrigeration can be costly but expenses can be reduced if factors such as the following are considered.

- Insulation is important in conserving energy. Polyurethane is the most efficient insulation. Generally, the thicker the insulation, the longer the cool temperature will be retained, increasing energy conservation because of reduced compressor running time.
- Larger compressors will do a better job of maintaining temperature and humidity levels in hot weather. A top-mounted compressor for reach-in refrigerators allows for relocation of the cabinet and is easier to clean and maintain.
- Capillary and expansion valves control the flow of the refrigerant into the evaporator coil. While capillary tubes may be more maintenance free and less expensive, expansion valves have a high recovery rate and can effectively cool over a wide ambient temperature range.
- Shelves should support at least 30 pounds each. Shelving generally is chrome or zinc-plated because of its low cost; however, stainless steel or plastic coated shelving can be specified if high durability is desired. Polygard (an Amco Corporation trademarked product) is a highly durable plastic resin coating.
- Handles should be evaluated for durability and should have a safety grip. Vertical handles may be easier to open as they allow for a natural grip; however, horizontal handles may be more durable under heavy kitchen traffic. Recessed handles are advisable when they are subject to battering.
- Metal door liners tend to conduct heat more readily, thus increasing compressor running time. Metal door liners also may dent and become marred; reinforced fiberglass or durable plastic liners are recommended because of their durability and reduced tendency to conduct heat.
- Door gaskets should be magnetic to produce a positive seal and prevent air leakage.
- Condensate vaporizers may be thermostatically controlled, containing an electric heating element to turn condensate into steam, or may consist of a hot gasline system that evaporates the condensate through the heat emitted from the condensing coil. The thermostatically controlled vaporizer requires a floor drain and uses energy, whereas the hot gasline system is energy efficient, requiring no additional electricity or floor drain.

- Legs should be at least six inches high; adjustable legs offer versatility to assure proper leveling upon installation.
- Warning systems should identify unsafe cabinet temperatures, blown fuses, or interruption in the electric current.
- Cord, plugs, and casters should be specified if relocation of the cabinet is a consideration.
- Proper airflow is essential in assuring uniform humidity and temperature levels. Multiple air outlets are recommended to provide maximum circulation. Shelves fully loaded close to the cabinet ceiling can block air distribution if vents are in the ceiling. Blockage of vents results in increased compressor running time, increased energy consumption and decreased shelf life of stored food items. A refrigerator that is too small for storage needs can cost more money in the long run.
- Two to four extra shelves per full door compartment should be specified to maximize refrigerated storage capacity and energy use.
- Interior liners may either be seamless or welded. While seamless liners are easy to clean, welded liners generally provide greater strength.

Walk-In Refrigeration

Walk-in cold rooms or refrigerating rooms involve elements such as the following:

- Insulation should be poured-foam rather than frothed-in-place polyurethane to assure more even distribution of insulation.
- Doors should have cam-lift, self-closing hinges so that they close and seal with a gentle nudge. Magnetic door gaskets ensure a tight seal, and the wiper gasket seals the bottom. Inside safety releases should be checked for ease of operation. Heater wires in the door prevent accumulation of frost, ice, or condensate.
- Doorcaps, the U-channel frame surrounding the door, prevent damage to the unit from heavy traffic.
- Door closers (spring-loaded or hydraulic) are an additional guarantee that doors will close automatically and produce a tight seal.
- Indicators for power and inside lights can be helpful in controlling energy. Some units provide alarms to alert employees of power failure and/or temperature rise. An exterior thermometer provides a quick, visual confirmation of inside temperature.
- Floor panels must be durable; floors should be flush with existing floors, or ramps should be provided. Floor screeds are necessary when an existing floor is utilized. Existing facilities should consider installing a metal floor to cope with possible uneven conditions. New construction units can consider installing quarry tile floors in walk-in units.
- Pressure relief ports are essential for proper operation of walk-in freezers to prevent compression damages. These ports should be an integral part of the construction of the unit.
- Vision panels offer the opportunity to evaluate freezer contents without the energy-wasting efforts of opening the door.

- Foot treadles are effective motion economy devices when loads are delivered frequently.
- Outdoor freezers must have a roof cap, winterized compressor controls, and an effective compressor cover.
- Shelving may be built in or specified separately but should be easy to clean to prevent rust.
- Panels should be at least 22-gauge galvanized steel, 20-gauge stainless steel, or .042-stucco aluminum with at least four inches of insulation.
- Locking assemblies should be located at least every 24 inches horizontally and 36 inches vertically.
- Spring-loaded or hydraulic door closer and self-closing hinges should be provided.
- There should be a five-year compressor warranty and a two-year one on parts and labor.
- The freezer space ratio should be one cubic foot per 35 pounds of food to be stored on a minimum of 1.5 cubic feet per meal served per day.
- Plastic-strip thermal-retention curtains in door opening are energy savers.
- Stainless steel, louvered shelving is helpful for air circulation and easy cleaning. Shelving also should be on casters to facilitate storage and cleaning. Polygard, as noted, provides a durable shelving finish that prevents rust.

Dishmachines

Low-temperature dishmachines were designed to sanitize dishes through the use of chemicals rather than heat. The use of 140° F. final rinse temperature eliminates the need for the energy-intensive booster heat and ventilation system, which can save as much as $15,000 a year in energy costs (for a large dishmachine, such as a flight type machine).

The chlorine-based sanitizer actually produces dishes that are more bacteria free than those cleaned by the traditional heat-sanitization method of 180° F. rinse.

Other points to consider:

- When evaluating racks per hour, individual needs such as peak workloads and available labor should be studied.
- Gallons per minute, as well as gallons per rack, should be determined, as adequate water flow is necessary to flush the dishes with sanitizer. Water—even at 140° F.—is costly, and an optimum flow must be determined.
- Nearly all models are available with a prewash option. Types of soiled dishes received (heavy grease or caked-on soil) determine the need for a prewash cycle.
- Close observation of the wash and rinse spray arms, both in use and dismantled, helps evaluate types of nozzles and ease of cleaning.
- A properly located electric control panel can prevent operator abuse or easy dislocation.
- Only a small booster heater is needed. However, it must be adequate for the rinse temperature to reach 140° F. Low-water cutoff prevents burnout.
- Cleanout brushes are not always necessary, depending on nozzle configuration.

- The automatic fill function prevents operator negligence in underfilling or overfilling the tanks.
- Backflow protection in food service operations maintains sanitary standards.
- Blowers can induce proper air drying of dishes.
- Idle-pump shutoff ensures that the conveyor is not in motion when no racks are in the machine, and water is not being utilized unnecessarily.

Low-temperature machines do, however, have limitations. High-volume applications may require blowers to aid drying. For low-temperature single-tank machines, a clean dishtable of ten feet is recommended. If space is limited, an alternative such as an open rack cart (for draining clean, wet dishes) pulled over a drain will replace the ten-foot clean dishtable. Chlorine sanitizers, when injected improperly, provide too much chlorine (more than 50 parts per million) and may damage certain glazes and finishes. Chlorine should not be used for silver or pewter as it will turn them permanently black.

WARRANTIES

Equipment warranties are one of the most commonly overlooked features in food service. A warranty gives a defined degree of protection against the risks of defects in equipment and should be a major factor in purchasing.

The warranty, combined with the way the law is written, protects the purchaser beyond the day the equipment is used. Manufacturers, as a rule, have a standard warranty to define the quality of performance of their merchandise. The law also requires them to make sure the item meets basic standards.

Many manufacturers and contractors who install equipment offer service contracts to provide preventive maintenance and extend warranty-type protection beyond the original contract warranty.

In a warranty, the manufacturer usually guarantees the equipment against defects but may not guarantee that it will survive normal wear and tear for the duration of the warranty period. The manufacturer may guarantee it will perform up to a certain industry standard for the defined period.

The cost of the warranty's assuming the risk of wear and tear for the equipment should be included in the contract price. This type of warranty may have many of the characteristics of a service contract. Service contracts can extend the type of coverage after an initial period for an additional cost.

Warranties involve at least two major areas: (1) coverage (labor and parts) and (2) duration (length and daily effectiveness).

The definition of parts may or may not include all elements of the equipment. The warranty may omit some attachments that are necessary if the equipment is to be used, such as thermostats, motors, thermometers, etc. Any add-on devices that must meet specific demands should be stated in the contract; otherwise, the warranty may be invalidated. Major parts, such as motors and compressors, may be excluded.

Some warranties cover only replacement of defective parts, not the labor needed to replace them. The documents should be examined to determine whether they include all labor, travel time, and service calls outside normal working hours. Location, dependability, and skill of the designated service representative is an important consideration. Checking references with other owners of the same type of equipment under consideration is recommended.

291

The length of coverage varies widely—as little as 90 days or as long as 10 years. The date the coverage begins also varies: on the date of shipment, on the date the equipment is received, or on the date installation is complete. This difference in time can be significant.

Although manufacturers must meet their own warranty standards, the legal system requires a further standard be met as well. These are known as implied warranties and may have a greater scope and longer duration than the written warranties. Under the Uniform Commercial Code, implied warranties provide uniform protection that a piece of equipment is able to meet the purpose for which it was intended. In other words, a dishwasher must be able to wash dishes as designed and represented to do. A manufacturer may be liable beyond the limitations of the written warranty if the equipment does not work.

SERVICE AGREEMENTS

There are several advantages to a service agreement:

- The food service does not have to set up and monitor its own preventive maintenance program.
- It can be sure the equipment will be kept in good working order.
- It can extend the life of its equipment by keeping it well cared for.
- It can budget a fixed amount for maintenance knowing it will not have unexpected repair expenses.

There are two kinds of service agreements—warranties and contracts. A service warranty may be included in the cost of purchase and installation. The manufacturer guarantees the equipment's performance for a certain period. If the equipment breaks down or functions improperly during this time, the manufacturer will repair it at no charge.

Service Contracts

A service contract may be purchased at the end of the warranty period or it may be an addition to a service warranty covering defects in material and workmanship but excluding labor costs, breakdowns, or some other repair item. There are four types of service contracts: (1) inspection, (2) time and materials, (3) full labor, and (4) full coverage.

Inspection Contract

An inspection contract provides only labor and miscellaneous materials such as lubricants needed at regular inspection calls. It usually includes a detailed schedule of visits and an explanation of tasks that will be completed on each visit.

The manufacturer may require this type of contract if the buyer is to make a claim under a defects warranty. Any problems found during inspection are subject to payment, although the contractor may provide labor and materials at a discount. If problems occur after an inspection because the contractor was negligent, the contractor is responsible for these repairs.

Time-and-Materials Contract

Under a time-and-materials contract, the contractor normally provides a discount on labor and materials during the contract time. There usually is a lump sum price for inspections as well. Discounts as well as prompt inspections are provided, but protection against major equipment failure is not.

Full-Labor Service Contract

A full-labor service contract often is a companion to a long-term manufacturer's warranty against defects. This contract provides the food service employer with all labor required for maintenance and repairs at a fixed price.

Full-Coverage Service Contract

The full-coverage service contract is perhaps the most widely used. For a fixed price, it offers inspection, preventive maintenance, and all labor and parts for repairs and emergency service during the term of the agreement. The contract also may contain a promise to keep the equipment in good working order. The full-coverage contract may exclude replacements of certain high-risk components such as compressors. Of course, all this makes it more expensive than other types.

With the proper combination of service warranty and service contract, food service equipment will be maintained at the most productive level in the most cost-efficient and economical way possible.

NOTES

1. Carl Vail, "Get The Most From Your Microwave Oven," *The Stokes Report* (May 1983):35.
2. "Radiation Emission Standards," Health & Safety Act of 1968, 21 C.F.R. Subchapter J.

REFERENCES

American Gas Association. "Maintenance Tips That Will Help Conserve Energy and Improve Your Food Service Operation." Catalogue No. R01023.

"Desktop Computers Emerge as Energy Management Tools," *Energy User News* 7, no. 41.

Hospitals 54, no. 20 (October 1980).

Janco, John W.; Krouner, Robert D.; and McConnell, Charles R. *The Hospital Energy Management Manual*. Rockville, Md.: Aspen Systems Corporation, 1980.

Chapter 14

Energy Management Systems: Pro and Cons

An effective energy management program can be initiated through the use of effective building surveys and through the thoughtful and efficient purchase of food service equipment. Continuing evaluation and maintenance, however, is a key in continuing energy conservation efforts. Preventive maintenance programs, active employee participation, and evaluation of new energy management equipment all are important parts of the effort.

PREVENTIVE MAINTENANCE

Establishing an efficient, regularized preventive maintenance program is a low-cost method to control energy costs. Such a program is required by the Joint Commission on Accreditation of Hospitals; however, it should be a regular part of any facility's approach to energy conservation.

One of the best sources of maintenance information is the operation manual provided with each piece of equipment. It is recommended when new equipment is purchased, the manuals be filed carefully after being reviewed by the food service director and employees so they will be readily available when needed. (However, manufacturers generally will provide replacements if they are misplaced.)

Equipment must be identified as to its maintenance needs—weekly, monthly, quarterly or annually. A tickler file using index cards or other monitoring systems should be established for each item. Details on maintenance checks, repairs, part orders, etc., can be documented for ready reference. Such information is invaluable when considering equipment replacement or purchase. Equipment that requires frequent repair should be reevaluated, and the availability of ready service and parts should be an important consideration when purchasing new equipment.

The following methods of preventive maintenance should be used for each of the following equipment items.

- Ranges and ovens should be evaluated monthly for proper door sealing and cleanliness of heating elements and walls, especially for self-cleaning and continuous-cleaning ovens.
- Convection oven fan blades should be cleaned monthly, and the motor should be inspected quarterly. A qualified service representative should calibrate

thermostats, inspect burners, and evaluate air-to-gas ratio quarterly. An oven thermometer should be used to verify temperature maintenance periodically.

- Vent hoods should be cleaned at least monthly, removing filters and cleaning with a grease-cutting detergent. Heavy grease deposits result in inefficient operation of the hood in exhausting cooking fumes. Water-wash hoods require additional preventive maintenance of the wash system and detergent and water flow must be evaluated at least on a monthly basis.

- Dishwashers require a monthly maintenance check of nozzles to clean out lime deposits and daily to remove food particles to ensure operational efficiency. Conveyor motors must be checked for proper lubrication. Feed and drain valves, as well as pumps, must be inspected for energy-wasting water leakage.

- Steamers must be checked at least monthly for proper seals, lime deposits, and thermostat accuracy. Boilers should be flushed weekly, following manufacturer's instructions. Steam lines and insulation must be checked monthly. Even small steam leaks can increase the load on the HVAC system and should be repaired immediately so that additional energy will not be used unnecessarily.

- Refrigerators and freezers must be evaluated monthly to lubricate hinges (be sure to use food grade oil), calibrate thermometers, clean fins and plates, check gaskets for cracks and damage, and clean compressors of dirt and lint. By feeling the outside walls of the refrigerator and/or freezer unit, cold spots (which may signal shifting insulation) can be detected. The manufacturer should be contacted if cold spots occur. Compressor units for walk-in refrigerators and freezers often are forgotten, as they may be located outside the kitchen area. Many compressors are on the roof or in an HVAC control area. Compressors should be covered if located outside to prevent dirt accumulation, and fans must be cleaned regularly to assure proper air circulation.

Exhibit 14–1 is a sample of a preventive maintenance form.

It is important that food service employees be familiar with each piece of equipment, including its operation and cleaning procedures. Regular inservice education programs on the proper care, cleaning, operation, and maintenance for each piece are essential to an effective energy management program. Job breakdown cards should be initiated, maintained, and updated annually (Exhibit 14–2).

Drafting and maintaining a preventive maintenance program is a vital component in energy conservation. Regular evaluation of equipment, as well as documentation of a "life history" of each article, along with the names and addresses of dealers and service representatives, is an important part of the operation.

ENERGY-EFFICIENT LAYOUT AND DESIGN

The layout and design of a food service operation are essential components in providing proper energy management. Effective conservation design should be considered when planning new construction, renovating, or even purchasing a single piece of equipment. Layout plans should be reevaluated periodically to determine possible use of recent innovations designed to conserve utilities. Initial expenditures must be weighed against long-term cost benefits. The following are areas of design where energy savings can be most effective:

Food preparation equipment

Griddles, rangetops, and broilers

- Check gas units for uneven or yellow flames. Check preheating times on electric equipment. Contact utility representatives should a problem be identified.
- Clean burners and coils, removing encrusted matter from cooled heating elements and burners. Soak in water and a good grease solvent.
- Scrape excess food and fat from griddles with a flexible spatula.
- Clean grease troughs, removing all grease and food. Wash with detergent, rinse, and sanitize.
- Clean griddle surface with soft cloth, wiping with grain while surface is warm.
- Clean gas burners with stiff wire to remove food particles (clogged burners slow cooking times).

Ovens

- Evaluate door gaskets regularly to be certain doors seal correctly. Keep lower edge of door free of crumbs to assure it will close evenly.
- Keep interior walls and heating elements free of food particles to provide maximum heat transfer.
- Be certain interior walls are free from dents if interior is continuous cleaning or self-cleaning.
- Have thermostat calibrated annually by a qualified service representative.
- Have convection oven fan motors checked at least annually. Keep fan blades free from dust and lint.

Fryers

- Clean heating elements regularly. Do not permit sediment build-up; it limits heat transfer.
- Inspect and clean interior walls to prevent grease and carbon deposits.
- Check the temperature of fat while the fryer is operating to evaluate accuracy of thermostat and heating elements.

Steam cooking equipment

- Check steam lines for leaks and repair all leaks—even small leaks can cost significantly.
- Check door seals to ensure adequate closure.
- Evaluate steam line insulation and replace where damaged.
- Flush boilers, following manufacturer's instructions, to remove mineral deposits caused by hard water. Use lime-removing chemicals in areas where water is especially hard.

Refrigeration

- Clean condenser fins and plates to remove grease and lint that may block airflow.
- Check door gaskets for cracks or other damage to ensure proper sealing. A 3″ × 5″ piece of paper should resist withdrawal if placed between the gasket and the closed door. Units should be level to allow proper door closure.
- Lubricate hinges and latches. Tighten hinges if loosening occurs to prevent air leaks.
- Check thermometer calibration to assure optimum temperature maintenance.
- Feel outside walls to check for cold spots, indicators that the insulation has settled or become waterlogged.
- Have the automatic defrost cycle evaluated and adjusted by a trained refrigeration service technician.

Exhibit 14-1 continued

- Be certain coils are kept free from ice buildup if unit does not have an automatic defrost cycle.
- Inspect and service electrical motors regularly.
- Maintain proper tension on compressor belts. Inspect regularly and replace worn out damaged belts.

Dishwashers

- Clean spray nozzles to remove mineral deposits caused by hard water.
- Remove scrap trays after each use to clean and remove food particles.
- Check rinse water temperatures to ensure accuracy. Excessive temperatures waste energy and accelerate lime deposits.
- Inspect feed and drain valves for leaks, which should be repaired immediately.
- Pumps should be regularly inspected for leaks.
- Check settings of power dryers to be certain that heated air is delivered just long enough to dry dishes. Consider the use of wetting agent in the final rinse to reduce the need for a power dryer.

- Lighting: The fewer windows in a building, the greater the heat efficiency, as clear glass conducts up to ten times more heat than an insulated wall. Tinted glass and draperies do not reduce the heat transfer significantly; however, heat-absorbing, reflective, or double-glazed glass can control solar heat gain. Strategic placement of windows can provide more natural light while reducing heat gain. Estimates show that as much as 30 percent of present lighting can be reduced with no significant effect on job performance.

- Placement of Equipment: A simple rearrangement of equipment may result in significant energy savings. A range near a refrigerator will produce high ambient temperature, causing a condenser overload. Moving the range can improve the efficiency of the refrigerator and saving as much as 50 percent.

- Energy-Efficient Design: Plans for new buildings that offer new concepts in orientation of the structure, wind velocity, climatic conditions, shape and size, and exterior materials are available. Feasibility studies as to program, scope, cost estimates, and conceptual design in terms of energy efficiency should be evaluated before any new construction. Geographical location is an important factor in considering the solar load on the heating and cooling systems. Window location can be effective when designed to reduce the amount of artificial illumination required. Prevailing winds also must be considered in placing entrances and exits. Food services, as heat-producing departments, generally are on the west or north side of the structure so that the area can be cooled by natural ventilation of prevailing winds.

Other seemingly minor construction features can result in energy efficiency, including bright, light interior walls to reduce lighting required; insulation in relation to heating and cooling areas, and location of heat-producing items such as refrigeration condensers.

Careful consideration and advance planning will produce an efficient, well-managed building.

Exhibit 14–2 Job breakdown card

*Energy Management
Systems: Pro and Cons*

HOW TO CLEAN A BUNNOMATIC

Equipment and Supplies Needed: Cleaning Products Needed:
2 cloths: Detergent:
  1 to wash   In amount needed to make one gal solution
  1 to dry   Proportion: 1 oz to 1 gal water
2 - 1 gallon containers   Sanitizing Agent: Bleach
                                  1/4 oz per gallon water
                    Approximate Time: 10 minutes
                    Frequency of cleaning: After each use
                    Approximate Cost: Labor _____
                                      Supplies _____

What To Do	How To Do It
1. Turn off.	1a. Black switch on left.
2. Remove basket and filter.	2a. Throw away filter.
3. Wash basket.	3a. Wash. Rinse. Sanitize.
4. Clean inside of unit.	4a. Press brew button once.
	b. With pot underneath.
5. Clean glass pot.	5a. Wash. Rinse. Sanitize.
6. Clean outside of unit.	6a. With water and detergent.
	b. Rinse.
	c. Dry.

HOW TO OPERATE A BUNNOMATIC

1. Turn on.	1a. Black switch on left.
2. Remove basket from coffee maker.	2a. Pull handle on front.
3. Place paper filter in basket.	
4. Empty coffee packet into filter.	
5. Return basket to position.	5a. Into slots
	b. Under the top of coffee maker in front.
6. Set glass pot on unit.	6a. After rinsing with hot water.
	b. Under the basket.
7. Push brew button.	7a. On right hand side of coffee maker.
8. Turn on warmer units as necessary.	

ENERGY MANAGEMENT INNOVATIONS

The use of computers and other systems to control the entire energy load of a building has mushroomed in recent years. Basically, most such systems monitor all equipment serviced by utilities within the building. In peak loading (as described in Chapter 12), a facility's utility rate often is based on the maximum amount of energy utilized at any given time. A sudden surge of power can determine the rate for months to come. Therefore, the energy management system may act as a load shedder, reducing utilization of energy-intensive equipment when a predefined peak load is reached. Savings of thousands of dollars a year have been identified in hospitals, colleges, and industries by taking advantage of computerized energy management systems.

Heat recovery systems are designed to use "wasted" heat to reduce utility expenditures. By recapturing heat produced from such daily operations as fuel combustion; engine exhaust; or heat exhaust from other equipment, heating, air conditioning, or steam production can operate with greater efficiency at reduced cost. Many heat recovery systems have unique capabilities.

For that reason, an energy audit is a must. Qualified engineers should determine areas of potential energy conservation and conduct a complete evaluation of building construction, including heating, ventilation, and air-conditioning equipment and operational efficiencies of major equipment. Before purchasing a heat recovery system, it is necessary to apply other energy conservation measures that may require only simple administrative policy changes.

For example, reducing building temperatures at night or domestic hot water temperatures will increase efficiency with no investment. Noninvestment conservation measures should be taken so that heat recovery equipment can be evaluated properly. Only then can the energy audit identify unused heat production. The amount of heat lost or wasted can be categorized as follows:

- Heat temperature loss: 1,200° to 3,000° F. caused by fuel consumed by such equipment as industrial refining services can be used to produce steam for turbine operation.
- Medium temperature loss: 450° to 1,200° F. caused primarily by large engine exhaust can be used to produce steam.
- Low temperature loss: below 450° F. results from such equipment as air-conditioning refrigeration condensers. Small internal combustion engines and pumps can be used to preheat domestic water supply to decrease the load of the water heater. Most food service equipment heat recovery devices rely on low temperature heat production; however, the heat created from a compressor for a walk-in cooler or freezer still is enough to preheat dish water, thereby possibly avoiding the use of a booster heater. Conserving this energy by use of the low temperature chemical method of sanitizing will result in even higher savings.

Many commercial heat recovery systems apply proved technology. It is important, therefore, to organize the process of identifying wasted heat and opportunities of heat recovery as well as evaluating manufacturers' proposals in determining economic benefits. The important thing to keep in mind is that any system must be adapted to a facility's specific needs. Examples of systems available include:

A thermal wheel is a large drum of heat-absorbing material. As it rotates in the air duct, heat is transferred from outgoing air to cooler incoming air.

Advantages: Heat recovery efficiency is high—as much as 90 percent—and initial and operating costs are low.

Disadvantages: Exhaust and supply airstreams must be adjacent and parallel. Cross-contamination of airstreams is possible. Preventive maintenance must be regular and thorough.

A heat pipe also transfers heat between adjacent air ducts but is composed of copper tubing containing refrigerant. The heat pipe tilts and the refrigeration vaporizes as it absorbs heat, then flows to the cold, incoming air, where it gives up heat and condenses, then repeats the cycle.

Advantages: There is no cross-contamination of airstreams, and no moving parts to require maintenance. Energy required is low.

Disadvantages: The exhaust and supply airstreams must be adjacent and parallel, and a preheat coil may be required if outside temperatures are below 18° F. to prevent freezing the condensate.

Heat pumps extract heat from air or water, compressing concentrated heat, and transporting extracted heat to a point where it can be used. Although it requires some energy, an efficient heat pump can save up to three times the energy it uses. Heat pumps can be used, for example, to transfer heat from waste dish water to domestic hot water supply. A unit such as this can save more than $2,000 a year.

Advantages: Flexibility in locating heat pumps is high as exposure to outside air is possible but not required. The temperature of each area can be controlled independently.

Disadvantages: Energy is required, and some heat is lost in the transfer from one unit to another.

Incinerators produce large amounts of heat that can be captured and used to heat incoming air or domestic hot water. Typically, incinerators in food service institutions and hospitals have up to 70 percent moisture and a heating value of 2,500 BTUs per pound.

Advantages: Heat sources are readily available.

Disadvantages: Heat from more than 1,000 pounds of garbage per day must be generated regularly and pollution regulations must be followed.

COMPUTERIZED ENERGY MANAGEMENT

Since the development of the thermostat, energy utilization in building HVAC units has been automatic. The use of computers now has streamlined this concept even further to provide control of air and water temperatures, boiler and chiller sequencing, and load shed/demand limiting. Computer systems have the advantage of being accurate and versatile, and some units can be added to systems already in use. Even desktop computers, which are used for accounting or inventory control, may be programmed to perform calculations or control monitors. While this cannot compare to sophisticated monitoring systems designed for building HVAC units, they may help determine energy utilization.

The latest technology involves the use of microprocessors to decentralize energy management systems' function. "Intelligent" field units scan and monitor demand for electricity and gas, then communicate the information to a central display terminal, thus eliminating the need for a front-end computer to evaluate information before being displayed.

Exhibit 14–3 Determining equipment payback using Life Cycle Costing (LCC) system

	Compensation 80/20 type vent hood	Conventional vent hood
Period of analysis	10 yrs.	10 yrs.
1. Initial investment cost salvage	$3,700.00	$2,800.00
2. Salvage	1,850.00	1,400.00
3. Present value of savings	714.00	540.40
4. Maintenance and repair costs	200.10	800.00
5. Present value* of maintenance & repair	1,562.40	6,249.60
6. Base-year energy costs	233.75	561.00
7. Present value of energy costs*	1,826.05	4,382.53
Total costs	6,374.35	8,028.13

Equation: LCC = #1 − #3 + #5 + #7

*Present values are calculated with a modified uniform present worth formula at a 10 percent discount rate, allowing for a 5 percent rate of energy price escalation. (This also applies to Exhibits 14–4, 14–5, 14–6, and 14–7.)

Source: Reprinted with permission of Lynn R. Hall.

DETERMINING COST BENEFITS

To determine payback for energy conservation equipment, proposed investments must be evaluated carefully for economic as well as energy efficiency. Several analytical tools are available to determine whether the proposed investment best meets the department's needs.

- The life cycle costing system determines the cost of purchase, installation, maintenance, and repair as well as replacement costs, energy costs, and salvage cost of an investment over the generally accepted life of the equipment. Investment that demonstrates the lowest total life cycle cost while maintaining the institution's quality standards is the most desirable. Exhibit 14–3 illustrates equipment payback using the life cycle costing system.

Exhibit 14–4 Determining equipment payback using benefit cost (BC) system

Compensation vs. Conventional vent hoods	
Period of analysis	10 yrs.
1. Base year energy savings	$327.25
2. Differential investment cost	900.00
3. Present value of differential salvage value	173.70
4. Present value of differential maintenance costs	4,687.20
5. Present value of energy savings	1,653.78
Present value savings	5,564.68

Equation: BC = #5 − (#2 − #3 + #4)

Exhibit 14–5 Determining equipment payback using savings-to-investment ratio (SIR)*

Conventional vs. Compensating vent hoods	
1. Base year energy savings	$ 327.25
2. Present value of total energy savings	2,556.48
3. Differential investment costs	900.00
4. Present value of differential salvage value	173.70
5. Present value of differential maintenance costs	−4,687.20
SIR Numerator	7,243.68
SIR Denominator	726.30
SIR Ratio	9.9

Equation: SIR = (#2 − #5) ÷ (#3 − #4)

*SIR = Savings-to-Investment Ratio.

- The benefit cost system is a modification of the life cycle costing system and involves evaluating the net benefits of a purchase to compare investments (Exhibit 14–4). The differences in energy savings, salvage value, and maintenance cost of two systems are identified. Total net savings can be calculated in the life cycle cost of the alternatives.

- The system of savings-to-investment ratio involves dividing the difference in energy cost and management by the differences in purchase, installation, salvage, and replacement cost. The resulting ratio (Exhibit 14–5) shows at a glance the savings-versus-investment proportion: The higher the ratio, the greater the savings.

- Return on Investment (Exhibit 14–6) discounts cash flows over the expected life cycle of the investment to accommodate expected interest rates. For example, in evaluating the life cycle cost of a refrigerator, compressor replacement costs of $500 expected to be made in ten years should be discounted to account for the expected interest rate over that period. Therefore, a 10 percent discount rate to reflect inflation would mean that a $500 cost in ten years should be figured as $307.25 in current dollars. Uniform present worth values used in this calculation are found in tables of discount formulas.

Exhibit 14–6 Determining equipment payback using return on investment (ROI) system

Compensating v. Conventional vent hoods		
Trial Interest Rate	20%	25%
1. Present value of energy savings	$979.88	$834.72
2. Differential investment costs	3,772.80	3,213.90
3. Present value of differential salvage value	728.15	620.28
4. Present value of differential maintenance costs	2,515.20	−2,142.60
5. Net present value based on trial interest	450.33	383.70

Equation #1 − (#2 − #3 + #4)

Exhibit 14–7 Determining equipment payback using discounted payback system (DPS)

	Compensating vs. Conventional vent hoods		
Years into the investment	Present value of cumulative energy savings	Differential investment costs	Present value of net savings
1	$312.52	$900.00	− $587.48
2	610.97		− 289.03
3	895.02		− 4.98
4	1,166.97		266.97
5	1,426.15		526.15

- The discounted payback system (Exhibit 14–7) determines the time between the initial investment and accumulated savings. This method cannot accurately compare projects competing for the same funds but does allow the evaluation of investment turnover. This system is used most commonly when purchasing energy conservation equipment.

Tax advantages also should be considered when evaluating payback periods. Accelerated depreciation schedules were passed by Congress in 1981 that may shorten payback periods. Certain energy management systems are subject to faster depreciation rates if obsolescence can be demonstrated, or if the equipment is removable. Current rulings are made case by case. Industry standards have not yet been set.

Any investment requires complex decision making. Noneconomic benefits such as those to employees (in the form of more efficient heating) or, to the community (such as reduction in use of commonly available fuels) also should be considered.

TRENDS IN ENERGY CONSERVATION

The desire for conservation techniques increases dramatically when energy supplies become tight and/or expensive. It is important to realize that consumption of fossil fuels continues to be a major part of the current way of life. Natural resources are limited. But national conservation efforts have been effective in restraining demand for energy. Meanwhile, the search for alternative sources has involved a number of routes, including those discussed next.

Solar Energy

The interest in utilizing the sun's heat for energy has existed for centuries but cost and other obstacles continue to pose challenges in the development of solar energy as a reliable source.

The sun produces enough energy to provide one kilowatt for every square meter of the earth's surface (equivalent to the electricity required for ten 100-watt bulbs burning simultaneously). The use of the sun's energy striking the earth could meet needs for years to come. However, the jury is still out on the cost effectiveness of solar energy because the materials required to convert it to usable electricity involve large amounts of aluminum, copper, glass, and steel, which need large amounts of energy in their own production.

Despite large expenditures by the federal government and private enterprise on solar energy development, it is estimated that no more than 20 percent of the country's energy needs will be met by solar power by the year 2000.[1] Solar energy has been applied successfully to public buildings and private residences. For example, the Aspen, Colo., Municipal Airport uses solar energy as its sole source of heating. Solar heating is an attractive alternative in that it is continuing, fully renewable, and nonpolluting.

Solar heating also has been used successfully in heating large amounts of water through use of solar collector panels. A back-up heating system usually is required to boost water temperature, if necessary. Solar water heating has been used successfully in Camp Pendleton, Calif., and in other sites throughout the Sun Belt.

Geothermal Energy

The heat naturally lying within the earth—hot water, dry steam, hot rock, etc.—offers an attractive energy alternative. Of course, this is limited to just a few regions and the technology required for widespread use is lacking.

Wind Power

The use of windmills and other wind power devices is another alternative. Although this, too, is limited to certain regions, wind power has the advantage of being inexpensive although not a totally dependable source. Current use of wind power has been limited to small facilities.

Hydroelectric Power

The use of running water to create electrical energy has long been recognized but the cost of building large dams is enormous. As compared with burning fossil fuels, hydroelectric power plants are a more feasible energy-producing source of the future.

Tidal Power

The use of tidal power to generate electricity also is an alternative. This force can be captured in areas where tides rise at least 30 feet, so feasible locations are limited. Plants in Brittany and near the Bering Sea in the Soviet Union have been successful.

EMPLOYEE PARTICIPATION

Food service employees are the key to implementing any workable plan for energy management. In such an energy-intensive area, they can help reduce costs significantly. Development and implementation of an action plan should be communicated to them to reinforce energy conservation goals. Feedback as to how conservation affects employees as well as obtaining their ideas is important. An employee energy committee can stimulate conservation. The committee should meet regularly with administration and act as the liaison in communicating and coordinating energy conservation goals. Daily work activities are high consumers of energy and regulating and monitoring them are important.

It also is important to make employees aware of energy costs. Graphs and charts are effective to illustrate the costs of energy on a month-to-month basis. The amount of energy used, as well as dollars required, should be emphasized. For example, the San Juan School District in Sacramento, Calif., realized a 49 percent reduction in gas consumption and a 32 percent drop in electricity use by involving students, teachers, and custodians in an energy management program. Energy conservation goals were identified for every school, and their success was compared each month. An energy advisory committee was established (membership voluntary) to critique, to modify energy conservation proposals, and to make recommendations. An energy management booklet also was developed for children in fourth through sixth grades to increase their awareness of conservation.

Hotels and hospitals must rely on housekeeping personnel to monitor energy conservation management. The Inn at the Park in Toronto reduced energy consumption by 10 percent simply by having housekeeping personnel turn off lights and air conditioners in empty rooms. Regular staff meetings also have been helpful.

Brainstorming sessions to develop ideas for conservation can be stimulating and fruitful and can encourage employees to become aware of energy utilization. Rewarding employees for ideas that have conserved energy can motivate additional savings. One school system based its "care about conserving" award on a percentage of dollars saved by the winning idea. A plaque honoring the achievement gave recognition to the individual as well as to the school.

A watchdog committee is another effective in-house tool. Selected employees make unannounced visits to each area of the facility to inspect working conditions based on a preestablished checklist. A quarterly award is then given to the department or area with the most energy-efficient operation. Recognition of employees who submit energy-saving ideas is effective. Rewards such as choice parking places or a special pin can be effective motivators. All suggestions by staff members should be answered personally by management and cost savings should be communicated. The secret of a successful program is staff motivation.

Energy management will continue to be of increasing importance as energy demands increase. Low-cost or no-cost programs, including effective preventive maintenance, equipment placement, and employee participation can result in significant benefits in cutting energy expenditures.

When sophisticated energy management equipment such as heat recovery systems or computerized energy management systems are being evaluated for possible purchase, the payback periods and possible tax advantages should be considered. Continuous new advancements in technology make it imperative that experts be consulted to determine the state of the art. Innovations in energy conservation have become a part of today's technology, and future advancements will be an exciting element of energy management programs.

Food service professionals can become food service pioneers and form an energy management team for the department.

NOTE

1. Jauco, John W.; Krouner, Robert D.; and McConnell, Charles R. *The Hospital Energy Management Manual.* Rockville, Md.: Aspen Systems Corporation, 1980.

REFERENCES

"Computers for Facilities & Energy Management." *Energy Engineering* 79, no. 1.

Donaho, Gary, and Rogers, Richard. *A Research Study: Waste Heat Recovery: Opportunities in Colorado*. Denver: Colorado Energy Conservation and Alternative Center for Commerce and Industry and Colorado Office of Energy Conservation, 1978.

"EMS Vendors Increasing or the Intelligence of Field Units." *Energy User News.* 8, no. 22.

"Employee Training, Incentives Boost Conservation Programs." *Energy User News.* 7, no. 40.

Federal Energy Administration. *Energy Management Workshops: Restaurants.*

Marshall, Harold E., and Ruegg, Rosalie T. *Simplified Energy Design Economics*. Washington, D.C.: U.S. Department of Commerce, 1980.

Appendix A

Menus

Legend
FF = fat free
SF = salt free
BU = buttered
D = diet

Exhibit A–1 Nonselective, Nursing Home, Western U.S.

WEEK NO. ONE DAY SUNDAY MENU CYCLE ___ FALL/WINTER

	800 Calories	1,000 Calories	1,200 Calories	1,500 Calories	1,800 Calories	2,000 Calories	2,200 Calories
Breakfast	½ c Orange Juice 1 FF Egg ½ c FF Ralston Coffee, Tea	½ c Orange Juice 1 FF Egg ½ c FF Ralston Coffee, Tea	½ c Orange Juice 1 FF Egg ½ c FF Ralston 1 Bacon 1 c 1% Milk Coffee, Tea	½ c Orange Juice 1 FF Egg ½ c FF Ralston 1 Bacon 1 c 1% Milk Coffee, Tea	½ c Orange Juice 1 FF Egg ½ c FF Ralston 1 Toast 2 Bacon 1 c 1% Milk Coffee, Tea	½ c Orange Juice 2 FF Eggs ½ c FF Ralston 1 Toast 1 Bacon 1 c 1% Milk Coffee, Tea	½ c Orange Juice 2 FF Eggs ½ c FF Ralston 2 Toast 1 Bacon 1 Oleo Coffee, Tea
Dinner	1 oz Turkey ¼ c FF Green Peas with Red Pepper ½ c FF Stuffing ½ c Sl Tomatoes ½ c FF Stewed Apples (no sugar) ½ c 1% Milk Coffee, Tea	1 oz Turkey ¼ c FF Green Peas with Red Pepper ½ c Sl Tomatoes ½ c FF Stewed Apples (no sugar) 1 c 1% Milk Coffee, Tea	2 oz Turkey ¼ c FF Green Peas with Red Pepper ½ c FF Stuffing ½ c Sl Tomatoes ½ c FF Stewed Apples (no sugar) 1 Oleo Coffee, Tea	2 oz Turkey ¼ c FF Green Peas with Red Pepper ½ c FF Stuffing ½ c Sl Tomatoes ½ c FF Stewed Apples (no sugar) 1 Roll, 1 Oleo Coffee, Tea	3 oz Turkey ¼ c FF Green Peas with Red Pepper ½ c FF Stuffing ½ c Sl Tomatoes ½ c FF Stewed Apples (no sugar) 1 Roll, 1 Oleo Coffee, Tea	3 oz Turkey ¼ c FF Green Peas with Red Pepper ½ c FF Stuffing ½ c Sl Tomatoes ½ c FF Stewed Apples (no sugar) 2 Rolls, 1 Oleo Coffee, Tea	3 oz Turkey ¼ c FF Green Peas with Red Pepper ½ c FF Stuffing ½ c Sl Tomatoes ½ c FF Stewed Apples (no sugar) 2 Rolls, 1 Oleo 1 c 1% Milk Coffee, Tea
Supper	2 oz Hamburger ½ c FF Mix Veg 8 Baked Fries ½ c Diet Frt Cockt ½ c 1% Milk Coffee, Tea	2 oz Hamburger ½ c FF Mix Veg 8 Baked Fries ½ c Diet Frt Cockt Coffee, Tea	2 oz Hamburger ½ c FF Mix Veg 8 Baked Fries Tomato/Lettuce 1 Oleo ½ c Diet Frt Cockt Coffee, Tea	3 oz Hamburger ½ c FF Mix Veg 8 Baked Fries Tomato/Lettuce 1 Bread, 1 Oleo ½ c Diet Frt Cockt Coffee, Tea	3 oz Hamburger ½ c FF Mix Veg 8 Baked Fries Tomato/Lettuce 1 Bread ½ c Diet Frt Cockt ½ c Ice Cream Coffee, Tea	3 oz Hamburger ½ c FF Mix Veg 8 Baked Fries Tomato/Lettuce 1 Bread ½ c Diet Frt Cockt ½ c Ice Cream Coffee, Tea	4 oz Hamburger ½ c FF Mix Veg 8 Baked Fries Tomato/Lettuce 1 Bread 1 c Diet Frt Cockt ½ c Ice Cream Coffee, Tea
Snack	1 c 1% Milk 2 Graham Crackers	1 c 1% Milk 2 Graham Crackers	1 c 1% Milk 2 Graham Crackers	1 c 1% Milk 2 Graham Crackers	1 c 1% Milk 2 Graham Crackers	1 c 1% Milk 4 Graham Crackers	1 c 1% Milk 4 Graham Crackers

CERTIFIED _____, R.D.

WEEK NO. ONE DAY MONDAY MENU CYCLE FALL/WINTER

	800 Calories	*1,000 Calories*	*1,200 Calories*	*1,500 Calories*	*1,800 Calories*	*2,000 Calories*	*2,200 Calories*
Breakfast	½ c Orange Juice 1 FF Egg, Scramb 1 Toast Coffee, Tea	½ c Orange Juice 1 FF Egg, Scramb 1 Toast 1 Oleo Coffee, Tea	½ c Orange Juice 1 FF Egg, Scramb 1 Toast 1 Oleo 1 c 1% Milk Coffee, Tea	½ c Orange Juice 1 FF Egg, Scramb 1 Toast 1 Oleo 1 c 1% Milk Coffee, Tea	½ c Orange Juice 1 FF Egg, Scramb 1 Toast ½ c FF Cr Wheat 2 Oleo 1 c 1% Milk Coffee, Tea	½ c Orange Juice 2 FF Eggs, Scramb 1 Toast ½ c FF Cr Wheat 1 Oleo 1 c 1% Milk Coffee, Tea	½ c Orange Juice 2 FF Eggs, Scramb 2 Toast ½ c FF Cr Wheat 2 Oleo Coffee, Tea
Dinner	1 oz Ham 1 c FF Greens ¼ c FF Yams ½ Banana ½ c 1% Milk Coffee, Tea	1 oz Ham 1 c FF Greens ½ Banana 1 c 1% Milk Coffee, Tea	2 oz Ham 1 c FF Greens ¼ c FF Yams ½ Banana 1 Oleo Coffee, Tea	2 oz Ham 1 c FF Greens ¼ c FF Yams 1-2″ Sq Cornbread ½ Banana Coffee, Tea	3 oz Ham 1 c FF Greens ¼ c FF Yams 1-2″ Sq Cornbread ½ Banana 1 Oleo Coffee, Tea	3 oz Ham 1 c FF Greens ¼ c FF Yams 2-2″ Sq Cornbread ½ Banana Coffee, Tea	3 oz Ham 1 c FF Greens ¼ c FF Yams 2-2″ Sq Cornbread ½ Banana 1 c 1% Milk Coffee, Tea
Supper	2 oz Beef ½ c FF Potatoes ½ c FF Zucchini ½ c Diet Frt Cockt ½ c 1% Milk Coffee, Tea	2 oz Beef ½ c FF Potatoes ½ c FF Zucchini ½ c Diet Frt Cockt Coffee, Tea	2 oz Beef ½ c FF Potatoes ½ c Zucchini ½ c Hot Tom Juice 1 Oleo ½ c Diet Frt Cockt Coffee, Tea	3 oz Beef ½ c FF Potatoes ½ c FF Zucchini ½ c Hot Tom Juice 1 Roll 1 Oleo ½ c Diet Frt Cockt Coffee, Tea	3 oz Beef ½ c FF Potatoes ½ c FF Zucchini ½ c Hot Tom Juice 2 Rolls 1 Oleo ½ c Diet Frt Cockt Coffee, Tea	3 oz Beef ½ c FF Potatoes ½ c FF Zucchini ½ c Hot Tom Juice 2 Rolls 1 Oleo ½ c Diet Frt Cockt Coffee, Tea	4 oz Beef ½ c FF Potatoes ½ c FF Zucchini ½ c Hot Tom Juice 2 Rolls 1 Oleo 1 c Diet Frt Cockt Coffee, Tea
Snack		1 c 1% Milk 2 Graham Crackers (Squares)	1 c 1% Milk 2 Graham Crackers	1 c 1% Milk 2 Graham Crackers	1 c 1% Milk 2 Graham Crackers	1 c 1% Milk 4 Graham Crackers	1 c 1% Milk 4 Graham Crackers

CERTIFIED ______________________, R.D.

Exhibit A–1 continued

WEEK NO. ONE   DAY TUESDAY   MENU CYCLE   FALL/WINTER

Meal	800 Calories	1,000 Calories	1,200 Calories	1,500 Calories	1,800 Calories	2,000 Calories	2,200 Calories
Breakfast	½ c Orange Juice	½ c Orange Juice	½ c Orange Juice	½ c Orange Juice	½ c Orange Juice	½ c Orange Juice	½ c Orange Juice
	1 FF Egg, Pchd	1 FF Egg, Pchd	1 FF Egg, Pchd	1 FF Egg, Pchd	1 FF Egg, Pchd	2 FF Eggs, Pchd	2 FF Eggs, Pchd
	½ c FF Oatmeal	½ c FF Oatmeal	½ c FF Oatmeal	½ c FF Oatmeal	½ c FF Oatmeal	½ c FF Oatmeal	½ c FF Oatmeal
		1 Oleo	1 Oleo	1 Oleo	1 Toast	1 Toast	2 Toast
					2 Oleo	1 Oleo	2 Oleo
			1 c 1% Milk	1 c 1% Milk	1 c 1% Milk	1 c 1% Milk	
	Coffee, Tea	Coffee, Tea	Coffee, Tea	Coffee, Tea	Coffee, Tea	Coffee, Tea	Coffee, Tea
Dinner	1 oz Bkd Chicken	1 oz Bkd Chicken	2 oz Bkd Chicken	2 oz Bkd Chicken	3 oz Bkd Chicken	3 oz Bkd Chicken	3 oz Bkd Chicken
	1 c FF Carrots	1 c FF Carrots	1 c FF Carrots	1 c FF Carrots	1 c FF Carrots	1 c FF Carrots	1 c FF Carrots
	½ c FF Potatoes		½ c FF Potatoes	½ c FF Potatoes	½ c FF Potatoes	½ c FF Potatoes	½ c FF Potatoes
			1 Oleo	1 2" Biscuit	1 2" Biscuit	2 2" Biscuits	2 2" Biscuits
					1 Oleo		
	½ c Diet Frt Cockt	½ c Diet Frt Cockt	½ c Diet Frt Cockt	½ c Diet Frt Cockt	½ c Diet Frt Cockt	½ c Diet Frt Cockt	½ c Diet Frt Cockt
	1 c 1% Milk	1 c 1% Milk					1 c 1% Milk
	Coffee, Tea	Coffee, Tea	Coffee, Tea	Coffee, Tea	Coffee, Tea	Coffee, Tea	Coffee, Tea
Supper	2 oz Beef	2 oz Beef	2 oz Beef	3 oz Beef	3 oz Beef	3 oz Beef	4 oz Beef
	½ c FF Tomatoes	½ c FF Tomatoes	½ c FF Tomatoes	½ c FF Tomatoes	½ c FF Tomatoes	½ c FF Tomatoes	½ c FF Tomatoes
			½ c FF Squash	½ c FF Squash	½ c FF Squash	½ c FF Squash	½ c FF Squash
	½ c FF Potatoes	½ c FF Potatoes	½ c FF Potatoes	½ c FF Potatoes	½ c FF Potatoes	½ c FF Potatoes	½ c FF Potatoes
				1 Bread	2 Bread	2 Bread	2 Bread
			1 Oleo	1 Oleo	1 Oleo	1 Oleo	1 Oleo
	½ c Diet Fruit	½ c Diet Fruit	½ c Diet Fruit	½ c Diet Fruit	½ c Diet Fruit	½ c Diet Fruit	1 c Diet Fruit
	1 c 1% Milk						
	Coffee, Tea	Coffee, Tea	Coffee, Tea	Coffee, Tea	Coffee, Tea	Coffee, Tea	Coffee, Tea
Snack		1 c 1% Milk	1 c 1% Milk	1 c 1% Milk	1 c 1% Milk	1 c 1% Milk	1 c 1% Milk
		2 Graham Crackers (Square)	2 Graham Crackers	2 Graham Crackers	2 Graham Crackers	4 Graham Crackers	4 Graham Crackers

CERTIFIED _____, R.D.

	800 Calories	1,000 Calories	1,200 Calories	1,500 Calories	1,800 Calories	2,000 Calories	2,200 Calories
Breakfast	½ c Orange Juice 1 FF Egg, Scrmb 1 Toast Coffee, Tea	½ c Orange Juice 1 FF Egg, Scrmb 1 Toast 1 Oleo Coffee, Tea	½ c Orange Juice 1 FF Egg, Scrmb 1 Toast 1 Oleo 1 c 1% Milk Coffee, Tea	½ c Orange Juice 1 FF Egg, Scrmb 1 Toast 1 Oleo 1 c 1% Milk Coffee, Tea	½ c Orange Juice 1 FF Egg, Scrmb 1 Toast 1 Oleo ½ c FF Malt-O-Meal 1 Bacon 1 c 1% Milk Coffee, Tea	½ c Orange Juice 2 FF Eggs, Scrmb 1 Toast ½ c FF Malt-O-Meal 1 Bacon 1 c 1% Milk Coffee, Tea	½ c Orange Juice 2 FF Eggs, Scrmb 2 Toast 1 Oleo ½ c FF Malt-o-Meal 1 Bacon Coffee, Tea
Dinner	1 oz Liver ½ c FF Gr Beans Lettuce Salad Zero Dressing ½ c FF Potatoes ½ c Diet Peaches ½ c 1% Milk Coffee, Tea	1 oz Liver ½ c FF Gr Beans Lettuce Salad Zero Dressing ½ c Diet Peaches 1 c 1% Milk Coffee, Tea	2 oz Liver ½ c FF Gr Beans Lettuce Salad Zero Dressing ½ c FF Potatoes 1 Oleo ½ c Diet Peaches Coffee, Tea	2 oz Liver ½ c FF Gr Beans Lettuce Salad Zero Dressing ½ c FF Potatoes 1 Roll ½ c Diet Peaches Coffee, Tea	3 oz Liver ½ c FF Gr Beans Lettuce Salad Zero Dressing ½ c FF Potatoes 1 Roll 1 Oleo ½ c Diet Peaches Coffee, Tea	3 oz Liver ½ c FF Gr Beans Lettuce Salad Zero Dressing ½ c FF Potatoes 2 Rolls 1 Oleo ½ c Diet Peaches Coffee, Tea	3 oz Liver ½ c FF Gr Beans Lettuce Salad Zero Dressing ½ c FF Potatoes 2 Rolls 1 Oleo ½ c Diet Peaches 1 c 1% Milk Coffee, Tea
Supper	2 oz Pork Cutlet ½ c Lettuce/Tom 1 Bread ½ c Diet Cinnamon Applesauce ½ c 1% Milk Coffee, Tea	2 oz Pork Cutlet ½ c Lettuce/Tom 1 Bread ½ c Diet Cinnamon Applesauce Coffee, Tea	2 oz Pork Cutlet ½ c FF Lettuce ½ c Sl Tomatoes 1 Bread ½ c Diet Cinnamon Applesauce 1 t Mayonnaise Coffee, Tea	3 oz Pork Cutlet ½ c FF Lettuce ½ c Sl Tomatoes 1 Bread ½ c Diet Cinnamon Applesauce ½ c Ice Cream Coffee, Tea	3 oz Pork Cutlet ½ c FF Lettuce ½ c Sl Tomatoes 2 Bread ½ c Diet Cinnamon Applesauce ½ c Ice Cream Coffee, Tea	3 oz Pork Cutlet ½ c FF Lettuce ½ c Sl Tomatoes 2 Bread ½ c Diet Cinnamon Applesauce ½ c Ice Cream Coffee, Tea	4 oz Pork Cutlet ½ c FF Lettuce ½ c Sl Tomatoes 2 Bread 1 c Diet Cinnamon Applesauce ½ c Ice Cream Coffee, Tea
Snack		1 c 1% Milk 2 Graham Crackers (Square)	2 c 1% Milk 2 Graham Crackers	1 c 1% Milk 2 Graham Crackers	1 c 1% Milk 2 Graham Crackers	1 c 1% Milk 4 Graham Crackers	1 c 1% Milk 4 Graham Crackers

CERTIFIED _____, R.D.

313

Exhibit A–1 continued

Meal	800 Calories	1,000 Calories	1,200 Calories	1,500 Calories	1,800 Calories	2,000 Calories	2,200 Calories
Breakfast	½ c Orange Juice 1 FF Egg ½ c FF Oatmeal Coffee, Tea	½ c Orange Juice 1 FF Egg ½ c FF Oatmeal 1 Oleo Coffee, Tea	½ c Orange Juice 1 FF Egg ½ c FF Oatmeal 1 Oleo 1 c 1% Milk Coffee, Tea	½ c Orange Juice 1 FF Egg ½ c FF Oatmeal 1 Oleo 1 c 1% Milk Coffee, Tea	½ c Orange Juice 1 FF Egg ½ c FF Oatmeal 1 Toast 2 Oleo 1 c 1% Milk Coffee, Tea	½ c Orange Juice 2 FF Eggs ½ c FF Oatmeal 1 Toast 1 Oleo 1 c 1% Milk Coffee, Tea	½ c Orange Juice 2 FF Eggs ½ c FF Oatmeal 2 Toast 2 Oleo Coffee, Tea
Dinner	1 oz Baked Meat ½ c Lettuce ½ Sl Tomatoes 1 Tortilla ½ c Diet Pineapple ½ c 1% Milk Coffee, Tea	1 oz Baked Meat ½ c Lettuce ½ Sl Tomatoes ½ c Diet Pineapple 1 c 1% Milk Coffee, Tea	2 oz Baked Meat ½ c Lettuce ½ Sl Tomatoes 1 Tortilla ½ c Diet Pineapple 1 t Mayonnaise Coffee, Tea	2 oz Baked Meat ½ c Lettuce ½ Sl Tomatoes ½ c FF Rice 1 Tortilla ½ c Diet Pineapple 1 Oleo or Mayo Coffee, Tea	3 oz Baked Meat ½ c Lettuce ½ Sl Tomatoes ½ c FF Rice 1 Tortilla ½ c Diet Pineapple 1 t Mayonnaise Coffee, Tea	3 oz Baked Meat ½ c Lettuce ½ Sl Tomatoes ½ c FF Rice 2 Tortillas ½ c Diet Pineapple 1 t Mayonnaise Coffee, Tea	3 oz Baked Meat ½ c Lettuce ½ c Sl Tomatoes ½ c FF Rice 2 Tortillas ½ c Diet Pineapple 1 t Mayonnaise 1 c 1% Milk Coffee, Tea
Supper	2 oz Turkey ½ c FF Br Sprouts ½ c FF Mash Potatoes 2 Diet Plums ½ c 1% Milk Coffee, Tea	2 oz Turkey ½ c FF Br Sprouts ½ c FF Mash Potatoes 2 Diet Plums Coffee, Tea	2 oz Turkey 1 c FF Br Sprouts ½ c FF Mash Potatoes 1 Oleo 2 Diet Plums Coffee, Tea	3 oz Turkey 1 c FF Br Sprouts ½ c FF Mash Potatoes 1 2" Biscuit 2 Diet Plums Coffee, Tea	3 oz Turkey 1 c FF Br Sprouts ½ c FF Mash Potatoes 2 2" Biscuits 2 Diet Plums Coffee, Tea	3 oz Turkey 1 c FF Br Sprouts ½ c FF Mash Potatoes 2 2" Biscuits 2 Diet Plums Coffee, Tea	4 oz Turkey 1 c FF Br Sprouts ½ c FF Mash Potatoes 2 2" Biscuits 4 Diet Plums Coffee, Tea
Snack		1 c 1% Milk 2 Graham Crackers (Square)	1 c 1% Milk 2 Graham Crackers	1 c 1% Milk 2 Graham Crackers	1 c 1% Milk 2 Graham Crackers	1 c 1% Milk 4 Graham Crackers	1 c 1% Milk 4 Graham Crackers

CERTIFIED _____, R.D.

314

	800 Calories	1,000 Calories	1,200 Calories	1,500 Calories	1,800 Calories	2,000 Calories	2,200 Calories
Breakfast	½ c Orange Juice 1 FF Egg 1 Toast Coffee, Tea	½ c Orange Juice 1 FF Egg 1 Toast Coffee, Tea	½ c Orange Juice 1 FF Egg 1 Pancake 1 c 1% Milk Coffee, Tea	½ c Orange Juice 1 FF Egg 1 Pancake 1 c 1% Milk Coffee, Tea	½ c Orange Juice 1 FF Egg 2 Pancakes 1 c 1% Milk Coffee, Tea	½ c Orange Juice 2 FF Eggs 1 Pancake ½ c FF Cr Wheat 1 Oleo 1 c 1% Milk Coffee, Tea	½ c Orange Juice 2 FF Eggs 2 Pancakes ½ c FF Cr Wheat Coffee, Tea
Dinner	1 oz Pork 1 c FF Cabbage ¼ c FF Swt Pot ½ c Diet Pineapple ½ c 1% Milk Coffee, Tea	1 oz Pork 1 c FF Cabbage ½ c Diet Pineapple 1 c 1% Milk Coffee, Tea	2 oz Pork 1 c FF Cabbage ¼ c FF Swt Pot 1 Oleo ½ c Diet Pineapple Coffee, Tea	2 oz Pork 1 c FF Cabbage ¼ c FF Swt Pot 1 Bread 1 Oleo ½ c Diet Pineapple Coffee, Tea	3 oz Pork 1 c FF Cabbage ¼ c FF Swt Pot 1 Bread 2 Oleo ½ c Diet Pineapple Coffee, Tea	3 oz Pork 1 c FF Cabbage ½ c FF Swt Pot 1 Bread 2 Oleo ½ c Diet Pineapple Coffee, Tea	3 oz Pork 1 c FF Cabbage ½ c FF Swt Pot 1 Bread 2 Oleo ½ c Diet Pineapple 1 c 1% Milk Coffee, Tea
Supper	2 oz Baked Fish ½ c FF Gr Beans ½ c FF Noodles 2 Diet Pear Hlvs ½ c 1% Milk Coffee, Tea	2 oz Baked Fish ½ c FF Gr Beans ½ c FF Noodles 2 Diet Pear Hlvs Coffee, Tea	2 oz Baked Fish ½ c FF Gr Beans ½ c FF Beets ½ c FF Noodles 1 Oleo 2 Diet Pear Hlvs Coffee, Tea	3 oz Baked Fish ½ c FF Gr Beans ½ c FF Beets ½ c FF Noodles 1 Bread 1 Oleo 2 Diet Pear Hlvs Coffee, Tea	3 oz Baked Fish ½ c FF Gr Beans ½ c FF Beets ½ c FF Noodles 2 Bread 1 Oleo 2 Diet Pear Hlvs Coffee, Tea	3 oz Baked Fish ½ c FF Gr Beans ½ c FF Beets ½ c FF Noodles 2 Bread 1 Oleo 2 Diet Pear Hlvs Coffee, Tea	4 oz Baked Fish ½ c FF Gr Beans ½ c FF Beets ½ c FF Noodles 2 Bread 1 Oleo 4 Diet Pear Hlvs Coffee, Tea
Snack	1 c 1% Milk 2 Graham Crackers (Square)	1 c 1% Milk 2 Graham Crackers (Square)	1 c 1% Milk 2 Graham Crackers	1 c 1% Milk 2 Graham Crackers	1 c 1% Milk 2 Graham Crackers	1 c 1% Milk 4 Graham Crackers	1 c 1% Milk 4 Graham Crackers

CERTIFIED _____, R.D.

315

Exhibit A–1 continued

WEEK NO. ONE DAY SATURDAY MENU CYCLE FALL/WINTER

	800 Calories	*1,000 Calories*	*1,200 Calories*	*1,500 Calories*	*1,800 Calories*	*2,000 Calories*	*2,200 Calories*
Breakfast	½ c Orange Juice 1 FF Egg, Scrmb ½ c FF Cr Rice Coffee, Tea	½ c Orange Juice 1 FF Egg, Scrmb ½ c FF Cr Rice 1 Oleo Coffee, Tea	½ c Orange Juice 1 FF Egg, Scrmb ½ c FF Cr Rice 1 Oleo 1 c 1% Milk Coffee, Tea	½ c Orange Juice 1 FF Egg, Scrmb ½ c FF Cr Rice 1 Oleo 1 c 1% Milk Coffee, Tea	½ c Orange Juice 1 FF Egg, Scrmb ½ c FF Cr Rice 1 Toast 2 Oleo 1 c 1% Milk Coffee, Tea	½ c Orange Juice 2 FF Eggs, Scrmb ½ c FF Cr Rice 1 Toast 1 Oleo 1 c 1% Milk Coffee, Tea	½ c Orange Juice 2 FF Eggs, Scrmb ½ c FF Cr Rice 2 Toast 2 Oleo Coffee, Tea
Dinner	1 oz Roast Beef 1 c FF Gr Beans ½ c Baked Potato 2 Diet Pear Hlvs ½ c 1% Milk Coffee, Tea	1 oz Roast Beef 1 c FF Gr Beans 2 Diet Pear Hlvs 1 c 1% Milk Coffee, Tea	2 oz Roast Beef 1 c FF Gr Beans 1 sm Baked Potato 1 Oleo 2 Diet Pear Hlvs Coffee, Tea	2 oz Roast Beef 1 c FF Gr Beans 1 sm Baked Potato 1 Roll or Bread 2 Diet Pear Hlvs Coffee, Tea	3 oz Roast Beef 1 c FF Gr Beans 1 sm Baked Potato 1 Roll or Bread 1 Oleo 2 Diet Pear Hlvs Coffee, Tea	3 oz Roast Beef 1 c FF Gr Beans 1 sm Baked Potato 2 Rolls or Bread 1 Oleo 2 Diet Pear Hlvs Coffee, Tea	3 oz Roast Beef 1 c FF Gr Beans 1 sm Baked Potato 2 Rolls or Bread 1 Oleo 2 Diet Pear Hlvs 1 c 1% Milk Coffee, Tea
Supper	2 oz Beef Cubes ½ c FF Broccoli ½ c FF Potatoes ½ c Diet Peaches ½ c 1% Milk Coffee, Tea	2 oz Beef Cubes ½ c FF Broccoli ½ c FF Potatoes ½ c Diet Peaches Coffee, Tea	2 oz Beef Cubes ½ c FF Broccoli ½ c FF Carrots ½ c FF Potatoes 1 Oleo ½ c Diet Peaches Coffee, Tea	3 oz Beef Cubes ½ c FF Broccoli ½ c FF Carrots ½ c FF Potatoes ½ c Diet Peaches ½ c Ice Cream Coffee, Tea	3 oz Beef Cubes ½ c FF Broccoli ½ c FF Carrots ½ c FF Potatoes 1 Roll ½ c Diet Peaches ½ c Ice Cream Coffee, Tea	3 oz Beef Cubes ½ c FF Broccoli ½ c FF Carrots ½ c FF Potatoes 1 Roll ½ c Diet Peaches ½ c Ice Cream Coffee, Tea	4 oz Beef Cubes ½ c FF Broccoli ½ c FF Carrots ½ c FF Potatoes 1 Roll 1 c Diet Peaches ½ c Ice Cream Coffee, Tea
Snack		1 c 1% Milk 2 Graham Crackers (Square)	1 c 1% Milk 2 Graham Crackers	1 c 1% Milk 2 Graham Crackers	1 c 1% Milk 2 Graham Crackers	1 c 1% Milk 4 Graham Crackers	1 c 1% Milk 4 Graham Crackers

CERTIFIED ______________________________, R.D.

	800 Calories	1,000 Calories	1,200 Calories	1,500 Calories	1,800 Calories	2,000 Calories	2,200 Calories
B r e a k f a s t	½ c Orange Juice 1 FF Egg 1 Toast Coffee, Tea	½ c Orange Juice 1 FF Egg 1 Toast 1 sl Bacon Coffee, Tea	½ c Orange Juice 1 FF Egg 1 Toast 1 sl Bacon 1 c 1% Milk Coffee, Tea	½ c Orange Juice 1 FF Egg 1 Toast 1 sl Bacon 1 c 1% Milk Coffee, Tea	½ c Orange Juice 1 FF Egg ½ c FF Oatmeal 1 Toast 1 sl Bacon 1 c 1% Milk Coffee, Tea	½ c Orange Juice 2 FF Eggs ½ c FF Oatmeal 1 Toast 1 sl Bacon 1 c 1% Milk Coffee, Tea	½ c Orange Juice 2 FF Eggs ½ c FF Oatmeal 2 Toast 1 sl Bacon 1 Oleo Coffee, Tea
D i n n e r	1 oz Bkd Steak 1 c FF Squash ½ c FF Potatoes ½ c Dt Applesauce ½ c 1% Milk Coffee, Tea	1 oz Bkd Steak 1 c FF Squash ½ c Dt Applesauce 1 c 1% Milk Coffee, Tea	2 oz Bkd Steak 1 c FF Squash ½ c FF Potatoes ½ c Dt Applesauce 1 Oleo Coffee, Tea	2 oz Bkd Steak 1 c FF Squash ½ c FF Potatoes 1 Roll ½ c Dt Applesauce 1 Oleo Coffee, Tea	3 oz Bkd Steak 1 c FF Squash ½ c FF Potatoes 1 Roll ½ c Dt Applesauce 2 Oleo Coffee, Tea	3 oz Bkd Steak 1 c FF Squash ½ c FF Potatoes 2 Rolls ½ c Dt Applesauce 2 Oleo Coffee, Tea	3 oz Bkd Steak 1 c FF Squash ½ c FF Potatoes 2 Rolls ½ c Dt Applesauce 2 Oleo 1 c 1% Milk Coffee, Tea
S u p p e r	2 oz Ham ½ c Bkd Noodles ½ c FF Beets 2 Diet Pear Hlvs ½ c 1% Milk Coffee, Tea	2 oz Ham ½ c Bkd Noodles ½ c FF Beets 2 Diet Pear Hlvs Coffee, Tea	2 oz Ham ½ c Bkd Noodles ¼ c Gr Peas ½ c FF Beets 1 Oleo 2 Diet Pear Hlvs Coffee, Tea	3 oz Ham ½ c Bkd Noodles ¼ c FF Gr Peas ½ c FF Beets 1 Bread 1 Oleo 2 Diet Pear Hlvs Coffee, Tea	3 oz Ham ½ c Bkd Noodles ¼ c FF Gr Peas ½ c FF Beets 2 Bread 1 Oleo 2 Diet Pear Hlvs Coffee, Tea	3 oz Ham ½ c Bkd Noodles ¼ c FF Gr Peas ½ c FF Beets 2 Bread 1 Oleo 2 Diet Pear Hlvs Coffee, Tea	4 oz Ham ½ c Bkd Noodles ¼ c FF Gr Peas ½ c FF Beets 2 Bread 1 Oleo 4 Diet Pear Hlvs Coffee, Tea
S n a c k		1 c 1% Milk 2 Graham Crackers (Square)	1 c 1% Milk 2 Graham Crackers	1 c 1% Milk 2 Graham Crackers	1 c 1% Milk 2 Graham Crackers	1 c 1% Milk 4 Graham Crackers	1 c 1% Milk 4 Graham Crackers

CERTIFIED _____, R.D.

317

Exhibit A–1 continued

WEEK NO. **TWO**   DAY **MONDAY**   MENU CYCLE **FALL/WINTER**

	800 Calories	1,000 Calories	1,200 Calories	1,500 Calories	1,800 Calories	2,000 Calories	2,200 Calories
Breakfast	½ c Orange Juice 1 FF Egg ½ c Malt-O-Meal Coffee, Tea	½ c Orange Juice 1 FF Egg ½ c Malt-O-Meal 1 Oleo Coffee, Tea	½ c Orange Juice 1 FF Egg ½ c Malt-O-Meal 1 Oleo 1 c 1% Milk Coffee, Tea	½ c Orange Juice 1 FF Egg ½ c Malt-O-Meal 1 Oleo 1 c 1% Milk Coffee, Tea	½ c Orange Juice 1 FF Egg ½ c Malt-O-Meal 1 sl Toast 2 Oleo 1 c 1% Milk Coffee, Tea	½ c Orange Juice 2 FF Eggs ½ c Malt-O-Meal 1 sl Toast 1 Oleo 1 c 1% Milk Coffee, Tea	½ c Orange Juice 2 FF Eggs ½ c Malt-O-Meal 1 sl Toast 2 Oleo Coffee, Tea
Dinner	1 oz Fish 1 c FF Broccoli ⅓ c FF Corn 2 Diet Pineapple Rings ½ c 1% Milk Coffee, Tea	1 oz Fish 1 c FF Broccoli 2 Diet Pineapple Rings 1 c 1% Milk Coffee, Tea	2 oz Fish 1 c FF Broccoli ⅓ c FF Corn 2 Diet Pineapple Rings 1 Oleo Coffee, Tea	2 oz Fish 1 c FF Broccoli ⅓ c FF Corn 1 W/W Bread 2 Diet Pineapple Rings 1 Oleo Coffee, Tea	3 oz Fish 1 c FF Broccoli ⅓ c FF Corn 1 W/W Bread 2 Diet Pineapple Rings 2 Oleo Coffee, Tea	3 oz Fish 1 c FF Broccoli ⅓ c FF Corn 2 W/W Bread 2 Diet Pineapple Rings 2 Oleo Coffee, Tea	3 oz Fish 1 c FF Broccoli ⅓ c FF Corn 2 W/W Bread 2 Diet Pineapple Rings 2 Oleo 1 c 1% Milk Coffee, Tea
Supper	2 oz Beef Patty ½ c FF Spinach ½ c FF Potatoes *⅓ c Carrot & Raisin Salad ½ c 1% Milk Coffee, Tea	2 oz Beef Patty ½ c FF Spinach ½ c FF Potatoes 1 Oleo *⅓ c Carrot & Raisin Salad Coffee, Tea	2 oz Beef Patty 1 c FF Spinach ½ c FF Potatoes 1 Oleo *⅓ c Carrot & Raisin Salad Coffee, Tea	3 oz Beef Patty 1 c FF Spinach ½ c FF Potatoes 1 sl Bread 1 Oleo *⅓ c Carrot & Raisin Salad Coffee, Tea	3 oz Beef Patty 1 c FF Spinach ½ c FF Potatoes 1 sl Bread 1 Oleo *⅓ c Carrot & Raisin Salad 5 Vanilla Wafers Coffee, Tea	3 oz Beef Patty 1 c FF Spinach ½ c FF Potatoes 1 sl Bread 1 Oleo *⅓ c Carrot & Raisin Salad 5 Vanilla Wafers Coffee, Tea	4 oz Beef Patty 1 c FF Spinach ½ c FF Potatoes 1 sl Bread *⅔ c Carrot & Raisin Salad 5 Vanilla Wafers Coffee, Tea
Snack	1 c 1% Milk 2 Graham Crackers	1 c 1% Milk 2 Graham Crackers (square)	1 c 1% Milk 2 Graham Crackers	1 c 1% Milk 2 Graham Crackers	1 c 1% Milk 2 Graham Crackers	1 c 1% Milk 4 Graham Crackers	1 c 1% Milk 4 Graham Crackers

*⅓ c Carrot & Raisin Salad = 1 Fruit Exchange

CERTIFIED _____ , R.D.

	800 Calories	1,000 Calories	1,200 Calories	1,500 Calories	1,800 Calories	2,000 Calories	2,200 Calories
Breakfast	½ c Orange Juice	½ c Orange Juice	½ c Orange Juice	½ c Orange Juice	½ c Orange Juice	½ c Orange Juice	½ c Orange Juice
	1 FF Egg	1 FF Egg	1 FF Egg	1 FF Egg	1 FF Egg	2 FF Eggs	2 FF Eggs
					½ c Cr of Wheat	½ c Cr of Wheat	½ c Cr of Wheat
	1 sl Toast	1 sl Toast	1 sl Toast	1 sl Toast	1 sl Toast	1 sl Toast	2 sl Toast
		1 Oleo	1 Oleo	1 Oleo	2 Oleo	1 Oleo	2 Oleo
			1 c 1% Milk	1 c 1% Milk	1 c 1% Milk	1 c 1% Milk	
	Coffee, Tea	Coffee, Tea	Coffee, Tea	Coffee, Tea	Coffee, Tea	Coffee, Tea	Coffee, Tea
Dinner	1 oz Chicken	1 oz Chicken	2 oz Chicken	2 oz Chicken	3 oz Chicken	3 oz Chicken	3 oz Chicken
	½ c FF Carrots	½ c FF Carrots	½ c FF Carrots	½ c FF Carrots	½ c FF Carrots	½ c FF Carrots	½ c FF Carrots
	¼ c FF Peas	¼ c FF Peas	¼ c FF Peas	¼ c FF Peas	¼ c FF Peas	¼ c FF Peas	¼ c FF Peas
	½ c FF Potatoes			½ c FF Potatoes	½ c FF Potatoes	½ c FF Potatoes	½ c FF Potatoes
			1 Biscuit	1 Biscuit	1 Biscuit	2 Biscuits	2 Biscuits
					1 Oleo		
	½ c Diet Peaches	½ c Diet Peaches	½ c Diet Peaches	½ c Diet Peaches	½ c Diet Peaches	½ c Diet Peaches	½ c Diet Peaches
	1 c 1% Milk	1 c 1% Milk					1 c 1% Milk
	Coffee, Tea	Coffee, Tea	Coffee, Tea	Coffee, Tea	Coffee, Tea	Coffee, Tea	Coffee, Tea
Supper	2 oz Beef	2 oz Beef	2 oz Beef	3 oz Beef	3 oz Beef	3 oz Beef	4 oz Beef
	1 Bread	1 Bread	1 Bread	2 Bread	2 Bread	2 Bread	2 Bread
			1 t Mayo or Oleo	1 t Mayo or Oleo	1 t Mayo or Oleo	1 t Mayo or Oleo	1 t Mayo or Oleo
			½ c FF Coleslaw	½ c FF Coleslaw	½ c FF Coleslaw	½ c FF Coleslaw	½ c FF Coleslaw
	½ c FF Mix Veg	½ c FF Mix Veg	½ c FF Mix Veg	½ c FF Mix Veg	½ c FF Mix Veg	½ c FF Mix Veg	½ c FF Mix Veg
					6 Saltines	6 Saltines	6 Saltines
	½ c Diet Frt Cockt	½ c Diet Frt Cockt	½ c Diet Frt Cockt	½ c Frt Cockt	½ c Frt Cockt	½ c Frt Cockt	1 c Frt Cockt
	1 c 1% Milk						
	Coffee, Tea	Coffee, Tea	Coffee, Tea	Coffee, Tea	Coffee, Tea	Coffee, Tea	Coffee, Tea
Snack		1 c 1% Milk	1 c 1% Milk	1 c 1% Milk	1 c 1% Milk	1 c 1% Milk	1 c 1% Milk
		2 Graham Crackers (Square)	2 Graham Crackers	2 Graham Crackers	2 Graham Crackers	4 Graham Crackers	4 Graham Crackers

CERTIFIED _____, R.D.

319

Exhibit A-1 continued

	800 Calories	1,000 Calories	1,200 Calories	1,500 Calories	1,800 Calories	2,000 Calories	2,200 Calories
Breakfast	½ c Orange Juice 1 FF Egg ½ c FF Oatmeal Coffee, Tea	½ c Orange Juice 1 FF Egg ½ c FF Oatmeal 1 Oleo Coffee, Tea	½ c Orange Juice 1 FF Egg ½ c FF Oatmeal 1 Oleo 1 c 1% Milk Coffee, Tea	½ c Orange Juice 1 FF Egg ½ c FF Oatmeal 1 Oleo 1 c 1% Milk Coffee, Tea	½ c Orange Juice 1 FF Egg ½ c FF Oatmeal 1 sl Toast 2 Oleo 1 c 1% Milk Coffee, Tea	½ c Orange Juice 2 FF Eggs ½ c FF Oatmeal 1 sl Toast 1 Oleo 1 c 1% Milk Coffee, Tea	½ c Orange Juice 2 FF Eggs ½ c FF Oatmeal 2 sl Toast 2 Oleo Coffee, Tea
Dinner	1 oz Pork 1 c FF Gr Beans ¼ c FF Sweet Potatoes ½ c Diet Applesauce ½ c 1% Milk Coffee, Tea	1 oz Pork 1 c FF Gr Beans ½ c Diet Applesauce 1 c 1% Milk Coffee, Tea	2 oz Pork 1 c FF Gr Beans ¼ c FF Sweet Potatoes 1 Oleo ½ c Diet Applesauce Coffee, Tea	2 oz Pork 1 c FF Gr Beans ¼ c FF Sweet Potatoes 1 Roll 1 Oleo ½ c Diet Applesauce Coffee, Tea	3 oz Pork 1 c FF Gr Beans ¼ c FF Sweet Potatoes 1 Roll 2 Oleo ½ c Diet Applesauce Coffee, Tea	3 oz Pork 1 c FF Gr Beans ¼ c FF Sweet Potatoes 2 Rolls 2 Oleo ½ c Diet Applesauce Coffee, Tea	3 oz Pork 1 c FF Gr Beans ¼ c FF Sweet Potatoes 2 Rolls 2 Oleo ½ c Diet Applesauce 1 c 1% Milk Coffee, Tea
Supper	2 FF Eggs ½ c Tomato Juice 1 sl Toast ½ c Diet Cinn Pineapple ½ c 1% Milk Coffee, Tea	2 FF Eggs ½ c Tomato Juice 1 sl Toast ½ c Diet Cinn Pineapple Coffee, Tea	2 FF Eggs 1 c Tomato Juice 1 sl Toast 1 Oleo ½ c Diet Cinn Pineapple Coffee, Tea	2 FF Eggs 1 oz Cheese 1 c Tomato Juice 2 sl Toast 1 Oleo ½ c Diet Cinn Pineapple Coffee, Tea	2 FF Eggs 1 oz Cheese 1 c Tomato Juice 3 sl Toast 1 Oleo ½ c Diet Cinn Pineapple Coffee, Tea	2 FF Eggs 1 oz Cheese 1 c Tomato Juice 3 sl Toast 1 Oleo ½ c Diet Cinn Pineapple Coffee, Tea	2 FF Eggs 2 oz Cheese 1 c Tomato Juice 3 sl Toast 1 Oleo 1 c Diet Cinn Pineapple Coffee, Tea
Snack		1 c 1% Milk 2 Graham Crackers (Square)	1 c 1% Milk 2 Graham Crackers	1 c 1% Milk 2 Graham Crackers	1 c 1% Milk 2 Graham Crackers	1 c 1% Milk 4 Graham Crackers	1 c 1% Milk 4 Graham Crackers

CERTIFIED _____, R.D.

320

WEEK NO. TWO DAY THURSDAY MENU CYCLE FALL/WINTER

	800 Calories	*1,000 Calories*	*1,200 Calories*	*1,500 Calories*	*1,800 Calories*	*2,000 Calories*	*2,200 Calories*
Breakfast	½ c Orange Juice 1 FF Egg 1 sl Toast Coffee, Tea	½ c Orange Juice 1 FF Egg 1 sl Toast 1 Oleo Coffee, Tea	½ c Orange Juice 1 FF Egg 1 sl Toast 1 Oleo 1 c 1% Milk Coffee, Tea	½ c Orange Juice 1 FF Egg 1 sl Toast 1 Oleo 1 c 1% Milk Coffee, Tea	½ c Orange Juice 1 FF Egg ½ c FF Cr of Rice 1 sl Toast 2 Oleo 1 c 1% Milk Coffee, Tea	½ c Orange Juice 2 FF Eggs ½ c Cr of Rice 1 sl Toast 1 Oleo 1 c 1% Milk Coffee, Tea	½ c Orange Juice 2 FF Eggs ½ c Cr of Rice 2 sl Toast 2 Oleo Coffee, Tea
Dinner	1 oz Steak ½ c FF Broc/Lemon ½ c FF Gr Beans ½ c FF Rice ½ c Diet Peaches ½ c 1% Milk Coffee, Tea	1 oz Steak ½ c FF Broc/Lemon ½ c FF Gr Beans ½ c Diet Peaches 1 c 1% Milk Coffee, Tea	2 oz Steak ½ c Broc/Lemon ½ c FF Gr Beans ½ c FF Rice 1 Oleo ½ c Diet Peaches Coffee, Tea	2 oz Steak ½ c Broc/Lemon ½ c FF Gr Beans ½ c FF Rice 1 Roll 1 Oleo ½ c Diet Peaches Coffee, Tea	3 oz Steak ½ c Broc/Lemon ½ c Gr Beans ½ c FF Rice 1 Roll 2 Oleo ½ c Diet Peaches Coffee, Tea	3 oz Steak ½ c Broc/Lemon ½ c Gr Beans ½ c FF Rice 2 Rolls 2 Oleo ½ c Diet Peaches Coffee, Tea	3 oz Steak ½ c Broc/Lemon ½ c Gr Beans ½ c FF Rice 2 Rolls 2 Oleo ½ c Diet Peaches 1 c 1% Milk Coffee, Tea
Supper	2 Hot Dogs ½ c FF Coleslaw 1 Bread ½ Banana ½ c 1% Milk Coffee, Tea	2 Hot Dogs ½ c FF Coleslaw 1 Bread ½ Banana Coffee, Tea	2 Hot Dogs ½ c FF Coleslaw ½ c FF Carrots 1 Bread 1 t Mayo or Oleo ½ Banana Coffee, Tea	2 Hot Dogs 1 oz Cheese ½ c FF Coleslaw ½ c FF Carrots 1 Hot Dog Bun 1 t Mayo or Oleo ½ Banana Coffee, Tea	2 Hot Dogs 1 oz Cheese ½ c FF Coleslaw ½ c FF Carrots 1 Hot Dog Bun 1 t Mayo or Oleo ½ Banana 5 Vanilla Wafers Coffee, Tea	2 Hot Dogs 1 oz Cheese ½ c FF Coleslaw ½ c FF Carrots 1 Hot Dog Bun 1 t Mayo or Oleo ½ Banana 5 Vanilla Wafers Coffee, Tea	2 Hot Dogs 2 oz Cheese ½ c FF Coleslaw ½ c FF Carrots 1 Hot Dog Bun 1 t Mayo or Oleo 1 Banana 5 Vanilla Wafers Coffee, Tea
Snack		1 c 1% Milk 2 Graham Crackers (Square)	1 c 1% Milk 2 Graham Crackers	1 c 1% Milk 2 Graham Crackers	1 c 1% Milk 2 Graham Crackers	1 c 1% Milk 4 Graham Crackers	1 c 1% Milk 4 Graham Crackers

CERTIFIED ______________________________, R.D.

Exhibit A–1 continued

WEEK NO. TWO DAY FRIDAY MENU CYCLE FALL/WINTER

	800 Calories	*1,000 Calories*	*1,200 Calories*	*1,500 Calories*	*1,800 Calories*	*2,000 Calories*	*2,200 Calories*
Breakfast	½ c Orange Juice 1 FF Egg ½ c FF Ralston Coffee, Tea	½ c Orange Juice 1 FF Egg ½ c FF Ralston 1 Oleo Coffee, Tea	½ c Orange Juice 1 FF Egg ½ c FF Ralston 1 Oleo 1 c 1% Milk Coffee, Tea	½ c Orange Juice 1 FF Egg ½ c FF Ralston 1 Oleo 1 c 1% Milk Coffee, Tea	½ c Orange Juice 1 FF Egg ½ c FF Ralston 1 sl Toast 2 Oleo 1 c 1% Milk Coffee, Tea	½ c Orange Juice 2 FF Eggs ½ c FF Ralston 1 sl Toast 1 Oleo 1 c 1% Milk Coffee, Tea	½ c Orange Juice 2 FF Eggs ½ c FF Ralston 2 sl Toast 2 Oleo Coffee, Tea
Dinner	1 oz Chicken #8 FF Veg Salad #8 FF Beets #8 FF Lima Beans 1 oz Zero Dressing #8 Dt Applesauce ½ c 1% Milk Coffee, Tea	1 oz Chicken ½ c FF Veg Salad ½ c FF Beets 1 oz Zero Dressing ½ c Dt Applesauce 1 c 1% Milk Coffee, Tea	2 oz Chicken ½ c FF Veg Salad ½ c FF Beets ½ c FF Lima Beans 1 oz Zero Dressing 1 Oleo ½ c Dt Applesauce Coffee, Tea	2 oz Chicken ½ c FF Veg Salad ½ c FF Beets ½ c FF Lima Beans 1 oz Zero Dressing 1 2″ Biscuit ½ c Dt Applesauce Coffee, Tea	3 oz Chicken ½ c FF Veg Salad ½ c FF Beets ½ c FF Lima Beans 1 oz Zero Dressing 1 2″ Biscuit 1 Oleo ½ c Dt Applesauce Coffee, Tea	3 oz Chicken ½ c FF Veg Salad ½ c FF Beets ½ c FF Lima Beans 1 oz Zero Dressing 2 2″ Biscuits ½ c Dt Applesauce Coffee, Tea	3 oz Chicken ½ c FF Veg Salad ½ c FF Beets ½ c FF Lima Beans 1 oz Zero Dressing 2 2″ Biscuits ½ c Dt Applesauce 1 c 1% Milk Coffee, Tea
Supper	2 oz Fish #8 FF Tomatoes #8 FF Potatoes # 8 Diet Fruit ½ c 1% Milk Coffee, Tea	2 oz Fish ½ c FF Tomatoes ½ c FF Potatoes ½ c Diet Fruit Coffee, Tea	2 oz Fish ½ c FF Tomatoes ½ c FF Zucchini ½ c FF Potatoes 1 Oleo ½ c Diet Fruit Coffee, Tea	3 oz Fish ½ c FF Tomatoes ½ c FF Zucchini ½ c FF Potatoes 1 Roll 1 Oleo ½ c Diet Fruit Coffee, Tea	3 oz Fish ½ c FF Tomatoes ½ c FF Zucchini ½ c FF Potatoes 2 Rolls 1 Oleo ½ c Diet Fruit Coffee, Tea	3 oz Fish ½ c FF Tomatoes ½ c FF Zucchini ½ c FF Potatoes 2 Rolls 1 Oleo ½ c Diet Fruit Coffee, Tea	4 oz Fish ½ c FF Tomatoes ½ c FF Zucchini ½ c FF Potatoes 2 Rolls 1 Oleo 1 c Diet Fruit Coffee, Tea
Snack		1 c 1% Milk 2 Graham Crackers (Square)	1 c 1% Milk 2 Graham Crackers	1 c 1% Milk 2 Graham Crackers	1 c 1% Milk 2 Graham Crackers	1 c 1% Milk 2 Graham Crackers	1 c 1% Milk 2 Graham Crackers

CERTIFIED ____________________, R.D.

WEEK NO. TWO DAY SATURDAY MENU CYCLE FALL/WINTER

	800 Calories	*1,000 Calories*	*1,200 Calories*	*1,500 Calories*	*1,800 Calories*	*2,000 Calories*	*2,200 Calories*
Breakfast	½ c Orange Juice 1 FF Egg 1 sl Toast Coffee, Tea	½ c Orange Juice 1 FF Egg 1 sl Toast 1 Oleo Coffee, Tea	½ c Orange Juice 1 FF Egg 1 sl Toast 1 Oleo 1 c 1% Milk Coffee, Tea	½ c Orange Juice 1 FF Egg 1 sl Toast 1 Oleo 1 c 1% Milk Coffee, Tea	½ c Orange Juice 1 FF Egg 1 sl Toast ½ c FF Oatmeal 2 Oleo 1 c 1% Milk Coffee, Tea	½ c Orange Juice 2 FF Eggs 1 sl Toast ½ c FF Oatmeal 1 Oleo 1 c 1% Milk Coffee, Tea	½ c Orange Juice 2 FF Eggs 2 sl Toast ½ c FF Oatmeal 2 Oleo Coffee, Tea
Dinner	1 oz Scrmb Beef ½ c FF Spaghetti ½ c FF Tomatoes ½ c Tossed Salad Zero Dressing ½ Banana ½ c 1% Milk Coffee, Tea	1 oz Scrmb Beef ½ c FF Tomatoes ½ c Tossed Salad Zero Dressing ½ Banana 1 c 1% Milk Coffee, Tea	2 oz Scrmb Beef ½ c FF Spaghetti ½ c FF Tomatoes ½ c Tossed Salad Zero Dressing 1 Oleo ½ Banana Coffee, Tea	2 oz Scrmb Beef ½ c FF Spaghetti ½ c FF Tomatoes ½ c Tossed Salad Zero Dressing 1 sl Toast 1 Oleo ½ Banana Coffee, Tea	3 oz Scrmb Beef ½ c FF Spaghetti ½ c FF Tomatoes ½ c Tossed Salad Zero Dressing 2 sl Toast 1 Oleo ½ Banana Coffee, Tea	3 oz Scrmb Beef ½ c FF Spaghetti ½ c FF Tomatoes ½ c Tossed Salad Zero Dressing 2 sl Toast 1 Oleo ½ Banana Coffee, Tea	3 oz Scrmb Beef ½ c FF Spaghetti ½ c FF Tomatoes ½ c Tossed Salad Zero Dressing 2 sl Toast 1 Oleo ½ Banana 1 c 1% Milk Coffee, Tea
Supper	2 FF Eggs ½ c Sliced Tomato ½ c FF Potatoes ½ c Diet Cinn Fruit Mix ½ c 1% Milk Coffee, Tea	2 FF Eggs ½ c Sliced Tomato ½ c FF Potatoes ½ c Diet Cinn Fruit Mix Coffee, Tea	2 FF Eggs ½ c Sliced Tomato ½ c FF Gr Beans ½ c FF Potatoes 1 Oleo ½ c Diet Cinn Fruit Mix Coffee, Tea	2 FF Eggs 1 oz Cheese ½ c Sliced Tomato ½ c FF Gr Beans ½ c FF Potatoes 1 sl Toast 1 Oleo ½ c Diet Cinn Fruit Mix Coffee, Tea	2 FF Eggs 1 oz Cheese ½ c Sliced Tomato ½ c FF Gr Beans ½ c FF Potatoes 1 sl Toast 2 Oleo ½ c Diet Cinn Fruit Mix Coffee, Tea	2 FF Eggs 1 oz Cheese ½ c Sliced Tomato ½ c FF Gr Beans ½ c FF Potatoes 2 sl Toast 2 Oleo ½ c Diet Cinn Fruit Mix Coffee, Tea	2 FF Eggs 2 oz Cheese ½ c Sliced Tomato ½ c FF Gr Beans ½ c FF Potatoes 2 sl Toast 2 Oleo ½ c Diet Cinn Fruit Mix Coffee, Tea
Snack		1 c 1% Milk 2 Graham Crackers (Square)	1 c 1% Milk 2 Graham Crackers	1 c 1% Milk 2 Graham Crackers	1 c 1% Milk 2 Graham Crackers	1 c 1% Milk 4 Graham Crackers	1 c 1% Milk 4 Graham Crackers

CERTIFIED ______________________________, R.D.

Exhibit A–1 continued

	800 Calories	1,000 Calories	1,200 Calories	1,500 Calories	1,800 Calories	2,000 Calories	2,200 Calories
Breakfast	½ c Orange Juice 1 FF Egg ½ c FF Malt-O-Meal 1 Bacon ½ c 1% Milk Coffee, Tea	½ c Orange Juice 1 FF Egg ½ c FF Malt-O-Meal 1 Bacon Coffee, Tea	½ c Orange Juice 1 FF Egg ½ c FF Malt-O-Meal 1 Bacon 1 c 1% Milk Coffee, Tea	½ c Orange Juice 1 FF Egg ½ c FF Malt-O-Meal 1 Bacon 1 c 1% Milk Coffee, Tea	½ c Orange Juice 1 FF Egg ½ c FF Malt-O-Meal 1 Toast 1 Bacon 1 Oleo 1 c 1% Milk Coffee, Tea	½ c Orange Juice 2 FF Eggs ½ c FF Malt-O-Meal 1 Toast 1 Bacon 1 c 1% Milk Coffee, Tea	½ c Orange Juice 2 FF Eggs ½ c FF Malt-O-Meal 2 Toast 1 Bacon 1 Oleo Coffee, Tea
Dinner	1 oz Ham 1 c FF Greens ¼ c FF Swt Potatoes ½ c Dt Applesauce ½ c 1% Milk Coffee, Tea	1 oz Ham 1 c FF Greens ½ c Dt Applesauce 1 c 1% Milk Coffee, Tea	2 oz Ham 1 c FF Greens ¼ c FF Swt Potatoes ½ c Dt Applesauce 1 Oleo Coffee, Tea	2 oz Ham 1 c FF Greens ¼ c FF Swt Potatoes ½ c Dt Applesauce 2" sq Cornbread Coffee, Tea	3 oz Ham 1 c FF Greens ¼ c FF Swt Potatoes ½ c Dt Applesauce 2" sq Cornbread 1 Oleo Coffee, Tea	3 oz Ham 1 c FF Greens ½ c FF Swt Potatoes ¼ c Dt Applesauce 2" sq Cornbread 1 Oleo Coffee, Tea	3 oz Ham 1 c FF Greens ½ c FF Swt Potatoes ½ c Dt Applesauce 2" sq Cornbread 1 Oleo 1 c 1% Milk Coffee, Tea
Supper	2 oz Scrmb Beef ½ c FF Tomatoes 8 Baked Fries ½ c Diet Pears ½ c 1% Milk Coffee, Tea	2 oz Scrmb Beef ½ c FF Tomatoes 8 Baked Fries ½ c Diet Pears Coffee, Tea	2 oz Scrmb Beef ½ c FF Tomatoes Lettuce Salad Buttermilk Dressing (3 T = Free) 8 Baked Fries 1 Oleo ½ c Diet Pears Coffee, Tea	3 oz Scrmb Beef ½ c FF Tomatoes Lettuce Salad 1 T Reg. Dressing 8 Baked Fries 1 Bread ½ c Diet Pears Coffee, Tea	3 oz Scrmb Beef ½ c FF Tomatoes Lettuce Salad 1 T Reg. Dressing 16 Baked Fries 1 Bread ½ c Diet Pears Coffee, Tea	3 oz Scrmb Beef ½ c FF Tomatoes Lettuce Salad 1 T Reg. Dressing 16 Baked Fries 1 Bread ½ c Diet Pears Coffee, Tea	4 oz Scrmb Beef ½ c FF Tomatoes Lettuce Salad 1 T Reg. Dressing 16 Baked Fries 1 Bread 1 c Diet Pears Coffee, Tea
Snack		1 c 1% Milk 2 Graham Crackers (Square)	1 c 1% Milk 2 Graham Crackers	1 c 1% Milk 2 Graham Crackers	1 c 1% Milk 2 Graham Crackers	1 c 1% Milk 4 Graham Crackers	1 c 1% Milk 4 Graham Crackers

CERTIFIED _____, R.D.

324

WEEK NO. THREE DAY MONDAY MENU CYCLE FALL/WINTER

	800 Calories	*1,000 Calories*	*1,200 Calories*	*1,500 Calories*	*1,800 Calories*	*2,000 Calories*	*2,200 Calories*
Breakfast	½ c Orange Juice 1 FF Egg 1 Toast Coffee, Tea	½ c Orange Juice 1 FF Egg 1 Toast 1 Oleo Coffee, Tea	½ c Orange Juice 1 FF Egg 1 Toast 1 Oleo 1 c 1% Milk Coffee, Tea	½ c Orange Juice 1 FF Egg 1 Toast 1 Oleo 1 c 1% Milk Coffee, Tea	½ c Orange Juice 1 FF Egg 1 Toast ½ c FF Cr of Wheat 2 Oleo 1 c 1% Milk Coffee, Tea	½ c Orange Juice 2 FF Eggs 1 Toast ½ c FF Cr of Wheat 1 Oleo 1 c 1% Milk Coffee, Tea	½ c Orange Juice 2 FF Eggs 2 Toast ½ c FF Cr of Wheat 2 Oleo Coffee, Tea
Dinner	1 oz Chicken ½ c FF Carrots ¼ c FF Peas ½ c FF Potatoes 2 Diet P/A Rings ½ c 1% Milk Coffee, Tea	1 oz Chicken ½ c FF Carrots ¼ c FF Peas 2 Diet P/A Rings 1 c 1% Milk Coffee, Tea	2 oz Chicken ½ c FF Carrots ¼ c FF Peas ½ c FF Potatoes 1 Oleo 2 Diet P/A Rings Coffee, Tea	2 oz Chicken ½ c FF Carrots ¼ c FF Peas ½ c FF Potatoes 1 Roll 1 Oleo 2 Diet P/A Rings Coffee, Tea	3 oz Chicken ½ c FF Carrots ¼ c FF Peas ½ c FF Potatoes 1 Roll 2 Oleo 2 Diet P/A Rings Coffee, Tea	3 oz Chicken ½ c FF Carrots ¼ c FF Peas ½ c FF Potatoes 2 Rolls 2 Oleo 2 Diet P/A Rings Coffee, Tea	3 oz Chicken ½ c FF Carrots ¼ c FF Peas ½ c FF Potatoes 2 Rolls 2 Oleo 2 Diet P/A Rings 1 c 1% Milk Coffee, Tea
Supper	2 oz Bkd Fish ½ c FF Gr Beans ½ c FF Mashed Potatoes ½ c Diet Frt Cockt 1 c 1% Milk Coffee, Tea	2 oz Bkd Fish ½ c FF Gr Beans ½ c FF Mashed Potatoes ½ c Diet Frt Cockt Coffee, Tea	2 oz Baked Fish ½ c FF Beets ½ c FF Gr Beans ½ c FF Mashed Potatoes 1 Oleo ½ c Diet Frt Cockt Coffee, Tea	3 oz Baked Fish ½ c FF Beets ½ c FF Gr Beans ½ c FF Mashed Potatoes 1 Bread 1 Oleo ½ c Diet Frt Cockt Coffee, Tea	3 oz Bkd Fish ½ c FF Beets ½ c FF Gr Beans ½ c FF Mashed Potatoes 2 Bread 1 Oleo ½ c Diet Frt Cockt Coffee, Tea	3 oz Bkd Fish ½ c FF Beets ½ c FF Gr Beans ½ c FF Mashed Potatoes 2 Bread 1 Oleo ½ c Diet Frt Cockt Coffee, Tea	4 oz Bkd Fish ½ c FF Beets ½ c FF Gr Beans ½ c FF Mashed Potatoes 2 Bread 1 Oleo 1 c Diet Frt Cockt Coffee, Tea
Snack		1 c 1% Milk 2 Graham Crackers (Square)	1 c 1% Milk 2 Graham Crackers	1 c 1% Milk 2 Graham Crackers	1 c 1% Milk 2 Graham Crackers	1 c 1% Milk 4 Graham Crackers	1 c 1% Milk 4 Graham Crackers

CERTIFIED ______________________________, R.D.

Exhibit A–1 continued

WEEK NO. THREE DAY TUESDAY MENU CYCLE FALL/WINTER

	800 Calories	*1,000 Calories*	*1,200 Calories*	*1,500 Calories*	*1,800 Calories*	*2,000 Calories*	*2,200 Calories*
Breakfast	½ c Orange Juice 1 FF Egg ½ c FF Oatmeal Coffee, Tea	½ c Orange Juice 1 FF Egg ½ c FF Oatmeal 1 Oleo Coffee, Tea	½ c Orange Juice 1 FF Egg ½ c FF Oatmeal 1 Oleo 1 c 1% Milk Coffee, Tea	½ c Orange Juice 1 FF Egg ½ c FF Oatmeal 1 Oleo 1 c 1% Milk Coffee, Tea	½ c Orange Juice 1 FF Egg ½ c FF Oatmeal 1 Toast 2 Oleo 1 c 1% Milk Coffee, Tea	½ c Orange Juice 2 FF Eggs ½ c FF Oatmeal 1 Toast 1 Oleo 1 c 1% Milk Coffee, Tea	½ c Orange Juice 2 FF Eggs ½ c FF Oatmeal 2 Toast 2 Oleo Coffee, Tea
Dinner	1 oz Steak 1 c FF Carrots ½ c FF Rice ½ c Diet Peaches ½ c 1% Milk Coffee, Tea	1 oz Steak 1 c FF Carrots ½ c Diet Peaches 1 c 1% Milk Coffee, Tea	2 oz Steak 1 c FF Carrots ½ c FF Rice 1 Oleo ½ c Diet Peaches Coffee, Tea	2 oz Steak 1 c FF Carrots ½ c FF Rice 1 Roll 1 Oleo ½ c Diet Peaches Coffee, Tea	3 oz Steak 1 c FF Carrots ½ c FF Rice 1 Roll 2 Oleo ½ c Diet Peaches Coffee, Tea	3 oz Steak 1 c FF Carrots ½ c FF Rice 2 Rolls 2 Oleo ½ c Diet Peaches Coffee, Tea	3 oz Steak 1 c FF Carrots ½ c FF Rice 2 Rolls 2 Oleo ½ c Diet Peaches 1 c 1% Milk Coffee, Tea
Supper	2 oz Meat ½ c FF Gr Beans 1 Tortilla ½ c Diet Pears ½ c 1% Milk Coffee, Tea	2 oz Meat ½ c FF Gr Beans 1 Tortilla ½ c Diet Pears Coffee, Tea	2 oz Meat 1 c FF Gr Beans 1 Tortilla 1 Oleo ½ c Diet Pears Coffee, Tea	3 oz Meat 1 c FF Gr Beans 2 Tortillas 1 Oleo ½ c Diet Pears Coffee, Tea	3 oz Meat 1 c FF Gr Beans 3 Tortillas 1 Oleo ½ c Diet Pears Coffee, Tea	3 oz Meat 1 c FF Gr Beans 3 Tortillas 1 Oleo ½ c Diet Pears Coffee, Tea	4 oz Meat 1 c FF Gr Beans 3 Tortillas 1 Oleo 1 c Diet Pears Coffee, Tea
Snack		1 c 1% Milk 2 Graham Crackers (Square)	1 c 1% Milk 2 Graham Crackers	1 c 1% Milk 2 Graham Crackers	1 c 1% Milk 2 Graham Crackers	1 c 1% Milk 4 Graham Crackers	1 c 1% Milk 4 Graham Crackers

CERTIFIED ____________________, R.D.

WEEK NO. THREE DAY WEDNESDAY MENU CYCLE FALL/WINTER

	800 Calories	*1,000 Calories*	*1,200 Calories*	*1,500 Calories*	*1,800 Calories*	*2,000 Calories*	*2,200 Calories*
Breakfast	½ c Orange Juice 1 FF Egg 1 Toast Coffee, Tea	½ c Orange Juice 1 FF Egg 1 Toast 1 Oleo Coffee, Tea	½ c Orange Juice 1 FF Egg 1 Toast 1 Oleo 1 c 1% Milk Coffee, Tea	½ c Orange Juice 1 FF Egg 1 Toast 1 Oleo 1 c 1% Milk Coffee, Tea	½ c Orange Juice 1 FF Egg 1 Toast ½ c FF Cr of Rice 2 Oleo 1 c 1% Milk Coffee, Tea	½ c Orange Juice 2 FF Eggs 1 Toast ½ c FF Cr of Rice 1 Oleo 1 c 1% Milk Coffee, Tea	½ c Orange Juice 2 FF Eggs 2 Toast ½ c FF Cr of Rice 2 Oleo Coffee, Tea
Dinner	1 oz Pork 1 c FF Tomatoes ½ c FF Mshd Pots ½ Banana ½ c 1% Milk Coffee, Tea	1 oz Pork 1 c FF Tomatoes ½ Banana 1 c 1% Milk Coffee, Tea	2 oz Pork 1 c FF Tomatoes ½ c FF Potatoes ½ Banana 1 Oleo Coffee, Tea	2 oz Pork 1 c FF Tomatoes ½ c FF Potatoes 1 2″ Biscuit ½ Banana Coffee, Tea	3 oz Pork 1 c FF Tomatoes ½ c FF Potatoes 1 2″ Biscuit ½ Banana 1 Oleo Coffee, Tea	3 oz Pork 1 c FF Tomatoes ½ c FF Potatoes 2 2″ Biscuits ½ Banana Coffee, Tea	3 oz Pork 1 c FF Tomatoes ½ c FF Potatoes 2 2″ Biscuits ½ Banana 1 c 1% Milk Coffee, Tea
Supper	2 oz Lunch Meat 1 Bread ½ c FF Mix Veg ½ c Diet Fruit ½ c 1% Milk Coffee, Tea	2 oz Lunch Meat 1 Bread ½ c FF Mix Veg ½ c Diet Fruit Coffee, Tea	2 oz Lunch Meat 1 Bread 1 t Mayo or Oleo ½ c FF Mix Veg ½ c Hot Tomato Jce ½ c Diet Fruit Coffee, Tea	2 oz Lunch Meat 1 oz Cheese 2 Bread 1 t Mayo or Oleo ½ c FF Mix Veg ½ c Hot Tomato Jce ½ c Diet Fruit Coffee, Tea	2 oz Lunch Meat 1 oz Cheese 2 Bread 1 t Mayo or Oleo ½ c FF Mix Veg ½ c Hot Tomato Jce ½ c Diet Fruit 5 Vanilla Wafers Coffee, Tea	2 oz Lunch Meat 1 oz Cheese 2 Bread 1 t Mayo or Oleo ½ c FF Mix Veg ½ c Hot Tomato Jce ½ c Diet Fruit 5 Vanilla Wafers Coffee, Tea	3 oz Lunch Meat 1 oz Cheese 2 Bread 1 t Mayo or Oleo ½ c FF Mix Veg ½ c Hot Tomato Jce 1 c Diet Fruit 5 Vanilla Wafers Coffee, Tea
Snack		1 c 1% Milk 2 Graham Crackers (Square)	1 c 1% Milk 2 Graham Crackers	1 c 1% Milk 2 Graham Crackers	1 c 1% Milk 2 Graham Crackers	1 c 1% Milk 4 Graham Crackers	1 c 1% Milk 4 Graham Crackers

CERTIFIED ______________________________, R.D.

Exhibit A–1 continued

	800 Calories	1,000 Calories	1,200 Calories	1,500 Calories	1,800 Calories	2,000 Calories	2,200 Calories
Breakfast	½ c Orange Juice 1 FF Egg ½ c FF Ralston 1 Oleo Coffee, Tea	½ c Orange Juice 1 FF Egg ½ c FF Ralston 1 Oleo Coffee, Tea	½ c Orange Juice 1 FF Egg ½ c FF Ralston 1 Oleo 1 c 1% Milk Coffee, Tea	½ c Orange Juice 1 FF Egg ½ c FF Ralston 1 Oleo 1 c 1% Milk Coffee, Tea	½ c Orange Juice 1 FF Egg ½ c FF Ralston 1 Toast 2 Oleo 1 c 1% Milk Coffee, Tea	½ c Orange Juice 2 FF Eggs ½ c FF Ralston 1 Toast 1 Oleo 1 c 1% Milk Coffee, Tea	½ c Orange Juice 2 FF Eggs ½ c FF Ralston 2 Toast 2 Oleo Coffee, Tea
Dinner	1 oz Beef Strips 1 c FF Broccoli ½ c FF Noodles ½ c Diet Apricots ½ c 1% Milk Coffee, Tea	1 oz Beef Strips 1 c FF Broccoli ½ c Diet Apricots 1 c 1% Milk Coffee, Tea	2 oz Beef Strips 1 c FF Broccoli ½ c FF Noodles 1 Oleo ½ c Diet Apricots Coffee, Tea	2 oz Beef Strips 1 c FF Broccoli ½ c FF Noodles 1 Roll 1 Oleo ½ c Diet Apricots Coffee, Tea	3 oz Beef Strips 1 c FF Broccoli ½ c FF Noodles 1 Roll 2 Oleo ½ c Diet Apricots Coffee, Tea	3 oz Beef Strips 1 c FF Broccoli ½ c FF Noodles 2 Rolls 2 Oleo ½ c Diet Apricots Coffee, Tea	3 oz Beef Strips 1 c FF Broccoli ½ c FF Noodles 2 Rolls 2 Oleo ½ c Diet Apricots 1 c 1% Milk Coffee, Tea
Supper	2 oz FF Chicken ½ c FF Mix Veg ½ c FF Potatoes ½ c Dt Applesauce ½ c 1% Milk Coffee, Tea	2 oz FF Chicken ½ c FF Mix Veg ½ c FF Potatoes ½ c Dt Applesauce Coffee, Tea	2 oz FF Chicken 1 c FF Mix Veg ½ c FF Potatoes 1 Oleo ½ c Dt Applesauce Coffee, Tea	3 oz FF Chicken 1 c FF Mix Veg ½ c FF Potatoes 1 Biscuit ½ c Dt Applesauce Coffee, Tea	3 oz FF Chicken 1 c FF Mix Veg ½ c FF Potatoes 1 Biscuit ½ c Dt Applesauce 5 Vanilla Wafers Coffee, Tea	3 oz FF Chicken 1 c FF Mix Veg ½ c FF Potatoes 1 Biscuit ½ c Dt Applesauce 5 Vanilla Wafers Coffee, Tea	4 oz FF Chicken 1 c FF Mix Veg ½ c FF Potatoes 1 Biscuit 1 c Dt Applesauce 5 Vanilla Wafers Coffee, Tea
Snack	1 c 1% Milk	1 c 1% Milk 2 Graham Crackers (Square)	1 c 1% Milk 2 Graham Crackers	1 c 1% Milk 2 Graham Crackers	1 c 1% Milk 2 Graham Crackers	1 c 1% Milk 4 Graham Crackers	1 c 1% Milk 4 Graham Crackers

CERTIFIED _____, R.D.

328

	800 Calories	1,000 Calories	1,200 Calories	1,500 Calories	1,800 Calories	2,000 Calories	2,200 Calories
Breakfast	½ c Orange Juice 1 FF Egg 1 Toast Coffee, Tea	½ c Orange Juice 1 FF Egg 1 Toast 1 Oleo Coffee, Tea	½ c Orange Juice 1 FF Egg 1 Toast 1 Oleo 1 c 1% Milk Coffee, Tea	½ c Orange Juice 1 FF Egg 1 Toast 1 Oleo 1 c 1% Milk Coffee, Tea	½ c Orange Juice 1 FF Egg 1 Toast ½ c FF Oatmeal 2 Oleo 1 c 1% Milk Coffee, Tea	½ c Orange Juice 2 FF Eggs 1 Toast ½ c FF Oatmeal 1 Oleo 1 c 1% Milk Coffee, Tea	½ c Orange Juice 2 FF Eggs 2 Toast ½ c FF Oatmeal 2 Oleo Coffee, Tea
Dinner	1 oz Bkd Fish ⅓ c FF Mex Corn 1 c FF Cauliflower ½ c Diet Frt Cockt ½ c 1% Milk Coffee, Tea	1 oz Bkd Fish 1 c FF Cauliflower ½ c Diet Frt Cockt 1 c 1% Milk Coffee, Tea	2 oz Bkd Fish ⅓ c FF Mex Corn 1 c FF Cauliflower 1 Oleo ½ c Diet Frt Cockt Coffee, Tea	2 oz Bkd Fish ⅓ c FF Mex Corn 1 c FF Cauliflower 1 W/W Bread 1 Oleo ½ c Diet Frt Cockt Coffee, Tea	3 oz Bkd Fish ⅓ c FF Mex Corn 1 c FF Cauliflower 1 W/W Bread 2 Oleo ½ c Diet Frt Cockt Coffee, Tea	3 oz Bkd Fish ⅓ c FF Mex Corn 1 c FF Cauliflower 2 W/W Bread 2 Oleo ½ c Diet Frt Cockt Coffee, Tea	3 oz Bkd Fish ⅓ c FF Mex Corn 1 c FF Cauliflower 2 W/W Bread 2 Oleo ½ c Diet Frt Cockt 1 c 1% Milk Coffee, Tea
Supper	2 oz Beef ½ c FF Carrots ½ c FF Macaroni ½ c Diet Pears ½ c 1% Milk Coffee, Tea	2 oz Beef ½ c FF Carrots ½ c FF Macaroni ½ c Diet Pears Coffee, Tea	2 oz Beef 1 c FF Carrots ½ c FF Macaroni 1 Oleo ½ c Diet Pears Coffee, Tea	3 oz Beef 1 c FF Carrots ½ c FF Macaroni 1 Roll 1 Oleo ½ c Diet Pears Coffee, Tea	3 oz Beef 1 c FF Carrots ½ c FF Macaroni 2 Rolls 1 Oleo ½ c Diet Pears Coffee, Tea	3 oz Beef 1 c FF Carrots ½ c FF Macaroni 2 Rolls 1 Oleo ½ c Diet Pears Coffee, Tea	4 oz Beef 1 c FF Carrots ½ c FF Macaroni 2 Rolls 1 Oleo 1 c Diet Pears Coffee, Tea
Snack		1 c 1% Milk 2 Graham Crackers (Square)	1 c 1% Milk 2 Graham Crackers	1 c 1% Milk 2 Graham Crackers	1 c 1% Milk 2 Graham Crackers	1 c 1% Milk 4 Graham Crackers	1 c 1% Milk 4 Graham Crackers

CERTIFIED _____, R.D.

329

Exhibit A–1 continued

WEEK NO. __THREE__   DAY __SATURDAY__   MENU CYCLE ____   FALL/WINTER

	800 Calories	1,000 Calories	1,200 Calories	1,500 Calories	1,800 Calories	2,000 Calories	2,200 Calories
Breakfast	½ c Orange Juice; 1 FF Egg; ½ c FF Malt-O-Meal; Coffee, Tea	½ c Orange Juice; 1 FF Egg; ½ c FF Malt-O-Meal; 1 Oleo; Coffee, Tea	½ c Orange Juice; 1 FF Egg; ½ c FF Malt-O-Meal; 1 Oleo; 1 c 1% Milk; Coffee, Tea	½ c Orange Juice; 1 FF Egg; ½ c FF Malt-O-Meal; 1 Oleo; 1 c 1% Milk; Coffee, Tea	½ c Orange Juice; 1 FF Egg; ½ c FF Malt-O-Meal; 1 Toast; 2 Oleo; 1 c 1% Milk; Coffee, Tea	½ c Orange Juice; 2 FF Eggs; ½ c FF Malt-O-Meal; 1 Toast; 1 Oleo; 1 c 1% Milk; Coffee, Tea	½ c Orange Juice; 2 FF Eggs; ½ c FF Malt-O-Meal; 2 Toast; 2 Oleo; Coffee, Tea
Dinner	1 oz Beef; 1 c Mix Veg; ¼ c FF Bkd Beans; ½ c Diet Peaches; ½ c 1% Milk; Coffee, Tea	1 oz Beef; 1 c FF Mix Veg; ½ c Diet Peaches; 1 c 1% Milk; Coffee, Tea	2 oz Beef; 1 c FF Mix Veg; ¼ c FF Bkd Beans; 1 Oleo; ½ c Diet Peaches; Coffee, Tea	2 oz Beef; 1 c FF Mix Veg; ¼ c FF Bkd Beans; 1 Roll; 1 Oleo; ½ c Diet Peaches; Coffee, Tea	3 oz Beef; 1 c FF Mix Veg; ¼ c FF Bkd Beans; 1 Roll; 2 Oleo; ½ c Diet Peaches; Coffee, Tea	3 oz Beef; 1 c FF Mix Veg; ¼ c FF Bkd Beans; 2 Rolls; 2 Oleo; ½ c Diet Peaches; Coffee, Tea	3 oz Beef; 1 c FF Mix Veg; ½ c FF Bkd Beans; 2 Rolls; 2 Oleo; ½ c Diet Peaches; 1 c 1% Milk; Coffee, Tea
Supper	2 oz Pork; ½ c FF Gr Beans; 1 Toast; ½ c Diet Fruit; ½ c 1% Milk; Coffee, Tea	2 oz Pork; ½ c FF Gr Beans; 1 Toast; ½ c Diet Fruit; Coffee, Tea	2 oz Pork; ½ c FF Gr Beans; Tossed Salad; Zero Dressing; 1 Toast; 1 Oleo; ½ c Diet Fruit; Coffee, Tea	3 oz Pork; ½ c FF Gr Beans; ½ c FF Mash Pots; Tossed Salad; Zero Dressing; 1 Toast; 1 Oleo; ½ c Diet Fruit; Coffee, Tea	3 oz Pork; ½ c FF Gr Beans; ½ c FF Mash Pots; Tossed Salad; Zero Dressing; 1 Toast; 1 Oleo; ½ c Diet Fruit; 5 Vanilla Wafers; Coffee, Tea	3 oz Pork; ½ c FF Gr Beans; ½ c FF Mash Pots; Tossed Salad; Zero Dressing; 1 Toast; 1 Oleo; ½ c Diet Fruit; 5 Vanilla Wafers; Coffee, Tea	4 oz Pork; ½ c FF Gr Beans; ½ c FF Mash Pots; Tossed Salad; Zero Dressing; 1 Toast; 1 Oleo; 1 c Diet Fruit; 5 Vanilla Wafers; Coffee, Tea
Snack	1 c 1% Milk; 2 Graham Crackers (Square)	1 c 1% Milk; 2 Graham Crackers	1 c 1% Milk; 2 Graham Crackers	1 c 1% Milk; 2 Graham Crackers	1 c 1% Milk; 2 Graham Crackers	1 c 1% Milk; 4 Graham Crackers	1 c 1% Milk; 4 Graham Crackers

CERTIFIED _____, R.D.

	800 Calories	1,000 Calories	1,200 Calories	1,500 Calories	1,800 Calories	2,000 Calories	2,200 Calories
Breakfast	½ c Orange Juice 1 FF Egg ½ c FF Oatmeal Coffee, Tea	½ c Orange Juice 1 FF Egg ½ c FF Oatmeal 1 Bacon Coffee, Tea	½ c Orange Juice 1 FF Egg ½ c FF Oatmeal 1 Bacon 1 c 1% Milk Coffee, Tea	½ c Orange Juice 1 FF Egg ½ c FF Oatmeal 1 Bacon 1 c 1% Milk Coffee, Tea	½ c Orange Juice 1 FF Egg ½ c FF Oatmeal 1 Toast 1 Bacon 1 Oleo 1 c 1% Milk Coffee, Tea	½ c Orange Juice 2 FF Eggs ½ c FF Oatmeal 1 Toast 1 Bacon 1 c 1% Milk Coffee, Tea	½ c Orange Juice 2 FF Eggs ½ c FF Oatmeal 2 Toast 1 Bacon 1 Oleo Coffee, Tea
Dinner	1 oz Bkd Chicken ½ c FF Peas ½ c FF Potatoes ½ c Diet Fruit ½ c 1% Milk Coffee, Tea	1 oz Bkd Chicken ½ c FF Peas ½ c Diet Fruit 1 c 1% Milk Coffee, Tea	2 oz Bkd Chicken ½ c FF Peas ½ c FF Potatoes 1 Oleo ½ c Diet Fruit Coffee, Tea	2 oz Bkd Chicken ½ c FF Peas ½ c FF Potatoes 1 Roll 1 Oleo ½ c Diet Fruit Coffee, Tea	3 oz Bkd Chicken ½ c FF Peas ½ c FF Potatoes 1 Roll 2 Oleo ½ c Diet Fruit Coffee, Tea	3 oz Bkd Chicken ½ c FF Peas ½ c FF Potatoes 2 Rolls 2 Oleo ½ c Diet Fruit Coffee, Tea	3 oz Bkd Chicken ½ c FF Peas ½ c FF Potatoes 2 Rolls 2 Oleo ½ c Diet Fruit 1 c 1% Milk Coffee, Tea
Supper	2 oz FF Beef ½ c Sl Tomatoes 1 Bread ½ c Diet Fruit ½ c 1% Milk Coffee, Tea	2 oz FF Beef ½ c Sl Tomatoes 1 Bread ½ c Diet Fruit Coffee, Tea	2 oz FF Beef ½ c Sl Tomatoes ½ c Gr Beans Ital 1 Bread 1 Oleo ½ c Diet Fruit Coffee, Tea	3 oz FF Beef ½ c Sl Tomatoes ½ c Gr Beans Ital 2 Bread 1 Oleo ½ c Diet Fruit Coffee, Tea	3 oz FF Beef ½ c FF Noodles ½ c Sl Tomatoes ½ c Gr Beans Ital 2 Bread 1 Oleo ½ c Diet Fruit Coffee, Tea	3 oz FF Beef ½ c FF Noodles ½ c Sl Tomatoes ½ c Gr Beans Ital 2 Bread 1 Oleo ½ c Diet Fruit Coffee, Tea	4 oz FF Beef ½ c FF Noodles ½ c Sl Tomatoes ½ c Gr Beans Ital 2 Bread 1 Oleo 1 c Diet Fruit Coffee, Tea
Snack		1 c 1% Milk 2 Graham Crackers (Square)	1 c 1% Milk 2 Graham Crackers	1 c 1% Milk 2 Graham Crackers	1 c 1% Milk 2 Graham Crackers	1 c 1% Milk 4 Graham Crackers	1 c 1% Milk 4 Graham Crackers

CERTIFIED ______________________________, R.D.

Exhibit A–1 continued

WEEK NO. FOUR DAY MONDAY MENU CYCLE FALL/WINTER

	800 Calories	*1,000 Calories*	*1,200 Calories*	*1,500 Calories*	*1,800 Calories*	*2,000 Calories*	*2,200 Calories*
Breakfast	½ c Orange Juice 1 FF Egg 1 Toast Coffee, Tea	½ c Orange Juice 1 FF Egg 1 Toast 1 Oleo Coffee, Tea	½ c Orange Juice 1 FF Egg 1 Toast 1 Oleo 1 c 1% Milk Coffee, Tea	½ c Orange Juice 1 FF Egg 1 Toast 1 Oleo 1 c 1% Milk Coffee, Tea	½ c Orange Juice 1 FF Egg 1 Toast ½ c FF Cr of Rice 2 Oleo 1 c 1% Milk Coffee, Tea	½ c Orange Juice 2 FF Eggs 1 Toast ½ c FF Cr of Rice 1 Oleo 1 c 1% Milk Coffee, Tea	½ c Orange Juice 2 FF Eggs 2 Toast ½ c FF Cr of Rice 2 Oleo Coffee, Tea
Dinner	1 oz Roast Beef ½ c FF Spinach Lettuce Salad Buttermilk Dress (= Free Exchange) ½ c FF Msh Pots ½ c Diet Peaches ½ c Snow Pudding (= Free Exchg) ½ c 1% Milk Coffee, Tea	1 oz Roast Beef ½ c FF Spinach Lettuce Salad Buttermilk Dress (= Free Exchange) ½ c Diet Peaches ½ c Snow Pudding (= Free Exchg) 1 c 1% Milk Coffee, Tea	2 oz Roast Beef ½ c FF Spinach Lettuce Salad Buttermilk Dress (= Free Exchange) ½ c FF Msh Pots 1 Oleo ½ c Diet Peaches ½ c Snow Pudding (= Free Exchg) Coffee, Tea	2 oz Roast Beef ½ c FF Spinach Lettuce Salad Buttermilk Dress (= Free Exchange) ½ c FF Msh Pots 1 Roll, 1 Oleo ½ c Diet Peaches ½ c Snow Pudding (= Free Exchg) Coffee, Tea	3 oz Roast Beef ½ c FF Spinach Lettuce Salad Buttermilk Dress (= Free Exchange) ½ c FF Msh Pots 1 Roll, 2 Oleo ½ c Diet Peaches ½ c Snow Pudding (= Free Exchg) Coffee, Tea	3 oz Roast Beef ½ c FF Spinach Lettuce Salad Buttermilk Dress (= Free Exchange) ½ c FF Msh Pots 2 Rolls, 2 Oleo ½ c Diet Peaches ½ c Snow Pudding (= Free Exchg) Coffee, Tea	3 oz Roast Beef ½ c FF Spinach Lettuce Salad Buttermilk Dress (= Free Exchange) ½ c FF Msh Pots 2 Rolls, 2 Oleo ½ c Diet Peaches ½ c Snow Pudding (= Free Exchg) 1 c 1% Milk Coffee, Tea
Supper	2 oz Pork ½ c FF Broccoli ½ c FF Noodles ½ c Dt Pineapple ½ c 1% Milk Coffee, Tea	2 oz Pork ½ c FF Broccoli ½ c FF Noodles ½ c Dt Pineapple Coffee, Tea	2 oz Pork 1 c FF Broccoli ½ c FF Noodles 1 Oleo ½ c Dt Pineapple Coffee, Tea	3 oz Pork 1 c FF Broccoli ½ c FF Noodles 1 W/W Bread 1 Oleo ½ c Dt Pineapple Coffee, Tea	3 oz Pork 1 c FF Broccoli ½ c FF Noodles 2 W/W Bread 1 Oleo ½ c Dt Pineapple Coffee, Tea	3 oz Pork 1 c FF Broccoli ½ c FF Noodles 2 W/W Bread 1 Oleo ½ c Dt Pineapple Coffee, Tea	4 oz Pork 1 c FF Broccoli ½ c FF Noodles 2 W/W Bread 1 Oleo 1 c Dt Pineapple Coffee, Tea
Snack		1 c 1% Milk 2 Graham Crackers (Square)	1 c 1% Milk 2 Graham Crackers	1 c 1% Milk 2 Graham Crackers	1 c 1% Milk 2 Graham Crackers	1 c 1% Milk 4 Graham Crackers	1 c 1% Milk 4 Graham Crackers

CERTIFIED ______________________________, R.D.

WEEK NO. FOUR DAY TUESDAY MENU CYCLE FALL/WINTER

	800 Calories	1,000 Calories	1,200 Calories	1,500 Calories	1,800 Calories	2,000 Calories	2,200 Calories
Breakfast	½ c Orange Juice 1 FF Egg ½ c FF Cr of Wheat Coffee, Tea	½ c Orange Juice 1 FF Egg ½ c FF Cr of Wheat 1 Oleo Coffee, Tea	½ c Orange Juice 1 FF Egg ½ c FF Cr of Wheat 1 Oleo 1 c 1% Milk Coffee, Tea	½ c Orange Juice 1 FF Egg ½ c FF Cr of Wheat 1 Oleo 1 c 1% Milk Coffee, Tea	½ c Orange Juice 1 FF Egg ½ c FF Cr of Wheat 1 Toast 2 Oleo 1 c 1% Milk Coffee, Tea	½ c Orange Juice 2 FF Eggs ½ c FF Cr of Wheat 1 Toast 1 Oleo 1 c 1% Milk Coffee, Tea	½ c Orange Juice 2 FF Eggs ½ c FF Cr of Wheat 2 Toast 2 Oleo Coffee, Tea
Dinner	1 oz Bkd Fish ½ c FF Carrots Tomato Slices 1 Roll ½ c Dt Pineapple ½ c 1% Milk Coffee, Tea	1 oz Bkd Fish ½ c FF Carrots Tomato Slices ½ c Dt Pineapple 1 c 1% Milk Coffee, Tea	2 oz Bkd Fish ½ c FF Carrots Tomato Slices 1 Roll, 1 Oleo ½ c Dt Pineapple Coffee, Tea	2 oz Bkd Fish ½ c FF Carrots Tomato Slices ½ c FF Potatoes 1 Roll, 1 Oleo ½ c Dt Pineapple Coffee, Tea	3 oz Bkd Fish ½ c FF Carrots Tomato Slices ½ c FF Potatoes 1 Roll, 2 Oleo ½ c Dt Pineapple Coffee, Tea	3 oz Bkd Fish ½ c FF Carrots Tomato Slices ½ c FF Potatoes 2 Rolls, 2 Oleo ½ c Dt Pineapple Coffee, Tea	3 oz Bkd Fish ½ c FF Carrots Tomato Slices ½ c FF Potatoes 2 Rolls, 2 Oleo ½ c Dt Pineapple 1 c 1% Milk Coffee, Tea
Supper	2 oz Ham ½ c FF Beets ½ c FF Potatoes ½ c Diet Pears ½ c 1% Milk Coffee, Tea	2 oz Ham ½ c FF Beets ½ c FF Potatoes ½ c Diet Pears Coffee, Tea	2 oz Ham ½ c FF Beets ½ c Lettuce/ Zero Dressing ½ c FF Potatoes 1 Oleo ½ c Diet Pears Coffee, Tea	3 oz Ham ½ c FF Beets ½ c Lettuce/ Zero Dressing ½ c FF Potatoes 1 Roll, 1 Oleo ½ c Diet Pears Coffee, Tea	3 oz Ham ½ c FF Beets ½ c Lettuce/ Zero Dressing ½ c FF Potatoes 2 Rolls, 1 Oleo ½ c Diet Pears Coffee, Tea	3 oz Ham ½ c FF Beets ½ c Lettuce/ Zero Dressing ½ c FF Potatoes 2 Rolls, 1 Oleo ½ c Diet Pears Coffee, Tea	4 oz Ham ½ c FF Beets ½ c Lettuce/ Zero Dressing ½ c FF Potatoes 2 Rolls, 1 Oleo 1 c Diet Pears Coffee, Tea
Snack		1 c 1% Milk 2 Graham Crackers (Square)	1 c 1% Milk 2 Graham Crackers	1 c 1% Milk 2 Graham Crackers	1 c 1% Milk 2 Graham Crackers	1 c 1% Milk 4 Graham Crackers	1 c 1% Milk 4 Graham Crackers

CERTIFIED ______________________ ______________________, R.D.

Exhibit A–1 continued

WEEK NO. FOUR DAY WEDNESDAY MENU CYCLE FALL/WINTER

	800 Calories	*1,000 Calories*	*1,200 Calories*	*1,500 Calories*	*1,800 Calories*	*2,000 Calories*	*2,200 Calories*
Breakfast	½ c Orange Juice 1 FF Egg 1 Toast Coffee, Tea	½ c Orange Juice 1 FF Egg 1 Toast 1 Oleo Coffee, Tea	½ c Orange Juice 1 FF Egg 1 Toast 1 Oleo 1 c 1% Milk Coffee, Tea	½ c Orange Juice 1 FF Egg 1 Toast 1 Oleo 1 c 1% Milk Coffee, Tea	½ c Orange Juice 1 FF Egg ½ c FF Malt-O-Meal 1 Toast 2 Oleo 1 c 1% Milk Coffee, Tea	½ c Orange Juice 2 FF Eggs ½ c FF Malt-O-Meal 1 Toast 1 Oleo 1 c 1% Milk Coffee, Tea	½ c Orange Juice 2 FF Eggs ½ c FF Malt-O-Meal 2 Toast 2 Oleo Coffee, Tea
Dinner	1 oz Meat Loaf ½ c FF Cabbage Tossed Salad Zero Dressing ½ c FF Potatoes ½ c Diet Apples ½ c 1% Milk Coffee, Tea	1 oz Meat Loaf ½ c FF Cabbage Tossed Salad Zero Dressing ½ c Diet Apples 1 c 1% Milk Coffee, Tea	2 oz Meat Loaf ½ c FF Cabbage Tossed Salad Zero Dressing ½ c FF Potatoes 1 Oleo ½ c Diet Apples Coffee, Tea	2 oz Meat Loaf ½ c FF Cabbage Tossed Salad Zero Dressing ½ c FF Potatoes 1 W/W Bread 1 Oleo ½ c Diet Apples Coffee, Tea	3 oz Meat Loaf ½ c FF Cabbage Tossed Salad Zero Dressing ½ c FF Potatoes 1 W/W Bread 2 Oleo ½ c Diet Apples Coffee, Tea	3 oz Meat Loaf ½ c FF Cabbage Tossed Salad Zero Dressing ½ c FF Potatoes 2 W/W Bread 2 Oleo ½ c Diet Apples Coffee, Tea	3 oz Meat Loaf ½ c FF Cabbage Tossed Salad Zero Dressing ½ c FF Potatoes 2 W/W Bread 2 Oleo ½ c Diet Apples 1 c 1% Milk Coffee, Tea
Supper	2 oz FF Chicken ½ c FF Gr Beans ½ c FF Potatoes ½ c Citrus Sec ½ c 1% Milk Coffee, Tea	2 oz FF Chicken ½ c FF Gr Beans ½ c FF Potatoes ½ c Citrus Sec Coffee, Tea	2 oz FF Chicken 1 c FF Gr Beans ½ c FF Potatoes 1 Oleo ½ c Citrus Sec Coffee, Tea	3 oz FF Chicken 1 c FF Gr Beans ½ c FF Potatoes 1 Bread, 1 Oleo ½ c Citrus Sec Coffee, Tea	3 oz FF Chicken 1 c FF Gr Beans ½ c FF Potatoes 2 Bread, 1 Oleo ½ c Citrus Sec Coffee, Tea	3 oz FF Chicken 1 c FF Gr Beans ½ c FF Potatoes 2 Bread, 1 Oleo ½ c Citrus Sec Coffee, Tea	4 oz FF Chicken 1 c FF Gr Beans ½ c FF Potatoes 2 Bread, 1 Oleo 1 c Citrus Sec Coffee, Tea
Snack		1 c 1% Milk 2 Graham Crackers (Square)	1 c 1% Milk 2 Graham Crackers	1 c 1% Milk 2 Graham Crackers	1 c 1% Milk 2 Graham Crackers	1 c 1% Milk 4 Graham Crackers	1 c 1% Milk 4 Graham Crackers

CERTIFIED ______________________________, R.D.

WEEK NO. FOUR DAY THURSDAY MENU CYCLE FALL/WINTER

	800 Calories	*1,000 Calories*	*1,200 Calories*	*1,500 Calories*	*1,800 Calories*	*2,000 Calories*	*2,200 Calories*
Breakfast	½ c Orange Juice 1 FF Egg 1 sl Toast Coffee, Tea	½ c Orange Juice 1 FF Egg 1 sl Toast 1 Oleo Coffee, Tea	½ c Orange Juice 1 FF Egg 1 sl Toast 1 Oleo 1 c 1% Milk Coffee, Tea	½ c Orange Juice 1 FF Egg 1 sl Toast 1 Oleo 1 c 1% Milk Coffee, Tea	½ c Orange Juice 1 FF Egg 1 sl Toast ½ c FF Ralston 2 Oleo 1 c 1% Milk Coffee, Tea	½ c Orange Juice 2 FF Eggs 1 sl Toast ½ c FF Ralston 1 Oleo 1 c 1% Milk Coffee, Tea	½ c Orange Juice 2 FF Eggs 2 sl Toast ½ c FF Ralston 2 Oleo Coffee, Tea
Dinner	1 oz Beef Patty 1 c Lettuce & Tom ½ c FF Potatoes ½ Banana ½ c 1% Milk Coffee, Tea	1 oz Beef Patty 1 c Lettuce & Tom ½ Banana 1 c 1% Milk Coffee, Tea	2 oz Beef Patty 1 c Lettuce & Tom ½ c FF Potatoes 1 Oleo ½ Banana Coffee, Tea	2 oz Beef Patty 1 c Lettuce & Tom ½ c FF Potatoes ½ Bun or 1 Bread 1 Oleo ½ Banana Coffee, Tea	3 oz Beef Patty 1 c Lettuce & Tom ½ c FF Potatoes ½ Bun 2 Oleo ½ Banana Coffee, Tea	3 oz Beef Patty 1 c Lettuce & Tom ½ c FF Potatoes 1 Bun 2 Oleo ½ Banana Coffee, Tea	3 oz Beef Patty 1 c Lettuce & Tom ½ c FF Potatoes 1 Bun 2 Oleo ½ Banana 1 c 1% Milk Coffee, Tea
Supper	2 oz Sliced Ham ½ c FF Dried Beans *½ c Hrty Veg Soup 2 Diet Plums ½ c 1% Milk Coffee, Tea	2 oz Sliced Ham ½ c FF Dried Beans *½ c Hrty Veg Soup 2 Diet Plums Coffee, Tea	2 oz Sliced Ham ½ c FF Dried Beans 1 Oleo *1 c Hrty Veg Soup 2 Diet Plums Coffee, Tea	3 oz Sliced Ham ½ c FF Dried Beans 1 t Oleo *1 c Hrty Veg Soup 1 Bread 2 Diet Plums Coffee, Tea	3 oz Sliced Ham ½ c FF Dried Beans 1 t Oleo *1 c Hrty Veg Soup 6 Saltines 1 Bread 2 Diet Plums Coffee, Tea	3 oz Sliced Ham ½ c FF Dried Beans 1 t Oleo *1 c Hrty Veg Soup 6 Saltines 1 Bread 2 Diet Plums Coffee, Tea	4 oz Sliced Ham ½ c FF Dried Beans 1 t Oleo *1 c Hrty Veg Soup 6 Saltines 1 Bread 4 Diet Plums Coffee, Tea
Snack		1 c 1% Milk 1 Graham Cracker (Square)	1 c 1% Milk 2 Graham Crackers	1 c 1% Milk 2 Graham Crackers	1 c 1% Milk 2 Graham Crackers	1 c 1% Milk 4 Graham Crackers	1 c 1% Milk 4 Graham Crackers

*See Recipe—1 Hearty Vegetable Soup = 2 Vegetable Exchanges

CERTIFIED ______________________________, R.D.

Exhibit A–1 continued

WEEK NO. FOUR DAY FRIDAY MENU CYCLE FALL/WINTER

	800 Calories	*1,000 Calories*	*1,200 Calories*	*1,500 Calories*	*1,800 Calories*	*2,000 Calories*	*2,200 Calories*
Breakfast	½ c Orange Juice 1 FF Egg ½ c FF Oatmeal Coffee, Tea	½ c Orange Juice 1 FF Egg ½ c FF Oatmeal 1 Oleo Coffee, Tea	½ c Orange Juice 1 FF Egg ½ c FF Oatmeal 1 Oleo 1 c 1% Milk Coffee, Tea	½ c Orange Juice 1 FF Egg ½ c FF Oatmeal 1 Oleo 1 c 1% Milk Coffee, Tea	½ c Orange Juice 1 FF Egg ½ c FF Oatmeal 1 sl Toast 2 Oleo 1 c 1% Milk Coffee, Tea	½ c Orange Juice 2 FF Eggs ½ c FF Oatmeal 1 sl Toast 1 Oleo 1 c 1% Milk Coffee, Tea	½ c Orange Juice 2 FF Eggs ½ c FF Oatmeal 2 sl Toast 2 Oleo Coffee, Tea
Dinner	1 oz Meatball 1 c FF Tomatoes ½ c FF Potatoes ½ c Dt Pear Hlvs ½ c 1% Milk Coffee, Tea	1 oz Meatball 1 c FF Tomatoes ½ c Dt Pear Hlvs 1 c 1% Milk Coffee, Tea	2 oz Meatballs 1 c FF Tomatoes ½ c FF Potatoes 1 Oleo ½ c Dt Pear Hlvs Coffee, Tea	2 oz Meatballs 1 c FF Tomatoes ½ c FF Potatoes 1 Bread 1 Oleo ½ c Dt Pear Hlvs Coffee, Tea	3 oz Meatballs 1 c FF Tomatoes ½ c FF Potatoes 1 Bread 1 Oleo ½ c Dt Pear Hlvs Coffee, Tea	3 oz Meatballs 1 c FF Tomatoes ½ c FF Potatoes 2 Bread 1 Oleo ½ c Dt Pear Hlvs Coffee, Tea	3 oz Meatballs 1 c FF Tomatoes ½ c FF Potatoes 2 Bread 1 Oleo ½ c Dt Pear Hlvs 1 c 1% Milk Coffee, Tea
Supper	1 Hard Ckd Egg ¼ c Cott Cheese ½ c FF Carrots ½ c FF Potatoes ½ c Dt Cinn Peach ½ c 1% Milk Coffee, Tea	1 Hard Ckd Egg ¼ c Cott Cheese ½ c FF Carrots ½ c FF Potatoes ½ c Dt Cinn Peach Coffee, Tea	1 Hard Ckd Egg ¼ c Cott Cheese 1 c FF Carrots ½ c FF Potatoes 1 Oleo ½ c Dt Cinn Peach Coffee, Tea	2 Hard Ckd Eggs ¼ c Cott Cheese 1 c FF Carrots ½ c FF Potatoes ½ c Dt Cinn Peach ½ c Ice Cream Coffee, Tea	2 Hard Ckd Eggs ¼ c Cott Cheese 1 c FF Carrots ½ c FF Potatoes 1 Bread ½ c Dt Cinn Peach ½ c Ice Cream Coffee, Tea	2 Hard Ckd Eggs ¼ c Cott Cheese 1 c FF Carrots ½ c FF Potatoes 1 Bread ½ c Dt Cinn Peach ½ c Ice Cream Coffee, Tea	2 Hard Ckd Eggs ½ c Cott Cheese 1 c FF Carrots ½ c FF Potatoes 1 Bread ½ c Dt Cinn Peach ½ c Ice Cream Coffee, Tea
Snack		1 c 1% Milk 2 Graham Crackers (Square)	1 c 1% Milk 2 Graham Crackers	1 c 1% Milk 2 Graham Crackers	1 c 1% Milk 2 Graham Crackers	1 c 1% Milk 4 Graham Crackers	1 c 1% Milk 4 Graham Crackers

CERTIFIED ______________________________, R.D.

	800 Calories	1,000 Calories	1,200 Calories	1,500 Calories	1,800 Calories	2,000 Calories	2,200 Calories
Breakfast	½ c Orange Juice 1 FF Egg ½ c FF Cr of Wheat Coffee, Tea	½ c Orange Juice 1 FF Egg ½ c FF Cr of Wheat 1 Oleo Coffee, Tea	½ c Orange Juice 1 FF Egg ½ c FF Cr of Wheat 1 Oleo 1 c 1% Milk Coffee, Tea	½ c Orange Juice 1 FF Egg ½ c Cr of Wheat 1 Oleo 1 c 1% Milk Coffee, Tea	½ c Orange Juice 1 FF Egg 1 sl Toast ½ c Cr of Wheat 2 Oleo 1 c 1% Milk Coffee, Tea	½ c Orange Juice 2 FF Eggs 1 sl Toast ½ c Cr of Wheat 1 Oleo 1 c 1% Milk Coffee, Tea	½ c Orange Juice 2 FF Eggs 2 sl Toast ½ c Cr of Wheat 2 Oleo Coffee, Tea
Dinner	1 oz Pork 1 c FF Winter Mix ½ c FF Rice ½ c Diet Fruit ½ c 1% Milk Coffee, Tea	1 oz Pork 1 c FF Winter Mix ½ c Diet Fruit 1 c 1% Milk Coffee, Tea	2 oz Pork 1 c FF Winter Mix ½ c FF Rice 1 Oleo ½ c Diet Fruit Coffee, Tea	2 oz Pork 1 c FF Winter Mix ½ c FF Rice 1 Roll 1 Oleo ½ c Diet Fruit Coffee, Tea	3 oz Pork 1 c FF Winter Mix ½ c FF Rice 1 Roll 2 Oleo ½ c Diet Fruit Coffee, Tea	3 oz Pork 1 c FF Winter Mix ½ c FF Rice 2 Rolls 2 Oleo ½ c Diet Fruit Coffee, Tea	3 oz Pork 1 c FF Winter Mix ½ c FF Rice 2 Rolls 2 Oleo ½ c Diet Fruit 1 c 1% Milk Coffee, Tea
Supper	2 oz FF Beef Cubes ½ c FF Carrots 1 Bread ½ c Diet Fruit ½ c 1% Milk Coffee, Tea	2 oz FF Beef Cubes ½ c FF Carrots 1 Bread ½ c Diet Fruit Coffee, Tea	2 oz FF Beef Cubes 1 c FF Carrots 1 Bread 1 Oleo ½ c Diet Fruit Coffee, Tea	3 oz FF Beef Cubes 1 c FF Carrots ½ c FF Potatoes 1 Bread 1 Oleo ½ c Diet Fruit Coffee, Tea	3 oz FF Beef Cubes 1 c FF Carrots ½ c FF Potatoes 2 Bread 1 Oleo ½ c Diet Fruit Coffee, Tea	3 oz FF Beef Cubes 1 c FF Carrots ½ c FF Potatoes 2 Bread 1 Oleo ½ c Diet Fruit Coffee, Tea	4 oz FF Beef Cubes 1 c FF Carrots 1 c FF Potatoes 2 Bread 1 Oleo 1 c Diet Fruit Coffee, Tea
Snack	1 c 1% Milk 2 Graham Crackers	1 c 1% Milk 2 Graham Crackers (Square)	1 c 1% Milk 2 Graham Crackers	1 c 1% Milk 2 Graham Crackers	1 c 1% Milk 2 Graham Crackers	1 c 1% Milk 4 Graham Crackers	1 c 1% Milk 4 Graham Crackers

CERTIFIED _____, R.D.

337

Exhibit A–2 Nonselective Nursing Home, Western U.S.

WEEK NO. __ONE__ DAY __SUNDAY__ MENU CYCLE __FALL/WINTER__

	Regular/Bland	Mechanical	2 Gram Sodium	4 Gram Sodium	Blended		
Breakfast	½ c Orange Juice #16 Egg, Scrmb #8 Hot Ralston 1 sl Bacon 1 Toast Oleo, Jelly 1 c Milk Coffee, Tea	Orange Juice Egg, Scrmb Hot Ralston Bacon Toast Oleo, Jelly Milk Coffee, Tea	Orange Juice Egg, Scrmb Hot Ralston Toast Oleo, Jelly ½ c Milk Coffee, Tea	Orange Juice Egg, Scrmb Hot Ralston Toast Oleo, Jelly ½ c Milk Coffee, Tea	Strain Orange Juice Blended Egg Strain Hot Ralston Toast or Bread Oleo, Jelly Milk Coffee, Tea		
Dinner	2 oz Rst Turkey Gravy #8 Bread Stuffing #16 Bu Green Peas Cranberry Sauce 1 Hot Roll, Oleo 1 tsp #8 Apple Crisp 1 c Milk Coffee, Tea, *Sanka	Grd Rst Turkey Gravy Bread Stuffing Bu Green Peas Cranberry Sauce Hot Roll, Oleo Apple Crisp Milk Coffee, Tea	SF Rst Turkey SF Bread Stuffing SF Gr Peas/Red Pepper Cranberry Sauce Hot Roll, Oleo Apple Crisp ½ c Milk Coffee, Tea	SF Rst Turkey Bread Stuffing Bu Gr Peas/Red Pepper Cranberry Sauce Hot Roll, Oleo Apple Crisp ½ c Milk Coffee, Tea	Bl Rst Turkey #12 Bl Stuffing #12 Bl Gr Peas #12 Cranberry Sauce Roll, Oleo Applesauce #8 Milk Coffee, Tea		
Supper	2 oz Hamb/Bun #8 Tater Tots ½ c Lettuce/Tomato Condiments #8 Chill Frt Mix/ Grape Jubilee #8 Ice Cream *No Pepper 1 c Milk Coffee, Tea, *Sanka	Grd Beef/Bun Tater Tots Lettuce/Tomato Condiments Chill Fruit Mix/ Grape Jubilee Ice Cream Milk Coffee, Tea	SF Hamburger/Bun SF Tater Tots Lettuce/Tomato Chill Frt Mix/Grape Jubilee Ice Cream ½ c Milk Coffee, Tea	SF Hamburger/Bun Tater Tots Lettuce/Tomato Chill Frt Mix/Grape Jubilee Ice Cream ½ c Milk Coffee, Tea ½ t salt to be added	Bl Hamburger #12 Bl Tater Tots #12 Tomato Juice 4 oz Bread Bl Frt Mix #8 Ice Cream Milk Coffee, Tea		

*For Bland diet.
Portion sizes are same as for Regular unless otherwise specified.
Bran is to be added to one menu item per day.

CERTIFIED _____, R.D.

338

	Regular/Bland	Mechanical	2 Gram Sodium	4 Gram Sodium	Blended		
B r e a k f a s t	½ c Orange Juice #16 Egg, Scrmb #8 Cr of Wheat 1 Toast 1 t Oleo, Jelly 1 c Milk Coffee, Tea, *Sanka	Orange Juice Egg, Scrmb Cr of Wheat Toast/Bread Oleo, Jelly Milk Coffee, Tea	Orange Juice Egg, Scrmb Cr of Wheat Toast Oleo, Jelly ½ c Milk Coffee, Tea	Orange Juice Egg, Scrmb Cr of Wheat Toast Oleo, Jelly ½ c Milk Coffee, Tea	Strain Orange Juice Blended Egg Str Cr of Wheat Toast/Bread Oleo, Jelly Milk Coffee, Tea		
D i n n e r	2 oz Ham/PA Sauce #8 Yams #16 Seas Greens 1 2" sq Cornbread, Oleo Fruit Split Cake (½ c fruit) 1 c Milk Coffee, Tea, *Sanka	Grd Ham/PA Sauce Yams Seasoned Greens Cornbread, Oleo Fruit Split Cake Milk Coffee, Tea	SF Pork Yams SF Greens Roll, Oleo Fruit Split Cake ½ c Milk Coffee, Tea	SF Pork Yams Seas Greens Cornbread, Oleo Fruit Split Cake ½ c Milk Coffee, Tea	Bl Ham/PA Sauce #12 Bl Yams #12 Bl Greens #12 Bread, Oleo Bl Frt Cockt #8 Milk Coffee, Tea		
S u p p e r	2 oz Meat Loaf/ Sauce #8 Potatoes O'Brien #16 Bu Zucchini Hot Roll, Oleo #8 Lemon Pudding 1 c Milk Coffee, Tea, *Sanka	Grd Meat Loaf/ Sauce Potatoes O'Brien Buttered Zucchini Hot Roll, Oleo Lemon Pudding Milk Coffee, Tea	SF Meat Loaf/ Sauce SF Potatoes O'Brien SF Zucchini Hot Roll, Oleo Fruit in Season ½ c Milk Coffee, Tea	SF Meat Loaf/Sce Potatoes O'Brien Buttered Zucchini Hot Roll, Oleo Lemon Pudding ½ c Milk Coffee, Tea ½ t salt to be added	Bl Meat Loaf #12 Bl Potatoes #12 Bl Zucchini #12 Bread, Oleo Lemon Pudding #8 Milk Coffee, Tea		

*For Bland diet.
Portion sizes are same as for Regular unless otherwise specified.
Bran is to be added to one menu item per day.

CERTIFIED _____, R.D.

339

Exhibit A-2 continued

	Regular/Bland	Mechanical	2 Gram Sodium	4 Gram Sodium	Blended		
B **r** **e** **a** **k** **f** **a** **s** **t**	½ c Orange Juice 1 Egg, Pchd ½ c Hot Oatmeal 1 Toast 1 t Oleo, Jelly 1 c Milk Coffee, Tea, *Sanka	Orange Juice Egg, Pchd Hot Oatmeal Toast Oleo, Jelly Milk Coffee, Tea	Orange Juice Egg, Pchd Hot Oatmeal Toast Oleo, Jelly ½ c Milk Coffee, Tea	Orange Juice Egg, Pchd Hot Oatmeal Toast Oleo, Jelly ½ c Milk Coffee, Tea	Strain Orange Juice Bl Egg Strain Hot Oatmeal Toast or Bread Oleo, Jelly Milk Coffee, Tea		
D **i** **n** **n** **e** **r**	2 oz Fried Chicken #8 Msh Potatoes/ Gravy #16 Parsl Bu Carrots Hot Biscuit Oleo 1 sl Choc Pan Pie *Peaches (no choc pie) 1 c Milk Coffee, Tea, *Sanka	Grd Chicken Msh Potatoes/ Gravy Parsl Bu Carrots Hot Biscuit Oleo Choc Pan Pie Milk Coffee, Tea	SF Fried Chicken SF Potatoes SF Gravy SF Parsl Carrots Bread Oleo Peaches #8 ½ c Milk Coffee, Tea	SF Fried Chicken Msh Potatoes/ Gravy Parsl Bu Carrots Hot Biscuit Oleo Choc Pan Pie ½ c Milk Coffee, Tea	Bl Chicken #12 Bl Potatoes #12 Bl Carrots #12 Biscuit/Bread Oleo Bl Peaches #8 Milk Coffee, Tea		
S **u** **p** **p** **e** **r**	2 oz Veal #16 Bu Yellow Squash #8 Lime Perfection Salad 1 sl Bread, 1 t Oleo Cherry Cake Milk Coffee, Tea, *Sanka	Veal Bu Yellow Squash Lime Perfection Salad Bread, Oleo Cherry Cake Milk Coffee, Tea	SF Veal SF Yellow Squash Lime Perfection Salad Bread, Oleo Cherry Cake 1 c Milk Coffee, Tea	SF Veal Bu Yellow Squash Lime Perfection Salad Bread, Oleo Cherry Cake 1 c Milk Coffee, Tea ½ t salt to be added	Bl Veal #12 Bl Squash #12 Lime Jello #8 Bread, Oleo Ice Cream Milk Coffee, Tea		

*For Bland diet.

Portion sizes are same as for Regular unless otherwise specified.

Bran is to be added to one menu item per day.

CERTIFIED _____, R.D.

340

	Regular/Bland	Mechanical	2 Gram Sodium	4 Gram Sodium	Blended	
B r e a k f a s t	½ c Orange Juice #16 Egg, Scrmb/ Bacon Bits ½ c Malt-O-Meal 1 Toast 1 t Oleo, Jelly Milk Coffee, Tea, *Sanka	Orange Juice Egg, Scrmb/Bacon Bits Malt-O-Meal Toast/Bread Oleo, Jelly Milk Coffee, Tea	Orange Juice Egg, Scrmb Malt-O-Meal Toast Oleo, Jelly ½ c Milk Coffee, Tea	Orange Juice Egg, Scrmb Malt-O-Meal Toast Oleo, Jelly ½ c Milk Coffee, Tea	Strain Orange Juice Bl Egg Malt-O-Meal Toast/Bread Oleo, Jelly Milk Coffee, Tea	
D i n n e r	2 oz Liver/Onions #8 Scall Potatoes #16 Bu Gr Beans 1 Hot Roll, 1 t Oleo #8 Cape Cod Fruit Dessert/Topping 1 c Milk Coffee, Tea, *Sanka	Liver/Onions Scall Potatoes Bu Gr Beans Hot Roll, Oleo Cape Cod Fruit Dessert/Topping Milk Coffee, Tea	SF Liver/SF Onions SF Msh Potatoes SF Gr Beans Hot Roll, Oleo Cape Cod Fruit Dessert/Topping ½ c Milk Coffee, Tea	SF Liver/Reg Onions Msh Potatoes Bu Gr Beans Hot Roll, Oleo Cape Cod Fruit Dessert/Topping ½ c Milk Coffee, Tea	Bl Liver/Bl Onions #12 Msh Potatoes #12 Bl Gr Beans #12 Roll/Bread, Oleo Bl Fruit #8 Milk Coffee, Tea	
S u p p e r	6 oz Broccoli Soup 2 oz Pork Cutlet Sdw ½ c Sl Tom/Lettuce Condiments #8 Cinn Applesauce 1 c Milk Coffee, Tea, *Sanka	Broccoli Soup Pork Cutlet Sand Sl Tom/Lettuce Condiments Cinn Applesauce Milk Coffee, Tea	SF Broccoli Soup SF Pork Cutlet Sl Tom/Lettuce Cinn Applesauce ½ c Milk Coffee, Tea	Broccoli Soup SF Pork Cutlet Sand Sl Tom/Lettuce Cinn Applesauce ½ c Milk Coffee, Tea ½ t salt to be added	Str Broccoli Soup Bl Pork Cutlet #12 Bl Tom/Lettuce Bread Bl Cinn Applesauce #8 Milk Coffee, Tea	

*For Bland diet.

Portion sizes are same as for Regular unless otherwise specified.

Bran is to be added to one menu item per day.

CERTIFIED _____ , R.D.

341

Exhibit A-2 continued

WEEK NO. ONE   DAY THURSDAY   MENU CYCLE FALL/WINTER

	Regular/Bland	Mechanical	2 Gram Sodium	4 Gram Sodium	Blended			
Breakfast	½ c Orange Juice 1 Egg, Fried ½ c Oatmeal 1 Toast 1 t Oleo, Jelly 1 c Milk Coffee, Tea, *Sanka	Orange Juice Egg, Fried Oatmeal Toast/Bread Oleo, Jelly Milk Coffee, Tea	Orange Juice Egg, Fried Oatmeal Toast Oleo, Jelly ½ c Milk Coffee, Tea	Orange Juice Egg, Fried Oatmeal Toast Oleo, Jelly ½ c Milk Coffee, Tea	Strain Orange Juice Bl Egg Strain Oatmeal Toast/Bread Oleo, Jelly Milk Coffee, Tea			
Dinner	2 oz Enchiladas *No Chili Pwd #16 Refried Beans #8 Spanish Rice ½ c Shred Lettuce 3 oz Sherbet 1 c Milk Coffee, Tea, *Sanka	Enchiladas Refried Beans Spanish Rice Shred Lettuce Sherbet Milk Coffee, Tea	SF Enchiladas SF Refried Beans Spanish Rice Shred Lettuce Sherbet ½ c Milk Coffee, Tea	SF Enchiladas SF Refried Beans Spanish Rice Shred Lettuce Sherbet ½ c Milk Coffee, Tea	Bl Beef #12 Bl Rice #12 Bl Lettuce Bl Fruit #8 Sherbet Milk Coffee, Tea			
Supper	6 oz Turkey ala King (2 oz meat) on Msh Potatoes #16 Bu Brussel Sprts #8 Apple Ring Hot Roll, Oleo #8 Peach Sunshine Surprise (½ c Fruit) 1 c Milk Coffee, Tea, *Sanka	Turkey ala King on Msh Potatoes Bu Brussel Sprts Apple Ring Hot Roll, Oleo Peach Sunshine Surprise Milk Coffee, Tea	SF Turkey ala King on SF Potatoes SF Brussel Sprts Apple Ring Hot Roll, Oleo Peach Sunshine Surprise 1 c Milk Coffee, Tea	SF Turkey ala King on Msh Potatoes Bu Brussel Sprts Apple Ring Hot Roll, Oleo Peach Sunshine Surprise 1 c Milk Coffee, Tea	Bl Turkey #12 Bl Potatoes #12 Bl Brussel Sprts #12 Bl Peaches #8 Bread, Oleo Milk Coffee, Tea			

*For Bland diet.
Portion sizes are same as for Regular unless otherwise specified.
Bran is to be added to one menu item per day.

CERTIFIED _____, R.D.

342

	Regular/Bland	Mechanical	2 Gram Sodium	4 Gram Sodium	Blended	
B r e a k f a s t	½ c Orange Juice 1 Pancake or Waffle Syrup 1 oz Sausage #8 Cr of Wheat Oleo 1 c Milk Coffee, Tea, *Sanka	Orange Juice Pancake or Waffle Syrup Egg or Sausage Cr of Wheat Oleo Milk Coffee, Tea	Orange Juice Egg Toast Cr of Wheat Oleo, Jelly ½ c Milk Coffee, Tea	Orange Juice Egg Toast Cr of Wheat Oleo, Jelly ½ c Milk Coffee, Tea	Strain Orange Juice Bl Egg Strain Cr of Wheat Toast or Bread Oleo, Jelly Milk Coffee, Tea	
D i n n e r	2 oz Pork Chop #8 Sw Potatoes #16 Cabbage 1 Bread, 1 t Oleo Pineapple Upside Down Cake 1 c Milk Coffee, Tea, *Sanka	Grd Pork Chop Sw Potatoes Cabbage Bread, Oleo Pineapple Upside Down Cake Milk Coffee, Tea	SF Pork Chop SF Sw Potatoes SF Cabbage Bread, Oleo Pineapple Chunks ½ c Milk Coffee, Tea	SF Pork Chop Sw Potatoes Cabbage Bread, Oleo Pineapple Upside Down Cake ½ c Milk Coffee, Tea	Bl Pork Chop #12 Bl Sw Potatoes #12 Bl Cabbage #12 Bread, Oleo Bl Pineapple #8 Milk Coffee, Tea	
S u p p e r	6 oz Tuna Casserole/ Noodles (2 oz Meat) #16 Harvard Beets Hot Roll, Oleo #8 Tinted Pear 1 c Milk Coffee, Tea, *Sanka	Tuna Casserole/ Noodles Harvard Beets Hot Roll, Oleo Tinted Pear Milk Coffee, Tea	SF Tuna Casserole/ SF Noodles SF Beets Hot Roll, Oleo Tinted Pear 1 c Milk Coffee, Tea	SF Tuna Casserole/ SF Noodles Harvard Beets Hot Roll, Oleo Tinted Pear 1 c Milk Coffee, Tea ½ t salt to be added	Bl Tuna Casserole #12/Bl Noodles Bl Beets #12 Roll/Bread, Oleo Bl Pear #8 Milk Coffee, Tea	

*For Bland diet.
Portion sizes are same as for Regular unless otherwise specified.
Bran is to be added to one menu item per day.

CERTIFIED _____, R.D.

Exhibit A–2 continued

WEEK NO. ___ONE___ DAY ___SATURDAY___

	Regular/Bland	Mechanical	2 Gram Sodium	4 Gram Sodium	Blended	
B r e a k f a s t	½ c Orange Juice #16 Egg, Scrmb ½ c Cr of Rice 1 Toast 1 t Oleo, Jelly 1 c Milk Coffee, Tea, *Sanka	Orange Juice Egg, Scrmb Cr of Rice Toast Oleo, Jelly Milk Coffee, Tea	Orange Juice Egg, Scrmb Cr of Rice Toast Oleo, Jelly ½ c Milk Coffee, Tea	Orange Juice Egg, Scrmb Cr of Rice Toast Oleo, Jelly ½ c Milk Coffee, Tea	Strain Orange Juice Bl Egg Strain Cr of Rice Toast/Bread Oleo, Jelly Milk Coffee, Tea	
D i n n e r	2 oz Rst Beef/Gravy #8 Bkd Potatoes #16 Gr Beans 1 Bread, Oleo 1 t #8 Pear Crisp 1 c Milk Coffee, Tea, *Sanka	Rst Beef/Gravy Bkd Potatoes Gr Beans Bread, Oleo Pear Crisp Milk Coffee, Tea	SF Rst Beef/Gravy SF Bkd Potatoes SF Gr Beans Bread, Oleo Pear Crisp ½ c Milk Coffee, Tea	SF Rst Beef/Gravy Bkd Potatoes Gr Beans Bread, Oleo Pear Crisp ½ c Milk Coffee, Tea	Bl Beef #12 Bl Potatoes #12 Bl Gr Beans #12 Bread, Oleo Bl Pears #8 Milk Coffee, Tea	
S u p p e r	6 oz Beef Veg Soup Crackers Pimento Ch Sand (2 oz cheese) ½ Deviled Egg #8 Mix Fruit Cookies 1 c Milk Coffee, Tea, *Sanka	Beef Veg Soup Crackers Pimento Ch Sand ½ Deviled Egg ½ c Mix Fruit Cookies Milk Coffee, Tea	SF Beef Veg Soup SF Crackers SF Pimento Ch Sand ½ Deviled Egg ½ c Mix Fruit Cookies ½ c Milk Coffee, Tea	Beef Veg Soup SF Crackers Pimento Ch Sand ½ Deviled Egg ½ c Mix Fruit Cookies ½ c Milk Coffee, Tea ½ t salt to be added	Str Beef Veg Soup 2 oz Bl Beef in Soup #8 Bl Veg in Soup Bl Mix Fruit #8 Jello #8 Milk Coffee, Tea	

*For Bland diet.

Portion sizes are same as for Regular unless otherwise specified.

Bran to be added to one menu item per day.

CERTIFIED _____, R.D.

344

	Regular/Bland	Mechanical	2 Gram Sodium	4 Gram Sodium	Blended		
B r e a k f a s t	½ c Orange Juice 1 Egg, Fried ½ c Oatmeal 1 sl Bacon 1 Toast 1 t Oleo, Jelly 1 c Milk 1 c Coffee, Tea, *Sanka	Orange Juice Egg, Fried Oatmeal Bacon Toast or Bread Oleo, Jelly Milk Coffee, Tea	Orange Juice Egg, Fried Oatmeal Toast Oleo, Jelly ½ c Milk Coffee, Tea	Orange Juice Egg, Fried Oatmeal Toast Oleo, Jelly ½ c Milk Coffee, Tea	Strain Orange Juice Bl Egg Strain Oatmeal Toast or Bread Oleo, Jelly Milk Coffee, Tea		

D i n n e r	2 oz Country Fried
	   Steak
	#8 Ov Br Potatoes
	#16 Bu Squash
	1 Hot Roll, Oleo
	Strawberry Short-
	   cake/Topping
	1 c Milk
	1 c Coffee, Tea,
	   *Sanka
		Grd Country Fried
		   Steak
		Ov Br Potatoes
		Bu Squash
		Hot Roll, Oleo
		Strawberry Short-
		   cake/Topping
		Milk
		Coffee, Tea
			SF Country Fried
			   Steak
			SF Potatoes
			SF Squash
			Hot Roll, Oleo
			Strawberry Short-
			   cake/Topping
			½ c Milk
			Coffee, Tea
				SF Country Fried
				   Steak
				Ov Br Potatoes
				Bu Squash
				Hot Roll, Oleo
				Strawberry Short-
				   cake/Topping
				½ c Milk
				Coffee, Tea
					Bl Country Fried
					   Steak #12
					Bl Potatoes #12
					Bl Squash #12
					Roll or Bread, Oleo
					Bl Strawberries #8
					Milk
					Coffee, Tea		

S u p p e r	1 c Ham in Mac &
	   Cheese
	#16 Bu Gr Peas
	#16 Pickled Beets
	1 sl Bread, Oleo 1 t
	#8 Peaches
	1 c Milk
	Coffee, Tea, *Sanka
		Grd Ham in Mac &
		   Cheese
		Buttered Gr Peas
		Pickled Beets
		Bread, Oleo
		Peaches
		Milk
		Coffee, Tea
			½ c Macaroni
			2 oz SF Cheese
			SF Gr Peas
			SF Beets
			Bread, Oleo
			Peaches
			1 c Milk
			Coffee, Tea
				6 oz Mac & Cheese
				Bu Gr Peas
				Pickled Beets
				Bread, Oleo
				Peaches
				1 c Milk
				Coffee, Tea
				½ t salt to be added
					Bl Ham in Mac &
					   Cheese
					Bl Gr Peas #12
					Bl Beets #12
					Bread, Oleo
					Bl Peaches #8
					Milk
					Coffee, Tea		

*For Bland diet.
Portion sizes are same as for Regular unless otherwise specified.
Bran is to be added to one menu item per day.

CERTIFIED _____ , R.D.

345

Exhibit A-2 continued

	Regular/Bland	Mechanical	2 Gram Sodium	4 Gram Sodium	Blended
Breakfast	½ c Orange Juice 1 Egg, Pchd #8 Malt-O-Meal 1 Toast 1 t Oleo, Jelly 1 c Milk Coffee, Tea, *Sanka	Orange Juice Egg, Pchd Malt-O-Meal Toast Oleo, Jelly Milk Coffee, Tea	Orange Juice Egg, Pchd Malt-O-Meal Toast Oleo, Jelly ½ c Milk Coffee, Tea	Orange Juice Egg, Pchd Malt-O-Meal Toast Oleo, Jelly ½ c Milk Coffee, Tea	Strain Orange Juice Bl Egg Strain Malt-O-Meal Toast or Bread Oleo, Jelly Milk Coffee, Tea
Dinner	6 oz Tamale Pie** (2 oz meat) #16 Bu Broccoli #16 Pineapple/¼ c Cott Ch Salad W/W Bread Oleo Frosted Cake Sq*** 1 c Milk Coffee, Tea, *Sanka	Tamale Pie Bu Broccoli Peach/Cott Ch Salad W/W Bread Oleo Frosted Cake Sq Milk Coffee, Tea	SF Tamale Pie SF Broccoli Pineapple/Cott Ch Salad W/W Bread Oleo Frosted Cake Sq ½ c Milk Coffee, Tea	SF Tamale Pie Bu Broccoli Pineapple/Cott Ch Salad W/W Bread Oleo Frosted Cake Sq ½ c Milk Coffee, Tea	Bl Tamale Pie #12 Bl Broccoli #12 Bl Pineapple #8 Bl Cott Cheese #16 Bread Oleo Bl Cake Milk Coffee, Tea
Supper	2 oz Patty Melt #8 Tater Tots #8 Carrot/Raisin Salad Rye Bread #8 Fruit in Season 1 c Milk Coffee, Tea, *Sanka	Grd Patty/Melt Ch Tater Tots Carrot/Raisin Salad Rye Bread Soft Fruit in Season Milk Coffee, Tea	SF Patty/SF Cheese SF Tater Tots Carrot/Raisin Salad Rye Bread Fruit in Season ½ c Milk Coffee, Tea	SF Patty/Reg Cheese Tater Tots Carrot/Raisin Salad Rye Bread Fruit in Season ½ c Milk Coffee, Tea	Bl Patty Melt #12 Bl Tater Tots #12 Bl Ckd Carrots #12 Bread Bl Fruit #8 Milk Coffee, Tea

*For Bland diet.

Portion sizes are same as for Regular unless otherwise specified.

Bran is to be added to one menu item per day.

**Bland, no chili.

***Bland, no choc.

CERTIFIED _____, R.D.

346

	Regular/Bland	Mechanical	2 Gram Sodium	4 Gram Sodium	Blended		
B r e a k f a s t	½ c Orange Juice 1 Egg, Hd Ckd ½ c Cr of Wheat 1 Toast 1 t Oleo, Jelly 1 c Milk Coffee, Tea, *Sanka	Orange Juice Egg, Hd Ckd Cr of Wheat Toast or Bread Oleo, Jelly Milk Coffee, Tea	Orange Juice Egg, Hd Ckd Cr of Wheat Toast Oleo, Jelly ½ c Milk Coffee, Tea	Orange Juice Egg, Hd Ckd Cr of Wheat Toast Oleo, Jelly ½ c Milk Coffee, Tea	Strain Orange Juice Bl Egg Strain Cr of Wheat Toast or Bread Oleo, Jelly Milk Coffee, Tea		
D i n n e r	6 oz Chicken & Bisc #16 Peas/Carrots 1 Hot Roll, Oleo 1 sl Mock Pecan Pie 1 c Milk Coffee, Tea, *Sanka	Grd Chicken & Bisc Peas/Carrots Hot Roll, Oleo Mock Pecan Pie Milk Coffee, Tea	SF Chicken SF Peas/Carrots Hot Roll, Oleo Fruit in Season ½ c Milk Coffee, Tea	SF Chicken & Bisc Peas/Carrots Hot Roll, Oleo Fruit in Season ½ c Milk Coffee, Tea	Bl Chicken & Bisc Bl Peas/Carrots #12 Bread Bl Fruit #8 Milk Coffee, Tea		
S u p p e r	6 oz Minestrone Soup Crackers #16 Carrot/Celery 2 oz Egg—Egg Sld Sand #8 Fruit Jello Cubes/Lettuce #16 Cott Cheese Cookies 1 c Milk Coffee, Tea, *Sanka	Minestrone Soup Crackers Egg Salad Sand Fruit Jello Cubes/Lettuce Cott Cheese Cookies Milk Coffee, Tea	SF Beef-Veg Soup Crackers Peanut Bu/Jelly Sand Fruit Jello Cubes/Lettuce Dry Cott Cheese Cookie ½ c Milk Coffee, Tea	Minestrone Soup Crackers Peanut Bu/Jelly Sand Fruit Jello Cubes/Lettuce Cott Cheese Cookie ½ c Milk Coffee, Tea ½ t salt to be added	Str Minestrone Soup Bl Egg Salad #8 Bl Fruit #8 & Cott Cheese #16 Jello #8 Bread Milk Coffee, Tea		

*For Bland diet.
Portion sizes are same as for Regular unless otherwise specified.
Bran is to be added to one menu item per day.

CERTIFIED _____, R.D.

347

Exhibit A–2 continued

WEEK NO. __TWO__ DAY __WEDNESDAY__   MENU CYCLE ____ __FALL/WINTER__

	Regular/Bland	Mechanical	2 Gram Sodium	4 Gram Sodium	Blended		
B r e a k f a s t	½ c Orange Juice #16 Egg, Scrmb ½ c Oatmeal 1 Toast 1 t Oleo, Jelly 1 c Milk Coffee, Tea, *Sanka	Orange Juice Egg, Scrmb Oatmeal Toast or Bread Oleo, Jelly Milk Coffee, Tea	Orange Juice Egg, Scrmb Oatmeal Toast Oleo, Jelly ½ c Milk Coffee, Tea	Orange Juice Egg, Scrmb Oatmeal Toast Oleo, Jelly ½ c Milk Coffee, Tea	Orange Juice Bl Egg Oatmeal Toast or Bread Oleo, Jelly Milk Coffee, Tea		
D i n n e r	2 oz Roast Pork #8 Sw Potatoes #16 Gr Beans Cornbread, Oleo #8 Applesauce 1 c Milk Coffee, Tea, *Sanka	Grd Roast Pork Sw Potatoes Buttered Gr Beans Cornbread, Oleo Applesauce Milk Coffee, Tea	SF Roast Pork Sw Potatoes SF Gr Beans Bread, Oleo Applesauce ½ c Milk Coffee, Tea	SF Roast Pork Sw Potatoes Gr Beans Cornbread, Oleo Applesauce ½ c Milk Coffee, Tea	Bl Rst Pork #12 Bl Sw Potatoes #12 Bl Gr Beans #12 Bread, Oleo Applesauce #8 Milk Coffee, Tea		

S u p p e r	6 oz Ch Beef
	  Quiche
	  (2 oz Beef)
	Coleslaw/Tomato
	1 Bread, Oleo
	½ c Bu Cinn
	  Pineapple
	3 oz Ice Cream
	  (Bland-No Choc)
	1 c Milk
	Coffee, Tea, *Sanka
		Ch Beef Quiche
		Coleslaw/Tomato
		Bread, Oleo
		Bu Cinn Pineapple
		Ice Cream
		Milk
		Coffee, Tea
			SF Ch Beef Quiche
			SF Coleslaw/
			  Tomato
			Bread, Oleo
			Cinn Pineapple
			Ice Cream
			½ c Milk
			Coffee, Tea
				SF Ch Beef Quiche
				Coleslaw/Tomato
				Bread, Oleo
				Tomato Juice
				Ice Cream
				½ c Milk
				Coffee, Tea
					Bl Quiche #12
					Bl Slaw #12
					Bread
					Bl Pineapple #8
					Ice Cream
					Milk
					Coffee, Tea		

*For Bland diet.
Portion sizes are same as for Regular unless otherwise specified.
Bran is to be added to one menu item per day.

CERTIFIED _____, R.D.

348

	Regular/Bland	Mechanical	2 Gram Sodium	4 Gram Sodium	Blended		
B **r** **e** **a** **k** **f** **a** **s** **t**	½ c Orange Juice 1 sl Fr Toast/Syrup #16 Egg or 1 oz Sausage #8 Cr of Rice 1 t Oleo 1 c Milk Coffee, Tea, *Sanka	Orange Juice Fr Toast/Syrup Egg Cr of Rice Oleo Milk Coffee, Tea	Orange Juice Fr Toast/Syrup Egg Cr of Rice Oleo ½ c Milk Coffee, Tea	Orange Juice Fr Toast/Syrup Egg Cr of Rice Oleo ½ c Milk Coffee, Tea	Orange Juice Bl Fr Toast/Syrup Bl Egg Strain Cr of Rice Oleo Milk Coffee, Tea		

D
i
n
n
e
r
	2 oz Mock Swiss
	  Steak
	#8 Steamed Rice
	#16 Bu Broccoli
	1 Hot Roll, Oleo
	Sunshine Ginger-
	  bread with #8
	  Peaches
	1 c Milk
	Coffee, Tea, *Sanka
		Grd Mock Sw Steak
		Steamed Rice
		Bu Broccoli
		Hot Roll, Oleo
		Sunshine Ginger-
		  bread with
		  Peaches
		Milk
		Coffee, Tea
			SF Mock Sw Steak
			SF Rice
			SF Broccoli
			Hot Roll, Oleo
			Sunshine Ginger-
			  bread with
			  Peaches
			½ c Milk
			Coffee, Tea
				SF Mock Sw Steak
				Steamed Rice
				Bu Broccoli
				Hot Roll, Oleo
				Sunshine Ginger-
				  bread with
				  Peaches
				½ c Milk
				Coffee, Tea
					Bl Sw Steak #12
					Bl Rice #12
					Bl Broccoli #12
					Bread, Oleo
					Bl Peaches #8
					Milk
					Coffee, Tea		

S
u
p
p
e
r
	1 oz Hotdog/Bun
	6 oz Chili **Soup
	Pickle Strip
	Condiments
	#8 Coleslaw
	#8 Banana
	  Pudding/Topping
	1 c Milk
	Coffee, Tea, *Sanka
		Grd Hotdog/Bun
		Chili
		Pickle Strip
		Condiments
		Coleslaw
		Banana Pudding/
		  Topping
		Milk
		Coffee, Tea
			SF Tstd Ch Sand
			SF Chili
			Coleslaw
			Banana Pudding/
			  Topping
			½ c Milk
			Coffee, Tea
				SF Tstd Ch Sand
				Chili
				Coleslaw
				Banana Pudding/
				  Topping
				½ c Milk
				Coffee, Tea
					Bl Hotdog/Bun #12
					Bl Ckd Cabbage
					  #12
					Soup
					Soft Pudding/
					  Topping
					Milk
					Coffee, Tea		

*For Bland diet.
**1 c Tomato Soup.
Portion sizes are same as for Regular unless otherwise specified.
Bran is to be added to one menu item per day.

CERTIFIED _____, R.D.

Exhibit A-2 continued

WEEK NO. ___TWO___ DAY ___FRIDAY___   MENU CYCLE ___ FALL/WINTER ___

	Regular/Bland	Mechanical	2 Gram Sodium	4 Gram Sodium	Blended		
Breakfast	½ c Orange Juice 1 Egg Omelet #8 Ralston 1 Toast 1 t Oleo, Jelly 1 c Milk Coffee, Tea, *Sanka	Orange Juice Egg Omelet Ralston Toast Oleo, Jelly Milk Coffee, Tea	Orange Juice Egg Omelet Ralston Toast Oleo, Jelly ½ c Milk Coffee, Tea	Orange Juice Egg Omelet Ralston Toast Oleo, Jelly ½ c Milk Coffee, Tea	Strain Orange Juice Bl Egg Strain Ralston Toast or Bread Oleo, Jelly Milk Coffee, Tea		
Dinner	2 oz Fried Chicken #16 Baby Lima Beans #16 Beets 1 2" Homemade Biscuit 1 t Oleo #8 Comb Veg Sal ½ c Apple Cobbler 1 c Milk Coffee, Tea, *Sanka	V-8 Juice Grd Chicken Baby Lima Beans Beets Homemade Bisc Oleo Comb Veg Salad Apple Cobbler Milk Coffee, Tea	SF Chicken SF Lima Beans SF Beets Roll Oleo Veg Salad Bkd Apples ½ c Milk Coffee, Tea	SF Chicken Baby Lima Beans Beets Homemade Bisc Oleo Veg Salad Apple Cobbler ½ c Milk Coffee, Tea	Bl Chicken #12 Bl Lima Beans #12 Bl Beets #12 Bread, Oleo Bl Apples or Juice #8 Milk Coffee, Tea		
Supper	2 oz Sea Burger/ 1 T Tartar Sauce #8 Potatoes Au Gratin #16 Zucchini & Tom 1 Steamed Bun 1 2" Cup Cake 1 c Milk Coffee, Tea, *Sanka	Grd Sea Burger/ Tartar Sauce Potatoes Au Gratin Zucchini & Tom Steamed Bun Cup Cake Milk Coffee, Tea	SF Sea Burger SF Potatoes Au Gratin SF Zucchini & Tom Steamed Bun Cup Cake 1 c Milk Coffee, Tea	SF Sea Burger Potatoes Au Gratin Zucchini & Tom Steamed Bun Cup Cake 1 c Milk Coffee, Tea	Bl Sea Burger #12 Bl Potatoes #12 Bl Zucchini & Tom #12 Bread Bl Fruit #8 Milk Coffee, Tea		

*For Bland diet.
Portion sizes are same as for Regular unless otherwise specified.
Bran is to be added to one menu item per day.

CERTIFIED_____, R.D.

350

	Regular/Bland	Mechanical	2 Gram Sodium	4 Gram Sodium	Blended		
B r e a k f a s t	½ c Orange Juice 1 Egg, Pchd ½ c Oatmeal Toast Oleo, Jelly 1 c Milk Coffee, Tea, *Sanka	Orange Juice Egg, Pchd Oatmeal Toast or Bread Oleo, Jelly Milk Coffee, Tea	Orange Juice Egg, Pchd Oatmeal Toast Oleo, Jelly ½ c Milk Coffee, Tea	Orange Juice Egg, Pchd Oatmeal Toast Oleo, Jelly ½ c Milk Coffee, Tea	Strain Orange Juice Bl Egg Strain Oatmeal Toast or Bread Oleo, Jelly Milk Coffee, Tea		
D i n n e r	#8 Spaghetti/ #16 Meat Sauce ½ c Shred Lettuce/ Dressing #16 Bu Gr Veg 1 Garlic Toast 1 Banana 1 c Milk Coffee, Tea, *Sanka	Spaghetti/Meat Sauce Shred Lettuce/ Dressing Bu Gr Veg Garlic Toast Banana Milk Coffee, Tea	SF Spaghetti/ SF Meat Sauce Shred Lettuce/SF Dressing SF Gr Veg Toast Banana 1 c Milk Coffee, Tea	Spaghetti/SF Meat Sauce Shred Lettuce/1 T Dressing Buttered Gr Veg Toast Banana 1 c Milk Coffee, Tea Add ½ t salt	Bl Spaghetti #12 Bl Meat Sauce Bl Gr Peas #12 Bread Bl Banana #8 Milk Coffee, Tea		
S u p p e r	6 oz Impossible Pie (2 oz meat) #16 Gr Beans Sliced Tomatoes 1 2" Biscuit, Oleo #8 Cinn Fruit Mix 1 c Milk Coffee, Tea, *Sanka	Impossible Pie Gr Beans Sliced Tomatoes Biscuit, Oleo Cinn Fruit Mix Milk Coffee, Tea	SF Impossible Pie SF Gr Beans Sliced Tomatoes Biscuit, Oleo Cinn Fruit Mix 1 c Milk Coffee, Tea	SF Impossible Pie Gr Beans Sliced Tomatoes Biscuit, Oleo Cinn Fruit Mix 1 c Milk Coffee, Tea	Bl Impossible Pie #12 Bl Gr Beans #12 Tomato Juice Biscuit, Oleo Bl Cinn Fruit #8 Milk Coffee, Tea		

*For Bland diet.
Portion sizes are same as for Regular unless otherwise specified.
Bran is to be added to one menu item per day.

CERTIFIED _____, R.D.

351

Exhibit A–2 continued

WEEK NO. ___THREE___ DAY ___SUNDAY___

MENU CYCLE ___FALL/WINTER___

	Regular/Bland	Mechanical	2 Gram Sodium	4 Gram Sodium	Blended		
B r e a k f a s t	½ c Orange Juice 1 Egg, Pchd 1 Bacon ½ c Malt-O-Meal 1 Toast 1 t Oleo, Jelly 1 c Milk Coffee, Tea, *Sanka	Orange Juice Egg, Pchd Bacon Malt-O-Meal Toast Oleo, Jelly Milk Coffee, Tea	Orange Juice Egg, Pchd Malt-O-Meal Toast Oleo, Jelly ½ c Milk Coffee, Tea	Orange Juice Egg, Pchd Malt-O-Meal Toast Oleo, Jelly ½ c Milk Coffee, Tea	Strain Orange Juice Bl Egg Strain Malt-O-Meal Toast or Bread Oleo, Jelly Milk Coffee, Tea		
D i n n e r	2 oz Bkd Ham #8 Sw Potatoes #16 Seas Greens 1 2" sq Cornbread, Oleo #8 Applesauce Autumn 3 oz Ice Cream 1 c Milk Coffee, Tea, *Sanka	Grd Bkd Ham Sw Potatoes Seas Greens Cornbread, Oleo Applesauce Autumn Ice Cream Milk Coffee, Tea	SF Pork SF Sw Potatoes SF Greens Bread, Oleo Applesauce Autumn Ice Cream ½ c Milk Coffee, Tea	SF Pork Sw Potatoes Seas Greens Cornbread, Oleo Applesauce Autumn Ice Cream ½ c Milk Coffee, Tea	Bl Bkd Ham #12 Bl Sw Potatoes #12 Bl Greens #12 Bread, Oleo Bl Applesauce #8 Ice Cream Milk Coffee, Tea		
S u p p e r	2 oz Sloppy Joe/ Bun *without chili pwd #16 Bu Mix Veg #8 Fr Fries #8 Pear in Jello on Lettuce Lemon Pie 1 c Milk Coffee, Tea, *Sanka	Sloppy Joe/Bun Bu Mix Veg Fr Fries Pear in Jello on Lettuce Lemon Pie Milk Coffee, Tea	SF Sloppy Joe/Bun SF Mix Veg SF Fr Fries Pear in Jello on Lettuce Lemon Pudding Coffee, Tea	SF Sloppy Joe/Bun Bu Mix Veg Fr Fries Pear in Jello on Lettuce Lemon Pudding Coffee, Tea ½ t salt to be added	Bl Sloppy Joe #12 Bl Bun Bl Potatoes #12 Bl Pear in Jello #12 Lemon Pudding #8 Milk Coffee, Tea		

*For Bland diet.
Portion sizes are same as for Regular unless otherwise specified.
Bran is to be added to one menu item per day.

CERTIFIED _____, R.D.

	Regular/Bland	Mechanical	2 Gram Sodium	4 Gram Sodium	Blended		
B r e a k f a s t	½ c Orange Juice 1 Egg, Fried ½ c Cr of Wheat 1 Toast 1 t Oleo, Jelly 1 c Milk Coffee, Tea, *Sanka	Orange Juice Egg, Fried Cr of Wheat Toast or Bread Oleo, Jelly Milk Coffee, Tea	Orange Juice Egg, Fried Cr of Wheat Toast Oleo, Jelly ½ c Milk Coffee, Tea	Orange Juice Egg, Fried Cr of Wheat Toast Oleo, Jelly ½ c Milk Coffee, Tea	Strain Orange Juice Bl Egg Strain Cr of Wheat Toast or Bread Oleo, Jelly Milk Coffee, Tea		

D i n n e r	2 oz BBQ Chicken
	*No chili pwd or
	   pepper
	#8 Parsl Pots
	#16 Bu Gr Peas
	#8 Pineapple sl/
	   Grape Jubilee
	Hot Roll, Oleo
	Choc Cake
	*White Cake
	1 c Milk
	Coffee, Tea, *Sanka
		Grd BBQ Chicken
		Parsl Potatoes
		Bu Gr Peas
		Pineapple Slice/
		   Grape Jubilee
		Hot Roll, Oleo
		Choc Cake
		Milk, Coffee, Tea
			SF BBQ Chicken
			SF Potatoes
			SF Gr Peas
			Pineapple Slice/
			   Grape Jubilee
			Hot Roll, Oleo
			White Cake
			½ c Milk
			Coffee, Tea
				BBQ Chicken
				Parsl Potatoes
				Bu Gr Peas
				Pineapple Slice/
				   Grape Jubilee
				Hot Roll, Oleo
				White Cake
				½ c Milk
				Coffee, Tea
					Bl BBQ Chicken
					   #12
					Bl Potatoes #12
					Bl Gr Peas #12
					Bl Pineapple Slice/
					   Grape Jubilee #8
					Bread
					Jello #8
					Milk
					Coffee, Tea		

S u p p e r	2 oz Salmon Patty/
	   Cheese Sauce
	#16 Msh Potatoes
	#16 Ly Gr Beans
	Bread, Oleo
	½ c Fruited Vanilla
	   Pudd/Topping
	1 c Milk
	Coffee, Tea, *Sanka
		Flaked Salmon
		   Patty/Ch Sce
		Msh Potatoes
		Lyonnaise Gr
		   Beans
		Bread, Oleo
		Frtd Van Pud/Top
		Milk
		Coffee, Tea
			SF Salmon Patty
			SF Potatoes
			SF Gr Beans
			Bread, Oleo
			Fruited Vanilla
			   Pudd/Topping
			½ c Milk
			Coffee, Tea
				SF Salmon Patty
				Msh Potatoes
				Ly Gr Beans
				Bread, Oleo
				Fruited Vanilla
				   Pudd/Topping
				½ c Milk
				Coffee, Tea
				½ t salt to be added
					Bl Salmon Patty
					   #12
					Bl Potatoes #12
					Bl Gr Beans #12
					Bread, Oleo
					Bl Fruited Vanilla
					   Pudd #8
					Milk
					Coffee, Tea		

*For Bland diet.
Portion sizes are same as for Regular unless otherwise specified.
Bran is to be added to one menu item per day.

CERTIFIED _____, R.D.

353

Exhibit A–2 continued

WEEK NO. ___THREE___ DAY ___TUESDAY___   MENU CYCLE ___FALL/WINTER___

	Regular/Bland	Mechanical	2 Gram Sodium	4 Gram Sodium	Blended		
B r e a k f a s t	½ c Orange Juice 1 Hard Ckd Egg ½ c Oatmeal 1 Toast 1 t Oleo, Jelly 1 c Milk Coffee, Tea, *Sanka	Orange Juice Hard Ckd Egg Oatmeal Toast Oleo, Jelly Milk Coffee, Tea	Orange Juice Hard Ckd Egg Oatmeal Toast Oleo, Jelly ½ c Milk Coffee, Tea	Orange Juice Hard Ckd Egg Oatmeal Toast Oleo, Jelly ½ c Milk Coffee, Tea	Strain Orange Juice Bl Egg Strain Oatmeal Toast or Bread Oleo, Jelly Milk Coffee, Tea		

D i n n e r	2 oz Mushroom
	  Steak
	#16 Stm Rice
	½ c Glzd Carrots
	1 Hot Roll, Oleo 1 t
	#8 Peach Cobbler
	1 c Milk
	Coffee, Tea, *Sanka
		Grd Mushroom
		  Steak
		Stm Rice
		Glzd Carrots
		Hot Roll, Oleo
		Peach Cobbler
		Milk
		Coffee, Tea
			SF Mushroom
			  Steak
			SF Rice
			SF Carrots
			Hot Roll, Oleo
			Peaches
			½ c Milk
			Coffee, Tea
				SF Mushroom
				  Steak
				Rice
				Carrots
				Hot Roll, Oleo
				Peaches
				½ c Milk
				Coffee, Tea
					Bl Mushroom Steak
					  #12
					Bl Rice #12
					Bl Carrots #12
					Bread, Oleo
					Bl Peaches #8
					Milk
					Coffee, Tea		

S u p p e r	2 oz Chili Relleno
	#8 Ital Gr Beans
	1 Tortilla, Oleo 1 t
	#16 Cott Cheese
	  Mexicali
	#8 Fruit in Season
	Milk
	Coffee, Tea, *Sanka
		Chili Relleno
		Ital Gr Beans
		Tortilla, Oleo
		Cott Cheese
		  Mexicali
		Soft Fruit in Season
		Milk
		Coffee, Tea
			SF Chili
			SF Gr Beans
			Tortilla, Oleo
			Fruit in Season
			Milk
			Coffee, Tea
				SF Chili
				Ital Gr Beans
				Tortilla, Oleo
				Cott Cheese
				Fruit in Season
				Milk
				Coffee, Tea
					Bl Chili #12
					Bl Gr Beans #12
					Bread
					Bl Cott Cheese #16
					Bl Fruit #8
					Milk
					Coffee, Tea		

*For Bland diet.
Portion sizes are same as for Regular unless otherwise specified.
Bran is to be added to one menu item per day.

CERTIFIED _____, R.D.

	Regular/Bland	Mechanical	2 Gram Sodium	4 Gram Sodium	Blended		
B **r** **e** **a** **k** **f** **a** **s** **t**	½ c Orange Juice #16 Egg, Scrmb/ 　Bacon Bits ½ c Cr of Rice 1 Toast 1 t Oleo, Jelly 1 c Milk Coffee, Tea, *Sanka	Orange Juice Egg, Scrmb/Bacon 　Bits Cr of Rice Toast or Bread Oleo, Jelly Milk Coffee, Tea	Orange Juice Egg, Scrmb Cr of Rice Toast Oleo, Jelly ½ c Milk Coffee, Tea	Orange Juice Egg, Scrmb Cr of Rice Toast Oleo, Jelly ½ c Milk Coffee, Tea	Strain Orange Juice Bl Egg Strain Cr of Rice Toast or Bread Oleo, Jelly Milk Coffee, Tea		
D **i** **n** **n** **e** **r**	2 oz Pork Cutlets/ 　Gravy #8 Parsl Potatoes #16 Brd Tomatoes 1 Bread, 1 t Oleo Spice Cake 1 c Milk Coffee, Tea, *Sanka	Grd Pork Cutlet Parsl Potatoes Brd Tomatoes Bread, Oleo Spice Cake Milk Coffee, Tea	SF Pork Cutlet SF Potatoes SF Tomatoes Bread, Oleo Fruit in Season Milk Coffee, Tea	SF Pork Cutlet Parsl Potatoes Brd Tomatoes Bread, Oleo Spice Cake Milk Coffee, Tea ½ t salt to be added	Bl Pork Cutlet #12 Bl Potatoes #12 Bl Tomatoes #12 Bread Bl Fruit #8 Milk Coffee, Tea		
S **u** **p** **p** **e** **r**	6 oz Cr Tomato 　Soup 4 Crackers Lunch Meat & 　Cheese Sand 　2 oz #16 Carrots & 　Celery #8 Ambrosia 　Cookies 1 c Milk Coffee, Tea, *Sanka	Cr Tomato Soup Crackers Lunch Meat & 　Cheese Sand Stm Carrots Ambrosia Cookies Milk Coffee, Tea	SF Tomato Soup SF Crackers SF Cheese Sand Carrots Ambrosia Cookie Milk Coffee, Tea	Cr Tomato Soup SF Crackers Cheese Sand 2 oz Carrots Ambrosia Cookie Milk Coffee, Tea ½ t salt to be added	Cr Tomato Soup Bl Lunch Meat #12 　& Cheese Sand Bl Ckd Carrots #12 Ambrosia #8 Milk Coffee, Tea		

*For Bland diet.
Portion sizes are same as for Regular unless otherwise specified.
Bran is to be added to one menu item per day.

CERTIFIED _____, R.D.

355

Exhibit A-2 continued

WEEK NO. THREE DAY THURSDAY MENU CYCLE FALL/WINTER

	Regular/Bland	Mechanical	2 Gram Sodium	4 Gram Sodium	Blended		
Breakfast	½ c Orange Juice 1 Egg, Pchd ½ c Ralston 1 Toast 1 t Oleo, Jelly 1 c Milk Coffee, Tea, *Sanka	Orange Juice Egg, Pchd Ralston Toast or Bread Oleo, Jelly Milk Coffee, Tea	Orange Juice Egg, Pchd Ralston Toast Oleo, Jelly ½ c Milk Coffee, Tea	Orange Juice Egg, Pchd Ralston Toast Oleo, Jelly ½ c Milk Coffee, Tea	Strain Orange Juice Bl Egg Strain Ralston Toast or Bread Oleo, Jelly Milk		
Dinner	#8 Beef Strog (2 oz Meat) #8 Stm Noodles #16 Bu Broccoli Hot Roll, Oleo 4 Apricot Hlvs 1 c Milk Coffee, Tea, *Sanka	Grd Beef Strog Stm Noodles Bu Broccoli Hot Roll, Oleo Apricot Hlvs Milk Coffee, Tea	SF Beef Strog SF Noodles SF Broccoli Hot Roll, Oleo Apricot Hlvs ½ c Milk Coffee, Tea	SF Beef Strog Noodles Broccoli Hot Roll, Oleo Apricot Hlvs ½ c Milk Coffee, Tea	Bl Beef Strog #12 Bl Noodles #12 Bl Broccoli #12 Bread, Oleo Bl Apricot Hlvs #8 Milk Coffee, Tea		
Supper	2 oz Lemon Bkd Chicken #8 Whip Potatoes #16 Mix Veg 1 2" Homemade Biscuit Oleo 1 t 3 oz Sherbet 1 c Milk Coffee, Tea, *Sanka	Grd Lemon Bkd Chicken Whip Potatoes Mix Veg Biscuit, Oleo Sherbet Milk Coffee, Tea	SF Bkd Chicken SF Potatoes SF Mix Veg Roll, Oleo Sherbet ½ c Milk Coffee, Tea	SF Bkd Chicken Potatoes Mix Veg Biscuit, Oleo Sherbet ½ c Milk Coffee, Tea	Bl Chicken #12 Potatoes #12 Bl Mix Veg #12 Bread, Oleo Bl Prunes #8 Milk Coffee, Tea		

*For Bland diet.
Portion sizes are same as for Regular unless otherwise specified.
Bran is to be added to one menu item per day.

CERTIFIED _____, R.D.

356

	Regular/Bland	Mechanical	2 Gram Sodium	4 Gram Sodium	Blended	

B r e a k f a s t	½ c Orange Juice
	Pancakes or
	  Waffles 2/Syrup
	1 oz Saus Pattie
	½ c Oatmeal
	1 t Oleo
	1 c Milk
	Coffee, Tea, *Sanka
		Orange Juice
		Pancakes or
		  Waffles/Syrup
		Egg
		Oatmeal
		Oleo
		Milk
		Coffee, Tea
			Orange Juice
			Egg
			Toast
			Oatmeal
			Oleo, Jelly
			½ c Milk
			Coffee, Tea
				Orange Juice
				Pancakes or
				  Waffles/Syrup
				Egg
				Oatmeal
				Oleo
				½ c Milk
				Coffee, Tea
					Strain Orange Juice
					Bl Pancakes or
					  Waffles/Syrup
					Bl Egg
					Strain Oatmeal
					Oleo
					Milk
					Coffee, Tea	

D i n n e r	2 oz Frd Fish/Tartar
	  Sauce
	#8 Mex Corn
	#16 Cauliflower
	1 W/W Bread, Oleo
	  1 t
	#8 Fruit Brd Pudd
	1 c Milk
	Coffee, Tea, *Sanka
		Flaked Fish/Tartar
		  Sauce
		Potatoes or Mex
		  Corn
		Cauliflower
		W/W Bread, Oleo
		Fruit Brd Pudd
		Milk
		Coffee, Tea
			SF Fish
			SF Mex Corn
			Cauliflower
			W/W Bread, Oleo
			Fruit
			½ c Milk
			Coffee, Tea
				SF Fish
				Mex Corn
				Cauliflower
				W/W Bread, Oleo
				Fruit Brd Pudd
				½ c Milk
				Coffee, Tea
					Bl Fish #12
					Bl Potatoes #12
					Bl Cauliflower #12
					Bread, Oleo
					Bl Fruit Brd Pudd
					  #8
					Milk
					Coffee, Tea	

S u p p e r	6 oz Hung Goulash
	  (2 oz Meat)
	#16 Parsl Bu
	  Carrots
	#8 Bu Macaroni
	1 Hot Roll, 1 t Oleo
	#8 Blush Pear
	  Salad
	Poke Cake
	Milk
	Coffee, Tea, *Sanka
		Grd Hung Goulash
		Parsl Bu Carrots
		Bu Macaroni
		Hot Roll, Oleo
		Blush Pear Salad
		Poke Cake
		Milk
		Coffee, Tea
			SF Beef
			SF Macaroni
			SF Bu Carrots
			Hot Roll, Oleo
			Blush Pear Salad
			Poke Cake
			1 c Milk
			Coffee, Tea
				SF Beef
				SF Macaroni
				SF Bu Carrots
				Hot Roll, Oleo
				Blush Pear Salad
				Poke Cake
				1 c Milk
				Coffee, Tea
				½ t salt to be added
					Bl Beef #12
					Bl Macaroni #12
					Bl Carrots #12
					Roll
					Bl Pear & Prunes
					  #8
					Milk
					Coffee, Tea	

*For Bland diet.
Portion sizes are same as for Regular unless otherwise specified.
Bran is to be added to one menu item per day.

CERTIFIED _____, R.D.

357

Exhibit A-2 continued

	Regular/Bland	Mechanical	2 Gram Sodium	4 Gram Sodium	Blended		
B	½ c Orange Juice	Orange Juice	Orange Juice	Orange Juice	Strain Orange Juice		
r	1 Egg, Fried	Egg, Fried	Egg, Fried	Egg, Fried	Bl Egg		
e	½ c Malt-O-Meal	Malt-O-Meal	Malt-O-Meal	Malt-O-Meal	Strain Malt-O-Meal		
a	1 Toast	Toast or Bread	Toast	Toast	Toast or Bread		
k	1 t Oleo, Jelly	Oleo, Jelly	Oleo, Jelly	Oleo, Jelly	Oleo, Jelly		
f	1 c Milk	Milk	½ c Milk	½ c Milk	Milk		
a	Coffee, Tea, *Sanka	Coffee, Tea	Coffee, Tea	Coffee, Tea	Coffee, Tea		
s							
t							
D	2 oz Shrt Ribs Beef	Grd Beef	SF Shrt Ribs Beef	SF Shrt Ribs Beef	Bl Beef #12		
i	#8 Bkd Beans	Bkd Beans	SF Bkd Beans	Bkd Beans	Bl Bkd Beans #12		
n	#16 Mix Veg	Mix Veg	SF Mix Veg	Mix Veg	Bl Mix Veg #12		
n	1 Hot Roll, 1 t Oleo	Hot Roll, Oleo	Hot Roll, Oleo	Hot Roll, Oleo	Bread, Oleo		
e	Choc Brownie	Choc Brownie	Fresh Fruit in	Choc Brownie	Bl Fruit #8		
r	*Blond Brownie		Season				
	1 c Milk	Milk	½ c Milk	½ c Milk	Milk		
	Coffee, Tea, *Sanka	Coffee, Tea	Coffee, Tea	Coffee, Tea	Coffee, Tea		
S	2 oz Pork/Gravy	Grd Pork/Gravy	SF Pork/SF Gravy	SF Pork/SF Gravy	Bl Pork/Gravy #12		
u	#8 Msh Potatoes	Msh Potatoes	SF Msh Potatoes	Msh Potatoes	Msh Potatoes #12		
p	#16 Bu Gr Beans	Bu Gr Beans	SF Gr Beans	Bu Gr Beans	Bl Gr Beans #12		
p	½ c Tomato	Tomato Wedges	Tomato Wedges	Tomato Wedges	Bl Tomato #12		
e	Wedges	Bread, Oleo	Bread, Oleo	Bread, Oleo	Bread, Oleo		
r	Bread, Oleo	Peachy Creamy	Peaches	Peachy Creamy	Bl Peaches #8		
	#8 Peachy Creamy	Milk	Milk	Milk	Milk		
	1 c Milk	Coffee, Tea	Coffee, Tea	Coffee, Tea	Coffee, Tea		
	Coffee, Tea, *Sanka			½ t salt to be added			

*For Bland diet.
Portion sizes are same as for Regular unless otherwise specified.
Bran is to be added to one menu item per day.

CERTIFIED _____, R.D.

358

	Regular/Bland	Mechanical	2 Gram Sodium	4 Gram Sodium	Blended		
B r e a k f a s t	½ c Orange Juice #16 Egg, Scrmb ½ c Oatmeal 1 sl Bacon Toast Oleo, Jelly 1 c Milk Coffee, Tea, *Sanka	Orange Juice Egg, Scrmb Oatmeal Crisp Bacon Toast Oleo, Jelly Milk Coffee, Tea	Orange Juice Egg, Scrmb Oatmeal Toast Oleo, Jelly Milk Coffee, Tea	Orange Juice Egg, Scrmb Oatmeal Toast Oleo, Jelly Milk Coffee, Tea	Strain Orange Juice Egg, Pureed Strain Oatmeal Bread Oleo, Jelly Milk Coffee, Tea		
D i n n e r	2 oz Crumb Chicken #8 Ranch Potato #16 Bu Peas 1 Hot Roll, Oleo 1 t #8 Bkd Custard 1 c Milk Coffee, Tea, *Sanka	Grd Chicken Potatoes Bu Peas Hot Roll, Oleo Bkd Custard Milk Coffee, Tea	SF Chicken SF Potatoes SF Peas Reg Bread, Oleo Fruit in Season ½ c Milk Coffee, Tea	SF Chicken SF Potatoes SF Peas Roll, Oleo Bkd Custard ½ c Milk Coffee, Tea	Bl Chicken #12 Bl Potatoes #12 Bl Peas #12 Roll, Oleo Bkd Custard #8 Milk Coffee, Tea		

S u p p e r	6 oz Lasagna
	  (2 oz Meat)
	Garlic Toast
	#8 Three Bean
	  Salad
	#8 Heavenly Hash
	1 c Milk
	Coffee, Tea, *Sanka
		Lasagna
		Garlic Toast
		Three Bean Salad
		Heavenly Hash
		Milk
		Coffee, Tea
			SF Lasagna
			SF Toast
			SF Three Bean
			  Salad
			Heavenly Hash
			Milk
			Coffee, Tea
				SF Lasagna
				Toast
				SF Three Bean
				  Salad
				Heavenly Hash
				Milk
				Coffee, Tea
				½ t salt to be added
				  by patient
					Bl Beef #12
					Bl Noodles #12
					Bl Bean Salad #12
					Bread
					Bl Fruit #8
					Milk
					Coffee, Tea		

*For Bland diet.
Portion sizes are same as for Regular unless otherwise specified.
Bran is to be added to one menu item per day.

CERTIFIED _____, R.D.

359

Exhibit A-2 continued

WEEK NO. ___FOUR___ DAY ___MONDAY___   MENU CYCLE ___FALL/WINTER___

	Regular/Bland	Mechanical	2 Gram Sodium	4 Gram Sodium	Blended		
B r e a k f a s t	½ c Orange Juice 1 Egg, Pchd ½ c Cr of Rice 1 Toast 1 t Oleo, Jelly 1 c Milk Coffee, Tea, *Sanka	Orange Juice Egg, Pchd Cr of Rice Toast/Bread Oleo, Jelly Milk Coffee, Tea	Orange Juice Egg, Pchd Cr of Rice Toast Oleo, Jelly ½ c Milk Coffee, Tea	Orange Juice Egg, Pchd Cr of Rice Toast Oleo, Jelly ½ c Milk Coffee, Tea	Strain Orange Juice Bl Egg Strain Cr of Rice Toast/Bread Oleo, Jelly Milk Coffee, Tea		
D i n n e r	Hot Rst Beef Sand (2 oz Beef) #8 Msh Potatoes/ Gravy #16 Bu Spinach/ Lemon Carrot/Raisin Cake 1 c Milk Coffee, Tea, *Sanka	Hot Rst Beef Sand Msh Potatoes/ Gravy Bu Spinach/Lemon Carrot/Raisin Cake Milk Coffee, Tea	SF Rst Beef Sand SF Msh Potatoes SF Spinach/Lemon Carrot/Raisin Cake ½ c Milk Coffee, Tea	SF Rst Beef Sand Msh Potatoes Spinach/Lemon Carrot/Raisin Cake ½ c Milk Coffee, Tea	Bl Rst Beef #12 Bl Msh Potatoes #12/Gravy Bl Spinach #12/ Lemon Bread Ice Cream Milk Coffee, Tea		
S u p p e r	6 oz Pork Chop Suey #8 Rice #16 Bu Broccoli W/W Bread, Oleo #8 Fruit in Season 1 c Milk Coffee, Tea, *Sanka	2 oz Grd Pork Rice Bu Broccoli W/W Bread, Oleo Soft Fruit in Season 1 c Milk Coffee, Tea	2 oz SF Pork SF Rice SF Broccoli W/W Bread, Oleo Fruit in Season 1 c Milk Coffee, Tea	2 oz SF Pork Rice Bu Broccoli W/W Bread, Oleo Fruit in Season 1 c Milk Coffee, Tea ½ t salt to be added	Bl Pork #12 Bl Rice #12 Bl Broccoli #12 Bread, Oleo Bl Fruit #8 1 c Milk Coffee, Tea		

*For Bland diet.
Portion sizes are same as for Regular unless otherwise specified.
Bran is to be added to one menu item per day.

CERTIFIED _____, R.D.

360

	Regular/Bland	Mechanical	2 Gram Sodium	4 Gram Sodium	Blended		
B r e a k f a s t	½ c Orange Juice 1 French Toast #16/Syrup 1 oz Saus Pattie ½ c Cr of Wheat Oleo 1 c Milk Coffee, Tea, *Sanka	Orange Juice French Toast/Syrup Egg Cr of Wheat Oleo Milk Coffee, Tea	Orange Juice French Toast/Syrup Egg Cr of Wheat Oleo ½ c Milk Coffee, Tea	Orange Juice French Toast/Syrup Egg Cr of Wheat Oleo ½ c Milk Coffee, Tea	Strain Orange Juice Bl Egg Strain Cr of Wheat Bread Oleo Milk Coffee, Tea		
D i n n e r	2 oz Bkd Fish/Dill Sauce #8 Tater Tots #16 Glzd Carrots 1 Bran Muffin, Oleo 1 t 1 2" Rice Krispie Sq 1 c Milk Coffee, Tea, *Sanka	Flaked Fish/Dill Sauce Tater Tots Glzd Carrots Bran Muffin, Oleo Rice Krispie sq Milk Coffee, Tea	SF Bkd Fish SF Tater Tots SF Glzd Carrots Roll, Oleo Rice Krispie Sq ½ c Milk Coffee, Tea	SF Bkd Fish Tater Tots Glzd Carrots Bran Muffin, Oleo Rice Krispie Sq ½ c Milk Coffee, Tea	Bl Fish #12 Bl Potatoes #12 Bl Carrots #12 Muffin, Oleo Vanilla Pudd #8 Milk Coffee, Tea		
S u p p e r	6 oz Ham/Scall Pot Egg Bake (2 oz Meat) #16 Bu Beets 1 Hot Roll, Oleo 1 t #8 Green Minted Pear 1 c Milk Coffee, Tea, *Sanka	Grd Ham/Scall Pot Egg Bake Bu Beets Hot Roll, Oleo Green Minted Pear Milk Coffee, Tea	SF Chicken SF Scall Potatoes SF Beets Hot Roll, Oleo Green Minted Pear 1 c Milk Coffee, Tea	SF Chicken Scall Potatoes Bu Beets Hot Roll, Oleo Green Minted Pear 1 c Milk Coffee, Tea ½ t salt to be added	Bl Ham #12 Bl Potatoes #12 Bl Beets #12 Roll, Oleo Bl Minted Pear #8 Milk Coffee, Tea		

*For Bland diet.
Portion sizes are same as for Regular unless otherwise specified.
Bran is to be added to one menu item per day.

CERTIFIED _____ , R.D.

361

Exhibit A-2 continued

WEEK NO. ___FOUR___ DAY ___WEDNESDAY___   MENU CYCLE ___FALL/WINTER___

	Regular/Bland	Mechanical	2 Gram Sodium	4 Gram Sodium	Blended	
B r e a k f a s t	½ c Orange Juice #16 Egg, Scrmb ½ c Malt-O-Meal 1 Toast Oleo 1 t, Jelly 1 c Milk Coffee, Tea, *Sanka	Orange Juice Egg, Scrmb Malt-O-Meal Toast/Bread Oleo, Jelly Milk Coffee, Tea	Orange Juice Egg, Scrmb Malt-O-Meal Toast Oleo, Jelly ½ c Milk Coffee, Tea	Orange Juice Egg, Scrmb Malt-O-Meal Toast Oleo, Jelly ½ c Milk Coffee, Tea	Strain Orange Juice Bl Egg Strain Malt-O-Meal Bread Oleo, Jelly Milk Coffee, Tea	
D i n n e r	2 oz Meat Loaf #8 Boil Potatoes #16 Bu Cabbage 1 W/W Bread, Oleo 1 t #8 Fruit Cobbler ½ c Milk Coffee, Tea, *Sanka	Grd Meat Loaf Boil Potatoes Bu Cabbage W/W Bread, Oleo Fruit Cobbler Milk Coffee, Tea	SF Meat Loaf SF Potatoes SF Bu Cabbage W/W Bread, Oleo Fruit ½ c Milk Coffee, Tea	SF Meat Loaf Boil Potatoes Bu Cabbage W/W Bread, Oleo Fruit ½ c Milk Coffee, Tea	Bl Meat Loaf #12 Bl Potatoes #12 Bl Cabbage #12 Bread Bl Fruit #8 Milk Coffee, Tea	
S u p p e r	2 oz Chicken Romano #8 Snow Flake Potatoes #16 Bu Gr Beans Bread, Oleo 1 t Lemon Pudd Cake 1 c Milk Coffee, Tea, *Sanka	Grd Chicken Snow Flake Potatoes Bu Gr Beans Bread, Oleo Lemon Pudd Cake Milk Coffee, Tea	SF Chicken SF Potatoes SF Gr Beans Bread, Oleo Lemon Pudd Cake ½ c Milk Coffee, Tea	SF Chicken SF Potatoes Bu Gr Beans Bread, Oleo Lemon Pudd Cake ½ c Milk Coffee, Tea	Bl Chicken #12 Bl Potatoes #12 Bl Gr Beans #12 Bread Lemon Pudd #8 Milk Coffee, Tea	

*For Bland diet.
Portion sizes are same as for Regular unless otherwise specified.
Bran is to be added to one menu item per day.

CERTIFIED _____, R.D.

362

	Regular/Bland	Mechanical	2 Gram Sodium	4 Gram Sodium	Blended		
B r e a k f a s t	½ c Orange Juice 1 Omelet #8 Hot Ralston 1 Toast Oleo 1 t, Jelly 1 c Milk Coffee, Tea, *Sanka	Orange Juice Omelet Hot Ralston Toast/Bread Oleo, Jelly Milk Coffee, Tea	Orange Juice Omelet Hot Ralston Toast Oleo, Jelly ½ c Milk Coffee, Tea	Orange Juice Omelet Hot Ralston Toast Oleo, Jelly ½ c Milk Coffee, Tea	Strain Orange Juice Bl Egg Strain Ralston Bread Oleo, Jelly Milk Coffee, Tea		
D i n n e r	2 oz Cheeseburger/ Bun #8 Potato Salad Condiments ½ c Lettuce/Tom #8 Tapioca Pudd 1 c Milk Coffee, Tea, *Sanka	Grd Beef/Cheese/ Bun Potato Salad Condiments Lettuce/Tom Tapioca Pudd Milk Coffee, Tea	SF Cheeseburger/ Bun SF Potato Salad Lettuce/Tom Tapioca Pudd Coffee, Tea	SF Cheeseburger/ Bun Potato Salad Lettuce/Tom Tapioca Pudd Coffee, Tea	Bl Beef #12 Bl Potatoes #12 Tomato Juice Bl Fruit #8 Milk Coffee, Tea		
S u p p e r	Ham & Dried Beans (2 oz Ham) 1 2" Mexican Corn- bread/1 t Oleo #8 Chef Salad (Lettuce/Cheese) #8 Fruit Cup Cookies 1 c Milk Coffee, Tea, *Sanka	Grd Ham & Dried Beans Bu Squash Plain Cornbread Oleo Soft Fruit Cup Cookies Milk Coffee, Tea	SF Pork SF Lima Beans SF Squash Hot Roll, Oleo Lettuce Salad Fruit Cup Coffee, Tea	SF Pork SF Lima Beans Bu Squash Hot Roll, Oleo Lettuce Salad Fruit Cup Coffee, Tea	Bl Ham #12 Bl Lima Beans #12 Bl Squash #12 Bread Bl Fruit #8 Milk Coffee, Tea		

*For Bland diet.
Portion sizes are same as for Regular unless otherwise specified.
Bran is to be added to one menu item per day.

CERTIFIED _____, R.D.

363

Exhibit A–2 continued

WEEK NO. ___FOUR___ DAY ___FRIDAY___

	Regular/Bland	Mechanical	2 Gram Sodium	4 Gram Sodium	Blended		
B r e a k f a s t	½ c Orange Juice 1 Egg, Fried ½ c Oatmeal 1 Toast Oleo 1 t, Jelly 1 c Milk Coffee, Tea, *Sanka	Orange Juice Egg, Fried Oatmeal Toast Oleo, Jelly Milk Coffee, Tea	Orange Juice Egg, Fried Oatmeal Toast Oleo, Jelly ½ c Milk Coffee, Tea	Orange Juice Egg, Fried Oatmeal Toast Oleo, Jelly ½ c Milk Coffee, Tea	Strain Orange Juice Bl Egg Strain Oatmeal Bread Oleo, Jelly Milk Coffee, Tea		
D i n n e r	2 oz Meatballs/ Gravy #8 Scall Potatoes #16 Stw Tomatoes 1 Bread, Oleo 1 t Cheesecake 1 c Milk Coffee, Tea, *Sanka	Grd Beef/Gravy Scall Potatoes Stw Tomatoes Bread, Oleo Cheesecake Milk Coffee, Tea	SF Meatballs SF Potatoes SF Tomatoes Bread, Oleo Cheesecake ½ c Milk Coffee, Tea	SF Meatballs Potatoes Stw Tomatoes Bread, Oleo Cheesecake ½ c Milk Coffee, Tea	Bl Meatballs #12 Bl Potatoes #12 Bl Tomatoes #12 Bread Bl Fruit #8 Milk Coffee, Tea		
S u p p e r	6 oz Cr Pea Soup Egg Salad Sand on W/W & White Bread (#16 Egg Salad) #16 Cott Cheese Salad on #8 Peach/Pear Cookies 1 c Milk Coffee, Tea, *Sanka	Cr Pea Soup Egg Salad Sand on W/W & White Bread Cott Cheese Salad Cookies Milk Coffee, Tea	SF Cr Pea Soup SF Chicken Salad Sand on Bread Peach/Pear Half Salad 1 c Milk Coffee, Tea	Cr Pea Soup SF Chicken Salad Sand on Bread Peach/Pear Half Salad Cookies 1 c Milk Coffee, Tea	Bl Cr Pea Soup Bl Egg Salad #12 Bread Bl Cott Cheese #12 Bl Peach/Pear #8 Milk Coffee, Tea		

*For Bland diet.
Portion sizes are same as for Regular unless otherwise specified.
Bran is to be added to one menu item per day.

CERTIFIED_____, R.D.

364

	Regular/Bland	Mechanical	2 Gram Sodium	4 Gram Sodium	Blended	
B r e a k f a s t	½ c Orange Juice ½ Egg, Pchd ½ c Cr of Wheat 1 Toast Oleo 1 t, Jelly 1 c Milk Coffee, Tea, *Sanka	Orange Juice Egg, Pchd Cr of Wheat Toast/Bread Oleo, Jelly Milk Coffee, Tea	Orange Juice Egg, Pchd Cr of Wheat Toast Oleo, Jelly ½ c Milk Coffee, Tea	Orange Juice Egg, Pchd Cr of Wheat Toast Oleo, Jelly ½ c Milk Coffee, Tea	Strain Orange Juice Bl Egg Strain Cr of Wheat Bread Oleo, Jelly Milk Coffee, Tea	
D i n n e r	2 oz Sw/Sour Pork #8 Stm Rice #16 Winter Mix 1 Bread, Oleo 1 t 3 oz Sherbet Cookies 1 c Milk Coffee, Tea, *Sanka	Grd Sw/Sour Pork Stm Rice Winter Mix Bread, Oleo Sherbet Soft Cookies Milk Coffee, Tea	SF Pork SF Rice SF Winter Mix Bread, Oleo Sherbet ½ c Milk Coffee, Tea	SF Pork SF Rice Winter Mix Bread, Oleo Sherbet Cookies ½ c Milk Coffee, Tea	Bl Pork #12 Bl Rice #12 Bl Winter Mix #12 Bread, Oleo Soft Sherbet Milk Coffee, Tea	
S u p p e r	6 oz Beef Stew/ Potatoes/#16 Carrots 1 Hot Biscuit, Oleo 1 t #8 Cinn Bkd Apple Slices 1 c Milk Coffee, Tea, *Sanka	Grd Beef Stew/ Potatoes/Carrots Hot Biscuit, Oleo Cinn Bkd Apple Slices Milk Coffee, Tea	SF Beef Stew/SF Potatoes/SF Carrots Bread, Oleo Cinn Bkd Apple Slices 1 c Milk Coffee, Tea	SF Beef Stew/ Potatoes/Carrots Bread, Oleo Cinn Bkd Apple Slices 1 c Milk Coffee, Tea	Bl Beef Stew #12/ Potatoes #12/ Carrots #12 Bread, Oleo Bl Apple Slices #8 Milk Coffee, Tea	

*For Bland diet.
Portion sizes are same as for Regular unless otherwise specified.
Bran is to be added to one menu item per day.

CERTIFIED _____ , R.D.

365

Exhibit A–3 Selective, Private, Southeastern U.S. Hospital

WEEK NO. ONE

	Wednesday	Thursday	Friday	Saturday	Sunday	Monday	Tuesday
B r e a k f a s t	Assorted Juice 4oz / Scrmb Eggs #16 / Bacon-1 or Sausage-1 / Toast or Hot Biscuit or Sweet Rolls / Margarine / Assorted Cereal ¾c / Coffee/Tea/Milk	Assorted Juice 4oz / Scrmb Eggs #16 / Bacon-1 or Sausage-1 / Toast or Sweet Roll / Margarine / Assorted Cereal ¾c / Coffee/Tea/Milk	Assorted Juice 4oz / Fried Eggs #16 / Bacon-1 or Sausage-1 / Toast or Hot Biscuit or Bran Muffin / Margarine / Assorted Cereal ¾c / Coffee/Tea/Milk	Assorted Juice 4oz / Scrmb Eggs #16 / Bacon-1 or Sausage-1 / Toast or Sweet Rolls / Margarine / Assorted Cereal ¾c / Coffee/Tea/Milk	Assorted Juice 4oz / Scrmb Eggs #16 / Bacon-1 or Sausage-1 / Toast & Asst'd Bread / Margarine / Assorted Cereal* ¾c / Coffee/Tea/Milk	Assorted Juice 4oz / Boiled Egg 1 / Bacon-1 or Sausage-1 / Toast or Hot Biscuit or Eng. Muffin* or Sweet Rolls / Margarine / Assorted Cereal ¾c / Coffee/Tea/Milk	Assorted Juice 4oz / Scrmb Eggs / Bacon-1 or Sausage-1 / Toast or Eng. Muffin or Sweet Rolls / Margarine / Assorted Cereal ¾c / Coffee/Tea/Milk
D i n n e r	Beef Stroganoff 3oz / Fried Fish 3oz / *Noodles #8 / Lima Beans #8 / *Winter Mix #8 / Beets #8 / Assorted Breads, Salads, and Desserts / Coffee, Tea or Milk	Chicken Livers 3oz / *Hamburger Steak 3oz / *French Fries #8 / *Peas #8 / Turnip Greens #8 / Sweet Potatoes #8 / Assorted Breads, Salads, and Desserts / Coffee, Tea or Milk	Polish Sausage 3oz / *Fried Chicken 3oz / Spinach #8 / *Noodles #8 / *Beets #8 / Mix Vegetables #8 / Assorted Breads, Salads, and Desserts / Coffee, Tea or Milk	*Crepes Florentine/Tacos* 1 / Whole Potato #8 / *Zucchini/Tomatoes #8 / Collard Greens #8 / *Cauliflower/Chs. #8 / Assorted Breads, Salads, and Desserts / Coffee, Tea or Milk	Hungarian Stew 6oz / *Turkey 3oz / *Dressing #8 / *Green Beans #8 / Beets #8 / *Glazed Carrots #8 / Assorted Breads, Salads, and Desserts / Coffee, Tea or Milk	Baked Fish 3oz / *BBQ Beef Ribs 3oz / *Oven Baked Pot. / *Spinach #8 / Mix Vegetable #8 / Peas/Onion #8 / Assorted Breads, Salads, and Desserts / Coffee, Tea or Milk	Corned Beef 3oz / *Pork Roast 3oz / *Cabbage #8 / *Northern Beans #8 / Collard Greens #8 / Carrots #8 / Assorted Breads, Salads, and Desserts / Coffee, Tea or Milk
S u p p e r	Baked Chicken 3oz / *Veal Cutlet/3oz / Mushrooms / *Green Beans #8 / *Squash Casserole #8 / Mashed Potatoes #8 / Glazed Carrots #8 / Assorted Breads, Salads, and Desserts / Coffee, Tea or Milk	Pork Chops 3oz / *Spaghetti 6oz / Sauerkraut #8 / Rice #8 / Okra/Tomatoes #8 / Brussels Sprouts #8 / *Succotash #8 / Assorted Breads, Salads, and Desserts / Coffee, Tea or Milk	*Pepper Steak 3oz / Shrimp/Clams 3oz / French Fries #8 / Green Beans #8 / *Rice #8 / *Broccoli #8 / Assorted Breads, Salads, and Desserts / Coffee, Tea or Milk	Veal 3oz / Pizza 1 sl / Ham 3oz / Peas/Carrots #8 / *Brussels Sprouts #8 / Hot German Potatoes #8 / *Italian Vegetable Medley #8 / Assorted Breads, Salad, and Desserts / Coffee, Tea or Milk	Swiss Steak 3oz / *Sweet/Sour Pork 3oz / *Steamed Rice #8 / Spinach #8 / *Oriental Veg/ Chinese Noodles #8 / Assorted Breads, Salads, and Desserts / Coffee, Tea or Milk	Manicotti / *Roast Beef 3oz / *Mashed Potatoes #8 / *Green Beans #8 / Apple Sticks / Squash #8 / Assorted Bread, Salads, and Desserts / Coffee, Tea or Milk	*Turkey Divan 3oz / Flank Steak / Blackeyed Peas #8 / Noodles #8 / Squash Cass. #8 / *Beets #8 / Assorted Breads, Salads, and Desserts / Coffee, Tea or Milk

*Items on the extended menus for modified diets.

CERTIFIED _____, R.D.

	Bland (No Pepper)	4 Gm Na (No Salt)	2 Gm Na (No Salt)	Low Fat/Low Chol	Low Fiber/Low Residue	High Fiber	
B r e a k f a s t	Orange Juice *Scrmb Eggs Crisp Bacon Grits Toast Margarine/Jelly Milk Cereal Beverage	Orange Juice 1 Scrmb Egg 1 sl Bacon Grits Toast Margarine/Jelly Milk Tea/Coffee	Orange Juice 1 Scrmb Egg SF Grits Toast 2 tsp Margarine/ Jelly Milk Tea/Coffee	Orange Juice *1 FF Egg Cereal (Assorted) Toast/Jelly Skim Milk Coffee	Orange Juice Scramb Egg Bacon or Sausage Rice Krispies Toast Margarine/Jelly Milk Coffee/Tea	Orange Juice Scrmb Eggs Bacon or Sausage Shredded Wheat Whole Grain Bread or Muffin Margarine/Jelly Coffee/Tea/Milk	
D i n n e r	Beef Stroganoff 3 oz Noodles #8 Beets #8 Roll/Margarine 1 tsp Sugar Cookies Juice/Milk	Beef Stroganoff Noodles Beets Tossed Salad Roll/Margarine Assorted Dessert Milk/Tea/Coffee	SF Beef Stroganoff SF Noodles SF Beets Tossed Salad Roll/Margarine Sugar Cookies Tea/Coffee	FF Boiled Fish 2oz FF Noodles FF Winter Mix FF Garden Salad 1T Low Cal Dressing Roll Angel Food Cake Coffee/Tea/Skim Milk	Beef Stroganoff Beets Gr Beans Roll/Margarine Canned or Cooked Fruit Coffee/Tea/Milk	Beef Stroganoff Winter Mix Raw Veg. Salad Whole Grain Bread Margarine Dessert or Fruit Coffee/Tea/Milk	
S u p p e r	Bkd Chicken 3oz Mashed Potatoes #8 Gr Beans #8 Roll/Margarine 1 tsp Applesauce #8 Juice/Milk Cereal Beverage	Bkd Chicken Mashed Potatoes Gr Beans Roll/Margarine Assorted Dessert Milk/Tea/Coffee	Bkd Chicken SF Potatoes ½ c Gr Beans Roll/Margarine 2 tsp Fresh Fruit/Pudding 1c Milk/Tea/Coffee	Bkd Chicken 2oz (no skin) FF Mashed Potatoes FF Gr Beans Sliced Tomatoes 1 Roll 1 tsp Margarine** Sherbet Coffee/Tea/Milk	Bkd Chicken Mashed Potatoes Gr Beans Canned Fruit Roll/Margarine Iced Cake Coffee/Tea/Milk	Veal Cutlet w/ Mushroom Bkd Pot./Skin Squash Casserole Raw Veg. Salad Whole Grain Bread/ Margarine Dessert or Fruit Coffee/Tea/Milk	

*Egg Substitute
**Margarine must be veg liquid oil

CERTIFIED _____, R.D.

367

Exhibit A–3 continued

MENU CYCLE ___ SPRING/SUMMER ___

	Bland (No Pepper)	4 Gm Na (No Salt)	2 Gm Na (No Salt)	Low Fat/Low Chol	Low Fiber/Low Residue	High Fiber	
B r e a k f a s t	Orange Juice Scrmb Egg Crisp Bacon Assorted Cereal 1 English Muffin Margarine/Jelly Milk/ Cereal Beverage	Orange Juice Scrmb Egg 1 sl Bacon Assorted Cereal 1 English Muffin Margarine/Jelly Milk/Tea/Coffee	Orange Juice 1 SF Scrmb Egg SF Dry Cereal ½ English Muffin 2tsp Margarine 1c Milk/Tea/ Coffee	Orange Juice *Boiled FF Egg Cereal-Assorted Toast Margarine/Jelly Coffee/Tea/Skim Milk	Orange Juice Scrmb Eggs Bacon or Sausage Puffed Cereal Toast Margarine/Jelly Coffee/Tea/Milk	Orange Juice Scrmb Eggs Bacon or Sausage Bran Flakes Whole Grain Toast or Muffin Margarine/Jelly Coffee/Tea/Milk	
D i n n e r	Hamburger Steak 3oz French Fries #8 Turnip Greens #8 Roll/Margarine 1 tsp Angel Food Cake Milk Fruit Drink	Hamburger Steak French Fries Peas Tossed Salad Roll/Margarine Assorted Desserts Milk/Tea/Coffee	SF Hamburger Steak SF French Fries SF Peas Tossed Salad Roll/Margarine-2tsp Angel Food Cake Tea/Coffee	FF Hamburger Steak FF Oven Bkd Fries FF Turnip Greens Garden Salad Roll/Margarine 1T Low Cal Dressing Jello Coffee/Tea/Skim Milk	Hamburger Steak French Fries Gr Beans Roll/Margarine Canned or Cooked Fruit Coffee/Tea/Milk	Hamburger Steak Bkd Pot/skin Turnip Greens Cornbread/ Margarine Raw Veg. Salad Fruit or Dessert Coffee/Tea/Milk	
S u p p e r	Bkd Pork Chops 3oz Rice #8 Okra/Tomatoes #8 Roll/Margarine 1 tsp Canned Peaches #8 Milk Fruit Drink Cereal Beverage	Bkd Pork Chops Rice Brussel Sprouts Tossed Salad Roll/Margarine Assorted Desserts Milk/Tea/Coffee	SF Bkd Pork Chops SF Rice SF Brussel Sprouts Tossed Salad Roll/Margarine 2 tsp Sherbet 1c Milk/Tea/Coffee	FF Bkd Pork Chops 2oz FF Rice FF Brussel Sprouts Sliced Tomatoes 1 Roll 1 tsp Margarine Fresh Fruit Coffee/Tea/Skim Milk	Bkd Pork Chops Rice Beets Potato Salad Roll/Margarine Jello or Canned Fruit Coffee/Tea/Milk**	Pork Chops Okra/Tomatoes Brussel Sprouts Raw Veg. Salad Whole Grain Bread Margarine Fruit or Dessert Coffee/Tea/Milk	

*Egg Substitute
**Limit Milk to 2 × day

CERTIFIED _____ , R.D.

368

	Bland (No Pepper)	4 Gm Na (No Salt)	2 Gm Na (No Salt)	Low Fat/Low Chol	Low Fiber/ Low Residue	High Fiber
B r e a k f a s t	Orange Juice Scrmb Eggs Hot Biscuit Margarine Crisp Bacon Grits Jelly Milk Cereal Beverage	Orange Juice Fried Eggs Toast Margarine 1 sl Bacon Grits Jelly Milk/Tea/Coffee	Orange Juice 1 SF Fried Egg Toast 2 tsp Margarine SF Grits Jelly 1c Milk/Tea/Coffee	Orange Juice *FF Eggs (Boiled) FF Cereal Toast/Margarine & Jelly Coffee/Tea/Skim Milk	Orange Juice Fried Eggs Rice Krispies Toast/Margarine & Jelly Bacon or Sausage Coffee/Tea/Milk	Orange Juice Fried Eggs Granola Whole Grain Bread Margarine/Jelly Bacon or Sausage Coffee/Tea/Milk
D i n n e r	Bkd Chicken 3oz Noodles #8 Spinach #8 Roll/Margarine 1 tsp Vanilla Pudding #8 Milk Fruit Drink	SF Bkd Chicken SF Noodles SF Spinach Roll/Margarine Salad Assorted Dessert Milk/Tea/Coffee	FF Bkd Chic 2oz Noodles ½c Canned Spinach Roll/2tsp Margarine Salad Fruit Tea/Coffee	Bkd Chicken 2oz (no skin) FF Noodles FF Spinach Carrot & Raisin Salad/No Mayo. Roll/1 tsp Margarine Fruit Coffee/Tea/Skim Milk	Fried Chicken 4oz Noodles Beets Roll/Margarine Macaroni Salad Plain Cake or Cookie Coffee/Tea/Milk	Fried Chicken 4oz Noodles Spinach Raw Veg. Salad Whole Grain Bread Margarine Fruit or Dessert Coffee/Tea/Milk
S u p p e r	Pepper Steak 3oz Mashed Potatoes #8 Carrots #8 Broccoli #8 Roll/Margarine 1 tsp Sherbet 3oz Milk Fruit Drink/Cereal Beverage	Pepper Steak Mashed Potatoes Carrots Broccoli Roll/Margarine Assorted Desserts Milk/Tea/Coffee	SF Pepper Steak SF Mashed Potatoes SF Carrots SF Fresh Broccoli Roll/2 tsp Margarine Plain Cake 1c Milk/Tea/Coffee	FF Pepper Steak FF Mashed Potato FF Gr Beans FF Cole Slaw Roll/Margarine 1tsp Sherbet Coffee/Tea/Skim Milk *Egg Substitute	Pepper Steak Mashed Potato Gr Beans Roll/Margarine Ice Cream or Plain Cake Coffee/Tea/Milk Limit milk to 2× day for low residue	Pepper Steak Bkd Pot. w/Skin Broccoli Raw Veg. Salad Whole Grain Bread Margarine Fresh Fruit or Dessert Coffee/Tea/Milk

CERTIFIED _____, R.D.

369

Exhibit A-3 continued

	Bland (No Pepper)	4Gm Na (No Salt)	2 Gm Na (No Salt)	Low Fat/Low Chol	Low Fiber/ Low Residue	High Fiber		
B r e a k f a s t	Orange Juice Scrmb Eggs Toast Margarine Jelly Crisp Bacon Cereal Milk/ Cereal Beverage	Orange Juice Scrmb Eggs Toast Margarine Jelly 1 sl Bacon Cereal Milk/Tea/Coffee	Orange Juice 1 SF Scrmb Egg Toast 2 tsp Margarine Jelly SF Grits 1c Milk/Tea/Coffee	Orange Juice *FF Egg Toast/Margarine Jelly FF Cereal Coffee/Tea/Skim Milk	Orange Juice Scrmb Egg Sausage or Bacon Biscuit/Margarine Jelly Corn Flakes Coffee/Tea/Milk	Orange Juice Scrmb Eggs Bacon or Sausage Bran Muffin or Wheat Toast Shredded Wheat Margarine/Jelly Coffee/Tea/Milk		
D i n n e r	Crepes Florentine Whole Potato #8 Zucchini/Tomatoes #8 Roll/Margarine 1 tsp Sugar Cookies Milk Fruit Drinks	Tacos Whole Potato Zucchini/Tomatoes Salad Roll/Margarine Assorted Dessert Milk/Tea/Coffee	SF Broiled Beef Patty SF Whole Potato SF Zucchini/ Tomatoes Salad Roll/2 tsp Margarine Sugar Cookies Tea/Coffee	FF Br Beef Patty 2oz FF Whole Potato FF Zucchini/ Tomatoes Tomato Slices Roll/Margarine Fruit Coffee/Tea/Skim Milk	Crepes Florentine Whole Potatoe w/o skins Gr Beans Roll/Margarine Canned or Cooked Fruit or Ice Cream Coffee/Tea/Milk	Tacos Collards Raw Vegetable Salad Whole Grain Bread Margarine Fruit or Dessert Coffee/Tea/Milk		
S u p p e r	Veal Rolls 3oz Boiled Potatoes #8 Brussels Sprouts #8 Roll/Margarine 1 tsp Fruit/Jello #8 Milk/water/ Fruit Drink/ Cereal Beverage	Veal Rolls Boiled Potatoes Brussels Sprouts Roll/Margarine Salad Assorted Desserts Milk/Tea/Coffee	SF Veal Rolls 4oz SF Boiled Potatoes SF Brussels Sprouts Roll/ Margarine 2 tsp Salad Fruit/Jello 1c Milk/Tea/Coffee	FF Veal Rolls 2oz FF Boiled Potatoes FF Brussel Sprouts FF Coleslaw Roll/ 1 tsp Margarine Jello Coffee/Tea/Skim Milk	Veal Rolls Boiled Potatoes Carrots Roll/Margarine Plain Cake Cooked or Canned Fruit Coffee/Tea/Milk Limit Milk to 2× day	Veal Rolls or Pizza Italian Veg. Medley Raw Vegetable Salad Whole Grain Bread Margarine Fruit or Dessert Coffee/Tea/Milk		

*Egg Substitute

CERTIFIED _____, R.D.

370

	Bland (No Pepper)	4 Gm Na (No Salt)	2 Gm Na (No Salt)	Low Fat/Low Chol	Low Fiber/ Low Residue	High Fiber		
Br**e**a**k**f**a**s**t**	Orange Juice Scrmb Eggs Sweet Roll Cooked Cereal Margarine/Jelly Crisp Bacon Milk/Water/ Cereal Beverage	Orange Juice Scrmb Eggs Sweet Roll Cooked Cereal Margarine/Jelly 1 sl Bacon Milk/Tea/Coffee	Orange Juice 1 SF Scrmb Egg Sweet Roll SF Cooked Cereal 2 tsp. Margarine/ Jelly 1c Milk/Tea/Coffee	Orange Juice FF Eggs Cereal Toast/1 tsp Margarine/Jelly Coffee/Tea/Skim Milk	Orange Juice Scrmb Eggs Rice Krispies Toast/Margarine/ Jelly Sausage or Bacon Coffee/Tea/Milk	Orange Juice Scrmb Eggs Raisin Bran Whole Grain Toast/Margarine/ Jelly Sausage or Bacon Coffee/Tea/Milk		
Di**n**n**e**r**	Turkey 3oz Dressing #8 Beets #8 Roll/Margarine 1 tsp Sherbet 3oz Milk Fruit Drink	Turkey Dressing Beets Roll/Margarine Salad Assorted Desserts Milk/Tea/Coffee	SF Turkey SF Noodles SF Beets Roll/2 tsp Margarine Salad Sherbet Tea/Coffee	FF Baked Turkey 2oz FF Broccoli FF Beets FF Carrot Salad Roll/1 tsp Margarine Sherbet Coffee/Tea/Skim Milk	Turkey Dressing Gr Beans Beets Roll/Margarine Canned or Cooked Fruit or Jello Coffee/Tea/Milk	Turkey Dressing Broccoli Raw Veg. Salad Whole Grain Bread Margarine Fruit or Dessert Coffee/Tea/Milk		
Su**p**p**e**r**	Broiled Beef Patty 3oz Steamed Rice #8 Oriental Vegetable #8 Roll/Margarine 1 tsp Angel Food Cake Milk/Fruit Drink/Cereal Beverage	Swiss Steak Steamed Rice Oriental Vegetable Salad Roll/Margarine Assorted Desserts Milk/Tea/Coffee	SF Swiss Steak SF Steamed Rice ½c SF Oriental Veg. SF Salad Roll/2 tsp Margarine Plain Cake 1c Milk/Tea/Coffee	FF Beef Patty 2oz FF Steamed Rice FF Spinach Tomato Slices Roll/1 tsp Margarine Fruit Coffee/Tea/Skim Milk	Swiss Steak Steamed Rice Spinach Roll/Margarine Ice Cream or Plain Cake Coffee/Tea/Milk Limit Milk to 2× day	Swiss Steak Steamed Rice Spinach Raw Veg. Salad Whole Grain Bread Fruit or Dessert Margarine Coffee/Tea/Milk		

CERTIFIED _____, R.D.

Exhibit A-3 continued

	Bland (No Pepper)	4 Gm Na (No Salt)	2 Gm Na (No Salt)	Low Fat/Low Chol	Low Fiber/ Low Residue	High Fiber		
B r e a k f a s t	Orange Juice Boiled Egg Crisp Bacon Hot Biscuit Margarine/Jelly Cereal Milk Cereal Beverage	Orange Juice Boiled Eggs 1 sl Bacon Hot Biscuit Margarine/Jelly Cereal Milk/Tea/Coffee	Orange Juice 1 Boiled Egg Toast 2 tsp Margarine/ Jelly SF Cereal 1c Milk/Tea/Coffee	Orange Juice *FF Eggs Cereal Toast/Margarine/ Jelly Coffee/Tea/Skim Milk	Orange Juice Boiled Egg Bacon or Sausage Corn Flakes Toast/Margarine/ Jelly Coffee/Tea/Milk	Orange Juice Boiled Eggs Bacon or Sausage Shredded Wheat Whole Grain Toast Margarine/Jelly Coffee/Tea/Milk		
D i n n e r	Baked Fish 3oz Oven Baked Pot. #8 Peas/Onions #8 Roll/Margarine 1 tsp Pudding #8 Milk Fruit Drink	Baked Fish Oven Baked Pot. Peas/Onions Roll/Margarine Salad Assorted Dessert Milk/Tea/Coffee	SF Baked Fish SF Oven Baked Pot. SF Peas/Onions Roll/2 tsp Margarine Salad Plain Cake Tea/Coffee	FF Baked Fish 2oz FF Baked Potato FF Peas/Onions Roll Garden Salad 1T Low Cal Dressing Fruit Coffee/Tea/Skim Milk	Baked Fish *Baked Potato *Peas/No Onions Roll/Margarine Canned or Cooked Fruit Plain Cookie Coffee/Tea/Milk	BBQ Beef Ribs Baked Pot. w/Skins Mixed Vegetables Whole Grain Bread Margarine Fruit or Dessert Coffee/Tea/Milk		
S u p p e r	Roast Beef 3oz Rice #8 Green Beans #8 Roll/Margarine 1 tsp Fruit Jello #8 Milk Fruit Drink/Cereal Beverage	Roast Beef Rice Gr Beans Salad Assorted Dessert Milk/Tea/Coffee	SF Roast Beef SF Rice ½c SF Gr Beans SF Salad Roll/2 tsp Margarine Fruit — Jello 1c Milk/Tea/Coffee	FF Roast Beef 2oz FF Rice FF Gr Beans FF Salad Roll/1 tsp Margarine Jello Coffee/Tea/Skim Milk *Egg Substitute	Roast Beef Rice Gr Beans Roll/Margarine Canned or Cooked Fruit Jello Coffee/Tea/Milk *Subs Mashed Pot/ Gr Bean for low residue Limit Milk to 2× day	Roast Beef or Burritos Rice Gr Beans Raw Veg. Salad Whole Grain Roll Margarine Fruit or Dessert Coffee/Tea/Milk		

CERTIFIED _____ , R.D.

372

	Bland (No Pepper)	4Gm Na (No Salt)	2 Gm Na (No Salt)	Low Fat/Low Chol	Low Fiber/Low Residue	High Fiber	
B r e a k f a s t	Orange Juice Crisp Bacon Scrmb Egg English Muffin Margarine/Jelly Cereal Milk Cereal Beverage	Orange Juice 1 sl Bacon Scrmb Egg English Muffin Margarine/Jelly Cereal Milk/Coffee/Tea	Orange Juice 1 SF Scrmb Egg ½ Muffin 2 t. Margarine SF Cereal 1c Milk/Coffee/Tea	Orange Juice *FF Eggs (Poached) Toast/1 tsp Margarine Jelly Cereal Skim Milk/Coffee/ Tea	Orange Juice Scrmb Eggs Sausage or Bacon Toast/ 1 tsp Margarine/Jelly Rice Krispies Coffee/Tea/Milk	Orange Juice Scrmb Eggs Bacon or Sausage Raisin Bran Whole Grain Toast Margarine/Jelly Coffee/Tea/Milk	
D i n n e r	Pork Roast 3oz Boiled Potatoes #8 Cabbage #8 Roll/Margarine 1 tsp Sugar Cookies Milk Fruit Drink	Pork Roast Boiled Potatoes Cabbage Roll/Margarine Salad Dessert Coffee/Tea	SF Pork Roast SF Boiled Potatoes SF Cabbage Roll/2 tsp Margarine SF Salad Dessert Water/Coffee/Tea	FF Pork Roast 2oz FF Boiled Potatoes FF Cabbage FF Salad Roll/1 tsp Margarine Sherbet Coffee/Tea/Skim Milk	Pork Roast Potatoes Carrots Roll/Margarine Canned or Cooked Fruit Coffee/Tea/Milk	Pork Roast North Beans Collard Greens Raw Veg. Salad Whole Grain Bread Margarine Fruit or Dessert Coffee/Tea/Milk	
S u p p e r	Flank Steak 3oz Potatoes #8 Squash Casserole #8 Roll/Margarine 1 tsp Plain Ice Cream 3oz Milk/ Fruit Drink/Cereal Beverage	Flank Steak Potatoes Beets Salad Roll/Margarine Coffee/Tea/Milk	SF Flank Steak SF Potatoes SF Beets SF Salad Roll/2 tsp Margarine 1c Milk/Coffee/Tea	FF Flank Steak 2oz FF Potatoes FF Beets Garden Salad w/ 1T Low Cal Dressing Roll Fruit Coffee/Tea/Skim Milk *Egg Substitute	Flank Steak Potatoes Beets Roll/Margarine Ice Cream Coffee/Tea/Milk Limit Milk to 2× day	Turkey Divan BE Peas Squash Casserole Raw Veg. Salad Whole Grain Bread w/Margarine Fruit or Dessert Coffee/Tea/Milk	

CERTIFIED _____ , R.D.

373

Exhibit A–4 Selective, Hospital, Southeastern U.S.

WEEK NO. ONE   DAY WEDNESDAY

MENU CYCLE SPRING/SUMMER

	1,000 Calories	1,200 Calories	1,500 Calories	1,800 Calories	2,000 Calories	2,200 Calories
Breakfast	½c Orange Juice 1 FF Egg 1 sl W. Wheat Toast 1 tsp Margarine 1c Skim Milk Tea/Coffee	½c Orange Juice 1 FF Egg 1 sl W. Wheat Toast 1c Skim Milk 1 tsp Margarine Tea/Coffee	½c Orange Juice 1 FF Egg 1 sl W. Wheat Toast 1c Skim Milk 2 tsp Margarine Tea/Coffee	½c Orange Juice 1 FF Egg 2 sl Wh. Grain Toast 1c Skim Milk 2 tsp Margarine Tea/Coffee	½c Orange Juice 2 FF Eggs 2 sl Wh. Grain Toast 1c Skim Milk 2 tsp Margarine Tea/Coffee	½c Orange Juice 2 FF Eggs 2 sl Wh. Grain Toast ½c FF Grits 1c Skim Milk 2 tsp Margarine Tea/Coffee
Dinner	1oz Baked Fish ½c FF Beets ½c FF Winter Mix 1 tsp Margarine 1 Small Apple Tea/Coffee	2oz Baked Fish ½c FF Beets ½c FF Winter Mix 1 Roll 1 tsp Margarine 1 Small Apple Tea/Coffee	2oz Baked Fish ½c FF Beets ½c FF Winter Mix 1 Roll ½c FF Lima Beans 1 tsp Margarine 1 Small Apple Tea/Coffee	3oz Baked Fish ½c FF Beets ½c FF Winter Mix 1 Roll ½c FF Lima Beans 2 tsp Margarine 1 Small Apple Tea/Coffee	3oz Baked Fish ½c FF Beets ½c FF Winter Mix 2 Rolls ½c FF Lima Beans 2 tsp Margarine 1 Small Apple Tea/Coffee	3oz Baked Fish ½c FF Beets ½c FF Winter Mix 2 Rolls ½c FF Lima Beans 2 tsp Margarine 1 Small Apple Tea/Coffee
Supper	2oz Baked Chicken ½c FF Green Beans ½c FF Mashed Pot. ½c Diet Fruit Tea/Coffee	2oz Baked Chicken ½c FF Green Beans ½c FF Squash ½c FF Mshd Potatoes ½c Diet Fruit 1 tsp Margarine Tea/Coffee	3oz Baked Chicken ½c FF Green Beans ½c FF Squash ½c FF Mshd Potatoes 1 Roll ½c Diet Fruit 1 tsp Margarine Tea/Coffee	3oz Baked Chicken ½c FF Green Beans ½c FF Squash ½c FF Mshd Potatoes 2 Rolls ½c Diet Fruit 2 tsp Margarine Tea/Coffee	3oz Baked Chicken ½c FF Green Beans ½c FF Squash ½c Mashed Potatoes 2 Rolls ½c Diet Fruit 2 tsp Margarine Tea/Coffee	4oz Baked Chicken ½c FF Green Beans ½c FF Squash ½c Mashed Potatoes 2 Rolls 1c Diet Fruit 2 tsp Margarine Tea/Coffee
Snack	1c Skim Milk	1c Skim Milk 2 Gr Crackers	1c Skim Milk 2 Gr Crackers	1c Skim Milk 2 Gr Crackers	1c Skim Milk 4 Gr Crackers	1c Skim Milk 4 Gr Crackers

CERTIFIED _____, R.D.

374

	1,000 Calories	1,200 Calories	1,500 Calories	1,800 Calories	2,000 Calories	2,200 Calories
Breakfast	½c Orange Juice 1 FF Egg ½ English Muffin 1 tsp Margarine 1c Skim Milk Coffee/Tea	½c Orange Juice 1 FF Egg ½ English Muffin 1 tsp Margarine 1c Skim Milk Coffee/Tea	½c Orange Juice 1 FF Egg ½ English Muffin 1 tsp Margarine 1c Skim Milk Coffee/Tea	½c Orange Juice 1 FF Egg ½ English Muffin 1 tsp Margarine 1c Skim Milk Coffee/Tea	½c Orange Juice 2 FF Eggs ½ English Muffin 2 tsp Margarine 1c Skim Milk Coffee/Tea	½c Orange Juice 2 FF Eggs 1 English Muffin 2 tsp Margarine 1c Skim Milk ½c FF Cooked Cereal Coffee/Tea
Dinner	1oz Baked Chicken Livers ½c FF Turnip Greens ½c Sliced Tomatoes ½c FF Noodles 1tsp Margarine ¼ Cantaloupe Coffee/Tea	2oz Baked Chicken Livers ½c FF Turnip Greens ½c Sliced Tomatoes ½c FF Noodles 1 tsp Margarine ¼ Cantaloupe Coffee/Tea	2oz Baked Chicken Livers ½c FF Turnip Greens ½c Sliced Tomatoes ½c FF Noodles 1 Roll 1 tsp Margarine ¼ Cantaloupe Coffee/Tea	3oz Baked Chicken Livers ½c FF Turnip Greens ½c Sliced Tomatoes ½c FF Noodles 1 Roll 2 tsp Margarine ¼ Cantaloupe Coffee/Tea	3oz Baked Chicken Livers ½c FF Turnip Greens ½c Sliced Tomatoes ½c FF Noodles 2 Rolls 2 tsp Margarine ¼ Cantaloupe Coffee/Tea	3oz Baked Chicken Livers ½c FF Turnip Greens ½c Sliced Tomatoes ½c FF Noodles 2 Rolls 2 tsp Margarine ¼ Cantaloupe Coffee/Tea
Supper	2oz Pork Chop ½c FF Brussels Sprouts ½c FF Rice ½ Banana Coffee/Tea	2oz Pork Chop ½c FF Brussels Sprouts ½c FF Okra/Tomatoes ½c FF Rice 1 tsp Margarine ½ Banana Coffee/Tea	3oz Pork Chop ½c FF Brussels Sprouts ½c FF Okra/Tom ½c FF Rice 1 Roll 1 tsp Margarine ½ Banana Coffee/Tea	3oz Pork Chop ½c FF Brussels Sprouts ½c FF Okra/Tom ½c FF Rice 2 Rolls 2 tsp Margarine ½ Banana Coffee/Tea	3oz Pork Chop ½c FF Brussels Sprouts ½c FF Okra/Tom ½c FF Rice 2 Rolls 2 tsp Margarine ½ Banana Coffee/Tea	4oz Pork Chop ½c FF Brussels Sprouts ½c FF Okra/Tom ½c FF Rice 2 Rolls 2 tsp Margarine 1 Banana Coffee/Tea
Snack	1c Skim Milk	1c Skim Milk 2 Gr Crackers	1c Skim Milk 2 Gr Crackers	1c Skim Milk 2 Gr Crackers	1c Skim Milk 4 Gr Crackers	1c Skim Milk 4 Gr Crackers

CERTIFIED _____, R.D.

375

Exhibit A–4 continued

	1,000 Calories	1,200 Calories	1,500 Calories	1,800 Calories	2,000 Calories	2,200 Calories	
B r e a k f a s t		½c Orange Juice 1 Boiled Egg 1 W. Wheat Bread 1c Skim Milk 1 tsp Margarine Tea/Coffee	½c Orange Juice 1 Boiled Egg 1 W. Wheat Bread 1c Skim Milk 2 tsp Margarine Tea/Coffee	½c Orange Juice 1 Boiled Egg 1 W. Wheat Bread ½c FF Grits 1c Skim Milk 2 tsp Margarine Tea/Coffee	½c Orange Juice 2 Boiled Eggs 1 W. Wheat Bread ½ c FF Grits 1c Skim Milk 2 tsp Margarine Tea/Coffee	½c Orange Juice 2 Boiled Eggs 2 W. Wheat Bread ½c FF Grits 1c Skim Milk 2 tsp Margarine Tea/Coffee	
D i n n e r	1oz Bkd Chicken ½c FF Spinach ½c FF Beets 1 tsp Margarine ½c Fresh Fruit Tea/Coffee	2oz Bkd Chicken ½c FF Spinach ½c FF Beets ½c FF Noodles 1 tsp Margarine ½c Fresh Fruit Tea/Coffee	2oz Bkd Chicken ½c FF Spinach ½c FF Beets ½c FF Noodles 1 Roll 1 tsp Margarine ½c Fresh Fruit Tea/Coffee	3oz Bkd Chicken ½c FF Spinach ½c FF Beets ½c FF Noodles 1 Roll 2 tsp Margarine ½c Fresh Fruit Tea/Coffee	3oz Bkd Chicken ½c FF Spinach ½c FF Beets 1c FF Noodles 1 Roll 2 tsp Margarine ½c Fresh Fruit Tea/Coffee	3oz Bkd Chicken ½c FF Spinach ½c FF Beets 1c FF Noodles 1 Roll 2 tsp Margarine ½c Fresh Fruit Tea/Coffee	
S u p p e r	2oz Peppersteak ½c FF Broccoli ½c Bkd F. Fries ½c Diet Fruit Tea/Coffee	2oz Peppersteak ½c FF Broccoli ½c FF Carrots ½c Bkd F. Fries 1 tsp Margarine ½c Diet Fruit Tea/Coffee	3oz Peppersteak ½c FF Broccoli ½c FF Carrots ½c Baked F. Fries 1 Roll 2 tsp Margarine ½c Diet Fruit Tea/Coffee	3oz Peppersteak ½c FF Broccoli ½c FF Carrots 1c Bkd F. Fries 1 Roll 2 tsp Margarine ½c Diet Fruit Tea/Coffee	3oz Peppersteak ½c FF Broccoli ½c FF Carrots 1c Bkd F. Fries 1 Roll 2 tsp Margarine ½c Diet Fruit Tea/Coffee	4oz Peppersteak ½c FF Broccoli ½c FF Carrots 1c Bkd F. Fries 1 Roll 2 tsp Margarine ½c Diet Fruit Tea/Coffee	
S n a c k	1c Skim Milk ¾c Dry Cereal	1c Skim Milk ¾c Dry Cereal	1c Skim Milk ¾c Dry Cereal	1c Skim Milk ¾c Dry Cereal	1c Skim Milk ¾c Cereal 2 Gr Crackers	1c Skim Milk ¾c Cereal 2 Gr Crackers	

	1,000 Calories	1,200 Calories	1,500 Calories	1,800 Calories	2,000 Calories	2,200 Calories
Breakfast	1/2c Orange Juice 1 FF Egg 1 sl W. Wheat Toast 1c Skim Milk 1 sl Crisp Bacon Tea/Coffee	1/2c Orange Juice 1 FF Egg 1 sl W. Wheat Toast 1c Skim Milk 1 sl Crisp Bacon Tea/Coffee	1/2c Orange Juice 1 FF Egg 1 sl W. Wheat Taost 1c Skim Milk 1 sl Crisp Bacon 1 tsp Margarine Tea/Coffee	1/2c Orange Juice 3/4c Dry Cereal 1 FF Egg 1 sl W. Wheat Toast 1c Skim Milk 1 sl Crisp Bacon 1 tsp Margarine Tea/Coffee	1/2c Orange Juice 3/4c Dry Cereal 2 FF Egg 1 sl W. Wheat Toast 1c Skim Milk 1 sl Crisp Bacon 1 tsp Margarine Tea/Coffee	1/2c Orange Juice 3/4c Dry Cereal 2 FF Egg 2 sl W. Wheat Toast 1c Skim Milk 1 sl Crisp Bacon 1 tsp Margarine Tea/Coffee
Dinner	1oz Beef 1/2c Zucchini/Tom. 1T Reg. Salad Dress. 1c Tossed Salad 1/4 Cantaloupe Tea/Coffee	Taco 2oz Meat 1/2c Zucchini/Tom. 1 Taco Shell 1T Reg. Salad Dress. 1c Tossed Salad 1/4 Cantaloupe Tea/Coffee	Taco 2oz Meat 1/2c Zucchini/Tom. 2 Taco Shell 1T Reg. Salad Dress. 1c Tossed Salad 1/4 Cantaloupe Tea/Coffee	Taco 3oz Meat 1/2c Zucchini/Tom. 2 Taco Shell 2T Reg. Salad Dress. 1c Tossed Salad 1/4 Cantaloupe Tea/Coffee	Taco 3oz Meat 1/2c Zucchini/Tom. 2 Taco Shell 1/2c Boiled Potatoes 2T Reg. Salad Dress. 1c Tossed Salad 1/4 Cantaloupe Tea/Coffee	Taco 3oz Meat 1/2c Zucchini/Tom. 2 Taco Shell 1/2c Boiled Potatoes 2T Reg. Salad Dress. 1c Tossed Salad 1/4 Cantaloupe Tea/Coffee
Supper	2oz Baked Ham 1/2c FF Itl. Veg Medley 1 Roll 1/2c Diet Applesauce Tea/Coffee	2oz Baked Ham 1/2c FF Itl. Veg Medley 1c FF Brussels Sprouts 1/2c Potatoes 1 tsp Margarine 1/2c Diet Applesauce Tea/Coffee	3oz Baked Ham 1/2c FF Itl. Veg Medley 1c FF Brussels Sprouts 1c Potatoes 1 Roll 1 tsp Margarine 1/2c Diet Applesauce Tea/Coffee	3oz Baked Ham 1/2c FF Itl. Veg Medley 1c FF Brussels Sprouts 1/2c Potatoes 1 Roll 2 tsp Margarine 1/2c Diet Applesauce Tea/Coffee	3oz Baked Ham 1/2c FF Itl. Veg Medley 1c FF Brussels Sprouts 1c Potatoes 1 Roll 2 tsp Margarine 1/2c Diet Applesauce Tea/Coffee	4oz Baked Ham 1/2c FF Itl. Veg Medley 1c FF Brussels Sprouts 1c Potatoes 1 Roll 2 tsp Margarine 1c Diet Applesauce Tea/Coffee
Snack	1c Skim Milk	1c Skim Milk 2 Gr Crackers	1c Skim Milk 2 Gr Crackers	1c Skim Milk 2 Gr Crackers	1c Skim Milk 4 Gr Crackers	1c Skim Milk 4 Gr Crackers

CERTIFIED _____, R.D.

Exhibit A–4 continued

WEEK NO. ONE   DAY SUNDAY

MENU CYCLE   SPRING/SUMMER

	1,000 Calories	1,200 Calories	1,500 Calories	1,800 Calories	2,000 Calories	2,200 Calories	
Breakfast	½c Orange Juice 1 FF Egg 1 Biscuit 1c Skim Milk Tea/Coffee	½c Orange Juice 1 FF Egg 1 Biscuit 1c Skim Milk Tea/Coffee	½c Orange Juice 1 FF Egg 1 Biscuit 1 tsp Margarine 1c Skim Milk Tea/Coffee	½c Orange Juice 1 FF Egg 2 Biscuits 1c Skim Milk Tea/Coffee	½c Orange Juice 2 FF Eggs 2 Biscuits 1c Skim Milk Tea/Coffee	½c Orange Juice 2 FF Eggs 2 Biscuits ¾c Dry Cereal 1c Skim Milk Tea/Coffee	
Dinner	1oz Turkey ½c FF Gr Beans ½c FF Beets 1 tsp Margarine ½c Diet Fruit Tea/Coffee	2oz Turkey ½c FF Gr Beans ½c FF Beets ¼c Turkey Dress. 1 tsp Margarine ½c Diet Fruit Tea/Coffee	2oz Turkey ½c FF Gr Beans ½c FF Beets ¼c Turkey Dress. 1 Roll 1 tsp Margarine ½c Diet Fruit Tea/Coffee	3oz Turkey ½c FF Gr Beans ½c FF Beets ¼c Turkey Dress. 1 Roll 2 tsp Margarine ½c Diet Fruit Tea/Coffee	3oz Turkey ½c FF Gr Beans ½c FF Beets ¼c Turkey Dress. 2 Rolls 2 tsp Margarine ½c Diet Fruit Tea/Coffee	3oz Turkey ½c FF Gr Beans ½c FF Beets ¼c Turkey Dress. 2 Rolls 2 tsp Margarine ½c Diet Fruit Tea/Coffee	
Supper	2oz Hamburger Steak ½c FF Spinach ½c FF Steamed Rice ½c Diet Pineapple Tea/Coffee	2oz Hamburger Steak ½c FF Oriental Veg. ½c FF Spinach ½c FF Steamed Rice 1 tsp Margarine ½c Diet Pineapple Tea/Coffee	3oz Hamburger Steak ½c FF Oriental Veg. ½c FF Spinach ½c FF Steamed Rice 1 Roll 1 tsp Margarine ½c Diet Pineapple Tea/Coffee	3oz Hamburger Steak ½c FF Oriental Veg. ½c FF Spinach ½c FF Steamed Rice 2 Rolls 2 tsp Margarine ½c Diet Pineapple Tea/Coffee	3oz Hamburger Steak ½c FF Oriental Veg. ½c FF Spinach ½c FF Steamed Rice 2 Rolls 2 tsp Margarine ½c Diet Pineapple Tea/Coffee	4oz Hamburger Steak ½c FF Oriental Veg. ½c FF Spinach ½c FF Steamed Rice 2 Rolls 2 tsp Margarine 1c Diet Pineapple Tea/Coffee	
Snack	1c Skim Milk	1c Skim Milk ¾c Dry Cereal	1c Skim Milk ¾c Dry Cereal	1c Skim Milk ¾c Dry Cereal	1c Skim Milk ¾c Dry Cereal 2 Gr Crackers	1c Skim Milk ¾c Dry Cereal 2 Gr Crackers	

CERTIFIED _____, R.D.

378

	1,000 Calories	1,200 Calories	1,500 Calories	1,800 Calories	2,000 Calories	2,200 Calories	
B r e a k f a s t	½c Orange Juice 1 FF Egg ¾c Dry Cereal 1 sl Crisp Bacon 1c Skim Milk Tea/Coffee	½c Orange Juice 1 FF Egg ¾c Dry Cereal 1 sl Crisp Bacon 1c Skim Milk Tea/Coffee	½c Orange Juice 1 FF Egg ¾c Dry Cereal 1 sl Crisp Bacon 1 tsp Margarine 1c Skim Milk Tea/Coffee	½c Orange Juice 1 FF Egg ¾c Dry Cereal 1 sl W. Wheat Toast 1 sl Crisp Bacon 1 tsp Margarine 1c Skim Milk Tea/Coffee	½c Orange Juice 2 FF Eggs ¾c Dry Cereal 1 sl W. Wheat Toast 1 sl Crisp Bacon 1 tsp Margarine 1c Skim Milk Tea/Coffee	½c Orange Juice 2 FF Eggs ¾c Dry Cereal 2 sl W. Wheat Toast 1 sl Crisp Bacon 1 tsp Margarine 1c Skim Milk Tea/Coffee	
D i n n e r	1oz Bkd Fish ½c FF Spinach ½c FF Carrots 1 tsp Margarine ½c Fresh Fruit Salad Tea/Coffee	2oz Bkd Fish ½c FF Spinach ½c FF Carrots 1 Small Oven B. Pot. 1 tsp Margarine ½c Fresh Fruit Salad Tea/Coffee	2oz Bkd Fish ½c FF Spinach ½c FF Carrots 1 Small Oven B. Pot. 1 Roll 1 tsp Margarine ½c Fresh Fruit Salad Tea/Coffee	3oz Bkd Fish ½c FF Spinach ½c FF Carrots 1 Small Oven B. Pot. 1 Roll 2 tsp Margarine ½c Fresh Fruit Salad Tea/Coffee	3oz Bkd Fish ½c FF Spinach ½c FF Carrots 1 Small Oven B. Pot. 2 Rolls 2 tsp Margarine ½c Fresh Fruit Salad Tea/Coffee	3oz Bkd Fish ½c FF Spinach ½c FF Carrots 1 Small Oven B. Pot. 2 Rolls 2 tsp Margarine ½c Fresh Fruit Salad Tea/Coffee	
S u p p e r	2oz Roast Beef ½c FF Gr Beans ½c FF Mashed Potatoes ½c Diet Fruit Tea/Coffee	2oz Roast Beef ½c FF Gr Beans ½c FF Squash ½c FF Mashed Potatoes 1 tsp Margarine ½c Diet Fruit Tea/Coffee	3oz Roast Beef ½c FF Gr Beans ½c FF Squash ½c FF Mashed Potatoes 1 Roll 1 tsp Margarine ½c Diet Fruit Tea/Coffee	3oz Roast Beef ½c FF Gr Beans ½c FF Squash ½c FF Mashed Potatoes 2 Rolls 2 tsp Margarine ½c Diet Fruit Tea/Coffee	3oz Roast Beef ½c FF Gr Beans ½c FF Squash ½c FF Mashed Potatoes 2 Rolls 2 tsp Margarine ½c Diet Fruit Tea/Coffee	4oz Roast Beef ½c FF Gr Beans ½c FF Squash ½c FF Mashed Potatoes 2 Rolls 2 tsp Margarine 1c Diet Fruit Tea/Coffee	
S n a c k	1c Skim Milk	1c Skim Milk 6 Saltines	1c Skim Milk 6 Saltines	1c Skim Milk 6 Saltines	1c Skim Milk 12 Saltines	1c Skim Milk 12 Saltines	

379

Exhibit A–4 continued

WEEK NO. ONE DAY TUESDAY MENU CYCLE SPRING/SUMMER

	1,000 Calories	*1,200 Calories*	*1,500 Calories*	*1,800 Calories*	*2,000 Calories*	*2,200 Calories*	
Breakfast	½c Orange Juice 1 Poached Egg ½ English Muffin 1 tsp Margarine 1c Skim Milk Tea/Coffee	½c Orange Juice 1 Poached Egg ½ English Muffin 1 tsp Margarine 1c Skim Milk Tea/Coffee	½c Orange Juice 1 Poached Egg ½ English Muffin 2 tsp Margarine 1c Skim Milk Tea/Coffee	½c Orange Juice 1 Poached Egg 1 Muffin 1 tsp Margarine 1 sl Crisp Bacon 1c Skim Milk Tea/Coffee	½c Orange Juice 2 Eggs 1 Muffin 1 tsp Margarine 1 sl Crisp Bacon 1c Skim Milk Tea/Coffee	½c Orange Juice 2 Eggs 1 Muffin 1 tsp Margarine ¾c Dry Cereal 1 sl Crisp Bacon 1c Skim Milk Tea/Coffee	
Dinner	Chef Salad: 1oz Cheese ½c Lettuce ½c Tomato 1T French Dressing 12 Grapes Tea/Coffee	2oz Pork Roast ½c FF Cabbage ½c FF Carrots ½c FF Northern Beans 1 tsp Margarine 12 Grapes Tea/Coffee	2oz Pork Roast ½c FF Cabbage ½c FF Carrots ½c FF Northern Beans 1 Roll 1 tsp Margarine 12 Grapes Tea/Coffee	3oz Pork Roast ½c FF Cabbage ½c FF Carrots ½c FF Northern Beans 1 Roll 2 tsp Margarine 12 Grapes Tea/Coffee	3oz Pork Roast ½c FF Cabbage ½c FF Carrots ½c FF Northern Beans 2 Rolls 2 tsp Margarine 12 Grapes Tea/Coffee	3oz Pork Roast ½c FF Cabbage ½c FF Carrots ½c FF Northern Beans 2 Rolls 2 tsp Margarine 12 Grapes Tea/Coffee	
Supper	2oz Flank Steak ½c FF Squash ½c FF Noodles ½c D. Fruit Cockt Tea/Coffee	2oz Flank Steak ½c FF Squash ½c FF Beets ½c FF Noodles 1 tsp Margarine ½c D. Fruit Cockt Tea/Coffee	3oz Flank Steak ½c FF Squash ½c FF Beets ½c FF Noodles 1 Roll 1 tsp Margarine ½c D. Fruit Cockt Tea/Coffee	3oz Flank Steak ½c FF Squash ½c FF Beets ½c FF Noodles 2 Rolls 2 tsp Margarine ½c D. Fruit Cockt Tea/Coffee	3oz Flank Steak ½c FF Squash ½c FF Beets ½c FF Noodles 2 Rolls 2 tsp Margarine ½c D. Fruit Cockt Tea/Coffee	4oz Flank Steak ½c FF Squash ½c FF Beets ½c FF Noodles 2 Rolls 2 tsp Margarine 1c D. Fruit Cockt Tea/Coffee	
Snack	1c Skim Milk	1c Skim Milk 5 Vanilla Wafers	1c Skim Milk 5 Vanilla Wafers	1c Skim Milk 5 Vanilla Wafers	1c Skim Milk 10 Vanilla Wafers	1c Skim Milk 10 Vanilla Wafers	

CERTIFIED ______________________________, R.D.

	Wednesday	Thursday	Friday	Saturday	Sunday	Monday	Tuesday
B r e a k f a s t	Assorted Juice 4oz Eggs #16 Bacon/Sausage 1 Toast or Biscuit 2" Sweet Roll Assorted Cereal ¾c Pancakes/Syrup	Assorted Juice Eggs* Bacon/Sausage Toast or Biscuit Sweet Roll Assorted Cereal Pancakes/Syrup 1	Assorted Juice Eggs Bacon/Sausage Toast or Biscuit Sweet Roll/Bran M 1 Assorted Cereal French Toast/Syrup 1	Assorted Juice Eggs Bacon/Sausage Toast or Biscuit Sweet Roll Assorted Cereal Pancakes/Syrup 1	Assorted Juice Eggs* Bacon/Sausage Toast or Biscuit Sweet Roll Assorted Cereal Pancakes/Syrup 1	Assorted Juice Eggs Bacon/Sausage Toast or Biscuit Sweet Roll Assorted Cereal Pancakes/Syrup 1	Assorted Juice Eggs Bacon/Sausage Toast or Biscuit* Sweet Roll Assorted Cereal Pancakes/Syrup 1
D i n n e r	Roast Beef 3oz *Chicken/Dumplings 3oz Oven Browned Pot #8 Baby Limas #8 *Veg. Florentine #8 Steamed Squash #8 Assorted Breads, Desserts, Salad Coffee/Tea/Milk	Spaghetti 6oz *Fish Filet 3oz Steamed Rice #8 Whipped Potatoes #8 *Stewed Tomatoes #8 *Steamed Spinach #8 Assorted Breads, Desserts, Salad Coffee/Tea/Milk	*Meat Loaf 3oz Pork Chops 3oz *Sweet Potatoes #8 *Gr Beans #8 Steamed Cabbage #8 Vegetable Medley #8 Assorted Breads, Desserts, Salad Coffee/Tea/Milk	*Cheeseburgers Omelets *Hash Browns #8 Okra/Tomatoes #8 Broccoli #8 *Veg. of Choice #8 Assorted Breads, Desserts, Salad Coffee/Tea/Milk	*Roast Beef Au Jus 3oz Chicken Gems 3oz *Bkd Potato #8 Gr Beans #8 Squash Casserole #8 *Green Peas #8 Assorted Breads, Desserts, Salad Coffee/Tea/Milk	*Beef Stew 6oz Baked Fish 3oz *Oven Brn Potatoes #8 Parsleyed Noodles #8 Broccoli #8 *Carrots #8 Assorted Breads, Desserts, Salad Coffee/Tea/Milk	Rigatone 6oz *Fried Chicken 3oz *Steamed Rice #8 Sweet Potatoes #8 *Seasoned Greens #8 Harvard Beets #8 Assorted Breads, Desserts, Salad Coffee/Tea/Milk
S u p p e r	*Sliced Veal 3oz Corn Beef Hash 3oz Green Beans #8 *Broccoli #8 Hot Mixed Fruit #8 *Tater Tots #8 Assorted Breads, Desserts, Salad Coffee/Tea/Milk	BBQ Pork Ribs 3oz *Roast Lamb 3oz *Green Peas #8 Brussel Sprouts #8 *French Fries #8 Carrots #8 Assorted Breads, Desserts, Salad Coffee/Tea/Milk	Chicken Filet 3oz *Mac. Cheese/Ham 6oz Mashed Potatoes #8 Spinach #8 *Scalloped Apples #8 Vegetable Juice 4oz Assorted Breads, Desserts, Salad Coffee/Tea/Milk	*Lasagne 6oz Cubed Steak 3oz Steamed Rice #8 *Glazed Beets #8 Zucchini/#8 *Summer Squash #8 Assorted Breads, Desserts, Salad Coffee/Tea/Milk	Pork/Mushrooms 3oz *Quiche #8 Tater Tots #8 Green Peas #8 *Vegetable Florentine *2½"sl Tomatoes Assorted Breads, Desserts, Salad Coffee/Tea/Milk	*Hamburger Steak 3oz Polish Sausage 3oz Sauerkraut #8 Mixed Vegetables #8 *Scalloped Potatoes #8 *French Green Beans #8 Assorted Breads, Desserts, Salad Coffee/Tea/Milk	*Sal Croquettes 3oz Sliced Turkey 3oz Potatoe Salad #8 *Fried Okra #8 Zucchini & #8 *Tomatoes Cranberry Sauce Veg. of Choice #8 Assorted Breads, Desserts, Salad Coffee/Tea/Milk

*Items on the extended menus for modified diets.

CERTIFIED _____, R.D.

381

Exhibit A-5 continued

WEEK NO. TWO DAY WEDNESDAY

Breakfast (B r e a k f a s t)

Bland (No Pepper)	4Gm Na (No Salt)	2 Gm Na (No Salt)	Low Fat/Low Chol	Low Fiber/Low Residue	High Fiber
Orange Juice 4oz	Orange Juice	Orange Juice	Orange Juice	Orange Juice	Orange Juice
Scrmb Eggs #16	Scrmb Eggs	1 Egg	1 FF Egg*	Scrmb Eggs	Scrmb Eggs
Crisp Bacon 1	1 sl Bacon	SF Cereal	FF Cereal	Bacon/Sausage	Bacon/Sausage
Assorted Cereal ¾c	Assorted Cereal	Toast	Toast	Assorted Cereal	Bran Cereal
Toast/Biscuit	Toast/Biscuit	2 tsp Margarine	1 tsp Margarine	Toast/Biscuit	Whole Grain Bread
Margarine 1 tsp/ Jelly	Margarine/Jelly	1c Milk	Skim Milk	Margarine/Jelly	Margarine/Jelly
Milk	Milk	Coffee/Tea/Sanka	Coffee/Tea/Sanka	Milk	Milk
Cereal Beverage	Coffee/Tea/Sanka			Coffee/Tea/Sanka	Coffee/Tea/Sanka

Dinner (D i n n e r)

Bland (No Pepper)	4Gm Na (No Salt)	2 Gm Na (No Salt)	Low Fat/Low Chol	Low Fiber/Low Residue	High Fiber
Roast Beef 3oz	Roast Beef	Roast Beef 4oz	Roast Beef	Roast Beef	Roast Beef
Browned Potatoes #8	Browned Potatoes	SF Potatoes	FF Potatoes	Browned Potatoes	Browned Potatoes
Baby Limas #8	Baby Limas	½c Frozen or Canned	Baby Limas	Green Beans	Baby Limas
Steamed Squash #8	Steamed Squash	Steamed Squash	Steamed Squash	Strained Squash	Steamed Squash
Dinner Roll	Assorted Salad	SF Salad	Tossed Salad	Macaroni Salad	Raw Salad
Margarine 1 tsp	Dinner Roll	Dinner Roll	Dinner Roll	Dinner Roll	Whole Wheat Roll
Pudding #8	Margarine 1 tsp	Margarine 2 tsp	Margarine 1 tsp	Margarine	Margarine
Milk	Assorted Desserts	Sherbet	S. Milk Pudding	Pudding	Coconut Pie
Cereal Beverage	Milk	Milk	Skim Milk	Milk	Milk
	Coffee/Tea/Sanka	Coffee/Tea/Sanka	Coffee/Tea/Sanka	Coffee/Tea/Sanka	Coffee/Tea/Sanka

Supper (S u p p e r)

Bland (No Pepper)	4Gm Na (No Salt)	2 Gm Na (No Salt)	Low Fat/Low Chol	Low Fiber/Low Residue	High Fiber
Corned Beef Hash 6oz	Baked Chicken	4oz Bkd Chicken	Bkd Chicken & Skin	Bkd Chicken	Beef Pot Pie
Tater Tots #8	Tater Tots	SF Tater Tots	Baked Potato	Tater Tots	Bkd Potato w/Skin
Gr Beans #8	Green Beans	SF Gr Beans	FF Gr Beans	Gr Beans	Gr Beans
Canned Asparagus #8	Broccoli	SF Broccoli	FF Broccoli	Canned Asparagus	Broccoli
Dinner Roll	Dinner Roll	Dinner Roll	Dinner Roll	Dinner Roll	Whole Grain Roll
Margarine 1 tsp	Margarine	Margarine 2 tsp	Margarine 1 tsp	Margarine	Margarine
Hot Mixed Fruit #8	Hot Mixed Fruit	Hot Mixed Fruit	Hot Mixed Fruit	Hot Mixed Fruit	Hot Mixed Fruit
Milk	Milk	1c Milk	Skim Milk	Milk	Milk
Cereal Beverage	Cereal/Tea/Sanka	Coffee/Tea/Sanka	Coffee/Tea/Sanka	Coffee/Tea/Sanka	Coffee/Tea/Sanka
			*Egg Substitute	Limit Milk to 2c/day	

	Bland (No Pepper)	4Gm Na (No Salt)	2 Gm Na (No Salt)	Low Fat/Low Chol	Low Fiber/Low Residue	High Fiber
B r e a k f a s t	Grape Fruit Juice 4oz Eggs #16 Crisp bacon 1 Assorted Cereal ¾c Toast/Biscuit Margarine 1 tsp/ Jelly Milk Cereal Beverage	Grape Fruit Juice Eggs 1 sl Bacon Assorted Cereal Toast/Biscuit Margarine/Jelly Milk Coffee/Tea/Sanka	Grape Fruit Juice Eggs SF Cereal Toast 2 tsp Margarine 1c Milk Coffee/Tea/Sanka	Grape Fruit Juice FF Egg* Assorted Cereal Toast 1 tsp Margarine Skim Milk Coffee/Tea/Sanka	Grape Fruit Juice Eggs Bacon/Sausage Assorted Cereal Toast/Biscuit Margarine/Jelly Milk Coffee/Tea/Sanka	Grape Fruit Juice Eggs Bacon/Sausage Bran Cereal Whole Grain Bread Margarine/Jelly Milk Coffee/Tea/Sanka
D i n n e r	Fish 3oz Whipped Potatoes #8 Stewed Tomatoes #8 Steamed Spinach #8 Bread 1 sl Margarine 1 tsp Angel Food Cake Milk Cereal Beverage	Fish Whipped Potatoes Stewed Tomatoes Steamed Spinach Bread Margarine Assorted Desserts Milk Coffee/Tea/Sanka	SF Fish SF Whipped Potatoes ½c Tomatoes ½c Steamed Spinach Bread Margarine 2 tsp Angel Food Cake Milk Coffee/Tea/Sanka	FF Fish FF Whipped Potatoes FF Tomatoes FF Steamed Spinach Bread 1 tsp Margarine Angel Food Cake Skim Milk Coffee/Tea/Sanka	Fish Whipped Potatoes Stewed Tomatoes Steamed Spinach Bread Margarine Angel Food Cake Milk Coffee/Tea/Sanka	Fish Baked Potato/Skin Fresh Tomato Slices Steamed Spinach Whole Wheat Bread Margarine Fresh Fruit Raw Salad Coffee/Tea/Sanka
S u p p e r	Roast Lamb 3oz Green Peas #8 Carrots #8 Oven Baked FF #8 Roll 1 Margarine 1 tsp Fruit Jello #8 Milk Cereal Beverage	Roast Lamb Brussels Sprouts Carrots French Fries Roll Margarine Assorted Dessrts Milk Coffee/Tea/Sanka	SF Roast Lamb Brussels Sprouts ½c Canned Carrots SF French Fries Roll Margarine 2 tsp Fruit Jello 1c Milk Coffee/Tea/Sanka	FF Roast Lamb FF Brussels Sprouts FF Carrots FF O Bkd Potatoes Roll Margarine 1 tsp Fruit Jello Skim Milk Coffee/Tea/Sanka *Egg Substitute	Roast Lamb *Green Peas Carrots French Fries Roll Margarine Fruit Jello Milk Coffee/Tea/Sanka *Subs. Green Beans Limit milk to 2c/day	BBQ Pork Ribs Brussel Sprouts Raw Carrots Fr. Fries/Skin Whole Wheat Roll Raw Salad Banana Bread Milk Coffee/Tea/Sanka

CERTIFIED _____, R.D.

383

Exhibit A–5 continued

	Bland (No Pepper)	4Gm Na (No Salt)	2Gm Na (No Salt)	Low Fat/Low Chol	Low Fiber/ Low Residue**	High Fiber	
B r e a k f a s t	Orange Juice 4oz	Orange Juice	Orange Juice	Orange Juice	Orange Juice	Orange Juice	
	Eggs #16	Eggs	1 Egg	*1 FF Egg	Eggs	Eggs	
	Crisp Bacon 1sl	1 sl Bacon	SF Cereal	Assorted Cereals	Bacon/Sausage	Bacon/Sausage	
	Asrtd Cereals ¾c	Assorted Cereals	Toast	Toast	Assorted Cereals	Bran Cereal	
	Toast/Biscuit	Toast/Biscuit	Margarine 2 tsp	Margarine 1 tsp	Toast/Biscuit	Whole Wheat Bread	
	Marg 1 tsp/Jelly	Margarine/Jelly	1c Milk	Skim Milk	Margarine/Jelly	Margarine/Jelly	
	Milk	Milk	Coffee/Tea/Sanka	Coffee/Tea/Sanka	Milk	Milk	
	Cereal Beverage	Coffee/Tea/Sanka	French Toast/Syrup	French Toast/Syrup	Coffee/Tea/Sanka	Coffee/Tea/Sanka	
	French Toast/Syrup	French Toast/Syrup			French Toast/Syrup	W.W. Toast/Syrup	
D i n n e r	Pork Chops 3oz	Pork Chops	Pork Chops	Pork Chops	Pork Chops	Pork Chops	
	Sweet Potatoes #8	Sweet Potatoes	Sweet Potatoes	FF Sweet Potatoes	Sweet Potatoes	Potatoes/Skin	
	Gr Beans #8	Green Beans	Green Beans	FF Gr Beans	Gr Beans	Gr Beans	
	Steamed	Steamed Cabbage	SF Steamed	FF Steamed	Asparagus	Asparagus	
	Cabbage #8	Tossed Salad/Dr.	Cabbage	Cabbage	Bread	Raw Salad/Dres.	
	Bread 1 sl	Bread	Bread	Bread	Margarine	Whole Wheat Bread	
	Margarine 1 tsp	Margarine	Margarine 2 tsp	Margarine 1 tsp	*Egg Custard	Margarine	
	Egg Custard #8	Assorted Desserts	Sugar Cookies	Fresh Fruit Salad	Milk	Fresh Fruit Salad	
	Milk	Milk	Milk	Skim Milk	Coffee/Tea/Sanka	Milk	
	Cereal Beverage	Coffee/Tea/Sanka	Coffee/Tea/Sanka	Coffee/Tea/Sanka		Coffee/Tea/Sanka	
S u p p e r	Mac. Cheese/Ham 6oz	Chicken Filet	Chicken Filet	Chicken Filet	Chicken Filet	Chicken Filet	
	Spinach Souffle #8	Mashed Potatoes	SF Mashed Potatoes	FF Mashed Potatoes	Mashed Potatoes	Bkd Potato/Skin	
	Scalloped	Spinach Souffle	½c Reg. Spinach	FF Spinach Souffle	Spinach Souffle	Spinach Souffle	
	Apples #8	Scalloped Apples	Scalloped Apples	Scalloped Apples	Scalloped Apples	Scalloped App/Skin	
	Gelatin Salad #8	Assorted Salad	SF Tossed Salad	Gelatin Salad	Gelatin Salad	Raw Salad/ Dressing	
	Vegetable Juice 4oz	Assorted Dessert	Plain Cake	Plain Cake	Plain Cake	Coconut Pie	
	Plain Cake	Roll	Roll	Roll	Roll	Whole Wheat Roll	
	Roll	Margarine	Margarine 2 tsp	Margarine 1 tsp	Margarine	Margarine	
	Margarine 1 tsp	Milk	1c Milk	Skim Milk	Milk	Milk	
	Milk	Coffee/Tea/Sanka	Coffee/Tea/Sanka	Coffee/Tea/Sanka	Coffee/Tea/Sanka	Coffee/Tea/Sanka	
	Cereal Beverage			*Egg Substitute	Limit Milk to 2c/day		

**Low Residue: Sub Clear Broth for Cream Soup; Sub Fresh Fruit Salad for Custard.

CERTIFIED _____ , R.D.

384

	Bland (No Pepper)	4Gm Na (No Salt)	2Gm Na (No Salt)	Low Fat/Low Chol	Low Fiber/ Low Residue	High Fiber
B r e a k f a s t	Grapefruit Juice 4oz Eggs #16 Crisp Bacon 1sl Puffed Rice 1c Toast/Biscuit 1 Margarine 1 tsp/ Jelly Milk Cereal Beverage	Grapefruit Juice Eggs 1 sl Bacon Assorted Cereal Toast/Biscuit Margarine/Jelly Milk Coffee/Tea/Sanka	Grapefruit Juice 1 Egg SF Cereal Toast Margarine 2 tsp 1c Milk Coffee/Tea/Sanka	Grapefruit Juice *1 FF Egg Assorted Cereal Toast Margarine 1 tsp Skim Milk Coffee/Tea/Sanka	Grapefruit Juice Eggs Bacon/Sausage Assorted Cereal Toast/Biscuit Margarine Milk Coffee/Tea/Sanka	Grapefruit Juice Eggs Bacon/Sausage Bran Cereal Whole Wheat Toast Margarine Milk Coffee/Tea/Sanka

D i n n e r	Cheese Omelet
	Hash Browns #8
	Okra &
	  Tomatoes #8
	Green Beans #8
	Roll
	Margarine 1 tsp
	Milk
	Cereal Beverage
		Plain Omelet
		Hash Browns
		Okra & Tomatoes
		Broccoli
		Roll
		Margarine
		Milk
		Coffee/Tea/Sanka
			SF Plain Omelet
			SF Hash Browns
			SF Okra &
			  Tomatoes
			SF Broccoli
			Roll
			Margarine 2 tsp
			Milk
			Coffee/Tea/Sanka
				FF Beef Pattie 2oz
				Oven Bkd F.F.
				FF Okra &
				  Tomatoes
				FF Broccoli
				Roll
				Margarine 1 tsp
				Skim Milk
				Coffee/Tea/Sanka
					Cheese Omelet
					Hash Browns
					Applesauce
					Green Beans
					Roll
					Margarine
					Milk
					Coffee/Tea/Sanka
						Cheese Omelet
						Potatoes/Skins
						Applesauce
						Broccoli
						Raw Salad/Dress.
						Whole Wheat Roll
						Margarine
						Coffee/Tea/Sanka

S u p p e r	Cubed Steak 3oz
	Steamed Rice #8
	Glazed Beets #8
	Zucchini/S.
	  Squash #8
	Macaroni Salad #8
	Roll
	Margarine 1 tsp
	Milk
	Cereal Beverage
		Cubed Steak
		Steamed Rice
		Glazed Beets
		Zucchini/S. Squash
		Assorted Salad
		Roll
		Margarine
		Milk
		Coffee/Tea/Sanka
			Cubed Steak
			SF Steamed Rice
			SF Glazed Beets
			SF Zucc./S. Squash
			SF Macaroni Salad
			Roll
			Margarine 2 tsp
			1c Milk
			Coffee/Tea/Sanka
				Cubed Steak
				FF Steamed Rice
				FF Glazed Beets
				FF Zucc./S. Squash
				Tossed Salad
				Roll
				Margarine 1 tsp
				Skim Milk
				Coffee/Tea/Sanka
				
				*Egg Substitute
					Cubed Steak
					Steamed Rice
					Glazed Beets
					Wax Beans
					Macaroni Salad
					Roll
					Margarine
					Milk
					Coffee/Tea/Sanka
					Limit Milk to 2c/day
						Cubed Steak
						Brown Rice
						Glazed Beets
						Sweet Potato
						Raw Salad/
						  Dressing
						Whole Wheat Roll
						Margarine
						Milk
						Coffee/Tea/Sanka

CERTIFIED _____, R.D.

385

Exhibit A-5 continued

	Bland (No Pepper)	4Gm Na (No Salt)	2Gm Na (No Salt)	Low Fat/Low Chol	Low Fiber/Low Residue	High Fiber		
B r e a k f a s t	Orange Juice 4oz Eggs #16 Crisp Bacon 1 sl Grits ½c Toast/Biscuit Margarine 1 tsp/ Jelly Milk Cereal Beverage	Orange Juice Eggs 1 sl Bacon Assorted Cereal Toast/Biscuit Margarine/Jelly Milk Coffee/Tea/Sanka	Orange Juice 1 Egg Shredded Wheat Toast Margarine 2 tsp 1c Milk Coffee/Tea/Sanka	Orange Juice 1 FF Egg Assorted Cereal Toast Margarine 1 tsp Milk Coffee/Tea/Sanka	Orange Juice Eggs Bacon/Sausage Assorted Cereal Toast/Biscuit Margarine/Jelly Milk Coffee/Tea/Sanka	Orange Juice Eggs Bacon/Sausage Bran Cereal Whole Wheat Toast Margarine/Jelly Milk Coffee/Tea/Sanka		
D i n n e r	Roast Beef Au Jus 3oz Baked Potato 1 Green Beans #8 Squash Casserole #8 Roll Margarine/Sour Cr. 1 tsp Angel Food Cake Milk Cereal Beverage	Roast Beef Au Jus Bkd Potato Green Beans Squash Casserole Roll Margarine/Sour Cr. Assorted Dessert Milk Coffee/Tea/Sanka	Roast Beef Au Jus Bkd Potato ½c Canned Green Beans SF Squash Casserole Roll Margarine 2 tsp Angel Food Cake Milk Coffee/Tea/Sanka	Roast Beef Au Jus Bkd Potato FF Gr Beans FF Squash Casserole Roll Margarine 1 tsp Angel Food Cake Milk Coffee/Tea/Sanka	Roast Beef Au Jus Bkd Potato w/o skin Green Beans Carrots Roll Margarine/Sour Cr. Angel Food Cake Milk Coffee/Tea/Sanka	Roast Beef Au Jus Bkd Potato Green Beans Squash Casserole Raw Salad/ Dressing Roll Margarine/Sour Cr. Fresh Fruit Milk Coffee/Tea/Sanka		
S u p p e r	Quiche Tater Tots #8 Green Peas #8 2-1/2" Sliced Tomatoes Tossed Salad Roll Margarine 1 tsp Milk Pudding #8 Cereal Beverage	Pork/Mushrooms Tater Tots Baked Beans Veg. Florentine Assorted Salad Roll Margarine Milk Assorted Dessert Coffee/Tea/Sanka	Pork/Mushrooms Tater Tots ½c Canned Beans Veg. Florentine Tossed Salad/SF Dressing Margarine 2 tsp 1c Milk Assorted Dessert Coffee/Tea/Sanka	Pork/Mushrooms Tater Tots FF Bkd Beans Veg. Florentine 1T Low Cal Dress. Crackers Skim Milk Skim M. Pudding Coffee/Tea/Sanka	Quiche Tater Tots Mushrooms Spinach Macaroni Salad Roll Margarine Milk *Pudding Coffee/Tea/Sanka *Sub Sherbet Limit Milk to 2c/day	Pork/Mushrooms Tater Tots Bkd Beans Veg. Florentine Cole Slaw Whole Wheat Roll Margarine Milk Assorted Dessert Coffee/Tea/Sanka		

CERTIFIED _____, R.D.

	Bland (No Pepper)	4Gm Na (No Salt)	2 Gm Na (No Salt)	Low Fat/Low Chol	Low Fiber/Low Residue	High Fiber	
B r e a k f a s t	Grapefruit Juice 4oz Eggs 1 Crisp Bacon 1 Assorted Cereal ¾c Toast/Biscuit Margarine 1 tsp/ Jelly Milk Cereal Beverage	Grapefruit Juice Eggs 1 sl Bacon Assorted Cereal Toast/Biscuit Margarine/Jelly Milk Coffee/Tea/Sanka	Grapefruit Juice 1 Egg Puffed Wheat Toast Margarine 2 tsp 1c Milk Coffee/Tea/Sanka	Grapefruit Juice *1 FF Egg Assorted Cereals Toast Margarine 1 tsp Skim Milk Coffee/Tea/Sanka	Grapefruit Juice Eggs Bacon/Sausage Puffed Wheat Toast/Biscuit Margarine Milk Coffee/Tea/Sanka	Grapefruit Juice Eggs Bacon/Sausage Bran Cereal Whole Wheat Toast Margarine Milk Coffee/Tea/Sanka	
D i n n e r	Bkd Fish 3oz Ovn Brown Potatoes #8 Broccoli #8 Carrots #8 Roll 1 Margarine 1 tsp Sugar Cookies Milk Cereal Beverage	Bkd Fish Ovn Brown Potatoes Broccoli Carrots Roll Margarine Assorted Dessert Milk Coffee/Tea/Sanka	Baked Fish SF Ovn Brown Potatoes SF Broccoli Carrots Roll Margarine 2 tsp Assorted Dessert Milk Coffee/Tea/Sanka	Baked Fish FF Ovn Brown Potatoes FF Broccoli Carrots Roll Margarine 1 tsp Gelatin Dessert Milk Coffee/Tea/Sanka	Baked Fish Ovn Brown Potatoes Broccoli Carrots Roll Margarine Gelatin Dessert Milk Coffee/Tea/Sanka	Beef Stew Ovn Brown Potatoes/skin Broccoli Raw Carrots Whole Wheat Roll Margarine Assorted Dessert Milk Coffee/Tea/Sanka	
S u p p e r	Hamburger Steak 3oz Mixed Veg #8 Scal Pots #8 French Gr Beans #8 Macaroni Salad #8 Roll 1 Margarine 1 tsp Plain Cake Milk Cereal Beverage	Hamburger Steak Mixed Vegetable Scalloped Potatoes French Gr Beans Assorted Salad Roll Margarine Assorted Dessert Milk Coffee/Tea/Sanka	SF Hamburger Steak ½c SF Canned Vegetable SF Scal Pots SF Fr Gr Beans Tossed Salad Roll Margarine 2 tsp Plain Cake 1c Milk Coffee/Tea/Sanka	FF Hamburger Steak FF Mixed Vegetable FF Scal Pots FF Fr Green Beans Tossed Salad Crackers Margarine 1T low ca. Plain Cake Skim Milk Coffee/Tea/Sanka *Egg Substitute	Hamburger Steak Mixed Vegetable French Gr Beans Gelatin Salad Roll Margarine Plain Cake Milk Coffee/Tea/Sanka Limit Milk to 2c/day	Hamburger Steak Mixed Vegetable Fr Gr Beans Raw Veg. Salad Roll Margarine Fresh Fruit Milk Coffee/Tea/Sanka	

CERTIFIED _____, R.D.

387

Exhibit A–5 continued

	Bland (No Pepper)	4Gm Na (No Salt)	2Gm Na (No Salt)	Low Fat/Low Chol	Low Fiber/Low Residue	High Fiber	
B r e a k f a s t	Orange Juice 4oz Egg 1 Crisp Bacon 1 sl Assorted Cereal ¾c Toast/Biscuit Margarine 1 tsp/ Jelly Milk Cereal Beverage	Orange Juice Egg 1 sl Bacon Assorted Cereal Toast/Biscuit Margarine/Jelly Milk Coffee/Tea/Sanka	Orange Juice 1 Egg Puffed Rice Toast Margarine 2 tsp 1c Milk Coffee/Tea/Sanka	Orange Juice 1 FF Egg Assorted Cereal Toast Margarine 1 tsp Skim Milk Coffee/Tea/Sanka	Orange Juice Eggs Bacon/Sausage Puffed Rice Toast/Biscuit Margarine Milk Coffee/Tea/Sanka	Orange Juice Eggs Bacon/Sausage Bran Cereal Whole Wheat Toast Margarine Milk Coffee/Tea/Sanka	
D i n n e r	Bkd Chicken 3oz Steamed Rice #8 Sweet Potato #8 Harvard Beets #8 Roll Margarine 1 tsp Stewed Fruit #8 Milk Cereal Beverage	Bkd Chicken Steamed Rice Sweet Potato Seasoned Greens Roll Margarine Stewed Fruit Milk Coffee/Tea/Sanka	SF Bkd Chicken Steamed Rice Sweet Potato Harvard Beets Roll Margarine 2 tsp Stewed Fruit 1c Milk Coffee/Tea/Sanka	FF Bkd Chicken Steamed Rice Sweet Potato Harvard Beets Roll Margarine 1 tsp Stewed Fruit Skim Milk Coffee/Tea/Sanka	Bkd Chicken Steamed Rice Parsleyed Noodles Harvard Beets Roll Margarine Angel Food Cake Milk Coffee/Tea/Sanka	Rigatoni Brown Rice Parsleyed Noodles Seasoned Greens Whole Wheat Roll Margarine Fresh Fruit Milk Coffee/Tea/Sanka	

S u p p e r	3oz Sliced Turkey
	  w/ Cranberry
	  Sauce
	Potato Salad
	Zucchini/Tomatoes
	Carrots
	Gelatin Salad
	Roll
	Margarine
	Plain Cookies
	Milk
	Cereal Beverage
		Sliced Turkey w/
		  Cranberry Sauce
		Potato Salad
		Zucchini/Tomatoes
		Carrots
		Assorted Salad
		Roll
		Margarine
		Assorted Dessert
		Milk
		Coffee/Tea/Sanka
			SF Sliced Turkey w/
			  Cranberry Sauce
			SF Potato Salad
			Zucchini/Tomatoes
			Carrots
			Tossed Salad
			Roll
			1 tsp Margarine
			Plain Cookies
			1c Milk
			Coffee/Tea/Sanka
				FF Sliced Turkey w/
				  Cranberry Sauce
				Corn
				Zucchini/Tomatoes
				Carrots
				Tossed Salad
				Crackers
				1T low Cal Dressing
				Fresh Fruit
				Skim Milk
				Coffee/Tea/Sanka
					Sliced Turkey w/
					  Cranberry Sauce
					Potato Salad
					Green Beans
					Carrots
					Gelatin Salad
					Roll
					Margarine
					Plain Cookies
					Milk
					Coffee/Tea/Sanka
					Limit Milk to 2c/day
						Sliced Turkey w/
						  Cranberry Sauce
						Potato Salad
						Zucchini/Tomatoes
						Carrots
						Tossed Salad
						Whole Wheat Roll
						Margarine
						Assorted Desserts
						Milk
						Coffee/Tea/Sanka	

CERTIFIED _____, R.D.

Exhibit A–6 Selective, Hospital, Southeastern U.S.

	1,000 Calories	1,200 Calories	1,500 Calories	1,800 Calories	2,000 Calories	2,200 Calories	
B r e a k f a s t	½c Orange Juice 1 FF Egg 1 sl Toast 1 tsp Margarine 1c Skim Milk Coffee/Tea	½c Orange Juice 1 FF Egg 1 sl W. Wheat Toast 1 tsp Margarine 1c Skim Milk Coffee/Tea	½c Orange Juice 1 FF Egg 1 sl W Wheat Toast 2 tsp Margarine 1c Skim Milk Coffee/Tea	½c Orange Juice 1 FF Egg 2 sl Toast 2 tsp Margarine 1c Skim Milk Coffee/Tea	½c Orange Juice 2 FF Eggs 2 sl Toast 2 tsp Margarine 1c Skim Milk Coffee/Tea	½c Orange Juice 2 FF Eggs 2 sl Toast ¾c Cereal 2 tsp Margarine 1c Skim Milk Coffee/Tea	
D i n n e r	1oz Roast Beef ½c FF Veg. Florentine ½c FF Squash ½c O. Brown Pot. 1 tsp Margarine ¼ Cantaloupe Coffee/Tea	2oz Roast Beef ½c FF Veg. Florentine ½c FF Squash ½c O. Brown Pot. 1 tsp Margarine ¼ Cantaloupe Coffee/Tea	2oz Roast Beef ½c FF Veg. Florentine ½c FF Squash ½c O. Brown Pot. 1 Roll 1 tsp Margarine ¼ Cantaloupe Coffee/Tea	3oz Roast Beef ½c FF Veg. Florentine ½c FF Squash ½c O. Brown Pot. 1 Roll 2 tsp Margarine ¼ Cantaloupe Coffee/Tea	3oz Roast Beef ½c FF Veg. Florentine ½c FF Squash ½c O. Brown Pot. 2 Rolls 2 tsp Margarine ¼ Cantaloupe Coffee/Tea	3oz Roast Beef ½c FF Veg. Florentine ½c FF Squash ½c O. Brown Pot. 2 Rolls 2 tsp Margarine ¼ Cantaloupe Coffee/Tea	
S u p p e r	2oz Baked Chicken ½c FF Broccoli 1 Roll ½c Diet Mixed Fruit Coffee/Tea	2oz Bkd Chicken ½c FF Broccoli ½c FF Green Beans 1 Roll 1 tsp Margarine ½c Diet Mixed Fruit Coffee/Tea	3oz Bkd Chicken ½c FF Broccoli ½c FF Gr Beans ½c Tater Tots 1 Roll 1 tsp Margarine ½c Diet Mixed Fruit Coffee/Tea	3oz Bkd Chicken ½c FF Broccoli ½c FF Gr Beans ½c Tater Tots 2 Rolls 2 tsp Margarine ½c Diet Mixed Fruit Coffee/Tea	3oz Bkd Chicken ½c FF Broccoli ½c FF Gr Beans ½c Tater Tots 2 Rolls 2 tsp Margarine ½c Diet Mixed Fruit Coffee/Tea	4oz Bkd Chicken ½c FF Broccoli ½c FF Gr Beans ½c Tater Tots 2 Rolls 2 tsp Margarine ½c Diet Mixed Fruit Coffee/Tea ½c Cranberry Juice	
S n a c k	1c Skim Milk	1c Skim Milk 2 Graham Crackers	1c Skim Milk 2 Gr Crackers	1c Skim Milk 2 Gr Crackers	1c Skim Milk 4 Gr Crackers	1c Skim Milk 4 Gr Crackers	

Exhibit A-6 continued

WEEK NO. TWO   DAY THURSDAY

MENU CYCLE   SPRING/SUMMER

	1,000 Calories	1,200 Calories	1,500 Calories	1,800 Calories	2,000 Calories	2,200 Calories
Breakfast	½c Orange Juice 1 FF Egg 1 sl W. Grain Toast 1 tsp Margarine 1c Skim Milk Coffee/Tea	½c Orange Juice 1 FF Egg 1 sl W. Grain Toast 1 tsp Margarine 1c Skim Milk Coffee/Tea	½c Orange Juice 1 FF Egg 1 sl W. Grain Toast 2 tsp Margarine 1c Skim Milk Coffee/Tea	½c Orange Juice 1 FF Egg 2 sl W. Grain Toast 2 tsp Margarine 1c Skim Milk Coffee/Tea	½c Orange Juice 2 FF Eggs 2 sl W. Grain Toast 2 tsp Margarine 1c Skim Milk Coffee/Tea	½c Orange Juice 2 FF Eggs ¾c Dry Cereal 2 sl W. Grain Toast 2 tsp Margarine 1c Skim Milk Coffee/Tea
Dinner	Chef Salad: 1oz Cheese ½c Tomatoes ½c Lettuce 1T French Dressing ½c Diet Fruit Coffee/Tea	2oz Beef Patty ½c FF St. Tomatoes ½c FF Spinach 1 Roll 1 tsp Margarine ½c Diet Fruit Coffee/Tea	2oz Beef Patty ½c FF St. Tomatoes ½c FF Spinach ½c FF Rice 1 Roll 1 tsp Margarine ½c Diet Fruit Coffee/Tea	3oz Beef Patty ½c FF St. Tomatoes ½c FF St. Spinach ½c FF Rice 1 Roll 2 tsp Margarine ½c Diet Fruit Coffee/Tea	3oz Beef Patty ½c FF St. Tomatoes ½c FF St. Spinach ½c FF Rice 2 Rolls 2 tsp Margarine ½c Diet Fruit Coffee/Tea	3oz Beef Patty ½c FF St. Tomatoes ½c FF St. Spinach ½c FF Rice 2 Rolls 2 tsp Margarine ½c Diet Fruit Coffee/Tea
Supper	2oz Sliced Veal ½c FF Brussel Sprouts ½c FF Green Peas ½c Diet Peaches Coffee/Tea	2oz Sliced Veal ½c FF Brussel Sprouts ½c FF Carrots 1 Roll 1 tsp Margarine ½c Diet Peaches Coffee/Tea	3oz Sliced Veal ½c FF Brussel Sprouts ½c FF Carrots 2 Rolls 1 tsp Margarine ½c Diet Peaches Coffee/Tea	3oz Sliced Veal ½c FF Brussel Sprouts ½c FF Carrots ½c FF Green Peas 2 Rolls 2 tsp Margarine ½c Diet Peaches Coffee/Tea	3oz Sliced Veal ½c FF Brussel Sprouts ½c FF Carrots ½c FF Green Peas 2 Rolls 2 tsp Margarine ½c Diet Peaches Coffee/Tea	4oz Sliced Veal ½c FF Brussel Sprouts ½c FF Carrots ½c FF Green Peas 2 Rolls 2 tsp Margarine 1c Diet Peaches Coffee/Tea
Snack	1c Skim Milk	1c Skim Milk 2 Gr Crackers	1c Skim Milk 2 Gr Crackers	1c Skim Milk 2 Gr Crackers	1c Skim Milk 4 Gr Crackers	1c Skim Milk 4 Gr Crackers

CERTIFIED _____, R.D.

390

	1,000 Calories	1,200 Calories	1,500 Calories	1,800 Calories	2,000 Calories	2,200 Calories	
Breakfast	½c Orange Juice 1 FF Egg 1 sl W Wheat Toast 1 tsp Margarine 1c Skim Milk Coffee/Tea	½c Orange Juice 1 FF Egg 1 sl W Wheat Toast 1 tsp Margarine 1c Skim Milk Coffee/Tea	½c Orange Juice 1 FF Egg 2 sl W Wheat Toast 2 tsp Margarine 1c Skim Milk Coffee/Tea	½c Orange Juice 1 FF Egg 2 sl W Wheat Toast 2 tsp Margarine 1c Skim Milk Coffee/Tea	½c Orange Juice 2 FF Eggs 2 sl W Wheat Toast 2 tsp Margarine 1c Skim Milk Coffee/Tea	½c Orange Juice 2 FF Eggs 2 sl W Wheat Toast 2 tsp Margarine ¾c Dry Cereal 1c Skim Milk Coffee/Tea	
Dinner	1oz Pork Chops ½c FF Steamed Cabbage ½c FF Veg. Medley 1 tsp Margarine ½c Diet Cockt Coffee/Tea	2oz Pork Chops ½c FF Steamed Cabbage ½c FF Veg. Medley ¼c Sweet Potato 1 tsp Margarine ½c Diet Cockt Coffee/Tea	2oz Pork Chops ½c FF Steamed Cabbage ½c FF Veg. Medley ¼c Sweet Potato Roll 1 tsp Margarine ½c Diet Cockt Coffee/Tea	3oz Pork Chops ½c FF Steamed Cabbage ½c FF Veg. Medley ¼c Sweet Potato Roll 2 tsp Margarine ½c Diet Cockt Coffee/Tea	3oz Pork Chops ½c FF Steamed Cabbage ½c FF Veg. Medley ½c Sweet Potato Roll 2 tsp Margarine ½c Diet Cockt Coffee/Tea	3oz Pork Chops ½c FF Steamed Cabbage ½c FF Veg. Medley ½c Sweet Potato Roll 2 tsp Margarine ½c Diet Cocktail Coffee/Tea	
Supper	2oz Meat Loaf ½c FF Gr Beans ½c FF Boiled Potato 1 Small Apple Coffee/Tea	2oz Meat Loaf ½c FF Gr Beans ½c FF Spinach ½c FF Boiled Potato 1 tsp Margarine 1 Small Apple Coffee/Tea	3oz Meat Loaf ½c FF Gr Beans ½c FF Spinach ½c FF Boiled Potato Roll 1 tsp Margarine 1 Small Apple Coffee/Tea	3oz Meat Loaf ½c FF Gr Beans ½c FF Spinach ½c FF Boiled Potato 2 Rolls 2 tsp Margarine 1 Small Apple Coffee/Tea	3oz Meat Loaf ½c FF Gr Beans ½c FF Spinach ½c FF Boiled Potato 2 Rolls 2 tsp Margarine 1 Small Apple Coffee/Tea	4oz Meat Loaf ½c FF Gr Beans ½c FF Spinach ½c FF Boiled Potato 2 Rolls 2 tsp Margarine 1 Small Apple Coffee/Tea ½c Apple Juice	
Snack	1c Skim Milk	1c Skim Milk 2 Gr Crackers	1c Skim Milk 2 Gr Crackers	1c Skim Milk 2 Gr Crackers	1c Skim Milk 4 Gr Crackers	1c Skim Milk 4 Gr Crackers	

CERTIFIED _____, R.D.

Exhibit A–6 continued

WEEK NO. ___TWO___ DAY ___SATURDAY___   MENU CYCLE ___SPRING/SUMMER___

	1,000 Calories	1,200 Calories	1,500 Calories	1,800 Calories	2,000 Calories	2,200 Calories	
B r e a k f a s t	½c Orange Juice 1 FF Egg 1 Biscuit 1c Skim Milk Coffee/Tea	½c Orange Juice 1 FF Egg 1 Biscuit 1c Skim Milk Coffee/Tea	½c Orange Juice 1 FF Egg 1 Biscuit 1 tsp Margarine 1c Skim Milk Coffee/Tea	½c Orange Juice 1 FF Egg 2 Biscuits 1c Skim Milk Coffee/Tea	½c Orange Juice 2 FF Eggs 2 Biscuits 1c Skim Milk Coffee/Tea	½c Orange Juice 2 FF Eggs 2 Biscuits ¾c Dry Cereal 1c Skim Milk Coffee/Tea	
D i n n e r	¼c Cottage Cheese ½c Sliced Tomatoes 1 tsp Mayonnaise ½c Raw Carrots ½c Diet Peaches Coffee/Tea	2oz Meat Patty ½c FF Potatoes ½c FF Broccoli ½c Tomato Slices ½c Diet Peaches 1 tsp Mayonnaise Coffee/Tea	2oz Meat Patty 1 Bun ½c FF Broccoli ½c Tomato Slices ½c Diet Peaches 1 tsp Mayonnaise Coffee/Tea	3oz Meat Patty 1 Bun ½c FF Broccoli ½c Tomato Slices ½c Diet Peaches 2 tsp Mayonnaise Coffee/Tea	3oz Meat Patty 1 Bun ½c FF Broccoli ½c Tomato Slices ½c O Baked Fr. Fries ½c Diet Peaches 2 tsp Mayonnaise Coffee/Tea	3oz Meat Patty 1 Bun ½c FF Broccoli ½c Tomato Slices ½c O Baked Fr. Fries ½c Diet Peaches 2 tsp Mayonnaise Coffee/Tea	
S u p p e r	2oz Br. Cube Steak ½c FF Summer Squash ½c Steamed Rice ½ Banana Coffee/Tea	2oz Br. Cube Steak ½c FF Summer Squash ½c FF Beets ½c Steamed Rice 1 tsp Margarine ½ Banana Coffee/Tea	3oz Br. Cube Steak ½c FF Summer Squash ½c FF Beets ½c Steamed Rice Roll 1 tsp Margarine ½ Banana Coffee/Tea	3oz Br. Cube Steak ½c FF Summer Squash ½c FF Beets ½c Steamed Rice 2 Rolls 2 tsp Margarine ½ Banana Coffee/Tea	3oz Br. Cube Steak ½c FF Summer Squash ½c FF Beets ½c Steamed Rice 2 Rolls 2 tsp Margarine ½ Banana Coffee/Tea	4oz Br. Cube Steak ½c FF Summer Squash ½c FF Beets ½c Steamed Rice 2 Rolls 2 tsp Margarine 1 Banana Coffee/Tea	
S n a c k	1c Skim Milk	1c Skim Milk 5 Vanilla Wafers	1c Skim Milk 5 Vanilla Wafers	1c Skim Milk 5 Vanilla Wafers	1c Skim Milk 10 Vanilla Wafers	1c Skim Milk 10 Vanilla Wafers	

CERTIFIED _____, R.D.

392

WEEK NO. TWO DAY SUNDAY MENU CYCLE SPRING/SUMMER

	1,000 Calories	*1,200 Calories*	*1,500 Calories*	*1,800 Calories*	*2,000 Calories*	*2,200 Calories*	
Breakfast	½c Orange Juice 1 FF Scrmb Egg 1 sl Toast 1 tsp Margarine 1c Skim Milk Coffee/Tea	½c Orange Juice 1 FF Scrmb Egg 1 sl W Wheat Toast 1 tsp Margarine 1c Skim Milk Coffee/Tea	½c Orange Juice 1 FF Scrmb Egg 1 sl W Wheat Toast 2 tsp Margarine 1c Skim Milk Coffee/Tea	½c Orange Juice 1 FF Scrmb Egg 2 sl W Wheat Toast 2 tsp Margarine 1c Skim Milk Coffee/Tea	½c Orange Juice 2 FF Scrmb Eggs 2 sl W Wheat Toast 2 tsp Margarine 1c Skim Milk Coffee/Tea	½c Orange Juice 2 FF Scrmb Eggs 2 sl W Wheat Toast 2 tsp Margarine ¾c Dry Cereal 1c Skim Milk Coffee/Tea	
Dinner	1oz Roast Beef ½c FF Gr Beans ½c Sliced Tomatoes 1 tsp Margarine ½c Mixed Fruit Salad Coffee/Tea	2oz Roast Beef ½c FF Gr Beans ½c Sliced Tomatoes 1 Sm. Bkd Potato 1 tsp Margarine ½c Mixed Fruit Salad Coffee/Tea	2oz Roast Beef ½c FF Gr Beans ½c Sliced Tomatoes 1 Sm. Bkd Potato Roll 1 tsp Margarine ½c Mixed Fruit Salad Coffee/Tea	3oz Roast Beef ½c FF Gr Beans ½c Sliced Tomatoes 1 Sm. Bkd Potato Roll 2 tsp Margarine ½c Mixed Fruit Salad Coffee/Tea	3oz Roast Beef ½c FF Gr Beans ½c Sliced Tomatoes 1 Sm. Bkd Potato 2 Rolls 2 tsp Margarine ½c Mixed Fruit Salad Coffee/Tea	3oz Roast Beef ½c FF Gr Beans ½c Sliced Tomatoes 1 Sm. Bkd Potato 2 Rolls 2 tsp Margarine ½c Mixed Fruit Salad Coffee/Tea	
Supper	2oz Pork ¼c Baked Beans ½c Tossed Salad w/ Vinegar 1 FF Baked Apple Coffee/Tea	2oz Pork ½c FF S Tomatoes ¼c Baked Beans ½c Tossed Salad 1T Salad Dressing 1 FF Baked Apple Coffee/Tea	3oz Pork ½c FF S Tomatoes ¼c Baked Beans ½c Tossed Salad 1T Salad Dressing Roll 1 FF Baked Apple Coffee/Tea	3oz Pork ½c FF S Tomatoes ½c Baked Beans ½c Tossed Salad 1T Salad Dressing Roll 1 tsp Margarine 1 FF Baked Apple Coffee/Tea	3oz Pork ½c FF S Tomatoes ½c Baked Beans ½c Tossed Salad 1T Salad Dressing Roll 1 tsp Margarine 1 FF Baked Apple Coffee/Tea	4oz Pork ½c FF S Tomatoes ½c Baked Beans ½c Tossed Salad 1T Salad Dressing Roll 1 tsp Margarine 1 FF Baked Apple ½c Diet Fruit Coffee/Tea	
Snack	1c Skim Milk	1c Skim Milk 5 Ritz Crackers	1c Skim Milk 5 Ritz Crackers	1c Skim Milk 5 Ritz Crackers	1c Skim Milk 10 Ritz Crackers	1c Skim Milk 10 Ritz Crackers	

CERTIFIED ______________________________, R.D.

Exhibit A–6 continued

MENU CYCLE   SPRING/SUMMER

	1,000 Calories	1,200 Calories	1,500 Calories	1,800 Calories	2,000 Calories	2,200 Calories
Breakfast	½c Orange Juice 1 FF Egg ½ English Muffin 1 sl Bacon 1c Skim Milk Coffee/Tea	½c Orange Juice 1 FF Egg ½ English Muffin 1 sl Bacon 1c Skim Milk Coffee/Tea	½c Orange Juice 1 FF Egg ½ English Muffin 1 sl Bacon 1 tsp Margarine 1c Skim Milk Coffee/Tea	½c Orange Juice 1 FF Egg 1 English Muffin 1 sl Bacon 1 tsp Margarine 1c Skim Milk Coffee/Tea	½c Orange Juice 2 FF Eggs 1 English Muffin 1 sl Bacon 1 tsp Margarine 1c Skim Milk Coffee/Tea	½c Orange Juice 2 FF Eggs 1 English Muffin 1 sl Bacon ¾c Dry Cereal 1 tsp Margarine 1c Skim Milk Coffee/Tea
Dinner	1oz Baked Fish ½c FF Broccoli ½c FF Carrots 1 tsp Margarine ½c Diet Fruit Coffee/Tea	2oz Baked Fish ½c FF Broccoli ½c FF Carrots ½c Parsleyed Noodles 1 tsp Margarine ½c Diet Fruit Coffee/Tea	2oz Baked Fish ½c FF Broccoli ½c FF Carrots ½c Parsleyed Noodles Roll 1 tsp Margarine ½c Diet Fruit Coffee/Tea	3oz Baked Fish ½c FF Broccoli ½c FF Carrots ½c Parsleyed Noodles Roll 2 tsp Margarine ½c Diet Fruit Coffee/Tea	3oz Baked Fish ½c FF Broccoli ½c FF Carrots ½c Parsleyed Noodles 2 Rolls 2 tsp Margarine ½c Diet Fruit Coffee/Tea	3oz Baked Fish ½c FF Broccoli ½c FF Carrots ½c Parsleyed Noodles 2 Rolls 2 tsp Margarine ½c Diet Fruit Coffee/Tea
Supper	2oz Hamburger Steak ½c FF Gr Beans ½c FF O Br. Potato ½c Fresh Fruit Coffee/Tea	2oz Hamburger Steak ½c FF Gr Beans ½c FF Mixed Veg. ½c FF O Br. Potato 1 tsp Margarine ½c Fresh Fruit Coffee/Tea	3oz Hamburger Steak ½c FF Gr Beans ½c FF Mixed Veg. ½c FF O Br. Potato Roll 1 tsp Margarine ½c Fresh Fruit Coffee/Tea	3oz Hamburger Steak ½c FF Gr Beans ½c FF Mixed Veg. ½c FF O Br. Potato 2 Rolls 2 tsp Margarine ½c Fresh Fruit Coffee/Tea	3oz Hamburger Steak ½c FF Gr Beans ½c FF Mixed Veg. ½c FF O Br. Potato 2 Rolls 2 tsp Margarine ½c Fresh Fruit Coffee/Tea	4oz Hamburger Steak ½c FF Gr Beans ½c FF Mixed Veg. ½c FF O Br. Potato 2 Rolls 2 tsp Margarine 1c Diet Fruit Coffee/Tea
Snack	1c Skim Milk	1c Skim Milk 2 Gr Crackers	1c Skim Milk 2 Gr Crackers	1c Skim Milk 2 Gr Crackers	1c Skim Milk 4 Gr Crackers	1c Skim Milk 4 Gr Crackers

CERTIFIED _____, R.D.

	1,000 Calories	1,200 Calories	1,500 Calories	1,800 Calories	2,000 Calories	2,200 Calories	
Breakfast	½c Orange Juice 1 FF Egg 1 tsp Margarine ½c Cooked Cereal 1c Skim Milk Coffee/Tea	½c Orange Juice 1 FF Egg 1 tsp Margarine ½c Cooked Cereal 1c Skim Milk Coffee/Tea	½c Orange Juice 1 FF Egg 2 tsp Margarine ½c Cooked Cereal 1c Skim Milk Coffee/Tea	½c Orange Juice 1 FF Egg 2 tsp Margarine ½c Cooked Cereal 1 sl Toast 1c Skim Milk Coffee/Tea	½c Orange Juice 2 FF Eggs 2 tsp Margarine ½c Cooked Cereal 1 sl Toast 1c Skim Milk Coffee/Tea	½c Orange Juice 2 FF Eggs 2 tsp Margarine ½c Cooked Cereal 2 sl Toast 1c Skim Milk Coffee/Tea	
Dinner	Chef Salad: 1oz Egg Chopped ½c Tomato ½c Lettuce ½c Diet Fruit 1T Salad Dressing Coffee/Tea	2oz Baked Chicken ½c FF Greens ½c FF Beets ¼c FF Sweet Potato ½c Diet Fruit 1 tsp Margarine Coffee/Tea	2oz Baked Chicken ½c FF Greens ½c FF Beets ½c FF Sweet Potato ½c Diet Fruit 1 tsp Margarine Coffee/Tea	3oz Baked Chicken ½c FF Greens ½c FF Beets ½c FF Sweet Potato ½c Diet Fruit 2 tsp Margarine Coffee/Tea	3oz Baked Chicken ½c FF Greens ½c FF Beets ½c FF Sweet Potato ½c Diet Fruit Roll 2 tsp Margarine Coffee/Tea	3oz Baked Chicken ½c FF Greens ½c FF Beets ½c FF Sweet Potato ½c Diet Fruit Roll 2 tsp Margarine Coffee/Tea	
Supper	2oz Sliced Ham ½c FF Zucchini/Tom. ½c FF Potatoes ½c Diet Pineapple Coffee/Tea	2oz Sliced Ham ½c FF Zucchini/Tom. ½c FF Collards ½c FF Potatoes 1 tsp Margarine ½c Diet Pineapple Coffee/Tea	3oz Sliced Ham ½c FF Zucchini/Tom. ½c FF Collards ½c FF Potatoes Roll 1 tsp Margarine ½c Diet Pineapple Coffee/Tea	3oz Sliced Ham ½c FF Zucchini/Tom. ½c FF Collards ½c FF Potatoes 2 Rolls 2 tsp Margarine ½c Diet Pineapple Coffee/Tea	3oz Sliced Ham ½c FF Zucchini/Tom. ½c FF Collards ½c FF Potatoes 2 Rolls 2 tsp Margarine ½c Diet Pineapple Coffee/Tea	4oz Sliced Ham ½c FF Zucchini/Tom. ½c FF Collards ½c FF Potatoes 2 Rolls 2 tsp Margarine 1c Diet Pineapple Coffee/Tea	
Snack	1c Skim Milk	1c Skim Milk 2 Gr Crackers	1c Skim Milk 2 Gr Crackers	1c Skim Milk 2 Gr Crackers	1c Skim Milk 4 Gr Crackers	1c Skim Milk 4 Gr Crackers	

CERTIFIED _____, R.D.

395

Exhibit A-7 Selective, Hospital, Southeastern U.S.

WEEK NO. __THREE__

MENU CYCLE ___ SPRING/SUMMER

	Wednesday	Thursday	Friday	Saturday	Sunday	Monday	Tuesday
Breakfast	Asst Juice 4 oz	Asst Juice	Asst Juice	Asst Juice	Asst Juice	Asst Juice	Asst Juice
	Scrmb Eggs 1	Scrmb Eggs	Scrmb Eggs	Scrmb Eggs	Scrmb Eggs	Fried Eggs	Scrmb Eggs
	Asst Cereal ¾ c	Asst Cereal	Asst Cereal	Asst Cereal	Asst Cereal	Asst Cereal	*Asst Cereal
	Toast/Asst Breads 1	Toast/Asst Bread	Toast/Asst Breads	Toast/Asst Breads	Toast/*Asst Breads	Toast/Asst Breads	Toast/Asst Bread
	Bacon 1 sl	Bran Muffins	Bacon	Bacon	Bacon	Bacon	Bacon
	Sausage 1	Bacon	Sausage	Sausage	Sausage	Sausage	Sausage
	Fr Toast/Syrup	Sausage	Coffee/Tea/Milk	Pancakes/Syrup	Coffee/Tea/Milk	Coffee/Tea/Milk	Coffee/Tea/Milk
	Coffee/Tea/Milk	Coffee/Tea/Milk		Coffee/Tea/Milk			
Dinner	Fried Chicken 3 oz	Steamship Round 3 oz	*Ham/Cherry Sauce	*BBQ Pork 3 oz	Turkey 3 oz	Salisbury Steak 3 oz	Chix Fil/Gravy 3 oz
	*Pepper Steak 3 oz	*Chix Pot Pie 3 oz	*Lasagne 6 oz	Lemon Bkd Fish 3 oz	*Omelets	*Manicotti 3 oz	*Tuna Salad 3 oz
	Msh Potatoes #8	Potatoes #8	Sw Potatoes #8	*Potato Gems #8	Noodles Romanoff #8	Rice #8	*Corn-on-Cob #8
	Collards #8	Cauliflower #8	*Turnip Greens #8	Squash #8	Dressing #8	*Squash #8	*Spinach #8
	*Gr Peas/Onions #8	*Beets #8	*Blackeyed Peas #8	Winter Mix #8	Gr Peas #8	Okra/Tomatoes #8	Scall Potatoes #8
	Carrots #8	*Gr Beans #8	Breaded Okra #8	*French Gr Beans #8	*Eggplant #8	*Turnip Greens #8	Cauliflower #8
	*Mix Veg #8	Asst Breads	Gr Beans #8	Asst Breads	*Spinach #8	Asst Breads	Asst Breads
	Asst Breads	Asst Salads	Asst Breads	Asst Salads	Asst Breads	Asst Salads	Asst Salads
	Asst Salads	Asst Desserts	Asst Salads	Asst Desserts	Asst Salads	Asst Desserts	Asst Desserts
	Asst Desserts	Coffee/Tea/Milk	Asst Desserts	Coffee/Tea/Milk	Asst Desserts	Coffee/Tea/Milk	Coffee/Tea/Milk
	Coffee/Tea/Milk		Coffee/Tea/Milk		Coffee/Tea/Milk		
Supper	*Shrimp Chow Mein 3 oz	*Beef Strog 3 oz	*Steak 3 oz	Spaghetti 3 oz	*Cubed Steaks 3 oz	*Bkd Cod 3 oz	Rst Beef 3 oz
	Meatloaf/Gravy 3 oz	Cornish Hens 3 oz	Ital Sausage	*Fish Platter 3 oz	Ham/Mac/Cheese 3 oz	Polish Sausage	*Ham/Sw & Sour Sauce
	Rice #8	Squash #8	*Bkd Potatoes #8	Corn #8	*Bu Potatoes #8	Pinto Beans #8	*Parsl Bu Potatoes #8
	Stw Tomatoes #8	*Brussel Sprts #8	Onion Rings #8	Beets #8	Broccoli #8	*French Fries #8	Beets #8
	*Chow Mein Noodles #8	*Noodles #8	Spinach #8	Crowder Peas #8	*Lima Beans #8	*Mix Vegs #8	Yellow Squash #8
	*Oriental Vegs #8	*Veg Sticks	Cauliflower #8	*Ital Vegs #8	Carrots #8	Gr Beans #8	*Gr Peas/Onions #8
	Msh Potatoes #8	Asst Breads	*Mix Veg #8	Asst Breads	Asst Breads	Asst Breads	Asst Breads
	Asst Breads	Asst Salads	Asst Breads	Asst Salads	Asst Salads	Asst Salads	Asst Salads
	Asst Salads	Asst Desserts	Asst Salads	Asst Desserts	Asst Desserts	Asst Desserts	Asst Desserts
	Asst Desserts	Coffee/Tea/Milk	Asst Desserts	Coffee/Tea/Milk	Coffee/Tea/Milk	Coffee/Tea/Milk	Coffee/Tea/Milk
	Coffee/Tea/Milk		Coffee/Tea/Milk				

*Items on the extended menus for modified diets

CERTIFIED _____, R.D.

396

	Bland (No Pepper)	4 Gm Na (No Salt)	2 Gm Na (No Salt)	Low Fat/Low Chol	Low Fiber/Low Residue	High Fiber	
B r e a k f a s t	Orange Juice 4 oz Scrmb Eggs 1 Crisp Bacon 1 sl Toast-1/Margarine 1 tsp Jelly Dry Cereal ¾ c Milk Cereal Beverage	Orange Juice Scrmb Eggs 1 Sl Bacon Toast/Margarine Jelly Dry Cereal Milk/Coffee/Tea	Orange Juice 1 SF Scrmb Egg Roll 2 tsp Margarine Jelly SF Dry Cereal 1 c Milk/Coffee/Tea	Orange Juice *1 FF Fr Toast 1 tsp Margarine/ Jelly FF Cereal Coffee/Tea/Skim Milk	Orange Juice Fr Toast/Syrup Rice Krispies Coffee/Tea/Milk	Orange Juice Fr Toast (W/W Bread) Syrup Bacon Bran Flakes Coffee/Tea/Milk	
D i n n e r	Bkd Chicken 3 oz Msh Potatoes #8 Collards #8 Roll Margarine 1 tsp Pudding #8 Milk/Fruit Drink	Fried Chicken Msh Potatoes Collards Roll Margarine Asst Dessert Milk/Tea/Coffee	SF Fried Chicken SF Msh Potatoes ½ c SF Collards Roll 2 tsp Margarine Fruit Tea/Coffee	FF Bkd Chicken 2 oz (no skin) FF Msh Potatoes FF Collards Sliced Tomatoes Coffee/Tea/Skim Milk	Bkd Chicken Msh Potatoes Gr Beans Roll Margarine Cooked Fruit Coffee/Tea/Milk	Fried Chicken Potatoes w/Skins Collards Salad Whole Grain Roll Dessert Coffee/Tea/Milk	
S u p p e r	Shrimp Chow Mein 2 oz Rice #8 Oriental Vegs #8 Roll Margarine 1 tsp Cake—No Choc Milk/Fruit Drink Cereal Beverage	Shrimp Chow Mein Rice Oriental Vegs Salad Roll Margarine Cake—No Choc Milk/Coffee/Tea	SF Shrimp Chow Mein SF Rice SF Oriental Vegs Salad Roll 2 tsp Margarine SF Cake 1 c Milk/Coffee/Tea	FF Shrimp Chow Mein 2 oz FF Rice FF Oriental Vegs Chow Mein Noodles Garden Salad 1 T FF Dressing Jello Coffee/Tea/Skim Milk *Low Chol Fr Tst made w/Egg Substitute	Shrimp Chow Mein Rice Carrots Chow Mein Noodles Plain or Pnd Cake Coffee/Tea/Milk Limit Milk to 2c/day	Meatloaf/Gravy Rice Oriental Vegs Chow Mein Noodles Salad Whole Grain Bread Dessert Coffee/Tea/Milk	

CERTIFIED _____ R.D.

397

Exhibit A–7 continued

	Bland (No Pepper)	4 Gm Na (No Salt)	2 Gm Na (No Salt)	Low Fat/Low Chol	Low Fiber/Low Residue	High Fiber
B r e a k f a s t	Orange Juice 4 oz Boiled Eggs 1 Crisp Bacon 1 sl Sweet Roll 1 Margarine 1 tsp Dry Cereal ¾ c Milk Cereal Beverage	Orange Juice Boil Eggs Crisp Bacon Swt Roll Milk/Tea/Coffee	Orange Juice 1 Boil Egg Toast 2 tsp Margarine/ Jelly SF Dry Cereal 1 c Milk/Tea/Coffee	Orange Juice FF Eggs (Boil) Toast 1 tsp Margarine/ Jelly Coffee/Tea/Skim Milk	Orange Juice Scrmb Eggs Bacon or Saus Toast 1 tsp Margarine/ Jelly Coffee/Tea/Milk	Orange Juice Scrmb Eggs Bacon or Saus Whole Grain Bread Margarine/Jelly Coffee/Tea/Milk
D i n n e r	Steamship Rnd 3 oz Potatoes #8 Beets #8 Roll Margarine 1 tsp Sherbet #8 Milk/Water/Fruit Drink	Steamship Rnd Potatoes Beets Roll Margarine Asst Dessert Milk/Tea/Coffee	SF Steamship Rnd ½ c SF Potatoes ½ c SF Beets Roll 2 tsp Margarine Plain Cake Tea/Coffee/Fruit Drink	FF Steamship Rnd 2 oz FF Potatoes FF Beets Toss Salad/Vinegar Roll Margarine Jello Coffee/Tea/Skim Milk	Steamship Round Potatoes Gr Beans Roll Margarine Plain Cake Coffee/Tea/Milk	Steamship Rnd Potatoes w/Skins Gr Beans Raw Veg Salad Whole Grain Bread Dessert Coffee/Tea/Milk
S u p p e r	Cornish Hen 2 oz Noodles #8 Squash #8 Roll Margarine 1 tsp Cake—No Choc Milk/Fruit Drink Cereal Beverage	Cornish Hen Noodles Squash Salad Roll Margarine Cake—No Choc Milk/Coffee/Tea	SF Cornish Hen ½ c SF Noodles ½ c SF Squash Salad Roll 2 tsp Margarine Cake—No Choc 1 c Milk/Tea/Coffee	FF Cornish Hen 2 oz (no skin) FF Noodles FF Squash Roll 1 tsp Margarine Sherbet Coffee/Tea/Skim Milk	Cornish Hen Noodles Beets Roll Margarine Can or Ckd Fruit Coffee/Tea/Milk Limit Milk to 2c/day	Beef Strog Brussel Sprts Squash Raw Veg Salad Whole Grain Bread Dessert Coffee/Tea/Milk

CERTIFIED _____, R.D.

398

	Bland (No Pepper)	4 Gm Na (No Salt)	2 Gm Na (No Salt)	Low Fat/Low Chol	Low Fiber/ Low Residue	High Fiber

B r e a k f a s t	Orange Juice 4 oz
	Scrmb Eggs 1
	Bacon 1 sl
	Dry Cereal ¾ c
	Toast
	Margarine 1 tsp/
	  Jelly
	Milk
	Cereal Beverage
		Orange Juice
		Scrmb Eggs
		Bacon
		Dry Cereal
		Toast
		Margarine/Jelly
		Milk/Tea/Coffee
			Orange Juice
			SF Scrmb Eggs
			SF Cereal
			Toast
			2 tsp Margarine/
			  Jelly
			1 c Milk/Tea/Coffee
				Orange Juice
				*1 FF Egg
				FF Cereal
				Toast
				Margarine/Jelly
				Coffee/Tea/Skim
				  Milk
					Orange Juice
					Fried Egg
					Bacon or Saus
					Rice Krispies
					Toast
					Margarine/Jelly
					Coffee/Tea/Milk
						Orange Juice
						Fried Egg
						Bacon or Saus
						Shred Wheat
						Whole Grain Bread
						  or Muffin
						Margarine/Jelly
						Coffee/Tea/Milk

D i n n e r	Lasagna 6 oz
	Turnip Greens #8
	Roll
	Margarine 1 tsp
	Sugar Cookies
	Milk/Fruit Drink
		Lasagna
		Turnip Greens
		Roll
		Margarine
		Asst Dessert
		Milk/Tea/Coffee
			SF Lasagna
			½ c SF Turnip
			  Greens
			Roll
			2 tsp Margarine
			Jello/Fruit
			Tea/Coffee
				FF Beef Patty 2 oz
				FF Turnip Greens
				FF Swt Potatoes
				Roll
				1 tsp Margarine
				Fruit
				Coffee/Tea/Skim
				  Milk
					Lasagne
					Gr Beans
					Roll
					Margarine
					Ckd or Can Fruit
					Coffee/Tea/Milk
						Ham/Cherry Sauce
						Turnip Greens
						Swt Potatoes
						Raw Veg Salad
						Roll
						Margarine
						Fruit or Dessert
						Coffee/Tea/Milk

S u p p e r	Steak 3 oz Bkd Potatoes #8 Spinach #8 Roll Margarine 1 tsp Fruit Jello #8 Milk/Fruit Drink Cereal Beverage	Steak Bkd Potatoes Spinach Salad Roll Margarine Asst Dessert Milk/Tea/Coffee	SF Steak Bkd Potatoes ½ c SF Spinach SF Salad Roll 2 tsp Margarine Sherbet 1 c Milk/Tea/Coffee	FF Steak 2 oz Bkd Potatoes FF Spinach Salad/1 T FF Dress Roll Sherbet Coffee/Tea/Skim Milk *Egg Substitute	FF Steak Bkd Potatoes Spinach Roll Margarine Plain Cookie Coffee/Tea/Milk Limit Milk to 2c/day	Ital Sausage Bkd Potato w/Skins Mix Vegs Raw Veg Salad Roll Margarine Fruit or Dessert Coffee/Tea/Milk

CERTIFIED _____ _____ R.D.

Exhibit A-7 continued

WEEK NO. THREE   DAY SATURDAY   MENU CYCLE SPRING/SUMMER

Bland (No Pepper)	4 Gm Na (No Salt)	2 Gm Na (No Salt)	Low Fat/Low Chol	Low Fiber/Low Residue	High Fiber
B r e a k f a s t					
Orange Juice 4 oz	Orange Juice	Orange Juice	Orange Juice	Orange Juice	Orange Juice
Scrmb Eggs 1	Fried Egg	Fried Egg	*1 FF Egg	Scrmb Egg	Scrmb Egg
Crisp Bacon 1 sl	1 sl Bacon	SF Cereal	FF Cereal	Bacon or Saus	Bacon or Saus
Pancakes/Syrup 1	Dry Cereal	2 tsp Margarine	Toast	Corn Flakes	Raisin Bran
Margarine 1 tsp	Margarine	1 c Milk/Tea/Coffee	1 tsp Margarine/ Jelly	Toast	Whole Grain Bread or Muffin
Milk/Cereal	Milk/Tea/Coffee		Coffee/Tea/Skim Milk	Coffee/Tea/Milk	Margarine/Jelly
Beverage					Coffee/Tea/Milk
D i n n e r					
Lemon Bkd Fish 3 oz	Lemon Bkd Fish	SF Lemon Bkd Fish	FF Top Round 2 oz	Lemon Bkd Fish	Top Round
Potato Gems #8	Potato Gems	SF Potato Gems	FF Potatoes	Potato Gems	Potato Gems
French Gr Beans #8	French Gr Beans Salad	SF French Gr Beans	FF French Gr Beans	Gr Beans	French Gr Beans
Roll	Roll	SF Salad	FF Salad	Roll	Raw Veg Salad
Margarine 1 tsp	Margarine	Roll	Roll	Margarine	Whole Grain Bread
Pudding #8	Asst Dessert	2 tsp Margarine	Margarine	Ice Cream	Margarine
Milk/Fruit Drink	Milk/Tea/Coffee	Pudding	Fruit	Coffee/Tea/Milk	Fruit or Dessert
		Tea/Coffee	Coffee/Tea/Skim Milk		Coffee/Tea/Milk
S u p p e r					
Spaghetti 4 oz	Spaghetti	SF Spaghetti	FF Spaghetti (2 oz Meat)	Spaghetti	Spaghetti
Ital Vegs #8	Ital Vegs	SF Ital Vegs	FF Ital Vegs	Ital Vegs	Corn
Chop Lettuce #8	Asst Salad	Toss Salad/Vinegar	Green Salad	Bread	Raw Veg Salad
Roll	Roll	Roll	Roll	Margarine	Whole Grain Bread
Margarine 1 tsp	Margarine	1 tsp Margarine	1 T Low Cal Dress	Can or Ckd Fruit	Margarine
Vanilla Ice Crm #8	Asst Dessert	Ice Cream	Jello	Jello	Fruit or Dessert
Vanilla Wafers	Milk/Tea/Coffee	Vanilla Wafers	Coffee/Tea/Skim Milk	Coffee/Tea/Milk	Coffee/Tea/Milk
Milk/Fruit Drink		1 c Milk/Tea/Coffee	*Egg Substitute	Limit Milk to 2c/day	
Cereal Beverage					

CERTIFIED _____ , R.D.

	Bland (No Pepper)	4 Gm Na (No Salt)	2 Gm Na (No Salt)	Low Fat/Low Chol	Low Fiber/ Low Residue	High Fiber	
B r e a k f a s t	Orange Juice Scrmb Eggs Crisp Bacon Hot Biscuit Margarine/Jelly Cereal Milk/Cereal Beverage	Orange Juice Scrmb Eggs 1 Sl Bacon Hot Biscuit Margarine/Jelly Cereal Milk/Tea/Coffee	Orange Juice FF Scrmb Eggs Toast 2 tsp Margarine/ Jelly SF Dry Cereal 1 c Milk/Tea/Coffee	Orange Juice 1 FF Egg (Pchd) Toast/Asst Breads 1 tsp Margarine/ Jelly FF Cereal Coffee/Tea/Skim Milk	Orange Juice Scrmb Egg Toast Margarine/Jelly Corn Flakes Coffee/Tea/Milk	Orange Juice Scrmb Egg Whole Grain Toast or Muffin Margarine/Jelly Shred Wheat Coffee/Tea/Milk	
D i n n e r	Sliced Turkey 2 oz Dressing #8 Spinach #8 Roll Margarine 1 tsp Sherbet #8 Milk/Fruit Drink	Sliced Turkey Dressing Spinach Salad Roll Margarine Asst Dessert Milk/Tea/Coffee	SF Sliced Turkey SF Dressing SF Spinach Salad Roll 2 tsp Margarine Sherbet Tea/Coffee	FF Sliced Turkey FF Dressing FF Spinach FF Salad 1 Roll 1 tsp Margarine Sherbet Coffee/Tea/Skim Milk	Sliced Turkey Dressing Spinach Roll Margarine Pl Cake or Cookie Coffee/Tea/Milk	Sliced Turkey Dressing Spinach Raw Veg Salad Whole Grain Bread Margarine Fruit or Dessert Coffee/Tea/Milk	
S u p p e r	Cubed Steak 3 oz Bu Potatoes #8 Broccoli #8 Roll Margarine 1 tsp Plain Cake Milk/Fruit Drink Cereal Beverage	Cubed Steak Bu Potatoes Broccoli Salad Roll Margarine Asst Dessert Milk/Tea/Coffee	Cubed Steak SF Potatoes SF Broccoli SF Salad Roll 2 tsp Margarine Plain Cake 1 c Milk/Tea/Coffee	FF Cubed Steaks 2 oz FF Potatoes FF Broccoli Sliced Tomatoes Roll 1 tsp Margarine Fruit Coffee/Tea/Skim Milk	Cubed Steak Bu Potatoes Carrots Fruit Coffee/Tea/Milk Limit Milk to 2c/day	Cubed Steak Bu Potatoes Broccoli Raw Veg Salad Whole Grain Bread Margarine Fruit or Dessert Coffee/Tea/Milk	

CERTIFIED _____, R.D.

401

Exhibit A–7 continued

WEEK NO. ___THREE___   DAY ___MONDAY___

MENU CYCLE ___SPRING/SUMMER___

	Bland (No Pepper)	4 Gm Na (No Salt)	2 Gm Na (No Salt)	Low Fat/Low Chol	Low Fiber/Low Residue	High Fiber	
B r e a k f a s t	Orange Juice 4 oz Boil Eggs 1 Crisp Bacon 1 sl Toast 1 Margarine 1 tsp/ Jelly Dry Cereal ¾ c Milk/Cereal Beverage	Orange Juice Boiled Eggs 1 Sl Bacon Toast Margarine/Jelly Dry Cereal Milk/Tea/Coffee	Orange Juice Boiled Eggs Toast Margarine/Jelly SF Dry Cereal 1 c Milk/Tea/Coffee	Orange Juice *FF Egg Toast 1 tsp Margarine/ Jelly Cereal Coffee/Tea/Skim Milk	Orange Juice Scrmb Egg Bacon or Saus Toast Rice Krispies Coffee/Tea/Milk	Orange Juice Scrmb Egg Bacon or Saus Whole Grain Bread Margarine/Jelly Raisin Bran Coffee/Tea/Milk	
D i n n e r	Salisb Steak 2 oz Rice #8 Okra/Tomatoes #8 Roll Margarine 1 tsp Sugar Cookies Milk/Fruit Drink	Salisbury Steak Rice Okra/Tomatoes Salad Roll Margarine Asst Desserts Milk/Tea/Coffee	SF Salisb Steak SF Rice ½ c SF Turnip Greens Salad 2 tsp Margarine Sugar Cookies Tea/Coffee	FF Salisb Steak 2 oz (No Gravy) FF Rice FF Okra/Tomatoes Salad/1 T Low Cal Dress 1 Roll Fruit Coffee/Tea/Skim Milk	Salisb Steak Rice Carrots Roll Margarine Jello Coffee/Tea/Milk	Veg Lasagna Rice Okra/Tomatoes Raw Veg Salad Whole Grain Bread Margarine Fruit or Dessert Coffee/Tea/Milk	
S u p p e r	Bkd Cod 2 oz Msh Potatoes #8 Gr Beans #8 Roll Margarine 1 tsp Pudd—No Choc Milk/Fruit Drink Cereal Beverage	Baked Cod Msh Potatoes Green Beans Roll Margarine Asst Desserts Milk/Tea/Coffee	SF Bkd Cod SF Msh Potatoes ½ c SF Can Gr Beans Roll 2 tsp Margarine Pudd/Fresh Fruit 1 c Milk/Tea/Coffee	FF Bkd Cod 2 oz FF Msh Potatoes FF Gr Beans Sliced Tomatoes Roll 1 tsp Margarine Sherbet Coffee/Tea/Skim Milk *Egg Substitute	Bkd Cod Msh Potatoes Gr Beans Potato Salad 1 Roll Margarine Can or Ckd Fruit Coffee/Tea/Milk Limit Milk to 2c/day	Bkd Cod Pinto Beans Gr Beans Raw Veg Salad Whole Grain Bread Margarine Fruit or Dessert Coffee/Tea/Milk	

CERTIFIED _____, R.D.

402

	Bland (No Pepper)	4 Gm Na (No Salt)	2 Gm Na (No Salt)	Low Fat/Low Chol	Low Fiber/Low Residue	High Fiber	
B r e a k f a s t	Orange Juice 4 oz / Scrmb Egg 1 / Dry Cereal ¾ c / English Muffin 1 / Margarine 1 tsp/ Jelly / Crisp Bacon 1 sl / Milk/Cereal Beverage	Orange Juice / Scrmb Egg / Dry Cereal / English Muffin / Margarine/Jelly / Crisp Bacon / Milk/Tea/Coffee	Orange Juice / Scrmb Eggs / SF Dry Cereal / 1 Toast / 2 tsp Margarine/ Jelly / Coffee/Skim Milk/ Tea	Orange Juice / *FF Egg / FF Dry Cereal / 1 Toast / 1 tsp Margarine / Coffee/Tea/Milk	Orange Juice / Scrmb Egg / 1 Toast / Corn Flakes / Coffee/Tea/Milk	Orange Juice / Scrmb Egg / Bacon or Saus / Shred Wheat / Whole Grain Bread or Muffin / Margarine / Coffee/Tea/Milk	
D i n n e r	Chicken Fillet 2 oz / Scall Potatoes #8 / Spinach #8 / Roll / Margarine 1 tsp / Cake / Milk/Fruit Drink	Chicken Fillet / Scall Potatoes / Spinach / Roll / Margarine / Salad / Asst Desserts / Milk/Tea/Coffee	SF Chicken / SF Scall Potatoes / ½ c Can or Froz Spinach SF / Roll / 2 tsp Margarine / Salad / Plain Cake / Tea/Coffee	FF Chicken 2 oz / FF Scall Potatoes / FF Spinach / 1 tsp Margarine / Carrot Salad/No Mayo / Jello / Coffee/Tea/Skim Milk	Chicken Fillet / Scall Potatoes / Spinach / Roll / Margarine / Can or Ckd Fruits / Coffee/Tea/Milk	Chicken Fillet / Scall Potatoes / Spinach / Whole Grain Bread / Margarine / Raw Veg Salad / Coffee/Tea/Milk	
S u p p e r	Roast Beef 2 oz / Parsl Bu Potatoes #8 / Gr Peas/Onions #8 / Roll / Margarine 1 tsp / Ice Cream / Milk/Fruit Drink / Cereal Beverage	Roast Beef / Parsl Bu Potatoes / Gr Peas/Onions / Roll / Margarine / Asst Desserts / Milk/Tea/Coffee	SF Rst Beef / SF Parsl Bu Potatoes / ½ c Gr Peas/ Onions / Tomatoes, Sliced / Roll / 2 tsp Margarine / Ice Cream / 1 c Milk/Tea/Coffee	FF Rst Beef 2 oz / FF Parsl Potatoes / FF Gr Peas/Onions / Garden Salad/Low Cal Dress / 1 Roll / Fruit / Coffee/Tea/Skim Milk / *Egg Substitute	Rst Beef / Potatoes/Parsley / Beets / Roll / Margarine / Plain Cake / Ice Cream / Coffee/Tea/Milk / Limit Milk to 2c/day	Rst Beef / Potatoes/Parsley / Yellow Squash / Raw Veg Salad / Whole Grain Bread / Margarine / Coffee/Tea/Milk	

CERTIFIED _____, R.D.

403

Exhibit A–7 continued

	1,000 Calorie	1,200 Calorie	1,500 Calorie	1,800 Calorie	2,000 Calorie	2,200 Calorie
Breakfast	½ c Orange Juice 1 FF Egg 1 tsp Margarine ¾ c Dry Cereal 1 c Skim Milk Coffee	½ c Orange Juice 1 FF Egg 1 Whole Grain Toast 1 tsp Margarine 1 c Skim Milk Coffee	½ c Orange Juice 1 FF Egg 1 Whole Grain Toast 2 tsp Margarine 1 c Skim Milk Coffee	½ c Orange Juice 1 FF Egg 2 Sl Whole Grain Toast 2 tsp Margarine 1 c Skim Milk Coffee	½ c Orange Juice 2 FF Eggs 2 Sl Whole Grain Toast 2 tsp Margarine 1 c Skim Milk Coffee	½ c Orange Juice 2 FF Eggs 2 Sl Whole Grain Toast 2 tsp Margarine ¾ c Dry Cereal 1 c Skim Milk Coffee
Dinner	1 oz Bkd Chicken ½ c FF Collards ½ c FF Carrots 1 tsp Margarine 1 sm Sliced Apple Coffee/Tea	2 oz Bkd Chicken ½ c Msh Potatoes ½ c FF Collards ½ c FF Carrots 1 tsp Margarine 1 sm Sliced Apple Coffee/Tea	2 oz Bkd Chicken ½ c Msh Potatoes ½ c FF Collards ½ c FF Carrots Roll 1 tsp Margarine 1 sm Sliced Apple Coffee/Tea	3 oz Bkd Chicken ½ c Msh Potatoes ½ c FF Collards ½ c FF Carrots Roll 2 tsp Margarine 1 sm Sliced Apple Coffee/Tea	3 oz Bkd Chicken 1 c Msh Potatoes ½ c FF Collards ½ c FF Carrots Roll 2 tsp Margarine 1 sm Sliced Apple Coffee/Tea	3 oz Bkd Chicken 1 c Msh Potatoes ½ c FF Collards ½ c FF Carrots Roll 2 tsp Margarine 1 sm Sliced Apple Coffee/Tea
Supper	2 oz Meatloaf ½ c FF Rice ½ c FF Stw Tomatoes ½ c Diet Frt Cockt Coffee/Tea	2 oz Meatloaf ½ c FF Rice ½ c FF Stw Tomatoes ½ c FF Oriental Veg 1 tsp Margarine ½ c Diet Frt Cockt Coffee/Tea	3 oz Meatloaf ½ c FF Rice ½ c FF Stw Tomatoes ½ c FF Oriental Veg Roll 1 tsp Margarine ½ c Diet Frt Cockt Coffee/Tea	3 oz Meatloaf ½ c FF Rice ½ c FF Stw Tomatoes ½ c FF Oriental Veg 2 Rolls 2 tsp Margarine ½ c Diet Frt Cockt Coffee/Tea	3 oz Meatloaf ½ c FF Rice ½ c FF Stw Tomatoes ½ c FF Oriental Veg 2 Rolls 2 tsp Margarine ½ c Diet Frt Cockt Coffee/Tea	4 oz Meatloaf ½ c FF Rice ½ c FF Stw Tomatoes ½ c FF Oriental Veg 2 Rolls 2 tsp Margarine 1 c Diet Frt Cockt Coffee/Tea
Snack	1 c Skim Milk	1 c Skim Milk 2 Graham Crackers	1 c Skim Milk 2 Graham Crackers	1 c Skim Milk 2 Graham Crackers	1 c Skim Milk 4 Graham Crackers	1 c Skim Milk 4 Graham Crackers

CERTIFIED _____, R.D.

404

	1,000 Calorie	1,200 Calorie	1,500 Calorie	1,800 Calorie	2,000 Calorie	2,200 Calorie	
B r e a k f a s t	½ c Orange Juice 1 FF Egg ½ Eng Muffin 1 tsp Margarine 1 c Skim Milk Coffee/Tea	½ c Orange Juice 1 FF Egg ½ Eng Muffin 1 tsp Margarine 1 c Skim Milk Coffee/Tea	½ c Orange Juice 1 FF Egg ½ Eng Muffin 2 tsp Margarine 1 c Skim Milk Coffee/Tea	½ c Orange Juice 1 FF Egg 1 Eng Muffin 2 tsp Margarine 1 c Skim Milk Coffee/Tea	½ c Orange Juice 2 FF Eggs 1 Eng Muffin 2 tsp Margarine 1 c Skim Milk Coffee/Tea	½ c Orange Juice 2 FF Eggs 1 Eng Muffin 2 tsp Margarine ¾ c Dry Cereal 1 c Skim Milk Coffee/Tea	
D i n n e r	1 oz Steamship Rnd ½ c FF Cauliflower ½ c FF Gr Beans ¼ c Cantaloupe 1 tsp Margarine Coffee/Tea	2 oz Steamship Rnd ½ c FF Cauliflower ½ c FF Gr Beans ½ c FF Potatoes ¼ c Cantaloupe 1 tsp Margarine Coffee/Tea	2 oz Steamship Rnd ½ c FF Cauliflower ½ c FF Gr Beans ½ c FF Potatoes ¼ c Cantaloupe Roll 1 tsp Margarine Coffee/Tea	3 oz Steamship Rnd ½ c FF Cauliflower ½ c FF Gr Beans ½ c FF Potatoes ¼ c Cantaloupe Roll 2 tsp Margarine Coffee/Tea	3 oz Steamship Rnd ½ c FF Cauliflower ½ c FF Gr Beans ½ c FF Potatoes ¼ c Cantaloupe 2 Rolls 2 tsp Margarine Coffee/Tea	3 oz Steamship Rnd ½ c FF Cauliflower ½ c FF Gr Beans ½ c FF Potatoes ¼ c Cantaloupe 2 Rolls 2 tsp Margarine Coffee/Tea	
S u p p e r	2 oz Cornish Hen ½ c FF Squash ½ c FF Noodles ½ c Diet Fruit Coffee/Tea	2 oz Cornish Hen ½ c FF Squash ½ c FF Brussel Sprts ½ c FF Noodles ½ c Diet Fruit 1 tsp Margarine Coffee/Tea	3 oz Cornish Hen ½ c FF Squash ½ c FF Brussel Sprts ½ c FF Noodles ½ c Diet Fruit Roll 1 tsp Margarine Coffee/Tea	3 oz Cornish Hen ½ c FF Squash ½ c FF Brussel Sprts ½ c FF Noodles ½ c Diet Fruit 2 Rolls 2 tsp Margarine Coffee/Tea	3 oz Cornish Hen ½ c FF Squash ½ c FF Brussel Sprts ½ c FF Noodles ½ c Diet Fruit 2 Rolls 2 tsp Margarine Coffee/Tea	4 oz Cornish Hen ½ c FF Squash ½ c FF Brussel Sprts ½ c FF Noodles 1 c Diet Fruit 2 Rolls 2 tsp Margarine Coffee/Tea	
S n a c k	1 c Skim Milk	1 c Skim Milk ¾ c Dry Cereal	1 c Skim Milk ¾ c Dry Cereal	1 c Skim Milk ¾ c Dry Cereal	1 c Skim Milk ¾ c Dry Cereal 2 Graham Crackers	1 c Skim Milk ¾ c Dry Cereal 2 Graham Crackers	

CERTIFIED _____, R.D.

405

Exhibit A-7 continued

	1,000 Calorie	1,200 Calorie	1,500 Calorie	1,800 Calorie	2,000 Calorie	2,200 Calorie	
B r e a k f a s t	½ c Orange Juice 1 FF Scrmb Egg 1 sl Toast 1 t Margarine 1 c Skim Milk Coffee/Tea	½ c Orange Juice 1 FF Scrmb Egg 1 sl Toast 1 t Margarine 1 c Skim Milk Coffee/Tea	½ c Orange Juice 1 FF Scrmb Egg 1 sl Toast 2 t Margarine 1 c Skim Milk Coffee/Tea	½ c Orange Juice 1 FF Scrmb Egg 2 sl Toast 2 t Margarine 1 c Skim Milk Coffee/Tea	½ c Orange Juice 2 FF Eggs 2 sl Toast 2 t Margarine 1 c Skim Milk Coffee/Tea	½ c Orange Juice 2 FF Eggs 2 sl Toast 2 t Margarine ¾ c Dry Cereal 1 c Skim Milk Coffee/Tea	
D i n n e r	1 oz Sliced Ham ½ c FF Turnip Greens ½ c FF Gr Beans 1 t Margarine ½ c Diet Peaches Coffee/Tea	2 oz Sliced Ham ½ c FF Turnip Greens ½ c FF Gr Beans ¼ c Sw Potatoes 1 t Margarine ½ c Diet Peaches Coffee/Tea	2 oz Sliced Ham ½ c FF Turnip Greens ½ c FF Gr Beans ¼ c Sw Potatoes Roll 1 t Margarine ½ c Diet Peaches Coffee/Tea	3 oz Sliced Ham ½ c FF Turnip Greens ½ c FF Gr Beans ¼ c Sw Potatoes Roll 2 t Margarine ½ c Diet Peaches Coffee/Tea	3 oz Sliced Ham ½ c FF Turnip Greens ½ c FF Gr Beans ¼ c Sw Potatoes 2 Rolls 2 t Margarine ½ c Diet Peaches Coffee/Tea	3 oz Sliced Ham ½ c FF Turnip Greens ½ c FF Gr Beans ¼ c Sw Potatoes 2 Rolls 2 t Margarine ½ c Diet Peaches Coffee/Tea	
S u p p e r	2 oz Steak 1 sm FF Bkd Potato ½ c FF Cauliflower ½ c Diet Mix Fruit Coffee/Tea	2 oz Steak 1 sm FF Bkd Potato ½ c FF Cauliflower ½ c FF Spinach 1 t Margarine ½ c Diet Mix Fruit Coffee/Tea	3 oz Steak 1 sm FF Bkd Potato ½ c FF Cauliflower ½ c FF Spinach Roll 1 t Margarine ½ c Diet Mix Fruit Coffee/Tea	3 oz Steak 1 sm FF Bkd Potato ½ c FF Cauliflower ½ c FF Spinach 2 Rolls 2 t Margarine ½ c Diet Mix Fruit Coffee/Tea	3 oz Steak 1 sm FF Bkd Potato ½ c FF Cauliflower ½ c FF Spinach 2 Rolls 2 t Margarine ½ c Diet Mix Fruit Coffee/Tea	4 oz Steak 1 sm FF Bkd Potato ½ c FF Cauliflower ½ c FF Spinach 2 Rolls 2 t Margarine 1 c Diet Fruit Coffee/Tea	
S n a c k	1 c Skim Milk	1 c Skim Milk 2 Graham Crackers	1 c Skim Milk 2 Graham Crackers	1 c Skim Milk 2 Graham Crackers	1 c Skim Milk 4 Graham Crackers	1 c Skim Milk 4 Graham Crackers	

CERTIFIED _____, R.D.

	1,000 Calorie	1,200 Calorie	1,500 Calorie	1,800 Calorie	2,000 Calorie	2,200 Calorie	
Breakfast	½ c Orange Juice 1 FF Egg 1 Biscuit 1 c Skim Milk Coffee/Tea	½ c Orange Juice 1 FF Egg 1 Biscuit 1 c Skim Milk Coffee/Tea	½ c Orange Juice 1 FF Egg 1 Biscuit 1 t Margarine 1 c Skim Milk Coffee/Tea	½ c Orange Juice 1 FF Egg 2 Biscuits 1 c Skim Milk Coffee/Tea	½ c Orange Juice 2 FF Eggs 2 Biscuits 1 c Skim Milk Coffee/Tea	½ c Orange Juice 2 FF Eggs 2 Biscuits ¾ c Dry Cereal 1 c Skim Milk Coffee/Tea	
Dinner	1 oz Lemon Bkd Fish ½ c FF Squash ½ c FF Fr Gr Beans 1 t Margarine ½ c Diet Pears Coffee/Tea	2 oz Lemon Bkd Fish ½ c FF Squash ½ c FF Fr Gr Beans ½ c FF Potato Gems 1 t Margarine ½ c Diet Pears Coffee/Tea	2 oz Lemon Bkd Fish ½ c FF Squash ½ c FF Fr Gr Beans ½ c FF Potato Gems Roll 1 t Margarine ½ c Diet Pears Coffee/Tea	3 oz Lemon Bkd Fish ½ c FF Squash ½ c FF Fr Gr Beans ½ c FF Potato Gems Roll 2 t Margarine ½ c Diet Pears Coffee/Tea	3 oz Lemon Bkd Fish ½ c FF Squash ½ c FF Fr Gr Beans ½ c FF Potato Gems 2 Rolls 2 t Margarine ½ c Diet Pears Coffee/Tea	3 oz Lemon Bkd Fish ½ c FF Squash ½ c FF Fr Gr Beans ½ c FF Potato Gems 2 Rolls 2 t Margarine ½ c Diet Pears Coffee/Tea	
Supper	2 oz Meat Patty ½ c FF Ital Veg ⅓ c FF Corn ½ c Fresh Fruit Coffee/Tea	2 oz Meat Patty ½ c FF Ital Veg ½ c FF Beets ⅓ c FF Corn 1 t Margarine ½ c Fresh Fruit Coffee/Tea	3 oz Meat Patty ½ c FF Ital Veg ½ c FF Beets ⅓ c FF Corn Roll 1 t Margarine ½ c Fresh Fruit Coffee/Tea	3 oz Meat Patty ½ c FF Ital Veg ½ c FF Beets ⅓ c FF Corn 2 Rolls 2 t Margarine ½ c Fresh Fruit Coffee/Tea	3 oz Meat Patty ½ c FF Ital Veg ½ c FF Beets ⅓ c FF Corn 2 Rolls 2 t Margarine ½ c Fresh Fruit Coffee/Tea	4 oz Meat Patty ½ c FF Ital Veg ½ c FF Beets ⅓ c FF Corn 2 Rolls 2 t Margarine 1 c Fresh Fruit Coffee/Tea	
Snack	1 c Skim Milk	1 c Skim Milk 2 Graham Crackers	1 c Skim Milk 2 Graham Crackers	1 c Skim Milk 2 Graham Crackers	1 c Skim Milk 4 Graham Crackers	1 c Skim Milk 4 Graham Crackers	

CERTIFIED _____, R.D.

407

Exhibit A–7 continued

WEEK NO. ___THREE___   DAY ___SUNDAY___   MENU CYCLE ___SPRING/SUMMER___

	1,000 Calorie	1,200 Calorie	1,500 Calorie	1,800 Calorie	2,000 Calorie	2,200 Calorie	
B r e a k f a s t	½ c Orange Juice 1 FF Egg 1 Biscuit 1 c Skim Milk Coffee/Tea	½ c Orange Juice 1 FF Egg 1 Biscuit 1 c Skim Milk Coffee/Tea	½ c Orange Juice 1 FF Egg 1 Biscuit 1 t Margarine 1 c Skim Milk Coffee/Tea	½ c Orange Juice 1 FF Egg 2 Biscuits 1 c Skim Milk Coffee/Tea	½ c Orange Juice 2 FF Eggs 2 Biscuits 1 c Skim Milk Coffee/Tea	½ c Orange Juice 2 FF Eggs 2 Biscuits ¾ c Dry Cereal 1 c Skim Milk Coffee/Tea	
D i n n e r	1 oz FF Turkey ½ c FF Spinach ½ c Sliced Tomatoes 1 t Margarine ½ c Diet Fruit Coffee/Tea	2 oz FF Turkey ¼ c Dressing ½ c FF Spinach ½ c Sliced Tomatoes 1 t Margarine ½ c Diet Fruit Coffee/Tea	2 oz FF Turkey ½ c Dressing ½ c FF Spinach ½ c Sliced Tomatoes 1 t Margarine ½ c Diet Fruit Coffee/Tea	3 oz FF Turkey ½ c Dressing ½ c FF Spinach ½ c Sliced Tomatoes 2 t Margarine ½ c Diet Fruit Coffee/Tea	3 oz FF Turkey ½ c Dressing ½ c FF Spinach ½ c Sliced Tomatoes Roll 2 t Margarine ½ c Diet Fruit Coffee/Tea	3 oz FF Turkey ½ c Dressing ½ c FF Spinach ½ c Sliced Tomatoes Roll 2 t Margarine ½ c Diet Fruit Coffee/Tea	
S u p p e r	2 oz FF Cube Steak ½ c FF Broccoli Roll ½ c Diet Fruit Coffee/Tea	2 oz FF Cube Steak ½ c FF Broccoli ½ c FF Carrots ½ c FF Potatoes 1 t Margarine ½ c Diet Fruit Coffee/Tea	3 oz FF Cube Steak ½ c FF Broccoli ½ c FF Carrots ½ c FF Potatoes Roll 1 t Margarine ½ c Diet Fruit Coffee/Tea	3 oz FF Cube Steak ½ c FF Broccoli ½ c FF Carrots ½ c FF Potatoes 2 Rolls 2 t Margarine ½ c Diet Fruit Coffee/Tea	3 oz FF Cube Steak ½ c FF Broccoli ½ c FF Carrots ½ c FF Potatoes 2 Rolls 2 t Margarine ½ c Diet Fruit Coffee/Tea	4 oz FF Cube Steak ½ c FF Broccoli ½ c FF Carrots ½ c FF Potatoes 2 Rolls 2 t Margarine 1 c Diet Fruit Coffee/Tea	
S n a c k	1 c Skim Milk	1 c Skim Milk 5 Vanilla Wafers	1 c Skim Milk 5 Vanilla Wafers	1 c Skim Milk 5 Vanilla Wafers	1 c Skim Milk 10 Vanilla Wafers	1 c Skim Milk 10 Vanilla Wafers	

CERTIFIED _____, R.D.

408

	1,000 Calorie	1,200 Calorie	1,500 Calorie	1,800 Calorie	2,000 Calorie	2,200 Calorie
Breakfast	½ c Orange Juice 1 FF Egg 1 sl Toast 1 t Margarine 1 c Skim Milk Coffee/Tea	½ c Orange Juice 1 FF Egg 1 sl Toast 1 t Margarine 1 c Skim Milk Coffee/Tea	½ c Orange Juice 1 FF Egg 1 sl Toast 2 t Margarine 1 c Skim Milk Coffee/Tea	½ c Orange Juice 1 FF Egg 2 sl Toast 2 t Margarine 1 c Skim Milk Coffee/Tea	½ c Orange Juice 2 FF Eggs 2 sl Toast 2 t Margarine 1 c Skim Milk Coffee/Tea	½ c Orange Juice 2 FF Eggs 2 sl Toast 2 t Margarine ¾ c Dry Cereal 1 c Skim Milk Coffee/Tea
Dinner	Chef Salad 1 oz Cheese 1 c Lettuce ½ c Tomato 1 T Dressing ½ c Diet Fruit Coffee/Tea	2 oz Bkd Chicken ½ c FF Okra/ Tomato ½ c FF Squash ½ c FF Rice 1 t Margarine ½ c Diet Fruit Coffee/Tea	2 oz Bkd Chicken ½ c FF Okra/ Tomato ½ c FF Squash ½ c FF Rice Roll 1 t Margarine ½ c Diet Fruit Coffee/Tea	3 oz Bkd Chicken ½ c FF Okra/ Tomato ½ c FF Squash ½ c FF Rice Roll 2 t Margarine ½ c Diet Fruit Coffee/Tea	3 oz Bkd Chicken ½ c FF Okra/ Tomato ½ c FF Squash ½ c FF Rice 2 Rolls 2 t Margarine ½ c Diet Fruit Coffee/Tea	3 oz Bkd Chicken ½ c FF Okra/ Tomato ½ c FF Squash ½ c FF Rice 2 Rolls 2 t Margarine ½ c Diet Fruit Coffee/Tea
Supper	2 oz Baked Cod ½ c FF Gr Beans ½ c FF Pinto Beans 1 sm Apple Coffee/Tea	2 oz Bkd Cod ½ c FF Gr Beans ½ c FF Squash ½ c FF Pinto Beans 1 t Margarine ½ c Diet Fruit Coffee/Tea	3 oz Bkd Cod ½ c FF Gr Beans ½ c FF Squash ½ c FF Pinto Beans Roll 1 t Margarine ½ c Diet Fruit Coffee/Tea	3 oz Bkd Cod ½ c FF Gr Beans ½ c FF Squash ½ c FF Pinto Beans 2 Rolls 2 t Margarine ½ c Diet Fruit Coffee/Tea	3 oz Bkd Cod ½ c FF Gr Beans ½ c FF Squash ½ c FF Pinto Beans 2 Rolls 2 t Margarine ½ c Diet Fruit Coffee/Tea	4 oz Bkd Cod ½ c FF Gr Beans ½ c FF Squash ½ c FF Pinto Beans 2 Rolls 2 t Margarine 1 c Diet Fruit Coffee/Tea
Snack	1 c Skim Milk	1 c Skim Milk 6 Saltines	1 c Skim Milk 6 Saltines	1 c Skim Milk 6 Saltines	1 c Skim Milk 12 Saltines	1 c Skim Milk 12 Saltines

CERTIFIED _____, R.D.

409

Exhibit A–7 continued

WEEK NO. ___THREE___ DAY ___TUESDAY___ MENU CYCLE ___SPRING/SUMMER___

	1,000 Calorie	1,200 Calorie	1,500 Calorie	1,800 Calorie	2,000 Calorie	2,200 Calorie	
Breakfast	½ c Orange Juice 1 FF Egg ½ Eng Muffin 1 t Margarine 1 c Skim Milk Coffee/Tea	½ c Orange Juice 1 FF Egg ½ Eng Muffin 1 t Margarine 1 c Skim Milk Coffee/Tea	½ c Orange Juice 1 FF Egg ½ Eng Muffin 2 t Margarine 1 c Skim Milk Coffee/Tea	½ c Orange Juice 1 FF Egg 1 Eng Muffin 2 t Margarine 1 c Skim Milk Coffee/Tea	½ c Orange Juice 2 FF Eggs 1 Eng Muffin 2 t Margarine 1 c Skim Milk Coffee/Tea	½ c Orange Juice 2 FF Eggs 1 Eng Muffin 2 t Margarine ¾ c Dry Cereal 1 c Skim Milk Coffee/Tea	
Dinner	1 oz Meatloaf ½ c FF Spinach ½ c FF Cauliflower 1 t Margarine ½ c Diet Fruit Coffee/Tea	2 oz Meatloaf ½ c FF Spinach ½ c FF Cauliflower ½ c FF Potatoes 1 t Margarine ½ c Diet Fruit Coffee/Tea	2 oz Meatloaf ½ c FF Spinach ½ c FF Cauliflower ½ c FF Potatoes Roll 1 t Margarine ½ c Diet Fruit Coffee/Tea	3 oz Meatloaf ½ c FF Spinach ½ c FF Cauliflower ½ c FF Potatoes Roll 2 t Margarine ½ c Diet Fruit Coffee/Tea	3 oz Meatloaf ½ c FF Spinach ½ c FF Cauliflower ½ c FF Potatoes 2 Rolls 2 t Margarine ½ c Diet Fruit Coffee/Tea	3 oz Meatloaf ½ c FF Spinach ½ c FF Cauliflower ½ c FF Potatoes 2 Rolls 2 t Margarine ½ c Diet Fruit Coffee/Tea	
Supper	2 oz Roast Beef ½ c FF Yel Squash ½ c FF Potatoes ½ c Fresh Fruit Coffee/Tea	2 oz Rst Beef ½ c FF Yel Squash ½ c FF Beets ½ c FF Potatoes 1 t Margarine ½ c Fresh Fruit Coffee/Tea	3 oz Rst Beef ½ c FF Yel Squash ½ c FF Beets ½ c FF Potatoes Roll 1 t Margarine ½ c Fresh Fruit Coffee/Tea	3 oz Rst Beef ½ c FF Yel Squash ½ c FF Beets ½ c FF Potatoes 2 Rolls 2 t Margarine ½ c Fresh Fruit Coffee/Tea	3 oz Rst Beef ½ c FF Yel Squash ½ c FF Beets ½ c FF Potatoes 2 Rolls 2 t Margarine ½ c Fresh Fruit Coffee/Tea	4 oz Rst Beef ½ c FF Yel Squash ½ c FF Beets ½ c FF Potatoes 2 Rolls 2 t Margarine 1 c Fresh Fruit Coffee/Tea	
Snack	1 c Skim Milk	1 c Skim Milk 5 Ritz Crackers	1 c Skim Milk 5 Ritz Crackers	1 c Skim Milk 5 Ritz Crackers	1 c Skim Milk 10 Ritz Crackers	1 c Skim Milk 10 Ritz Crackers	

CERTIFIED _____, R.D.

410

Purchasing/Production Guide

SELECTIVE, HOSPITAL, SPRING/SUMMER CYCLE

Southeastern U.S.

Table B–1 Meats/Entrees

Item*	Size of purchase unit	Portion control size	Service utensil used**	#Serv./ purchase unit	#Times offered on Cycle 1	Cycle 2	Cycle 3	Serving extensions: 20	60	100	150	200	300
Beef*													
Gooseneck	per lb.	3 oz.	Spatula	5	1	2	2	8 lb.	24 lb.	40 lb.	60 lb.	80 lb.	120 lb.
Chuck roast	per lb.	2 oz.	Spatula	6	—	—	—	4 lb.	10 lb.	17 lb.	26 lb.	34 lb.	51 lb.
Flank steak	per lb.	2 oz.	Tongs	6	1	—	1	5 lb.	15 lb.	25 lb.	37.5 lb.	50 lb.	75 lb.
Cubes/tips	per lb.	2 oz.	#16 Scoop	6	3	1	1	4 lb.	10 lb.	17 lb.	25.5 lb.	34 lb.	51 lb.
Ground	per lb.	2 oz.	#16 Scoop	6	4	3	4	4 lb.	10 lb.	17 lb.	25.5 lb.	34 lb.	51 lb.
Ribs	per lb.	2 oz.	Tongs	8	1	—	—	15 lb.	45 lb.	75 lb.	112.5 lb.	150 lb.	225 lb.
Liver	per lb.	2 oz.	Spatula	8	—	—	—	2.5 lb.	7.5 lb.	12.5 lb.	19 lb.	25 lb.	37.5 lb.
Corned beef	per lb.	2 oz.	Tongs	8	1	1	0	10 lb.	30 lb.	50 lb.	75 lb.	100 lb.	150 lb.
Steaks:													
Chuckwagon	per lb.	2 oz.	Tongs	6	1	1	—	4 lb.	10 lb.	17 lb.	25.5 lb.	34 lb.	51 lb.
Cubed	per lb.	2 oz.	Tongs	6	—	—	1	4 lb.	10 lb.	17 lb.	25.5 lb.	34 lb.	51 lb.
Patty, H.B.	per lb.	2 oz.	Tongs	6	—	2	—	4 lb.	10 lb.	17 lb.	25.5 lb.	34 lb.	51 lb.
Salisbury	per lb.	2 oz.	Spatula	6	1	0	1	4 lb.	10 lb.	17 lb.	25.5 lb.	34 lb.	51 lb.
Veal cutlet	per lb.	2 oz.	Tongs	6	1	—	—	4 lb.	10 lb.	17 lb.	25.5 lb.	34 lb.	51 lb.
Chicken													
1/8 Whole fryer	per lb.	1/8 Chicken	Tongs	5 fry/15 lbs.	2	1	1	3 frys.	9 frys.	15 frys.	23 frys.	30 frys.	45 frys.
Fillet, brd.	per lb.	2 oz.	Tongs	8	—	1	1	2.5 lb.	7.5 lb.	12.5 lb.	18.75 lb.	25 lb.	50 lb.
Turkey, whole	per lb.	2 oz.	Tongs	8	—	—	—	15 lb.	45 lb.	75 lb.	112.5 lb.	150 lb.	225 lb.
Nuggets			#16 Scoop		—	1	1						
Hens, whole	per lb.	2 oz.	Tongs	4	—	1	—	5 lb.	15 lb.	25 lb.	37.5 lb.	50 lb.	75 lb.
Turkey breast	per lb.	2 oz.	Tongs	4	1	1	—	7 lb.	21 lb.	35 lb.	52.5 lb.	70 lb.	105 lb.

Item	Purchase Unit	Portion	Utensil	Servings									
Turkey roll	per lb.	2 oz.	Tongs	8	1	—	—	2.5 lb.	7.5 lb.	12.5 lb.	18.75 lb.	25 lb.	37.5 lb.
Cornish hens	per lb.	3 oz.	Tongs	5	—	—	1	4 lb.	12 lb.	20 lb.	30 lb.	40 lb.	60 lb.
Livers	per lb.	3 oz.	Tongs		1	—	—	—	—	—	—	—	—
Fish													
Fillet	per lb.	2 oz.	Spatula	8	2	2	2	2.5 lb.	7.5 lb.	12.5 lb.	18.75 lb.	25 lb.	37.5 lb.
Tuna	6-66.5 oz.	2 oz.	#16 Scoop	3¾ lb.-2.5 oz.	—	—	1	1 can	2 can	3 can	5 can	6 can	9 can
Pork													
Chops	per lb.	2 oz.	Tongs	5/lb.	—	1	—	4 lb.	12 lb.	20 lb.	30 lb.	40 lb.	30 lb.
Bacon	per lb.	1 oz.	Tongs	6	7	7	7	4 lb.	10 lb.	17 lb.	25.5 lb.	34 lb.	51 lb.
Sausage-link/patty	per lb.	2 oz.			7	7	7	3 lb.	9 lb.	15 lb.	23 lb.	30 lb.	45 lb.
Bologna, beef	per lb.	2 oz.	Tongs	8	—	—	—	2.5 lb.	7.5 lb.	12.5 lb.	18.75 lb.	25 lb.	37.5 lb.
Italian sausage	per lb.	2 oz.	Tongs	8	1	1	1	2.5 lb.	7.5 lb.	12.5 lb.	18.75 lb.	25 lb.	37.5 lb.
Ham	per lb.	2 oz.	Tongs	6	—	—	3	4 lb.	10 lb.	17 lb.	25.5 lb.	34 lb.	51 lb.
Ribs	per lb.		Tongs		—	1	—	12 lb.	36 lb.	60 lb.	90 lb.	120 lb.	180 lb.
Wieners, beef	per lb.	2 oz.	Tongs	8	—	—	—	2.5 lb.	7.5 lb.	12.5 lb.	18.75 lb.	25 lb.	37.5 lb.
Roast	per lb.	2 oz.	Tongs	8	2	1	1	4 lb.	10 lb.	17 lb.	25.5 lb.	34 lb.	51 lb.
Other													
Eggs, fresh	per doz.	2 oz.	#16 Scoop	6	7	8	8	4 dz.	10 dz.	17 dz.	25.5 dz.	34 dz.	51 dz.
Cheese	per lb.	2 oz.	Tongs	8	1	1	2	2.5 lb.	7.5 lb.	12.5 lb.	18.75 lb.	25 lb.	37.5 lb.
Veal cutlet	per lb.	2 oz.	Tongs	8	1	—	—	2.5 lb.	7.5 lb.	12.5 lb.	18.75 lb.	25 lb.	37.5 lb.
Polish sausage	per lb.	2 oz.	Tongs	8	1	—	1	2.5 lb.	7.5 lb.	12.5 lb.	18.75 lb.	25 lb.	37.5 lb.
Shrimp	per lb.	2 oz.	Tongs	8	—	—	1	2.5 lb.					
Clams	per lb.	2 oz.	Tongs	8	—	—	—						
Lamb roast	per lb.	3 oz.	Tongs	5	—	1	—						
Salmon					—	—	—	7.2 lb.	22 lb.	36 lb.	54 lb.	72 lb.	108 lb.
Pancake					1	6	1						

*.25% shrinkage figured in when six 2 oz. servings are identified per lb. purchase.
**Where a service utensil other than a #16 scoop is used, a portion control scale must be utilized.

413

Table B–2 Vegetables

Item*	Size of purchase unit	Portion control size	Service utensil used**	#Serv./ purchase unit	#Times offered on Cycle 1	Cycle 2	Cycle 3	Serving extensions: 20	60	100	150	200	300
Cans													
Beets													
Sliced	6-#10	2 oz.	#16 Scoop	46-#10	—	1	3	1-#10	2-#10	2-#10	3-#10	4-#10	6-#10
Diced	6-#10	2 oz.	#16 Scoop	46-#10	4	1	—	1-#10	2-#10	2-#10	3-#10	4-#10	6-#10
Beans													
Brown	6-#10	2 oz.	#16 Scoop	48-#10	0	0	0	1-#10	2-#10	2-#10	3-#10	4-#10	6-#10
Northern	6-#10	2 oz.	#16 Scoop	46-#10	1	0	0	1-#10	2-#10	2-#10	3-#10	4-#10	6-#10
Green	6-#10	2 oz.	#16 Scoop	46-#10	4	4	4	1-#10	2-#10	2-#10	3-#10	4-#10	6-#10
Kidney	6-#10	2 oz.	#16 Scoop	46-#10	—	0	0	1-#10	2-#10	2-#10	3-#10	4-#10	6-#10
Lima	6-#10	2 oz.	#16 Scoop	46-#10	1	1	1	1-#10	2-#10	2-#10	3-#10	4-#10	6-#10
Wax	6-#10	2 oz.	#16 Scoop	46-#10	—	0	—	1-#10	2-#10	2-#10	3-#10	4-#10	6-#10
Carrots	6-#10	2 oz.	#16 Scoop	46-#10	4½	2½	2	1-#10	2-#10	2-#10	3-#10	4-#10	6-#10
Corn	6-#10	2 oz.	#16 Scoop	46-#10	—	0	3	1-#10	2-#10	2-#10	3-#10	4-#10	6-#10
Greens	6-#10	2 oz.	#16 Scoop	46-#10	—	1	0	1-#10	2-#10	2-#10	3-#10	4-#10	6-#10
Hominy	6-#10	2 oz.	#16 Scoop	42-#10	—	0	0	1-#10	2-#10	2-#10	3-#10	4-#10	6-#10
Mixed vegetables	6-#10	2 oz.	#16 Scoop	46-#10	2	3	3	1-#10	2-#10	2-#10	3-#10	4-#10	6-#10
Peas													
Crowder	6-#10	2 oz.	#16 Scoop	46-#10	—	0	1	1-#10	2-#10	2-#10	3-#10	4-#10	6-#10
Green	6-#10	2 oz.	#16 Scoop	46-#10	2½	2	2	1-#10	2-#10	2-#10	3-#10	4-#10	6-#10
Potato													
Mashed	6-#10	2 oz.	#16 Scoop	280-#10	2	2	2	Less than 1-#10—Follow Label Directions					
Dehydrated					—	1	1						
Sweet	6-#10	2 oz.	#16 Scoop	40-#10	3	2	2	1-#10	2-#10	2-#10	3-#10	4-#10	6-#10
Whole	6-#10	2 oz.	#16 Scoop	46-#10	1	2	1	1-#10	2-#10	2-#10	3-#10	4-#10	6-#10
Sauerkraut	6-#10	2 oz.	#16 Scoop	42-#10	1	1	—	1-#10	2-#10	2-#10	3-#10	4-#10	6-#10
Spinach	6-#10	2 oz.	#16 Scoop	42-#10	3	2	2	1-#10	2-#10	2-#10	3-#10	4-#10	6-#10

Tomatoes

Item	Pack	Serving	Utensil	Yield									
Diced	6-#10	2 oz.	#16 Scoop	46-#10	—	2	—	1-#10	2-#10	2-#10	3-#10	4-#10	6-#10
Sauce	6-#10	2 oz.	#16 Scoop	46-#10	—	3	—	2-#10	2-#10	2-#10	3-#10	4-#10	6-#10
Stewed	6-#10	2 oz.	#16 Scoop	46-#10	—	—	1	1-#10	2-#10	2-#10	3-#10	4-#10	6-#10
Squash, yellow	6-#10	2 oz.	#16 Scoop	46-#10	1	2	1	1-#10	2-#10	2-#10	3-#10	4-#10	6-#10
Okra, tomatoes					—	1/0	1						
Zucchini, tomatoes	6-#10	2 oz.	#16 Scoop	42-#10	—	2/0	0	1-#10	2-#10	2-#10	3-#10	4-#10	6-#10

Frozen

Item	Pack	Serving	Utensil	Yield									
Beans, lima	20 lb.	2 oz.	#16 Scoop	8 lb.	—	0	—	2.6 lb.	7.5 lb.	12.5 lb.	18 lb.	25 lb.	37.5 lb.
Broccoli	12-2 lb.	2 oz.	#16 Scoop	8 lb.	2	3	1	2.6 lb.	7.5 lb.	12.5 lb.	18 lb.	25 lb.	37.5 lb.
Brussel sprouts	12-3 lb.	2 oz.	#16 Scoop	8 lb.	2	1	1	2.6 lb.	7.5 lb.	12.5 lb.	18 lb.	25 lb.	37.5 lb.
Carrots	20 lb.	2 oz.	#16 Scoop	8 lb.	—	0	0	2.6 lb.	7.5 lb.	12.5 lb.	18 lb.	25 lb.	37.5 lb.
Cauliflower	12-2 lb.	2 oz.	#16 Scoop	8 lb.	1	0	3	2.6 lb.	7.5 lb.	12.5 lb.	18 lb.	25 lb.	37.5 lb.
Corn	20 lb.	2 oz.	#16 Scoop	8 lb.	—	0	0	2.6 lb.	7.5 lb.	12.5 lb.	18 lb.	25 lb.	37.5 lb.
Greens	12-3 lb.	2 oz.	#16 Scoop	8 lb.	2	1	0	2.6 lb.	7.5 lb.	12.5 lb.	18 lb.	25 lb.	37.5 lb.
Mixed vegetables	20 lb.	2 oz.	#16 Scoop	8 lb.	—	0	1	2.6 lb.	7.5 lb.	12.5 lb.	18 lb.	25 lb.	37.5 lb.
Italian winter vegs.	20 lb.	2 oz.	#16 Scoop	8 lb.	1	1	0	2.6 lb.	7.5 lb.	12.5 lb.	18 lb.	25 lb.	37.5 lb.
Okra, breaded	20 lb.	2 oz.	#16 Scoop	8 lb.	1	1	1	2.6 lb.	7.5 lb.	12.5 lb.	18 lb.	25 lb.	37.5 lb.
Peas, green	20 lb.	2 oz.	#16 Scoop	8 lb.	—	0	0	2.6 lb.	7.5 lb.	12.5 lb.	18 lb.	25 lb.	37.5 lb.
Onion rings	20 lb.	2 oz.	Tongs	8 lb.	—	—	1	2.6 lb.	7.5 lb.	12.5 lb.	18 lb.	25 lb.	37.5 lb.
Potatoes													
Hash browns	18 lb.	2 oz.	#16 Scoop	8 lb.	—	1	1	2.6 lb.	7.5 lb.	12.5 lb.	18 lb.	25 lb.	37.5 lb.
Tater Tots	6-5 lb.	6–8	Tongs	8 lb.	—	2	1	2.6 lb.	7.5 lb.	12.5 lb.	18 lb.	25 lb.	37.5 lb.
Steak fries	168-2 oz.	2 oz. (1 Patty)	Spatula	168	1	1	1	2.6 lb.	7.5 lb.	12.5 lb.	18 lb.	25 lb.	37.5 lb.
Sweet, patties					—	0	0	20	60	100	150	200	300
Spinach	12-3 lb.	2 oz.	#16 Scoop	8 lb.	—	0	0	2.6 lb.	7.5 lb.	12.5 lb.	18 lb.	25 lb.	37.5 lb.
Succotash	12-2 lb.	2 oz.	#16 Scoop	8 lb.	1	0	0	2.6 lb.	7.5 lb.	12.5 lb.	18 lb.	25 lb.	37.5 lb.
Summer squash	12-3 lb.	2 oz.	#16 Scoop	8 lb.	—	1	0	2.6 lb.	7.5 lb.	12.5 lb.	18 lb.	25 lb.	37.5 lb.
Zucchini					—	—	1	2.6 lb.	7.5 lb.	12.5 lb.	18 lb.	25 lb.	37.5 lb.

*When vegetables can be purchased either canned or frozen, "# Times offered" section is identified for the canned category only to avoid redundancies.
**#8 scoop is used for KCAL-controlled diets (4 oz.); #16 scoop is used for all other diets (2 oz.)

415

Table B-2 Vegetables, continued

Item*	Size of purchase unit	Portion control size	Service utensil used**	#Serv./ purchase unit	#Times offered on Cycle 1	#Times offered on Cycle 2	#Times offered on Cycle 3	Serving extensions: 20	60	100	150	200	300
Fresh													
Cabbage	per lb.	2 oz.	#16 Scoop	7	1	1	0	3 lb.	8.5 lb.	14 lb.	21 lb.	28 lb.	42 lb.
Carrots (for salad)	per lb.	Used in salads		See recipe	—	—	1	See recipe					
Cucumbers	per lb.	Used in salads		See recipe	—	—	0	See recipe					
Eggplant	per lb.	2 oz.	Tongs		—	—	1						
Lettuce	per head	Used in salads		See recipe	—	—	—	See recipe					
Potatoes:													
Baking	per lb.	2 oz.	Tongs	8	2	2	1	2.5 lb.	7.5 lb.	12.5 lb.	18 lb.	25 lb.	37.5 lb.
Boiling	per lb.	2 oz.	#16 Scoop	7	—	—	—	3 lb.	8.5 lb.	14 lb.	21 lb.	28 lb.	42 lb.
Tomatoes (slices)	per lb.	2½" sls.	Tongs	12–16 sl.	14	14	14	3 lb.	8.5 lb.	14 lb.	21 lb.	28 lb.	42 lb.
Turnips (for salad)	per lb.	Used in salads		See recipe	—	—	—	See recipe					
Dry													
Beans:													
Navy	per lb.	2 oz.	#16 Scoop	24 lb.	—	0	—	1 lb.	1.5 lb.	4.5 lb.	7 lb.	9 lb.	13.5 lb.
Blackeye peas	per lb.	2 oz.	#16 Scoop	24 lb.	1	0	1	1 lb.	1.5 lb.	4.5 lb.	7 lb.	9 lb.	13.5 lb.
Pinto	per lb.	2 oz.	#16 Scoop	24 lb.	—	0	1	1 lb.	1.5 lb.	4.5 lb.	7 lb.	9 lb.	13.5 lb.
Chinese Noodles	per lb.	4 oz.	#8 Scoop	4	1	0	1	1 lb.	1.5 lb.	4.5 lb.	7 lb.	9 lb.	13.5 lb.

Table B-3 Fruits

Item*	Size of purchase unit	Portion control size	Service utensil used**	#Serv./ purchase unit**	#Times offered on† Cycle 1	Cycle 2	Cycle 3	Serving extensions: 20	60	100	150	200	300
Canned													
Apples													
A-butter	6-#10	Used in A-butter cake		See recipe	—	—	—	See recipe					
A-sauce	6-#10	4 oz.	#8 Scoop	52-#10	—	—	—	1-#10	2-#10	2-#10	3-#10	4-#10	6-#10
Sliced	6-#10	4 oz.	#8 Scoop	42-#10	—	—	—	1-#10	2-#10	2-#10	3-#10	4-#10	6-#10
Citrus sections	6-#10	4 oz.	#8 Scoop	42-#10	—	—	—	1-#10	2-#10	2-#10	3-#10	4-#10	6-#10
Fruit cocktail	6-#10	4 oz.	#8 Scoop	46-#10	—	—	—	1-#10	2-#10	2-#10	3-#10	4-#10	6-#10
Pears, diced	6-#10	4 oz.	#8 Scoop	46-#10	—	—	—	1-#10	2-#10	2-#10	3-#10	4-#10	6-#10
Peaches, diced	6-#10	4 oz.	#8 Scoop	46-#10	—	—	—	1-#10	2-#10	2-#10	3-#10	4-#10	6-#10
Pineapple													
Chunks	6-#10	4 oz.	#8 Scoop	46-#10	—	—	—	1-#10	2-#10	2-#10	3-#10	4-#10	6-#10
Crushed	6-#10	4 oz.	#8 Scoop	48-#10	—	—	—	1-#10	2-#10	2-#10	3-#10	4-#10	6-#10
Plums													
Dried (prunes)	6-#10	4 oz.	#8 Scoop	40-#10	—	—	—	1-#10	2-#10	2-#10	3-#10	4-#10	6-#10
Purple	6-#10	4 oz.	#8 Scoop	40-#10	—	—	—	1-#10	2-#10	2-#10	3-#10	4-#10	6-#10
Water packed††													
Apples	6-#10	4 oz.	#8 Scoop	42-#10	—	1	—	1-#10	2-#10	2-#10	3-#10	4-#10	6-#10
Apricots	6-#10	4 oz.	#8 Scoop	42-#10	—	—	—	1-#10	2-#10	2-#10	3-#10	4-#10	6-#10
Citrus sections	6-#10	4 oz.	#8 Scoop	42-#10	—	—	—	1-#10	2-#10	2-#10	3-#10	4-#10	6-#10
Fruit cocktail	6-#10	4 oz.	#8 Scoop	46-#10	—	1	—	1-#10	2-#10	2-#10	3-#10	4-#10	6-#10
Pears, diced	6-#10	4 oz.	#8 Scoop	46-#10	—	—	—	1-#10	2-#10	2-#10	3-#10	4-#10	6-#10

*During harvest season, it is recommended that fresh fruits, rather than canned or frozen, be purchased as much as possible.
**#8 scoop is used for KCAL-controlled diets (4 oz.); #16 scoop is used for all other diets (2 oz.).
†When vegetables can be purchased either canned or frozen, "# Times offered" section is identified for the canned category, only to avoid redundancies.
††For KCAL-controlled diets.

417

Table B-3 Fruits, continued

Item*	Size of purchase unit	Portion control size	Service utensil used**	#Serv./ purchase unit**	#Times offered on†			Serving extensions:					
					Cycle 1	Cycle 2	Cycle 3	20	60	100	150	200	300
Peaches, diced	6-#10	4 oz.	#8 Scoop	46-#10	—	—	—	1-#10	2-#10	2-#10	3-#10	4-#10	6-#10
Pineapple, chunks	6-#10	4 oz.	#8 Scoop	46-#10	—	—	—	1-#10	2-#10	2-#10	3-#10	4-#10	6-#10
Plums													
Dried (prunes)	6-#10	2 ea.	#8 Scoop	40-#10	—	—	—	1-#10	2-#10	2-#10	3-#10	4-#10	6-#10
Purple	6-#10	2 ea.	#8 Scoop	40-#10	—	—	—	1-#10	2-#10	2-#10	3-#10	4-#10	6-#10
Frozen													
Strawberries	per pt.	Used in pie & as sauce		See recipe	—	—	—	See recipe					
Rhubarb	per pt.	Used in pie		See recipe	—	—	—	See recipe					
Fresh††													
Apples	per lb.	Used in fruit mixes & salads		See recipe	1 At breakfast	—	—	See recipe					
Bananas	per lb.	1	Plastic glove	5-7				3 bun.	10 bun.	15 bun.	22 bun.	30 bun.	45 bun.

Table B-4 Bread/Starches

Item	Size of purchase unit	Portion control size	Service utensil used*	#Serv./ purchase unit	#Times offered on			Serving extensions:					
					Cycle 1	Cycle 2	Cycle 3	20	60	100	150	200	300
Bread													
Biscuit	per lb. (mixed)	1	Tongs	18 lb.	7	7	7	1.1 lb.	3.3 lb.	5.5 lb.	8.25 lb.	11 lb.	16.5 lb.
Cornbread	per lb. (meal)	1	Tongs	16 lb.	—	—	—	1.25 lb.	3.75 lb.	6.25 lb.	9.4 lb.	12.5 lb.	18.75 lb.
Cornmeal muffin	per lb. (meal)	1	Tongs	18 lb.	—	1	—	1.1 lb.	3.3 lb.	5.5 lb.	8.25 lb.	11 lb.	16.5 lb.
French	1# Loaf	1 sl.	Tongs	15	—	—	1	2 lvs.	4 lvs.	7 lvs.	10.5 lvs.	14 lvs.	21 lvs.
HB buns	per doz.	1	Tongs	12	1	1	1	2 dz.	5 dz.	9 dz.	13.5 dz.	18 dz.	27 dz.
HD buns	per doz.	1	Tongs	12	—	—	1	2 dz.	5 dz.	9 dz.	13.5 dz.	18 dz.	27 dz.
Dressing	per lb.	½ cup	#8 Scoop	4	1	1	1						
Loaf	1½# Loaf	1 sl.	Tongs	24	21	21	21	1 lf.	3 lvs.	4 lvs.	6 lvs.	8 lvs.	12 lvs.
Roll	per doz.	1	Tongs	12	21	21	21	2 dz.	5 dz.	9 dz.	13.5 dz.	18 dz.	27 dz.

*#8 scoop is used for KCAL-controlled diets (4 oz.); #16 scoop is used for all other diets (2 oz.).

419

Table B-5 Cereal

Item	Size of purchase unit	Portion control size	Service utensil used*	#Serv./ purchase unit	#Times offered on			Serving extensions:					
					Cycle 1	Cycle 2	Cycle 3	20	60	100	150	200	300
Cooked (Oatmeal)	per 42 oz.	½ C.	4 oz. dipper	50 bx.	—	—	—	4 bx.	1.2 bx.	2 bx.	3 bx.	4 bx.	6 bx.
Dry	per 16 oz.	¾ C.	Measuring cup	21 bx.	7	7	7	1 bx.	2.8 bx.	4.8 bx.	7.2 bx.	9.6 bx.	14.4 bx.
Cookies	per doz.	1	Tongs	6 dz.	—	—	—	1.75 dz.	5 dz.	8.3 dz.	12.5 dz.	16.6 dz.	24.9 dz.
Manicotti shells					1	1	2						
Rice	per lb.	2 oz.	#16 Scoop	38 lb.	3	3	2	5 lb.	1.6 lb.	2.6 lb.			
Dumplings	per lb.	2 oz.	#16 Scoop	8 lb.	1	1	1						
Spaghetti	per lb.	2 oz.	#16 Scoop	7 lb.	1	1	1	3 lb.	8.5 lb.	14 lb.			
Noodles	per lb.	½ C.	#8 Scoop		3	1	2						
Taco shells					1	—	1						
Assorted soups		6 oz.	6 oz. ladle		—	—	1						
Mushrooms					—	1	—						
Rigatoni					—	1	—						

*#8 scoop is used for KCAL-controlled diets (4 oz.); #16 scoop is used for all other diets (2 oz.)

NONSELECTIVE, NURSING HOME, FALL/WINTER CYCLE

Western U.S.

Table B-6 Meats/Entrees

Item	Size of purchase unit	Portion control size	Service utensil used	#Serv./ purchase unit	#Times offered on: Cycle 1	Cycle 2	Cycle 3	Cycle 4	Serving extensions: 50	100	200	300
Beef												
1. Gooseneck round or chuck roast	per lb.	2 oz.	Spatula	6	1	0	0	1	10.5 lb.	20.9 lb.	41.8 lb.	62.7 lb.
2. Short ribs	per lb.	4 oz.	Tongs	4	—	0	1	—	30 lb.	60 lb.	120 lb.	180 lb.
3. Cubes/tips	per lb.	2 oz.	#16 Scoop	6	½	1½	1	1	8.5 lb.	17 lb.	34 lb.	51 lb.
4. Ground	per lb.	2 oz.	#16 Scoop	6	3	4½	3	4	8.5 lb.	17 lb.	34 lb.	51 lb.
5. Liver	per lb.	2 oz.	Spatula	8	1	—	0	—	8.5 lb.	17 lb.	34 lb.	51 lb.
6. Steaks, salisbury	per lb.	2 oz.	Spatula	6	0	1	0	—	8.5 lb.	17 lb.	34 lb.	51 lb.
7. Veal	per lb.	2 oz.	Tongs	6	1	—	0	—	8.5 lb.	17 lb.	34 lb.	51 lb.
Chicken												
1. Hens, whole	per lb.	2 oz.	#16 Scoop or tongs	4	0	1	—	—	7.0 lb.	14 lb.	28 lb.	42 lb.
2. Turkey	per lb.	2 oz.	Tongs	8	1½	0	—	¼	6.8 lb.	13.6 lb.	27.2 lb.	40.8 lb.
3. ⅙ Cut fresh/frozen	Fryer/hen	2-3 oz.	Tongs	8	1	1	2	2	8.3 lb.	16.7 lb. or 43.1	33.4 lb.	50.1 lb.
Fish												
1. Salmon	6-64 oz.	2 oz.	Spatula	25	—	—	1	4	2 lb.	4 cans	8 lb.	12 lb.
2. Fillet	per lb.	2 oz.	Spatula	8	0	0	1	1	6.2 lb.	12.5 lb.	25 lb.	37.5 lb.
3. Tuna	6-66.5 oz.	2 oz.	#16 Scoop	3¾ lb.-2.5 oz.	1	1	0	—	1.5 lb.	3 Cans	6 lb.	9 lb.
4. Square	per lb.	2 oz.	Spatula	8	0	1	0	—	6.2 lb.	12.5 lb.	25 lb.	37.5 lb.

421

Table B-6 Meats/entrees, continued

Item	Size of purchase unit	Portion control size	Service utensil used	#Serv./purchase unit	#Times offered on Cycle 1	Cycle 2	Cycle 3	Cycle 4	Serving extensions: 50	100	200	300
Pork												
1. Roast (w/bone)	per lb.	2 oz.	Tongs	4.38	0	1	1	2	11.5 lb.	23 lb.	46 lb.	69 lb.
2. Pork chops	per lb.	2 oz.	Tongs	4	1	1	0	—	12.5 lb.	25 lb.	50 lb.	75 lb.
3. Bacon	per lb.	1 oz.	Tongs	6	1	0	1	1	8.5 lb.	17 lb.	34 lb.	51 lb.
4. Ham	per lb.	2 oz.	Tongs	6	1	1	1	1¼	8.5 lb.	17 lb.	34 lb.	51 lb.
5. Wieners	per lb.	2 oz.	Tongs	8	—	1	1	—	6.2 lb.	12.5 lb.	25 lb.	37.5 lb.
6. Sausage link/patty	per lb.	1½ oz. Patty	Tongs	10	1	1	1	1	12.3 lb.	24.6 lb.	49.2 lb.	73.8 lb.
7. Cutlet	per lb.	1½ oz. Patty	Tongs		1	—	1	—				
8. Luncheon meat	per lb.	1 oz.	Tongs		—	—	1	—				

Table B-7 Other

Item	Size of purchase unit	Portion control size	Service utensil used	#Serv./purchase unit	#Times offered on Cycle 1	Cycle 2	Cycle 3	Cycle 4	Serving extensions: 50	100	200	300
1. Eggs, fresh												
a. Deviled					1	0	1	—				
b. Breakfast	per doz.	1 oz.	#16 Scoop	12	6	6	6	6				
c. Other meals					½	1½	½	1				
2. Cheese	per lb.	2 oz.	Tongs	8	1	3	1½	3	6.2 lb.	12.5 lb.	25 lb.	37.5 lb.
3. Cottage cheese	per lb.	¼ cup	#16 Scoop	8	—	2	1	2	6.2 lb.	12.5 lb.	25 lb.	37.5 lb.

Table B-8 Vegetables

Item	Size of purchase unit	Portion control size	Service utensil used	#Serv./ purchase unit	#Times offered on Cycle 1	Cycle 2	Cycle 3	Cycle 4	Serving extensions: 50	100	200	300
Canned												
1. Beets, sliced	6-#10	2 oz.	#16 Scoop	46/#10	1	2	0	1	1-#10	2-#10	4-#10	6-#10
2. Beans:												
a. Green	6-#10	2 oz.	#16 Scoop	46/#10	1½	2	2	1½	1-#10	2-#10	4-#10	6-#10
b. Wax	6-#10	2 oz.	#16 Scoop	46/#10	1½	—	0	½	1-#10	2-#10	4-#10	6-#10
c. Baked	6-#10	2 oz.	#16 Scoop	46/#10	—	0	1	—				
3. Carrots, sliced	6-#10	4 oz.	#8 Scoop	23/#10	1	½	2	2	2-#10	4-#10	8-#10	12-#10
4. Corn	6-#10	2 oz.	#16 Scoop	46/#10	0	1	2	2	1-#10	2-#10	4-#10	6-#10
5. Mixed vegetables	6-#10	2 oz.	#16 Scoop	46/#10	1	1	3	—	1-#10	2-#10	4-#10	6-#10
6. Vegs. for stew	6-#10				1	—	—	1	1-#10	2-#10	4-#10	6-#10
7. Peas, green	6-#10	2 oz.	#16 Scoop	46/#10	1	1½	1	1	1-#10	2-#10	4-#10	6-#10
8. Potato												
a. Sliced dehyd.	per lb.	2 oz.	#16 Scoop	40/#10	1	1	0	2	1.25-#10	2.5-#10	5-#10	7.5-#10
b. Mashed	6-#10	2 oz.	#16 Scoop	280/#10	2	1	3	2	label directions			
c. Sweet	6-#10	2 oz.	#16 Scoop	40/#10	2	1	2	1	1-#10	2-#10	4-#10	6-#10
d. Whole	6-#10	2 oz.	#16 Scoop		—	1	0	1	1-#10	2-#10	4-#10	6-#10
9. Refried beans	6-#10	2 oz.	See recipe	42/#10	—	1	0	½	1-#10	2-#10	4-#10	6-#10
10. Kidney beans	6-#10	2 oz.	#16 Scoop	42/#10	—	—	0	—	1-#10	2-#10	4-#10	6-#10
11. Sauerkraut	6-#10	2 oz.	#16 Scoop	46/#10	—	1½	1½	2	1-#10	2-#10	4-#10	6-#10
12. Spinach	6-#10	2 oz.	#16 Scoop	46/#10	2	1	1	1	1-#10	2-#10	4-#10	6-#10
13. Tomato sauce	6-#10	2 oz.	#16 Scoop	42/#10	1	1	1½	—	1-#10	2-#10	4-#10	6-#10
14. Squash, yellow	6-#10	2 oz.	#16 Scoop		1	—	1	1				
15. Zucchini	6-#10	2 oz.	#16 Scoop		1	1½	1	—				
16. Greens	6-#10	2 oz.	#16 Scoop		1	1	1	1				
17. Stewed tomatoes	6-#10	2 oz.	#16 Scoop		—	1	1	0				
18. Tomato soup	6-#10	6 oz.	6 oz. Ladle		1	1	—	1				
19. Cream of pea soup	6-#10	6 oz.	6 oz. Ladle									

Table B-8 Vegetables, continued

Item	Size of purchase unit	Portion control size	Service utensil used	#Serv./ purchase unit	# Times offered on				Serving extensions:			
					Cycle 1	Cycle 2	Cycle 3	Cycle 4	50	100	200	300
Frozen												
1. Broccoli	12-2 lb.	2 oz.	#16 Scoop	8/lb.	1	—	1	1½	6.2 lb.	12.5 lb.	25 lb.	37.5 lb.
2. Carrots*	20 lb.	2 oz.	#16 Scoop	11.7/lb.	—	—	1	½	4.4 lb.	8.85 lb.	17.7 lb.	20.5 lb.
3. Mixed vegetables	20 lb.	2 oz.	#16 Scoop	8/lb.	0	1	1	—	6.2 lb.	12.5 lb.	25 lb.	37.5 lb.
4. Chinese vegetables	20 lb.	4 oz.	#8 Scoop	111/20#	0	1	—	1	6.2 lb.	12.5 lb.	25 lb.	37.5 lb.
5. Peas, green*	20 lb.	2 oz.	#16 Scoop	10/lb.	—	1½	0	—	5.0 lb.	10 lb.	20 lb.	30 lb.
6. Potatoes												
a. Hash browns	18 lb.	2 oz.	#16 Scoop	96/Case	—	—	1	1	.52 cs.	1.05 cs.	2.1 cs.	3.1 cs.
b. Tater Tots	6-5 lb.	6-8	Tongs	8/lb.	1	1	1	1	6.5 lb.	12.5 lb.	25 lb.	37.5 lb.
c. Potato wedges	6-5 lb.	6-8	Tongs	8/lb.	—	1	1	—				
d. French fries												
7. Spinach*	12-3 lb.	2 oz.	#16 Scoop	6.8 lb.	—	—	1	—	7.4 lb.	14.8 lb.	29.6 lb.	44.4 lb.
8. Brussels sprouts					1	—	—	—				
9. Baby limas	12-3 lb.	2 oz.	#16 Scoop		—	1	—	—				
10. Italian green beans	12-3 lb.	2 oz.	#16 Scoop		—	—	1	—				
Fresh												
1. Cabbage	per lb.	2 oz.	#16 Scoop	8.6/3.14	2	2	—	1	6.6 lb.	13.3 lb.	26.6 lb.	39.9 lb.
2. Carrots (for salad)	per lb.	Used in salads	Used in salads	2	1	½	1 recipe	—				
3. Lettuce	per head	Used in salads	Spoon	See recipe	2	2	2	2	Recipe			
4. Onion	per lb.	2 oz.		8	1	1	—	1	6.5 lb.	13 lb.	26 lb.	39 lb.
5. Peppers	per lb.	Used in casserole		See recipe	—	0	—	—	Recipe			
6. Potatoes												
a. Baking	per lb.	2 oz.	Tongs	8	2	—	0	0	6.2 lb.	12.5 lb.	25 lb.	37.5 lb.
b. Boiling	per lb.	2 oz.	#16 Scoop	7	—	0	0	1	7.0 lb.	14 lb.	28 lb.	42 lb.

*See canned vegetable listing to identify number of times each appears per cycle.

Item	Size of purchase unit	Portion control size	Service utensil used	#Serv./ purchase unit	Cycle 1	Cycle 2	Cycle 3	Cycle 4	50	100	200	300
7. Tomatoes												
a. Slices	per lb.	2-½" sls.	Tongs	12–16 sl.	2	2	1	1				
b. Wedges	per lb.		Tongs	See recipe	0	0	1	1				
8. Celery	per lb.	2 oz.	Used in salad	See recipe	1	1	1	—				
9. Zucchini	per lb.	2 oz.	Used in salad	See recipe	—	1	0	—				

Table B-9 Breads/Starches

	Size of purchase unit	Portion control size	Service utensil used	#Serv./ purchase unit	#Times offered on Cycle 1	#Times offered on Cycle 2	#Times offered on Cycle 3	#Times offered on Cycle 4	Serving extensions: 50	100	200	300
Item												
Bread												
1. Crackers	300 pkgs/cs	(2)			1	1	1	1	1.5 pkg.	3 pkg.	6 pkg.	9 pkg.
2. Biscuits	5#	1	Tongs	18/lb.	1	3	1	1	2.7#	5.5#	11#	16.5#
3. Brown bread-w/w	1½# Loaf	1 Slice	Tongs	24/lb.	—	1	1	2½	2 lvs.	4 lvs.	8 lvs.	12 lvs.
4. Cornbread	5#	1	Tongs	16/lb.	1	1	1	1	3.1 lb.	6.25 lb.	12.5 lb.	18.7 lb.
5. Bran muffin	5#	1	Tongs	16/lb.	0	0	—	1	2.7 lb.	5.5 lb.	11 lb.	16.5 lb.
6. Blueberry muffin	5#	1	Tongs	16/lb.	—	—	—	—	2.7 lb.	5.5 lb.	11 lb.	16.5 lb.
7. Pancake	5#	1	Spatula	18/lb.	1	0	0	1	2.7 lb.	5.5 lb.	11 lb.	16.5 lb.
8. French	1# Loaf	1 Slice	Tongs	15/lb.	—	1	0	1	3.5 lvs.	7 lvs.	14 lvs.	21 lvs.
9. Garlic	1# Loaf	1 Slice	Tongs	15/lb.	—	1	1	1	3.5 lvs.	7 lvs.	14 lvs.	21 lvs.
10. HB Buns	Per dozen	1	Tongs	12	1	1	0	1	4.5 dz.	9 dz.	18 dz.	27 dz.
11. Dressing	1½# Loaf	See recipe	Tongs		1	1	—	—	Recipe			
12. Loaf												
a. Breakfast toast	1½# Loaf	1 Slice	Tongs	24/lb.	6	6	6	6	2 lvs.	4 lvs.	8 lvs.	12 lvs.
b. For other meals	1½# Loaf	1 Slice	Tongs	24/lb.	7	4	5½	5½	2 lvs.	4 lvs.	8 lvs.	12 lvs.
c. Texas toast												
13. Roll	per dozen	1	Tongs	12	5	3	0	2	4.5 dz.	9 dz.	18 dz.	27 dz.
14. Danish	Per pkg.	1	Tongs		0	0	0	0	Per package			
15. Hot dog buns	per dozen	1	Tongs	12	—	1	0	0				
16. Rye bread	1# Loaf	1	Tongs		—	1	0	0				

425

Table B-10 Cereal

Item*	Size of purchase unit	Portion control size	Service utensil used	#Serv./ purchase unit	#Times offered on				Serving extensions:			
					Cycle 1	Cycle 2	Cycle 3	Cycle 4	50	100	200	300
1. Cooked												
a. Cream of Rice	1#	½ cup	4 oz. dipper	50/box	1	1	1	1	1 box	2 box	4 box	6 box
b. Cream of Wheat	1# 12 oz.	½ cup	4 oz. dipper	50/box	2	1	1	2	1 box	2 box	4 box	6 box
c. Oatmeal	5# per 42	½ cup	4 oz. dipper	50/box	2	3	2	2	1 box	2 box	4 box	6 box
d. Farina	5#	½ cup	4 oz. dipper	50/box	—	0	—	—	1 box	2 box	4 box	6 box
e. Malt O Meal	5#	½ cup	4 oz. dipper	50/box	1	1	1	1				
f. Ralston	5#	½ cup	4 oz. dipper	50/box	1	1	1	1				
2. Dry	¾ cup	¾ cup	Measuring cup	21/box	—	—	—	1	2.4 box	4.8 box	9.6 box	14.4 box
3. Cookies	6 Pkg. = #10	1	Tongs	6/dozen	1	1	1	3	4.15 dz.	8.3 dz.	16.6 dz.	24.9 dz.
4. Rice	per lb.	2 oz.	#16 Scoop	38/lb.	0	1	0	2	1.5 lb.	3.1 lb.	6.2 lb.	9.3 lb.
5. Chinese noodles	per lb.	⅔ cup	Tongs	32/lb.	—	0	0	—	7 lb.	14 lb.	28 lb.	42 lb.
6. Spaghetti	per lb.	2 oz.	#16 Scoop	7/lb.	—	1	0	—	2.8 lb.	5.7 lb.	11.4 lb.	17.1 lb.
7. Noodles												
a. Ribbon	per lb.	4 oz.	#8 Scoop	18/lb.	1	—	1	—	2.2 lb.	4.45 lb.	8.9 lb.	13.3 lb.
b. Elbow macaroni	per lb.	4 oz.	#8 Scoop	23/lb.	—	1	0	—	2.2 lb.	4.45 lb.	8.9 lb.	13.3 lb.
8. Flour tortilla					1	—	1	—				
9. Lasagne noodles	per lb.	4 oz.	Use in recipe		—	—	—	1				

*As per facility's needs.

Table B-11 Fruits

Item	Size of purchase unit	Portion control size	Service utensil used	#Serv./ purchase unit	# Times offered on Cycle 1	Cycle 2	Cycle 3	Cycle 4	Serving extensions: 50	100	200	300
Canned*												
1. Apples												
a. Sauce	6-#10	4 oz.	#8 Scoop	52/#10	1	1	1	—	1-#10	2-#10	4-#10	6-#10
b. Sliced	6-#10	Used in recipe		See recipe	1	1	—	1	Recipe			
c. Rings	6-#10	Each			1	0	1	1				
2. Citrus sections	6-#10	4 oz.	#8 Scoop	42/#10	—	—	1	1	1-#10	2-#10	4-#10	6-#10
3. Cranberry sauce	6-#10	2 oz.	Recipe		1½	2	1	1	1-#10	2-#10	4-#10	6-#10
4. Lite fruit mix	6-#10	4 oz.	#8 Scoop	46/#10	3	2	1½	1	1-#10	2-#10	4-#10	6-#10
5. Pears												
a. Diced	6-#10	4 oz.	#8 Scoop	46/#10	1	0	1	—	1-#10	2-#10	4-#10	6-#10
b. Halve	6-#10	4 oz.	#8 Scoop	46/#10	1	0	1	1½	1-#10	2-#10	4-#10	6-#10
6. Peaches												
a. Diced	6-#10	4 oz.	#8 Scoop	46/#10	—	—	—	—	1-#10	2-#10	4-#10	6-#10
b. Halve	6-#10	4 oz.	#8 Scoop	46/#10	1	2	1	—	1-#10	2-#10	4-#10	6-#10
c. Slice	6-#10	4 oz.	#8 Scoop	46/#10	—	—	1	½	1-#10	2-#10	4-#10	6-#10
7. Pineapple												
a. Sliced	6-#10	4 oz.	#8 Scoop	46/#10	—	2	1	—	1-#10	2-#10	4-#10	6-#10
b. Chunks	6-#10	4 oz.	#8 Scoop	46/#10	1	—	—	—	1-#10	2-#10	4-#10	6-#10
c. Lite pineapple	6-#10	4 oz.	#8 Scoop	46/#10	—	½	—	—	1-#10	2-#10	4-#10	6-#10
d. Crushed	6-#10	4 oz.	#8 Scoop	46/#10	—	—	—	—	1-#10	2-#10	4-#10	6-#10
8. Mandarin oranges	6-#10	4 oz.	#8 Scoop	40/#10	1	—	1	1	1-#10	2-#10	4-#10	6-#10
9. Apricots, halves	6-#10				—	—	—	1	1-#10	2-#10	4-#10	6-#10

*Vari-Care homes will be using Lite Fruit for all diets. Count in with Regulars.

Table B–11 Fruits, continued

Item	Size of purchase unit	Portion control size	Service utensil used	#Serv./ purchase unit	#Times offered on				Serving extensions:			
					Cycle 1	Cycle 2	Cycle 3	Cycle 4	50	100	200	300
Frozen												
1. Strawberries	6-#10	Used in pie and as sauce		See recipe	1	1	—	—	Recipe			
Fresh												
1. Apples	per lb.	Used in fruit mixes and salads		See recipe	0	1	1	—	Recipe			
2. Bananas	per lb.	1	Plastic gloves	5-7	0	1	—	—	7.5 bds.	15 bds.	30 bds.	45 bds.
3. Melon	per lb.	4 oz.	Plastic gloves		0	0	1	1				
4. Fresh fruit	per lb.	4 oz.	Plastic gloves		—	1	1	1				
5. Lemons	dozen	⅙ of lemon	Plastic gloves		—	—	—	1				
Misc.												
1. Tartar sauce	individual	1T			—	1	1	—				
2. Whip topping/ Miracle top					—	—	3	—				
3. Barbecue sauce	4-1 gal.				—	1	1	—				

428

Table B-12 Mixes

Item	Size of purchase unit	Portion control size	Service utensil used	#Serv./ purchase unit	#Times offered on				Serving extensions:			
					Cycle 1	Cycle 2	Cycle 3	Cycle 4	50	100	200	300
1. Chocolate pudding					1	0	1	—				
2. White cake					3	2	2	—				
3. Lemon pudding					1	—	1	—				
4. Gingerbread					—	1	—	—				
5. Banana pudding					1	1	—	—				
6. Cherry cake					—	—	3	1				
7. Pie crust					—	1	—	1				
8. Brownie					—	—	1	1				
9. Vanilla Pudding					—	—	1	1				
10. Chocolate cake					—	—	—	—				
11. Butterscotch brownie					—	—	—	—				
12. Custard					—	—	—	—				
13. Tapioca					—	—	—	—				
14. Cheesecake					—	—	—	—				
15. Carrot raisin cake					—	—	—	—				

Preparation Practicalities

The following pointers should improve cooks' productivity and experience.

EGGS

- Add salt to water when boiling eggs; it reduces cracking and makes them easier to peel.
- Crack hard-cooked eggs when hot and put in cold water to cool, then peel.
- Peel hard-cooked eggs by slipping spoon under cracked shell at large end.
- Cover unused egg yolks with cold water before storing in refrigerator; they will not dry out.
- Break eggs into small funnel to separate yolks from whites.
- Have pan ready in which to drop shells when opening eggs. This saves rehandling shells when you are ready to dispose of them. (Break an egg in each hand simultaneously.)
- Spin a whole egg. If it spins like a top, it is hard-cooked.
- Prepare scrambled eggs in double boiler for a tender, fluffy product. This seems to increase labor efficiency by reducing necessity for continuous supervision of product.
- Prepare following recipes to eliminate necessity of purchasing commercial whipped topping.

Yes, one egg white does yield one gallon of Miracle Topping.

Miracle Topping

(Yield: One gallon, serves 125)

1 Egg White
1 Cup Granulated Sugar
1 Cup Heavy Fruit Syrup (from can of peaches, fruit cocktail, or plums)
  1. Place all ingredients in mixing bowl at same time.
  2. Mix at high speed for 5 to 7 minutes or until topping forms stiff, white peaks.

431

This topping may be browned (for banana pudding). Topping also may be used as a complete dessert by folding or whipping in drained fruit pieces. Adding leftover cake crumbs, graham cracker crumbs, or broken cookie pieces makes a delightful dessert treat as well. Jello cubes folded with the topping are excellent as a "Jello Fluff."

Prepare Miracle Topping before serving. Tripling recipe facilitates whipping and will provide topping for the future. Cover and store in refrigerator. Whip again, and it is ready to use.

CHEESE

- Store cheddar cheese, grated or cubed, in plastic bags and freeze. Thaw and use as needed for such dishes as scrambled eggs and casseroles. Be sure to mark amount of cheese in each bag.
- Apply thin coat of butter to cut surface of cheese to prevent it from drying out under refrigeration.
- Dip loaf of cheese in hot water for easy removal of wrapper.
- Use dry vegetable brush for removing cheese from hand grater before washing it. This also works well for lemon and orange rind.
- Alternate corners of sliced cheese or meat when stacking slices for easy separation.
- Grate cheese and add to mayonnaise to give zip to salads made with peaches, pears, or apples.

MILK AND CREAM

- Coat inside of steam-jacketed kettle with butter when heating milk. This will prevent milk deposits and scorching, making cleaning job easier.
- Prevent formation of skin on milk during heating by:

  1. covering pan,
  2. floating small amount of butter or cream on surface of milk, or
  3. beating milk during heating time.

- Do not add salt to large quantities of milk or cream sauce until last minute or it will curdle.
- Mix sugar with egg rather than milk for best results when making custards or other dishes that call for hot milk to be added to eggs. Add hot liquids to beaten egg and sugar a little at a time. Do not overcook.
- Chill bowl, beater, and cream when whipping cream—cream will whip in half the time. Should cream seem too thin to whip, put chilled dish in pan of hot water, then whip.

CEREALS AND PASTAS

- Butter sides and bottom of pan in which noodles, spaghetti, or rice is to be cooked. This prevents them from boiling over and/or from sticking to pan.
- Add butter or cooking oil to boiling water before adding macaroni or spaghetti. Bring to boil and turn off heat. Keep covered to finish cooking.

- Heat only enough liquid to dissolve gelatin when using flavored gelatin for molded salads or desserts. To hasten congealing, use ice water to make up total amount of liquid.
- Do not soften plain gelatin if there is sugar in recipe. Simply mix gelatin and sugar together and dissolve in hot liquid.
- Use dried fruit-flavored gelatin granules as a garnish for salads, puddings, and cookies, and in combination with shredded coconut.
- Dip individual molds of gelatin salad in warm water, turn out trays, and place in refrigerator to firm before serving.
- Grease Jell-O molds with mayonnaise rather than oil before pouring in gelatin. This gives "frosted" appearance.

Pureed Diet Survey

Table D–1 Fruits

ITEM	Amt. Blended (Drained Wt.)	Amt. of Liquid Added	Blending Time Required	Yield	Volume Decrease
APRICOTS (H.S.)	3 c.	½ c.	30 sec.	2½ c.	29%
FRUIT COCKTAIL (H.S.)	3 c.	¼ c.	30 sec.	2½ c.	23%
PEACHES, Halves or Sliced (H.S. or L.S.)	3 c.	½ c.	30 sec.	3 c.	14%
PEACHES, Pie Pack	3 c.	—	30 sec.	3 c.	0%
PEARS, Halves (35/40) (H.S.)	3 c.	½ c.	20 sec.	2¾ c.	21%
FRUIT MIX (L.S.)	3 c.	—	30 sec.	3 c.	0%
PEAR HALVES (40/50) (L.S.)	3 c.	½ c.	30 sec.	2½ c.	29%
APRICOTS (W.P.)	3 c.	½ c.	30 sec.	3 c.	14%
FRUIT COCKTAIL (W.P.)	3 c.	—	30 sec.	3 c.	0%
PEACH HALVES (W.P.)	3 c.	½ c.	30 sec.	3 c.	14%
PEAR HALVES (W.P.)	3 c.	½ c.	30 sec.	2 c.	43%

H.S. = Heavy Syrup
L.S. = Light Syrup
W.P. = Water Pack

Table D–2 Pureed diet production guide—Fruit

| Item | 5 Servings | | | | | |
| | #12 Scoop (2.67 ounces) | | | #10 Scoop (3.2 ounces) | | |
	Amt. Solid Food	Amt. Liquid	Amt. Yield	Amt. Solid Food	Amt. Liquid	Amt. Yield
Apricots (H.S.)	17 oz	3+ oz	13+ oz	21 oz	3+ oz	16 oz
	2c 1 oz	3+ oz	1c 5+oz	2c 5 oz	3+ oz	2c
Fruit Cocktail (H.S.)	16 oz	1+ oz	13+ oz	20 oz	2 oz	16 oz
	2c	1+ oz	1c 5+oz	2c 4 oz	2 oz	2c
Peaches, Halves or (H.S.) Sliced (L.S.)	15 oz	2+ oz	13+ oz	18+ oz	3 oz	16 oz
	1c 7 oz	2+ oz	1c 5+oz	2c 2+oz	3 oz	2c
Peaches, Pie Pack	13+ oz		13+ oz	16 oz		16 oz
	1c 5+oz		1c 5+oz	2c		2c
Pears, Halves (35/40), (H.S.)	16 oz	2 oz	13+ oz	19 oz	3+ oz	16 oz
	2c	2 oz	1c 5+oz	2c 3 oz	3+ oz	2c
Fruit Mix (L.S.)	13+ oz		13+ oz	16 oz		16 oz
	1c 5+oz		1c 5+oz	2c		2c
Pear Halves (40/50)(L.S.)	17 oz	3+ oz	13+ oz	21 oz	3+ oz	16 oz
	2c 1 oz	3+ oz	1c 5+oz	2c 5 oz	3+ oz	2c
Apricots (W.P.)	15 oz	2+ oz	13+ oz	18 oz	3 oz	16 oz
	1c 7 oz	2+ oz	1c 5+oz	2c 2 oz	3 oz	2c
Fruit Cocktail (W.P.)	13+ oz		13+ oz	16 oz		16 oz
	1c 5+oz		1c 5+oz	2c		2c
Peach Halves (W.P.)	15 oz	2+ oz	13+ oz	18 oz	3 oz	16 oz
	1c 7 oz	2+ oz	1c 5+oz	2c 2 oz	3 oz	2c
Pear Halves (W.P.)	19 oz	3+ oz	13+ oz	23 oz	4 oz	16 oz
	2c 3 oz	3+ oz	1c 5+oz	2c 7 oz	4 oz	2c

| Item | 10 Servings | | | | | |
| | #12 Scoop (2.67 ounces) | | | #10 Scoop (3.2 ounces) | | |
	Amt. Solid Food	Amt. Liquid	Amt. Yield	Amt. Solid Food	Amt. Liquid	Amt. Yield
Apricots (H.S.)	35 oz	6 oz	27 oz	41 oz	7 oz	32 oz
	4c 3 oz	6 oz	3c 3 oz	5c 1 oz	7 oz	4c
Fruit Cocktail (H.S.)	33 oz	3 oz	27 oz	39 oz	3+ oz	32 oz
	4c 1 oz	3 oz	3c 3 oz	4c 7 oz	3+ oz	4c
Peaches, Halves or (H.S.) Sliced (L.S.)	31 oz	5+ oz	27 oz	36+ oz	6 oz	32 oz
	3c 7 oz	5+ oz	3c 3 oz	4c 4+oz	6 oz	4c
Peaches, Pie Pack	27 oz		27 oz	32 oz		32 oz
	3c 3 oz		3c 3 oz	4c		4c
Pears, Halves (35/40), (H.S.)	33 oz	5+ oz	27 oz	39 oz	7 oz	32 oz
	4c 1 oz	5+ oz	3c 3 oz	4c 7 oz	7 oz	4c
Fruit Mix (L.S.)	27 oz		27 oz	32 oz		32 oz
	3c 3 oz		3c 3 oz	4c		4c
Pear Halves (40/50)(L.S.)	35 oz	6 oz	27 oz	41 oz	7 oz	32 oz
	4c 3 oz	6 oz	3c 3 oz	5c 1 oz	7 oz	4c
Apricots (W.P.)	31 oz	5 oz	27 oz	36 oz	6 oz	32 oz
	3c 7 oz	5 oz	3c 3 oz	4c 4 oz	6 oz	4c

Table D–2 Fruit, continued

Item	#12 Scoop (2.67 ounces)			#10 Scoop (3.2 ounces)		
10 Servings	Amt. Solid Food	Amt. Liquid	Amt. Yield	Amt. Solid Food	Amt. Liquid	Amt. Yield
Fruit Cocktail (W.P.)	27 oz		27 oz	32 oz		32 oz
	3c 3 oz		3c 3 oz	4c		4c
Peach Halves (W.P.)	31 oz	5 oz	27 oz	36 oz	6 oz	32 oz
	3c 7 oz	5 oz	3c 3 oz	4c 4 oz	6 oz	4c
Pear Halves (W.P.)	39 oz	7 oz	27 oz	46 oz	8 oz	32 oz
	4c 7 oz	7 oz	3c 3 oz	5c 6 oz	1c	4c

Item	#12 Scoop (2.67 ounces)			#10 Scoop (3.2 ounces)		
15 Servings	Amt. Solid Food	Amt. Liquid	Amt. Yield	Amt. Solid Food	Amt. Liquid	Amt. Yield
Apricots (H.S.)	52 oz	9 oz	40 oz	62 oz	10+ oz	48 oz
	6c 4 oz	1c 1 oz	5c	7c 6 oz	1c 2+oz	6c
Fruit Cocktail (H.S.)	49 oz	4 oz	40 oz	59 oz	5 oz	48 oz
	6c 1 oz	4 oz	5c	7c 3 oz	5 oz	6c
Peaches, Halves or (H.S.)	46 oz	8 oz	40 oz	55 oz	9+oz	48 oz
Sliced (L.S.)	5c 6 oz	1c	5c	6c 7 oz	1c 1+oz	6c
Peaches, Pie Pack	40 oz		40 oz	48 oz		48 oz
	5c		5c	6c		6c
Pears, Halves (H.S.), (35/40)	48 oz	8 oz	40 oz	58 oz	10 oz	48 oz
	6c	1c	5c	7c 2 oz	1c 2 oz	6c
Fruit Mix (L.S.)	40 oz		40 oz	48 oz		48 oz
	5c		5c	6c		6c
Pear Halves (40/50)(L.S.)	52 oz	9 oz	40 oz	62 oz	12+oz	48 oz
	6c 4 oz	9 oz	5c	7c 6 oz	1c 4+oz	6c
Apricots (W.P.)	46 oz	8 oz	40 oz	55 oz	9+oz	48 oz
	5c 6 oz	8 oz	5c	6c 7 oz	1c 1+oz	6c
Fruit Cocktail (W.P.)	40 oz		40 oz	48 oz		48 oz
	5c		5c	6c		6c
Peach Halves (W.P.)	46 oz	8 oz	40 oz	55 oz	9+oz	48 oz
	5c 6 oz	8 oz	5c	6c 7 oz	1c 1+oz	6c
Pear Halves (W.P.)	57 oz	10 oz	40 oz	69 oz	12 oz	48 oz
	7c 1 oz	1c 2 oz	5c	8c 5 oz	1c 4 oz	6c

Item	#12 Scoop (2.67 ounces)			#10 Scoop (3.2 ounces)		
20 Servings	Amt. Solid Food	Amt. Liquid	Amt. Yield	Amt. Solid Food	Amt. Liquid	Amt. Yield
Apricots (H.S.)	68 oz	11+ oz	53+ oz	83 oz	14 oz	64 oz
	8c 4 oz	1c 3+oz	6c 5+oz	10c 3 oz	1c 6 oz	8c
Fruit Cocktail (H.S.)	65 oz	5+ oz	53+ oz	78 oz	6+ oz	64 oz
	8c 1 oz	5+ oz	6c 5+oz	9c 6 oz	6+ oz	8c
Peaches, Halves or (H.S.)	60+ oz	10 oz	53+ oz	73 oz	12+ oz	64 oz
Sliced (L.S.)	7c 4 oz	1c 2 oz	6c 5+oz	9c 1 oz	1c 4+oz	8c

437

Table D-2 Fruit, continued

| Item | 20 Servings | | | | | |
| | #12 Scoop (2.67 ounces) | | | #10 Scoop (3.2 ounces) | | |
	Amt. Solid Food	Amt. Liquid	Amt. Yield	Amt. Solid Food	Amt. Liquid	Amt. Yield
Peaches, Pie Pack	53+ oz		53+ oz	64 oz		64 oz
	6c 5 oz		6c 5+oz	8c		8c
Pears, Halves (35/40), (H.S.)	64 oz	11 oz	53+ oz	77 oz	13 oz	64 oz
	8c	1c 3 oz	6c 5+oz	9c 5 oz	1c 5 oz	8c
Fruit Mix (L.S.)	53+ oz		53+ oz	64 oz		64 oz
	6c 5+oz		6c 5+oz	8c		8c
Pear Halves (40/50)(L.S.)	68 oz	11+ oz	53+ oz	83 oz	14 oz	64 oz
	8c 4 oz	1c 3+oz	6c 5+oz	10c 3 oz	1c 6 oz	8c
Apricots (W.P.)	60 oz	10 oz	53+ oz	73 oz	12 oz	64 oz
	7c 4 oz	1c 2 oz	6c 5+oz	9c 1 oz	1c 4 oz	8c
Fruit Cocktail (W.P.)	53+ oz		53+ oz	64 oz		64 oz
	6c 5+oz		6c 5+oz	8c		8c
Peach Halves (W.P.)	60 oz	10 oz	53+ oz	73 oz	12 oz	64 oz
	7c 4 oz	1c 2 oz	6c 5+oz	9c 1 oz	1c 4 oz	8c
Pear Halves (W.P.)	76 oz	13 oz	53+ oz	92 oz	15+ oz	64 oz
	9c 4 oz	1c 5 oz	6c 5+oz	11c 4 oz	1c 7+oz	8c

| Item | 25 Servings | | | | | |
| | #12 Scoop (2.67 ounces) | | | #10 Scoop (3.2 ounces) | | |
	Amt. Solid Food	Amt. Liquid	Amt. Yield	Amt. Solid Food	Amt. Liquid	Amt. Yield
Apricots (H.S.)	86 oz	14+ oz	67 oz	103 oz	17 oz	80 oz
	10c 6 oz	1c 6 oz	8c 3 oz	12c 7 oz	2c 1 oz	10c
Fruit Cocktail (H.S.)	82 oz	7 oz	67 oz	98 oz	8 oz	80 oz
	10c 2 oz	7 oz	8c 3 oz	12c 2 oz	1c	10c
Peaches, Halves or (H.S.) Sliced (L.S.)	76 oz	13 oz	67 oz	91 oz	15+ oz	80 oz
	9c 4 oz	1c 5 oz	8c 3 oz	11c 3 oz	1c 7+oz	10c
Peaches, Pie Pack	67 oz		67 oz	80 oz		80 oz
	8c 3 oz		8c 3 oz	10c		10c
Pears, Halves (35/40), (H.S.)	81 oz	13+ oz	67 oz	97 oz	16+ oz	80 oz
	10c 1 oz	1c 5+oz	8c 3 oz	12c 1 oz	2c+	10c
Fruit Mix (L.S.)	67 oz		67 oz	80 oz		80 oz
	8c 3 oz		8c 3 oz	10c		10c
Pear Halves (40/50)(L.S.)	86 oz	14+ oz	67 oz	103 oz	17 oz	80 oz
	10c 6 oz	1c 6+oz	8c 3 oz	12c 7 oz	2c 1 oz	10c
Apricots (W.P.)	73 oz	12 oz	67 oz	91 oz	15+ oz	80 oz
	9c 1 oz	1c 4 oz	8c 3 oz	11c 3 oz	1c 7+oz	10c
Fruit Cocktail (W.P.)	67 oz		67 oz	80 oz		80 oz
	8c 3 oz		8c 3 oz	10c		10c
Peach Halves (W.P.)	73 oz	12 oz	67 oz	91 oz	15+ oz	80 oz
	9c 1 oz	1c 4 oz	8c 3 oz	11c 3 oz	1c 7+oz	10c
Pear Halves (W.P.)	96 oz	16 oz	67 oz	114 oz	19 oz	80 oz
	12c	2c	8c 3 oz	14c 2 oz	2c 3 oz	10c

438

Table D–2 Fruit, continued

Item	#12 Scoop (2.67 ounces) Amt. Solid Food	Amt. Liquid	Amt. Yield	#10 Scoop (3.2 ounces) Amt. Solid Food	Amt. Liquid	Amt. Yield
Apricots (H.S.)	103 oz	17 oz	80+ oz	124 oz	21 oz	96 oz
	12c 7 oz	2c 1 oz	10+c	15c 4 oz	2c 5 oz	12c
Fruit Cocktail (H.S.)	98 oz	8 oz	80+ oz	118 oz	20 oz	96 oz
	12c 2 oz	1c	10+c	14c 6 oz	2c 4 oz	12c
Peaches, Halves or (H.S.) Sliced (L.S.)	91 oz	15+ oz	80+ oz	109 oz	18 oz	96 oz
	11c 3 oz	1c 7+oz	10+c	13c 5 oz	2c 2 oz	12c
Peaches, Pie Pack	80+ oz		80+ oz	96 oz		96 oz
	10+c		10+c	12c		12c
Pears, Halves (H.S.), (35/40)	97 oz	16+ oz	80+ oz	116 oz	19 oz	96 oz
	12c 1 oz	2+c	10+c	14c 4 oz	2c 3 oz	12c
Fruit Mix (L.S.)	80+ oz		80+ oz	96 oz		96 oz
	10+c		10+c	12c		12c
Pear Halves (40/50)(L.S.)	103 oz	17 oz	80+ oz	124 oz	21 oz	96 oz
	12c 7 oz	2c 1 oz	10+c	15c 4 oz	2c 5 oz	12c
Apricots (W.P.)	91 oz	15+ oz	80+ oz	109 oz	18+ oz	96 oz
	11c 3 oz	1c 7+oz	10+c	13c 5 oz	2c 2+oz	12c
Fruit Cocktail (W.P.)	80+ oz		80+ oz	96 oz		96 oz
	10+c		10+c	12c		12c
Peach Halves (W.P.)	91 oz	15+ oz	80+ oz	109 oz	18+ oz	96 oz
	11c 3 oz	1c 7+oz	10+c	13c 5 oz	2c 2+oz	12c
Pear Halves (W.P.)	114 oz	19 oz	80+ oz	137 oz	23 oz	96 oz
	14c 2 oz	2c 3 oz	10+c	17c 1 oz	2c 7 oz	12c

Table D–3 Vegetables

ITEM	AMT. BLENDED (DRAINED WGT.)	AMT. OF LIQUID ADDED*	BLENDING TIME REQUIRED	YIELD	VOLUME DECREASE
Beets, sliced	3 c.	½ c.	30 sec.	2 c.	43%
Carrots, sliced	3 c.	½ c.	60 sec.	2 c.	43%
Green Beans	3 c.	½ c.	30 sec.	2 c.	43%
Green Peas (3 sieve)	3 c.	½ c.	30 sec.	2½ c.	29%
Mixed Vegetables	3 c.	½ c.	60 sec.	2¼ c.	36%
Peas, Blackeyed	3 c.	½c.	30 sec.	3 c.	14%
Potatoes, Whole New	3 c.	1 c.	90 sec.	2½ c.	38%
Spinach	3 c.	½ c.	30 sec.	3 c.	14%
Squash	3 c.	½ c.	30 sec.	2¾ c.	21%
Tomatoes** (whole, diced, crushed)	3 c.	—	20 sec.	3 c.	0%
Turnip Greens	3 c.	1 c.	60 sec.	3 c.	25%

*Liquid from canned vegetables was used.
**Results were the same with whole, diced, and crushed tomatoes.
Mean % decrease in volume = 25%

Table D-4 Pureed diet production guide—Vegetables

Item	5 Servings #12 Scoop (2.67 ounces) Amt. Solid Food	Amt. Liquid	Amt. Yield	5 Servings #10 Scoop (3.2 ounces) Amt. Solid Food	Amt. Liquid	Amt. Yield
Beets, Sliced	19 oz	3+ oz	13+ oz	23 oz	4 oz	16 oz
	2c 3 oz	3+ oz	1c 5+oz	2c 7 oz	4 oz	2c
Carrots, Sliced	19 oz	3+ oz	13+ oz	23 oz	4 oz	16 oz
	2c 3 oz	3+ oz	1c 5+oz	2c 7 oz	4 oz	2c
Green Beans	19 oz	3+ oz	13+ oz	23 oz	4 oz	16 oz
	2c 3 oz	3+ oz	1c 5+oz	2c 7 oz	4 oz	2c
Green Peas (3 Sieve)	17 oz	3 oz	13+ oz	21 oz	3+ oz	16 oz
	2c 1 oz	3 oz	1c 5+oz	2c 5 oz	3+ oz	2c
Mixed Vegetables	12 oz	3 oz	13+ oz	22 oz	4 oz	16 oz
	2c 5 oz	3 oz	1c 5+oz	2c 6 oz	4 oz	2c
Peas, Blackeyed	15 oz	2+ oz	13+ oz	18+ oz	3 oz	16 oz
	1c 7 oz	2+ oz	1c 5+oz	2c 2+oz	3 oz	2c
Potatoes, Whole New	18 oz	6 oz	13+ oz	22+ oz	7+ oz	16 oz
	2c 2 oz	6 oz	1c 5+oz	2c 6+oz	7+ oz	2c
Spinach	15 oz	2+ oz	13+ oz	18+ oz	3 oz	16 oz
	1c 7 oz	2+ oz	1c 5+oz	2c 2+oz	3 oz	2c
Squash	16 oz	3 oz	13 oz	19 oz	3+ oz	16 oz
	2c	3 oz	1c 5+oz	2c 3 oz	3+ oz	2c
Tomatoes (Diced, Crushed or Whole)	13+ oz		13+ oz	16 oz		16 oz
	1c 5+oz		1c 5+oz	2c		2c
Turnip Greens	16 oz	5+ oz	13+ oz	22 oz	7+ oz	16 oz
	2c	5+ oz	1c 5+oz	2c 6 oz	7+ oz	2c

Item	10 Servings #12 Scoop (2.67 ounces) Amt. Solid Food	Amt. Liquid	Amt. Yield	10 Servings #10 Scoop (3.2 ounces) Amt. Solid Food	Amt. Liquid	Amt. Yield
Beets, Sliced	39 oz	6+ oz	27 oz	46 oz	8 oz	32 oz
	4c 7 oz	6+ oz	3c 3 oz	5c 6 oz	1c	4c
Carrots, Sliced	39 oz	6+ oz	27 oz	46 oz	8 oz	32 oz
	4c 7 oz	6+ oz	3 c 3 oz	5c 6 oz	1c	4c
Green Beans	39 oz	6+ oz	27 oz	46 oz	8 oz	32 oz
	4c 7 oz	6+ oz	3c 3 oz	5c 6 oz	1c	4c
Green Peas (3 Sieve)	35 oz	6 oz	27 oz	41+ oz	7 oz	32 oz
	4c 3 oz	6 oz	3c 3 oz	5c 1+oz	7 oz	4c
Mixed Vegetables	37 oz	6+ oz	27 oz	44 oz	7+ oz	32 oz
	4c 5 oz	6+ oz	3c 3 oz	5c 4 oz	7+ oz	4c
Peas, Blackeyed	31 oz	5+ oz	27 oz	36+ oz	6 oz	32 oz
	3c 7 oz	5+ oz	3c 3 oz	4c 4+oz	6 oz	4c
Potatoes, Whole New	37+ oz	12+ oz	27 oz	44 oz	15 oz	32 oz
	4c 5+oz	1c 4+oz	3c 3 oz	5c 4 oz	1c 7 oz	4c
Spinach	31 oz	5+ oz	27 oz	36+ oz	6 oz	32 oz
	3c 7 oz	5+ oz	3c 3 oz	4c 4+oz	6 oz	4c

Table D–4 Vegetables, continued

Item	10 Servings					
	#12 Scoop (2.67 ounces)			#10 Scoop (3.2 ounces)		
	Amt. Solid Food	Amt. Liquid	Amt. Yield	Amt. Solid Food	Amt. Liquid	Amt. Yield
Squash	33 oz	5+ oz	27 oz	40 oz	7 oz	32 oz
	4c 1 oz	5+ oz	3c 3 oz	5c	7 oz	4c
Tomatoes (Diced, Crushed or Whole)	27 oz		27 oz	32 oz		32 oz
	3c 3 oz		3c 3oz	4c		4c
Turnip Greens	37 oz	12 oz	27 oz	40 oz	13+ oz	32 oz
	4c 5 oz	1c 4 oz	3c 3 oz	5c	13+ oz	4c

Item	15 Servings					
	#12 Scoop (2.67 ounces)			#10 Scoop (3.2 ounces)		
	Amt. Solid Food	Amt. Liquid	Amt. Yield	Amt. Solid Food	Amt. Liquid	Amt. Yield
Beets, Sliced	57 oz	9+ oz	40 oz	69 oz	11+ oz	48 oz
	7c 1 oz	1c 1+oz	5c	8c 5 oz	1c 3 oz	6c
Carrots, Sliced	57 oz	9+ oz	40 oz	69 oz	11+ oz	48 oz
	7c 1oz	1c 1+oz	5c	8c 5 oz	1c 3 oz	6c
Green Beans	57 oz	9+ oz	40+ oz	69 oz	11+ oz	48 oz
	7c 1 oz	1c 1+oz	5+c	8c 5 oz	1c 3 oz	6c
Green Peas (3 Sieve)	52 oz	9 oz	40 oz	62 oz	10+ oz	48 oz
	6c 4 oz	1c 1 oz	5c	7c 6 oz	1c 2 oz	6c
Mixed Vegetables	54 oz	9 oz	40 oz	65 oz	11 oz	48 oz
	6c 6 oz	1c 1 oz	5c	8c 1 oz	1c 3 oz	6c
Peas, Blackeyed	46 oz	8 oz	40 oz	55 oz	9+ oz	48 oz
	5c 6 oz	1c	5c	6c 7 oz	1c 1+oz	6c
Potatoes, Whole New	65 oz	22 oz	40 oz	66 oz	22 oz	48 oz
	8c 1 oz	2c 6 oz	5c	8c 2 oz	2c 6 oz	6c
Spinach	46 oz	8 oz	40 oz	55 oz	9+ oz	48 oz
	5c 6 oz	1c	5c	6c 7 oz	1c 1+oz	6c
Squash	48+ oz	8 oz	40 oz	58 oz	10 oz	48 oz
	6c	1c	5c	7c 2 oz	1c 2 oz	6c
Tomatoes (Diced, Crushed or Whole)	40 oz		40 oz	48 oz		48 oz
	5c		5c	6c		6c
Turnip Greens	50 oz	17 oz	40 oz	60 oz	20 oz	48 oz
	6c 2 oz	2c 1 oz	5c	7c 4 oz	2c 4 oz	6c

Item	20 Servings					
	#12 Scoop (2.67 ounces)			#10 Scoop (3.2 ounces)		
	Amt. Solid Food	Amt. Liquid	Amt. Yield	Amt. Solid Food	Amt. Liquid	Amt. Yield
Beets, Sliced	76 oz	13 oz	53+ oz	92 oz	15 oz	64 oz
	9c 4 oz	1c 5 oz	6c 5+oz	11c 4 oz	1c 7 oz	8c
Carrots, Sliced	76 oz	13 oz	53+ oz	92 oz	15+ oz	64 oz
	9c 4 oz	1c 5 oz	6c 5+oz	11c 4 oz	1c 7+oz	8c
Green Beans	76 oz	13 oz	53+ oz	92 oz	15+ oz	64 oz
	9c 4 oz	1c 5 oz	6c 5+oz	11c 4 oz	1c 7 oz	8c

Table D–4 Vegetables, continued

Item	20 Servings					
	#12 Scoop (2.67 ounces)			#10 Scoop (3.2 ounces)		
	Amt. Solid Food	Amt. Liquid	Amt. Yield	Amt. Solid Food	Amt. Liquid	Amt. Yield
Green Peas (3 Sieve)	74+ oz	12+ oz	53+ oz	87 oz	14 oz	64 oz
	9c 2 oz	1c 4 oz	6c 5+ oz	10c 7 oz	1c 6 oz	8c
Mixed Vegetables	72 oz	12 oz	53+ oz	87 oz	14+ oz	64 oz
	9c	1c 4 oz	6c 5+oz	10c 7 oz	1c 6+oz	8c
Peas, Blackeyed	60+ oz	10 oz	53+ oz	73 oz	12+ oz	64 oz
	7c 4+oz	1c 2 oz	6c 5+oz	9c 1 oz	1c 4 oz	8c
Potatoes, Whole New	73 oz	24+ oz	53+ oz	88 oz	29 oz	64 oz
	9c 1 oz	3c+	6c 5+oz	11c	3c 5 oz	8c
Spinach	60+ oz	10 oz	53+ oz	88 oz	29 oz	64 oz
	7c 4 oz	1c 2 oz	6c 5+oz	11c 1 oz	3c 5 oz	8c
Squash	64 oz	11 oz	53+ oz	77+ oz	13 oz	64 oz
	8c	1c 3 oz	6c 5+oz	9c 5 oz	1c 5 oz	8c
Tomatoes (Diced, Crushed or Whole)	53+ oz		53+ oz	64 oz		64 oz
	6c 5+oz		6c 5+oz	8c		8c
Turnip Greens	66 oz	22 oz	53+ oz	80 oz	27 oz	64 oz
	8c 2 oz	2c 6 oz	6c 5+oz	10c	3c 3 oz	8c

Item	25 Servings					
	#12 Scoop (2.67 ounces)			#10 Scoop (3.2 ounces)		
	Amt. Solid Food	Amt. Liquid	Amt. Yield	Amt. Solid Food	Amt. Liquid	Amt. Yield
Beets, Sliced	96 oz	16 oz	67 oz	114 oz	19 oz	80 oz
	12c	2c	8c 3 oz	14c 2 oz	2c 3 oz	10c
Carrots, Sliced	96 oz	16 oz	67 oz	114 oz	19 oz	80 oz
	12c	2c	8c 3 oz	14c 2 oz	2c 3 oz	10c
Green Beans	96 oz	16 oz	67 oz	114 oz	19 oz	80 oz
	12c	2c	8c 3 oz	14c 2 oz	2c 3 oz	10c
Green Peas (3 Sieve)	86 oz	14+ oz	67 oz	103+ oz	17+ oz	80 oz
	10c 6 oz	1c 6+oz	8c 3 oz	12c 7+oz	2c 1+oz	10c
Mixed Vegetables	91 oz	15 oz	67 oz	109 oz	18+ oz	80 oz
	11c 3 oz	1c 7 oz	8c 3 oz	13c 5 oz	2c 2+oz	10c
Peas, Blackeyed	76 oz	13 oz	67 oz	91 oz	15+ oz	80 oz
	9c 4 oz	1c 5 oz	8c 3 oz	11c 3 oz	1c 7+oz	10c
Potatoes, Whole New	92 oz	31 oz	67 oz	30 oz	10 oz	80 oz
	11c 4 oz	3c 7 oz	8c 3 oz	3c 6 oz	1c 2 oz	10c
Spinach	76 oz	13 oz	67 oz	91 oz	15+ oz	80 oz
	9c 4 oz	1c 5 oz	8c 3 oz	11c 3 oz	1c 7+oz	10c
Squash	81 oz	13+ oz	67 oz	97 oz	16+ oz	80 oz
	10c 1 oz	1c 5+oz	8c 3 oz	12c 1 oz	2+c	10c
Tomatoes (Diced, Crushed or Whole)	67 oz		67 oz	80 oz		80 oz
	8c 3 oz		8c 3 oz	10c		10c
Turnip Greens	84 oz	28 oz	67 oz	100 oz	33+ oz	80 oz
	10c 4 oz	3c 4 oz	8c 3 oz	12c 4 oz	4c 1 oz	10c

Table D–4 Vegetables, continued

| Item | 30 Servings | | | | | |
| | #12 Scoop (2.67 ounces) | | | #10 Scoop (3.2 ounces) | | |
	Amt. Solid Food	Amt. Liquid	Amt. Yield	Amt. Solid Food	Amt. Liquid	Amt. Yield
Beets, Sliced	114+ oz	19+ oz	80+ oz	137 oz	23 oz	96 oz
	14c 2+oz	2c 3+oz	10+c	17c 1 oz	2c 7 oz	12c
Carrots, Sliced	114+ oz	19+ oz	80+ oz	137 oz	23 oz	96 oz
	14c 2+oz	2c 3+oz	10+c	17c 1 oz	2c 7 oz	12c
Green Beans	114+ oz	19+ oz	80+ oz	137 oz	23 oz	96 oz
	14c 2+oz	2c 3+oz	10+c	17c 1 oz	2c 7 oz	12c
Green Peas (3 Sieve)	103+ oz	17+ oz	80+ oz	124 oz	21 oz	96 oz
	12c 7+oz	2c 1+oz	10+c	15c 4 oz	2c 5 oz	12c
Mixed Vegetables	109 oz	18+ oz	80+ oz	131 oz	6 oz	96 oz
	13c 5 oz	2c 2+oz	10+c	16c 3 oz	6 oz	12c
Peas, Blackeyed	91 oz	15+ oz	80+ oz	109 oz	18 oz	96 oz
	11c 3 oz	1c 7+oz	10+c	13c 5 oz	2c 2 oz	12c
Potatoes, Whole New	30 oz	10 oz	80+ oz	132 oz	12 oz	96 oz
	3c 6 oz	1c 2 oz	10+c	16c 4 oz	1c 4 oz	12c
Spinach	91 oz	15+ oz	80+ oz	109 oz	18 oz	96 oz
	11c 3 oz	1c 7+oz	10+c	13c 5 oz	2c 2 oz	12c
Squash	97 oz	16+ oz	80+ oz	116 oz	19+ oz	96 oz
	12c 1 oz	2+c	10+c	14c 4 oz	2c 3+oz	12c
Tomatoes (Diced, Crushed or Whole)	80+ oz		80+ oz	96 oz		96 oz
	10+c		10+c	12c		12c
Turnip Greens	100 oz	33+ oz	80+ oz	120 oz	40 oz	96 oz
	12c 4 oz	4c 1+oz	10+c	15c	5c	12c

443

Restaurant-Style Menus

Patients are given a meal card on which to write their selections. Generally, the menu items are numbered and the patient writes the number on the card rather than the name of the food or beverage. In some facilities, patients simply circle numbered menu items to minimize potential confusion.

The meal card should include at least the patient's name, room number, date, diet order, and a space for the selected items. The card usually is placed on the tray to ensure accuracy of the meal sent to the patient.

Meals for _____
(day of the week)

Breakfast

Juice # _____
Fruit # _____

Cereal# _____	Bread# _____
Egg# _____	Other# _____
Beverage# _____	

Dinner

Appetizer# _____	Salad# _____
Entree# _____	Veg.# _____
Veg.# _____	Bread# _____
Sand.# _____	
Dessert# _____	Beverage# _____

Supper

Appetizer# _____	Salad# _____
Entree# _____	Veg.# _____
Veg.# _____	Bread# _____
Sand.# _____	
Dessert# _____	Beverage# _____

Diet Order _____

Name _____Room # _____

Breakfast

Fruits/Juices

#1 Orange Juice
#2 Apple Juice
#3 Grapefruit Juice
#4 Pineapple Juice

#5 Citrus Sections
#6 Banana
#7 Prunes
#8 Melon in Season

Cereals

#9 Raisin Bran
#10 Total
#11 Granola
#12 Cheerios
#13 Grits
#14 Cream of Wheat
#15 Oatmeal

Breads & Starch

#16 Toast with Marg. and Jelly
#17 Whole Wheat Toast with
    Marg. & Jelly
#18 Hot Danish
#19 Pancakes with Marg. & Syrup
#20 Waffles with Marg. &
    Blueberry Syrup
#21 Bagel with Marg. & Cream
    Cheese
#22 Croissant
#23 Biscuit with Marg. & Jelly

Eggs

#24 Scrambled Eggs(2)
#25 Poached Egg
#26 Cheese Omelet
#27 Hard Cooked Egg
#28 Fried Egg

Other

#29 Bacon
#30 Sausage
#31 Ham
#32 Hash Browns
#33 Cheese Toast

Beverages

#34 Whole Milk
#35 2% Milk
#36 Skim Milk
#37 Coffee

#38 Decaf. Coffee
#39 Hot Tea
#40 Hot Chocolate
#41 Chocolate Milk

Dinner/Supper

Appetizer

#101 Beef Broth
#102 Chicken Broth
#103 Vegetable Cocktail
#104 Tomato Juice

#105 Vegetable Soup
#106 Chix & Noodle Soup
#107 Cream of Broccoli Soup
#108 Stuffed Celery

Salads

#109 Large Chef's
#110 Small Chef's
#111 Tossed Salad

#112 Fruit Cups
#113 Cottage Cheese & Fruit Plate
#114 Tomato & Cucumbers

Dressings: 115 Creamy Italian, 116 Ranch, 117 Blue Cheese, 118 French,
           119 Low Cal

#120 Potato Salad
#121 Coleslaw

#122 Macaroni Salad

Entrees

#123 Southern Fried Chicken
#124 Roast Beef with Mashed Potatoes
#125 Broiled Fish Almondine
#126 Baked Chicken with Wild Rice
#127 Creamy Macaroni & Cheese
#128 Sugar-Cured Ham
#129 Stuffed Peppers
#130 Sauteed Liver & Onions
#131 Fried Chicken Livers
#132 Spaghetti & Meatballs
#133 Rib-Eye

Vegetables

#134 Asparagus Tips
#135 Broccoli
#136 Brussel Sprouts
#137 Steamed Cabbage
#138 Corn
#139 Cauliflower
#140 English Peas
#141 Green Beans
#142 Hawad Beets
#143 Carrots
#144 Squash Casserole
#145 Sauteed Mushrooms
#146 Stewed Tomatoes
#147 Lima Beans

Potatoes

#148 Baked Potato with Marg.
#149 Stuffed Potatoes
#150 Cheese & Mushrooms
#151 Bacon & Cheese
#152 Sour Cream & Chives
#153 Baked Sweet Potato
#154 Candied Yams
#155 French Fries
#156 Mashed Potatoes
#157 Parsleyed New Potatoes

Sandwiches

#158 BLT
#159 Roast Beef
#160 Chicken Salad on white
      bread - #-A
#161 Tuna Salad
#162 Egg Salad
#163 Grilled Cheese
#164 Ham & Swiss on whole wheat -
      #-B

Breads

#165 Hot Roll
#166 Hot Biscuit
#167 Onion Roll
#168 White Bread
#169 Whole Wheat Bread
#170 Crescent Roll

Desserts

#171 Apple Pie
#172 Ice Cream
#173 Sherbet
#174 Mixed Fruit
#175 Applesauce
#176 Angel Food Cake
#177 Custard

Beverages

#178 Whole Milk
#179 Skim Milk
#180 Chocolate Milk
#181 Ice Tea
#182 Hot Tea
#183 Coffee

#184 Decaf. Coffee
#185 Fruit Punch
#186 Orange Juice

447

Diet Equivalents

HOSPITALS

Component	Average selling price/Svg.*
Regular Diet	
Entree	$1.25
Starchy vegetable	.50
Second vegetable	.50
Bread	.10
Margarine	.05
Salad	.65
Dessert	.75
Beverage	.10
Total	$3.90
Soft Diet	
Entree	$1.25
Starchy vegetable	.50
Second vegetable	.50
Bread	.10
Margarine	.05
Salad	.65
Dessert	.75
Beverage	.10
Total	$3.90

Percent of Regular—100%
Meal Equivalent—1.0

---

*Includes raw food cost and labor, overhead (including equipment depreciation and utilities), and small percent of profit, as determined by a Stokes Report reader survey, July 1982.

449

Component	Average selling price/Svg.*

Bland Diet

Entree	$1.25
Starchy vegetable	.50
Second vegetable	.50
Bread	.10
Margarine	.05
Salad	.65
Dessert	.75
Beverage	.10
Total	$3.90

Percent of Regular—100%
Meal Equivalent—1.0

Low Residue

Entree	$1.25
Starchy vegetable	.50
Second vegetable	.50
Bread	.10
Margarine	.05
Fruit for salad	.40
Low-residue dessert	.75
Beverage	.10
Total	$3.65

Percent of Regular—93%
Meal Equivalent—1.0

High Residue

Entree	$1.25
Starchy vegetable	.50
Second vegetable	.50
Whole grain bread	.15
Margarine	.05
Salad	.65
Dessert	.75
Beverage	.10
Total	$3.95

Percent of Regular—101%
Meal Equivalent—1.0

Component	Average selling price/Svg.*

Salt Restricted

Entree	$1.25
Starchy vegetable	.50
Low-sodium vegetable	.75
Bread	.10
Low-sodium margarine	.10
Salad	.65
Dessert (fruit)	.40
Beverage	.10
Total	$3.85

Percent of Regular—99%
Meal Equivalent—1.0

Fat Restricted

Entree	$1.25
Starchy vegetable	.50
Second vegetable	.50
Bread	.10
Corn oil margarine	.10
Salad	.65
Dessert (fruit)	.40
Beverage	.10
Total	$3.60

Percent of Regular—93%
Meal Equivalent—1.0

Clear Liquid

Broth bouillon	.15
Clear gelatin	.15
Clear fruit juice	.50
Supplemental beverage (soft drinks, etc.)	.90
Total	$1.70

Percent of Regular—43%
Meal Equivalent—.4

Full Liquid

Cream soup	.65
Juice	.50
Milk	.40
Milk-based dessert	.65
Total	$2.20

Percent of Regular—56%
Meal Equivalent—.5

451

Component	Average selling price/Svg.*
Diabetic Diet	
a. 800 calories	
1 oz Meat	.40
1 Vegetable	.50
1 Fruit (water-pack)	.50
1 Bread	.10
1 Margarine	.05
Beverage	.10
Total	$1.65
Percent of Regular—42%	
Meal Equivalent—.4	
b. 1,000 calories	
2 oz Meat	.80
2 Vegetables	1.00
1 Fruit (water-pack)	.50
1 Margarine	.05
Beverage	.10
Total	$2.45
Percent of Regular—63%	
Meal Equivalent—.6	
c. 1,200 calories	
2 oz. Meat	.80
2 Vegetables	1.00
1 Fruit (water-pack)	.50
1 Bread	.10
1 Margarine	.05
Beverage	.10
Total	$2.55
Percent of Regular—65%	
Meal Equivalent—.6	
d. 1,500 calories	
2 oz Meat	$ .80
1 Starchy vegetable	.50
Second vegetable	.50
Salad	.65
Bread	.10
Margarine	.05
Fruit (water-pack)	.50
Beverage	.10
Total	$3.20
Percent of Regular—87%	
Meal Equivalent—.9	

Component	Average selling price/Svg.*

e. 1,800 calories

3 oz Meat	$1.25
1 Starchy vegetable	.50
Second vegetable	.50
Salad	.65
Bread	.10
Margarine—2 tsp.	.10
Fruit (water-pack)	.50
Beverage	.10
Total	$3.70

Percent of Regular—95%
Meal Equivalent—1.0

f. 2,000 calories

3 oz Meat	$1.25
1 Starchy vegetable	.50
Second vegetable	.50
Salad	.65
Bread—2 slices	.20
Margarine—2 tsp.	.10
Fruit (water-pack)	.50
Beverage	.10
Total	$3.80

Percent of Regular—97%
Meal Equivalent—1.0

Protein-Restricted (40 gram)

2 oz. Entree	.75
Starchy vegetable	.50
Second vegetable	.50
Low-protein bread	.92
Fruit	.65
Beverage	.10
Total	$3.42

Percent of Regular—87%
Meal Equivalent—1.0

Tube Feeding

Cost for 2,000cc per day	$4.00

Percent of regular—25%
Meal Equivalent—.25

453

NURSING HOMES

Component	Raw food cost	Total cost*
Regular Diet		
Entree	$ .35	
Starchy vegetable	.10	
Second vegetable	.10	
Bread	.03	
Margarine	.02	
Dessert	.10	
Beverage	.05	
Total	$ .75	$1.50
Soft Diet		
Entree	$ .35	
Starchy vegetable	.10	
Second vegetable	.10	
Bread	.03	
Margarine	.02	
Dessert	.10	
Beverage	.05	
Total	$ .75	$1.50

Percent of Regular—100%
Meal Equivalent—1.0

Bland Diet		
Entree	$ .35	
Starchy vegetable	.10	
Second vegetable	.10	
Bread	.03	
Margarine	.02	
Dessert	.10	
Beverage	.05	
Total	$ .75	$1.50

Percent of Regular—100%
Meal Equivalent—1.0

---

*Includes labor, overhead, equipment, and building depreciation and utilities as determined by a Stokes Report reader survey, July, 1982.

Low-Residue Diet

Entree	.35	
Starchy vegetable	.10	
Second vegetable	.10	
Bread	.03	
Margarine	.02	
Fruit or low-residue dessert	.10	
Beverage	.05	
Total	$ .75	$1.50

Percent of Regular—100%
Meal Equivalent—1.0

High-Residue Diet

Entree	.35	
Starchy vegetable	.10	
Second vegetable	.10	
Whole grain bread	.03	
Margarine	.02	
Dessert	.10	
Beverage	.05	
Total	$ .75	$1.50

Percent of Regular—100%
Meal Equivalent—1.0

Salt Restricted

Entree	.35	
Starchy vegetable	.10	
Second vegetable	.10	
Bread	.03	
Margarine	.02	
Dessert	.10	
Beverage	.05	
Total	$ .75	$1.50

Percent of Regular—100%
Meal Equivalent—1.0

Component	Raw food cost	Total cost*

Fat Restricted

Entree	$ .35	
Starchy vegetable	.10	
Second vegetable	.10	
Bread	.03	
Margarine	.02	
Dessert	.10	
Beverage	.05	
Total	$ .75	$1.50

Percent of Regular—100%
Meal Equivalent—1.0

Clear Liquid

Broth/bouillon	$ .05	
Clear gelatin	.05	
Clear fruit juice	.20	
Total	.30	$.60

Percent of Regular—40%
Meal Equivalent—.4

Full Liquid

Cream soup	.15	
Juice	.20	
Milk	.15	
Milk-based dessert	.20	
Total	.70	$1.40

Percent of Regular—93%
Meal Equivalent—.9

Diabetic

a. 800 calories

1 oz Meat	.12	
1 Vegetable	.10	
1 Fruit (water-pack)	.15	
1 Bread	.03	
1 Margarine	.02	
Beverage	.05	
Total	.47	$ .94

Percent of Regular—63%
Meal Equivalent—.6

Component	Raw food cost	Total cost*

b. 1,000 calories

2 oz Meat	.24	
2 Vegetables	.20	
1 Fruit (water-pack)	.15	
1 Margarine	.02	
Beverage	.05	
Total	.66	$1.32

Percent of Regular—87%
Meal Equivalent—.9

c. 1,200 calories

2 oz Meat	.24	
2 Vegetables	.20	
1 Fruit (water-pack)	.15	
1 Bread	.03	
1 Margarine	.02	
Beverage	.05	
Total	.69	$1.38

Percent of Regular—92%
Meal Equivalent—.9

d. 1,500 calories

2 oz Meat	.24	
1 Starchy vegetable	.10	
2 Second vegetables	.20	
1 Fruit (water-pack)	.15	
1 Bread	.03	
1 Margarine	.02	
Beverage	.05	
Total	.79	$1.58

Percent of Regular—105%
Meal Equivalent—1.0

e. 1,800 calories

3 oz Meat	.35	
1 Starchy vegetable	.10	
2 Second vegetables	.20	
1 Fruit (water-pack)	.15	
1 Bread	.03	
2 Margarine	.04	
Beverage	.05	
Total	.92	$1.84

Percent of Regular—123%
Meal Equivalent—1.2

457

Component	Raw food cost	Total cost*
f. 2,000 calories		
3 oz Meat	.35	
1 Starchy vegetable	.10	
2 Second vegetables	.20	
1 Fruit (water-pack)	.15	
2 Bread	.06	
2 Margarine	.04	
Beverage	.05	
Total	.95	$1.90

Percent of Regular—127%
Meal Equivalent—1.3

Energy Analysis

100-BED NURSING HOME

Food Preparation Equipment

I. Identify the preparation equipment utilized:

EXAMPLE:

Type of equipment	Number	Make & model	Energy usage	Hours use/day
Convection Oven	1	Blodgett GZ-120	11 KW	8 hrs
Fryers	1	Keating TS-14	120,000 BTU	2 hrs
Ranges	1	South Bend	180,000 BTU	8 hrs
Microwave Ovens	0			
Griddles	0			
Broilers	0			
Steam Cookers	1	Market Forge	14 KW	6 hrs
Others				

II. Operating Procedures

Are proper preheating procedures followed?　　　　Yes _____　　No __XX__
Comments _The range requires at least one hour to preheat._ _____

Is temperature reduced or equipment turned off during　Yes _____　　No __XX__
slack periods?
Comments _Because the oven takes so long to heat, we leave it on all day._ _____

Is full production capacity of equipment being used?　　Yes _____　　No __XX__
Comments _Because the oven is on all day, we use it whenever we need it._ _____

Is the equipment utilized the correct size for tasks com-　Yes __XX__　　No _____
pleted?
Comments _____

Is equipment used correctly:

Are pots and pans grouped on the range tops? Yes __XX__ No _____

Are pans spaced properly in ovens to avoid crippled runs? Yes __XX__ No _____

Is a timer used to avoid opening oven door? Yes _____ No __XX__

Are microwave ovens used for heating or secondary rather than large primary cooking functions? Yes _____ No __XX__

Comments _We rely upon opening the oven door to determine if cooking time has been adequate._

III. Cleaning and Maintenance

Is a detailed cleaning schedule posted and followed? Yes _____ No __XX__

Comments _A cleaning schedule is posted but not followed._

Are thermostats checked periodically to verify accuracy? Yes __XX__ No _____

Comments _____

Have thermostats been calibrated? Yes _____ No __XX__

Comments _____

Do oven doors close properly? Yes _____ No __XX__

Comments _Oven door beneath range will fall open unexpectedly unless balanced._

Are indicator lights working properly? Yes __XX__ No _____

Comments _____

Is a preventive maintenance program in operation and up to date? Yes _____ No __XX__

Comments _No formal program has been established; the maintenance department_
checks food service equipment when repairs are required.

Is equipment clean?

Are spills cleaned as they occur? Yes __XX__ No _____

Are oven interiors and heating elements free from grease? Yes __XX__ No _____

Are griddles, burners and broiler grates kept clean? Yes __XX__ No _____

Are fryer heating elements clean? Yes __XX__ No _____

Is steam equipment free from mineral deposits? Yes _____ No __XX__

Are grease pans removed and cleaned? Yes _____ No __XX__

Comments _Lime deposits have built up in the steam equipment from the soft water_
in our area. Grease pans beneath the range top are cleaned on an irregular basis.

Refrigeration Equipment

I. Identify the refrigeration equipment utilized:

EXAMPLE:

Type of equipment	Number	Make & model	Energy usage
Reach-in refrigerator	1	McCall 1045	4 KW
Reach-in freezer	1	Nor-Lake	6 KW
Walk-in cooler	1	Koch	½ HP
Walk-in freezer			
Roll-in refrigerator			
Others			

II. Operating Procedures

Do door gaskets fit snugly?   Yes __XX__   No _____
Comments _____

Is refrigerator equipment located in a cool environment?   Yes _____   No __XX__
Comments _Reach-in refrigerator is located next to preparation equipment._

Are the number of times the door is opened limited?   Yes _____   No __XX__
Comments _Because so many people prepare the food, door openings are not regulated._

Are temperatures recorded twice daily?   Yes __XX__   No _____
Comments _____

III. Cleaning and Maintenance

Are evaporator coils kept free of excess frost?   Yes _____   No __XX__
Comments _Dust and lint had accumulated on the evaporator coils._

Are condenser coils kept free of lint, dust, and other obstructions?   Yes _____   No __XX__
Comments _____

Is there proper air circulation around condensers and condenser motors?   Yes __XX__   No _____
Comments _____

Are drive belts in good condition and properly adjusted?   Yes __XX__   No _____
Comments _____

Are suspension springs in good condition?   Yes __XX__   No _____
Comments _____

Are there cold spots on the outside walls of equipment?   Yes _____   No __XX__
Comments _____

Are door gaskets in good repair?   Yes __XX__   No _____
Comments _____

Warewashing Equipment

I. Identify warewashing equipment utilized:

EXAMPLE:

Type of equipment	Number	Make & model	Energy usage
Two Tank Dishwasher	1	Hobart C-44	1½ HP, 15 KW
Disposer			
Pot Washer			
Other			

461

II. Operating Procedures

Is machine turned on just before needed?   Yes __XX__   No _____
Comments _____

Is machine fully loaded each cycle?   Yes __XX__   No _____
Comments _____

Is cool water used when operating disposal?   Yes _____   No __XX__
Comments <u>Only hot water connections have been made to the disposer.</u>

Is equipment flushed after each meal period?   Yes __XX__   No _____
Comments _____

III. Cleaning and Maintenance

Is machine washed thoroughly after each day's
operation?   Yes __XX__   No _____
Comments _____

Are mineral deposits removed regularly?   Yes _____   No __XX__
Comments <u>We have multiple mineral deposits from soft water.</u>

Is machine oiled and lubricated on a regular schedule?   Yes __XX__   No _____
Comments _____

Are wash and rinse temperatures checked and recorded
daily?   Yes _____   No __XX__
Comments _____

Is water pressure evaluated regularly?   Yes _____   No __XX__
Comments _____

Lighting

I. Identify all lighting in food service area.

EXAMPLE:

Area	Type of light	Number	Wattage	Hours of use
Storage room	Incandescent	12	100	10 hours/day
Dining room	Incandescent	40	75	12 hours/day
Preparation area	Fluorescent	20	60	12 hours/day
Walk-in refrigeration	Incandescent	1	75	12 hours/day
Dishwashing area	N/A			
Offices and restrooms	Incandescent	10	75	12 hours/day
Other				

II. Operating Procedures

Are there adequate light switches to limit lighting to small
areas?   Yes _____   No __XX__
Comments <u>One light switch controls the entire kitchen.</u>

Are there transformer-type dimmer switches available for dining areas?   Yes _____   No __XX__

Comments _____

Are there timers available for lighting of large areas?   Yes _____   No __XX__

Comments _____

Are lights in offices and restrooms turned off when not in use?   Yes _____   No __XX__

Comments _____

Are walls and ceilings painted in a light color?   Yes __XX__   No _____

Comments _____

III. Cleaning and Maintenance

Are all bulbs replaced with the lowest wattage feasible?   Yes _____   No __XX__

Comments <u>Bulbs are replaced with the wattage originally in the fixture.</u>

Are unused fluorescent and incandescent fixtures de-lamped?   Yes _____   No __XX__

Comments _____

Are light fixtures cleaned regularly?   Yes _____   No __XX__

Comments _____

Water Heating

I. Identify capacity and energy usage of water heaters:

EXAMPLE:

Water heaters:

Capacity   Energy Usage   Temperature setting

Primary heater
Booster heaters

II. Operating Procedures

Are water heaters located close to the point of most frequent use?   Yes __XX__   No _____

Comments _____

Are storage tanks properly sized?   Yes __XX__   No _____

Comments _____

III. Cleaning and Maintenance

Are hot water pipes checked for leaks on a regularly scheduled basis?   Yes _____   No __XX__

Comments <u>Leaks are repaired as they occur.</u>

463

Are heaters and pipes insulated?   Yes _____   No _XX_

Comments _____

Are water pressure regulators used?   Yes _____   No _XX_

Comments _____

Is a heat recovery system utilized?   Yes _____   No _XX_

Comments _____

Heating, Ventilation, and Air Conditioning

I. Identify Ventilation Equipment: one wall-mounted vent hood, 8 feet long
Number of exhaust fans: two
Method of grease extraction: screen filters

II. Operating Procedures

Are fans used only when needed?   Yes _____   No _XX_

Comments Ventilation is on during the operating hours of the kitchen.

Are thermostats set at lowest setting?   Yes _XX_   No _____

Comments _____

Are doors and windows kept closed?   Yes _____   No _XX_

Comments Windows are kept closed but the back door often remains open.

III. Cleaning and Maintenance

Are vent filters cleaned and/or replaced regularly?   Yes _XX_   No _____

Comments _____

Are exhaust fan speeds evaluated regularly?   Yes _____   No _XX_

Comments _____

Are HVAC systems inspected regularly, including fans and ducts?   Yes _____   No _XX_

Comments _____

Is a heat recovery system utilized?   Yes _____   No _XX_

Comments _____

Recommendations:

1. Consider replacement of range and oven with a more efficient model.
2. Use a timer to determine whether cooking time has been adequate.
3. Enforce a cleaning schedule.
4. Repair oven door.
5. Establish preventive maintenance program.
6. Remove mineral deposits from steam and dishwashing equipment.
7. Use only cold-water connections to the disposer.
8. Consider installation of multiple light switches to control small areas of the kitchen.

Food Preparation Equipment

I. Identify the preparation equipment utilized:

EXAMPLE:

Type of equipment	Number	Make & model	Energy usage	Hours use/day
Convection Oven	2	Garland	11 KW	8 hrs
Low Temp Oven	1	Alto-Shaam	4 KW	8 hrs
Fryers	2	Pitco	120,000 BTU	2 hrs
Ranges	2	South Bend	180,000 BTU	8 hrs
Microwave Ovens	1	Amana		
Griddles	1	Keating		
Broilers				
Steam Cookers	2	Cleveland	36 KW	4 hrs
Others				

II. Operating Procedures

Are proper preheating procedures followed? Yes __XX__ No __XX__
Comments _Older equipment (ranges and convection ovens) require more heat up time._

Is temperature reduced or equipment turned off during slack periods? Yes __XX__ No _____
Comments _Temperature is reduced._

Is full production capacity of equipment being used? Yes __XX__ No _____
Comments _____

Is the equipment utilized the correct size for tasks completed? Yes __XX__ No _____
Comments _____

Is equipment used correctly:

Are pots and pans grouped on the range tops? Yes _____ No __XX__
Are pans spaced properly in ovens to avoid crippled runs? Yes __XX__ No _____
Is a timer used to avoid opening oven door? Yes _____ No __XX__
Are microwave ovens used for heating or secondary rather than large primary cooking functions? Yes __XX__ No _____
Comments _Cooks tend to utilize the entire range top rather than grouping pots and pans._

III. Cleaning and Maintenance

Is a detailed cleaning schedule posted and followed? Yes __XX__ No _____
Comments _____

Are thermostats checked periodically to verify accuracy? Yes _____ No __XX__
Comments _____

Have thermostats been calibrated? Yes _____ No __XX__
Comments _____

465

Do oven doors close properly? Yes __XX__ No _____
Comments _____
_____

Are indicator lights working properly? Yes __XX__ No _____
Comments _____
_____

Is a preventive maintenance program in operation and up Yes __XX__ No _____
to date?
Comments _The Maintenance Department keeps a preventive maintenance program up to date_
_in compliance with JCAH regulations._____

Is equipment clean?
    Are spills cleaned as they occur? Yes __XX__ No _____
    Are oven interiors and heating elements free from Yes __XX__ No _____
      grease?
    Are griddles, burners and broiler grates kept clean? Yes __XX__ No _____
    Are fryer heating elements clean? Yes __XX__ No _____
    Is steam equipment free from mineral deposits? Yes __XX__ No _____
    Are grease pans removed and cleaned? Yes __XX__ No _____
Comments _All of these items are detailed on the cleaning schedule._____

Refrigeration Equipment

I. Identify the refrigeration equipment utilized:

EXAMPLE:

Type of equipment	Number	Make & model	Energy usage
Reach-in refrigerator	1	Traulsen	4 KW
Reach-in freezer			
Walk-in cooler	2	Vollrath	1½ HP each
Walk-in freezer	1	Vollrath	2 HP
Roll-in refrigerator			
Others			

II. Operating Procedures

Do door gaskets fit snugly? Yes _____ No __XX__
Comments _Door gaskets have cracked on the reach-in._____

Is refrigerator equipment located in a cool environment? Yes __XX__ No _____
Comments _____
_____

Are the number of times the door is opened limited? Yes _____ No __XX__
Comments _____
_____

Are temperatures recorded twice daily? Yes __XX__ No _____
Comments _____
_____

III. Cleaning and Maintenance

Are evaporator coils kept free of excess frost? Yes __XX__ No _____
Comments _____
_____

Are condenser coils kept free of lint, dust, and other obstructions?	Yes __XX__	No _____

Comments _____

Is there proper air circulation around condensers and condenser motors?	Yes __XX__	No _____

Comments _____

Are drive belts in good condition and properly adjusted?	Yes __XX__	No _____

Comments _____

Are suspension springs in good condition?	Yes __XX__	No _____

Comments _____

Are there cold spots on the outside walls of equipment?	Yes _____	No __XX__

Comments _____

Are door gaskets in good repair?	Yes _____	No __XX__

Comments Rubber door gaskets have cracked. _____

Warewashing Equipment

I. Identify warewashing equipment utilized:

EXAMPLE:

Type of equipment	Number	Make & model	Energy usage
Flight type dishmachine with booster heater	1	Hobart F-700	8 HP, 60 KW
Disposer	1	Red Goat	2 HP
Pot Washer			
Other			

II. Operating Procedures

Is machine turned on just before needed?	Yes __XX__	No _____

Comments _____

Is machine fully loaded each cycle?	Yes _____	No _____

Comments Flight type machine has a continuous cycle; however the conveyor doesn't run if we don't load it.

Is cool water used when operating disposal?	Yes __XX__	No _____

Comments _____

Is equipment flushed after each meal period?	Yes __XX__	No _____

Comments _____

III. Cleaning and Maintenance

Is machine washed thoroughly after each day's operation?	Yes __XX__	No _____

Comments _____

467

Are mineral deposits removed regularly?   Yes __XX__   No _____
Comments _____

Is machine oiled and lubricated on a regular schedule?   Yes __XX__   No _____
Comments This is part of the preventive maintenance program. _____

Are wash and rinse temperatures checked and recorded   Yes __XX__   No _____
daily?
Comments _____

Is water pressure evaluated regularly?   Yes __XX__   No _____
Comments _____

Lighting

I. Identify all lighting in food service area.

EXAMPLE:

Area	Type of light	Number	Wattage	Hours of use
Storage room	Incandescent	12	100	10 hours/day
Dining room	Fluorescent	25	100	10 hours/day
Preparation area	Fluorescent	18	100	12 hours/day
Walk-in refrigeration	Incandescent	2	60	12 hours/day
Dishwashing area	Fluorescent	8	100	10 hours/day
Offices and restrooms	Fluorescent	4	100	12 hours/day
Other				

II. Operating Procedures

Are there adequate light switches to limit lighting to small   Yes _____   No __XX__
areas?
Comments Two main light switches service the entire department. _____

Are there transformer-type dimmer switches available for   Yes _____   No __XX__
dining areas?
Comments _____

Are there timers available for lighting of large areas?   Yes _____   No __XX__
Comments _____

Are lights in offices and restrooms turned off when not in   Yes _____   No __XX__
use?
Comments _____

Are walls and ceilings painted in a light color?   Yes __XX__   No _____
Comments _____

III. Cleaning and Maintenance

Are all bulbs replaced with the lowest wattage feasible?   Yes _____   No __XX__
Comments All bulbs are replaced with the wattage previously in the fixture. _____

| Are unused fluorescent and incandescent fixtures de-lamped? | Yes _____ | No __XX__ |

Comments _____

_____

| Are light fixtures cleaned regularly? | Yes _____ | No __XX__ |

Comments _____

_____

Water Heating

I. Identify capacity and energy usage of water heaters:

EXAMPLE:

Water heaters:

Capacity   Energy Usage   Temperature Setting

Primary heater
Booster heaters

II. Operating Procedures

| Are water heaters located close to the point of most frequent use? | Yes __XX__ | No _____ |

Comments _____

_____

| Are storage tanks properly sized? | Yes __XX__ | No _____ |

Comments _____

_____

III. Cleaning and Maintenance

| Are hot water pipes checked for leaks on a regularly scheduled basis? | Yes __XX__ | No _____ |

Comments _____

_____

| Are heaters and pipes insulated? | Yes __XX__ | No _____ |

Comments _____

_____

| Are water pressure regulators used? | Yes __XX__ | No _____ |

Comments _____

_____

| Is a heat recovery system utilized? | Yes __XX__ | No _____ |

Comments A heat recovery system is used for the building HVAC system but not in the Dietary Department per se.

Heating, Ventilation, and Air Conditioning

I. Identify Ventilation Equipment: One island-type vent hood, 20 feet long
Number of exhaust fans: 4
Method of grease extraction: Baffle type filters

II. Operating Procedures

| Are fans used only when needed? | Yes _____ | No __XX__ |

Comments The ventilation system is used during the entire operating time of the department.

_____

469

Are thermostats set at lowest setting?   Yes __XX__   No _____
Comments _____
_____

Are doors and windows kept closed?   Yes __XX__   No _____
Comments _____
_____

III. Cleaning and Maintenance

Are vent filters cleaned and/or replaced regularly?   Yes __XX__   No _____
Comments _____
_____

Are exhaust fan speeds evaluated regularly?   Yes _____   No __XX__
Comments _____
_____

Are HVAC systems inspected regularly, including fans   Yes __XX__   No _____
and ducts?
Comments _____
_____

Is a heat recovery system utilized?   Yes __XX__   No _____
Comments Only for the entire building. _____
_____

Recommendations:
1. Evaluate effectiveness of older preparation equipment and make long-range plans for replacement.
2. Utilize a timer to avoid opening oven door.
3. Utilize range top only when needed; consider replacing a range with a tilting braising pan.
4. Replace refrigerator door gaskets.
5. Consider use of a heat recovery system to capture lost heat from discarded dishwasher.
6. Consider installing multiple light switches to limit lighting to a small area. Consider use of timers for large areas.

Energy Conservation Ideas
to Save More Than $40,000

Dishwashing

A. Use a low temperature dishmachine, utilizing 140°F rinse water to eliminate the need for a booster heater.

Recommendation	Present	Proposed	Saving
Single Tank (Door Type)			
Booster	30 KW	N/A	
Sustainer	5 KW	N/A	
Pump motor	2 KW	2 KW	
Total KW/hr.	37 KW	2 KW	
Cost per hour (KW × $.055)	$2.04	$.11	
Hours used per day	6	6	
Cost per day (hours used × cost per hour)	$12.24	$.66	($11.58/day)
Cost per year (cost per day × 365)	$4,467.60	$240.90	$4,226.70/year
Multitank (Conveyor Type)			
Booster	58 KW	N/A	
Sustainer	20 KW	10 KW	
Tank Heater	20 KW	20 KW	
Motors & Controls	5 KW	5 KW	
Total KW/hr.	103 KW	35 KW	
Cost/hr. (KW × $.055)	$5.67	$1.93	
Hrs. used per day	6	6	
Cost per day (hours used × cost per hour)	$33.99	$11.58	($22.41/day)
Cost per year (cost per day × 365)	$12,406.35	$4,226.70	$8,179.65/year

472

B. Detergent/dishwasher cutoff devices to turn off the conveyor motor and wash, rinse, and final rinse booster heaters when there are no dishes on the conveyor to be washed.

Single-Tank Conveyor

Daily hours of operation	8.5	4.7
Cost per hour (37 KW × $.055)	$2.04	$2.04
Cost per day	$17.34	$9.59
Cost per year	$6,329.10	$3,500.35
		($7.75/day)
		$2,828.75

Multitank Conveyor

Daily hours of operation	7.2	4.5
Cost per hour (103 KW × $.055)	$5.67	$5.67
Cost per day	$40.82	$25.52
Cost per year	$14,897.30	$9,314.80
		($15.30/day)
		$5,584.50*

C. Strip curtains on flight-type machines prevent heat and steam escape, resulting in a 10% reduction in energy expenditures.

Cost of operation per hour	$5.67	$5.10 (Less 10%)
Daily cost of operation (cost per hour × 6 hrs. use per day)	$34.02	$30.60
Cost per year	$12,417.30	$11,169.00
		($3.42/day)
		$1,248.30*

D. Water softening agents can improve efficiency 30% by reducing mineral deposits that clog valves and pipes.

Single-Tank Machine

Cost of operation per hour	$2.04	$1.43 (Less 30%)
Daily cost of operation (cost per hour × 6 hrs. used per day)	$12.24	$8.58
Cost per year	$4,467.60	$3,131.70
		($3.66/day)
		$1,335.90

*indicates items added together for total.

Recommendation	Present	Proposed	Saving
Multitank Machine			
Cost of operation per hour	$5.67	$3.97	
	(103 KW × $.055)	(Less 30%)	
Daily cost of operation (cost per hour × 6 hrs. used per day)	$34.02	$23.82	($10.20/day)
Cost per year	$12,417.30	$8,694.30	$3,723.00*
E. Run only full racks of dishes to decrease running time by one-third.			
Single-Tank Machine			
Cost of operation per hour	$2.04	$1.43	
	(37 KW × $.055)	(Less 30%)	
Daily cost of operation (cost per hour × 6 hrs. used per day)	$12.24	$8.58	($3.66/day)
Cost per year	$4,467.60	$3,131.70	$1,335.90*
Multitank Machine			
Cost of operation per hour	$5.67	$3.97	
	(103 KW × $.055)	(Less 30%)	
Daily cost of operation (cost per hour × 6 hrs. used per day)	$34.02	$23.82	($10.20/day)
Cost per year	$12,417.30	$8,694.30	$3,723.00*
F. Use wetting agent rather than a power dryer (⅓ HP) to air-dry dishes adequately.			
Energy use for ⅓ HP motor (⅓ HP × .660 KW/HP)	.22 KW	wetting agent in lieu of power dryer	
Cost per hour (KW × $.055)	$.01	wetting agent in lieu of power dryer	
Cost per day (cost per hour × 6 hrs. used per day)	$.06/day		
Cost per year	$21.90		$21.90*

Preparation Equipment

A. Limit preheat times to 15 minutes. Turning on equipment an hour before it is needed is costly. Preheating to a higher temperature than is needed will not speed up preheating times.

Electric: Cost of oven use
(16 KW × $.055/hr.)

	Preheat time = 1 hr.	Preheat time = 15 min.
	$.88	$.22
		(.25 hr)
Cost per year	$321.20	$80.30

Gas: Cost of oven use
(120,000 BTU or 1.2 therms
× $.47/therm (therm = 100,000 BTU)

	Preheat time = 1 hr.	Preheat time = 15 min.
	$.56	$.14
		(.25 hr.)
Cost per year	$204.40	$51.10

($.66/day)
$240.90

($.42/day)
$153.30*

B. Reduce oven use time:

• Begin cooking as ovens warm up. Unless baked goods such as cakes or souffles are being made, preheating to desired temperature before cooking is unnecessary.

• Bake several items at once. Plan production so that as many menu items as possible can be baked at the same time. Partially cook items a day in advance to maximize oven space.

• Turn ovens off when not in use. If oven is not to be used within two hours, turn it off. Plan ahead to use ovens only once per day.

• Plan menu to maximize oven use. Include several menu items per day that require the oven, so that all items can be cooked at once. Consider planning a day requiring *no* oven use, especially in summer months. Salad and sandwich plates or cold meat platters can be refreshing during hot weather.

475

Recommendation	Present	Proposed	Saving
Electric: Cost per day (16 KW × $.055 = $.88/hr.)	$10.56/day (12 hrs. use)	$3.52/day (4 hrs. use)	($7.04/day)
Cost per year	$3,854.40	$1284.80	$2,569.60
Gas: Cost per day (120,000 BTU or 1.2 therms × $.47 therm = $.56)	$6.72/day (12 hrs. use)	$2.24/day (4 hrs. use)	($4.48/day)
Cost per year	$2,452.80	$817.60	$1,635.20*
C. Calibrate oven to 350 degrees. Quickbreads and other specialty items may require higher temperatures; however, most ovens should be calibrated to prevent excessive temperatures.			
KW required for 10 hrs. of operation (11 KW oven)	18.3 KW (450°) $1.01	16.4 KW (350°) $.90	$40.15*
(450° = 11 KW × 1 hr. + .8 KW × 9 hrs.) (350° = 11 KW × 1 hr. + .6 KW × 9 hrs.)			
D. Use timers to reduce opening oven door. Use an in-the-meat thermometer with outside gauge. Every second the oven door is open, the temperature drops one degree.			
Cost of opening door of 11 KW convection oven for 60 seconds (11 KW – 15 min. = .733 KW/min. to heat oven to 350°) .733 KW × $.055 = $.04			
Cost of opening door four times during cooking cycle	$.16	not opening door during cooking cycle	($.16/day)
Cost per year	$58.40		$58.40*

E. Utilize a low-temperature cook-and-hold oven for roasting meats. Meat yield is increased, waste is reduced, and a more desirable product results.

22 KW double-deck convection oven = 29.2 KW/10 hrs. use × $.055 (22 KW/hr. and .8 KW/hr. to maintain)	$1.61/10 hrs./day		
Cost per year	$587.65		
10 KW low temp oven = 15.4 KW/10 hrs. use × $.055 (10 KW/hr. and .6 KW/hr. to maintain)		$.85/10 hrs./day	($.76/day)
Cost per year		$310.25	$277.40*

Vent Hoods

A. Use compensation type 80/20 vent hoods [Example: 12' × 4' hood—4,800 cubic feet per minute (CFM)]. By installing a supply fan to provide compensating air beneath the vent hood, heating and air conditioning costs are reduced.

Cost of heating/air conditioning = **1.08 × CFM × T (temp. change) = Total BTU content of air (Based on 30° temperature change) (**Standard conversion factor)	4,800 CFM/hr. (100% reconditioned air)	960 CFM/hr. (20% reconditioned air)

$$\frac{1.08 \times 4{,}800 \text{ CFM} \times 30° \times 10 \text{ hrs./day} \times \$.47/\text{therm}}{100{,}000 \text{ BTU/therm}} = \quad \$7.31/\text{day}$$

Cost per year = $7.30 × 365 = $2,668.15/yr.

$$\frac{1.08 \times 960 \text{ CFM} \times 30° \times 10 \text{ hrs./day} \times \$.47/\text{therm}}{100{,}000 \text{ BTU/therm}} = \quad 1.46/\text{day}$$

Cost per year	$532.90/yr.	$2,135.25*

B. Increase efficiency by 20% by cleaning filters regularly.

Cost/day of operation	$7.31	$5.85 (Less 20%)	($1.46/day)
Cost/year	$2,668.15	$2,135.25	$532.90*

477

Recommendation	Present	Proposed	Saving
Refrigeration			
A. Use plastic strip curtains for walk-in units to increase efficiency by 30%. Heavy-duty plastic minimizes loss of cold air, even when door is open.			
Cost of operation/day for 8' × 10' walk-in cooler	$3.79	$2.65 (Less 30%)	($1.14/day)
Cost/year	$1,383.35	$967.25	$416.10*
B. Improve efficiency by 30% through keeping compressor free of dust and lint. Make this practice part of preventive maintenance program.			
Cost per day for 8' × 10' walk-in cooler	$3.79	$2.65 (Less 30%)	($1.14/day)
Cost per year	$1,383.35	$967.25	$416.10*
C. Disconnect reach-in refrigerators while on vacation or when not in use for three weeks or more.			
Cost per day of operation	$.86	$.86	
Cost per year	$313.90	$253.70 (Less 70 days or 10 wks.)	$60.20*
Lighting			
A. Change incandescent lighting to fluorescent.			
Cost per day of lighting (KW × $.055)	Incandescent: 40 × 100 W bulbs (4 KW) $.22/hr.	Fluorescent: 10 × 100 W bulbs (1 KW) $.055/hr.	
Cost per day (10 hrs. of operation)	$2.20	$.55	($1.65/day)
Cost per year	$803.00	$200.75	$602.25*

478

B. Reduce bulb wattage when possible. Using simple light meter, determine the foot/candles (measure of light) in the institution.

	20 100W bulbs	20 60W bulbs	
Cost per day (KW × 12 hrs. of use × $.055)	(2 KW) $1.32	(1.2 KW) $.79	
Cost per year	$481.80	$288.35	($.53/day) $193.45*

C. Turn off lights in areas not in use (i.e., walk-in refrigeration, storeroom)

Cost per day: 2 100W bulbs (.2 KW × $.055 = $.01)	$.13 (12 hrs.)	$.01 (1 hr.)	
Cost per year	$47.45	$3.65	($.12/day) $43.80*

Heat, Ventilation and Air Conditioning

Evaluation of HVAC savings was made through the following formula:

$1.08 \times CFM \times T$ (temperature change) = Total BTU content of air/hr.

Total BTU − 3413 = KW

KW × hrs. of operation = KWH × $.055 = cost of operation

Food service size: 20,000 cubic feet × .3 air changes per minute = 6,000 CFM

Average temperature change = 30°   Hours of operation = 12

A. Lower thermostat from 72° to 68° in winter (5 months), reducing average temperature differential to which internal air is heated from 30° to 26°F.

479

Recommendation	Present	Proposed	Saving
Electricity:			
Present			
$\dfrac{1.08 \times 6{,}000 \text{ CFM} \times 30° \times 12 \text{ hrs./day} \times 365 \text{ days/yr.} \times \$.055/\text{KWH}}{3413 \text{ BTU/KW}} =$	$13,721.35		
Proposed			
$\dfrac{1.08 \times 6{,}000 \text{ CFM} \times 26° \times 12 \text{ hrs./day} \times 365 \text{ days/yr.} \times \$.055/\text{KWH}}{3413 \text{ BTU/KW}} =$		$11,891.83	$1,829.52
Gas:			
Present			
$\dfrac{1.08 \times 6{,}000 \text{ CFM} \times 30° \times 12 \text{ hrs./day} \times 365 \text{ days/yr.} \times \$.47/\text{therm}}{100{,}000 \text{ BTU/therm}} =$	$4,001.92		
Proposed			
$\dfrac{1.08 \times 6{,}000 \text{ CFM} \times 26° \times 12 \text{ hrs./day} \times 365 \text{ days/yr.} \times \$.47/\text{therm}}{100{,}000 \text{ BTU/therm}} =$		$3,468.33	$533.59

B. Permanently—per season—calibrate thermostat to 68° in winter,
76° in summer to prevent employees from changing it.

Average temperature change due to thermostat adjustment =
10°F.

$$\dfrac{1.08 \times 10° \times 6{,}000 \text{ CFM} \times \$.055/\text{KW}}{3413 \text{ BTU/KW}} =$$

| | | | ($1.04/day) |
| | | | $379.60* |

C. Lower heat by 10° at night and on holidays in nonpatient areas.

$$\frac{1.08 \times 10° \times 6{,}000 \text{ CFM} \times \$.055 \text{ KW}}{3413 \text{ BTU/KW}} =$$

(\$1.04/day)
\$379.60*

D. Consider a heat recovery system.
A heat exchanger can transfer waste heat from dishwasher use to preheat domestic hot water.

$$\frac{T \times 8.34 \text{ lbs /gal} \times \# \text{ cycles/day} \times \text{gal/cycle} \times \$/\text{KW} \times \text{days/year}}{3413 \text{ BTU/KW}}$$

$$\frac{**56° \times 8.34 \text{ lbs/gal} \times 260 \text{ cycles/day} \times 4.0 \text{ gal/cycle} \times \$.055/\text{KW} \times 365 \text{ days/year}}{3413 \text{ BTU/KW}}$$

\$2,856.98*

(**Temperature recaptured from low-temperature dishwasher)

E. Utilize a heat recovery system that uses exhaust ventilation to preheat or precool incoming air. (Based on 20' × 4'6" hood and 30° temperature differential)

$$\frac{1.08 \times 9{,}000 \text{ CFM} \times 30° \times \$.47/\text{therm} \times 18 \text{ hrs./day}}{100{,}000 \text{ BTU/therm}} =$$

(\$24.67/day)
\$9,004.55*

F. Utilize a high velocity water saving prerinse spray.

$$3.6 \text{ gal/rack} \times 260 \text{ racks/day} \times \$.011/\text{gal (to heat water)} =$$

\$10.30/day
\$3,759.50/yr.

$$2.3 \text{ gal/rack} \times 260 \text{ racks/day} \times \$.011/\text{gal (to heat water)} =$$

\$6.58/day
\$2,401.70/yr.

G. Many local ventilation codes have changed, decreasing minimum standards for volume changes of air per hour. Decrease current fan size and motor size to reduce the ventilation rate to minimum standards. (Based on 20,000 cubic feet, 9' ceilings)

(\$3.72/day)
\$1,357.80

Recommendation	Present	Proposed	Saving
$\dfrac{18 \text{ volume changes/hr.} \times 20,000 \text{ cubic feet}}{60 \text{ minutes}} = 6000 \text{ CFM}$			
$\dfrac{2 \text{ HP} \times 2546 \text{ BTU/HP} \times 365 \text{ days/yr.} \times 24 \text{ hrs./day} \times \$.47/\text{therm}}{100,000 \text{ BTU/therm}} =$	$209.65		
$\dfrac{12 \text{ volume changes/hr.} \times 20,000 \text{ cubic feet}}{60 \text{ minutes}} = 6000 \text{ CFM}$			
$\dfrac{\frac{3}{4} \text{ HP} \times 2456 \text{ BTU/HP} \times 365 \text{ days/yr.} \times 24 \text{ hrs./day} \times \$.47/\text{therm}}{100,000 \text{ BTU/therm}} =$		$78.62	$131.03*
Reduced volume changes of air result in savings in loss of conditioned (heated or cooled) air.			
$\dfrac{4,700 \text{ normal annual degree days (per National Weather Service)}}{240 \text{ days/yr.}} = 19.6°F$			
65°F − 19.6°F = 45.4°F average outside temperature			
70°F (indoor temperature) − 45.4°F (outdoor temperature) = 24.6° average temperature difference			
$\dfrac{1.08 \times 2,000 \text{ CFM} \times 24.6°F \times 24 \text{ hrs./day} \times 365 \text{ days/yr.} \times \$.47/\text{therm}}{100,000 \text{ BTU/therm}} =$			$2,187.72*
Maximum total yearly savings			$48,576.90

Index

Note: Page numbers in italics indicate exhibits or tables.

E

About the Author

Judy Ford Stokes, FCSI, R.D., is President of Judy Ford Stokes & Associates, Inc., a food management/design consultant firm servicing health care, educational, correctional, and hospitality clients throughout the country. Ms. Stokes is known for her practical approach to food service operation, integrating over 20 years experience into food service design and management consulting.

Judy Ford Stokes is a widely acclaimed speaker providing presentations on strategic planning, cost effectiveness, food service design, managing, marketing and motivating, purchasing programs, energy conservation, equipment comparison and selection, as well as computer cost analysis.

Ms. Stokes is the author of *Cost Effective Quality Food Service,* first edition, Editor of *Atlanta Cooks for Company*, Publisher of *The Stokes Report* and *Clinical Management*, and she has had numerous articles published in publications including *Food Management, Harvard Business Review, Cooking for Profit, Atlanta Women's News, The Stokes Report*, the *American Health Care Association Journal, Southern Hospitals*, and others.

She is active in the food service industry, serving as Chairman of the Consultant Dietitians in Health Care Facilities (1985–86), representing approximately 4000 members, the largest and oldest practice group of the American Dietetic Association. She was named Outstanding Dietitian in Georgia for 1985 and was selected as the Outstanding Consultant Dietitian in Georgia in 1984. Ms. Stokes also serves as one of 17 ADA Ambassadors, and she has been named to Who's Who in Health Care in 1976. Judy also has been identified in 1978 as one of 10 Outstanding Young People in Atlanta and as one of the 10 Leading Ladies of Atlanta in 1976.

In addition to a busy travel schedule, Judy is a wife and also the mother of two active teenagers.